Chinese Justice, the Fiction

Chinese Justice, the Fiction

LAW AND LITERATURE
IN MODERN CHINA

Jeffrey C. Kinkley

STANFORD UNIVERSITY PRESS

STANFORD, CALIFORNIA

Stanford University Press
Stanford, California
© 2000 by the Board of Trustees of the Leland Stanford Junior University

Printed in the United States of America
CIP data appear at the end of the book

Dedicated to

Benjamin I. Schwartz and
Alexander Woodside

Acknowledgments

I am greatly indebted to those who sat for interviews; they are listed at the beginning of Interviews and Works Cited. Special thanks are due the Chinese Academy of Social Sciences, the Committee on Scholarly Communication with China, and the National Endowment for the Humanities, which hosted and funded my 1990 and 1991 trips to China; St. John's University, New York, which provided two research leaves, research teaching reductions, and a summer research grant; and the Chiang Ching-kuo Foundation for International Educational Exchange, whose 1996–97 research grant aided this project and an intended sequel.

Patrick Hanan, Robert Hegel, Leo Ou-fan Lee, Shao-chuan Leng, Patricia Laurence, Perry Link, Brian E. McKnight, Jonathan Ocko, James St. André, Phil Williams, Timothy Wong, and Mrs. C. F. Woo (nee Cheng Yuzhen) reviewed chapters of the book for accuracy. Alice Cheang, Jay Rubin, Mark Silver, and Tomoji Ohta provided research leads. Helen Tartar, Peter Kahn, Stacey Lynn, and Janet Mowery at Stanford University Press provided expert help with the text.

The following friends and colleagues helped while I was in China and since then as well: Ai Qun, Chen Mengxiong, Chen Mingqing, Dong Dexing, Fu Guangming, Gao Tao, Hao Min, Hua Jian, Li Hui and Ying Hong, Li Jian, Li Rui, Liu Binyan, Liu Huiying, Liu Yangti, Liu Zaifu, Liu Zongdai, Lü Haiyan, Ma Liangchun, Nie Jianguo, Shen Yingci, Wang Meng, Wang Shuo, Wang Yonghong, Wang Zengqi, Wei Dongsheng, Wu Ningkun, Wu Xiaoling, Xiao Qian and Wen Jieruo, Xu Heqi and Lü Yuanyi, Yang Xianyi and Gladys Yang, Ye Yonglie (who lent me a scrapbook of newspaper clippings for a popular history of Chinese crime fiction he was preparing), Yu Fenggao, Yu Hua, Zhang Xinxin, Zeng Zhennan, Zhou

Yunfa, Zou Dehua. Special thanks are owed the Guo Zijian, Modern Chinese Literature Institute, Shanghai Municipal Library, as well as the library staff at Columbia University, including Fran LaFleur; Princeton University; and the Bernardsville, New Jersey, public library.

At St. John's, I thank Tony Bonaparte, provost; deans Rev. David O'Connell, C. M., and Willard Gingerich; Shen Jianming and Margaret Turano of the Law School; Larry Egan and Eugene Orlowski; Louise McKenzie and staff, who prepared the graphics; and Rocco Mirro, who designed the book jacket and the table. Unless otherwise noted, all translations are my own. The Harvard University Asia Center kindly allowed me to quote from my article "Chinese Crime Fiction and Its Formulas" in my edited book *After Mao: Chinese Literature and Society, 1978–1981* (Cambridge, Mass.: Council on East Asian Studies, Harvard University, 1985).

My family, Chuchu Kinkley and Matthew Kang Kinkley, were very patient. The Shanghai cartoonists who created the "Black Cat Police Chief" (Heimao Jingzhang) may or may not want to know that Matthew, age four, viewed their creations on video cassette and loved them. The views in this book reflect my opinion only.

J.K.
Bernardsville, N.J.

Contents

Abbreviations

The following abbreviations are used in this book:

CCP: Chinese Communist Party
KMT: Kuomintang (Nationalist Party of China)
MPS: Ministry of Public Security
PLA: People's Liberation Army
PRC: People's Republic of China
CXQWJ: Cheng Xiaoqing, *Cheng Xiaoqing wen ji*
HSTAJ: Cheng Xiaoqing, *Huo Sang tan'an ji*
XDLP: Sun Liaohong, *Xia dao Lu Ping qi'an*
Int.:   Interview (in the Notes)

Chinese Justice, the Fiction

The Revival of Law and Literature in China

Three modern mysteries and a field of criticism called "law and literature" inspired this book. The story begins in the late 1970s, when fiction about crime and the law suddenly returned to China. The first mystery is how it could revive so quickly and in such good form after a nearly 30-year ban on reading or writing anything of the sort.[1] A second occasion for puzzlement arose in 1984. On the heels of still more suppressions, writing about crime enjoyed an abrupt reversal of fortune; it was officially extolled and ennobled as a "Chinese legal system literature." But this too put China's authorities at odds with the public. Most people thought it quite proper to affect superiority—in public—toward this subject matter that titillated them in private. And in private they did not consider association with the Chinese legal system nearly as glorious as the government did. Then the police emerged as crime fiction's most fervent backers. What that meant was a third mystery. The police were used to ridding society of dubious publications (and people), usually without recourse to any legal system. While investigating enigmas like these, this book means to lay out modern Chinese fiction about crime and the law as a field for critical analysis and to examine the interrelations of Chinese law and literature as such.

Things were different under Mao. Perhaps no work of fiction published in the People's Republic of China (PRC) between 1949 and 1977 told of common, apolitical crimes committed by ordinary PRC citizens.[2] The press did not report on crime; socialism was not supposed to produce it.[3] Major trespasses were political offenses, "contradictions between the enemy and the people."[4] In fiction, suspense was contraband,[5] and so therefore were many crime stories of no possible reflection on the New China. In 1956 the Masses' Press, publishing arm of the Ministry of Public Security (MPS; "the police"),[6] began to reprint the complete Sherlock Holmes. That effort was soon halted.[7] Holmes did figure in a 1961 dictionary. It defined detective fiction as "a kind of popular fiction that was produced and flourished in capitalist societies of Europe and America. . . . Most works of this type are low-grade, arousing base passions for sex and violence and propagandizing for the bourgeois view of morality. A noted example is the collected tales of Sherlock Holmes, by England's Conan Doyle."[8] The curious implication was that stories of crime and detection were foreign to China.

Crime was rare, by our standards. Beijing's first armed bank robbery since the revolution was in 1980.[9] But rarity does not diminish curiosity. Few stories in Mao's day told even of routine crime *fighting* by PRC judges, jailers, prosecutors, or police. To be sure, judges were not civic leaders under the proletarian or even the people's democratic dictatorship (the term used in Deng Xiaoping's era). The lawyer's profession and the Ministry of Justice were abolished outright from 1959 to 1979. Meantime, the MPS, with its household registration branches, civilian informers, and campaign-style policing, organized comprehensive surveillance of the public. Judges and procurators (public prosecutors) yielded to the police in the formal justice system, and they continue to do so. Yet most Chinese despise the police. In comparison with the glorious People's Liberation Army (PLA), the police are second-raters in their own eyes.

How then could even a new crime fiction in a country with such weak legal institutions be dignified as legal system fiction (*fazhi xiaoshuo*)? Indeed, the preferred term was legal system *literature* (*fazhi wenxue*), including legal system poetry, crime reportage, and works about civil conflicts. Whether law and literature go together naturally in China is a major concern of this book; so is the "rectification of names" by officials. A short explanation is that police work and euphemism go together naturally. The police detective fiction of Émile Gaboriau (1833–73) that paved the way for Sherlock Holmes was originally styled *le roman judiciaire* (French for "legal system fiction").[10] China calls its police a judicial organ (*sifa jiguan*).[11]

Yet China's legal system literature is not just a literature *about* the legal system, and still less just about cops, robbers, and detection. The concept has always suggested a literature of, by, and for China's new post-Mao legal system—something needing "advocates" in all walks of life. Legal system literature was supposed to "use literary forms to propagandize the legal system, and the content of the legal system to fructify literature."[12] Although police were the typical heroes, judges and procurators stood out in many works. "Law without lawyers" was a Chinese tradition,[13] but not Mao's kind of law, without courts. To most Chinese, "law" still conjured up visions of courtroom spectacle, an accused pleading for mercy, and severe sentencing. Such images underlie China's "purely detective" stories even now. Lore, imagination, and history can fill in.

Perhaps it was to be expected that the police would get involved in China's new fiction about crime and the law.[14] But they had to compromise with reform, human rights, and commercial interests, as well as a revived Ministry of Justice. Competition for "leadership" over crime fiction reflected broader struggles in Chinese literature and even the legal system. It helped that everyone was making a good deal of money—particularly the police— and that Yu Haocheng, who oversaw MPS publications from 1984 to 1986, was himself a human rights advocate.[15]

The 1989 massacre in Beijing changed the relationship between China's officials and its people, reminding everyone that Chinese legal institutions could function as instruments of terror. The massacre also marked a watershed in writing. "Legal system literature" was superseded, for some years, by a less progressive-sounding term: "police" or "public security literature" (*gōng'ān wénxúe*). (It is to be distinguished from China's ancient and respected *gōng'àn wénxúe* or "court case literature," though the police may like the linguistic similarity.) The term "literature of the new era," referring to all post-Mao writing, likewise expired for a time after 1989. When it reappeared in the 1990s, often it was as a historical term for a decade of productivity past: 1979– 89.[16] But bigger changes were in store. China was headed for an era when anything could be printed—sub rosa, for a price—when some judges and lawyers took bribes, and when the police cooperated with Triads in joint ventures.

Hence 1989 is the general, though not absolute, termination point for this study. Reading for amusement was in decline and foreign TV cop shows were ascendant. The adversary law of Perry Mason and *The People's Court* are absent from Chinese TV even now, when many Western detectives and Hollywood action heroes have become household names.[17] Yet writing about crime and civil cases goes on, and it appears to be substantially reviving. Zhang Yimou's justice-seeking 1992 film heroine Qiuju became a household name among intellectual filmgoers in the West. It is Chinese crime fiction that remains unknown in the West and unavailable in translation.[18]

In this book I attempt to fill the gap. I analyze Chinese crime and court case fiction's works, authors, genres, subgenres, levels, themes, characters, and plots. And I have theoretical aspirations. Through crime fiction, I hope to illuminate China's new legal culture (the thought and habits affecting legal behavior) and the predicament of all modern Chinese literature. Relevant to the latter are its historical and social contexts, modes of genre formation, and social levels; buffeting by party, state, and patriotic norms; and relations to other institutions and ideas, above all legal ones. The works discussed in this book are legally less sophisticated than Chinese academic articles, but the latter still give lip-service to Marxist theory. Creative writing now defers at most to vague "socialist" values.

Even so, Chinese officials tried to "legislate" whole genres into existence. This is not to say that genre is of necessity an artificial construct from above that overrides social and historical values. Nor need genre be so culturally idiosyncratic as to seem random and nonsensical to outside observers, like the categories of animals that Jorge Borges and Michel Foucault were amused to think had appeared in an ancient Chinese encyclopedia: "those that belong to the Emperor; embalmed ones; those that are trained; suckling pigs; mermaids"; and so forth.[19] Like many a book on detective fiction, with this one I hope to elicit interest, pleasure, and pedagogic utility from ideas of genre.[20] It is near the end, when the book catches up again to the communist era, that ideologically planned genres loom large. "To be a modern writer and to write generically is a contradiction in terms," Adena Rosmarin avers.[21] Recent studies, even of detective fiction, stress genre fluidity.[22] But genres can be confounded only if readers know them.[23] Borges's and Umberto Eco's self-conscious "crossovers" from the detective to the philosophical novel are themselves, in a word, generic.[24]

Subject-matter classification and taxonomy are still poorer relations of genre criticism in the West,[25] but not in China. Late Qing scholars spoke of "navigation fiction" and "constitution fiction."[26] Current enthusiasts of premodern Chinese *gongan* (court case) fiction, such as Huang Yanbo and Meng Liye, tend to include in the category any work with a crime and case in it.[27] Codified Chinese law, classified in the Qing dynasty according to the jurisdictions of China's Six Boards, likewise fell into subject-matter categories, although the number of them may reflect ancient cosmological theories of musical harmony.[28] The literatus Zhang Xuecheng (1738–1801) opined that both law and literature were originally created and kept in ancient China by government offices.[29] Likewise, the MPS and Ministry of Justice vied for oversight in the 1980s of what they preferred to call "police literature" and "legal system literature," respectively.

In fact, the West also defines genres according to "form or technique or, sometimes, subject matter,"[30] or by "formal structure (sonnet, picaresque novel), length (novella, epigram), intention (satire), effect (comedy), origin (folktale), and subject-matter (pastoral, science fiction)."[31] Crime fiction might claim at least three possible ambits.

CRIME FICTION IN THE BROADEST SENSE

"Crime fiction" may be defined as a broad subject-matter category encompassing any work showing crime or law enforcement, including Shakespeare's *The Merchant of Venice* and Wu Jianren's *Eyewitness Reports on Strange Things Seen in the Past Twenty Years*, according to some Chinese opinion. Western critics tend to doubt the literary importance of such an inclusive category, but it can be useful if the object of analysis is themes and contexts. This book examines, for instance, China's "literature of introspection" (*fansi wenxue*). Chinese crime aficionados do not claim stories in that category for their favorite genre, but certain works do illuminate their country's legal and literary culture. Moreover, quite a few of them employ generic crime themes and detective devices. The seriousness of the works' political critique blinds some readers to that fact, or perhaps compensates for it, in the view of others.

Crime fiction in the broadest sense is of special importance because it has an alter ego that looms very large in Chinese criticism, namely "legal system literature" itself. It is a category potentially so capacious that many of its enthusiasts cite Tolstoy's *Resurrection* and Hugo's *Les Misérables* as model works.[32] Police bureaucrats approve; the bigger the category, the more works they can supervise, and what a coup to have authority over China's Hugos and Tolstoys. But legitimate Chinese critics also take subject matter seriously.

CRIME FICTION AS WE KNOW IT: AN INTERMEDIATE CONCEPTION

"Crime fiction" in plain English, which perforce is the main usage in this book, is "fiction about crime and the law." The concept betrays an assumption, common to China and the West, that crime is inextricably bound up with law and punishment. Crime fiction is said to appeal to something "deeper" than "interest in crime itself." It triggers hidden biological, moral, social—in a word, mythic—hopes and fears.[33] So this is a narrower if less precise category than the previous one, though still a subject-matter class more than a genre. Yet this idea of crime fiction is concretized in distinct "genre fiction" types or subgenres—detective stories, courtroom dramas, thrillers, and so forth. Adding them all up does not define a whole,[34] but to many Chinese, doing so was preferable to giving the police license to intervene in every work that mentioned crime. Yet the police could use the narrower concept too: if legal system literature were both a giant subject-matter category (a lenient entry gatekeeper) *and* a genre (narrow in deciding which works could "get out"), the genre prescriptions could rein in lots of errant works. Still, the crime (sub)genres all seemed so "low," whereas *Resurrection* was too high for any generic categorization.

"Crime fiction" (*zuian xiaoshuo*) as such is a term seldom heard in China.[35] The lack of such a term—a modern counterpart of the old "court case" fiction—was the vacuum that the new concept, "legal system literature," filled.[36] "Genre fiction" has no Chinese equivalent either, but the concept cannot be difficult in a culture that so delights in naming subgenres, like the "mid-length love story of the everyday type," or "mid-length [historical] martial-arts story invoking the uncanny." Any work whose subject is so generic is thought to be outside of what in Chinese is called "pure literature."

In fact, critics everywhere, with exceptions like the formalist Viktor Shklovsky, tend to exclude fiction about crime and the law from the canon. Conversely, Kafka's *The Trial* (of which Auden said "it is the guilt that is certain and the crime that is uncertain")[37] is not called crime or law fiction, nor is Dostoevski's *Crime and Punishment*, despite its focus on crime—and punishment.[38] Evidently criminal, even legal themes, are trumped by moral, religious, philosophical, ideological, or psychological ones, including revenge; crime and even law are "low," with the result that any nonformulaic work with the "higher" themes is not "crime fiction" or "law fiction." It is not that fiction with crime themes cannot be considered serious, or even literature (canonical literature).[39] But crime, and even law, with its discourse of literalness and sanctioning,[40] appear low in comparison with more abstract and symbolic discourses.

Melville's *Billy Budd*, which is about a trial, is a favorite of "law and literature" analysis. But critics at large find its theme of law distinctly subordinate to themes of morality (Is Billy good, even if criminally responsible?), religion (Did Capt. Vere the Father sacrifice Billy the Son?), and philosophy (Is Billy "natural man"? How is law related to morality?). Few call it crime fiction or legal drama.[41] The theme of bad law in Dickens's *Bleak House* likewise strikes most readers as subordinate to the theme of defects in society, as well as in human nature. The crime and legal themes in Dostoevski and Tolstoy also are felt to pale beside the guilt, suffering, and redemption that they treat. Richard Posner's truism that no novel is great because it treats the law may not go far enough—though it does not follow that a great novel can be about law only insofar as law symbolizes a higher discourse—and that we must all therefore be, like him, "an intentionalist when it comes to reading statutes and the Constitution but a New Critic when it comes to reading works of literature."[42]

Julian Symons offers a discerning explanation. He thinks of crime fiction as a hybrid of literature and sensational literature, artistically positioned like Restoration comedy in relation to Jacobean drama—limited by its form, but its best works literary rather than "popular," and the very best worthy of being in the canon.[43] In England, "sensation" meant a turning away from interest in character development and morality. Before "crime fiction," there were Gothic, *The Newgate Calendar*, broadsides, biographies of criminals, and romances.[44] China had an old sensational fiction about court cases (criminals humbled by justice), scholar-beauty romance, ghosts, the uncanny, and finally the imported Western whodunits that some very well read Chinese still think smutty.[45] Both East and West also had old novels glorifying outlaws—picaros in the West;[46] men with their own code in China. They were not, however, "popular" if that means mostly read by the lower classes. Modernist literary histories of the age of Sherlock Holmes, when literacy was widespread in the West, slight not only fantasy, mystery, and adventure but also "the 'novel with a purpose,' the feminist, socialist, or otherwise political fiction that had a wide following in the 1890s and still proves fascinating today"[47]—as if it were sensational too. China's highly political modern fiction is driven all the more to slough off the "popular."

France's pioneering mysteries were also hybrids of "literature" and popular forms. Often they were about avengers—as in melodrama, the *roman d'aventure* (preceded by "serious" children's fiction), and the *roman-feuilleton*. Or are the many canonized novels by Dumas, Sand, and Balzac hybrids of romanticism ("modern literature") and "the novel," which was once a low form telling sensational tales about "the dangerous classes"?[48]

These views are indebted to a social and normative concept of "high," "serious," or just plain "literature" being different from "popular literature" (or "popular fiction," or just "fiction," to those who consider "popular literature" an oxymoron). Particularly in this age of capitalist diversity and deliberate crossovers and postmodern mixtures, it is easy to "problematize" the high/low distinction. There is not and never has been an absolute distinction between high and popular literature in audience, form, or subject matter.[49] A story can be elevated by different criteria—the explicitness of its social critique, or conversely the ambiguity of its figurative language. And, alternatively—or simultaneously—it can be accorded "low" or "popular" status by many different factors, from vulgar language to a notably titillating—or contrarily, familiar—plot. It is interesting to think of popular literature as that which does not bear reading twice, with detective stories as the model, for once one knows whodunit, the suspense is over. But this too fails in practice, since even television reruns are viewed with pleasure. The authors Boileau-Narcejac conjecture that a detective novel is too structurally predetermined to discover itself to the *author* during the writing process.[50] But again, some popular writers claim that their characters "create" the plot. Most people still think of literature as "high" and "low." We let social prestige affect our evaluations of works and feel torn between high and low tastes within ourselves, reading works we consider not just low but aesthetically *bad*.[51] The distinction between high and low is all in the mind, but no less real for that. This book finds the distinction to be endemic in China.

"Crime fiction" as defined by and taken as the main subject of this book refers to stories about crime and law that readers perceive not necessarily as low, but as having *roots* in the sensational. There are sensational subjects, like crimes, arrests, and trials. There is the formerly forbidden fruit of suspense. And there are sensational ideas, like strangers on a train committing murder for each other,[52] or the commoner idea of a respectable person being exposed as evil. The crime interest may be sublimated or "aestheticized," but formulaic elements recall a literary past in sensation. Crime fiction (above all its least sensational kind, armchair analytic detective fiction) is self-referential when not parodic, ever cannibalizing earlier texts. A mysterious murder, a series detective, and local color or "information" (often diverting attention from the crime) are clear signals.[53] A hint of them drags down a religious theme, keeps it from trumping a crime or legal theme as it would otherwise—hence G. K. Chesterton's Father Brown, who fits the category of "detective," fails to achieve the transcendence to which the author aspired.[54]

Critics may of course see roots in sensational fiction that most readers do not, just as I see crime fiction formulas in China's "literature of introspection." In this book I even argue, in Chapter Four, that most of China's "serious" fiction today is in fact "popular" by Chinese readers' own criteria; it is, for one thing, easy to read. Fixed ideas and social factors block acknowledgment of this. "Crossovers," by contrast, are works with overt crime story devices that just as deliberately sabotage their generic uses. At least Alain Robbe-Grillet does this; Borges and Eco may be too enmeshed in their own devices to have fully crossed over from the "detective novel." Crossovers are rare in China, although the mixing of genres, sometimes haphazardly, is very common.

CRIME OR LAW FICTION
IN A NARROWER SENSE

Crime fiction narrowly defined—about the commission of crime itself, as in the serial-murderer subgenre—is a concept of little use in this book. Chinese fiction usually avoids delving into a killer's psychology from his point of view. It is taboo, politically and perhaps morally. The 1980s did expose many instances of real corruption, and Wang Shuo's cynical and Liu Heng's sociological stories of hoodlums also appeared in that decade. Historically, crime without law enforcement has always been a minor theme in Chinese literature.[55]

However, China claims that the best part of its legal system literature is about the law itself. This "narrower" category is in fact yet another capacious subject-matter class. In China it is as old as the term *gongan*; reinforcing the concept are ancient, May Fourth, and communist ideas that literature on any subject is edifying and socially constructive. Yet most Chinese fiction about the law is melodramatic: faults of the system turn out to be awful *crimes*. American legal mystery can be sensational too, like that of Erle Stanley Gardner, John Grisham, Scott Turow, Brad Meltzer, Steven Paul Martini, John T. Lescroart, David Baldacci, and Lisa Scottoline. It is just that the formulaic and sensational roots of fictionalized misprision of justice are very old in China, and they do pose fundamental questions about the legal system. Relatively modest and low-key works of "capitalist legal system fiction" by Louis Auchincloss and Harper Lee (*To Kill a Mockingbird*) might well have exemplified just the sort of fiction that Chinese critics and officials hoped China would create in the 1980s, but all of the aforementioned authors and works were unavailable in the PRC.[56] Have Chinese authors now produced works of quality or insight comparable to *To Kill a Mockingbird*? Chapter Five offers candidates for consideration, but any conclusion is bound to be subjective.

THE STATE OF CHINESE CRIME FICTION

Chapter One begins with the new crime fiction that seemed to arise *ab ovo* just after Mao's death; this chapter's method is total immersion in literary works, but its philosophy, unlike Berlitz's, is to isolate the "grammar": the genres and archetypes that immediately occurred to Chinese authors writing about crime. "Philology" is saved for Chapter Two; it treats historical antecedents of China's modern taste in both law and literature. This chapter also considers common problems and mutual influences of Chinese law and literature, and not just in self-consciously fictional works, for fiction can be dressed up as nonfiction. Chapter Three addresses the invasion and conquest of China in the early twentieth century by literary forms and concepts from the West. The theme of Chapter Four is the role of politics, specifically communist politics.

The usual suspects are here: traditional bureaucratism and morality, Western dominance, and the authoritarian state, all conspiring to murder Chinese crime fiction, just as in the Agatha Christie novel loved by Chinese early in the post-Mao era, *Murder on the Orient Express*. So where is the surprise? At the end, of course, in Chapter Five, which is entitled "Fruition." Chinese crime-and-law fiction refused to stay murdered. Many of the survivors were "modern court case" works mixing Western and traditional Chinese elements and genuinely reflecting on the law. Three major fictional works and a film are presented as evidence, as summation. They are relatively unfettered by, though still indebted to, popular conceptions not just of genre but of society, politics, and decorum. Western film audiences already have found "for" *The Story of Qiuju*. But the fact that Chinese art seems always to be on trial in the West, or so the Chinese think, suggests that "postcolonial" criticism may be of use.

Some will question whether a fiction about crime, detection, and "bourgeois legal right" can exist outside of capitalist society. When Germany and Italy banned mysteries before World War II, many observers already thought of detective fiction as "not likely to be popular in societies where an individual's rights under the law are not recognized or where they are flagrantly repressed," and that such fiction must be post-Enlightenment, since detectives cannot flourish "while a common criminal procedure is arrest, torture, confession, and death."[57] This is already directly although not unconditionally refuted by China's premodern "court case" fiction. The many ordinary Chinese who understandably say that their country has no law may still wonder if their country can at this time produce a genuine fiction about crime and the law.[58] The answer is yes. Most Chinese crime fiction is mediocre or worse, but some works have everything an aficionado could want.[59]

Can Chinese crime fiction, under any name, find its own canon, readers, and critics, in a society whose values are in turmoil and where one fad follows another? Can Chinese *literature* do so? Chinese crime fiction has no "canon" as yet; trying to figure out which works to read, since one can hardly read them all, was an obstacle to research.[60] Loyal readers are numerous. Whether crime authors and readers can ever regard published criticisms as good-faith critiques is another question. In this, the predicament of China's crime fiction differs little from that of its "pure literature."

Still, some may say: Granted that crime fiction is amusing and needs no further justification, is it not too conservative, if only because it tries to satisfy formula tastes, to comment on the state of the law in any depth (as aficionados claim), much less challenge the status quo?[61] In this book I argue that crime fiction as such is upsetting to the Chinese status quo, even when the police manipulate it. Crime fiction does leave many social commonplaces unexamined, notably gender relations. But sometimes it is not after all clear what is "progressive." China's fragile new property rights are already in conflict with equally new and fragile human rights.

ADVERSARIAL AND PATERNALISTIC LAW AND LITERATURE

This study does not, then, intend to leave all the social questions dangling; it is not just about genre. It finds that Chinese ideas of law and literature illuminate age-old tensions between paternalistic and adversarial human relations and that the latter have been gaining since 1978.[62]

Although justifying individual rights against the party and state is an important project that will be contested for a long time, in this book I do not erect that paradigm into a telos. And the main question is not whether China has "rule of law"—not because the concept is anathema to critical legal studies, but because it is so protean and has moreover been studied before.[63] Nor does this study even invoke the "discourse of liberation" espoused by liberals and radicals alike (with the exception of Foucault).[64] It subsumes all such questions within a search for paternalistic and adversarial *forms* in China's legal culture and literature, starting with its crime-and-law fiction.

Paternalism is easy to identify, as when the Shanghai Lawyers' Association preached, in 1990: "the legal adviser is not competing with the procuratorial and court personnel to see who comes out on top; it is a propaganda effort, directed at citizens, to condemn vice and praise justice."[65] The old way was for the defendant to seek mercy from the state; there was "leniency for those who confess, severity for those who resist."

"Adversarialism" is more subject to interpretation. It can mean either a fight to the death or a "limited war" within a structured agreement to disagree. The two are related, but the latter is rarer. China's history is littered with rebels and dissidents, righteous and criminal, but in an adversary system the framework of contestation lives on. Prosecutors and defenders are "argumentative" coprofessionals, each understanding "that what [their practice] permits or requires depends on the truth of certain propositions that are given sense only by and within the practice."[66] This actually builds community. American lawyers argue on behalf of their clients in ways still inconceivable in China, even when they think them guilty, even when the clients' interests contradict the state's. That is adversarial and often indecorous; yet in setting precedents, adversarial lawyers serve collective interests.

One can view literature, too, as contentious, but within "argumentative" limits. In the broadest sense, adversarialism means tolerance of variant versions of the truth during a "trial" period. A trial or a literary work (a detective story, surely) suggests that truth potentially has many versions, even if the legal or epistemological system is constitutionally unitary. Contestation brings demands for more freedom to contest. A "thematics of opposites" prized by the late novelist Stanley Elkin, in which truth and human character emerge dialectically, not from precise rules correctly and unambiguously applied, "deconstructs" law itself, if law is merely rules.[67] Rule of law does not simply mean deciding everything "by laws."

Indeed, Ian Watt has written that "the novel's mode of imitating reality" may be "well summarized in terms of the procedures of another group of specialists in epistemology, the jury in a court of law." Both insist on all the facts from clearly identified witnesses, and in their own words: they take "the circumstantial view of life."[68]

The Chinese legal system is the paternal extreme—having no juries, being more inquisitorial than continental Europe's, and sometimes functioning as a mere tool of state administration. Chinese law has anciently entailed, besides control of expression, "rule of man" over "rule of law," discouragement (effectively or not) of lawsuits in favor of mediation imposed from above, relatively unrestrained power of the state (and within the state, the sovereign), no open argument of opposing positions by legal counsel in court, and lack of a tradition that Jerome A. Cohen has called an adversary system's crux: "providing a fair opportunity to defend himself to an individual accused by the state of some infraction or offense."[69]

China's rulers traditionally kept quotidian social conflict quiet and even showed ambivalence about how much law commoners should know. In the PRC, some laws were secret; secrecy helped the state control society. (When the state in the new era became intent on controlling businesses, a new ploy was to charge them a fee for disclosure of the law.)[70] Only in November 1988 did the state decide that all laws, though not all regulations with the force of law, must be published.[71] Law in Mao's era was even more paternalistic than law in the USSR, which Harold J. Berman called "parental" because of "its emphasis upon the role of law in educating a new type of man."[72] The PRC did people's legal thinking for them. In such trials as there were, the state came to a final (or rather a prior) gnostic account of events and proclaimed the truth.

Post-Mao China not only liberated public and literary expression; it finally gave knowledge of law and lawsuits to the people. That this was done at the state's behest meant that Chinese law became "parental" in Berman's sense: a tool by which the state socialized the masses through their passive but legally informed participation. But soon it went further than that. Bringing laws into the open became necessary for business. There have been many disappointments, and one cannot predict the outcome. This study does not embrace adversarialism as an ultimate end; even benign adversarial legal practice can go too far, as it no doubt has in America today, where so much social energy is expended in lawsuits. Adversarial literary practice in prewar China was benign too, but it likewise generated too many polemics and too few creative works. Gaps between ideals and reality can defeat any system. Yet one can agree with William Alford and others who believe that putting adversarial legal ideals in the public domain in China today—even hypocritically, as in kangaroo-court trials of dissidents—is a double-edged sword.[73] Like poems, laws can give people "ideas." Lawyers are back, and now they—like writers, who were slightly ahead of them—may seek out their own truths and be paid by the public instead of the state. Already, lawyers and jurists are becoming a professional lobby for the law. The state had to keep lawyers away from the trials of the June 4 democracy advocates. Lawyers were becoming loose cannons, willing and able to point out trumped-up cases.[74]

Law in China is not yet "juridical," an autonomous field playing by its own rules, but it is no longer a fully instrumental tool of the state either. It is becoming like a "force field," as Pierre Bourdieu and the legal pluralists might put it, pulling social disputes into its realm like a magnet, despite subcurrents reflecting political, social, and intellectual divisions among its own professionals, and between itself and other fields like politics and academic life.[75]

Literature has a similar history in China as a tool of paternalism, but it became notably adversarial against the state—and rival blocs of writers—from about 1917 until the communist revolution. The solemn role of literature as gadfly was not forgotten by certain writers during the strictest days of Maoism. In an age when individualism was considered an erroneous tendency, literature could still represent the interests of groups. Or did May Fourth adversarialism leave no room for argument, and was Hundred Flowers–era writing (1956–57) only respectful pleading to the patriarch? Crime fiction of the early twentieth century was not especially supportive of the modernizing legal innovations of the era; it may have embodied a "post-colonial" backlash because these innovations were so Western. Yet writers of the Republic treated the West as an adversary to be bested in its own terms and genres instead of simply denouncing it for cultural imperialism.[76]

In post-Mao times, creative writing and reportage became notoriously adversarial again, often with the Chinese state as the respondent. The truly dissident writing may well mean to engage the state in a fight to the death. But the freer buying and selling of books and magazines after 1984 allowed writers in all genres to "compete" like prosecutors and defenders, with each other and with the state, and yet live to argue another polemic another day.[77]

In the new legal system literature, even before that name was coined, the latent adversarial power of Chinese law and literature combined. It was a fiction that challenged communist complacency and often pleaded for the institution of adversary law, not for obedience or revolution. Yet as of old, this new fiction was despised by people of culture. Many who enjoyed crime and law enforcement themes had internalized enough of the orthodox values to feel guilty just reading about trials. Others naturally feared that the new recombination of law and literature was just another tool of the state. Literature has been so powerful in China that it is much easier to theorize it, rather than law, as a field in Bourdieu's sense.[78] For all its great poets, China

never had a Shelley who thought it a compliment to liken poets to legislators.[79] Yet today, Chinese literature is weakening, even as the Chinese legal
system gathers strength.

A coordinate theme of this work is that truth and morality in China,
though from ancient times conceived absolutely, have also been thought to
be graspable in less than perfect forms at different levels of insight. The paternalism in Chinese law and literature are manifest in explicit recognition
of "high" and "low" codes of behavior and forms of literature. Low forms of
law and literature are less respectable, yet because they are after all less perfect versions of "high" literature and morality, the low forms are not to be neglected. Human nature and society have their high and low—their distance
from the ideal—and thus the civilizing influence of law and literature is for
everyone. There may even be an implication that the truth depends on less
perfect forms of it at lower levels. The stratification of law and literature be-
tokens an ambivalence toward both that was not so problematic in imperial
times. But under the modern empirical, adversarial, egalitarian, and individualist philosophical bases of Chinese law and literature today it cannot be
disguised.

This book therefore reflects on Chinese law and literature's shared paradoxes and ambiguities. China's "legal system literature," so very "low" and
yet at other times so mischievously "high," is not a campy cultural outlier
but a suitable metonym for all modern Chinese literature. It is even a bell-
wether for the modern Chinese legal system. We usually think of law as a
state discourse and literature as belonging to individuals, but law may be
built on the adversary principle, as America is all too aware, and in China,
literature often expresses collective ideals. Law and literature can be
metaphors for each other, and their paradigms can interpenetrate.

This is not the first book to say so. The field of "law and literature" (sometimes "law and humanities") in its present incarnation in the law schools and
law reviews of North America, Europe, Australia, and beyond, is not much
older than the post-Mao Chinese legal system, literary avant-garde, and legal
system literature of which this book speaks.[80] Some scholars have derided the
law and literature field as just an amorphous, preprofessional curriculum to
humanize lawyers.[81] Others have called it a cause. One of the first books on
the subject to achieve a high profile among general readers, by Richard
Posner, was a brief against the significance of much of what had been writ-

ten on the subject.[82] In fact most writers in the field have pursued abstract questions in opposition to Judge Posner's "law and economics" field, which tends to see a "market reality" of realized individual preferences as the best of all possible worlds, regardless of where those preferences lead. Literature envisions better worlds that might be. If it can help a society whose citizens see social justice often stymied by overreliance on markets and individualism, maybe it can work for a society stymied by overreliance on collectivist utopias and the state. In legalistic America, Robin West points out, morality itself is so shaped by the sanctity of the law that it is essential to establish moral views independent of the law, as in literary texts; otherwise, law is difficult to criticize.[83] Law hardly has such a position China, but the sanctity of Chinese morality, which enfolds the law into itself, presents a similar problem. Chinese writers recognize this; in times of freedom, their criticisms of social norms go for the moral jugular: the Dao, or the state ideology. These works are not just critical but adversarial.

LAW IN LITERATURE

Law *in* literature is an obvious enough subject. The Western field asks, How do we understand arrests, trials, lawyers, police, and prisons through Melville, Dickens, and Kafka? Indeed, the public reads John Grisham for concrete "information" about the tactics of noble lawyers (in *The Street Lawyer*) and of crooked lawyers (in *The Partner*), much as *E.R.* fans watch that program to learn about medicine and hospitals.[84] Chinese crime fiction fills this role because China's world of trials, arrests, and prisons seems so professional and yet so inaccessible.

The state calls Chinese trials open, but they are open only to small, pre-elected audiences.[85] And although "cases" loom large in popular imagination, Chinese trained in comparative law deny that China even has casebooks. Instead of cases, 1980s law students read treatises on legal theory. There were a few collections, often classified, of sample cases. In the 1990s the Supreme People's Court and Procuratorate finally published bulky compendiums. But most such casebooks are digests—in law school parlance, hornbooks. Some may even have been conceived as moral admonitions to the public: Do not break these laws. Hence tabloidized case write-ups similar to popular fiction flourish. They serve general readers starved for information about social conflict and the legal system. Some are still admonitory.[86]

One looks in vain for regularly published Chinese case law. The Supreme People's Court was allowed to publish communiques for public consumption only in 1985. These are condensed opinions from lower courts rewritten by the highest court, sometimes with a notation of "correct" or "absolutely correct," rather like an emperor's rejoinder in vermilion ink. They "usually include little or no legal reasoning" and are not to be cited in later decisions.[87] (Lower courts may write to the Supreme People's Court for guidance.) Prior cases and decisions have three possible fates: to be communicated publicly in gazettes, conveyed to lower courts through internal (classified) channels, or kept secret.

Court opinions in China are in general terser and less given to legal justifications than in common law countries, and there are no dissenting opinions.[88] Indeed, "Chinese legal doctrine insists that courts cannot and do not make law."[89] Some scholars feel that they do not even adjudicate.[90] That has always been for the sovereign legislator, which is today in principle the National People's Congress and its Standing Committee, which pass major laws. The State Council enacts less permanent rules—sometimes jointly with the *Party* Central Committee. Sundry state organs freely make up lesser rules in their bailiwicks. In reality, party committees that supervise courts do much of China's adjudication. China really has no case law.

However, many major cases not reported on turned up in another anomaly of the publishing world, besides popular fiction: the monthly periodical *Minzhu yu fazhi* (Democracy and legal system), founded in 1979 by the Shanghai Law Society and East China Institute of Politics and Law but run by veteran journalists with a nose for news, from major corruption cases too hot for the press to human interest stories about two-timing and wife-beating. They were printed in monthly columns with names like "Daode fating" (The court of morality) that resemble articles in the *National Enquirer*. In the absence of official case write-ups, Carlos Wing-hung Lo was able to analyze China's 1980s jurisprudence by using *Democracy and Legal System* as his main source.[91]

In any event, "law," in life as in literature, is not just a compilation of statutes and cases. It includes our broad and conflicting concepts of justice, or what James Boyd White calls "enacted experience."[92] This book examines both kinds of law in Chinese literature: depictions of the police and legal system, and broader revelations of China's multifarious conceptions of just what "law" may be.

LAW AS LITERATURE

Study of law *as* literature finds new ways of reading statutes and legal opinions, either to interpret them for use or to "deconstruct" them. This can be done with Chinese law. Robin West again points out a methodological problem: if one assumes that adjudication is simply interpretation of texts of statutes (a hermeneutic exercise familiar to literary critics), one might overlook the element of political choice made by the judge. This could lead to a misleading conclusion that adjudication is either natural (objectively made—the school of Owen Fiss) or arbitrary (subjective—the school of Stanley Fish).[93]

Analyzing Chinese law as an implementation of politics is all too easy; addressing its literariness is more challenging. China's own conceit about its law is that all eventualities have been foreseen by legislation, obviating interpretation. Hence one could follow Robin West and subject Chinese jurisprudence to the aesthetics of myth criticism: jurisprudentially, Chinese law is "natural" or God-given (Dao-given) and so, aesthetically, it is "romantic." Most Chinese fiction about the law popularly seen as "traditional" does indeed tend toward the romantic, the chivalric, and the melodramatic—it is either respectful of authority or opposed to it—revolutionary, "outlaw."[94]

However that may be, Chinese codes, statutes, and cases (which were of importance before communism) have a narrative aspect; Chinese law and literature may have influenced each other since ancient times. Popular case narratives that are neither clearly fiction nor nonfiction are but the tip of the iceberg.

Chapter One begins with the suspenseful but derivative forms of crime fiction that emerged at the very start of the post-Mao thaw and their relatively simple perspectives on crime and the law. Chapters Two through Four indicate the march of time up to and past the post-Mao thaw, and they are also thematic. They deal with tradition, the problem of being in the shadow of the West, and communist politics, three successive forces potentially lethal to adversary law and adversarial literature. Yet the conclusion, Chapter Five, finds as a legacy of the Deng Xiaoping era major works that are of artistic merit *and* support a lively adversarialism in both law and literature. The works selected were written after 1984, the year that George Orwell made into a symbol of Big Brother and the very year that China's police and judiciary began to realize the ultimate police-state fantasy: writing China's crime fiction themselves.

CHAPTER ONE

Origins

What was a good PRC crime story like in the early thaw, 1978–80? It was a rare moment: the first time public interest in crime and official misconduct could hold its own against communism, and the last time communist pieties could hold their own in Chinese popular fiction. The wonder is that any good crime stories were written after so long a ban. This chapter finds a partial explanation in the stories' generic nature. Old kinds of plots and heroes provided sure formulas for pleasing audiences.

There were two major genres or subgenres, here termed the "whodunit with Chinese characteristics" and the "penal law melodrama." As the names imply, Western and ancient Chinese formulas loom larger in them than "social reality." Maybe that is how they gained popularity while standing so firmly on the side of the police. Yet the police were still not satisfied. They would intervene later to make Chinese crime fiction more "realistic."

PRC writing about crime in 1978–80 was frankly imitative, but then, much of the world—Europe, Latin America, Japan—had originally taken up Poe and Conan Doyle as foreign imports to be copied. It was later that Latin American detective fiction found its own modernist path under Jorge

Borges, Carlos Fuentes, and others,[1] and that postwar Japan, Holland, and Sweden developed the "social" detective novel or police procedural. Post-Mao China is unique because of the speed with which it recapitulated the passage from imitation to differentiation, and because its authors had a native tradition to consider. The latter was once itself an international standard; it inspired Japanese imitations as early as the seventeenth century.

Some Soviet "KGB" stories were available in Chinese before the Sino-Soviet split. Exemplary "social detective stories" by Matsumoto Seichō and other postwar Japanese writers were also introduced in the 1950s and early 1960s. Their police heroes seemed less capitalistic and less alien than Sherlock Holmes. That was only natural; the Chinese police organization today still reflects certain practices originally perfected in Meiji Japan and by the darker regimes that followed. But postwar Soviet and Japanese mysteries were themselves influenced by the whodunit formula, and it is unclear how deep an impression they left on China after they were banned during the Cultural Revolution, so they are not necessarily responsible for the peculiarities of China's new post-Mao crime fiction.[2]

Chinese crime stories also provide bearings on PRC legal realities. Some works might be called, in law-school parlance, "law stories":[3] tales about the law outside the legal system's own discourse. The state sanctioned them in the early 1980s, when there was still an ancien régime to defeat. It may also have hoped that fiction, as propaganda, might take the place of lawsuits—be another Court of Morality like the sensational and accusatory human interest and letters-to-the-editor columns that harped on social wrongdoing in the press. Accusation—"exposure"—was the sine qua non of non-Maoist "realistic" fiction in China. In court, accusation could be tantamount to conviction. A distinctive feature of Chinese courts today is that they have special offices to receive petitioning visitors and complaint letters, even from litigants whose trials and appeals are over.[4]

The state miscalculated. It was dissident writers like Bai Hua and Liu Binyan who revived literature as the people's "most illustrious tribunal," with themselves as the "supreme impartial judges."[5] Yet stories cannot replace open trials, and pressure on verdicts from any quarter, even "the masses," is still pressure. By the late 1980s, Bai Hua and Liu Binyan's old kind of adversarialism, addressed to the Chinese Communist Party (CCP) itself, was passé. Many later writers simply left the party out of it.

THE SETTING

Deng Xiaoping acceded to power at the Third Plenum of the Eleventh Central Committee of the CCP, 1978, consequent upon the death in September 1976 of Mao and the arrest a month later of the Gang of Four, a metonym for the radicalism ascendant since the Cultural Revolution. It was Deng's virtual coup d'état that allowed a new Chinese literature and a new Chinese legal system.

Literature, ideological education, and culture—all branches of propaganda, in the CCP view—seemed to have two paradigms of change. One envisioned gradual liberation. As Deng gathered power, anything seemed possible; perhaps Mao himself would be repudiated (though in the end he was declared only 30 percent incorrect). Crime reporters point to 1980 as the year when the press began to report on common crimes.[6] Creative literature was already far ahead. Some works were shocking because they were politically dissident; their young authors vied to become "groundbreaking heroes" in taboo realms of subject matter. Other works shocked because they had no evident politics, no "point." That made them avant-garde or difficult, officially unfriendly to "workers, peasants, and soldiers." The first non-Maoist fiction with a "point"—the "literature of the wounded" written in 1977–78—blamed nearly all problems on influence from the Gang of Four. By 1979 those works had already yielded to a "literature of introspection" censuring current policies, foundational state myths, and the communist system. Eroticism, the last frontier, was breached in 1986.[7]

The other paradigm was of alternating periods of clampdown and latitude, in synchronization with political campaigns as in Mao's era. Writers reluctantly admitted the continuation of this pattern after Democracy Wall and its unofficial magazines were put out of action beginning in 1979. Deng Xiaoping began 1980 by criticizing "bourgeois liberalization" and announcing that four kinds of freedom of expression would be deleted from the state constitution. A campaign was waged against a screenplay by Bai Hua in 1981, and a bigger one against "spiritual pollution" opened in late 1983. Yet that movement was unsuccessful in mobilizing intellectuals to attack each other. Marxist ideology was quickly expiring. However, the June 4, 1989, massacre led to a longer cultural freeze.[8]

Reform in the legal sphere was more complex, for it impinged directly on

China's governance. The changes seemed dramatic because so many previous attempts to establish legal institutions in the PRC had been reversed. In 1949, the PRC repealed all Nationalist (Kuomintang, or KMT) laws—the "Six Codes." No replacement ever came in Mao's lifetime: no code of criminal, civil, or administrative law, just a constitution, finally, in 1954 (the first of four so far), and statutes such as the Marriage Law. A criminal code reached its thirty-third draft in 1963. It was never enacted owing to another wave of political zeal that culminated in the Cultural Revolution.[9]

With Soviet influence had come lawyers and a more active procuracy in 1953–57. Trial judges were mostly just army veterans, their verdicts decided for them by court presidents in a collegial "adjudication committee" before the trial. (Such a committee is described below, in the film scenario *Before the Bench and Behind the Scenes*.) Only a fraction of China's judges had postsecondary education; legal training was not compulsory for them until 1983. Citizens had always feared judges, but they were and are lesser administrative cadres in the communist bureaucracy, of insecure tenure and not much more exalted than local traffic court judges in the West. The government does not yet deem courts important enough to give them their own budget.[10]

In name, and only in name, the procuracy and judiciary had originally been "independent," though only from police and other state organs at their own level, not from organs above—or from the party committee at the same level. Individual judges could not act independently of their court president. Even the theoretical independence of judicial bodies from other organs at their level was judged incorrect in the Anti-Rightist campaign of 1957–58. In 1959 the Ministry of Justice was abolished outright. The number of lawyers dwindled from 3,000 in 1957 to precisely four in 1958–80, says jurist Ma Rongjie. The USSR had 100,000 lawyers in 1970.[11]

In the late 1950s, police, judiciary, and procuracy (prosecutorial) functions were simply merged in a unitary law enforcement apparatus typically housed at police headquarters and commanded from above by local political-legal cadres of the Chinese Communist Party. They were the party's finest, but only because the former Nationalist regime's concept of "political-legal" work had evolved into the sacred communist duty of protecting the revolution: security, not jurisprudence.[12] Enemies of the people were tried in batches at mass trials.[13]

In the Cultural Revolution, procuracy was abolished; it was deleted from the 1975 state constitution. Courts "still existed but functioned only sparingly";[14] many disappeared. That left the police, whom Mao attacked, commanding Red Guards to "smash the public security, procuracy, and judiciary." *People's Daily* editorialized "In Praise of Lawlessness." The police regrouped in the 1970s, replacing ad hoc rebel and army-led security, militia, and judicial organs like those depicted in stories by Yang Rongfang and Pang Taixi (related below). But police morale hit an all-time low in 1978–79, when they were blamed for suppressing the (first) Tiananmen Incident of April 5, 1976, which ended in the second purge of Deng Xiaoping.[15]

Once in power, Deng suddenly rebuilt legal institutions back to 1965, or even beyond 1955 standards. The PRC passed its first criminal and criminal procedure codes in 1979. The Supreme People's Procuratorate was refounded, as was the Ministry of Justice. It was to assist the courts, oversee mediation and lawyers, and promote lay and professional legal education. More codes followed, including a revised criminal code and a Lawyers Law in 1996.[16] Law schools and law departments reopened, though lawyers in the 1980s were paid by the state and were also state cadres, bound by the same velvet chains of access to privileged information as any cadre.[17] Defendants in criminal trials could ask a friend or relative to be their "defense," but only a small fraction retain a lawyer even today. Training lawyers took time; only 73 were at work in Beijing in 1981, and they had to work in mediation and serve party and state organs and enterprises besides criminal defendants. The number of lawyers in China finally passed the 100,000 mark in 1997.[18]

In 1982 the state promulgated a civil procedure code (rev. 1991), though it gave up on a full civil code, settling for 1986 General Provisions that left huge gaps, particularly on property. Yet fundamental uncodified concepts were taught at law schools in treatises from the same German tradition as Nationalist China's, which is still used on Taiwan. Says William C. Jones, these assume that "society is composed of discrete entities called persons (natural and juristic). . . . The law enforces their individual decisions and holds them responsible for their individual acts."[19]

Still, many laws were instrumental, one more device by which the state could work its will on people.[20] Officials did foster a new legal culture. Propaganda after 1979 emphasized legal consciousness, equality before the law (which was not, however, reinscribed in the constitution until 1982), and more trials for criminals. "Redressing mishandled cases" (*pingfan*) was a ubiquitous theme in the early 1980s; plays and operas about final justice for the legally aggrieved were enjoyed even by conservatives as symbolic of their victimization under and turning the tables on the Gang of Four by "legal" redress. "Rule of law" was praised, not only against crime and social disorder but also against legal amateurism, the identification of offenders by class background, and "rule of man," meaning local or national rule by strongmen. At first that simply meant the Gang of Four; Red Guards claimed that Mao had said "depend on the rule of man, not the rule of law"; precepts of the ancient Legalist school that Mao had praised were not taken to heart. Deng, in contrast, spoke up for "democracy and rule of law," though Red Guards ("Li Yizhe") had preceded the leaders on this too, calling in 1973 for "socialist democracy and legal system" and "rule of law." Recognizing that unchecked cadre power had given the masses a "hunger for law," the party and state in post-Mao times increasingly draped their acts in legal symbolism.[21]

Enactment of true rule of law still required changes in politics and ideology transcending even legal culture. Law was in theory a tool of dictatorship by which one class ruled another, and China's "rule of law" was said to be part of its "socialist spiritual civilization."[22] Indeed, state-promulgated *laws* were not society's only "laws." Lower-level rules and regulations adopted and enforced by bureaucracies did not always have less legal force than laws of the state.[23] Party "policy" was still called "the soul of law"; bureaucracies treated it as an imperial edict, as if it were law.[24] Major policies were at least publicized, unlike regulations, some of which were secret until one broke them. What direction would law take? Without *stare decisis* (the tradition of following juristic precedents), who would apply the law in specific cases? Chinese fiction would offer some suggestions.

MODERN STORIES ABOUT CRIME STORIES, CHINESE AND WESTERN

Post-Mao fiction is of mixed origins. The marvel is the formulaic purity of the era's first crime stories—how fully they embody, typically without parody, either the Judge Bao or the Sherlock Holmes tradition.

Before 1984, China had no regular genre magazines or full-length novels of crime fiction. It was not the subject of theoretical criticism (*pinglun*), the sine qua non of Chinese genre formation in the view of critics.[25] Contents pages of journals did not tag stories by genre; there was uncertainty about what to call crime stories even in the mid-1980s. It was by story titles that readers found their favorite reading matter. "The Case of the Three Front Teeth," "The Death of Bai Yingying," and "The Murder Happened Late on a Saturday Night" signaled the Sherlock Holmes tradition. Even an ellipsis like "The Lady Who Knocked at Dusk" might tip off an aficionado. "The Female Head Judge," "Public Procurator from Beijing," and "Upholder of the Law" evoked latter-day Judge Baos. "Save Her" was in a subgenre about youthful offenders. "Fellow Prisoner" and "Blood-Stained Magnolias Below the Big Wall" promised exposure of prison conditions ("Big Wall" is the Chinese equivalent of "Big House").[26] "The Strange Case on Taoyuan Street" suggested a Western-style whodunit, but "strange" sent mixed signals about possible ghosts or manifestations of the uncanny familiar in ancient Chinese fiction. Some stories had illustrations that gave them away—showing uniformed police, judges on the bench, or "perps" in handcuffs. The time was not yet ripe to show criminals as armed and dangerous, but a common grabber on the first page was a line-drawing montage of "crime scene photographs," usually with one of a body on the floor.

Meantime, information and modern myths about native and foreign crime fiction were gaining currency. Let us examine these "stories of the stories" before addressing scholarly refinements. The popular-culture history of the Western whodunit was soon as well known in China as in the West.

"The story goes" that Edgar Allan Poe invented modern Western crime fiction in the form of the analytical detective story. Sir Arthur Conan Doyle brought it worldwide acclaim. Agatha Christie, Dorothy Sayers, Ngaio Marsh, Margery Allingham, S. S. Van Dine, and a host of others created its Golden Age. Meanwhile followers of Conan Doyle created a Golden Age for the selfsame genre in Chinese after the turn of the century, and Edogawa Rampō fathered Japan's version in 1923. It was one great chain of master plot-makers, linking all Western-style crime fiction to intellect, science, and individual creative genius. Ellery Queen gave this ostensible straight-line development a tidy historicist twist when he put Edogawa Rampo's work in the period between Agatha Christie and Edgar Wallace.[27]

Crime fiction in English subsequently splayed out in many directions:

into the hard-boiled private-eye detection of Hammett and Chandler, the police procedural, detective comedy of manners, metaphysical detection, and true crime. When Latin American detective fiction pursued parodic, antiheroic, and antidetective angles, that was a common international reaction to the mainstream. North American readers in an age of commercialism and postmodernism went on to legal thrillers, pathologists' memoirs, serial murderer mysteries, and thrilling or socially edifying adventures of gritty, humorous, mystical, sensitive, gay, politically conscious, female, and ethnic minority detectives.[28] Meanwhile, Simenon, Jack Webb, and Ed McBain created a taste for lower-middle-class antibureaucratic bureaucrats.[29] At the other end were historical mysteries and re-evocations of interwar classics considered nostalgic even in their own day. They became a subgenre, "the cozy."[30] From the standpoint of a China suddenly obsessed with modernization and catch-up, this too was a tale of linear development, of scientific analysis spreading to an ever wider variety of modern subject matter—informative subject matter.[31]

China's traditional crime fiction was ancient. It could not be attributed to individual geniuses, for its authors were anonymous, but it could be traced to the collective genius of the Chinese folk—hypothetical creators, in the Song dynasty or earlier, of a nonextant oral crime literature. This old crime fiction was now valued in modern terms—as a "popular" genre embodying popular justice.

What linked late imperial crime fiction to ancient times was a name passed down in history: *gongan* or "court case" literature—or such was its meaning in the Ming dynasty. In the Song, *gongan* referred to a genre of puppet drama and a genre of oral fiction. Specimens do not survive, but aficionados like to think that they were about crimes and cases. This takes a leap of faith. There were Yuan dramas featuring crime themes and Judge Bao himself, but they were probably not called *gongan* in their day. "*Gongan*" has not always referred to court case plots in modern times, not to speak of the ancient and middle imperial eras.

One can still imagine that the subject matter of crimes and cases, if not necessarily Yuan and Ming plots and forms, have ancient Chinese origins. Three early stories of the *huaben* type, which may date from the Yuan and perhaps have Song origins, have good crime case plots and even a concealed perpetrator—though one can turn it around and note that the pleasures of these stories are not formulaic.[32] Absorbing plots about crimes and cases are found again in northern dramas (*zaju*) of the Yuan and early Ming, and in chantefables (narratives that intersperse songs with prose) of the fifteenth century. From the later part of the sixteenth century come the famous collections of short court case stories that were called *gongan* in their era.

They have savior judges, most famously Judge Bao: in Chinese, Bao Gong (Lord Bao) or Bao Longtu (Academician Bao, of the Longtu Pavilion). Both clever and virtuous, both detective and avenger—hero to the humble— this character is based on the historical figure Bao Zheng (999–1062), who served as prefect at the capital, censor, and fiscal intendant for the Song emperor Renzong. Some of Bao Zheng's memorials are extant, and he appears in ancient histories and casebooks.[33] But it is his legend that was elaborated in the Yuan dramas and Ming fiction, most famously the late Ming story collection *Longtu gongan* (Longtu's cases).

In the Qing, stories about Lord Bao circulated in *baojuan* (precious scrolls), oral performances called *zidishu* and *tanci*, operas, folklore, and finally in epic swashbuckling novels of the late nineteenth century.[34] The novels were called *gongan*, but they so differ in genre and subject matter from any Ming story that readers now call them *wuxia xiaoshuo* (chivalric, knight-errant, or martial-arts novels).[35] The first to feature Lord Bao was *San xia wu yi* (Three heroes and five gallants, 1879), revised as *Qi xia wu yi* (Seven heroes and five gallants, 1889), with sequels. To the modern scholar Hu Shi, Lord Bao was simply an icon who picked up kudos and legends like lint.[36]

Judges Peng, Li, and others likewise became famous in the later Qing, in long "*gongan*" (here, "martial-arts") novels bearing their names, and in Peking operas that often predated the novels. Most novels were knockoffs. *Shi gongan* or *Judge Shi's Cases* (1798) seems to be the earliest, though Wilt Idema and Lloyd Haft identify Judge Bao's own *Three Heroes and Five Gallants* as the watershed, since it was printed with lithography and enjoyed a greatly expanded readership.[37] In most such works, the judge in the title is one of many heroes, symbolizing top-down justice like an imperial figurehead. Crime interests are crowded out by adventure, intrigue, and fighting. Before the Qing was over, readers associated astute detection more with Sherlock Holmes than with any Chinese judge save Lord Bao, thanks to translations and imitations of Conan Doyle in classical Chinese. Martial-arts novels continued on their own path in the first half of the twentieth century, until all the genres were indiscriminately banned after 1949.

THE "REAL STORIES" OF CRIME FICTION

Scholarship has modified the popular culture accounts of these traditions, without always changing the main narrative or the genealogical impulse itself. Tracing analytical detection to the Old Testament and *Oedipus Rex* may be a stretch, but crime and detection did not begin with Poe.[38] Stephen Knight feels that crime fiction's social function (ideological consolation that criminals will be identified) entered literature before detection did.[39]

Some argue that the classical Western detective genre early on bifurcated into the detective story and the detective novel.[40] When Conan Doyle revived analytical detection as the main generic interest, Wilkie Collins, in *The Woman in White*, had already created the detective novel with character development and social interest. Many genre boundaries were crossed before Poe (between fiction and nonfiction, for instance) and after Ellery Queen (indeed, we call them crossovers). The French (Eugène François Vidocq, Émile Gaboriau, Honoré de Balzac, Victor Hugo), especially, blurred the boundary between fact and fiction, criminal and detective. Holmes was not the first Victorian detective; women figured among his contemporary rivals. And analytical detection in fiction appears, upon examination, really to be intuitive and solipsistic.[41]

English and American writings, which dominated the world through their large native readership and copious translations, were only part of the picture. Arsène Lupin, Maurice Leblanc's French gentleman-burglar turned detective, played a close second fiddle to Sherlock Holmes in precommunist China and in Taiwan, as he did in Francophone nations and perhaps briefly in the United States.[42] The Chinese are now better informed than most Westerners about Japanese and Russian detectives too.

There is even more to debunk in the long Chinese genealogies of *gongan* and hero judges. "*Gongan*" does not refer to one genre, tradition, or even a single kind of subject matter. It is hard to think of written texts as "popular" in a mostly illiterate society, or as uninfluenced by narratives about crimes and judges in the classical language. Oral sources for stories may be recent.

Chinese folklorists still collected oral tales about Lord Bao in the 1980s.[43] To many Chinese, he was a deity, and at least one temple dedicated to him reopened in the 1980s.[44] Mao Zedong's own 1927 "Report on an Investigation of the Peasant Movement in Hunan," which extols idol-smashing, adds that peasants spared icons of Lord Bao only. Ghostwriters who made Mao's writings more politically correct did not delete this favorable reference to the "feudal judge."[45]

The relations between even the earliest extant *huaben* and Song storytelling are problematic. China's greatest talents imitated the storytellers' style as a convention. As to serial collections of stories about particular judges, the Ming had them, but it also had collections featuring several good officials. Famous literary judges had their ups and downs from century to century, and they exchanged stories. The character of Judge Bao himself is inconsistent. In some works he is simply wise and incorruptible, even subject to ridicule; in others he is superhuman and divine, an immortal judge of dead souls.[46] In the late Qing novels he retains powers in the other world but sometimes has to be prompted by his friends, his protectors, and even his wife.

Apart from the late Qing chivalric novels, most fiction about Bao that is read today dates to a mere twenty-year boom in court case publication in the late Ming, Patrick Hanan notes.[47] It was not repeated (nor were all its works kept in print) until Sherlock Holmes translations stimulated something similar after 1900. A Chinese crime story editor who sees shades of Judge Bao in China's new popular fiction likens *him* to the sheriff in American Westerns: a brave and trustworthy marshal, judge, and jury all rolled up in one man![48]

The genre concept is diffuse even in the briefer Western tradition. It was only in the Golden Age, thanks to the theologically inclined Dorothy Sayers and Msgr. Ronald Knox, that detective-story writers were enjoined to play fair with the reader, ultimately leading to commandments grouped by tens—"decalogues."[49] That term was facetious, but Golden Age plots grew ever more ingenious in order to dance in the authors' self-imposed chains. Conan Doyle, the master, was never so fettered. Some of his mysteries involved conspiracies, like the Ku Klux Klan in "The Five Orange Pips," or a surrogate for the Italian-American Black Hand brotherhood in "The Adventure of the Red Circle." He resorted to a criminal mastermind, Moriarty, and let Holmes go in disguise—taboo to Golden Age strict constructionists. Many of his plots are simply not whodunits. But so strong is the aura of his detective, Holmes, that one thinks of his adventures as the classic "detective stories" between Poe and Christie anyway.[50]

Indeed, the archetypes were plain enough to inspire imitations. Post-structuralist and postmodernist theoreticians attempt to "destabilize" or "problematize" literary types,[51] but detective fiction is relatively immune, as "the most frequently and most intensively theorized of all popular genres."[52] It was self-referential already in the time of Poe, each story alluding to or cannibalizing its predecessors. Defensive battles against critics like Edmund Wilson and purifications through decalogues made the genre still more self-conscious about its form.[53]

With its neat division between what the Russian formalists called *syuzhet* (plot) and *fabula* (story line), wrapped up in a recapitulation of the true story, the *fabula*, at the end, its doubly conceived plots made detective fiction a paradigm of narratology to structuralists, as it was of psychological workings to Lacan. The semiotician Umberto Eco and the French culture theorist and psychoanalyst Julia Kristeva have written detective fiction.[54] Poe is seen as a precursor of Jacques Derrida for his interest in codes and the "play of language."[55] Poststructuralists laud not only popular culture, but also writing without symbolic or ironic hidden content, and metonymy above metaphor. Detective fiction exemplifies all of that;[56] Michael Holquist and Stefano Tani argue that detective fiction inspired much of postmodern creativity.[57] "Cultural studies" and ideological critiques use the genre for their project of finding common elite and popular "signifying practices."[58] Chinese crime stories should be grist for their mills.

FORMULA ONE:
THE WESTERN CLASSICAL DETECTIVE STORY

The Sherlock Holmes tradition is really that of Edgar Allan Poe, who as far as many later writers are concerned did "invent" what is variously called the whodunit, the puzzle story, or the classical, Anglo-American, or analytical detective story. By one count, 32 genre conventions originated in the three C. August Dupin stories: "The Murders in the Rue Morgue" (1841), "The Mystery of Marie Rogêt" (1842), and "The Purloined Letter" (1844). Here are eight of twenty found in "The Rue Morgue" alone:[59]

[1] the eccentric private detective with a genius for applying pure inductive and deductive reasoning to human behavior, [2] the less acute friend who narrates the story, [3] an extraordinary crime such as, in this case, a locked-room mystery, [4] the open display of clues giving the reader a fair chance to solve the puzzle before the detective does, [5] the need to relieve an innocent person of suspicion, [6] the detective's visit to the scene of the crime, [7] the battle of wits with the official police, [8] and the final summary scene in which the surprising but satisfactory solution is revealed.

Scholars have noted the incongruous Gothic origins of this rationalistic genre and the interest of the later master, Conan Doyle, in spiritualism.[60] It was odd that Dupin, the first series detective, was so respectable, since detectives in life and in popular European fiction originated as spies and "thief-takers."[61] David Der-wei Wang marvels that a good name was the most precious asset of ancient Chinese series detectives like Judge Bao, yet in late Qing novels they stooped to enlist knights-errant in their cause.[62] In the West, the two sides of the law switched places earlier, but the order was reversed: the peacemakers went from "compromised" to "pure and detached." Later, hard-boiled dicks would walk on the other side of the law again.

It remained for Conan Doyle to make the Great Detective a true mythic character, more eccentric than before, and add conventions like the opening gambit or "preamble" in which he deduces amazingly detailed and perfectly irrelevant facts before the game is afoot, establishing his genius in advance.[63] Conan Doyle also gave the less-acute friend and narrator a personality and a name: Watson. Holmes certainly promoted an adversarial style of truth-seeking. Yet as feminists point out, socially he was paternalistic.[64]

Late Victorian "MacGuffins," to use Alfred Hitchcock's term for plot-generative devices, were typically lost or stolen precious objects and irreplaceable documents leading to them, like wills.[65] By the interwar Golden Age, though, murder was the obligatory crime—shocking murder, described in grisly, clinical terms, the more out of place because of the idyllic setting, most famously a vicarage or English country estate. An aristocratic (in America, upper-middle-class) setting is often probed by its own class, or by middle- or lower-middle-class cops and private eyes who are no longer coded *amateurs* in the upper-class sense.[66] Readers selected favorite subgenres and authors for their style, their specialized social and geographical settings (dialects and local color), and their apparent expertise—from campanology (bell-changing, in Sayers's *The Nine Tailors*) to esoterica of poisons (in

Christie, who knew her pharmacology).[67] Today, readers are loyal to Chicago and Boston settings (Sara Paretsky, David J. Walker, Robert B. Parker), high-tech international crime (Tom Clancy), even lawyering (Scott Turow, John Grisham).

Ruth Rendell and a few others provided psychological interests, but for many authors, character development languished while plots grew ever more complicated, making detective fiction, in the words of Frye, "a ritual drama around a corpse in which a wavering finger of social condemnation passes over a group of 'suspects' and finally settles on one."[68] Delineation of character—that is, of the suspects—became just another avenue for exploring occupations, hobbies, quirks, legal motives (e.g., inheriting a legacy), and exotic technologies. It was a direction bound to appeal to a Chinese popular reader in an age when technology, gadgets, and foreign things were new.

Let us "deduce," then, how a whodunit with turn-of-the-1980s "Chinese characteristics" might differ. This is to be sure a conceit, as in the fiction itself, because these are deductions after the fact.

First, one would expect more politics, or engagement. Suspense, analytical focus, and fine detail in the Anglo-American classics so overshadow the social criticism found in "higher" nineteenth-century European novels that social comment was once thought to be excess baggage in the whodunit. It was held that it attenuated suspense and distracted the reader from the puzzle—from matching wits with the author. G. D. H. Cole, a famous Labour Movement leader in England, ignored social themes in the whodunits he wrote.[69] In China too, Liang Qichao differentiated the detective story and the political novel in the 1890s, and they became rivals. The political novel lost. But the Japanese, Dutch, and others have created strong modern mysteries with social themes; Victorian, Edwardian, and interwar whodunit writers must have eschewed higher social-political criticism for their own reasons.[70] As the classics become dated, period pieces, their rich atmosphere actually accentuates their social nature as comedies of manners.[71]

Chinese writers, like other detective writers, had three options when it came to politics. They could put jarring, status-quo communist politics into their story. That was the only fully nondissident option. They could, like Cole, forbear to manipulate reader interest in politics, though that interest was already so well cultivated in China. That option was dissident like "misty poetry"—"putting art above politics." Or they could deploy a little non-communist politics: social criticism that hurt, from the Chinese discourse of "realism." That was deliberate political dissidence.

As Westernized stories, in which the comedy of manners is trained on a gallery of suspects, Chinese whodunits could represent political wounds with simple points of description, like scars and limps. Political stereotypes in conventional (Maoist) circles, which already found people suspect on grounds of wealth, occupation, and class background, could be amplified to make a red herring, or, contrarily, a very, very Red "least likely suspect." These conventional class stereotypes were being turned upside down (verdicts reversed, *pingfan*) in life and in vanguard serious fiction, so anything was possible. Former heroes like communist cadres were now all too plausible culprits—or material for red herrings. Under Maoist literary policy it had been an offense just to make an innocent person look guilty or to exonerate someone who by all outer ("objective") signs "ought" to be guilty. This used to make sense to the public, since real crime was so rare. In the words of the police interrogator remembered by so many formerly imprisoned Chinese memoirists: "If you're not guilty, what are you doing in jail?" It was the mission of the whodunit to question that commonplace, if only as a matter of form.

As works of social criticism in a more Japanese-style whodunit tradition, Chinese authors might focus on cadre corruption and the social decadence of major suspects. Or they could use it only as "social background," "local color," part of the "information dividend." Instead of disquisitions on toxicology, they could offer a little putative inside information on persecutions by the Gang of Four, or something stronger and more contemporary. But it was Cole's apolitical option that most Chinese whodunit writers chose.

The genre still requires banishing moral sentiment. John Cawelti builds a wall between the detective tradition, which aestheticizes murder even as it describes the corpse in shocking detail, and melodrama, which manipulates moral sentiments. So does the team of Boileau-Narcejac. They characterize the sentiments as "not lived but dreamed—fabricated, thanks to situations that run counter to nature: the father cursing his son and so forth" (a very Chinese nightmare, that).[72] This book follows those critics' example by separating post-Mao whodunits from penal melodramas. But sentimentalism and didacticism are so strong in twentieth-century Chinese fiction, including Maoist formulas, that one can expect to see traces of them even in whodunits.

Another expected Chinese modification would be "chapter-driven" suspense: division of the story, however short, into chapters, each perhaps with an intriguing title, and each ending in a cliffhanger. It is a traditional device from China's great Ming and Qing vernacular novels, perhaps so strong in China's modern whodunits (whose biggest surprise is at the end) because Cheng Xiaoqing and other precommunist purveyors of the classical Western detective story had so well combined the two devices before.

Any whodunit, East or West, needs a Great Detective. Perhaps because the window of creative freedom was so short, beginning to close already in 1980, Chinese series detectives were rare. And Chinese detection is done by the police. There were no private detectives until 1993, when a few retired policemen set up an agency.[73] George Dove reminds us that few Americans have ever seen a private eye either.[74] But imagination and the media can fill in.[75] The main Western impact is on the depiction of the police heroes. Contrary to what one might expect, hardly any turn-of-the-1980s Chinese story is a generic "police procedural" whose main interest is interrogations, lab work, stakeouts, and tailings by rotating teams, or that other staple of Chinese police routine, meetings, endless meetings (though they appear in some stories). Authors say that dramatizing the use of informants (*ermu*, "eyes and ears") is forbidden.[76] Then again, most real police work is boring, and murders are seldom clever or even premeditated.

And yet the Chinese Great Police Detective acts like a private eye. He is a hero, which is after all legitimated by traditional and communist values. Formulaic writing erases the low social repute of the police. Chinese cops in fiction can be seen to ratiocinate, act on one case at a time, and follow leads seemingly on their own initiative. T. J. Binyon has called such individualistic cop heroes in Western fiction "professional amateurs."[77] The post-Mao solution was to make the hero cop head of his department, allowing the realism of paramilitary command to dilute the socialist myth of teamwork. The subordinate cops rarely become well-developed characters (any more than they do in the Western whodunit or in socialist realism); neither are they likely to resemble Dr. Watson in becoming an equal or a friend of the head cop.

Post-Mao Chinese society limited some opportunities for fiction while expanding others. Citizens were not very mobile, socially or geographically. There were few guns to murder with, few rare goods to steal, few cars to make a getaway in (or for the police to give chase in), few open but unobserved places to perpetrate a crime or stash a body, and few fortunes to finance a private smuggling operation. There were no vicarages or country estates. Most people still lived in rural villages, while urbanites resided in look-alike apartment blocks. If one had a friend or accomplice over in the evening, the neighborhood granny with surveillance responsibilities over the stairwell might file a report immediately, leading to a visit from a household registration cop. But the Chinese family still offered infinite possibilities. And, early in the 1980s, so did one's work unit, a quasi family in itself.

Murder is the typical crime, but in a China newly captivated by private property, theft is enough to motivate a plot, as in Victorian England. Private fortunes were still rare in the 1980s, so the MacGuffin really *had* better be a rare bauble stolen from a museum, antique shop, or state-owned vault. And society was too prelegal for the subject to be a will—but that era was past by the end of the decade.

Because China was so rural, or perhaps because so many writers originated in or had been sent down to the countryside, one finds a unique type of rural story of murder and detection, like "The Case of the Strange Yuan River Corpse" described below. Soil types, river currents, and crop varieties are clues to peasants. They can identify microregional subdialects and shoe prints; in their locale, shoes are expensive, even the ones made from discarded tires. The village, with its mutual suspicions and collective approach to crime, is a community even more closed than a group of aristocrats and holiday-makers stranded for the weekend on a British estate.

A Model Whodunit: Making Politics Serve the Plot, Not Vice Versa

Wang Hejun's 1980 novella "Mousha fasheng zai Xingqiliu yewan" (The murder happened late on a Saturday night) shows how close to the Western classical genre a Chinese story could get, even under communism.

Wang's mystery takes the apolitical option, "proving," like the Anglo-American classics, that "the social order is not responsible for the crime because it was the act of a particular individual with his own private motives."[78] In China under communism, even private motives might be political. But not this murderer's. The misleading suspects are the political ones—guilty-looking on the political surface of things. Much of the fun thus comes before the unmasking, while the author plays with his political red herrings: people Chinese readers loved to hate. The story deploys Maoist and post-Mao clichés about who makes a good villain but in the end overturns not just political stereotypes of guilty appearances but also the axiom that everything is political to begin with. Hence the real culprit is a genuine surprise, truly "least likely."

"The Murder Happened Late on a Saturday Night" opens with a hideous murder; the corpse of a 25-year-old man is found in a lake. The reader sees it under a bridge, face up and soaked to the bone, hair matted across the forehead and mouth open. In this nearly gunless society, both eyes have been gouged out and there is a hole where the right temple should be. The place whose serenity is so violated by this horrible crime is as close to the idyllic Edwardian estate as a communist society could come: a people's park in springtime, coincidentally the only public place in the late 1970s where one could be alone, as lovers knew. When police later investigate the scene, the narrative voice apostrophizes, "Oh passersby, so serene and composed, if only you knew what a terrible murder occurred in this place" (6).

The deceased is one Liu Zhi, a technician in the No. 4 Plastics Factory and a new party member in his probationary period, affianced to Jiang Yaorong, a dancer. We come upon the body in the company of Yaorong and her mother, Mrs. Jiang, as they are cutting through the park. They are on their way to visit Yaorong's future in-laws, whom they encounter just before they all see a commotion and police activity under the bridge. Liu Zhi had taken Jiang Yaorong to a movie the night before and had not returned; in this age of sexual innocence, his parents thought he might have stayed the night at his future in-laws'. (The young people were chaperoned, even in the theater.) The four relatives-to-be push through the crowd and recognize the corpse, Mrs. Jiang first. Liu's mother faints. His father stands still in shock; "only tears welling up in his eyes betrayed the fact that he was still among the living" (2). None of this escapes the notice of a Great Detective already watching silently nearby.

The tale is told in quasi-documentary style, like *Dragnet*, with each chapter headed by the date and time. The opening chapter is mostly dialogue, and the narration is not wholly omniscient, despite the apostrophe above.

When we first see the crowd gathered around the corpse, we, like the chief investigator, can identify some people only by their looks and actions; we learn their names and relationships later, as the police do. The second chapter ventures into police procedural territory, showing a meeting at the Public Security Bureau. Present are the three investigating cops, a uniformed female police cadre who barks "Report!" before presenting new results from the crime lab, and "concerned leaders" on high, presumably municipal party heads. The cop in charge of the investigation is the stereotypical middle-aged and overworked Gao Si (lit., "High"; "Thinking"). He will direct Li Zhengbin, a dashing young man, and a token young policewoman, Liang Hong. With responsibilities divided up, they can follow several lines of inquiry simultaneously.

Good police work has already turned up in the lake the knife that gouged out the eyes (blood samples have been matched) and lubricating oil that evidently was used to make the decedent slip, it having been found on his shoe soles and on the bridge, with his blood on top of it. The police have questioned park sanitation workers to confirm that the oil spill was new; this genre is realistic and loath to leave any loose ends. A second weapon, a hammer, has been deduced as the cause of the perforated temple, though it was not found at the crime scene. Li Zhengbin is a secondary detective, a "Watson," less seasoned to boot, but by old socialist convention he must be drawn as a Holmes in training; he deduces from the use of the oil that the murderer must not have been stronger than the decedent. Why else bother with the oil? His surmise is intelligent and, as it turns out, both correct and instructive, if only the reader could realize it at the time—though actually adventitious, when one thinks about it. But the "fallacy of the undistributed middle term" is characteristic of the classical genre, as mystery writer R. Austin Freeman pointed out long ago. The conclusion the detective reaches is not the only possible explanation.[79]

An anonymous cop deduces from the coroner's report that the time of death was about 9:00 P.M. But now, Great Detective Gao Si inserts a more brilliant deduction of his own (more brilliant because still more adventitious), and this steers the chapter away from police procedural and back onto the classical track. It also heightens suspense at the end of the chapter, fulfilling the expectations of a Chinese reader with tastes honed by traditional chapter-driven (*zhanghui*) fiction. Without any more evidence, using sheer brainpower, he pronounces that there were two assailants. Why would a person first gouge out Liu's eyes with a knife when he had a hammer to kill him in one blow? And if he had both weapons and did kill with the hammer first, why would he gouge out the eyes afterward? Moreover, why would he discard one weapon (the knife, found in the lake) and not the other? Maybe he meant to take the knife but accidentally dropped it, speculates Ms. Liang Hong. No, Gao Si corrects her, the knife was found so far from the bridge that we can be sure it was deliberately hurled away.[80]

So we are in the classical genre, and Gao Si is a Great Detective, but with "Chinese characteristics." Relations between him and his subordinates are not merely paramilitary but have a collegial quality, like the fictitious comradeship in socialist realism. They are even familial. Gao Si, familiarly called Ol' Gao even by his subordinates, acts as patriarch. He is commanding, all-seeing, rock-steady, quiet, but forgiving, nurturing, educating. He gently instructs and corrects his impetuous young wards, and they look up to him in awe. They delight in reading the signs of his conspicuous ratiocination. They know when he has had an insight, but not what it is or how he arrived at it. The signs are that he pulls at his cigarette or scratches a scar on his chin, a reminder of his rectitude, for he got it from being persecuted in the Cultural Revolution. In the Western genre such personal signs indicate withdrawal for purposes of seeing the world anew, says Elliott Gilbert, who traces them to Western romanticism.[81] Unfortunately, this burdening of smoking habits with psychological significance is so ubiquitous in 1980s Chinese crime stories—an inheritance perhaps from Cheng Xiaoqing's and Sun Liaohong's heroes if not from Holmes himself, with his pipe—that these actions provide at most textual punctuation, not mystery. And though there is much police work—evidence gathering, lab tests, interviewing—the word "clue" is overused. The best clues come from Gao's detached observation and deduction. In the end he solves the crime by calculating how long it takes to walk from one street to another.

The knife is identified as belonging to a fitter who worked in the same factory as the decedent. But he had lent it to one Yang Huting. Yang, victim Liu Zhi, and Liu's fiancée, Jiang Yaorong, had all been high school classmates. Yang is also an ex-boyfriend of Ms. Jiang, whom she left for Liu Zhi when Yang got into a fight and was sent to do a term of reform-through-labor. Yang thus becomes the first suspect. He makes a good one—a brawling hoodlum with a bad attitude who smokes, wears a dirty old army uni-form, and threatened Liu Zhi and Ms. Jiang's mother more than once to get his girl back. But before his subordinates get carried away with speculation, the Great Detective ends the chapter enigmatically yet coolly with the con-clusion: "Maybe Yang Huting is one of the murderers" (7).

At Yang's house, the suspect looks guilty four times over. He has a bad attitude, lies that he knows nothing about the knife, and has a hammer in his knapsack; then there is his prison record. Yang says he lent the dagger again, to one Hu Weijun, but by now his own mother suspects him. Why did *Yang* borrow the knife? Because the police took away his own, he ad-mits. Li Zhengbin pronounces him incorrigible. Yet the formula reader re-alizes it would be just too obvious, not to mention anticlimactic, for a punk like this to be the guilty one. With fate itself arrayed against him, he looks like a victim.

In fact it was not so fashionable for authors in 1980 to assume the worst of people with prison records, for they might have been incarcerated by the Gang of Four. And another dash of social-manners commentary adds to morally exculpatory sympathy for the wretch. His father was a cadre perse-cuted until he committed suicide in the Cultural Revolution, now posthu-mously rehabilitated (owing to a *pingfan* or reversal of the previous verdict on him). The boy himself was a good Communist Youth Leaguer in high school. He went bad only after being sent down to the countryside after graduation. Then again, when young Ms. Jiang is interviewed in the next chapter, she reveals that she was escorted home not by the deceased but only by her neighbor (since her mother was sick), and she ran into a suspi-cious person: Yang Huting. So maybe Yang lied about having given away the dagger?

Yet the finger of suspicion also begins to hover over Hu Weijun. He like-wise looks plenty guilty, first by circumstance: he too was spurned by Jiang Yaorong and had vowed to get her anyway. Mrs. Jiang had even promised her daughter's hand to him because he was such a good match. Hu is also marked by politics, only this time by the newborn stereotypes of *post*-Mao politics. They call for the reader to suspect the very worst of those in power, who might after all have been installed by the ancien régime. Hu Weijun is the son of a general—the deputy commander of the local military region. With such a father, Li Zhengbin thinks, even if Hu is guilty, no one will dare sign a warrant for his arrest. Twenty-five-year-old Hu Weijun was himself in the army (thanks to pull from his father, one assumes), entered the party, and is now working in the Organization Department of the Communist Youth League Municipal Committee just a year after his demobilization. Spoiled children of high cadres were stereotypical villains in 1979–80 "serious" fiction exposing political crimes of the ancien régime, and Hu Weijun fits the type, being arrogant, quick to lean on his family's clout, and spoiled by his mother, so the story goes. It makes him a good suspect, but the post-Mao politics is not milked for political purposes; it is simply used to make the character look suspicious. Gao Si is not ironic when he initially proclaims, with detachment: "His political bearing is good" (12). Moreover, a match of blood types just now reveals that the concealed hammer in Yang Huting's knapsack was the murder weapon. (Liang Hong returns to Yang's house on her own authority and in effect *steals* it for evidence, when no one is looking.) Yet Gao Si remains cool, loath to jump to conclusions.

A breakthrough comes when a servant at the Hu mansion testifies to having seen Hu leave before the time of the murder and come back afterward with the knife. Yang, for his part, was seen drinking in a bar, after having been spotted and called into Mrs. Jiang's home; she had tried to warn him off her daughter again. So the police go to interview Hu Weijun in jail. He wears a Western-cut suit (bad), lies about the knife (very bad), saying he does not recognize it, and is disdainful of the police (very, very bad). He challenges their "right" to detain him and asks to call military headquarters, which he assumes can get him released. Finally, in all arrogance, he admits that he gouged out Liu Zhi's eyes, adding that Liu had it coming to him. He still defies the police to put him away, since he did not actually kill the victim.

So who did kill the blinded Liu Zhi? Yang Huting and his mother claim that the murder hammer appeared in their courtyard the day after the murder. Ol' Gao sees Ms. Jiang and her mother out for a stroll and has a flash of insight. Subsequently, after pacing out some walking routes with a stopwatch, he has another insight, having evidently solved the case. We cannot tell whodunit, but on rereading the story, with the benefit of knowing who really did it, we can see retroactively what the clues were that stimulated him, if not the necessity of his deduction.

The story takes the classical whodunit's rationalistic nineteenth-century ethos, which allows an opportunity to commit murder to be deduced from railway timetables, to the final extreme. Ol' Gao deduces who could and could not have committed Liu Zhi's murder according to their last reported location, distance from the crime scene, and likely gait. He paces off the distances himself, with his stopwatch. Since people could run or bicycle even in 1980, this is hardly airtight, but here the author, providing large- and small-scale maps of the city and crime scene in the manner of the Western interwar classics, turns the dull boxiness of the Chinese communist city to good advantage. This is evidently a northern city with a limited number of broad avenues and vast apartment blocks in between, each avenue several minutes from the next on foot, without the complications of crisscrossing side streets or shortcuts through alleys. In this city of vast spaces the distances between each house, the murder scene, and the bar where Yang Huting had his drink are marked out on the map in pedestrian minutes. Gao Si thus figures out the identity of the murderer, who is truly an unlikely figure: a little old lady, quite apolitical, but greedily wanting a wealthier match for her daughter than Liu Zhi. The criminal is Jiang Yaorong's mother. True to the genre of Perry Mason and J. B. Fletcher (of TV's *Murder She Wrote*), Gao Si lures the culprit into giving herself away (into throwing the lubricating oil over the wall of the Yangs' house, as she had previously pushed the murder hammer under the door), and still her identity is not revealed to the reader until the next chapter, when Gao Si confronts her in jail.

This is not the end of the story; it leads to another generic formula, a double recap—a second and then a third narration of exactly how the murderer carried out each detail of her well-planned crime, and then of how Ol' Gao figured it out, in the chronology of his enlightenment. Mother Jiang stayed home from the movie, excusing herself because of illness. She invited Yang Huting into her house, to arouse his fury and steal his hammer. She let him go at 8:30, so that he would pass her daughter on the street and be observed in the flush of his anger. Then she ran to the bridge with the oil and the hammer to await Liu Zhi, knowing he would be coming home from the movie alone because she had prearranged for her daughter to take another route to get her medicine. Little did she know that Hu Weijun would also take out his revenge on Liu Zhi that night; it almost prevented Mrs. Jiang from returning home before her daughter. But Liu's blinding facilitated her mission, and the next night, on the excuse of diarrhea (indoor plumbing being scarce in 1980), she slipped out to return the incriminating hammer to the Yangs, as she did later, to plant the lubricating oil. Every detail is taken into account. Hence Gao Si's second recap, of how he put two and two together. He had noted the first day when the Lius and the Jiangs came upon the corpse that this woman, then unknown to him, was the first to recognize the corpse by the bridge. Later she had been happy to implicate Yang Huting, even as her daughter tried to cover up for her ex-beau. And why on earth would she invite Yang into her house? And so on, concluding with a pyrotechnics of clues worthy of Poirot or Holmes, presented with the same lack of humility. A talk with Jiang Yaorong had presented Ol' Gao with five discrete clues, about time, place, the frequency of her mother's trips to the latrine, and the odd fact that she was washing her clothes when her daughter returned from the movie—to wash off the sweat of hurrying back after Hu Weijun's assault delayed her murder plans, Gao figured out shrewdly. It was of course Gao who planted in Mother Jiang's mind the importance of the lubricating oil as incriminating evidence, and he who followed her when she threw it over the Yangs' wall.

The story ends. There is no need to see the guilty party locked up, made to write a confession, and tried, or for deep probing of Mrs. Jiang's psychology, once her simple motive—greed—is identified. Still, not only does every scrap of evidence, even irrelevant facts, find an explanation in retrospect, but every question previously asked by the cops is explained, to indicate what they were driving at. After a story like this, even a regular reader of popular fiction could doubt that there is any Fate left in the world. The last sentence reverts to Mao-style encomiums: "Li Zhengbin and Liang Hong listened together, sincerely convinced and admiring their superior from the bottom of their hearts" (37)—their teacher and father figure, Ol' Gao.

Sidekicks, Satire, Local Color, Manners

Other stories actually did address the social and political themes that Chinese readers of recent decades had come to expect (but with the political values reversed), and yet they remained militantly in genre territory by deploying formulaic elements such as loyal sidekicks, local color, comedy of manners, and ridicule of the bureaucratic police, all quite as extravagantly as in the Anglo-American originals. " 'San ke menya' anjian" (The case of the three front teeth) by Su Yunxiang and "Yuan Shui qi shi an" (The case of the strange Yuan River corpse) by Yang Rongfang manage even to graft Maoist themes of class struggle and politically motivated hatred onto the plot by confining the politics to the end and to the beginning, respectively. In "The Case of the Three Front Teeth," the political revenge motive of the murderer is such a surprise that this seemingly classical whodunit becomes a political tale only in retrospect—"on the last page."

The tale is notable for its satire of class manners even as it presents three stock characters. Ying Jie is a nearly perfect Watson, a recent "political-legal cadre school" graduate who narrates the story and reveres his superior, a middle-aged Great Detective he calls Ol' Zhao. Zhao is not high ranking but does have a scar on his cheek from the Cultural Revolution (like Ol' Gao), which he got in retribution for apprehending the criminal son of a powerful cop. Zhao tiresomely lectures his young ward, telling him to be exact and not jump to conclusions, but Ying Jie is only too happy to admit to the reader that he had the pointers coming. He exults that Zhao loves his work and ratiocinates in a rapture, "eyebrows dancing and face radiant" (40).

The stupid, pompous, vain, and sycophantic cop who heads the investigation, Ma Yucai, is eager to find a motive for murder in class struggle. He is right, but for the wrong reasons. What he means by "class struggle" is the old Maoist non sequitur that the murder of a man found stripped of his watch—an item most Chinese could not afford in 1980—must have been motivated by theft. Crimes against property reflect the class struggle. Here, Ma's mindless Maoism has a genre function—throwing the reader off the track, particularly since the real who- and whydunit are political in a more genuine sense. And, with Ma as the Lestrade figure, Zhao can show him up like a Sherlockian "professional amateur."

It is in a people's park again that the bodies of a young man and woman are found. At first they appear to be love suicides, but this is just a misleading plot twist. When Ol' Zhao and Ying Jie are summoned to the scene, they find a third body: a middle-aged cadre, hanging from a tree and missing his three front teeth. It turns out that the young people only fainted, after grazing the corpse's dangling feet. The cadre is the real corpse, and he is not a suicide. He is Long Zhenting, a department head in the provincial government, a mover and a shaker; the missing teeth could be the criminal's "signature." Ma's pronouncement, that this was a murder to cover up the theft of his watch and money, leads Ol' Zhao privately to denounce the inspector as a "cat that can't catch mice," a "dumbbell, an idiot, suffering from the after-effects of a cerebral inflammation. . . . If you played the lute to a cow, would he graze any faster and get any fatter?" To his protégé, Zhao proclaims, à la Hercule Poirot, "I've already formed an image of the criminal in my brain" (40). Then he proceeds to give a miraculously detailed description of the man—age, height, beard, and high paddy-field boots—manufactured in the Shenyang Rubber Shoe Factory in 1972. That this reflects Holmes and Poirot more than real police work is clear from his coy reluctance to "reveal all of his conjuring tricks," because that might spoil his "act." He calls his subordinate "Ol' Younger Bro' " (40).

Shades of Agatha Christie are successfully invoked when these two lowly municipal-level policemen go snooping around a "palace"—Ying's phrase is "edenic fairyland"—of the class above them, the home of the deceased provincial VIP. Like lower-middle-class cops everywhere, they have heard about the drawing rooms and manners of the aristocracy. Now is their chance to see how they really live. Ying Jie, the youth, finds himself smitten with a fragile "princess" they find there, to whom Ol' Zhao says straight off, with Sherlockian assurance, "You would be Long Zhenting's daughter" (41). But in deference evidently to her status and aristocratic delicacy, crusty Ol' Zhao humors the princess rather than press her too far with questions. Already he has found a clue in her remembrance that Long Zhenting fainted after encountering an uninvited visitor at a social affair. But just now Ma Yucai arrests his "thieves" and claims credit for cracking the case.

"It sounds easy, but it really wasn't," he says (41). Long Zhenting visited the home of his secretary the night of the murder. (Mrs. Long gave Ma that hot tip.) Zhao learns afterward that the wife's suspicions were not unfounded; her husband *had* had a dalliance with his secretary. She and her husband were also blackmailing department head Long, indeed had forced him to hand over his watch and wallet the night of the murder, before sending him home a drunk and broken man. But they did not of course murder their new cash cow. Inspector Ma is oblivious to such logic, only intent on ingratiating himself with his superiors:

> The longer I was there, the more I suspected them, and the longer I suspected them, the more questions I asked. Finally the woman began to cry. Her grief was my pleasure. We had them under the gun. With the help of a little trick,

I soon had them in the people's militia headquarters, which gave us the chance to search their house. Heaven smiled on us then! I found clothes inside the closet that contained a calendar watch and a leather wallet with a few bills in it. They were department head Long's. With the stolen goods in custody, we had an ironclad case that loomed up before us like a mountain! If we achieved anything whatsoever, it's all due to the gravity the leadership attached to this case, the joint efforts of everybody, and also thanks to the party, and Chairman Mao, yuk yuk. (42)

To the thunderous applause that follows, Ma nods and waves back "as if he were greeting foreign guests" (42). Yet this remains a detective story, even if it is in the subgenre "detective comedy of manners." The author does not draw melodramatic lessons about Ma's incompetence or corruption, or about Long's sybaritic and immoral lifestyle; nor does he describe such behavior in detail, as in a realistic or "introspective" tale of exposure—though the fact that Ma works for a people's militia rather than a public security bureau hints that the story is set in Maoist times, an era for which the present regime can pretend to have no responsibility.

The real murderer is a young man named Tong whose father Long had tortured until he committed suicide back in 1968, when Long was an ultra-leftist in power with command over several brigades enforcing the "masses' dictatorship." Long had struck the elder Tong in the mouth with a pickax and taken his three front teeth home as trophies. The luxurious home the cops searched was once the Tongs'; Long took it over.

Young Tong was incarcerated once Long convicted his father as a spy, no doubt groundlessly. But how did the boy regain enough freedom to murder Long and go to his own father's grave in Shenyang, where he made an offering of three front teeth from the man who had ruined him? It was thanks to a staple of the nineteenth-century novel—love across a class barrier. The younger Tong got temporary leave because he had a powerful girlfriend, the daughter of department head Long. She had fallen for Tong when he rescued her from an attack by hoodlums. She is still covering for him now, despite everything.

And so, with the murderer revealed to be an unjustly incarcerated young man whose act was a settling of scores with an evil minion of the Gang of Four—a filial son who avenged a criminally unjust death to boot—young Tong's act is on post-Mao political grounds and on traditional Chinese

moral grounds a possibly justifiable homicide. The story ends indetermi-
nately, with Ol' Zhao burying his face in the bushes in sorrow as he witnesses
the youth present the three front teeth on his father's grave. Still, the murder has been solved, after sufficient obfuscation and misleading turns, so the
classical genre reader is not disappointed and has moreover been treated to
good satire and a touch of the macabre along the way. It is at the very end
that the story turns into the other major 1978–80 genre, the penal law melodrama, exploring injustice and how to rectify it. The elder Tong is now
posthumously exonerated; he has had his *pingfan*. One thing is certain: neither the solution of Long's murder nor justice for the deceased Tong owes
anything at all to Inspector Ma's vaunted Mao Zedong Thought.

"The Case of the Strange Yuan River Corpse" by Yang Rongfang reverses
the strategy of "The Case of the Three Front Teeth" by outlining a highly
charged, morally repugnant Cultural Revolution political setting at the outset, then abandoning the potential political themes in the classical whodunit
plot that follows. One wonders if the opening misled readers about what
kind of story they were getting, though the title is generic enough. Or did
the author mean to attract readers in the local Hunanese periodical that
printed his story with a promise of a weepy or indignant post-Mao story
about horrors of the Cultural Revolution, then steer them into a detective
genre that was at the time still new to many readers?

In the story, an unidentified corpse has mysteriously washed up on the
riverbank in Yuanling, West Hunan. In the summer of 1967, the most frenzied period of the Cultural Revolution, the "police, procuracy, and judiciary"
have been "smashed" by ultraleft rebel forces, specifically a "Lin Biao–Jiang
Qing Military Corps" partly made up of radical Red Guards like Shen
Zhaozhang, a West Hunan native who has helped seize power here at home
after his university in Beijing shut down. Police investigations are impossible; the former police cadres are all designated capitalist roaders who must
clean toilets to reform themselves through labor. However, they are still in
town and under the supervision of the "masses"—that is, the Lin-Jiang
Corps. The story need not add that 1967 was a time of many political
killings.

Here the marvelous political shtick is a socially degraded Great Detective
and a "Watson" who is openly hostile to him. The detective, middle-aged
and of medium build as usual, was deputy head of the county public secu-

rity bureau until leftists overthrew the power structure. Like most cops of rank, he was once in the People's Liberation Army (PLA). Now he is just Zeng Jinian, under house arrest and round-the-clock observation. We meet this capitalist roader carrying a load of night soil under the direction of young Shen, who is in effect his warden and labor boss.

The rural brigade leader who discovers the corpse on the Yuan River bank rushes to consult "Deputy Bureau Head" Zeng, ignoring his reversal of status from cop to near-criminal. Zeng cannot of course resume his profession, go out on an investigation, or even elude his Red Guard controller. He contemplates going on the lam to investigate the case, which would take the story into hard-boiled or thriller territory. Indeed, as in the spy thriller, Zeng is motivated by a desire to "serve the people" and defeat the *enemy*. Moreover, he has a burning desire to ask for permission from his old boss (though he too is a capitalist roader condemned to reform-through-labor), so strongly does loyalty to the organization burn in his heart (161). This story is progressive for 1980; when the corpse is found, we see the evil Lin-Jiang Corps about to string up and beat the ex–county magistrate (the top capitalist roader formerly in power) into falsely confessing that he had the man murdered to divert attention from the class struggle. But the Red values of service and loyalty to the party apparatus mark the story as conservative by later 1980s standards. (A 1979 story blames the Gang of Four for having disrupted surveillance of people!)[82] These are indeed transitional "Chinese communist" whodunits.

As it happens, young Shen, who is after all a student, is curious and has visions of glory. Wanting in on the investigation, he is soon talked into traveling with Zeng so that they can crack the case together. Yet Shen will be in charge, though he is now Zeng's student. With neat satire of a typically Maoist travesty, the boy is at first seen maintaining his political superiority (and also getting knowledge from Zeng) by giving the ex-cadre an oral examination to "see if he really knows his profession." Was it murder or suicide, he asks?—Murder. Note the three punctures in the back made by a square pointed metal instrument. Was he killed here?—See the water in his lungs. He drowned, then floated down the You River, not the Yuan, judging by where he washed up. Shen begins secretly to admire the professional (161).

This admiration grows as Zeng uses his knowledge of Chinese medicine to heal a wound of Shen's. Zeng also proves himself through a Sherlockian "preamble": he "deduces" how far up the You River the decedent was when he drowned from the bloating of his body and his dress, for the victim belongs to the Tujia ethnic minority, like Shen. His skin is dark and scaly from sun and water; his hands are calloused and his chest is muscular; and his feet are also calloused, but not cut or cracked like a peasant's. Hence he is a boatman, used to rowing on deck. He is about 40 and has been in love for twenty years, Zeng deduces from the color of the embroidered Tujia betrothal pouch, a woman's gift, at his waist.

> "Then is he married?"
> "Married? Yes."
> "Does he have children?"
> "Probably one."
> "How, how can you possibly know?"
> "Later. Perhaps we'll even meet this child." (163)

That child is Shen himself, who was orphaned and abandoned in 1953, not far from the murder site. Zeng notices that he carries a relic of his dead mother in his pocket. So the boy has two sides to him.

Shen's respect for—and dependency on—Zeng grow. Soon he is no longer "Ol' Zeng's" taskmaster but his apprentice, a junior Watson like young cops in other stories—"Lil' Shen," Zeng calls him, with lèse-majesté toward the dictatorship of the proletariat.

The peace officers go upstream to the location Zeng deduced. The party branch secretary of the local production brigade there recognizes the deceased from a photo as one Hé Fengkui, who failed to return from a trip with Hè Laopeng. The locals found blood in the bottom of their boat and a suspected murder weapon, a punting pole; the discerning Zeng also noted the oddity of "a boat without a punting pole," which proved to be the one with the blood in it. The local peace officer has already jailed Hè on suspicion of murder, evidently after beating a confession out of him. Shen is convinced; the motive must have been theft. But not the Great Detective. Why wasn't the victim killed away from home? Hè Laopeng then spins for Zeng, as his alibi, a tale of bandit romance worthy of a traditional Chinese novel. The deceased married the local beauty, Locust Flower, in 1945, who bore him a son. Then, twenty years ago, as law and order deteriorated just before the communist revolution, a bandit named Shi abducted Locust Flower and the

boy forever. Hé had been abashed to think that he had questioned her loyalty when Bandit Shi first began hanging around; Locust Flower had
smashed her silver bracelet, swearing an oath that she might likewise be rent
in two if ever she were unfaithful. Little did Hé know that Locust Flower was
obliged to give away their son to save the boy's life from Shi. She had
smashed her remaining half of the bracelet once more, giving her infant son
a quarter of it to remember her by. Twenty years later, Hé Fengkui heard a
rumor that his beloved Locust Flower was alive, seen washing laundry by the
river. He journeyed to look for her but disappeared.

Suffice it to say that once the Great Detective from Yuanling is turned
loose on the evidence—a third set of fingerprints on the pole, and rubber-tire
shoe prints on the bank where the deceased was last seen when his travel
companion went to relieve himself (Hé and Hè were too poor to buy even
shoes made from tires), he is able miraculously to finger a third party and ex-
culpate the unlucky Hè Laopeng. He takes Lil' Shen back to Yuanling,
though Zeng is subject to immediate arrest by the fascist Lin-Jiang regime,
and Shen too must lie low for his bad judgment in letting a class enemy like
Zeng Jinian "escape." With ever more uncanny insight, Zeng deduces
Locust Flower's whereabouts and pins the murder on her second husband—
bandit Shi, who forced her to marry and changed both their names to Liu.
Moreover, Shi/Liu is none other than the head of the Lin-Jiang Army Corps
that has wrought such evil in Yuanling. Not only that, Lil' Shen is the lost
son, with the quarter-bracelet in his pocket. The Great Detective has of
course deduced all of this. He and an underground group of former cops
corner Shi/Liu and get him to confess. Worrying that Hé might find Locust
Flower, Shi/Liu had followed him to his home in the Tujia uplands and murdered him there, taking Hé's half of the bracelet. Lil' Shen is disabused of his
past allegiance to his father's murderer and the man's hypocritical politics.
He has lost a father (Hé) and a mentor (Liu/Shi) but gained a mother. He
has of course above all gained a "father" and true mentor: the Great
Detective, (ex-)Deputy Bureau Head Zeng.

In the denouement, young Shen rushes in to say that a posse means to
lynch the Great Detective and all his "capitalist roader" colleagues. The
story ends before we know whether they will be persuaded by the truth and
by Lil' Shen's conversion or go ahead and lynch the former magistrate for
murder and Zeng Jinian as his accessory. The sudden ending keeps the story

from veering into melodrama (were Zeng miraculously to defeat all the entrenched bad people) or a "serious" story damning society (if, realistically, the good people were lynched). In a whodunit, when the murderer is named the game is over; political though he is, Shi committed *this* murder for personal reasons, to control his wife and cover up his past. His identity is revealed too late for politics to sidetrack the mystery quest. There is the added, quintessentially Chinese subplot of a filial son being able to avenge his father's murderer and find a new patriarch, material for a *pingfan* melodrama. But that is just an unexpected bonus; revenge was not the object of his quest.

The main "extra dividend" this basically classical ("Anglo-American") story delivers, in addition to the traditional family reunion interest and the exposure of injustice (including criticism of the torture of Hè Laopeng up in the village, though it was done "sincerely"), is local color. As in interwar Anglo-American stories, much is made of local scenery, costume, and social manners—those of West Hunan, immortalized by Shen Congwen in the 1930s and Han Shaogong in the mid-1980s. There is dialect, footnoted for the general reader, and a short disquisition on Tujia courtship. Locust Flower was the pick of local maidens not only for her beauty but also for her songs. She and Hé Fengkui met by song, on the ancient site for boy-girl responsive vocalizing. Here, even politics is kept in its place as just one more kind of period local color.

A New World of Greed Instead of Politics

Before departing the classical genre, let us discuss two stories written with virtually no reference at all to politics or Maoist class analysis. Indeed, the first story employs conventional stereotypes of middle-class provenance, for in it a worldly and well-off scoundrel has run through his father's money and latched on to a petty thief to do his dirty work. These classic stories have extrapolitical "Chinese characteristics" worth investigating. They point the way to the future: to a crime world not of politics but of greed, lust, and concealment of sin.

"Bai Yingying zhi si" (The death of Bai Yingying) by Lin Xiao has a touch of Cantonese local color and all the other genre staples. The story begins with a corpse: the 23-year-old body of the beautiful Bai Yingying. She was raped, strangled, and sent to the bottom of a lotus pond by a rock tied on with a factory transmission belt. There is a Great Detective, Captain Zhang Ming, who has a preternatural command of forensics. There is an unerringly error-prone Dr. Watson / Captain Hastings fresh out of the police academy, Li Xiaofeng, who narrates the story in the first person as a tribute to his hero and never seems to tire of being proved wrong. And there are clues. Zhang Ming puts on a performance of his prowess up front, in a "preamble." At the end he explains, in a recap, how he had cracked the case by mid-story.

But this story also has a theft. A few days before the murder, 6,000 yuan disappeared from the till of a machine repair factory. Bai Yingying was the teller. Few others had a set of keys, so Ms. Bai is the prime suspect. Another unique feature of this rather short story is the insertion of pages from Ms. Bai's diary (a form much loved by Chinese readers), and it gives the deceased a voice. If she has been wrongly suspected, her good name must be restored and her ghost appeased (as Captain Zhang puts it). Thus *pingfan*, the belated exculpation of the innocent and accusation of the guilty, is the story's final "Chinese characteristic," a quest for posthumous vindication as ancient as that of Dou E.[83]

Bai Yingying was not the thief; her diary has subtle clues that only Captain Zhang can read. He is further aided by the transmission belt, which leads him to a factory, a female factory worker, and finally her brother, a professional hoodlum named The Cat. There is also a photo of The Cat and a friend (that this person is Ms. Bai's current boyfriend is hidden from the reader until Zhang Ming recites his train of deductions at the end—not "fair play"). The boyfriend is quite a piece of work. He "got something" on the hoodlum so he could use him, ultimately to commit the theft and then the murder, and beforehand, to stage the very bicycle accident by which the boyfriend first met Ms. Bai, whom he had already staked out as his factory's teller. So the evil "boyfriend" is motivated by greed and then by the need to cover up his crime. As the diary also indicates to Captain Zhang, Bai Yingying was beginning to suspect him. The boyfriend had money to live on, but he wanted to see Tibet, then the world. As for Bai Yingying, who surprisingly (for 1979) earns no opprobrium for having three boyfriends in succession (the other two are red herrings for the police to check out), she, like Lil' Shen of West Hunan, is an orphan. One begins to suspect that this is a neat way of separating Chinese characters from their families, so that they may be reduced to the kind of individually responsible existence that goes with the Western-derived genre.

"Yi zun jin foxiang" (A gold Buddha) by Cen Zhijing and Wang Wenjin, another story set in Canton, goes a step further than the previous story, presenting just a theft, without a murder. (Canton, with its trade fairs, was still the commercial frontier with the West in 1979–80; it was also a place of liberal literary standards.) Classical Edwardian and interwar Western stories seldom do without a murder; a common if unpersuasive explanation in the critical literature is that only the motivation of solving the ultimate crime can keep a reader focused on such a narrow case of puzzlement. A historicist might ask if there was more interest in crimes against property at this time in China, when private property was returning as an institution. The more probable explanation is that murders and major private thefts were still equally sensational and seldom reported in China in 1979, when "A Gold Buddha" was written. This may in turn reflect a lingering Maoist obsession with grand theft as sabotage of socialism, a conspiratorial subject of much Maoist fiction.

So who stole the Gold Buddha from an antique store? This is not the stuff of Maltese Falcon legends, but in 1979 antique shops were mostly closed except to foreigners, Overseas Chinese, and the privileged set. Again the story serves the old Agatha Christie whodunit function of letting readers behold the manners of the aristocracy. The sleuths quickly recognize the crime as an inside job by the girl on night duty who was found tied up the morning after the theft. But who was her accomplice, and how will he fence the Buddha?

The other special "Chinese characteristic" is division of the story into chapters, with suspense at the end of each. Otherwise, it is as full of classical "Western" conventions as one could devise in so short a space, including a recap of the Great Detective's ratiocination at the end. The detective, Ol' Tan, has the usual younger male sidekick and is spectacularly didactic. Tan pauses while relating his numbered deductions, so that his young partner can fill in the blanks, as in an exam. "What clues can we deduce from this?" he asks about a button found at the crime scene (48). "Clues" abound; tracing that button becomes a fetish that threatens to distract one from the theft itself.

There is an amateur detective in the story, dubbed by his friends "the Holmes of the seventies." The quixotic finger of suspicion hovers over his

head from time to time, for he informs on and then seems to have framed a
fellow worker. But he really did just have the incredible good luck to overhear a guilty secret conversation. Meanwhile the finger inculpates, then exculpates, and finally inculpates for good the manager of the store, a man
with connections in Hong Kong. The Great Detective, for his part, gathers
all suspects and witnesses into one room. He uses railroad timetables to ver-
ify that the guilty manager had time to make a quick trip to Hong Kong and
get back without being missed. And this story comes as close as any to Ellery
Queen's standard Challenge to the Reader to match wits with the detective
(51). There is also satire: Ol' Tan addresses the amateur sleuth facetiously as
"Comrade Holmes." There is everything but a locked-room mystery.

Like the Anglo-American classics, the Chinese whodunit introduces the
reading public to a world not of political evil but of sin (in the mode of comedy rather than melodrama), of greed, lust, and deception. Pure greed motivates the theft of the Buddha: a desire for funds to emigrate in search of a
better standard of living. The alibi of the worker who is framed is that he was
having an affair with a married woman. She succumbed because her husband, from Hong Kong, "cared more for money than for her." The woman
at first lies to cover up her affair, denying the framed worker his alibi. What
a tangled web they weave, always leading to Hong Kong. Hong Kong itself
is a corrupting force of elemental greed—not just of "capitalism." China's future in the 1990s—grand larceny, official malfeasance, and rampant cohabitation—is not far off.

FORMULA TWO:
THE CHINESE COURT CASE MELODRAMA

China's native crime story tradition is more diffuse. Its anonymous authors
worked in many centuries and in many genres, developing, rediscovering,
and plagiarizing plots, themes, and styles. *Gongan* fiction as Huang Yanbo
sees it is virtually all Chinese works with court cases, and they are numerous.
Indeed, for modern crime authors, tradition surely did not mean only Ming
court case stories, which were short, had few characters, and were not so colloquial. There was also the vernacular great novel tradition of *Water Margin*
and *Dream of the Red Chamber*. Some of those novels asked the reader from

time to time to close the book and guess what came next.[84] Like law codes, these works grew by accretion.

One cannot assume that crime authors in 1980 had read Ming or Qing fiction or attended Chinese operas about Judge Bao. What all Chinese knew were legends and anecdotes about him and other good officials. This chapter extracts common threads mostly from Yuan *zaju* and late Ming "Judge Bao tales," epitomized by those collected in the *Longtu gongan* (Longtu's cases), also known as *Bao gongan* (Bao's cases). It has 100 or 62 stories, depending on the edition, in a language neither wholly vernacular nor classical. The 62-story edition was streamlined into a semipunctuated 58-story collection, *Bao Gong qi'an* (Strange cases of Lord Bao), which printed cases as separate stories instead of as paired chapters, as if the work were a traditional episodic novel. Mass audiences still read the *Strange Cases* today.[85] Traditional Qing scholars would not have had access to as many versions of the Judge Bao legend as even the modern cursory analysis here, nor might they have been reconciled to all the conflicting images of him.[86]

In the twentieth century, the Judge Bao tales were compared with the West's classical detective tradition and found wanting, even by Chinese, since the first generation to take "popular" fiction seriously was antitraditional in ideology. The Chinese tales were held to Poe standards of analytical detection, rationalism, and plot. Hence the first celebrated distinction: the identity of the criminal in the prototypical Yuan drama or late Ming story is known from the start. (And yet, earlier crime tales sometimes conceal the culprit's identity.)[87] Though the criminal is usually known to the reader, there may still be a detective interest in seeing how the judge figures it out. This "inverted tale" formula, an interwar staple even in the West thanks to R. Austin Freeman (and later *Columbo* on TV), has its own suspense.[88] Yet detection need not be the focus in the Chinese tale; misprision of justice will do. A quest for justice is the theme in nearly every case, amid anxiety (especially in the plays) that it will not be done even after the facts are known. The original crime will not be shorn of its moral importance—the plotting and initial commission of it may well be dramatized, providing a *frisson*, though the didactic narratorial comment is less than in other Chinese fiction. At the end the judge sternly reads a long-winded formal verdict admonishing the guilty. The plot includes the punishment, proving that the criminal will not still "get away with it" after the case is solved. As in melodrama by Cawelti's definition,[89] one knows that justice will be done, despite the terrible obstacles. The judge guarantees it.

The original crime may be a theft or a swindle, a murder or a rape, as in a whodunit. It is premeditated and concealed, and for familiar motives: cupidity, lust, concealment of past sins—not for socially motivated revenge or rebellion.[90] The crime may be brutal, bizarre, interesting (a step, perhaps, toward aestheticization), like attempting to starve a person by imprisoning him under a several-ton temple bell. As in the Western form, the aberrational physical horror of a foul deed may be heightened by having it committed in quiet, elegant surroundings, perhaps a monastery or the boudoir of a scholar's wife. Again, the criminal is not likely a madman, fanatic, professional criminal, or even a tyrant, though perhaps of the monied or examination elite, especially their aspiring fringes; it may be a traveling merchant, a tradesman, a monk, or a woman. The *victim* may be humble. Social status may be at the heart of the plot, as in schemes to thwart a socially unsuitable marriage (no different from "The Murder Happened Late on a Saturday Night," a whodunit). It would be wrong to attribute the crime to a conspiracy, but often the murderer's comrades, his family, or his fellow monks are in on it. In the secondary crime, obstruction of justice, the rich and powerful are to blame. Hence the Chinese stories have not just moral but also political implications.

Other traits reflect the ancient Chinese cultural ethos. Chinese critics today, like Huang Yanbo, are still apologetic for the Chinese tales' "prerational" atmosphere. Judge Bao serves the emperor's Mandate of Heaven, the Dao (Tao), or the workings of *bao* (retribution, requital), sometimes even arranges situations beyond the grave. Gods tell him the true facts in his dreams.[91] In the Ming, Judge Bao himself enters the netherworld to get information. Rogues may be spirits in human form. A decedent may be heard from beyond the grave (famously in *Injustice to Dou E*, a drama outside the Bao tradition). In fact a concealed murder is exposed by a dream prophecy in *The Canterbury Tales*. *Iudium dei*, trial by a process that lets God deliver His verdict, occurs in Western medieval romances as it did in life. But the Enlightenment purged most of that; Poe gave us the rationalist, wide-awake modern detective tale.[92] However, when spirits in Chinese tales give mystery-solvers puzzles and rebuses to work that lead to the solution, that seems quite a good analogue for modern clues.

The Great Judge is the major Chinese tradition. He acts like an official on stage, and in late Qing novels the reader gets a chill—an enjoyable one—when horrible torture instruments are trotted out. It is the judge himself who personifies the law, or more broadly, "justice." Besides finding and punishing the guilty, he may have to engage in social engineering afterward: arrange a marriage between widowed survivors, provide for the funding of a survivor's education, or for the worship of wronged ancestral spirits without descendants of their own. (Wilkie Collins's *The Moonstone*, "the first detective novel," has as its denouement the marriage of two wronged suspects after the solution of the theft; so perhaps this Victorian novel is only borderline "detective fiction," like the Bao stories.) In the early plays and prosimetric works, Bao is famous for gaining equity for the common man, suffering for them by going in disguise as a commoner and being beaten by tyrants for his pains, even punishing his own bad kin. In the classic late Ming stories he solves some more ordinary domestic crimes, often coming on the scene only at the last minute—again, as a moral rather than an intellectual force. In *Three Heroes and Five Gallants*, Lord Bao's fate is personally linked to the emperor's again.

As detective, the judge prevails not so much by "analytical reasoning," though he may gather evidence and deduce facts from clues, as by using his wits, his powers of observation, and his ability to understand, interrogate, shape, and reshape human nature—and omens—the natural cunning of "detectives" in the Bible and Herodotus.[93] Bao tests not physical reality but people, to make them give themselves away. He is more detective than jurist because, for a Chinese magistrate, "finding the facts was regarded as much more difficult and important than finding the law—something that the magistrate tended anyway to leave to his clerk."[94] In life, as copious Qing case files[95] and cops of all nations attest, most murder cases are not so enigmatic.

But this is fiction; there must be enigmas. Bao can determine guilt from physiognomy. In fact the ancient Chinese reader saw Bao as brilliant, Y. W. Ma points out, for being able to rightly judge cases without need of investigation.[96] Likewise, the detective Eugène François Vidocq (1775–1857) resented the ghostwriters of his memoirs for making him seem too rational, instead of spontaneous and resourceful. This takes one full circle, to the uncanny deductions of Holmes in Conan Doyle's preambles. *Shen*, meaning "marvelous, divinely inspired" in reference to detection by intuition, is still used as a Chinese adjective even for modern detectives in the Western mold.[97] The Great Chinese Judge does detect, then, and with spectacular results, but that does not make every Judge Bao tale a "detective story." The punishments may be more ingenious than the criminal investigations.

If Lord Bao is not always our sort of analytical detective, neither is he a judge in our sense, rather "the means through which the Emperor governed at the lowest level . . . [and who] exercised all of the powers of the state at that level."[98] Judging is not a separate duty of the magistrate; applying penal law for the Board of Punishments is the same as enforcing law for any other branch of the bureaucracy. The official administers his flock as a "father-and-mother official." He judges in his yamen, not a court, and there are no "parties" to his trials.

Politically, the Chinese magistrate was indeed less than a judge in our tradition. The code was supposed to do his thinking for him. In truly important cases, "he could only propose decisions which could be (and often were) revised or reversed by superiors."[99] Lord Bao was something of an exception. He (the character, not the Bao Zheng of history) has an imperially bestowed sword and gold badge giving him license to execute any criminal of any social or political class on his own authority.[100] Truly he is a figure of wish fulfillment. But a traditional judge, unlike a communist judge, was not forever deferring to other magistrates and judicial services at his own level, much less to a court president who judged the case for him and only let him read the verdict. An imperial judge was often second-guessed, but by higher levels of administration. He could deliver the lightest punishments on his own authority.

The character of the judge also fits a society less Edwardian than hardboiled—or rather the lawless world of William Godwin (1756–1836) and Vidocq, minus the sympathy for criminals in their works. Without the savior judge, money would buy "justice" every time. Judge Bao's predecessor may have judged a case wrongly and corruptly. *Pingfan* is thus a major theme. There is so much judicial malpractice in the Yuan dramas that one might think society corrupt in principle—though they never spell out this conclusion, unlike their successors in post-Mao times. China's ancient court case tradition may have cleaned up the real situation even so. A magistrate's handbook paints a picture not just of subofficials with their hands out, but of conniving relatives of the victim blackmailing and generally victimizing the suspect and his kin if they sense a victory.[101]

Wits are more important to the Chinese judge than the physical prowess that America's hard-boiled detectives need. The Chinese judge has runners and guards, though he also goes to investigate himself, in disguise (taboo to the decaloguists, though not to Conan Doyle), and does not eschew the medieval custom of torturing people (even plaintiffs and witnesses) to get them to tell the truth, which is taboo in modern Western classics, excluding hard-boiled tales. Yet Bao transcends the ordinary Chinese good judge; he does not just get the facts and punish the guilty, but with Solomonic shrewdness and intuition figures out just solutions to unyielding social dilemmas. And in facing the secondary crime, the miscarriage of justice—which calls for the most courage—he must prevail not only through his wits but also through his probity and persistence, his willingness to overrule even relatives of the emperor. As to wearing disguises, to the Chinese reader the point was that Judge Bao did not assign all his leg work to subordinates.[102]

Though part of a cosmic chain and dedicated to the common man, the judge is alone. He has trusted regulars and minions to gather evidence, as well as yamen runners that in one legendary case deceive him.[103] But his assistants are of a lower class, not equals like Watson and Hastings. The Chinese helpers could never hope to succeed to the boss's position, like the young Great-Detectives-in-training of the 1979–80 police detective stories just analyzed. In *Three Heroes and Five Gallants*, Judge Bao is served by a stable of chivalrous knights who take charge of the plot as his role peters out by mid-novel; even as a symbolic plot motivator, he has a surrogate later in the novel, Yan Chasan.[104] Lord Bao, as he is referred to even as a child, does however have a companion from childhood, Bao Xing, whose loyalty is not unlike that of Dr. Watson or Captain Hastings.

The Judge Bao of Ming fiction was too lofty and divine to partake of such a mundane human relationship. Accounts of the judge spanning dynasties and genres depict him as stern and humorless. His law does not bring joy but functions as a terrible sword of justice. Even after saving a man from unjust execution, he may scold or punish him for getting into trouble. That does not diminish a Chinese father; he can be entrusted with one's welfare. Judge Bao's paternalism ranges in various stories and genres from that of the strict and terrible steward of the emperor's trust to that of a father with stern but paternal regard for his flock. The kind of fiction in which Judge Bao appears, however, does not allow the reader to analyze his psychology in depth, as has been done for the more eccentric Holmes. Bao's inner life is opaque.

One seeming consequence of Judge Bao's severity is that, although he does not undermine the class interests of the literati, neither does he embody their "amateur ideal." He does not waste his time on calligraphy, painting, poetry, and archery. This makes him seem a more "modern" detective, and more an instrument of state and otherworldly power than a person of his class. In fact, though Watson in *A Study in Scarlet* enumerates gaps in Holmes's knowledge, the later stories have left readers with an impression of Holmes as a man of Renaissance knowledge and talents. Probably even from a Chinese viewpoint, Holmes is more the ideal amateur gentryman than Bao.

It remains to be said that Judge Bao tales in Ming editions were paired and given chapter titles in couplets, like chapters in traditional full-length vernacular novels. And there was at least one well-developed novel about a wise judge, the historical Di Renjie (Judge Di, or "Dee," in Robert Van Gulik's spelling), in which the identity of the criminal(s) is revealed only at the end, when the judge solves the case. This novel came late to the Chinese tradition of crime fiction and is not typical of the extant part of it, but it may have been read by Chinese authors of the early twentieth century.[105] No doubt it influenced Robert Van Gulik, who translated the work and wrote his own whodunits: classical puzzlers rich in local color and social manners, with Judge Dee as the Great Detective and plot elements from old Chinese court case fiction. The original Chinese novel at least illustrated that traditional stylistics and whodunit mystery were not incompatible.

Let us now deduce how this tradition might have changed to appeal to reader taste in 1978–80, a taste brought up on domestic Maoist literature and little else. There appears to be a direct line of descent through the Judge Bao tradition to the penal law melodrama, whose uniformed heroes perform detection and solve mysteries but are above all incorruptible and sworn to overturn (*pingfan*) privileges and past injustices of the high and mighty in their lofty calling of law enforcement for the state. Why "melodrama"? Characters are black or white, and there is a sense of clear and present danger; the story unfolds in "a world that is purportedly full of violence and tragedy we associate with the 'real world' but that in this case seems to be governed by some benevolent moral principle."[106] The realization of that in a happy ending—or the possibility of a happy ending in the future, when all officials have graduated to the altruism of the hero—separates these works from contemporaneous "serious" stories about communist corruption. That the melodramas are not simply curious about whodunit differentiates them from the more Westernized popular subgenre previously discussed. The melodramas center on a benevolent, moral law enforcer; if they depart from traditional formula, it is because sometimes the final accomplishment of justice is left a little uncertain. Perhaps the author, as social critic, wants a dose of doubt for realism, to leave behind the rosy formulas of Maoism; or perhaps social criticism to change policy is a major purpose of the story, one that justifies melodramatic exaggeration.

The post-Mao era's slogan, "rule of law"—not a communist habit to begin with—should rest uneasily in stories indebted to Lord Bao's ancient "rule of man" ideal of dominion by a wise and upright man with a vision of justice less petty and arbitrary than any imprisoned in static law. (Bao, like Holmes, was morally, not legally, inflexible.) But the moral didacticism of both ancient and Maoist literary traditions leaves room for "rule of law" propaganda in commentary and parables. In the post-Mao era, with no gods, few heroes, and soon no Marxism, the old taste for heroism may lead to the contradiction of heroes *personifying* the new "rule of law."

The post-Mao political mandate of decriminalizing an avowedly unjust legal system (attributable to an ancien régime) and reversing its misjudged cases repeats the quest for justice in the ancient tradition, in which secondary political-legal cases (frame-ups, false imprisonments, murders of witnesses, torture) may eclipse an initial, mostly instrumental crime. Modern authoritarianism allows conspiracies only dreamed of in ancient times. Murders along the way will not be so graphically described as in a whodunit, but their moral and ideological meaning will not be aestheticized. Readers will be indignant, want to mount the barricades; in this, turn-of-the-1980s stories are even more melodramatic than ancient ones. Yet we expect a higher comparative, social-science consciousness of legal institutions than in the Ming, and our analysis of post-Mao law profits by them. These melodramas critique the system; they savage party paternalism itself.

In ancient stories the perpetrator of the initial crime may be ordinary, but in the modern age the political nature of villainy will likely be present from the start; the apolitical rape or murder that sets a subsequent miscarriage of justice in motion will be committed by the high and mighty: by leftover Maoists and their offspring. Yet as a crime story instead of an old Maoist political cautionary tale, the penal law melodrama will still focus on the evil of *crimes* uncovered by police and judicial detectives, which are best countered by individual trials rather than purges and political campaigns. There is a detective interest in learning who committed the initial crime (concealed from the reader, in whodunit fashion), or at least a mystery left for the end about whether the bad men will be brought to justice. There is also chapter-driven suspense in the modern melodramas, even though many are short—though, curiously, they tend to lack the chapter titles that are commonplace in contemporaneous Chinese whodunits. Perhaps Maoist fiction was the greater influence on the Chinese penal law melodramas, other whodunits more influential on latter-day Chinese classical whodunits.

Realism is the orthodox doctrinal commitment of nearly all Chinese literature in modern times. Unprettified subject matter, close observation of detail, believable dialogue, and the *technique* of nineteenth-century Western realism will surely distinguish modern melodramas from Judge Bao stories. The Western reader of course sees the realism of the modern stories compromised by unbelievable plots, overt ideology, cultural and intellectual blind spots, outsized heroes, and melodrama.

Lord Bao is still a good modern hero; there are hints and direct references to him in the modern fiction. Counterparts today will continue to be peace officers, perhaps with a smattering of lawyers and teachers, but they too are government employees authorized to serve society, not their clients.[107] They need not be personally stern; the terror of Judge Bao's justice now resides in the law itself, which remains merciless (*wuqing*). The test of the judge's mettle is not freeing the innocent but punishing the guilty. Modern heroes are still paternal, dispensing "tough love."

A difference from both ancient tradition and Maoism is the division of labor in the modern Chinese justice system. Harold Tanner points out that the standard order of naming the public security, procuracy, and judiciary (*gong jian fa*) reflects their relative power, importance, and prestige as the cadres see it, even their pay.[108] Citizens encounter only cops, fearing and despising their ill-mannered ("uncultured"), contemptuous ways; history, fantasy, and wish fulfillment make the public picture savior high cadres still as father-and-mother "judges." The three services are under a unitary communist system, but they still compete. They publish, perhaps commission stories about heroes wearing their own service's uniforms (all three do wear uniforms), and lobby for themselves, much like scientists, who write science fiction to get increased recognition and funds for their profession, Wagner points out.[109] Lawyers (who do not wear uniforms) were still too new and powerless to be a fourth force. One would not expect exposés of party VIPs "responsible for political-legal affairs" who overrule prosecutors and judges either, yet there are some. The reform ideology of the moment was professionalism and separation of the legal from the political, so heroes even in less daring stories will wear uniforms and uphold a universe of technicalities—of laws, not "policies."

The modern Judge Bao, whether a procurator, judge, or cop (in rural areas, a militia head or other peace officer), will surely make use of analytical detection and all other tricks of Holmes's and Bao's trade, as long as they are "scientific." He or she will have colleagues but get no advice from spirits. Ghosts, deified ancestors, reincarnation, divinity, physiognomy and preternatural insight, and spirit-sent dreams and omens were rooted out of fiction by a state that promulgated militant atheism, rationalism, and scientism. The state promoted tales about people who refused to believe in ghosts.[110] *Bao* (retribution) can be understood secularly, so plots with people miraculously getting their just deserts are fine; without afterlife, justice *must* come in this life. But even hunches will be defensively accounted for in contemporary stories. And these heroes are too professional to be father-and-mother Solomons, though they set an example, more like Bao than Holmes, in helping children cross the street.[111]

Also more like Bao than Holmes, their probity and perseverance will be tested, for society is corrupt, a world of Spade and Marlowe, not Holmes and Ol' Zhao. Some of the heroes' "detection" may be in court, as of old— or its modern, authoritarian substitute, the interrogation room. Their prowess may be tested, for "the enemy" now has guns and goons; but this is melodrama, not a story by Hammett, so martyrdom is also an honorable choice. The hero must not, however, ever use judicial torture, though Judge Bao did. That would be "feudal."

Judge Bao in Uniform

More than detection, more even than reversal of a verdict, a surrogate "Judge Bao" hero is the most formulaic aspect of the modern penal law melodrama. The range of characterization is narrow, though the service and rank varies.

The hero of the first story related below, a powerful official from the central government, must simply not give in to friendship. In the four narratives that follow, the hero or heroine is an underdog, obliged to incriminate superior officers and their kin—notably, indeed formulaically, their uncontrollable offspring. (Judge Bao had to indict the emperor's relatives.) A heroic cop in one story is forced to draw on genuine courage and fortitude. A female judge, in a more realistic work, faces subtle reprisals and rewards. A female judge in a film scenario finds herself caught in a web of conspiracy but acquires a young ally. And a procurator in another film scenario uncovers a conspiracy that reaches far above him, but he is protected by a paternal network of bureaucratic benevolence going even higher than the evil.

The savior legal cadre who lends his title to the first story, "Beijing lai de jianchaguan" (Public procurator from Beijing) by Su Dezhen, Li Yangui, and Lan Yangchun, is wise, incorruptible, and in his sixties—older than a cop hero in a Chinese whodunit. Like Judge Bao as known in operas, he has a dark, squarish face and eyes that gleam with a spirit that is "courageous and resolute" (17). And his name is Yang Qingtian, his given name homophonous with the classical honorific "Qingtian" or "Blue [or Clear] Skies," referring to the purity of an incorruptible judge—like Bao Qingtian, Lord Bao.

Again like Bao, Yang Qingtian travels far to make a case where previously there was silence, a one-year silence after a hushed-up crime and fundamental miscarriage of justice instigated by people in power. Moreover, Yang is moved to intervene by a nonroutine petition from the masses—a letter from a mere factory security chief. We learn that he used to be employed by the judiciary, but they sacked him when he got too conscientious about really doing justice. Procurator Yang will be the deus ex machina that sets things right. To be sure, this resonates both with Chinese tradition and with an old Maoist formula in which a traveling cadre walks into a seemingly intractable political problem at the grass roots and sees the right path chosen—melodrama of another kind. Yang Qingtian *is* a powerful outsider representing the king's law, though the locals have a home-court advantage in this era of decentralization. Yang is from the Supreme People's Procuratorate, which seems to give him power to intervene in any case authorized by Party Central, like Judge Bao on circuit tour. In keeping with socialist heroism, he eschews majesty for a low profile, traveling by train when he could fly, choosing spartan cadres' hostels over fancy hotels, and walking instead of riding in cars. It not only sets a good example; it is as good as going in disguise for a high cadre, who usually can be spotted by his perquisites. Lord Bao (in fiction) acted similarly, for the same reason.

The case is simple. Du Ping, secretary of the party municipal committee in a southern town and evidently its most powerful citizen, has succumbed to his special privileges. His son deliberately ran down and killed a young girl on a bicycle with his Toyota, and Du Ping got him off. (Toyota was a fancy make then. Automobiles represented power and privilege; even accidental death was not easily forgiven when a car was involved.) The chiefs of municipal security, procuracy, and judiciary—an interlocking directorate of three comrades—got telephone calls from Du Ping and then agreed unanimously that it was just an accident. No case was even recorded. Yang Qingtian must therefore stand up to Du Ping's perversion of justice. Remarkably, and supremely testing Yang's probity, it turns out that Du Ping was his former army commander. They were party members together, Long March survivors, then generals—first and second in command of an army that won the battle of Nanjing and helped found the PRC. Their favorite subordinate was Yu Zhong, the grieving father of the girl Du Ping's son murdered! Yu refused cash damages proffered by Du Ping in lieu of criminal punishment, a common resolution of wrongful death cases in old China (when the state was thankful not to have to intervene). Yu was prevailed upon to keep silent, to give his old army commander some "face."

Procurator Yang necessarily becomes an uncompromising Lord Bao figure, though he is not really stern, which might overstress the raw power of the central organs. He loves truth and justice—punitive justice—for their own sake, even more than he does social harmony, though he mouths topical, soon-to-be-dated propaganda about the legal system serving the Four Modernizations. He holds forth about the need for equality before the law not only to Du Ping and the judiciary head (court president) who toadies to Du Ping, but also to Yu Zhong. Now that his daughter is dead, Yu would rather forget the whole thing, out of fear as well as loyalty to his old commander. The great paternal judge figure must keep Yu's backbone stiff—whip him into standing up for his rights—so that justice may prevail, a good example may be set, and the reputation of the party and its modern, socialist Dao may be unblemished.

He performs a little detection too. No one ever figured out why Du Ping's son wanted to kill Yu's daughter. Procurator Yang finds her diary, pages of which are read into the story. The two young people had fallen in love while sent down to the countryside. Young Du took her by force after his father got them transferred back to town. Then he abandoned her for a prettier girl in the PLA, just as Ms. Yu became pregnant. Her intent to accuse young Du drove him to murder her so that she would not "ruin his life." At the end, Yang tells the whole story he has pieced together to the court president, like the recap in a whodunit or the final conclusion pronounced in court by Judge Bao. The cowardly local jurist still wants to be assured that Yang will stay and Du Ping will fall from power before opening the case. This is a dark but realistic comment about China and the nature of power. But Procurator Yang assures the judge that his work has just begun. He *is* from Party Central, so a successful outcome is ensured, even though the reader has not yet seen Du Ping demoted or his son cast into jail. Retribution will come full circle in this didactic morality play.

In the next four pieces, heroes and heroines must prosecute villains who outrank them; their position is risky but not unknown to Judge Bao.[112] The hero of "Zhifazhe" (Upholder of the law) by Shen Zhiwei is just a local cadre, a brave and gritty cop who finds that he must fight alone against the kind of corruption familiar to Sam Spade and Philip Marlowe, but without the freedom of action of a private eye. He is Bai Ping (lit., "White" or "Plain"; "Equal" or "Balanced"), another white-haired paragon with injuries from the Cultural Revolution. The story is relatively literary in technique and unlike a police procedural in its gut-wrenching action, but it does deliver a dose of procedural "realism."

Bai Ping is deputy chief of a municipal public security bureau. His son has grown up with the uncontrollable son of Bai Ping's boss, police chief Guo Weimin. One day the younger Guo, provoked by a common traffic cop, swears he will wring his head off. That night, Guo steals his father's revolver and shoots the man. Bai's son, ever the compliant companion, duly saws off the head. In a park.

There is no mystery about who did it. Bai Ping runs in his own son, then goes after the boss's, since the boss will not. Soon Bai is telephoning cops in their police boxes, telling them to stop any car with the chief's license plates. The police force reacts incredulously to this order to be insubordinate; Bai

Ping must remind them that their duty is to the law, not to the leading cadre. Meantime, Bai chases the chief's car, which may be taking the chief's son to a hideout or acting as a decoy for the real getaway. Melodramatic suspense and moral outrage climax as Bai, the stern cop who will not be moved, fruitlessly knocks on his boss's door, then interrogates his own son while Mrs. Bai and her mother wail and bang on the doors outside. The wife takes suicide pills and has to be removed to the hospital, but still the interrogation goes on; Bai finally brings in the chief's son for interrogation, as the chief and the chief's boss no doubt prepare to break down the door.

Arresting one's own son before he can get away may be heroic, but how many policemen would also mutiny against the captain and commandeer the whole ship in the name of the Crown while in port? The social truth here is one revealed inadvertently: that the justice system is not in the hands of procurators and judges at all, but the police. As supposed legal exemplars fighting higher-ups who "fear neither the Law below nor Heaven above," Bai Ping and his chief of detectives duly prepare a proper arrest warrant. Then Bai personally stamps the Public Security seal on it and signs it on his own authority, as a cop! Whether it will stick might depend on whether the chief and his party-boss friend can break down that door.

Ji Rong, heroine of "Nü tingzhang" (The female head judge) by Cao Yumo, has less need of courage than Bai Ping, but more need of Judge Bao's persistence and dedication to principle over career interests. Her world is not hard-boiled, but one in which justice is likened to a play; a veil of gauze ensures that "spectators can see the action only indistinctly" (10). The threat is not to Ji Rong's person but to her integrity, and it is delivered deftly and indirectly through her boss, Ol' Jiang, Eastern District court president (*yuanzhang*), a paternal figure who offers carrots and sticks ostensibly for Ji Rong's own good. But she is unreachable because, like Lord Bao, she is solitary—an aging spinster with no personal life to distract her from duty. Persecuted as a Rightist ever since 1957, for calling for an independent judiciary during the Hundred Flowers campaign, sent to a farm for penal labor under "supervision by the masses" for four years after the Cultural Revolution and left there without a new assignment for another six, she is now too old, 52, and has too unsavory a past for anyone to woo her. She accepts the role of loner, odd fish, and frustrated woman thrust upon her by colleagues, the better to keep her own counsel.

Ji Rong's vulnerability, and also her detachment and impartiality, are the greater because she was rehabilitated and returned to work in the legal system just months earlier. The boss hands her a heavy stack of files to encourage her to take a quiet teaching post. But among the complainants crying out to the law personified—"Oh Law, Sacred Law, protect us! Judge the true from the false for our sakes, and let justice prevail!" (10; cf. *Dou E*), one in particular catches Head Judge Ji Rong's attention. A worker named Chen raped a young girl, but his case file has been shuffled between courts, procuracy, and police for months without prosecution. She gets on her rusty bike to make a few inquiries with the boy's boss and designated people-watchers at the relevant neighborhood committees. Before Ji Rong can finish, the dust raised by her simply asking around brings the limousine of the deputy secretary of the party municipal committee—the committee member in charge of political-legal work—to the doorstep of her own unit's rundown offices. Out steps Deputy Secretary Xie himself, bearing gifts: a promise of appropriations for rebuilding courtrooms and offices, to repair decades of neglect and years of outright vandalism during the Cultural Revolution. The shadow play has begun.

Judge Ji is visited by her boss in her quarters; the local procuratorate wants the rapist's case file back. The rapist is just a boy led down the wrong path by the Gang of Four, he explains, best disciplined administratively by his factory rather than by the courts. Judge Ji has already learned that the rapist's father is a cadre and a war buddy, not to mention a relative by marriage, of Deputy Secretary Xie himself. The fix is in; the reward is the funds to repair the courthouse. Judge Ji refuses to compromise. She expedites the case and sentences the rapist to three years.

Three months later the rapist is already released and Judge Ji knows she must strip away a veil to find the reason. Chen moreover intends to settle scores by raping the same girl again (he also threatens the judge), but he is rearrested in the attempt—and released once more, before the female head judge can interview him in jail. The limousine pulls up again. Deputy Secretary Xie wants to add new blood to the judiciary and reward a long-persecuted cadre with early, full-pay retirement: Ji Rong. But her boss must "mobilize" (persuade) her. She of course only stiffens her spine and writes out a new complaint about Chen's latest crime. She visits the party secretary at the provincial level above, to deliver a personal petition for justice (*gaozhuang*)—after finally getting past army guards at the door and having to make a second trip to find the secretary "in." He handles the case. He sends it back down to Deputy Secretary Xie to deal with.

This story is generic; it arouses pity and anger, the case is stereotyped, and its hero is old Judge Bao in female form. But perhaps it is more than a melodrama. The outcome is not ensured, and the means by which evil is done, reaching down through the chain of command with a graduated array of bureaucratic rewards and punishments, is relatively subtle. A final paragraph showing the female judge forging ahead, giving a speech at a provincial-level political meeting, appears tacked on. The words of the raped girl's father, a teacher, strike a more realistic chord. Even he has an excuse for the rapist: "We haven't educated them right. . . . Better that we the innocent bear the sins of others in silence" (16). Someone, or some ideology, has got to him too.

Another female head judge, Shang Qin, is the heroine in *Fating neiwai* (Before the bench and behind the scenes), a film scenario by Song Yuexun and Chen Dunde that was in fact filmed.[113] The municipal intermediate court she "heads" is really under her feckless boss, Ol' Jing, though she pulls rank on a bought-off judge in the trial of first instance, District Court President Cao. She ultimately reverses Cao's ruling, rising above Ol' Jing, who stays home with a political illness just before the retrial. The tale ponders the same crimes as "Public Procurator from Beijing," but with the stakes and number of players raised on all sides. Here the Judge Bao figure sees through the gauze veil from the start.

As in "Public Procurator," a cadre's son, Xia, has slain an uncooperative girlfriend by premeditated vehicular homicide. This boy's father is the party secretary of a whole province, one giant level of government above Head Judge Shang Qin. Again the cover-up alleges that the death was accidental, and even that Xia was not driving. Once more, justice is set in motion not by ordinary legal investigation or a formal appeal of a lower court decision, but by "petitions" from the masses—an anonymous letter and a protest from a mere court recorder, Gan Chunqing ("Sweet"; "Pure"; "Clear"), who knows a trumped-up case when she records it. The car used in the crime has appropriately been upgraded to a Mercedes. And the secretary's family again buys the silence of the girlfriend's surviving family members. When Judge Shang investigates, they throw a few gifts her way.

Before the Bench is more complex than "Public Procurator"—more quasi realistic in details, more theatrical, more sinister in atmosphere, and with more references to laws and procedures. Members of the high-cadre family themselves are divided between the two camps, justice and injustice. And Shang Qin is not all alone. There are also love interests, as in other fiction of the period. One romance is between Shang Qin's son and a young woman who starts out as her gadfly, none other than Gan Chunqing, the court reporter. Middle-aged Shang Qin takes Ms. Gan along on her investigations and they become a crime-fighting team, though the young woman is always passing judgment on Judge Shang for not immediately carrying out "equality before the law"—that is, summary arrests of high cadres. The word is out, she says, "that our law is like a spider web. It only catches little flies and bugs. When the big guys test it, the web breaks" (44). Ms. Gan breaks off her engagement to Shang Qin's son until she has convinced herself that Judge Shang is a selfless enough cadre to be her future mother-in-law. A young activist and unreflective fighter for the right, Gan may be as much a type from Maoist as traditional fiction. The feminist message of Shang's and Gan's heroism is either negated or reinforced, depending on how one looks at it, by the choice of villain: the secretary's wife, Liu. It is she who masterminds the plot to save her son, in the name of her sick husband. He remains in the dark, indeed disowns his son and wife when he finds out. Ms. Liu resembles many a Chinese villainess who makes her way up in the world through her husband but is not controlled by him.[114]

But is Shang Qin a *Great* Judge? At first she is morally upstaged by Ms. Gan, who wears her righteousness on her sleeve. In the younger woman's mind, the judge is on trial. What China needs, Gan says, is a "black-faced Judge Bao," willing to take on crown princes (43–44). Yet that is Head Judge Shang Qin to a tee, in some ways even more than the "procurator from Beijing." She is truly stern (50). Although initially she is at sea—like Bao, in some Yuan plays—a kind of daydream, vision, or illumination brings her insight, not unlike the spirit visions that came to the Song dynasty judge in his dreams (51). In the end the judge, not Ms. Gan, turns out to be the wiser one when she admonishes Gan not to jump to conclusions but always to rely on evidence (46). Ms. Gan would indict the secretary himself, though he turns out to be outside the conspiracy. Shang Qin elevates the law into something sacred, surely more abstract than mere vengeance, and therein lies her greatness.

Through investigation, fearlessly and with superior technique and intuition, Judge Shang strips away one lie after another. She proves that the chauffeur could not have driven the car that ran down the victim; then, that the next one to confess, Xia's hoodlum friend Ji, was not driving either; and finally, through forensic evidence, that it was murder, not an accident, following attempted rape in the back seat of the car. She is a stickler for the full truth: when Ji confesses, young Xia is sentenced to one year in prison, as accessory after the fact to hit-and-run with a car he took out himself. But that is not enough, and of course it is improper that Ji should take a two-year rap for vehicular manslaughter when he was not driving. As her boss runs for cover, Shang Qin takes charge of the case herself. At the end, she dreams one night that Xia will go to jail for a long time. But the story ends before the trial, so one cannot know the actual outcome.

This dramatization, like traditional fiction, means to gain dramatic power from images of the *majesty* of the law—of courts with all their trappings—particularly in a scene at the outset. A judge and two people's assessors are seated majestically on a "very high" dais, looking down on the accused; there are judicial police and stern warnings, plus indictments and judgments read out verbatim in legalese. Perhaps inadvertently, the story is also surprisingly revealing about how courts are run. It is in several "meetings about the trial" before open sessions that Head Judge Shang shows her gumption, presumably the same sort of liaison meetings as those attended by Procurator Xu Li in a film scenario outlined below. *Before the Bench* shows judges and procurators deciding guilt and innocence, even sentences, before the trial has begun (50).

The sinister ways in which the provincial secretary's wife obstructs justice are the point of the story. Ms. Liu induces the chauffeur to conceive on his own the idea of taking the rap for her boy, though the chauffeur was not even in the car.[115] She appeals to his loyalty to her husband, who was so piteous in the Cultural Revolution. Then she disingenuously volunteers to have her son take the rap for the chauffeur (for his "crime" of giving away his car keys), threatening him and planting in his mind the idea of honor among thieves (45). She also works on Judge Shang Qin, reminding her that it was Secretary Xia who had her educated and got her this judgeship. Later, when Shang Qin commandeers a liaison meeting to push the final prosecution forward, she is interrupted by a personal visit from the vice director of the provincial revolutionary committee. She gets calls from the deputy provincial secretary (of the party), the head of the provincial Party Organization Department (enforcing "discipline" or compliance among party members like herself), and others, until Shang Qing pretends she is unavailable (58–60).

The piece is decidedly didactic about the danger of party cadres being above the law. It also delivers an explanation for juvenile delinquency: not only did the Cultural Revolution tolerate lawlessness and anarchy by destroying law enforcement institutions, as stories in all genres proclaim; it also deprived many young adolescents of the stabilizing moral influence of their fathers while the latter were in prison or cadre school (42). In a way, *Before the Bench* undermines its own message by showing that strong paternalistic relations bind all cadres, not only as an upper class but as one big family. The cadres in a given city know each other and have "raised" each other's young. Shang Qin herself once babysat Xia. She used to pick him up at school while his father did time in the countryside. Judge Shang Qin, the antidote for party patriarchalism, is a savior matriarch.

Realities and Fictions about the Legal System

A municipal-level procurator named Xu Li, far less exalted than the public procurator from Beijing in that story, performs as the savior legal cadre in the film scenario *Zhifazhe* (Upholder of the law) by Luo Huajun and Li Zaizhong, not to be confused with the story of the same title by Shen Zhiwei. Why did procurators in the early 1980s play a role in penal law melodramas so much larger than in life?

There was in 1980 a functional separation of the three services again. In criminal cases at the municipal level, the police were to investigate and detain suspects. Procurators were to examine the evidence, issue an arrest warrant for execution by the police, and prepare the indictment. A judge and two people's assessors, laypersons untrained in the law who virtually always concurred with the judge, heard the case and passed sentence.[116] The defendant might have a defender (a family member or lawyer) at the trial, and the state's case prepared by the procurator might be backed up by a complainant (e.g., a relative of the person murdered). The condemned would go to a jail or prison farm run by the Ministry of Public Security (MPS) until 1983, and by the Ministry of Justice after that. The Ministry of Supervision inspects jails and judicial management, but it did not at the time of these stories. It was abolished between 1959 and 1986.[117]

So judges are not the detective, judge, prosecutor, and jury as they were in imperial times. Since communism, that all-in-one role has typically belonged to the police. Today they may still on their own authority detain troublemakers for three months of "custody and investigation" to dig up facts, according to a classified (and even so, often abused) party dictum.[118] Indeed the police punish technically lesser offenses not named in the criminal code of *law*. In 1992, they handled seven times as many of these "administrative" cases as the courts did criminal ones, though the former could be as serious as drug use, running a brothel, or damaging telephone lines, and they could get an offender four years of "reeducation-through-labor" in penal camps. (In theory, these are now acknowledged police "verdicts" that one may appeal to a higher police station or even a court.)[119] Police can arrange for house or neighborhood arrest, or surveillance and punishment of an offender by his or her work unit. They enforce (or ignore) civil penalties as instructed, and lock people up during campaigns against pets and pornography (policy, not law).

These practices make the heroic fictional roles imputed to procurators and judges startling. In 1954 the procuracy was remodeled to resemble a comparable Soviet legal institution, theoretically with power to supervise the legality of actions by state organs at all levels, including the police. Local Chinese procuratorates were to authorize all arrests and prosecutions, and some actually ordered the release of detainees on technical grounds.[120] Procurators might have imagined themselves as inheritors of the mantle of the imperial censors, who could report corruption anywhere and remonstrated with the emperor himself. An old term for "censor" was *zhifa*, or "upholder of the law," whose personification in the film scenario by that name is Procurator Xu Li. After 1952 the procuracy put out citizen complaint boxes and recruited its own correspondents, some 20,000 "activists" (informers) by 1956.[121] But the Communist Party was, even in the state constitution, leader of the revolution, hence the top watchdog and leader over the government. Procurators who wanted to play that role, subordinate only to the Supreme People's Procuratorate, struck hard-liners of 1958 as rivals of the party. Saying that "the procuratorial organs are judicial organs, are only responsible to the law, should not be responsible to the party, and that the procuracy cannot be the yes-man of the Party committee," their "insolence" was "such that they want to supervise and put themselves above the Party committee."[122] That was the end of the procuracy's supervisory role; the Cultural Revolution ended its other duties. The 1975 state constitution (superseded in 1978) specified that "the functions and powers of procuratorial organs are exercised by the organs of public security at various levels."[123]

When the supreme and local procuratorates were reestablished after 1978, local procurators had lost the single-line leadership they enjoyed in 1954. Local procuratorates were now accountable to their superior offices and to local people's congresses—that is, the local CCP. They had also lost their blanket power of supervision over state organs; they were to go after state employees only when such employees acted *criminally*. However, they still had powers of investigation and the duty to oversee court trials and activities of the police in criminal matters. A 1979 procuratorial law restored their "independence."[124] One can thus imagine how a seasoned procurator or an author aware of the procuracy's glory days in the mid-1950s might aspire for the central procurators to accede to the role of the old imperial censors. (In those anti-Russian times they probably would have been reluctant to invoke the Soviet image of the procurator as "watchman" or "guardian of legality.")[125] In the early 1980s, model procurators who fought higher-ups were celebrated in newspaper articles, evidently to help relegitimize a "new" institution short on experienced and reputable cadres.[126] Yang Qingtian and "upholder of the law" Xu Li are precursors.

Just as surprising is the ability of the two women judges, the Beijing procurator, and Procurator Xu Li to take on Judge Bao's role in criminal investigation. Each of the three services had the duty to investigate, but a division of labor evolved so that procurators mostly investigated corruption and malfeasance, not ordinary criminal violations. Judges are to collect evidence for the trial, and in the field they are accompanied by a recorder to take notes, like the redoubtable Gan Chunqing.[127] But it is remarkable that these two female judges in fiction are so active in police-type investigation. Judges may initiate investigations on their own when they receive a complaint. But Judge Shang's staff do all the investigating, with a little help from the procurator's office; judicial staff, not the police, conduct the interrogation in prison that breaks Mr. Ji (57–58). The role of the police is fully censored.

In life, the judiciary and procuracy lacked the power and the staff to intervene so directly. Victor Li found that the "theoretical model of the legal process never became fully operational in China, and was perhaps hardly implemented at all,"[128] even in the 1950s. In a suburban county of Guangzhou,

> the procuracy did almost nothing, and the court often was little more than a rubber stamp in criminal cases. Thus, in practice, the administration of the criminal process was handled almost entirely by the public security apparatus without the active participation of the other two political-legal organs. The inactivity of the Hui-yang procuracy is fairly easy to demonstrate. Since its establishment in the latter part of 1955, the number of persons working there never exceeded five and dropped to as few as three.[129]

Cases were usually submitted to the procuratorate after the police had "completed their investigations and reviewed their findings several times. . . . The Hui-yang court did not fare much better than the procuracy."[130] And that was when procuracy was in its prime.

Many offenses were mediated or punished by mere discipline by the CCP, if the offender was a party member, or by an administrative measure carried out in the accused's work unit. Ji Rong's boss seeks the latter outcome for the rapist in "The Female Head Judge"; Xia's mother tries to arrange it for her son in *Before the Bench and Behind the Scenes*.

By all accounts, Chinese judicial organs are rubber stamps today; in Ji Rong's time (1979), most legal cadres had just been rehabilitated from outcast status themselves, after rustication and perhaps incarceration in "cow sheds" during the Cultural Revolution. Many of the new procurators suffered stage fright when they came to court.[131] The unimportance of trials in establishing facts may be determined from the official statistic that in the first nine months of 1979, 99.7 percent of the accused prosecuted at all levels were found guilty in people's courts.[132] Trials were stage dramas, rehearsed ritual enactments to educate and warn the masses.[133] The educational function is specified in the Organic Law of the People's Courts.[134] Even today, courts are seen by other organs as coordinate, indeed inferior branches of the bureaucracy. Courts so often defer to other branches (as by declining jurisdiction) that one scholar wonders if, "despite their superficial resemblance to the courts of Western nations, they can be regarded as functionally comparable institutions."[135] To invest a present-day procurator or judge with the authority, vigor, or prestige of Judge Bao is the act of a reformer, a dreamer, or a propagandist. Harold Tanner points out that the role of the new procurators is not so often to save the wrongly accused as to see that the guilty do not get off easy.[136] But that was also Lord Bao's main accomplishment.

The independence of China's judiciary that Ji Rong asked for in 1957 is compromised not just by the police but also by a dual chain of command to the CCP. Municipal judges, procurators, and police answer to courts, procuratorates, and security departments at the provincial level, on up to the Supreme People's Court, Supreme People's Procuratorate, and the MPS. But each organ also answers to the CCP authority at its own level, which really outranks it; a municipal judge must answer to the first secretary of the party's municipal committee, and often to a deputy secretary (like Xie) specifically charged with oversight of "political-legal affairs."

The municipal committee's line of communication goes straight up to the Party Central Committee and paramount leader. Du Ping, presumably the party's municipal first secretary in "Public Procurator from Beijing," thus commands the three local law enforcement services. Judge Shang Qin, in *Before the Bench*, is thwarted by the *wife* of a provincial first secretary. Ji Rong, of "The Female Head Judge," is stymied by a deputy municipal party secretary. And she appeals the Chen rape case not to higher courts but to the *party's* provincial committee. That is where power resides. She, the advocate of judicial independence, has circumvented her own judicial bureaucracy by appealing over its head to the party.

In the later 1980s, when party and state organs were supposed to be separated, to depict the CCP's control so clearly, as Liu Zongdai did in *Gongan hun* (The soul of public security), was to expose wrongdoing. But in 1959 "the model judge [was] one who consult[ed] the local party apparatus about any important case."[137] Still in 1979, "To decide if the facts of the case are in order, the evidence convincing, if the defendant should be subject to criminal sanction, and what criminal punishment should be imposed—all this must be sent to the secretary in charge of political-legal affairs of the local party committee at the same level for review and approval. This has a name, the system of approving cases by the secretary."[138] Party leadership was so taken for granted that authors did not cover it up. CCP "oversight" did in theory discourage the police from becoming an out-of-control KGB. And the more prestigious PLA handled more serious security matters. The police perspective was that they simply could not get any respect.

Xu Shaowu's "Jianchazhang renxuan" (The choice for head procurator) shows how a city's head procurator might be selected. The Organization Department of the municipal CCP committee, together with comrades responsible for politics and law in the municipal revolutionary committee (as municipal governments were called in the aftermath of the Cultural Revolution), has proposed three judges (that is, "personnel from the leading ranks" of the municipal intermediate-level people's courts) as candidates for the post. The first secretary of the municipal CCP committee is to choose ("nominate") one of them for election by the municipal-level people's congress. Here the Judge Bao figure is a party secretary, not even a uniformed professional. He is an admirable, poker-faced version of the archetype, and newly appointed—ready to clean up the city. Sure enough, his son has committed a crime and his wife is trying to cover it up. The secretary chances to overhear all three candidates discuss his son's case. Two have become wishy-washy about it, now that they know who the new secretary is. The secretary holds to his principles and promotes the third man, who wants to prosecute his son. The secretary is confirmed in his judgment when he later learns that he came to know and respect his candidate in an encounter years earlier.

The CCP has branch committees with their own separate party line of command infiltrating and leading (if not wholly staffing) state organs like public security bureaus and procuratorates; these party secretaries (heads) report directly to their municipal CCP committee. When Shen Zhiwei's heroic deputy police chief, Bai Ping, decides to mutiny against the police chief in order to arrest his son, he is also mutinying against the party, for the chief is concurrently the secretary of its branch within the police. Bai's subordinates advise him to first call a meeting of the party branch, evidently without the chief, to help Bai diffuse responsibility for authorizing his controversial arrest (9–10). Instead he argues that a cop who follows the law can arrest a lawbreaker on his own authority, without any instructions from (CCP) leaders. Those are the revolutionary implications of the rule of law when it is understood literally.

Upholder of the Law (by Luo Huajun and Li Zaizhong) is candid about the leadership role of the civilian party secretaries over uniformed professionals. The dramatic scene that opens the story and creates its mystery is a "security, procuracy, and judiciary liaison meeting" in which Deputy Head of the Municipal Public Security Bureau Liang Jing (i.e., chief of police), in charge of the criminal investigation at hand as one would expect, makes a report pinning the crime of attempted murder on young Zhang Hua. (The head of the security bureau is not shown; in a likely scenario, he would be a holdover appointment from the Maoist regime, not yet fired but with his power taken over by a newer or rehabilitated man from the ascendant Deng Xiaoping camp named as his deputy.) Stalwart head procurator Xu Li is then called on to deliver his report. Dramatically—unexpectedly to his fellow legal professionals!—he asks for permission to present his own version.

This opening liaison meeting frames the main narrative as a flashback. At the end, Liang Jing appears to be the top uniformed law officer (though not the top banana) in an evil conspiracy. Yet the paternal procurator hero has his own patriarch for protection. The one who chairs the meeting and calls on the Great Procurator to make his dissenting report is Ol' Zhao, the municipal party secretary "in charge of political and legal affairs." The "three chiefs" (of the public security bureau, procuratorate, and court, all of whom would be party members), with the municipal secretary above them, are the political-legal party group at their level.[139] As Procurator Xu Li homes in on the conspiracy, he goes to Secretary Zhao and gets authorization to seek out the root of the obstruction of justice, which must lie in the Leading Party Group for Political-Legal Affairs of the municipal party committee itself, which "leads" the police, procuratorates, and courts (105).

These stories in general may be wildly optimistic about how much a procurator can do, but this one, Xu Li, has authorization from above that is more telling than his job title. The interesting variation on the savior legal official hero in *Upholder of the Law* is that its conspiracy of evil faces a stronger paternal web of good. That extensive and hierarchical network of protection incorporates popular appeals that are more common in full-length vernacular novels than in typical Ming court case stories. There is something for every taste: a melodramatic fight against evil, family entanglements, detection, social criticism of the high and mighty, and miraculous coincidences.

Upholder of the Law, the film scenario, has a family melodrama interest because the coconspirator who carried out the murder attempt and whom the Great Procurator must accuse, without prejudice, turns out to be his own son, Xu Haitao. The most active conspirator dramatized in the text is the son's boss, a woman named Liao Qi, the party secretary exercising leadership over the Foreign Trade Bureau. The accused whom Procurator Xu Li exculpates, Zhang Hua, is a former Red Guard who was Xu Li's warder years earlier when Xu was incarcerated during the Cultural Revolution. He let Xu Li escape when leftists were coming to murder him. And the one whom Xu Haitao has just now tried to murder is his own ex-girlfriend, Tang Min, whom he had recently jilted in order to date his evil boss's daughter. Tang Min is also Zhang Hua's trusted friend. He gave her his evidence that Trade Bureau boss Liao Qi during the Cultural Revolution murdered someone (Tang Min's uncle!), and proof that Liao is now obstructing justice by having three gang members swear that Zhang Hua was their leader so that he can be put away.

Extended family? It was immoral for Xu Haitao to ditch his girlfriend. Tang Min was true to him, and she cannot see anyone else now, it being the obligation of young people at the turn of the 1980s to marry the first person they date. Hence the Great Procurator and his wife, having already accepted Tang Min into the family, never accept the breakup, though she is the niece of a class enemy who allegedly hanged himself to escape punishment. They grow daily closer to Tang Min and more distant from their son.

Melodrama? While a teenager during the Cultural Revolution, Tang Min shared the prejudices of the age and despised her uncle, though his "hatting" as an antiparty, antisocialist element was an error. Later she had time to think about the injustice done him when she was sent to the countryside herself. It was Zhang Hua, the ex–Red Guard, who brought about her final reconciliation with her uncle. Zhang was himself disillusioned with leftism, having been sentenced by the Red Guards to reform-through-labor after his rescue of the future Great Procurator. He was sent to the same Trade Bureau prison farm as the uncle. By chance, Tang Min lost her way one night while bicycling home; she came to this farm instead of her own. She met Zhang Hua and they became friends; her uncle was nearby, and she apologized to him. It was just in time, for the next day he "hanged himself" (he was actually murdered by Liao Qi).

Miraculous coincidence, family intrigues with reconciliations and betrayals, and fated meetings with strangers bringing their own requitals are customary fare in good traditional Chinese literature, though not so much in the shorter Judge Bao stories. In fact, *Upholder of the Law* is a bridge to the classical detective genre previously discussed. The themes are Chinese, but the plot owes much to the whodunit; it is only that the bad guys keep obstructing the investigation, requiring that the Great Procurator not only use his wits but also keep his wits about him, as in the hard-boiled subgenre. This is a power struggle seemingly for its own sake, without the political or class meaning of a Maoist melodrama. Although the authors of the story, if brought to task, would surely claim that the perverters of justice are holdovers appointed by the Gang of Four who represent their mistaken politics, nothing about the characters' policies, language, or work style suggests that. They committed their crimes simply out of greed and a need for cover-up. This is a crime story, not a crusade. There are didactic asides and personal histories that count against the Gang of Four, but that is all they are: social background.

The plot is a detection of a miscarriage of justice. As the story opens, Xu Li must first discover that there has been a crime. He is pressured into immediately signing an arrest warrant for "Hoodlum Zhang Hua" at the personal request of Deputy Chief of Police Liang Jing. Procurator Xu Li does not recognize Zhang Hua as the boy who saved him during the Cultural Revolution; he had never learned the name of his benefactor—a common enough device in fiction old and new. But he finds that the three confessions of Zhang's alleged fellow gang members are identical, hence evidently false. Still, on the further say-so of his son, head of security now for the Foreign Trade Bureau (a bureau through which much money flows), and Liao Qi, the procurator joins the search for fugitive Zhang Hua. Miraculously, Xu Li later runs into his former benefactor and invites him home, still not knowing that he is named Zhang Hua—until after his daughter-in-law-to-be Tang Min spirits him away. Just then the procurator is astounded to see his benefactor's photo on an all-points bulletin (APB) his son brings him. This chapter ends in suspense. Likewise, the next chapter, in which Xu Li learns that Zhang Hua has committed suicide, leaving a note protesting his innocence.

Xu Li continues to evaluate more clues: careless comments and signs of venality on the part of his son, the loyalty of Tang Min to her old friend Zhang Hua, and the very light sentences given to the "three hoodlums." He senses a conspiracy and now begins to amass evidence of it. He brilliantly (and unmotivatedly) deduces that Zhang Hua must still be alive, for the report of his suicide would be a great cover story to protect Liao Qi. After observing the procurator's conversion, Tang Min takes him to see Zhang Hua, who is in hiding. Now Xu Li is both detective and counterconspirator. But it is by his legal professionalism that he begins unraveling the miscarriage of justice. He shows the three "gang members" a photo of Zhang Hua and they do not recognize him. In a dramatic but very unrealistic scene, it is in court that they first learn that it is a photo of the man they accused. They are charged with perjury. (One imagines that in real life this would have all been handled in a cell, by the police, with beatings—administered by their favorite prisoner cell bosses.) The three conspirators reveal who put them up to it, but again they can only describe the young man, for they do not know his name. Their description is good enough for Xu Haitao's mother, who listens in court and faints. Then she begs her husband to spare their son.

But might the three have framed Xu Haitao? The case will not be closed until Xu Li finishes his detection and reveals the identities of everyone involved, giving *pingfan* to Zhang Hua and, who knows, maybe his son too. Now the detection turns on finding out who suppressed a letter Zhang Hua sent to the municipal party committee charging Liao Qi with persecuting Tang Min's uncle to cover up her other crimes. The finger of suspicion hovers for a time over Secretary Zhao himself, for he simply passed the letter down to the police to handle. Finally, after seeing himself spied upon, the procurator tails his own son and notes that he has snuck into Liao Qi's apartment with cop Liang Jing for a strategy session. The case is finally broken with a combination of wits *and* prowess. Someone breaks into Tang Min's apartment at night to get the evidence Zhang Hua secreted there—including evidence of Liao Qi's murder of Tang Min's uncle. The savior in Tang Min's inky room—who is not identified—is strong enough to prevent the murder and savvy enough to grab a button from the assailant's coat. Only at the end, as we return to the liaison meeting that opened the story, do we learn the identity of the savior (Procurator Xu Li) and the would-be murderer (Xu Haitao).

Like Judge Bao, Procurator Xu Li punishes the bad, whoever they may be. First, he pursued Zhang Hua, even after recognizing him as the man who saved his life. Duty must prevail over personal affections; Xu had threatened to lock up even his "daughter" Tang Min if she were harboring this fugitive. Second, once Zhang Hua is cleared to his satisfaction, Xu Li finds himself pursuing his own son, twice. He both gathers the evidence and actually fingers him. Third, and most dangerously, he must expose and make the case against party leaders who outrank him. Probably the corrupt cop will be punished; but, more like a serious story of exposure or indeed a whodunit, the story stops short of the punishments and the full political aftermath. We have to assume that Liao Qi will be jailed—and Liang Jing perhaps demoted?

Still, a melodramatic happy ending overturns the near disaster, and the story is heavily didactic. On behalf of rule of law, Xu Li reproves Liao Qi during the initial search of Zhang Hua's quarters (she wants the materials incriminating her): "Do you have a search warrant?" She smiles. Xu retorts, "According to legal procedure, searches must be authorized by organs upholding the law, and carried out by the public security" (92). She claims that a warrant is not needed in an emergency, and the authors get Xu Li out of that one by changing the subject.[140]

Xu Li's eyes continually alight on contemporary propaganda slogans: a bookstore flies a banner, "Strengthen Socialist Legal System and Democracy" (93), and a newspaper editorial is entitled "Vigorously Strengthen the Work of the People's Procuracy" (95). Perhaps these slogans were to get the story past censors. But are they not modern functional equivalents of heavenly signs that benevolent forces really are looking out for the procurator?

Class Background and the Law

Equality before the law was stated in the 1954 state constitution, denounced in the Anti-Rightist movement, then deleted from the 1975, even the 1978 constitution, under which the above stories were written. The famous Third Plenum of 1978 hailed the slogan again and it was put in the 1982 constitution.[141] The phrase meant that no one was supposed to be above the law, as the stories summarized above advocate. It could also mean that no one was beneath protection of the law, not even landlords or counterrevolutionaries.

The two stories related below, from 1979, condemn such prejudice. The system of class statuses was soon to collapse of its own absurdity; the newborn in a titularly classless society were inheriting the class status of their forebears. In post-Mao times, this injustice had a name: *xuetonglun*, "the principle of bloodlines," or "like father, like son." Class status had all the force of a legal category such as "married" or "single"; its existence may even have worked to discredit the idea of rule of "law" in Maoist times. Moreover, since a family tended to hold a common class status, in accord with China's age-old household economy, there was a reverberation with tradition quite unnerving to the individualistic modern mind: the old spectacle of "collective prosecution," of an accused together with kin.[142]

Both these stories stretch the genre, but they are far apart in setting. The first, a fable whose upright detective is an antihero, occurs in the countryside, which is primitive but unregimented and full of communal feeling. The second is set in the more complicated and confined space of a police interrogation room; its heroine is reborn as a righteous person only at the end. The heroes are morally alone but not free to act alone. More realistically than in the previous works, they are hemmed in by higher-ups. They may not prevail in the end, even after solving the mystery. Both stories also expose the use of judicial torture. And the victim becomes an important (not to say well-rounded) character. Still, the theme is a quest for justice, a fight between good and evil, through another familiar formula: upholding the law even if it means imperiling one's kin or, in the second story, oneself. But just when a certain authenticity about how the legal system really works is about to push the stories into the "serious" category, overwhelming moralism emphasizes the melodrama. Unlike the many less-generic post-Mao tales of injustice in the "feudal" countryside, however, here injustice is a matter not of politics and ideology, but of law.

Pang Taixi's "Poan zhi hou" (After cracking the case) unfolds at a rural level beneath the purview of uniformed professionals. But it is 1970, and Chairman Mao's villages have paramilitaries. The hero law enforcer, Shi Kanghua, is head of his production brigade's militia and concurrently director of security. He polishes (but does not use) his pride of office, a semiautomatic rifle. Born a peasant, Shi is now an "educated youth." He has completed high school in the city and returned to his old village to serve the people as a party member. But he has not yet joined the village cadre elite. The latter have just decided to reward him, at the opening of the story, by sending him to college. The party has a branch here at the brigade level, and its secretary is Shi's boss. In these years the commune leadership is above the brigade, and higher still are party and government organs of the county. Regular public security organs having been "smashed" in the Cultural Revolution, law enforcement in the county is under a *baoweizu* (security group) headed up by the imperious Lü Jinhong.

Like a savior jurist, Shi Kanghua is a model of decorum and disinterested public service. He acts heroically during a typhoon. So does his friend Lei Chun, who went to high school with Shi and now clerks in the production brigade store. This friendship is a millstone around Shi's neck, for Lei's father, a teacher at the school they attended, was like many teachers branded a capitalist roader and traitor by the leftists. He died of heat stroke in captivity during round-the-clock harassment. Shi's other millstone, in some cadres' view, is his reluctance to punish all counterrevolutionaries and their offspring as a category. He sanctions only those who refuse to reform themselves. Fortunately for him, the majority of local cadres so far have taken this only as evidence that he follows written party directives ("law," such as it was at the time).

A flood comes; the night it crests, while Shi and Lei nearly sacrifice their lives fighting it, the brigade store is broken into. Its old manager is bound, gagged, and blindfolded, and the then enormous amount of 3,100 yuan is stolen from the safe. The crime is reported to the commune and county. Down to the countryside come the city man, Lü Jinhong, and his "investigators." In order to "let the masses solve the case" (by informing on their neighbors' class motives, without need of evidence), Lü sets up a "three-way county-commune-brigade small group to break the case" (219). This at least lets the locals participate; Lü names himself head, and Shi deputy head, in view of his security enforcement posts. The brigade has never had a crime before.

It looks like an inside job, and Lü wants summarily to pin it on the young man with bad class ancestry: Shi's friend Lei, the store clerk. Lü's only evidence is that Lei procured traveling expenses of unknown provenance (Lei says they were borrowed) to go protest for posthumous redress of his father's case; and that Lei's brother, a possible confederate, visited Lei Chun at the store a few days earlier. Lü thinks it inevitable that filial sons of a counterrevolutionary would gang up to get vengeance on the dictatorship of the proletariat, which they must hate (220). His suspect in hand, Lü seeks more evidence through torture. He whips Lei, then beats his ankles with an iron bar. Shi Kanghua stops him before he strikes Lei in the mouth (221).

That night there is a search for the tortured victim, who has escaped. Shi Kanghua's own father, who returned the night of the flood, reports having seen Lei go in one direction, but Kanghua follows up a different lead and finds his friend in an abandoned house just before he succeeds in hanging himself. Lü Jinhua had tortured Lei again, making him drink kerosene until he confessed to the crime (222). Foreseeing that his life could only become more miserable, Lei thought he had no other way out. Shi Kanghua berates the tyrannical city man, promising to file a complaint with his bosses in the county committee—that is, with the party, not any legal organ. He resigns himself to not going to college after all, for there is sure to be fallout. Lü returns to the city in a huff, saying the investigation is now up to Shi.

So Shi Kanghua launches his own investigation in earnest, during the agricultural slack season. There are reports that Shi Dashou, the hero's own father, has been living high off the hog. His whereabouts the night of the burglary are unaccounted for. He has committed petty theft before, and Shi now realizes that his father had tried to keep him from saving Lei Chun from suicide.

Just as Shi is about to arrest his father, his militia are in crisis: a riot is brewing between them and county security (224). Lü Jinhua and his goons from the city have come to the village in a car, determined to drag off Lei Chun for a really thorough "investigation." The militia surround them, ready to neutralize the outside threat. Shi Kanghua keeps the peace by delivering up his father and the remaining loot. The county man congratulates the young idealist and beats a hasty retreat. Shi Kanghua is a hero, to his village above all. Even the leftists approve of him.

But there is a problem. Shi Kanghua has inadvertently changed his own class status to "family member of an active counterrevolutionary." He is disqualified for college or to be a peace officer, even in the village. He might as well have robbed the store himself. The story ends with an explicit didactic tag, like a Ming vernacular tale: "As the villagers bewailed the injustice to Shi Kanghua, in sympathy, in sorrow, in anger . . . they pondered this question: Why, in our socialist society, can't a good man get what he deserves? Party policy hasn't changed that much, has it?" (225).

"Yi ge nü yushenyuan de zishu" (Statement from a female preliminary hearing interrogator) by Xu Xiao has more description, physical and psychological—including stream-of-consciousness narration, appropriate to its more confined and rarefied universe. In 1976, before the death of Mao, a female police interrogator is assigned to break a slightly younger dissident woman named Su Ning. Much like the cop, the dissident is of cadre lineage, went on the rampage as a Red Guard during the Cultural Revolution, but then had a change of heart in her fallen state as a rusticated youth in the countryside, so much so that she fell in love with the son of a Rightist.

Su Ning is accused of distributing reactionary handbills. The slogan "Down with Executioner Jiang Qing, Who Framed Premier Zhou" alone could get her twenty years of hard labor. Yet the interrogator is moved to sympathy by the dignity and sense of righteousness Su Ning exudes—until she has been handcuffed behind the back for a few days in her cell, made to crouch over her food to eat like a dog, and suffers painful swelling in her wrists (216). This story too exposes torture. It is the interrogator's job to wring from Su Ning the names and addresses of her confederates.

From diaries, letters, and a love token, the interrogator learns that Su Ning's socially downtrodden lover is Liu Xiyi, none other than the Rightist's son whom the interrogator once pitied and loved herself but abandoned when her uncle got her into the army. (It was that which launched her on a civilian career in security—a typical track.) The female interrogator's uncle could have got Liu transferred to Beijing, too, if only Liu had denounced his father. But Liu stuck to his principles, principles that later attracted the affection of the same kind of confused girl from the privileged class: Su Ning. She is the interrogator's replacement. But she will stick by Liu Xiyi, who is now her confederate in dissidence.

A past connection with a dissident like Liu Xiyi could threaten more than the career of a public security cadre, so the interrogator fears for herself (214). But pity, sympathy, guilt, and belated loyalty to her former lover, heightened by envy of her righteous prisoner, well up in her heart. Seeking absolution, she identifies herself to Su Ning, who recognizes and forgives her. Morally, the jailer and prisoner trade places. However, the interrogator's boss learns the identity and whereabouts of Liu Xiyi from another source. Throwing caution to the winds, the interrogator goes to warn him, but too late. He is already in handcuffs.

The female police officer's conversion is remarkable—melodramatic. That a policewoman who turns and tries to save a "counterrevolutionary" could "live to tell the tale" is a gift of history, though in fiction it seems a cheap political coup de théâtre: Jiang Qing was arrested a few months later, and her enemies were mostly exonerated. And yet, much as the cast of political suspects in "The Murder Happened Late on a Saturday Night" frames the discovery that real guilt may lie with an old lady who has her own private motives, here too injustices under the Gang of Four lead to other conclusions. First, the "theory of bloodlines" is evil; so moralizes the story, in the interrogator's voice (214). Second, political prisoners are human and should be treated as such. But for the grace of God, there goest thou.

The interrogator has little claim to Judge Bao status, and perhaps few readers would shed a tear to see any preliminary hearing investigator go to jail. But we know the political wind will shift, and if Liu Xiyi and his lover are to be exonerated and reunited, surely this born-again heroine will be the instrument of their salvation. She has already committed herself to their case.

From Police Justice to Lawyer's Justice

Back in the genre proper, with its saviors and happy endings, "Shensheng de shiming" (Sacred duty; Sept. 1978) and "Bianhuren" (Defender; May 1980) may be called the penal law melodrama's alpha and omega. The former is primitive and propagandistic and has a brave cop as hero. The latter is convoluted, envisions a legal world that does not exist in China even today, and has a Judge Bao surrogate whose profession barely existed in 1980: a lawyer. Both stories are by Wang Yaping,[143] a brilliant young army writer and "ground breaking hero" who would soon retire from the Chinese literary scene. "Sacred Duty," printed in *People's Literature* and later filmed,[144] virtually founded the penal law melodrama genre, before Maoism was dead. Its title is generic, but in a Maoist, not a popular-fiction sense. The "sacred duty" of which it speaks is that of the police. Other professions in communist society have a sacred duty too, notably writers; law and literature are already linked in this story by the shared Maoist cliché. Initially, however, critics pigeonholed the story as "literature of the wounded."

That was because "Sacred Duty" is a focused attack on the Cultural Revolution. The story came so soon after Mao's death that Wang still felt obliged to praise the chairman and indeed the Cultural Revolution; evil is attributed to those who did not understand Mao's intentions. This story became the foundational work of the new generic penal law melodrama because of its self-conscious depiction of immorality and malfeasance as crimes, and its use, in the end, not of Mao and Zhou Enlai, or even of good men following correct political and historical principles, but of good men and women upholding the *law* to right China's wrongs—though the name of the party, and Mao, had to be invoked to make the new medicine go down.

The plot is one part suspense (an archenemy who will stop at nothing closes in, as in anti-spy stories) and one part suffering (the "tragedy" of "the wounded"; but really melodrama, for, as in socialist realism, good prevails in the end). The victims fit the social profile of types that the party, or the Deng Xiaoping faction within it, wanted to rehabilitate. The chief victim is Bai Shun, a factory technician and college graduate—an intellectual. In August 1967, as violence crested nationwide in the Cultural Revolution, he was framed for attempted rape of the daughter of his politically ambitious next-door neighbor. The police came, Bai was beaten, and his wife never saw him again. He was sentenced to fifteen years of hard labor on a farm, where with the connivance of camp administrators he was repeatedly beaten, until Chen, a good cadre of the pre–Cultural Revolution regime who was actually trained at a police academy, arrived to take charge of the work brigade housing Bai. (Security personnel and wardens appointed during the Cultural Revolution are by political convention presumed to be nonprofessionals.) Chen came in time to foil one last attempt by the bad guys to kill Bai before their control lapsed. Meantime, Bai's wife has been petitioning for redress and has been rewarded with persecution of herself. She has lost her housing permit and had repeatedly to move, until she and her son, now eight years old (in 1975) and never seen by his father, live in a hovel scarcely better than a prison themselves. The good warder Chen has also repeatedly petitioned for reduction of Bai's sentence, overly long for a rape not completed and subject to reduction for good behavior during time served (eight years). Yet an invisible force high in the police hierarchy (Fei Fanian) frustrates every appeal. With its exposure of prison camps as places for torturing and warehousing innocent political victims, "Sacred Duty" might be called the founder of China's prison-camp literature too. Bai Shun is a broken man—physically injured, old before his time, and psychologically hurt to the point of near muteness, without any hope or meaning in his life.

He is of course innocent. In 1967 he fell afoul of the Cultural Revolution leaders in town by overhearing their plan to bring down the good Lu Qing, the top cadre in the municipal government, by murdering Lu's aide and pinning the blame on him. (It succeeded; two more victims.) The real murderer was Bai Shun's neighbor, Yang Darong, a faction leader. His ultraleft co-conspirators on top are gradually and suspensefully revealed as Fei Fanian, in 1975 still deputy head of provincial public security, and Xu Runcheng, still deputy head of the provincial revolutionary committee on high. Fei directs the rehabilitation of wronged cadres like Bai Shun while in reality sabotaging it. Yang Darong's reward for his infamous Cultural Revolution deeds was a key job on Xu's staff.

In 1967 Bai Shun had sent a letter to the leaders exposing his neighbor Yang Darong as a murderer. So Yang had forced his own teenage daughter, Yang Qiong, to act out a scene in which she accused Bai Shun of attempted rape. Bai was called next door, where leftist thugs, as quasi cops, seized him and dragged him away. The Yang daughter had always liked the Bais, and she was old enough to understand what she had done. So she is a victim too, with deep psychological wounds from a crime she committed under duress. This is all uncovered gradually in investigations by the savior hero, whose return to the provincial public security department begins the story.[145] He is Wang Gongbo, a tough old cop (59 years old) fully worthy of Judge Bao's mantle. He will overcome every obstacle, every act of surveillance and sabotage directed by Xu Runcheng and Deputy Chief Fei, to exonerate Bai Shun and see justice done. In the end, he makes the ultimate sacrifice to save the only witness to Bai's innocence.

Wang Gongbo has four assets: personal courage, professional experience and pride, a good and caring boss (Provincial Security Department Chief Zheng), and "a sacred duty entrusted to public security and legal personnel by Chairman Mao and the Central Committee of the Party," "carrying out the dictatorship of the proletariat" (111–12), which to him means "justice."[146] Wang Gongbo's experience is telling because he too is a victim. At the outset of the story he is just returning to his police work from a term of "re-education" at a May Seventh Cadre School, a work farm and place of political reindoctrination. When Wang's investigation gets too close to uncovering the leftists' crimes, he is taken off the case and sent back to the farm for more reeducation. He "escapes" with a medical leave in the provincial capital, but actually he goes back to the case. Presumably his ill health too is due to the Cultural Revolution.

Suspense mounts because the enemies of justice, using surveillance directed by Xu Runcheng, are only one step behind in silencing witnesses and trying to liquidate the cop who will not quit. Wang Gongbo must do some detecting, for the neighbor's daughter who swore out the complaint against Bai Shun has changed her name. She is a school teacher—the teacher of Bai Shun's son, in fact, whom she in her guilt secretly protects from bullying by kids who despise the son's "class background." (Victims in melodrama are good—truly good.) She feels too guilty to let on that her father is a provincial cadre or to reveal her real name to her boyfriend—Bai's son's homeroom teacher, who besides Bai's downtrodden wife is the boy's best protector. In comes Wang Gongbo of the Clear Skies, a still more efficacious protector for the unlucky boy, as he who fathoms the secret connection between the two teacher-lovers, which the homeroom teacher himself does not know. He not only gets the female teacher to reveal in a teary scene her identity as Bai's past accuser to his wife, so she can beg forgiveness, but also marshals the girl's support to be his sole witness to the innocence of Bai Shun and the infamy of her own father and his supporters. She will bring down the whole Gang of Four as it exists in this provincial capital.

Zheng's good operatives and the opposing ones of the Xu/Fei clique race to the scene of Yang's daughter's revelation and conversion, each side relying on its own intelligence and aware of the enormous stakes. That exposure of injustice to a factory technician, or even of murder by a man who was a mere revolutionary rebel in the Cultural Revolution, could bring down the party leadership of a whole province requires a suspension of disbelief, but this is melodrama. The black hats try to run over Wang Gongbo's witness—the reformed Ms. Yang Qiong—with a car ("Sacred Duty" may be the archetype for vehicular homicide stories too), but the good cop pushes her out of the way, apparently suffering fatal injury in her place. Still, he has accomplished his sacred duty. One year later the Gang of Four are arrested, and so, thanks to the evidence developed by Wang Gongbo, are Xu, Fei, and Yang Darong. Bai Shun is released and reunited with his family, whose honorary member now includes the woman who as a little girl was forced to accuse him. Outdoing even Judge Bao, the cop has made a *family* out of adversaries.

At first glance, "Sacred Duty" reads like a throwback to Maoism, both in its direct propagandizing and in its chosen icons. Observing wounds on the head of Bai Shun's son, just back from a beating by school bullies, Wang Gongbo tries to comfort Bai's wife: "Don't worry, you must trust the Party and the Party's policies. No innocent person will remain falsely accused." She responds "with determination." "Chairman Mao is still alive and the Party's policy is clear. I'll never lose hope. I'm sure that one day the Party will pardon my husband" (119). Today a Chinese audience would guffaw at those lines. Justice is this melodrama's theme, but is it also a precursor of less formulaic *law* stories of the future?

The bad people have not just persecuted people and betrayed the revolution; they have framed their victims as criminals (Bai Shun as an attempted rapist, Lu Qing as a murderer), and they have themselves committed crimes: murder, attempted murder (of Yang Qiong), perjury, libel, misuse of public office. The hero is not just a loyal party member but a professional law enforcer. He sniffs out the injustice from the start, from *legal* irregularities in the case file—Bai Shun's confession does not bear his signature or fingerprints or the name of the cadre in charge of the case, only the red seal of an unnamed department (104). (Presumably a Cultural Revolution organ with police powers was in charge; clearly no judge or procurator had any part in the case.) Also, Wang's experience tells him that fifteen years is not a typical sentence for attempted rape. His sacred duty, even if it is called Maoist, is to go out alone like Judge Bao and right these legal wrongs. It is a duty for officers of public security and the courts.

That this is such an early and pathbreaking story may explain why Wang Yaping, a young army writer, took the safe road of finding his Lord Bao surrogate in the fraternal public security service, not the judiciary or procuracy, as seems to have been preferred in the later penal law melodramas of 1979–80. (China's jurists were still cowed in 1978; but then, how many lawyers were there when Wang Yaping wrote "Defender"? The political climate for literature moved faster than the legal system.) The public may have actually enjoyed seeing the Gang of Four "smash" targets like the police with their violent and secretive ways. When cops appear as heroes in later stories, it is often against other cops, or against their inner selves, as in "Statement from a Female Preliminary Hearing Interrogator." And the cop-heroes are too old and experienced to manhandle their prey.

Note, finally, that "Sacred Duty" represents a transition in the concept of legal protection as a paternal duty. Wang Gongbo is nearly a knight-errant, fighting on his own, seemingly picking his own battles and getting little direct help from his well-meaning but evidently not very powerful boss,

Zheng. He feels he has a direct line to God (Mao). But the relation of Mao to his flock is paternal; Wang acts not as a free righteous spirit but because he feels *authorized*. This story represents a stage when the supreme paternal authority of Chairman Mao is vested in Judge Bao–like police heroes. Mao's paternalism has been delegated downward, looking forward to the time of his death. And so Wang Gongbo's chief mission is that invoked by Lu Xun: "save the children."[147] Wang is the father who will save Yang Qiong, Bai Shun's son, and the new generation as a whole, who need to be brought up with the precepts of justice instead of the violence of the Cultural Revolution. He was once the teacher of the good warden Chen, for Wang was a "legal" specialist trained at a police academy when such institutions still functioned. China's police, of course, have a more parochial understanding of the story. To them the "sacred duty" is simply police work, whatever ultimate end it may serve.

"Defender," a real "legal system" melodrama fortified with the puzzlements of a whodunit, shows how far the genre had traveled since "Sacred Duty"— except for the denouement.

The paeans to the party and Chairman Mao of "Sacred Duty" are gone in the 1980 story, long passé, not to mention credits to Chairman Hua Guofeng and the Cultural Revolution that seemed antediluvian within months of the former story's publication. "Defender" chooses a lawyer as its paragon of justice. This is wishful thinking; Wang Yaping was once more ahead of his time. China's lawyers had abandoned their practice from 1958 to 1980. All six university law departments and four higher-education political-legal institutes closed in 1966; they had trained 19,000 personnel since 1949, but that included procurators, police chiefs, and political-legal staff in the party.

The right of the accused to defense (usually by a friend or relative) was not deleted from the constitution until 1975, but it was effectively negated, with other rights, after the Anti-Rightist furor of 1957–58. Defense counsel had to act "in the interests of the state and the people" and not "favor the defendant." It was asserted that the only purpose of the (pre-1975) constitutional right of defense was to assist law enforcement agencies in assessing evidence of the accused's crime and degree of repentance, to enable them "more fiercely, accurately and firmly to attack the enemy."[148]

Beginning in 1977, law departments, and in 1979, political-legal institutes, were gradually restored to train new political-legal cadres. Some cadres did become lawyers in legal advisory offices where they worked for the state. Still, some judges and party political-legal chiefs assumed that asking someone to defend you was prima facie evidence that you lacked remorse for your crimes. Quite a few regarded lawyers as "trouble-making and even traitorous"—"on the side of the enemy."[149] Through the 1980s, there were instances of lawyers being arrested for defending unpopular clients.[150] Still today, lawyers are usually passive at trials, speaking only during the concluding debate. Without the court's permission, they have no right to question witnesses or the police during a trial, introduce new evidence, or enter a plea of innocent for the accused. Mostly they try to minimize the damages alleged to have resulted from the defendant's crimes or give evidence of mitigating circumstances and remorse. In criminal cases, they are not bound to follow the defendant's wishes.[151] They also have little opportunity to shake up a case through investigation, being called into the process only when the court is about to proceed to trial. Until the law changed in 1996, the court did not have to give the defendant notice of his or her upcoming prosecution, or permission to hire a lawyer, until seven days before trial.[152] That occurred only after the three branches had completed their investigations and got their case airtight, to protect the 99.7 percent conviction rate. An official source says that before 1996, "Court trials were scheduled only when judges believed in the guilt of a defendant."[153] The defendants were addressed as "the criminal"; the accused in Wang Yaping's 1980 story is thus "Criminal Tang." It was this practice that was stopped in the 1996 "Decision on Revisions to the Law of Criminal Procedure," under the banner of "presumption of innocence." The burden of proof did not shift to the prosecution, and much less was reasonable doubt exculpatory.

Chinese lawyers in the early 1980s were loath to claim they were independent or even working *for* the accused. Their responsibility was not to help an accused criminal escape his legal debt to society. Lawyers saw themselves as a fourth service in the unitary, nonadversarial pursuit of justice. This makes Wang Yaping's lawyer hero, Lei Meng, all the more like Judge Bao.

One learns at the outset, from the at first anonymous first-person narrator,[154] that Lei Meng became a famous lawyer by righting injustices before the Cultural Revolution. Following his rehabilitation after the fall of the Gang of Four, he worked to establish a legal advisory office (presumably the main work was getting permission for it), and it has just now opened. The problem with lawyers, in Lei Meng's own words, is that people assume that they are "loyal to evil people with lots of power" (115). That was taken for granted well before communism tarred lawyers as bourgeois abominations (see discussion in Chapter Three). But Lei Meng has a veneer of legitimacy because he had the right enemies. In the Cultural Revolution his ribs were broken and he became permanently crippled in one leg. His wife was driven to suicide and his children were beaten to death.

Lei Meng plays the righteous hero by seeking justice wherever it may take him. He puts his reputation at risk by throwing a wrench in an open-and-shut case; he makes his own investigations (he gathers medical records of the deceased and surprises the prosecution with them the day of the trial—highly unlikely in life) and uses his forceful personality to get reluctant parties to the case to come clean with all they know.

The solemnity and majesty of the law are dramatically evoked in the packed courtroom where Lei Meng proves his mettle. On trial for murder is Tang Xiaobo, son of Tang Hanjiang, secretary of the party committee at the prefectural level (between province and county). Can such a high cadre's son be severely punished, perhaps with the death penalty? How will that affect the power structure? wonder the spectators. Lei Meng has been hired by the Tangs, the powerful ones, instead of by the family of the deceased young girl, Jiang Xiaofan, a mere typist at a grocery depot—one more strike against the image of lawyers. During the investigative part of the trial, before "debate," "Criminal Tang" acknowledges that the murder weapon and other physical evidence are his and bows his head in admission of guilt after the story narrator testifies that he witnessed Tang run from the crime scene. Tang must have killed the girl because he got her pregnant and did not want to marry her. Being a new party member in his probationary period, he could see his future going up in smoke. But during debate, the lawyer uses medical records to show that Ms. Jiang knew she was pregnant before ever meeting young Tang; she extorted hush money from him anyway. And she had been dismissed from her job for promiscuity a few months earlier. Had someone else plotted with her? Was she gunning for Tang Xiaobo when she met him, to solve her problem of pregnancy, foolishly unconcerned that she might drive him to the ultimate means of silencing her? The trial must adjourn for further investigation. Lei Meng has scored a brilliant, Perry Mason–style turnaround in mid-process. It is fantasy, to be sure; the conviction rate has already been noted. Prosecutors and police are not so careless as to overlook medical records, and lawyers who value their jobs share information with comrade court officers. But readers need to suspend their knowledge of reality to enjoy Perry Mason too.

Lei Meng looks cool and professional next to the flummoxed 38-year-old female procurator, Su Ning, who did have the guts years ago to divorce her husband, a trial judge, for helping the Gang of Four. Su Ning harbors such a prejudice against lawyers, particularly any who would help the Tangs, that when Lei Meng visits the first-person narrator, Su Ning assumes that Lei will try to bribe the narrator, perhaps ask him to say that he saw a second person also flee the crime scene. Because she is the narrator's relative, or perhaps because the latter is afraid of the lawyer, he lets her—the prosecutor—hide in a closet to eavesdrop ("as a witness") while the lawyer questions him!

The main suspense comes from the device of the first-person narrator himself, an "inadequate narrator." Before the trial he confides to the reader his terrible fear that the skillful lawyer will get a guilty secret out of him. Might the narrator even be the murderer? Tang Xiaobo soon confesses, but the nature of the narrator's misconduct remains a mystery. Was he an abettor? That mystery, along with gradual revelation of facts about the case and the parties to it, including a retrospective telling of the many crimes done to the decedent—all in the reverse order so appreciated by formalist and structuralist critics—recreates the pleasures of a classical detective story. The plot is multifarious, to say the least, even as a *fabula* related by the narrator to the lawyer at the end. The narrator knew Jiang Xiaofan before she died. In fact, he came upon her as she was attempting suicide and saved her. She was ruined because Luo, head of the food depot where she worked, had accused her of having an affair with his deputy and fired her. Luo by that means damaged both of them, particularly Ms. Jiang, whom he had raped but who refused to become his lover. Ms. Jiang had then impetuously informed on him to Tang Hancheng, the big cheese in the provincial committee. The narrator immediately realized what folly that was. Luo and Tang were fellow thieves. Tang had misappropriated antipollution funds, taken enough grain to create a famine in the countryside, and committed other misdeeds; he always got away with it by bribing central inspectors with feasts provided by

Luo the grocer. Ms. Jiang had tried suicide once before, been discovered and rescued by Tang's son, Xiaobo, then been raped by *him*, and pressured again to become *his* mistress. The *narrator* then conceived of charging Ms. Jiang's pregnancy to Tang Xiaobo, as a way out for Ms. Jiang and also a means of bringing down Tang's omnipotent and treacherous father. No one predicted that Xiaobo would resort to murder.

With this plot twist, the inadequate narrator is revealed as having morals. He may have acted illegally in abetting the framing of the younger Tang (it was Jiang, not he, who thought to ask for hush money), but he was fighting to exonerate Ms. Jiang while bringing down Tang Hanjiang, the root of all evil. Ms. Jiang could never have got justice against either Luo or the younger Tang with Tang Hanjiang still in power, and the younger Tang was guilty of rape anyway. So the narrator fights for justice beyond the law, with the biggest villain as his target. That, at least, is the story's logic and lawyer Lei's conclusion; all three judicial cadres brush off the fact that the narrator helped make Ms. Jiang a blackmailer and then a corpse.

Recognizing the greater justice that the narrator has fought for, Lei Meng shakes his hand, pronounces him not guilty, and offers to be his lawyer to get him off on any charges that may be preferred against him! Su Ning, convinced that *this* lawyer is a good lawyer, comes out of hiding to congratulate the startled Lei. She sees that he is indeed on her side—that of justice. Lei Meng, ever the lawyer, at least has the sense to warn the procurator that she has no evidence to convict Luo now that Ms. Jiang is dead, much less Tang Hanjiang, who has committed no crime under the law (he has only mismanaged funds he was authorized to spend). Never mind, says the procurator, she will use the trial to *educate* society, which is a higher duty of a socialist court. (It is a paternalistic duty, and it squelches needless adversarialism.) Perhaps Tang Xiaobo can be persuaded to give evidence against his father, to escape the death penalty, adds the lawyer hopefully. Lei Meng agrees to help Su Ning make her case, and they shake hands. In the last line, the narrator comes to a realization: "on our socialist judicial battle lines, lawyers and procurators true to their professions fight for a common goal: purveying justice and thoroughly extirpating evil" (115).

So the lawyer has merged with the procurator into a unitary icon of higher justice and synoptic wisdom. Lei began as an adversary, a foreign element in Chinese legal practice. Now even he is dissolved in the unitary jurisprudence of Lord Bao. Legal justice is still a higher morality of virtue and just deserts.

CONCLUSION

Chinese crime fiction just after the death of Mao had little to build on but old formulas. Yet it reconstituted itself very quickly. One genre successfully incorporated the intricate mystery plotting of the classical whodunit and must have struck readers as new and foreign. It offered the thrill of the unknown in an era that was frantic to Westernize and modernize. The other genre touched so many chords in China's premodern literature that it offered the comforts of nostalgia, of escape to a simpler time when men were good or bad and a wise judge made everything right. One can marvel at how faithfully foreign and traditional formulas were reproduced in the post-Mao years. Or one can marvel at how they were mixed and stretched, with Western-style mystery and detection for interest and Chinese-style morality for reassurance. Just what simpler time and place was sought was ambiguous. Maybe it was the orderly England of Holmes, the America of scientific technology, or the alluring if scandalous capitalist society of Hong Kong. Maybe it was Judge Bao's world, before the torments of communism. Perhaps it was as recent as 1954–57, a reputed "Golden Age" when crime was rare and good communist father-and-mother-officials could still be imagined to be keeping evil at bay.

China, of course, was deeply divided in 1978–80. Most citizens felt both gratitude and aversion to the society they were about to leave behind. The whodunit genre, with its simple, benevolent, pragmatic, and not particularly Maoist cops, may have appealed as much to conservative, "socialist" taste as to readers hungry for science and modernity. And the penal law melodramas, for all their obligatory paeans to the party and conventional morality, evoked such hatred for party-boss villains and their despised ex–Red Guard offspring that cynics and dissidents may have enjoyed them. These stories are transitional, a part of China's passage from communist to "postcommunist" society.

Strong heroines appear only in the melodramas, and perhaps more often in the early 1980s than later. Kathleen Klein notes that the Western classical

detective story (not to mention the hard-boiled story) is male-centered because of the kind of hero it calls for. It is in general conservative.[155] Certainly
policewomen play a supporting role to the paternal hero in the Chinese
whodunits. Some penal law melodramas cast women in the starring role, but
not in particularly feminist ways. Like Maoist fiction, the new legal melodramas ignore social realities of gender inequality by creating a gloriously
unsexed future world in the present. Judge Bao's legacy becomes a gender-
neutral patriarchalism/matriarchalism. A more positive harbinger is the
"Statement from a Female Preliminary Interrogator," narrated in the voice of
a woman—a complicated woman—who by the end of the story feels sister-
hood for her prey. But beautiful female corpses like Bai Yingying's are dis-
turbing. The connection between scantily clad female bodies and violence
becomes especially explicit on magazine covers once crime fiction is unfettered in 1984, as Chapter Four indicates.

Regardless of subgenre, most stories traffic in murder, rape, and theft, and
in suspense, detection, and moral exemplars. They are under the spell of the
habitual and doctrinal Chinese commitment to realism and social relevance,
and yet of didacticism too. The whodunits are meticulous about clues; the
melodramas are meticulous about laws. Neither is reliable about investigative procedure.

However complicated the plots, the crimes and their motives are simple,
and this simplicity offers the reader still more reassurance. Common crime
was skyrocketing at the time, in life and even more in public consciousness.
There were new kinds of crime, and uncertainties about what *was* a crime.
Was anything criminal, if officials could with impunity turn public assets
into private property? And was anything in the new economy *not* a crime in
somebody's eyes, if hard-liners could prosecute bosses who gave workers
bonuses on a charge of bribery? The most complicated murder was simple in
China's new age of economic crime.

The turn-of-the-1980s stories show early stirrings of the adversarial spirit,
and not just in Wang Yaping's "Defender," which is remarkably nonadversarial at the end. Both the melodramas and the whodunits feature heroes
who act from their own initiatives, as if they were alone. Cops predominate
in the whodunits, perhaps because they do not evoke a sense of threat there,
whereas they tend to be erased from the melodramas in favor of bureaucrats
who might restrain them. Both subgenres favor uniformed professionals as

their heroes. They well represent the spirit of China's first period of modernization under communism.

Still, the comforts of paternalism permeate both subgenres. Unlike Western or indeed Maoist fiction, there are few amateur heroes from below. "Comrade Holmes," the young worker who wants to be a private eye in "A Gold Buddha," is ridiculed. However cerebral and professional, the crime fighters have a paternal (or maternal) style. They assume responsibility for the security of all, or personify justice for all, like the father-and-mother officials of dynasties past. They are like parents as well as role models to their subordinates. Their chief concern, in an age frightened of the Red Guard generation, is to save the young. Even in the melodramas, where the archvillains are middle-aged men and women in power, their representative crime is covering up a criminal action committed by their spoiled offspring. The good judge, procurator, or cop takes the villain's place to punish and reform the offspring. One is not to take the law into one's own hands. And yet the heroes do not go through channels. They take evidence of crimes to the top, to the paternal bureaucratic equalizer, through petition. The "amateur heroes" on top, the party rulers, are paternal authority personified—unless they have become corrupted supercriminals who must be removed.

Chinese crime fiction in this era stood at a crossroads: between communism and postcommunism, and between paternalism and individual advocacy. The next chapter views comparable legal and literary themes in a longer historical perspective.

CHAPTER TWO

Tradition

How might post-Mao Chinese writing about crime and the law reflect pre-twentieth-century legal and literary practices? This chapter finds them in original works of the new era as well as in centuries-old writings about crime cases that won a new mass readership in the 1980s. Also noted are some shared forms and predicaments of code-making and fiction writing. Both activities are generally thought to have blossomed in the Tang dynasty or about a century before. They have likely influenced each other ever since, both ideologically and textually.[1] Some ancient "legal texts" have long been read for pleasure. Literary writing about true crime continues today in Chinese reportage.

This chapter therefore considers premodern Chinese law *in* literature—new literature—and *as* literature, in imperial-era works that may be read for pleasure. Law *of* literature, such as Ming and Qing literary bans and intellectual property law, is beyond the scope of this book, although Chapter Four concerns modern freedom of expression.[2] That has seldom been protected by law. In 1868 the famous governor-general Ding Richang wanted to ban the tales of Judge Bao's cases as an unhealthy influence![3]

This chapter draws force from a conservatism in Chinese legal and literary forms that is visible in attitudes and morals sometimes called Confucian, and in thirteen centuries of codes that have preserved certain laws "long after they had ceased to have any connection with social reality."[4] The code was modernized only in 1910, just a year before imperial rule expired.[5] There was more openness and adversarialism in law and literature in later decades, but in 1949 Mao reestablished a system in which the sovereign (the CCP) employed laws and literary propaganda—often for the same ends—without being subject to them.

ROOTS OF CHINESE AMBIVALENCE TOWARD LAW AND FICTION

Premodern China, like the premodern West, saw literary value and proper human behavior as holistic unities embodying transcendental principles (of the Dao, or Way). Morality, or *li* (Rites), overlapped, subsumed, and bettered the law from a state of higher perfection. Literature (*wen*; actually "writing," and more, as explained below) stood in a similar relation to writing for amusement. To state the common predicament of Chinese law and fiction in a phrase, law was to Rites as fiction was to Literature. Yet even the highest morality, however transcendent in theory, was rendered mundane and "legalistic" by the incessant codifying and intellectualizing of it in late imperial China.[6] High literary value was likewise evermore embodied in enjoyable works of dubious social reputation.

These polarities reversed in the modern West, without wholly overturning the underlying unities of value. When fiction became high literature, its values became the dominant literary ones. With the coming of secular and constitutional democratic rule, the sanctity of law began to trump and assimilate morality. Law professors implied that a legal education could mold a moral and socially beneficial mind, rather like Confucians who imputed similar benefits to the study of Rites.[7] It is partly for that reason that other law professors in the West have resorted to literature, indeed fiction—modern, canonized novels—to critique the law; morality no longer always provides sufficient leverage for that.[8]

Old dualisms have not completely expired in the West. Bookstores shelve "fiction" apart from "literature," and clergy are more revered than lawyers and judges. In literature, it is always law that allegorizes morality, not the reverse. Perhaps the law "excludes (or suppresses) other modes of discourse."[9] But these contradictions are not necessarily flash points for controversy in our time. James Boyd White has constructed the *law* as a moral, humanistic practice like literature, one capable of making citizens their best selves. To Ronald Dworkin, law is an interpretive practice in which judges, like composers of a chain novel, create law subject to the constraints of what went before. They make the law the best it can be within its genre, discovering its telos as they adjudicate.[10]

In China the paradigmatic law text is a code, not evolving opinion from the bench, and the old dualisms remain. Officially, literature and enforceable norms of behavior, many of which go beyond the law, were and are indivisible, incontestable, and nonadversarial; they have long embodied a unitary and moral truth that serves the sovereign—today, the CCP.[11] Literary works and legal advice were sold to commoners before modern times, but even then such transactions were déclassé and often of questionable legality. Under Mao, law and literature were wholly barred from becoming autonomous, fee-for-service professional callings. Some would say that legal and literary practice virtually disappeared, replaced by party rule and propaganda.

The traditional Chinese state and orthodox culture, by contrast, did allow a place for the low callings of law and "popular" amusement.[12] The fear was that knowledge of the law and fiction would spread uncontrolled among commoners and serve evil purposes.[13] The orthodox culture was, in short, ambivalent about law and fiction. Lawsuits and novels were not banned as a whole; they were themselves seen as vehicles for teaching.[14] It was in the early twentieth century that modern upward revaluations of law, popular culture, and the masses threw Chinese values into a tizzy. The cultural fields of law and fiction gained prestige and power, claiming value on their own terms. But the old ambivalence toward them reemerged. It continues in the post-Mao era, whose task is the undoing of three decades in which law and literature were diminished in ways unprecedented in China. The resulting ideological turmoil has greatly enlivened the new "Chinese legal system literature."

ENFORCEABLE NORMS: MORALITY AND LAW

Even before Rites were swept away in the 1911 revolution that brought down the empire, the word *falü* (law, laws) and its shorter form in classical Chinese, *fa* (law, laws), were close to synonyms for the English, though other Chinese terms could also be translated as "law."[15] In some ancient texts, "*fa*" was interchangeable with "*xing*," which meant punishment, specifically corporal punishments such as death and mutilation that may have existed before the writing down of *fa*.[16] In any case, Chinese *fa* has long been codified and subject to judicial review, and Western law for its part punishes infractions. The character *fa* originally meant "pattern," Derk Bodde says; hence the notion of law as "a model or standard imposed by superior authority, to which the people must conform."[17] "*Fa*" can also mean "magic," "dharma," "methods," indeed, "rules" for behavior[18]—or literary composition[19]—but those may be considered different words.

The majority of "penal" statutes in the code by Qing times were administrative laws instructing the emperor's officials; infractions of them were as severely punished as thefts and murders committed by civilians. However, what we think of as "criminal law," mostly under the Board of Punishments in China, defines a legal system as it is popularly understood, and it did to the Chinese as well.[20]

In the view of legal anthropology, the field of law also includes local rules below the state's law, even unwritten ones.[21] China had this substratum of local customary usages and clan and guild rules. Doubling, extending, or contradicting official codes, they assimilated to the term *falü* in the twentieth century to the extent that they were enforced by the state. Until recently, few Western scholars realized how often local magistrates even in imperial times had had to adjudicate civil disputes (what the emperor and literati called "minor" altercations), many of which were not covered in the code.[22] Still, most civil disputes did not come before the government. Many dynasties also had, outside their code but at the same level (some were in practice higher), imperial edicts, "precedents" (decisions on specific cases—though not all could be cited, or were published, in the Qing), administrative regulations, even statutes.[23]

It raises Chinese hackles to call the ancient *li* (Rites) a Chinese *super-stratum* of "law," and certainly they were not an ecclesiastical canon law. But they were codified no later than the Han and in certain times and places en-forced, although often by parties other than the state. The Rites' legitimacy in a mythologized primordial tradition is not wholly unlike that of higher customary law in other societies.[24] Morality, in the form of Rites, overlapped the law; ideally it subsumed law and obviated its punishments.[25] Many Chinese thought that Rites, music, *wen*, and law all imitated heavenly or natural patterns, though imperfectly.[26] Indeed, Jean Escarra depicts Chinese *fa* not really as "laws," but as models or behavioral standards whose punish-ments were "theoretical."[27] Others emphasize the many unenforced laws in Chinese codes, calling them moralistic, idealistic, or "symbolic," with the function of teaching, not adjudicating.[28] Certainly the imperial Chinese bu-reaucracy was too small to handle most offenses; local, "private justice" filled in.[29] One cannot understand the social position and functioning of the law as such (*fa*) without reference to the gravitational pull both of custom and of *li*.

Like other peoples, the Chinese also conceived of justice beyond all law, Rites, and custom: what Aristotle called equity. Anglo-American equity came from courts of chancery that remedied the severity of the law, though later they were absorbed by it.[30] In China, equitable ideas were influenced but not exhausted by ideas of *bao* (retribution, requital) and Buddhist karma. Punishments in hell were imagined to resemble punishment by the state law. Here law became entangled with unenforced and yet sometimes codified popular morality beyond the purview of orthodox belief and the state. Popular religious texts assigned proportionate merit and demerit points in lists of good and bad deeds; in late imperial times some common people and literati constructed personal ledgers anticipating final (transgen-erational, if need be) requital by "hidden laws" (*yinlü*).[31] But Chinese trea-tises on law as such do not speak of transcendental justice, abstract or hid-den, though it may have been so conceived millennia ago, in the Dao itself.[32]

"Law" per se (*fa*) was limited in scope, and embraced only ambivalently by literati and the state, for at least three overt reasons. First, it was com-monly believed that law was for the lower classes, indeed the lowest, crimi-nal element of the lower classes. In reality, nobles who committed offenses were brutally punished in all eras.[33] But the *Li ji* or *Book of Rites* says that "The rules of ceremony [*li*] do not go down to the common people. The penal statutes [*xing*] do not go up to great officers."[34] This is now received opinion among Chinese of diverse political persuasions; it may reflect not only the class consciousness of the twentieth century but also the clearer boundary between gentry and commoners that accompanied the rise of Confucian ritualism in late imperial China.[35]

A second weakness of law perceived since ancient times is its negativity. Laws can be applied only after they are broken; even then they might not reach the inner person. A Hong Kong barrister thus reproved Jerome A. Cohen in the 1960s: "The trouble with you Westerners is that you've never got beyond that primitive stage you call the 'rule of law.' You're all preoccupied with the 'rule of law.' China has always known that law is not enough to govern a society."[36] Codes tell bad sorts just what behavior they can get away with. Quoth the *Zuozhuan*, "When the people know what the penalties are, they lose their fear of authority and acquire a contentiousness which causes them to make their appeal to the written words, on the chance that this will bring them success [in court cases]."[37]

By the third century B.C. the Qin state, influenced by the Legalist school, published a harsh regimen of laws that applied, in theory though not in practice, to all classes. Subjects were meant to know and live in terror of law. The Legalist thinker Han Feizi spoke of laws as opposed to literary learning; he advocated clarifying the former and prohibiting the latter.[38] But it was Confucius, defender of the *li*, whose views later became orthodox: "I can try a lawsuit as well as other men; the important thing is for there to be no lawsuits."[39] Rites were attributed to sage kings, whereas *fa* were ascribed divine or semidivine origins in no extant text. Derk Bodde notes that the earliest surviving account of *fa*'s origins (in the *Classic of History*) attributes it to barbarians who, shunning "spiritual cultivation" for "the five oppressive punishments, which they called law (*fa*)," executed so many innocents that the supreme deity Shang Di was moved to exterminate them, one and all.[40]

Third, the state tried to suppress open social conflict and communicated a disdain of lawsuits to all subjects. The Kangxi emperor once in effect lauded injustice; he wrote that "lawsuits would tend to increase to a frightful amount if people were not afraid of the tribunals and if they felt confident of always finding in them ready and perfect justice. . . . I desire therefore that those who have recourse to the tribunals should be treated without any pity, and in such a manner that they shall be disgusted with the law, and tremble to appear before a magistrate."[41] Early-twentieth-century

Chinese proverbs about the law ran to "Win your lawsuit and lose your money," "Of the ten reasons by which a magistrate may decide a case, nine are unknown to the public," and "Nine lawsuits out of ten are decided by arbitration."[42]

China's civil service examinations did not stress legal knowledge, apart from special legal examinations in the Tang dynasty. Qing examinees had to write sample judicial decisions (*pan*), but only before 1756.[43] Modern scholars disagree about how much detailed legal knowledge Chinese magistrates possessed, but in Ming and Qing times they seem in practice to have relied on legal secretaries. Although would-be lawyers advised citizens on suits as early as the Tang, in late imperial times they were suspected of being "legal tricksters" who instigated lawsuits and aggravated false charges. That was punishable by the code; taking money for legal advice was particularly reprehensible.[44]

People went to court anyway, certainly in the Qing, and magistrates often tried civil disputes rather than always shuffle the litigants off to mediation, as would happen under communism. Hence Philip C. C. Huang sees dissonance between the Qing civil legal system's self-representation and its practice. Madeleine Zelin even speaks of a nascent "contract culture."[45] The Kangxi emperor's own *Sacred Edict*, which was read in public from 1670 until 1911, admonished subjects to "lecture on the laws, in order to warn the ignorant and obstinate."[46] There was a provision in the Ming and Qing codes that commoners able to explain the laws might be let off for an unintentional first offense.[47]

So the state was ambivalent about, not opposed to law. It was after all a tool of the sovereign's governance; over half the Qing code's statutes regulated the official activities of bureaucrats. There was detailed law about marriage because the family system was important to the polity.[48] Land rights and inheritance were regulated because they affected the stability of the realm and taxation. Laws were arranged under the central ministry governing the kind of behavior the laws regulated. And law was a tool for teaching; a certain majesty adhered to it in popular culture. Fiction and folklore showed judges saving the people with law, though in many cases they were also saving people *from* the law. Only under Mao did party norms above state law limit the force of state law in the eyes of the state itself.

The human or "positive" rather than "natural" origins of law were clear enough; the emperor's decisions became substatutes of the code in Ming and Qing times, and they took precedence. There were 1,800 substatutes by 1740, making the law convoluted.[49] Joseph Needham saw *li* as natural law, *fa* as positive law.[50] Yet, reasons one scholar, the emperor, having Heaven's Mandate, himself enacted "natural law."[51] Imperial amnesties suggested that the emperor could cleanse a wrongdoer of his taint, notes Brian McKnight. The law embodied cosmological principles that, for example, limited executions to autumn and winter, although the question of whether the law itself must thereby have been sanctified is disputed by scholars.[52]

A law code was seldom read as literature, and yet it was written in classical Chinese and could be regarded "as a treatise of sorts."[53] Statutes (articles), unlike substatutes, were relatively immutable, for the same reason as the Rites: they were handed down from of old. One could always adapt their interpretation with new substatutes and intertextual commentary, or leave the statutes as written without pretense of enforcement as a tribute to judicial ideals and ways of governance past. One scholar attributes to the immutable dynastic statutes, and to a lesser degree even the substatutes, a kind of "sanctity."[54]

Behind the ambivalence toward law lies, implicitly, another factor: the authority of the Rites as norms of society—enforced and codified, like law. Rites included, perhaps began as, rituals and ceremonies for the dead and for the heavens. They addressed many nonlegal matters and matters too trivial to be severely punished: how to dress, walk, bow, and speak, and taboos of personal deportment. They concerned duties to patriarchs and feudal lords, not just the sovereign. Being semisacred, they were not to be amended by him. They were originally recorded in different classic texts (the *Zhou li* or *Rites of Zhou*, the *Yi li* or *Book of Ceremonies and Rites*, and the *Book of Rites*), themselves composed from earlier texts, though unchangeable once put in final form, in the Han.[55] Yet the same state authority that promulgated the great Tang dynasty code of laws also published, in 732 A.D., a great code of Rites for the emperor and his bureaucracy, in 150 volumes. Subsequent dynasties followed suit.[56] The great orthodox Neo-Confucian Zhu Xi (1130–1200) in effect updated the Rites for popular practice in his era. A French missionary in the 1720s reported that his *Family Rituals* was in "every household."[57]

In fact, parts of the *Book of Rites* speak of prohibitions[58] and just punishments, some to be imposed by the noble man.[59] The classic specifies certain sanctions,[60] indicates in what month prisons are to be repaired, handcuffs and fetters provided, and criminals captured,[61] and tells how to hear a case requiring application of the five punishments. A modern scholar sees in the *Rites of Zhou* prescriptions for a use of imprisonment that amounts to "reform through labor."[62]

That the Rites included duties to the spirits simply attests to the blurred boundary between humans and spirits in ancient belief. Imperial sacrifices were also specified by law in Book Four of the Qing code: laws applying to the Board of Rites. The Rites prescribe behavior according to one's status in society and one's family, but so did the law. Transgression of the Rites might lead to sanctions by a patriarch or feudal lord rather than the monarch, but that is often true of law in feudal societies. Rites in the old books were recognized even in imperial times as utopian idealizations, but the ancients were thought to have behaved better than contemporaries.

Above all, the logic of the Rites was incorporated into the law code, as in heavier penalties for killing a father than a son. T'ung-tsu Ch'ü and Derk Bodde called this the Confucianization of the law (*fa*).[63] Ch'ü adds, "originally *li* were enforced by social sanction, and later by legal sanction. A rule of behavior enforced by social sanction is *li*; the same rule of behavior is law when legal sanction is introduced."[64] To quote Chen Chong, a first-century minister of justice, "What is left by *li* is covered by punishment. To go beyond *li* means to enter punishment. The two are but the outside and the inside of the same thing." The ancients used such terms as *lifa* and *lilü* (Rites and law). To Taizu, founder of the Ming, the law and Rites were like an outer garment and its inner lining.[65] The Qing code proper states that *fa* are sometimes directly derived from *li* and cites the *Rites of Zhou*.[66] The *Annotated Catalog of the Qing Complete Library of the Four Treasuries* proclaims the Tang code to be based entirely on Rites. Indeed, the code's subcommentary cites all three classics of Rites extensively.[67] The purging of *li* from the modern 1910 code was the major grounds on which conservatives attacked it.[68]

It was a paternal justice system. Moral teaching by the sovereign, men of nobility, and fathers should prevent disputes. Failing that, local notables might mediate. If courts had to be involved as a last resort, the complainant did not sue the other party but launched an accusation with the magistrate. The imperial authority did the questioning; there were no separate prosecutors or lawyers for the defense. The magistrate, however, was subject to close supervision and judicial review, by the Board of Punishments itself in capital cases. Subjects were to internalize both the Rites and the ideology that law prevailed not of its own excellence, but only through good judges and good sovereigns.

There is however an adversarial aspect to a trial absent in legislation: an implication of alternative versions of the truth. Official attitudes toward knights-errant were ambivalent too. Heroic opponents of evil and the legal system were suppressed in their time but praised in official histories. Knight-errantry was another form of local and customary justice that kept disputes out of the courts. Moreover, the righteousness that these figures enforced was a supermorality,[69] an extension of the *li*. Knights-errant enforced the filial obligations of other people to *their* fathers. That was the role of the law, with its attendant ritual strengths and weaknesses: a judge not related to the dis-putants—not the true patriarch—enforced a father's rights against his son that ideally he would have been able to enforce himself.

Chapter One noted that paternalism has survived in PRC legal practice. This chapter addresses the continuing tendency, even after Mao, for social-moral norms and laws to overlap, tending toward mutual identification and confusion, and yet also bifurcation into separate codes for higher and lower—or better rather than more criminal—members of society.

In the PRC, the ordinarily precise discourse of *fa* in the usage meaning "law" reverted to a broad sense of "norms" more familiar in legal anthropol-ogy and literature. The 1979 *Cihai* (Sea of words), China's new major dic-tionary of the time, defined *fa* ("law," or we might say, "rules with the force of law") thus:

> Legal term. 1. Overall designation for behavioral norms (*xingwei guize*) that embody the will of the ruling class, are formulated or approved by the state, and whose implementation is guaranteed by the state's coercive power. Into the sphere of "*fa*" fall all laws (*falü*), decrees (*faling*), rules (*tiaoli*), regulations (*guize*), resolutions (*jueding*), orders (*mingling*), precedents (*panli*), practices (*guanli*), etc. One of the instruments of class dictatorship . . . 2. Identical to "*falü*."[70]

A 1989 revision accords comparable breadth of meaning to "*falü* in the broadest sense," with "administrative laws and regulations" among its sub-species.[71] A 1990 book explains that the "legal system" is based on "laws" above and "rules and regulations" below. It adds that the legislature (National People's Congress) "vests the State Council with the power of en-acting 'quasi laws.' " Evidently temporary or experimental law is meant.[72]

But the new post-Mao legal system retains a more profound traditional dualism than that. Besides the laws and regulations promulgated and enforced by all levels of the bureaucracy—by the state—the party too has "norms": *zhengzhi luxian* (political lines), *fangzhen* (orientations, or "general policy"), and *zhengce* (policies),[73] enforced in that order. The party's norms are a codified (if changeable, and variably applied) Law above state law: the "real law" guaranteeing the coercive power of the ruling class. The communist slogan "policy is the soul of law" was in effect even in the 1990s. A 1980 book on "basic knowledge of the law" explains: "The spirit of statutory law and political norms is identical. If contradictions between statutory law and political norms arise, then the state shall repeal or revise statutory laws, or promulgate new statutory law."[74]

When extensive state law was enacted, beginning in 1979, party norms, in the form of policies and personal codes of behavior for party members, were not superseded, but assumed the superlegal position of the ancient Rites. Ad hoc mediation, education, and other "internal" means of social regulation had always supplemented the state's "exterior" governance.[75] But party norms duplicated or second-guessed the laws of the state. Like the Rites, they were separate but higher: codes for the ruling class, however weakly enforced, and yet in theory inextricably linked with the proletariat. Like Rites, they were thought to embody the masses' better nature, to which any of them might aspire, though bad class background in practice kept many from doing so. But at any given time there were still two kinds of people. Political and ideological study molded the "work style" of Communist Party members; laws were for the intractable. Only belatedly did they come into play to punish the transgressions of the better people—the party members.[76]

The task the party-state of the 1980s reluctantly set itself was to let the CCP's Rites, which true believers may really have felt to be holy models that changed the inner person, pass into history, so that state law might have the legal field to itself.

LITERATURE AND FICTION

The original meaning of *wen* is uncertain; it "came to mean something like what we now call 'literature' " in the second century B.C., notes James J. Y.

Liu. Previously it meant "pattern," and by the time of Confucius, "culture," "civilization," or "learning."[77] Like the patterns named *fa*, patterns named *wen* recalled those of nature. Liu Xie's discussion of *wen* in his *Wenxin diaolong* (The literary mind and the carving of dragons, completed before A.D. 502) thus finds "the origin of literary forms in the imitation of patterns observed in the natural world."[78] In literature as in law, closeness to the authority of established patterns was the means of evaluation and discrimination.

It was in the Han dynasty that the word *wen* came to be used for writings predominantly aesthetic rather than pragmatic. The modern word for literature, *wenxue*, originally meant "literary learning"; in the Six Dynasties period (222–589) it assimilated to the meaning of *wen*, and in the fifth century, as "literature," it was officially separated from scriptural scholarship (*jingxue*), philosophy (*xuanxue*), and history (*shixue*).[79] Literary criticism was mostly interpretation of poetry, but respect was accorded any competent writing in the classical language—less to writing seen as too utilitarian, such as legal documents and the "eight-legged essays" used in late imperial examinations. But Liu points out that pragmatic theories of literature were the most influential in premodern China; they critiqued literature as a vehicle of the Dao, and metaphysical theories also saw literature as a manifestation of the Dao.[80] This gave even creative writing a didactic purpose. Chinese authors before the Tang tended not to think of literature as being created, but of themselves as vehicles through which works of literature came into the world. Hence *chuanqi* (tales) of the Tang have been generally considered "the first consciously fictitious genre in Chinese literary history."[81] This causes a problem for those who seek the roots of Chinese fiction in our sense. Moreover, authors of fiction about the law were adept at passing it off as more important, nonfiction writing.

Fiction in the vernacular language, drama, and fanciful tales of all sorts were accorded low status (there were lower verse genres too). All were written by literati and often had nuances that only the highly educated could fully grasp—perhaps only the author's friends, if there was a single author. Still, fiction was generally considered incapable of expressing a writer's most delicate and profound feelings. It was because all writing was considered a tool of teaching that lofty morals were imparted to it.

After 1917 there came a reversal in the status of high and low literary genres in the eyes of intellectuals, as there had been in the relative statuses of

Rites and law. Ambivalence was manifest by 1902, when literary subgenres were already being "reshuffled."[82] The great reformer Liang Qichao called fiction "the highest genre of literature" owing to its presumed educative power, even as he blamed China's myriad social evils on all the dirty, unreformed fiction of the past.[83] Fiction would be deemed to have a demonic split personality for the rest of the century.

Contradictory modern concepts and concerns have complicated the idea of fiction and of what its premodern status really was. The history of China's fiction has been replayed in linguistic-genetic, formal, etymological, and aesthetic-normative terms. Let us briefly examine these four approaches. All of them ultimately reassert hierarchies of high and low. They do not, in the end, elevate fiction as a whole, but create a high and low within fiction itself, often in resonance with traditional Chinese genre conceptions that privilege subject matter and its presumed moral influence. Thus the deck was stacked against narratives about crime and the law. Moreover, since Chinese crime narratives were not always vernacular or even fiction, they did not wholly share in the modern upward revaluation of those once low forms. Chinese crime narratives had no way up.

The linguistic-genetic view takes fiction (today called *xiaoshuo*) and drama to be primarily an evolving tradition in the *vernacular* language since middle imperial times.[84] Vernacular fiction, even more than drama,[85] was an "outlaw" genre until the twentieth century.[86] Its colloquial language was denigrated as vulgar, its storytellers' conventions as reminiscent of their putative origins in humble marketplace storytelling, its subject matter as close to pornography and sedition (much as Maoists would later link Holmes to sex, violence, and bourgeois sedition). Some great novels were proscribed in late imperial times and today are still read under the covers in conservative households. Certain major works were not printed until after their authors had died. Vernacular novels were not to be read by literati—specifically, not by legal secretaries.[87] But fiction in classical Chinese was not considered important either.[88]

The upward revaluation of popular culture in the early twentieth century reversed the positions of the classical and vernacular languages. Vernacular fiction's presumed origin in storytelling and performances of acting and singing was celebrated as a living tradition of the folk, unlike the "dead" tradition of the literati. But the direct link of the great old vernacular fiction to

Song dynasty folk and oral forms has been largely exploded, as have been the popular origins of the presumed subgenre of *gongan*.[89] Indeed, it is now appreciated that by the sixteenth century some vernacular works could be fully enjoyed only by the upper classes. Connoisseurship arose in the mid-Ming, when "a broad public was assured for vernacular fiction, and the fiction itself became an institution," says Patrick Hanan.[90] The implied storyteller's conventions and episodic management of suspense were really an author's pose, at least in the late, great novels, an element of literary as much as popular attraction; to literati readers, they lent the Chinese novel an irony we associate with the Western novel, Andrew Plaks argues.[91] As David Rolston puts it, certain Ming literati elevated the great novels by rewriting them with implied authors, associating them with classics and belles lettres, and dignifying them with classical-Chinese interlinear commentaries and prefaces the same as they did for writings in the higher language.[92] The literati novel was born.[93]

Although still more ancient vernacular fiction from the Tang called *bianwen* has been discovered since Lu Xun wrote his classic history of vernacular fiction,[94] the upward revaluation of late imperial vernacular fiction by recent researchers and critics—in effect the third in history—has elevated it to a point that vitiates its onetime presumed status as an independent populist tradition. And yet the existence of a great or canonical stratum at the top, as it is appreciated in Western modernist terms, presumably leaves most vernacular fiction on the bottom.

A second approach seeks fiction not by its language but in the formal terms of comparatists, beginning with the older, classical-language tradition. By assimilating fiction to the general concept of narrative instead of to the growth of mass audiences, critics have found the origins of Western fiction, even the novel, in ancient Greece and Rome.[95] With a similar emphasis on fiction as "shaping"—even without the deliberate spinning of fictive tales— William Nienhauser sees Chinese fiction in parables of the Zhou and Han histories, in classics, and in ancient books of myth, philosophy, and fable.[96] Not all scholars agree that fiction is to be found so early.[97] The emphasis on fiction as mere shaping may seem a reaction to the Chinese reluctance to admit to invention.[98]

It is easier to see as fiction the short, classical-language narratives of the Six Dynasties period called *zhiguai* or "records of anomalies." They are of interest to this study, since ghosts and anomalies appear even in modern

Chinese detective stories, if only as red herrings. But the *zhiguai* as a category encompassed a variety of forms and content. Most were accounts of exceptional people and supernatural happenings overlooked or passed over by the official historians. Some were only one-line observations; it was in the sixth century that there were some recognizable short stories, followed by *chuanqi* tales in the Tang that clearly amounted to fiction. Even these stories, though they were in classical Chinese, were traditionally denied major literary status.[99] The *zhiguai* were distinct in their lack of authority—literally as creative pieces not authorized by the sovereign, and figuratively as accounts lacking the "authority" of orthodox history. Fiction, by this definition, is once again to be known by its departure from a standard. This is not a prestigious grounding for fiction, and indeed the great vernacular novels of the Ming and Qing are seldom linked to the *zhiguai*.

A third approach, used by Lu Xun, is to trace the Chinese expression "*xiaoshuo*" to see what kind of works it was applied to before the vernacular fiction (*xiaoshuo*) of Ming and Qing times appeared. But the meanings of words—like *gongan*—change, crippling many an etymological argument. The first *xiaoshuo*, listed by title in Ban Gu's *History of the Han Dynasty*, do not seem to have been well-shaped stories or necessarily antecedents of later fiction in classical language. They were "street talk and alley gossip," literally "petty talk" or "lesser discourse," including evidently historical fragments, sayings, argument, and odd records, all putatively collected by ancient kings to take the pulse of folk sentiment, and perhaps only reflecting a tendency to preserve any ancient writing.[100] Again the standard was historicity, or truthfulness more generally, and in this light "the term *xiaoshuo* emerged with the rather weak and unappealing sense of defective history."[101] Sheldon Lu argues that a major Chinese tendency is still to judge narrative in general by the standards of history-writing.[102]

In the late Ming, the term *xiaoshuo* took its modern meaning, referring mostly to vernacular fiction.[103] But at the end of the Qing, *xiaoshuo* could still be a confusing catchall for "classical tales; plays; novels and *huaben*; *tanci*; *guci*, etc. Probably in most cases only the bad examples are meant," claims Wilt Idema.[104] Tan Zhengbi found that official and private bibliographers of the sixteenth century seldom included any texts of vernacular fiction in their lists, under any category; when novels did pop up in later centuries, it was typically in lists of books to be banned.[105]

A fourth approach, that of Wilt Idema and Lloyd Haft, is to speak of "trivial literature" in premodern China, a term whose connotations are inevitably normative.[106] David Rolston notes that the classical/vernacular distinction reified by early-twentieth-century reformers and literary historians was already underlain by a more important distinction "between 'refined and ornamented' (*wenzao*) writing for an elite, educated audience rather than a more 'popular' (*tongsu*) style that included simplified and denotative literary Chinese."[107]

This is of interest to our study, for Idema takes *Three Heroes and Five Gallants* and other knockoffs of that Judge Bao novel and of *Judge Shi's Cases* (which was earlier) as the epitome of lower-tier schlock novels. He considers them to be written in a debased, unliterary classical Chinese lacking the ornamental gems in "impeccable" classical idiom that gave life and prestige—in certain circles—to the great vernacular novels.[108] Idema also classes *Longtu's Cases* as written in a simplified classical-Chinese "novelese"; this view is contested.[109]

Yet Idema and Haft also apply the concept of "trivial literature" differently, and persuasively, not only to marginal novels that have a pedestrian mix of classical and vernacular Chinese but also to (1) all vernacular fiction; (2) all unprestigious writing in classical Chinese, such as the *zhiguai*; and (3) anything called *xiaoshuo*. These three categories recapitulate the three conceptions of fiction discussed above. All three notions, which at least partly engage old Chinese values, are unkind to Chinese fiction. Fiction by any conception was known by its distance from something higher, better, or more important. That went double for fiction about crime.

Fiction was irremediably "low" until it was presumed to have superseded the old high literature, much as the "low" phenomenon of law superseded the anciently respected Rites. New fiction didactically embodied modern ideology, but even as a low form, premodern fiction was seen by society's upper strata as a vehicle for teaching—either implicitly, by showing the appropriate consequences of sordid behavior, or explicitly, through direct comment. Yet "the convention of proclaiming the utility of fiction in prefaces, postscripts, and moralizing commentaries, . . . echoing the earliest recorded statements on literature and its function in society"[110] must have indicated some doubt that such utility existed. Fiction became self-consciously "serious" in the twentieth century both in principle and in order to overcome its past.

The parallel revolution in the world of law began in 1910–12, when Rites, like classical literature, were overthrown. Yet it was only in post-Mao times that law, for late-twentieth-century Chinese, began to be elevated to fill the vacuum in fully public, codified norms. It is that time lag that occasions this book.

Chinese fiction in the twentieth century was reconceived as high; in the process, its values became dominant in literature, as in the West. But crime and law were low, and when they were combined with popular forms, fiction's disreputable associations came flooding back. One post-Mao solution was the traditional one: to write crime fiction in putatively nonfictional forms, as "true case" write-ups. In modern times it was not always easy to improve on the old casebooks and literati writings. This may explain the latter's renewed, post-Mao popularity. However, writers with journalistic skills found new ways of writing about cases in reportage.

As an institution, Chinese literature was paternalistic. And yet, just as lawsuits formally speaking had two sides, so literature developed ideas through dialogue—famous in the *Analects* of Confucius, the *Laozi*, the *Zhuangzi*, and Zhou and Han books of myth and history (some say fiction) like the *Intrigues of the Warring States*. These works embody Stanley Elkin's "thematics of opposites," or the dialogic discourse Bakhtin thought unique to the novel. Genuine dialogue—conversation as it really might have been spoken—was a strength particularly of China's great vernacular novels. The Judge Bao stories suffer from its absence.

LAW IN LITERATURE (I):
LEGAL PLEADING IN A SHORT STORY

China's voluminous premodern literature is a field for studies of law in literature hardly yet touched,[111] but more relevant to this book are traditional legal concepts that have struck a chord with post-Mao readers. It may be that "modern Chinese and Japanese jurists look at legal phenomena with minds trained in the categories and methods of Roman law."[112] Although party members above the law and class enemies below it are exceptions, in theory socialism brought to China very modern concepts of equality, whereas "the principle of legalized inequality" was "probably the most conspicuous single Confucian influence on imperial Chinese law."[113] Yet imperial China maintained an exacting legal system under a detailed code, and in that respect it was closer than Mao's China to modern legal practice. Maoism created a vacuum after which old legal ideas flooded back as if from repressed memory. Many of them are observable in the 1980 short story "Shenpan" (The trial) by Li Dong and Wang Yungao.

"The Trial" plays off competing abstract conceptions of law in a dialectical, indeed adversarial fashion. The plot and theme are as in a penal law melodrama: a high crime has been alleged and an upright procurator named Chen Zhe comes in from the outside to prosecute it. After overcoming temptations to shirk his duty—doing intellectual battle with a bevy of good old boys in the party and emotional battle with a previous benefactor, and finally with his own soul—he does the right thing by prosecuting the case to the fullest extent of the law and winning. Yet this is not a typical "upright official" genre story, for two reasons. The accused, Liu Lei, director of a big reservoir construction project whose physical collapse after torrential rains caused heavy losses of life and property, is a criminal by negligence, not intent. He is no villain, and at the end he in effect joins the procurator as a hero by accepting responsibility for the disaster. He smoothes the way for his own condemnation by law, vowing to serve the Four Modernizations after his rehabilitation through a five-year prison sentence. This rosy ending of conversion, self-sacrifice, and serving the people recalls Maoist formulas. It may even subvert its own legal message by suggesting a discourse of administrative rather than legal punishment: psychologically, the cadre is still managing to make the primary punishment the one he deals himself. His is a "perfect" trial, doing justice, educating the public, and rehabilitating a "criminal" all at once. The other departure is that the usual penal melodrama uses mystery, suspense, and other devices to entertain, whereas in "The Trial," discourse, indeed ideological argument, overshadows the action.

Liu Lei had cut too many corners in building his reservoir, over technical objections from his chief engineer. The ideological climate favored speed above all else in those days under the Gang of Four (soon to end). Liu's superiors in the standing committee of the local municipal party committee (the usual villains in more generic crime-and-law stories) surely pressured him to follow Chairman Mao's dictates in this matter. Liu was not bribed, and there is no hint of favors for subcontractors. But the political authority one rung higher, the standing committee of the prefectural party committee, has now investigated and put the chief blame on Liu. They have ordered the constitution of a "special court" to try this case because of the grave consequences of the project's collapse.

Procurator Chen Zhe, trained at a political-legal institute during a period of the 1950s when there was something of a legal system, answered the call to return to his home town when "the Central Committee, after the smashing of the 'Gang of Four,' in order to strengthen a socialist legal system, transferred a batch of political-legal cadres to the provinces to strengthen police, procuratorial, and judicial organs at every level" (7). This is his first grass-roots case. Whom should he be called on to prosecute but his foster father, Liu Lei—for Chen became a war orphan in 1944 when the Japanese captured and executed his parents, both underground CCP members. Liu Lei, a fellow party member and Eighth Route Army commander at a nearby base area, led a daring attempt to rescue their surviving eight-year-old son, Chen Zhe. Japanese agents had put the Chen house under surveillance, with little Chen Zhe as bait. By the ruse of replacing Chen with his only son, nine years old, Liu Lei liberated the hostage. The Japanese imprisoned his own son and smashed one of his feet, crippling him for life. After the war, Liu raised both boys as his own.

The authors have thus framed Chen's dilemma as a classic conflict of *qing* (human feelings; here, sentiments of sympathy, partiality, gratitude, and indebtedness, especially toward kin and other benefactors—in this case, Liu Lei) versus law, or really punishment. *Qing* is a moral obligation in Chinese society, like giving a gift in return for a gift. It is backed up by the old orthodox Confucian view of *qing* as inborn emotion, understood positively as that which distinguishes people from animals; one must feel and act on one's sentiments to be fully human. The authors of "The Trial," however, take a modern, anti-Confucian view of *qing* as primarily "partiality," a distorting and corrupting force negating reasonable, equal, and unselfinterested human relations.[114] By a paradox of history, progressive 1980s authors wanting to undo Maoism could not cite Legalism, the ancient anti-Confucian philosophy opposing partiality and emphasizing law, since Mao had praised Legalism during the Cultural Revolution. The story's attack on *qing* indeed resonates with latter-day vulgar "Confucian" antipathy toward emotions as such, which conflated *qing* with *yu* (human desires). Neo-Confucianism, like Buddhism, was wary of these feelings. But the contest between *qing* and *law*, each freighted with old connotations cutting both ways, is not wholly one-sided.

And yet, under this dichotomy, *law* as the inverse of *qing* is not an emotionally neutral force one would ever trust to judge a friend. It is by nature harsh and penal, like the punitive imperial *fa*, something to be visited only on evil people in a retributive spirit. Theoretically, *qing* might be given a juristic spin, as a traditional form of equity under the law deriving from the sense that application of statutes does not always serve justice. This equitable justice existed in traditional provisions for leniency, as in commutation and mitigation of sentences and lighter criminal penalties for juveniles, elders, the mentally impaired, and sole surviving sons, which often were written into the codes themselves, as they were in the *Rites of Zhou*.[115]

After weighing arguments for both sides, by having cadres, friends, superiors, and coworkers of Liu Lei's stage a debate at his house—where Chen Zhe also finds himself after strolling there unconsciously, since he was raised there—the story comes down in favor of law.

"The Trial" may be called propaganda for the "rule of law." Descriptive passages emphasize law's majesty (in the courtroom's awed hush) and its strict procedures, contrasting with the indignity of prison, which is for pornography merchants, smugglers, and spies for Vietnam, whom Liu Lei ruefully learns are on the other side of his cell walls.

Statutes are quoted verbatim with their number, as in many a law story of this era. This renders rule of law more self-conscious, "popularizes" (spreads the word about, makes universal) new citizen rights and procedures under the law—and also keeps faith with tradition, since citation of the relevant statute or substatute was "an absolute requirement at every judicial level" even in late imperial China.[116] However, one bit of legal information passed on here is inaccurate, although the aim is to assert the newly restored right of defense to the accused. The cop heading the preliminary interrogation department declaims to Liu in his cell that "According to the Constitution of the People's Republic of China, Article 76, 'The accused has the right to defense.' In addition to the right to defend yourself, you may appoint a lawyer to defend you. If you find that inconvenient, the court can appoint one for you, and he will appear in court." (6–7). Right to a trial defense was reinserted in the 1978 state constitution, after being deleted from the 1975 one, but it is Article 76 only, in the 1954 constitution, which was in 1980 already twice superseded. The right to retain a lawyer for defense, and the possibility, not the requirement, of a court appointing defense (not necessarily a lawyer), are in the 1979 Law of Criminal Procedure.[117] Like the melodramas, this story is more conscientious in sorting out political and administrative minutiae such as job titles than points of law.

In fact, the particular statute Liu Lei has broken is not divulged, and this uncovers, perhaps unintentionally, a real problem of the "rule of law." There had been few trials of massive official negligence at the time, and criminal negligence law was underdeveloped. Judicial review of administrative acts came only in 1986, or more formally in 1989. It is not clear under what statute Liu Lei might be assigned a "crime" in proportion to the degree of political mistrust he has stirred up for the party. The PRC code is revealed to be vague, especially next to the imperial ones.[118]

As of old, Liu Lei's offense was to betray the state and then the people. This is a model trial to show how the state fulfills its most sacred trust of governance. There is no move to prosecute Liu simply for multiple counts of "negligently killing" or injuring people (arts. 133, 135). Chinese criminal law (art. 53) also provides for supplementary civil suits by parties injured by a crime. Evidently law and legal system literature are didactic enough to prefer prosecutions with broader policy implications.

The 1979 criminal code, chap. 2, "Crimes of Endangering Public Security," like the even more ideologically important chap. 1, "Crimes of Counterrevolution," has origins in old socialist law. Its emphasis is on deliberate *sabotage*, with the breaching of dikes explicitly named (art. 106; the Qing code also devoted its art. 433 to it), and although the 1979 code tacks on a paragraph outlawing the difficult concept of negligently committed "sabotage," in this story it was nature that breached the dikes, not Liu.[119] Liu Lei has not taken bribes, misappropriated public property or funds, or taken advantage of his office to "engage in corruption involving articles of public property" (art. 155). Communist law, like traditional law, is much more concerned with punishing its officials' "private offenses" (intentionally committed, for profit or to gratify some passion) than their "public offenses" (negligent mistaken decisions in the course of their ordinary work).[120]

Art. 114 provides for lesser punishment of "staff and workers of factories . . . [and] construction enterprises . . . who do not submit to management and violate the rules . . . thereby giving rise to major accidents involving injury or death." This seems made to order but for the focus on following superiors' orders. Liu Lei *is* management, and he erred by not following the advice of a subordinate. Perhaps the state could do no better than to prosecute him under art. 187, for official "neglect of duty"—though a lawyer might point out that his fault lay in the misdirection of a fully engaged performance of duty.[121] This statute does not make explicit provision for loss of life—rather for causing "public property or the interests of the state or the people to suffer major losses." At the end of the story Liu is sentenced to five years, as if convicted under art. 187, but the story does not say so; it indicates instead that five years is a reduced sentence conditioned by Liu's (political, not legal) confession of guilt and current moral rehabilitation, as if he were originally convicted under art. 106 or 114 after all. His crime is mysterious for a legal system in which names are so important.[122]

Alarm bells set off by a Western legal outlook begin with the subjection of Liu Lei to a show trial. Regular courts do sometimes try cases at the place of the crime or dispute, for educative purposes; one hopes for Liu Lei that this is such an instance, not a "special court" like the one that tried the Gang of Four. Second, his good character and years of good service as a cadre (so often used in the past by other cadres for an end run around the legal process) are deemed irrelevant, since uncorrupted law must be harsh and show no pity. Third, there are conflicts of interest. The authors are aware that Chen Zhe might have recused himself from a case against a man who rescued and raised him, for they specify that Chen consciously decided that the lack of a direct kinship relation between himself and Liu meant that formally there was no conflict. They also finesse the problem by having Liu Lei told, both at the trial and in advance of it, that he has the right to ask for court officers to recuse themselves if he thinks there are grounds. Just as shocking, one of the people's assessors is from the flooded village; concurrently, he is asked to testify as a witness to the horrors. Assessors are citizens who usually just second the judge, but in theory their role is one that some Chinese dictionaries translate as "juror." The authors countenanced such conflicts of interest probably to enliven the plot with drama. Finally, one need not advocate a Nuremberg defense to point out that Liu Lei's bosses in the municipal CCP committee, even Chairman Mao, share his guilt. Liu was caught out by a shift in party line; evidently no written construction regulations were contravened. But people could not defend themselves in 1980 by saying that the Gang of Four made them do it, in law or in literature, and the point of the story is to build up rule of law, with the Gang of Four's antipathy to it as antithesis to the new post-Mao consensus.

The story tackles other legal conflicts as well, though, and they illustrate deep-seated ambivalence toward law. The intellectual debate is exactly that: friends and kin of the accused verbally spar with Chen Zhe about justice.

The authors want to "popularize" the rule of law, and the first antithesis is a Marxist-Leninist view expressed by an old party member on the standing committee of the municipal committee above Liu Lei. He notes that "everyone wants law, and everyone wants order," implying that law is law-and-order. "The problem is," he continues, "what kind of law do we want? The people's law ought to protect the people and be used to carry out dictatorship only against class enemies. But is Liu Lei a class enemy?" (8).

This viewpoint is easily dismissed in Chen Zhe's interior monologue. It was once orthodox that law was a tool of dictatorship by which one class ruled another, but ideology has changed. (In fact, on this point it had not.) Chen in any case takes the conflict to a deeper level. If the law is only for certain bad characters, this will create a class of people beyond the law. That was what the Gang of Four were, and it led to awful turmoil. The further implication, however, since the old cadre so stresses his party membership and his forgiveness as a *party* view, is that the CCP and its appointees are the class above the law.

Meantime, a related but more reasonable argument has been put forward by Liu Lei's son, the cripple: his father is entitled to a break, not because of his party membership but for his merit in service. This is a good argument in any legal system, though to Chen Zhe this can only mean another merit of Liu Lei's that Chen ought to ignore: Liu's saving of Chen's life. The simplification making law (impartial justice) the alternative to *qing* (partiality, or injustice as such) stacks the deck against Liu Lei, making law an inhumane juggernaut of punishment, as imagined by two millennia of anti-legalists. And the authors have further simplified the dilemma by polarizing the choice: either Liu Lei will be tried (under the law) or he will not be tried (because there is no law; *qing*). The alternative of giving him a criminal trial and introducing his character, motivation, and good service as mitigating circumstances is not mentioned—for the good old boys in the party do indeed have the all-or-nothing objective of wholly avoiding a criminal trial.

Behind the idea of law as something only to be visited on class enemies lies the traditional sentiment that law is only for bad people, and the related idea (and reality, under communism) that to be charged is as good as to be convicted. Cadres who have committed "mistakes" (not crimes) can always be sanctioned administratively and demoted if necessary.

Finally, another cadre pushes the idea of *qing* too far, from a personal, humane point of privilege to a blanket social protection, though based on status rather than class membership—on a bias, really, that finds cadres by nature too refined (like white-collar criminals in the West) for criminal status. This cadre represents literature rather than law; he is a fat, middle-aged novelist who has published several novels about Liu Lei as a model hero. He has been a frequent guest at the Liu household ever since, add the authors, who may be implying that their fellow professionals in literature are lap dogs of the ruling elite. "What is *qing*?" asks the novelist, in all his eloquence. "Another word for the will of the people, the wishes of the people! With such lofty will and ambition did Old Liu join the Revolution and go through hell and high water for decades on end. And now they want to deal with him through the legal system?" Besides confirming the old view that "law" is something so terrible that it is to be visited only on bad people, in extremis, when softer administrative sanctions are exhausted or inappropriate, this novelist has abstracted *qing* into something owed in principle by a category of people (the citizenry) to another category (the cadres who made the Revolution). But then he slyly brings *qing* back into the Confucian realm, asking the procurator why he of all people does not have the "conscience" (the old concept, *liangxin*) to recognize his personal debt to Liu Lei. This just proves to Chen Zhe, and to readers, who do not owe any of the characters anything, that *qing* distorts justice.

This is reinforced as Chen Zhe mentally rehearses lessons he learned at the political-legal institute ("law school") condemning the views of Confucius, who allegedly held gentlemen (*junzi*) to be above the law. Finally, at Liu Lei's trial, the losses caused by his negligence are brought forward in testimony to balance the merits of his previous life.[123] But then a witness meant to testify (objectively) to the awful damage of the flood has a change of heart when he learns, for the first time, that the negligent director he wants to castigate is none other than the 1940s army commander he had always (subjectively) esteemed under his secret code name. *Qing* overcomes the chief engineer too, who says on the stand that he must take some of Liu Lei's responsibility for him. *Qing* distorts reason.

"The Trial" abandons dramatization for legal discourse once again. Chen Zhe mentally rehearses other case histories of cadres who have done stupid and unforgivable things but with proper authority, so that they were in the end untouchable by the law. It all finishes with a grand authorial lament, still phrased within an interior monologue not too convincingly placed in Chen Zhe's voice, in a vocabulary that harks back to the classics to condemn blind respect and obedience to the rulers as an aspect of *qing*. It is disparagingly referred to as constituting an inescapable "web of *qing*."

Under attack here is a historical sense of law as inherently class-bound. The ruling class (today, the CCP) was in principle above the *criminal* punishment of imprisonment—cadres equated it with "legal" punishment, which was really reserved for a class even below the commoners, namely enemies and bad elements. This comes from a sense that the commoners, the nonparty members ("the masses"), have a code appropriate to themselves, which is law or lawfulness, and that party members have a higher code. Previously it would have been called the *li* or Rites, but now it is the Leninist concept of *dangxing* (adherence to party principle and one's proper nature as a party member; lit., "partyness"; *partinost'* in Russian). Offenses against it are punishable within the party by party discipline and administrative sanctions, such as self-criticism, "study," perhaps demotion. These sanctions are in Confucian terms "teaching," different in principle from "criminal punishments" (*xing*) under the law (*fa*), and less severe. This is the old bifurcation of morality or transcendental law (Rites, the self-cultivation of a communist) and "law" (penal law with punishments, criminal punishments—incarceration and the death penalty). "The Trial" does not attack *dangxing*, which would be to attack party rule, still unthinkable in 1980. Party nature as a supreme moral foundation is mentioned and exalted more than once. But in these post-Mao times, transcendental law is backed up by penal law like the outer coat and its inner lining, to echo the Ming founder. Earlier, the inner lining was enough. But now, a moral person—a party person (a gentleman)—would want to ensure that external laws are obeyed as a least condition. Even party members—they above all—must now be subject to law's minimal demands of good citizenship. Lately, some have taken advantage of their presumed superiority.

The authors' modern antipathy toward separate codes for rulers and commoners also supports their focus on the evils of *qing*. The Rites are dead, but not *qing*, the "human feelings" on which the Rites were based. This suggests that above the law the pernicious idea of a natural law for the sovereign only lives on.[124]

The story is adversarial in approach, yet the authors are not so committed to the adversary trial. When Liu Lei finally comes to understand his crime, through being tried, the indication of this is that he concedes the state's case, forgoing a defense. He refuses to let anyone speak for him. This follows antilegal social prejudice and is unfair to Liu, particularly under a conception of law that concedes rights even to the guilty and believes that the whole truth is heard only when all sides of a case find a voice.

An ironic turn of the plot is that Liu Lei is finally brought to a state of proper contrition by the revelation to him, at the trial, that the flood killed an old man, Dong, and his granddaughter. Dong had saved Liu Lei during the war by having his own daughter vacate a hiding place so that Liu Lei, then a soldier being sought by the Japanese, might occupy it. The girl was shot and Liu Lei lived. Now, as an official, Liu has outdone even the enemy—gone and wiped out the whole family line. Liu Lei's violation of *qing* to the Dongs is what allows him to see the enormity of his crime. This may seem also an ironic contradiction of the story's argumentative contraposition of law and *qing*, but perhaps the greater truth is that *qing*, as a web of human debts we all owe each other, does have a place—though not a controlling role—in the rule of law. Personal obligations, like rights, can be in mutual conflict. Getting them all out in the open is part of the adversarial process.

LAW IN LITERATURE (II):
LEGAL DUALISM DRAMATIZED

It is partly through its language that Xing Yixun's 1979 four-act play *Quan yu fa* (Power vs. law) provides perspective on the bifurcation of law into high and low under communism. A tocsin for "rule of law" and "equality before the law" actually staged in Beijing, it was one of the most popular plays of its day. Audiences clapped, wept, and "exulted" at the discomfiture of the public security chief at the end.[125] He is only a lackey; the real villain is a deputy secretary of the local municipal party committee named Cao, a classic type of villain in 1980 melodramas, but only because 1979 works like this one paved the way.[126]

In this melodrama one wants to see Secretary Cao punished for embezzling state famine-relief funds. He used them to build homes, offices, and facilities for himself and his cronies in the party. Then he blackmailed the accountant, Ding Mu, who had doctored the books for him, before she could confess to it (in wake of the fall of the Gang of Four). Cao now threatens to frame her for murdering her husband, but really leftists hounded him to death for his alleged Rightist deviations. Jailing Cao would be "law" countering his "power"; the title is however one of the few instances where the word "law" stands alone, instead of appearing as the second, subordinate element in the compound, "party discipline and the law of the state" (*dangji guofa*). Most exceptions accentuate the penal quality of the law or use the concept metaphorically. Examples are "The law is without pity (*qing*)" (81; a common saying echoing "The Trial");[127] "he should be sanctioned by law"; "the law is whatever he says it is"; and "he is his own law" ("he knows neither the Law below nor Heaven above").

"Law" precedes "discipline" mostly when it is negated: "violating law and [party] discipline" (*weifa luanji*). One could be excused for thinking that law and discipline, and maybe even economic regulations, are all the same thing. From Ding Mu, the repenter, to the villainous Secretary Cao: "You committed a grave mistake, violating party discipline and the state law, and destroying financial-economic discipline" (80). Cao to his lackey, director of the general office of the party municipal committee: "The Central Committee is just now tackling the problem of violations of law and discipline, and destruction of financial-economic discipline" (82). Zheng, editor of a party newspaper, to accountant Ding, ruefully: "I've not only ended up a bureaucrat, I've protected those who violated the law and discipline" (86). Accountant Ding to her daughter: "Oblivious to whether people in the disaster area lived or died, oblivious to party discipline and state law, Secretary Cao destroyed the party's financial-economic discipline" (90). The daughter of the party first secretary, Luo, the hero, who has just been transferred over Cao's head after being rehabilitated for his alleged misdeeds during the Cultural Revolution: "[Secretary Cao] ought to be punished by party discipline and state law; he ought to be sanctioned under the law" (96). First Secretary Luo on Deputy Secretary Cao, to Cao's wife—who is also Luo's sister: "He grew arrogant because of his good deeds in the past. He went in for special privileges, violated law and discipline, and committed all sorts of outrages" (97). The newspaper editor: "The party's municipal committee has decided to use this affair to launch a citywide study campaign against special privilege, bureaucratism, and violations of law and discipline, to rectify the party and its work style" (104). The editor to the chief of police, who, on Cao's orders, is about to arrest accountant Ding on the bogus murder rap: "Do you still believe in party discipline and the law of the state? Do you have a shred of the concept of legal system left in you?" (104).

Discipline and legal prosecution may have the same targets, but disciplinary commissions work secretly, punish more lightly, and judge their own good old boys. Yet in this play, where the key players are party members and the authorial viewpoint strongly praises the party for its idealism and potential to rectify its errors, party discipline seems a healthy supplement to the law.

The logic of the situation is otherwise. In "The Trial," the old *li*/law paradigm was criticized by pointing out the existence of a higher party standard of conduct or "code" in a metaphorical sense: partyness, available only to the ideological and moral elite, above mere lawfulness, which was just for the masses. The result was two unequal classes of people. *Power vs. Law* also conceptualizes a *li*/law dichotomy, but now the higher rules are not just a metaphorical "code" of conduct, they are a quasi *legal* code enforced by separate, extrajudiciary "courts." Secret disciplinary "courts" are competition for the genuine "people's courts," particularly given the myth (the reverse of reality) that discipline holds party members to a higher standard. If discipline has primacy and the party's own "law" above the law judges its man innocent, the masses may never have their say.

Why would a playwright champion as "rule of law" a quasi legal system competing with—prejudging and perhaps undermining—the real law? Because, sadly, the CCP's Central Discipline Inspection Commission was as "new" as the revived legal system just put in place to enforce state law. Disbanded in the Cultural Revolution, the commission began to meet again only in March 1979.[128] When all else failed, this was how the top, if so inclined, could finally rein in party malfeasance at the bottom. The commission also "led" the Supreme People's Court. Its powers only expanded in the 1990s.[129]

Lacking *fa*'s historical connection with punishment, party sanctions were "humane," aimed at rehabilitation, not retribution—remolding the party member so that he or she might return and serve the people. Contrarily, from Chinese penal codes, modern and premodern, one may infer principles of retribution and requital, from the subtle gradation of punishments according to the moral wickedness and amount of harm done by the infraction.[130] No one executed was ever rehabilitated.

And party discipline, like *li*, was used to enforce morality, including obedience. Did it not in fact call for a higher standard than mere legality—out of paternal concern? (Police authority, not criminal law as such, punished immorality, notably sexual offenses.) As Secretary Luo's daughter points out to her mother, and as one may well imagine from the family connections among the elite in this and other melodramas, party comradeship presents the same comforts and blinded vision as family ties: "Kinship ties (*guanxi*), workplace relations, inter-Party relations—they should be kept separate, not mixed together or merged, don't you think?" (95) says Ms. Luo.

The play never posits a law with fixed rules and separate authority that can rein in the power of the party; law must agree with, and thus is subordinate to, party discipline. Hence the party's *quan* is not just translatable as "power," but as "authority," if not "right." And the party not only has "eternal" *li* of morality—that is, discipline—but "flexible" policies for mundane regulation, again supposedly helping law by doubling it, but really second-guessing it. The good Secretary Luo himself slips into the habit of equating party policy and state law at the climax of the play, when he upbraids the police chief for blindly following Cao's self-serving orders: "Do you consider your superiors to be truth incarnate, their power tantamount to policy and law (*zhengce falü*)?" (106). But what really chastens the police chief is that Secretary Luo outranks him. Maybe the official translation of the title is wrong; perhaps "Authority *and* Law" is better. The contest is proper authority-and-law versus illegitimate authority and improper use of law.

Luo is Judge Bao—good incarnate—but he finally prevails because of his rank: his power and authority. He is the party first secretary. Cao for his part orders the police around not only from informal power he acquired as the previous first secretary, but because he is even now the municipal committee member in charge of political-legal affairs. But he is subordinate to Luo.

Power vs. Law mentions the new 1978 state constitution three times (91, 96, 104), as if to give state law primacy as the law of the land. Young people pin their hopes on it, and it is invoked in one instance, against the police chief's intended arrest of the reformed accountant. This may be in reference to the new freedoms in art. 47, "The citizens' freedom of person and their homes are inviolable," and "No citizen may be arrested except by a decision of a people's court or with the sanction of a people's procuratorate" (35). On the other hand, art. 1 of the state constitution declares China "a socialist state of the dictatorship of the proletariat." Article 2 states, "The CCP is the core leadership of the whole Chinese people. The working class exercises leadership over the state through its vanguard, the CCP." The party, too, has a constitution (there was a new one in 1982), and it is a foundational document of the polity.

The play never depicts party governance as opposing state law. When the newspaper editor seeks to stop the police chief from arresting the accountant, he asks him if he has "authorization from the municipal committee" (105). This is asking the state to seek permission from the party. But there was no procuracy yet, so what the editor seems to have in mind as rule of law really is proper procedure of any sort, instead of just acting out of political motives. Luo's logic is a bit different. He tells the police chief not to make arrests purely on someone's say-so—not evil Secretary Cao's, at the climax, not even on his own higher say-so—but to arrest according to *evidence*. This is the viewpoint of the Ming Judge Bao stories: justice means getting the real facts, not the cooked facts. It is not a matter of law as such. Ruling by law means finding out the truth, with all the optimism that implies. It is not following certain rules on the assumption that the truth may never reveal itself, or have contradictory sides.

Still, procedure must have something to do with it, as the editor sensed. But on this point, good Secretary Luo has his own Achilles' heel, even apart from the fact that his crusade for law is taking place during a political campaign, and through the press instead of the courts—without any visible input from a state justice system. It is all part of a power struggle to put good people on top and demote the bad people. At one point Luo wants to make an important decision without going through the usual process of a municipal CCP committee meeting to approve it (99). His wife reproves him for this and he is chastened. No one is perfect. And this is after all just political, not legal procedure. But what is the important matter? Authorization for a newspaper to print an article. In a world run by law, that should not require permission from the party. (It is an important article, to be sure—accountant Ding Mu's accusations of Secretary Cao and her own self-criticism.)

The central action thus revolves around machinations to get Ding Mu to come forward with her evidence in the press, or, on the other side, to get her to suppress it. It never seems to occur to anyone that she might still have to go to jail for her role in Secretary Cao's embezzlement, even if she has repented and confessed. But the playwright was perspicacious enough to foresee the objection to Luo's use of the press, even for good. He has Luo proclaim, "The press is not an organ of the law" (98). Still, the play has its head in the world of politics, which can *institute* rule of law. But that may be necessary under the circumstances. However low its legal consciousness, the play pleads, directly and indirectly, for citizens to speak up and do their own thinking. Besides Secretary Luo's reproof to the police chief to not follow his every order, one hears the formerly vacillating newspaper editor state, regretfully, "All these years, I found it easier, and safer, to follow instructions than to think for myself" (98).

LEGAL TOPICS IN POST-MAO FICTION

Whether these problems of law reflect ancient or Maoist habits—the far tradition or the "near" one—is moot. In a socialist state without much administrative law, party discipline had to fill in. China's imperial codes had long lists of administrative infractions and penalties for them. But officials had privileges of petition, reduction of punishment, and so forth that were unavailable to commoners. A 1725–27 Qing code revision made it so that "no offense, other than a light fault, committed by an official of any rank might be investigated without permission from the throne." Sentencing of an official also required imperial permission. "Thus, Ming and Qing law conferred on all officials a procedural privilege that removed them, where they had committed an offense, from subjection to the ordinary legal process. . . . [And] a much greater use was made of administrative punishments than in earlier times."[131]

The role of confession in law and literature, past and present, offers more grounds for investigation. It was so important a ritual that even petty offenders punished by the gentry rather than by the state might be forced to write a confession before, say, having their legs broken; Lu Xun's fictional character Kong Yiji is a famous example.[132] PRC police today sometimes still force citizens to write a self-criticism as a mild extralegal punishment.[133]

There is a taste for confession in any readership. "The Trial" ends with a confession both Maoist and judicial; Wang Yaping's "Defender" gets its story started with a dramatic courtroom confession by a murderer, then stupefies the reader at the end when the narrator himself confesses to complicated crimes. Getting the accused to confess and implicate others is of course key in police interrogation, though a confession is no longer necessary for conviction.[134] It can, however, be a pretext to suspend a sentence, and failure to confess can lengthen one's sentence. In the contentious cases written up in *Democracy and Legal System*, the "attitude" of the accused—a nonlegal factor—often appears to have been as important as any law in sentencing.[135]

False confession has long figured prominently in drama, fiction, and the Song dynasty collection of legendary cases, the *Tangyin bishi* or *Parallel Cases Solved by Just and Benevolent Officials* (lit., Parallel cases from under the pear tree). In Mao's era, "the fact that false confessions sometimes [went] undetected by the police [was] a subject of continuing concern."[136] The problem is exposed in post-Mao penal law melodramas, particularly those concerned with reversing verdicts. In *Before the Bench and Behind the Scenes*, Judge Shang Qin's job is to overturn false confessions made for a high cadre's son. In *Upholder of the Law*, the film scenario by Luo Huajun and Li Zaizhong, the key to hero procurator Xu Li's cracking of a giant municipal party conspiracy against justice is his discovery that three confessions framing the young hero Zhang Hua are suspiciously identical. Likewise, the hero cop of Wang Yaping's "Sacred Duty" is moved to restore justice to Bai Shun by the phoniness of a confession attributed to him. In a whodunit, proceeding with trial and confession once the case is solved is anticlimactic, except in "The Case of the Strange Yuan River Corpse," in which a false confession functions as a red herring.

Yet false confession, except as a formulaic prop to accuse politically bad characters, still seems censored. This goes with the censoring of police torture and the very role of police, which hardly appears in "The Trial." That case appears to be completely in the hands of a procurator. "After Cracking the Case" is an exception. It clarifies twin evils of torture: inhumanity to the innocent and distraction from finding the guilty. Torture is not a universal and unambiguous concept in China, however, as is indicated by oxymoronic official references to "excessive torture," implying that judicial torture as such is still tolerated.[137]

Also censored is the Maoist concept of a "preventive justice" like preventive medicine. The Maoist state preferred that resources be applied to political and ideological work among the masses so that they did not acquire the bug of criminality in the first place, rather than to tracking down criminals.[138] This is cold comfort to anyone who can imagine him- or herself a crime victim, and much popular fiction depends on that very attraction. Citizens want to see police on the case instead of knocking on the doors of innocent citizens. The concept of preventive justice also suggests the mass style of Maoist policing, which meant show trials, summary justice during campaigns, and household checks, though the idea that deterrence can reduce crime and therefore the need for trials also has traditional overtones. So does the conception, seen in "The Trial," "Defender," and Cao Yumo's "The Female Head Judge," that legal process is important as a means of educating the masses. To the extent that works such as these popularize "rule of law," literature may be conceived as obviating real practice of law in the form of arrests and trials.

Perhaps because much of it reflects perceived propaganda needs, the earliest post-Mao literature, like post-Mao prosecutions, focuses on "big cases," not minor civil matters like wife-beating, theft of inheritance, abuse of the elderly, or "illegal" sexual immorality. Workers in law and literature were to encourage the solution of civil disputes through mediation, not in courts. That was something journalism could also handle. Stories about corruption and administrative offenses necessarily pointed at public officials; big private enterprises were still scarce. These were "economic crimes," or if not that, a violation of "economic discipline" as in *Power vs. Law*. In the early 1990s there was no statute against embezzlement of private assets.

Let us conclude with four possibly traditional aspects of jurisprudence that the stories reveal indirectly. One is a fixation on the names of offenses. In imperial law, to find the name of the crime was to fit it into a preselected category shaped by the omniscience of all sovereigns and their codes since the Tang, and thus to know the proper graded punishment—and implicitly, the gravity of the moral trespass inherent in the offense.[139] The dramatic climax of act 1 in *Power vs. Law* is not when Secretary Cao in his evil hints that accountant Ding may have had an affair and killed her husband, but when Cao casually links the alleged offenses and names them as a generic crime: "You've committed the crime of 'adultery with murder of the aggrieved husband' (*tongjian shafu zui*)!" (81). This authoritatively plots Ding Mu's destiny in a hall of shame with moral offenders past. She faints. Such a specific crime is not found in a PRC code, but it is in the Qing code (art. 285). The punishment was death by slicing for the woman and the lesser one of beheading with delay for the lover, unless he killed the husband, in which case the wife would only be strangled with delay—whether or not she knew the circumstances.[140]

Second, the justification of modern Chinese law because of its utility rather than its justice is eyebrow-raising. Scholars have posited that imperial law was instrumental in the service of controlling the realm. It is still shocking to see law justified only for the sake of the economy and Four Modernizations, in "The Trial" (13):

> As part of the superstructure, law serves the economic basis of society and is to protect the interests of the people. . . . Our Party was taught many bitter lessons and paid for them dearly before it finally arrived at the comparatively correct ideological and political line of today, and understood that large-scale socialist production and implementation of the Four Modernizations were impossible using the methods of small-scale production. Thereupon [it] promulgated civil law and criminal law; just now [it] is experimenting with economic law, intending to establish courts of economic law that will use law to guarantee reconstruction under the Four Modernizations.

Literature too was justified instrumentally, as epitomized in the official 1980s promotion of a "literature of reform."

Third, the meaning of "law" was vague enough, yet this literature indicates that mere accusation—bringing wrongdoing to the attention of the authorities—is already "rule of law." Even language muddied the distinction between "filing suit" and "launching a complaint against someone with his boss," both of which were called *gaozhuang*. From the citizen's viewpoint, the two were much alike. The conflation of accusation and legal process began in imperial law, for one could not sue people directly; one had to file a complaint against them with the magistrate. In post-Mao as in Maoist times, the state's preferred role for citizens, exemplified in legal education campaigns, was to help the state ferret out criminals. That kept the state on top as the paternal judge, and the citizens from suing each other—and officials—as if everyone were a king and could pretend to a king's perspicacity. Hence it is natural to see *Power vs. Law* represent the exposure of crimes in the press as tantamount to "rule of law." It led to the demotion or firing of the guilty officials. Such administrative sanctions, in lieu of trials, were the state's preferred way of dealing with official malfeasance. The press and literature, through their information gathering and accusations, thus had the potential to replace judicial action. It is also natural for Judge Ji Rong in her story to protest the municipal party's interference with her duties not by suing them or appealing upward to higher courts—but by filing a complaint with their bosses, the party at the provincial level.

Finally, the penal law melodramas show that rule of law, or discipline, or policy—is unachievable without implementation by a truly exceptional person. But reliance on saviors fosters reliance on moral authority embodied in persons, not laws. Secretary Luo of *Power vs. Law* is the epitome. His commitment to justice thwarts the bogus indictment of accountant Ding Mu for murder, and at the end of the play he appears to have sent Secretary Cao down the road to the criminal trial he deserves. Yet he manages all this as a deus ex machina, as the party secretary. Without Luo at the helm, law would not prevail. Under the circumstances, the average Chinese reader and viewer were expected to take heart even in a solution such as this.

LAW AS LITERATURE

Codes and edicts are texts, and traditional China revered texts, whatever the subject matter. Furthermore, the indistinct line between fiction and recording was especially manifest in unofficial crime case "records," which were in classical Chinese. Thus reading traditional Chinese law as literature is not so new. The famous nineteenth chapter of Liu Xie's *Literary Mind and the Carving of Dragons* is genre criticism of royal edicts, focusing on their style and language. To Liu, edicts were "laws to all chieftains" and at the same time literary.[141]

The reputation of Chinese justice suffered not from its written norms or theories of adjudication but from the gap between them and the shocking reality. The latter is not absent from writings, including memoirs, case write-ups, handbooks for magistrates, and late Qing novels. Among the problems frequently noted are nonenforcement of laws and any rights a subject might enjoy by implication against the gentry and the sovereign; capricious arrests of suspects and witnesses; their imprisonment in appalling conditions and without procedural protections; judicial torture as an almost obligatory means of interrogation, during which the magistrate looked down imperiously on, without really being able to see (or judge) the one he was addressing; petty officials extorting bribes from family members; and pandemonium, even riots, outside the yamen.

Codes, legal treatises in dynastic histories, and case digests existed apart from reality as texts in a world of other texts. Officially, trials were preserved, if at all, in case files and summaries, not full transcripts of proceedings. The codes were so detailed, and the administration of them so bureaucratic and timorous, that basic-level magistrates' case files and reports even on murder were in a routinized language that recast crimes to fit statutes.[142] Such official distortions impel historians of China to consult literature. In recent centuries, contemporary Chinese have found themselves awash in unofficial accounts of cases. These might be counted as forerunners of Chinese reportage, although they seldom bear close scrutiny from a legal, archival, or historical point of view. Judges are given bureaucratic titles not yet invented, and recent cases look suspiciously like previous cases. But the unofficial cases are entertaining, and like pathologists' true-crime memoirs today, they are a step on the road to popular fiction and certainly an influence on it. They are read as popular fiction again now.

The American field, in contrast, faces a vast quantity of quite accessible texts, mundane and subliterary, including verbatim trial transcripts. Reading them as literature is new, and it can be practical in a system of pleading where lawyers need rhetorical skills and use case law instead of deductions from codes. From the many expansive but nondefinitive texts comes the impulse to study the words: for the original intentions of those who uttered them; to understand the words' internal relations, logical and aesthetic; or even to "deconstruct" them, whether to reformulate the principles of legal argument or "trash" the legal system.[143] Statutes, opinions, and trials become symbols or narratives of life or of ideologies of power, inviting the myriad readings and methodologies of literary critics.

Post-Mao China is poor in texts actually used in legal processes that have a strong narrative dimension as conventionally understood, or that even convey the evolution of legal thinking. American law professors have long analyzed "how judges speak," if only for their rhetoric; in China still today, judges do not "speak" their own words.[144] They do not tolerate "stories" or indeed most American defense strategies. Lawyers do not help make new law or add to legal concepts when they speak at all.

Premodern China did publish cases in digest form, and it had more elaborately codified bodies of law than China in the 1980s. It also had case files, though they were seldom read by the elite outside their government service. Dissent is recorded in the case digests, along with appeals to philosophic underpinnings, in epigrammatic form, but creativity and the addressing of future implications in opinion writing, which was done collectively at the Board of Punishments, contradicted the bureaucratic culture and was in effect lèse-majesté. The district magistrate might be more expansive in his opinions; he could write unofficially about the facts of a case, his investigations, and his speculations about motives, but not about the law's intent.[145]

The ancient and modern paucity of official discourse about judiciary legislation as process, and the lack of private-sector lawyerly discourse no doubt exaggerate the image of Chinese law as something statically fixed in texts. In the beginning and the end are the codes, with their commentaries. But they and model Qing casebooks are sophisticated and will reward analysis that uses techniques associated with literary criticism. Surely one can analyze them as narrative.[146] This chapter can only suggest the possibilities, leaving the main job to specialists.

Among the texts are ostensible case write-ups that look like fiction and must have been read for the pleasures of fiction even in their day. This fact averts a common objection to the study of law as literature, which is that the two have different functions—that literature has an aesthetic impact or amuses individual readers, whereas law directs social conduct and is uniquely backed by coercive power.[147] China does not draw so hard and fast a distinction, not even for the *Book of Rites*.

The *Book of Rites*, with its recitations and explications of transcendental rules, shows the problem of dividing law from literature on the basis of aesthetic and operative functions. Like the Bible and other canonical texts once viewed only through the prism of their sacredness, the *Book of Rites* is today read as philosophy, historical document, and literature.[148] Many read it as such in ancient times, as a utopian document, but that did not diminish it as a text of sacred norms. The old literati asked, in a sense, What did the original framers intend? The classic's content is the righteous and properly ceremonious rules and customs of life in some sense thought to have been followed and advocated by Confucius, the ancient Zhou kings before him, and the mythic sage kings before them. Although the idea that its precepts are laws would have offended the ancients, its current reputation as creative literature instead of as a sort of code is conditioned not by a view of its content as non-, super-, or meta-legal. Far more important is the general recognition that it is an idealization of Zhou rites—indeed adumbrated with some imaginative narrative, "fiction"—even if the latter did not come from a deliberately creative impulse. The idealizing character of the Rites, ridiculed by non-Confucian writers millennia ago, has long been recognized, like the dead-letter portions of imperial codes. The line between beautiful ideals taught and coercive norms enforced is not a hard and fast line, and not one between law and literature.

Traditional textual analysis of the *Book of Rites* as literature is not just defensible but necessary, since the classic is made up of books and chapters varying in length, content, date, and the process of their accretion. The classic, in separate chapters and within chapters, identifies the Rites and the institutions that embody them. It interprets particular Rites in their social or historical context. It discourses on the philosophical underpinnings of education and music as well as rituals and norms of conduct. And it provides anecdotes and dialogues featuring Confucius and his disciples expounding on the nature and meaning of Rites and other philosophical concepts, often in parabolic ways.[149] Hermeneutics—trying to figure out what Confucius and the ancient sages, the "original framers" of right conduct, really meant— was the orthodox approach to the text in ancient times. The classics were also lessons in rhetoric. Hermeneutical study remains dominant today, though the *Book of Rites* is a comparatively neglected text owing to its "lateness" and catholicity as an "encyclopedia" of Confucian doctrine in accreted chapters that are mutually inconsistent or repetitive.[150]

The classic may be critically analyzed in formal terms according to its language, which is often figurative and rich in natural images; the parallelism of its tropes and analogical reasoning; its humor, paradoxes, and modes of mix-

ing dialogue, discourse, anecdote, and parable; its plots; and perhaps its ordering of canons within chapters. When Cheng Xiaoqing, China's future
master of detective fiction, was writing undistinguished ghost stories at the
age of seventeen in 1911, an editor who saw promise in him advised that he
learn about style from the *Tan Gong* chapter of the *Book of Rites*.[151]

Thematic analysis may yield propositions about the relationships of the
religious Rites so meticulously prescribed to Rites of a more ethical, moral,
or political nature. The classic may also be analyzed, chapter by chapter, as
narrative. There are dialogues and anecdotes. Norms of behavior are sometimes related directly as canons, but other times by way of historical accounts
of what sacrifices and ceremonies were performed on specified occasions.
Chap. 8, *Wen Wang shi zi* (King Wen as son and heir), begins with a biographical account of a historical figure and the Rites he performed, before
launching into discourse on education. The following chapter, the *Li yun*
(Evolution of Rites), purports to tell the historical origin and development
of Rites. Other chapters tell of ancient Rites "in the imperfect tense" (by implication; Chinese has no tenses), as procedures and mandates followed and
commanded by certain rulers during their reigns as a general practice.
Sometimes the Rites are explicated as answers to rhetorical questions, as in
the *San nian wen* (Questions about the three-year mourning, chap. 38), or in
catechisms with Confucius, as in *Ai Gong wen* (Questions of Duke Ai, chap.
27). Often the text presents argument by way of alternative anecdotes and
pronouncements by Confucius; the constituent anecdotes and parables are
small narratives within discursive prose. That Rites, legendary actions, and
pronouncements of the past have a mandate as ideal codes for present behavior is understood by the reader.

The difficulty in training literary analysis on the *Book of Rites* lies not in
figuring out how to apply the methodologies of literary criticism, but in
doing so in a "law and literature mode"—retaining a view of the book, in all
its idealism, as somehow still connected to the regulation, ordering, and enforcement of codes in real life.[152]

The successive dynastic penal codes present an opposite problem for legal
literary study.[153] Their language is too unadorned and unwieldy to be considered literary by most standards. The new post-Mao codes are least elegant
of all, presenting interminable strings of offenses with punishments named

in legalese. Commentaries on the Tang code are interlarded with quotations and allusions from the classics, but that is reflected glory. Still, the Chinese quip that "one does not read the code" may have meant more to Western Sinologists of yesteryear than to Chinese literati;[154] a modern scholar argues that the codes "had a status rather like that of the Confucian classics, constituting a work with which succeeding rulers and even dynasties should not have the temerity to tamper."[155] What literary scholars today might see in the codes is a grand implied narrative, not with a linear plot but with a circular, seamless web of myriad plots, a net of spontaneously generating deviations from a comprehensive standard, all errors being brought back into line by counterforces precisely calibrated according to the deviation. The principles of what is right and wrong, why, and in what degree, are only implicit in the code. Yet because the laws have been made mutually consistent and reinforcing, one can read the code for "the spirit of the law" much more easily than one can the *Book of Rites* for the "spirit of the Rites," though many generations of Chinese literati have devoted themselves to precisely that.

In the code, crimes, often occurring in a series with follow-up crimes or preceding aggravating circumstances, are laid out in an implied conditional tense, followed by attendant penal consequences. There may be alternative courses of secondary crimes after the initial one, and alternative consequences. Within a given article or realm of activity, there is a comprehensiveness of infractions and outcomes listed that gives an impression that every contingency of human agency has been preimagined and its necessary recompense preordained—as if *bao* (retribution, requital), prime plot-mover and "moral grammar of interaction among men or between men and gods,"[156] were set to be played out whatever the path of the human player. In any matter recognized by law, a sanction will be found to fit it. Regarding theft, for instance, the draftsmen must have "started to make up hypotheticals about the basic fact pattern of theft and ask what happens if the thief obtains no property."[157]

When the criminal selects a path not preimagined by the code-maker (the emperor), that legislator (in today's language) takes the code into "hypertext," locating the appropriate article, then legislating a new punishment for the new offense. It becomes a substatute. Most subcontingencies have already been imagined or played out and given rise to a preexisting substatute, so the question is one of burrowing in and finding it. There was, for instance, a penalty for a daughter who caused her parents to commit suicide out of shame and indignation from learning that she had had illicit sexual relations *and* their having failed in an attempt to kill her seducer.[158] One substatute noteworthy for its implied narrative has details from a particular case. The substatute begins: "If a knavish fellow from outside [the capital], with a yellow square of cloth on his back, a yellow banner planted upon his head, and accusations issuing from his mouth, rushes into a government office in order to exercise coercion upon the officials there . . ."[159]

The code proper was immutable, but it sat atop an evolving stratum of substatutes (in effect, emperor's case law). And between its lines was the original Chinese hypertextual intervention in any literary endeavor: interlinear commentary—added, deleted, or preserved from a previous dynasty's code.

The code is cross-referenced—literally, in many instances, and also in a figurative sense, since the rules were refined and mutually harmonized over the centuries, general principles being "factored out."[160] Some general principles and definitions of terms are also outlined in an opening section, "Names and General Rules." The conscientiousness about fixing the identity of specific crimes through specific names as seen in the modern play *Power vs. Law* is primarily evident in the main bodies of laws, where the names of crimes and aggravating circumstances are repeated precisely and at full length, however monotonous this may be.

This hypothetical narrative has a precise point of view: that of the state, the emperor. The phrasing of how punishment is to be implemented is clearly that of the state to its magistrate. The matters recognized as of legal interest, and their placement in the larger structure of the code, indicate that the named crimes' importance is how they might diminish the interests of the state, not private parties. Laws against dangerous and heterodox religious practices are grouped with laws having to do with the Board of Rites, which manages the emperor's ritual regulation of the empire and punishes official errors in sacrifices, or junior officials at court audiences who speak before elder officials have spoken. Theft of landed property is listed under the Board of Revenue laws. The state wants proper land transactions because it taxes land and desires general peace and prosperity. Heading the Ten Abominations, crimes of surpassing wickedness singled out for harsh treatment at the opening (they are not to be commuted during amnesties), are rebellion and treason. Most of the code is laws for bureaucrats, enjoining them from hiring more than a specified number of clerks, using too many post-boats or horses, or mixing medicines for the emperor in nonapproved ways. The implied reader is the magistrate who must deal with a homicide, or the higher official who must discipline an astronomer who has failed to report a celestial phenomenon. Might the point of view be above the emperor him-self? Or was Chinese law merely his "disciplinary system"? Most observers feel that it made universal claims from above the sovereign's level, but it is doubtful that it governed him.[161]

True cases may be read as stories, but there are few official books of them. Most surviving are from the Qing. However, some of the latter are well known through Derk Bodde and Clarence Morris's marvelously annotated translations from the *Xing'an huilan*, or *Conspectus of Penal Cases*, as they called the original collection with its two sequels. Of 7,600 case digests writ-ten between 1736 and 1885, Bodde and Morris translated 190. In relating named crimes by named people, with some details of the commission, the write-ups provide narratives, if not refined literary interests. The interest is the greater because some crimes are bizarre, devious, sensational, or compli-cated by accidental interventions by third parties during a premeditated act. Sometimes there is a conspiracy, of lovers, family members against other family members, and the like. Bodde is moved to reflect on the content: A son protests his father's adultery and the father slits the son's throat, aided by the lover's husband, whom he had been paying off. Two men murder three peasants in a cave as they sleep. A 70-year-old is arrested for having over the years sucked bone marrow from sixteen baby girls. An innkeeper totes a sick man out of his inn and leaves him naked in the wilderness rather than have a death on his hands. A father forces his younger son to help bury the elder son alive. A Manchu officer commits suicide to serve his deceased teacher in the next world (after telling a superior, who had the legal duty to stop him).[162]

Despite the "tabloid" interest of such shocking deeds, and the appearance of the "strange," this is neither popular nor literary reading matter. Details not relevant to judgment are omitted, sometimes even including the social status of the parties. The interesting and shocking details given are often quantitative—how much money was stolen, how many babies were violated, how close a relation to the deceased were those who did him in? These are matters of legal interest in sentencing, a quantitative matter of how many lashes or what degree of severity the death penalty, according to degrees of mourning in the relationship between perpetrator and victim. The frustrating spareness of the accounts is not unrelated to the interest and complexity of the crimes; these are digests of cases referred up to the Board of Punishments and later summarized from its archives, worthy of judicial review because their complexity had resulted in contradictory rulings at lower levels. Or the case called for a reversal of verdict, or a precedent-setting ruling by analogy in the absence of a relevant statute. At the top of the system there was no time for human-interest details.

The overall narrative of a case in the *Conspectus* is not typically the story of the crime or the trial of first instance. It is a bureaucratic report, beginning with a summary of a memorial or report from a lower level (sometimes an edict), proceeding to the statutes relevant to the crimes at hand, a more detailed look at the facts, and a final recommendation by the board. There may be the interest of a rebuke at the end, perhaps moralizing by the emperor. It is a bureaucratic narrative. Some might have read it for curiosity, but one must go through much legal ore to get to scandalous metal that might be "diverting."

A quite different kind of law-case anthology is typified by the *Tangyin bishi* (Parallel cases solved by just and benevolent officials), a collection of 144 civil and criminal cases taken mostly from prior anthologies, shaped in A.D. 1211 by an obscure Southern Song police official, Gui Wanrong, and today available in Ming recensions. Numerous pre-Song and particularly Song, Ming, and Qing literati, into the twentieth century, dignified an individual case by writing it up as a short "literati essay" in classical Chinese, the latter a genre so amorphous and uncatalogued that it was called *biji*, "note-form" or "notational literature." The topic need not be a case. It might be a point of philology or history, or an encounter with a ghost, if it is given due evidentiary treatment. Works that might be considered short stories or fictionalized sketches, anecdotes, or notes are now called *biji xiaoshuo* ("note-form fiction" or "record-stories"), a term that is relatively new. What in these works is history and what is fiction is not clarified, individually or collectively. *Biji* case write-ups were often anthologized in miscellanea rather than in "casebooks."[163]

When in 1896 Liang Qichao's *Shiwubao* (The Chinese progress) serialized the first-ever Chinese translations of Sherlock Holmes tales, it cited as its source *The* Biji *of Sherlock Holmes*, or, in the later installments, *The* Biji *of Watson*. The translations of the tales are relatively faithful, yet the terse classical style and abridgment of the English originals' preambles and Watson's badinage with Holmes, delivered in the good doctor's own words, tend to strip the tales down to the bare essentials of *biji* case write-ups. Since the *Shiwubao* also published accounts of evidently true cases, including in its premier issue one solved by an English detective other than Holmes, readers not initiated into Sherlockiana might have been confused about whether Conan Doyle wrote up fictional or nonfiction cases—if indeed they realized that he was the author, since his name was never mentioned. But three of the four stories selected were from the book Conan Doyle called the *Memoirs of Sherlock Holmes* (one is from the *Adventures*), so the term "*biji*," stripped of its historical associations, might be considered a reasonable rendition.[164]

Ostensibly, the Song *Parallel Cases* is a handbook for administration of justice, a "manual of jurisprudence and detection," Robert Van Gulik, its translator, called it. Its prefaces suggest that magistrates read the cases so as not to fall into error when they judge. A version edited in the fifteenth century by Wu Na, who served as a judge in Nanjing, argues with some of the judges' decisions on contemporary (Ming dynasty) legal grounds.[165]

Wu Na's approach might strike readers today as pompous and beside the point, like criticizing the jurisprudence of the captain in *Billy Budd* (a topic in American law and literature studies).[166] As we read them now, the *Parallel Cases* appear to have been preserved for their plot interest, as fiction, or as historical fiction combining the interests of fiction, history, and legend. Books like the *Parallel Cases* served as prototypes for popular anthologies of historical cases that editors put together in the 1980s and 1990s, sometimes as "stories about righteous officials (*qingguan*)." Selected *Parallel Cases* themselves were reissued in 1983, with vocabularies and full translations into modern Mandarin, as leisure reading for Chinese of any level of education.[167] The original casebook would come to be seen as an ancient example of China's great tradition of "legal system literature," once that term was coined.

The *Parallel Cases* must have been considered "law as literature" by many of its original literati readers—indeed, as a "legal system literature." "Nearly all the plots found in Ming and later detective tales and crime novels are elaborations of themes occurring in old casebooks," opines Gulik, who used them for his own detective stories in English.[168]

The original sources of the cases that the *Parallel Cases* anthologized are literary and edifying. They include biographies in official dynastic histories, tomb inscriptions, and *biji*. Even the *biji* were written under the pretense of fact rather than fiction. Jaroslav Průšek considered the plethora of *biji* in the Song as the sign of a turn away, in classical-language narrative, from well-structured, Tang *chuanqi*-style fiction.[169] Yet crime and law cases by nature provide a story line, imparting to "true cases" recorded in *biji* a strong fictional appeal. Like any fiction in the Chinese tradition, the *biji* cases freely exchange plots, themes, and characters in a so far untraced line of literary influence.[170] Actual court cases, then, whether ever officially textualized or not, have fed into at least two streams of fiction. One includes *huaben*, *gongan* fiction, and vernacular novels. Another includes *biji xiaoshuo*, from Song exemplars to Wu Jianren in the late Qing,[171] and historical-fiction casebooks, from the *Parallel Cases* to the post-Mao anthologies of old cases examined below. No doubt the two streams have influenced each other, and also post-Mao crime stories and reportage.

The *Parallel Cases* stories are in classical Chinese and in very summary form, sometimes only three or four sentences. The compiler selected only material he considered authentic, but the cases selected come from a span of fourteen centuries, from about 300 B.C. to A.D. 1100. As one might suspect on those grounds alone, some cases have the scent of legend, including two in which the judge is Lord Bao.

The cases are arranged in 72 pairs. Each pair has a theme and is preceded by a rhyming couplet encapsulating the gist of each case. This arrangement is more literary than jurisprudential. There is such a paralleling of cases also in the *Longtu gongan* in the Ming. In each *Parallel Cases* anecdote the judge of history (and legend) is named, and sometimes the parties to the case are too. The entries are in narrative form, beginning with the offense or the presentation of it to the adjudicating official. The account proceeds to the discovery of the truth and ends in a confession, arrest, or judgment. Dialogues and details about the parties that are not necessary to the judging of the case are presented, but statutes are rarely cited.

In only about a dozen anecdotes is the point a matter of law, and typically it is on behalf of clemency. An exception is the case of an unfilial son who destroyed a portrait of his father; he was punished with an ingenious analogy to a law forbidding monks from destroying images of their deities (case no. 25A). Another lawyerly point evokes a conundrum that sounds like a more serious counterpart to our joke about the man who wanted to be exonerated from killing his parents because he was an orphan; in the Chinese case, a wife does not suffer guilt by association with her husband after he murdered her parents because the murder thankfully dissolved the marriage (no. 59A).

As in other Chinese "law fiction," old and modern, most often the point is uncovering hidden case facts—"detection." This may be as simple as looking up a date of birth, determining the quantity of destroyed objects by weighing them, verifying historical seal styles, or going down to the rice fields to investigate. It may hinge on the judge's observation of details, of whether a woman's cries for her deceased husband betray sadness or fear, or of ink stains on a monk's shoe that may mask bloodstains. The judge's observation of society may be the crucial thing: of the fact that a deceased man has a pretty wife, who might have a lover, or that a man without enemies might still have lent money. It may all hinge on "science"—moderns' "detection"—namely the judge's ability to test for the presence of agers on falsified documents, recognize spontaneous combustion (the official runs his own experiment), or calculate the weight of a quantity of yellow metal that mysteriously turned to brown clay, to see if it could ever really have been the gold it allegedly started out as (which would have been very heavy). Cracking the case may need surveillance, or occasionally a miraculous omen or presentation of a divinable hexagram in a dream (no. 29A). Above all, the successful judge will trip up lying witnesses and complainants with contradictions in their testimony. He also catches them with ruses and stings, as by offering a reward to all who bring in objects of the kind stolen.

Although a magistrate reading the *Parallel Cases* might learn a tad about poisons and agers (as one might from an Agatha Christie novel), part of the edification, and the pleasure, lies in getting to know a "legend": either a case known in historical lore or an inspirational judge. Beyond the cultural edification is the diversion of seeing an ingenious mind at work.

Literary indirection and a plot with a double surprise in the space of what is in English a five-sentence anecdote make no. 26B one of the most famous cases in the collection. A salt carrier and a wood carrier each claims that a lambskin cloak belongs to him. In the second line, the judge adds a conundrum of his own. "Question this skin under torture, then you will know its owner," he orders. Is he mad? He has the lambskin beaten. Grains of salt fall out, and in the fifth sentence the wood carrier confesses. The "beating" was not lunacy but a brilliant ploy dressed up in an ingenious figure of speech—one that also evokes the dread felt by any guilty (or innocent) person caught up in the judicial system. The theme of "putting the physical evidence on the rack" to see what it testifies to in a case of disputed ownership is an archetype in *biji xiaoshuo*, a literary model that transcends any one case.[172]

A fairly complex plot is developed in no. 70A, about a young woman killed at night by a robber who entered a door she left open for her lover; the lover arrived later and became the suspect. Besides describing how the lovers met, how the girl was stabbed, and how her beau was tracked down, the story relates two ruses of the judge. The first identifies the owner of the murder weapon and the second lures him back by spreading abroad the misimpression that the case is closed. As in many a Judge Bao story, and indeed as in the Chinese legal system, the beau does not, however, get off scot-free. He has still committed "night interloping."

Besides its aesthetic appeal, this "casebook" presents a plea for justice sure to strike a chord with the Chinese reader. The main concern is injustice, and the typical case requires clearing a person wrongly suspected. More than one crime is committed not to end a life or gain property as an end in itself, but to gain a corpse or booty to frame an enemy for murder or theft. The typical case has a false accusation, a slander, or a frame-up—in the worst instance, convincing one's own sick mother to let one murder her, so that blame for her homicide may be falsely imputed to one's enemy, to avenge one's father (no. 28A). Or, in dozens of examples, a suspect is in dire straits after wrongly confessing under torture. Clearly the technology existed to wring a confession of guilt from anyone. The judge's usual way of uncovering the typical mode of obstructing justice—lying and deceit—is through ruses of his own: proclaiming false contests, false procurements, nonexistent executions, or nonexistent words from nonexistent informers that lull the guilty party into false security or even play upon his greed to further capitalize on his ill-gotten gains.

In this view of Chinese justice, punishment often as not comes from a commoner's initiative. The suit is adversarial—more than that, often an act of war against a grudge foe, wrapped up in a false accusation. But the judge, therefore, in using his own deceitful ruses to expose the deceit of evil civilians, frequently saves the innocent *from the law*. That message is by no means revolutionary: lawsuits are launched to no good end, typically to deny rule of law; only a good, paternal judge can save you. Lawsuit appears to be as threatening to life and limb as crime itself. And the interest of these stories lies not only in the just solutions to cases, but in the ingenious crimes, frame-ups, and conspiracies behind them, as well as the awful injustices that might have been. The subject matter is lurid, and it holds some of the appeal of horror fiction.

Yet there is little moralizing. One hundred forty-four cases prove that one cannot survive the horrors of the law without the assistance of a good judge. Because no commentary is necessary from Gui Wanrong, the plots move right along. By comparison, other compilations of illustrative cases by officials directly admonish the official who is the more-than-implied reader that author and reader are meeting on the serious and sacred grounds of not making a mistake. Thus the *Xiyuan jilu* (Manual for redressing injustice) of Song Ci (1186–1249), China's first forensic medicine manual, continuously complains that magistrates in criminal cases leave investigation of the corpse to underlings. Lan Dingyuan's book of his own cases, the *Luzhou gongan* (Cases of [Lan] Luzhou, preface ca. 1729), inveighs against the pitfalls of subofficials and "litigation tricksters" and harps on familiar official themes about the evils of cult superstition. Yet even these didactic classics were good popular reading matter in the 1980s, reprinted with annotations and a translation into modern Mandarin. Lan Dingyuan's pompous disquisitions have also been collected in more fanciful "popular" anthologies of literati case write-ups for the less-educated reader.[173] The pleasures of these texts today include the satisfaction of cultural curiosity, even the gratification of nationalistic desires to see the ancients being very advanced in scientific fields the better part of a millennium ago. But that is partly an interest in the cases as jurisprudence.

LAW INTO LITERATURE

Surely law texts and fiction have influenced each other in Chinese history. William Nienhauser has highlighted the fashioning of a piece of ninth-century fiction from a now somewhat mysterious line of the *Book of Rites*, which occurs amid otherwise prosaic descriptions of royal sacrifice procedures.[174] Gulik cites the influence of old casebooks like the *Parallel Cases* on Ming stories. He gives a few examples, such as the theme of a wife murdering her husband without a scar by driving a nail into his head.[175] It reappeared in the detective novel *Wu Zetian si da qi'an* (Four strange cases during the reign of Wu Zetian), which Gulik translated under what he surmised was its original title, *Di gongan* or *Celebrated Cases of Judge Dee*. As the reading public expanded and authors remained unconcerned with taking credit for creating original plots, true cases were constantly written up for literary or subliterary purposes of amusement, always tempered by the putative aim of edification still apparent in the post-Mao examples provided below. A notable instance is Wu Jianren's *Jiuming qiyuan* (The strange case of nine murders; 1906), which borrows from Western whodunit conventions but reworks material from a crime novel or novels—and perhaps Cantonese ballads—which in turn were inspired by a famous murder case of 1738.[176]

Wilt Idema observes that the typical *huaben* consists of two stories, both exemplifying the same general law of retribution; the introductory tale is short and well known, whereas the second and main tale is more recent and complex. The exemplification of an explicit or implicit rule (a "law"—perhaps indeed a statute) in paired stories is seen in the *Parallel Cases*, Judge Bao stories from the Ming, and still in the popular modern casebooks described below. Y. W. Ma and Joseph S. M. Lau refer to the introductory tale in *huaben* as the preamble; the structural similarity to the preambles in Sherlock Holmes stories is striking, though surely coincidental.[177] The possibilities for cross-generic influences in Chinese writing remain.

Influences from the law on language is another area for research. Statutes and cases were hardly models for imitation, but they had their own legalese. So much upper-class aspiration was caught up in bureaucratic pursuits that it is hard perhaps to separate literary citations of legalese from the bureaucratese that was inevitable in all conversations about the state of the realm. Especially notable is the *Hai Gangfeng xiansheng juguan gongan zhuan* (Account of Mr. Hai Rui's court cases while in office; preface 1606), a literary and fictional collection of case write-ups in classical Chinese with individual tales often printed in quadripartite form, each of the last three elements masquerading as a legal document. After a narration of the facts, beginning with a mystery but continuing through to the solution of it, there may be a formal indictment in the voice of a person denoted as the *gaozhuangren* (accuser), such as the survivor of the person allegedly murdered; then, in some cases, a defense plea (a *su*, so named) in the voice of the accused (*suzhuangren*, pleader); and finally the verdict ("Hai Gong *pan*," Lord Hai finds . . .). Each quasi document is set apart in the text through elevation, and each *line* of the verdict is individually elevated. Apart from standard official terminology marking the close of an indictment and plea, however, the "documents" are not remarkably bureaucratic in tone. Some convey emotional distress.[178]

The familiar Judge Bao stories of the *Longtu gongan*, which likewise are not particularly vernacular to begin with, may have as many as two cut-and-paste embeddings in the main story of representations of legal reports, accusations, and indictments by plaintiffs, and an ostensible written judgment near the end in which Lord Bao summarizes the case, names the crimes, and pronounces sentence. The plaintiff's documents are set off at the start by a phrase such as *gao wei* (I hereby accuse) or *su wei* (I issue this indictment). They are realistically terminated by the respective bureaucratic formulas *shang cheng*, *shang su*, or *shang gao* ("respectfully is it thus reported"; "respectfully is this indictment thus preferred"; "respectfully is this accusation thus preferred"). The judge's pronouncement is preceded by *shen de* (we find that, it is judged that). One story notes that Judge Bao "took up his pen and pronounced" the ensuing judgment.[179] Another has a full explanatory confession by the culprit, ending with the phrase, "I am willing to submit to the death penalty [which I deserve]."[180]

The language of the plaintiffs' statements and Bao's judgments is more compact than that of the main text. Accusations invariably begin with the all-important naming of the crime or crimes, followed by a relation of the details of the case in the sparest prose possible. There is sometimes a bit of moralizing at the start ("there are no greater feelings than those between parent and child, and no greater matters than those of life and death"),[181] or a decrying of the injustice of it all at the end. One judgment of Bao's continues on past the formulaic statement of the facts, naming of the crime, and pronouncement of sentence, to include "the marriage,"[182] or coda—that bit of social engineering by which Lord Bao, having sentenced the guilty, acts as Confucian father to ensure satisfaction of the other world too. Typically this means finding a mate for orphans and widows (which he may have created with the death penalty!) from other case survivors, so that all will have companions and be able to propagate their line.

Though there may be some influence from actual courtroom practice in the judge's sentence, its grandly literary function is more evident. Judge Bao always manages to give a recap of all the salient facts, moral and material, from beginning to end, in the fewest words possible. It is the very image of the *fabula* noted by formalist theorists in the whodunit formula, even if the main plot line leading up to it is not some *syuzhet*. Hence Judge Bao stories share something after all with the classical Western whodunit form (something often lacking in real Sherlock Holmes stories), even if they are "wanting" in formal Sherlockian "detection"—Holmes's main link to the Poe formula.

Let us examine now the "new" anthologies of old cases compiled during the post-Mao era, which may be counted as an integral if subordinate branch of China's popular legal system literature, as it was called after 1984. By the late 1980s, ancient cases, historical fiction, modern true crime, and modern crime fiction were all mixed together in anthologies of designated "popular fiction," in magazines and books with titles like *Xin* Paian jingqi (The new *Slapping the Table in Amazement*; 1987), after the Ming collection of vernacular stories by Ling Mengchu. The reuse of diverse stories and genres by layering and mixing them, making them one's own and adding commentaries for different ends in different eras, was common in old Chinese fiction.[183] The success of the new editions encouraged publishers finally to do a mass reprinting, in 1985, of the *Longtu gongan*, in a form accessible to readers with a middling education. These old Judge Bao stories from the Ming were still in classical Chinese, but the syntax was subtly modernized or simplified in places, and the stories appeared in fully modern punctuation for the first time.[184]

There may well have been state propaganda purposes behind the propagation of these old cases. Many of the anthologies purport to give uplifting examples of "good officials," some of whom undid past injustices (*pingfan*); folklore journals of the early 1980s also ran sections on famous upright judges of history, notably Judge Bao and Kuang Zhong.[185] The theme of righteous powerholders supported Deng Xiaoping's attempt to restore confidence in old (pre–Cultural Revolution) cadres now rehabilitated;

some readers suspected a message that "only an official could solve all problems."[186]

But old cases also had a radical edge in the 1980s. Showing officials of "feudal times" in a good light ran counter to Marxism as it had long been interpreted in China. Some anthologies thus mount quaint defenses for having chosen pre-1949 cases for purposes other than condemning the old society.[187] A resurgence in the 1990s, after the Beijing massacre, of books about old cases from imperial times may again have answered the leadership's call to trust officials and stay in one's place. By then the stock of Confucius himself had risen, and the public interest in socially critical prose, which was otherwise suppressed after 1989, may have found an outlet by official design in stories about the distant past. But stories of good and bad officials in imperial China also provided a fertile field for allegory about good and bad communist officials of the present; during the crackdown after the massacre the intellectual reading public looked for such allegories everywhere, in books and magazines, and even in government accounts justifying the suppression of the demonstrators for democracy.

What the anthologies of the post-Mao era evidence is a constant concern for the entertainment value of their texts within a very broad range of reading levels. Though collected in the spirit of providing spare-time reading matter, some are too difficult to be "popular literature." Some case write-ups also ask the reader to tolerate moral commentary from dynastic authors that modern taste usually finds tiresome.

At the high end is *Biji xiaoshuo anli xuanbian* (Selected and edited cases from *biji xiaoshuo* [literati jottings]), a compilation of 128 cases from the Five Dynasties to Wu Jianren, with a 1981 preface by Liu Yeqiu, who worked with two colleagues. It is "high-end" since all pieces are in the original classical Chinese and the source of each is cited; annotations cover only proper nouns and obsolete characters. There is no modern Mandarin rendering.

This book and all the others are in simplified characters, but the language of some stories might tax an average worker's reading skills. It is not a page-turner compared to anthologies in vernacular Chinese with which it had to compete. Yet this little book with a 41,000-copy first printing was to be read for pleasure. After the usual pious words on how comrades in the security, procuracy, and judiciary might learn from the book (which may be twitting them), and how general readers may pick up some common and historical knowledge, Liu Yeqiu acknowledges that lovers of literature may read it as an ordinary anthology of stories. And, after apologizing for the repetitions and plagiarisms in this "genre," he ends his preface with the words, "This being a book of popular reading matter, such matters need not detain us anyway" (7). The stories are then grouped according to seven categories of plot interest: cases solved by clever observation; cases solved by ruses and stings; cases solved by magistrates' personal comings-down to the scene of the crime; cases judged corruptly or incompetently; cases resulting from clever crimes; cases with bizarre or convoluted circumstances; and misjudged cases. Discrimination between genuine cases and fiction was not a consideration. Several stories from Pu Songling's fictional *Strange Tales from a Chinese Studio* are included, undoubtedly because of their superior interest and literary style. This is leisure-time reading matter for China's modern educated classes—a book waiting to be reworked in a more vernacular form for the masses.

A step down the chain is the *Ming Qing anyu gushi xuan* (Selected tales of cases from the Ming and Qing), with a pious preface for Marxists by Xin Ziniu, who headed up a team of editors at Shanghai's East China Institute of Politics and Law. The 92 cases appear in the original classical Chinese, but with much annotation and complete translations into modern Mandarin without affected archaisms (e.g., "he said" is rendered by the contemporary word *shuo*, not the *dao* of the great Ming and Qing vernacular novels). The first print run, in December 1983, was 100,000 copies; sixteen months later, another 185,000 were printed. One could skip right to the translations and read them as popular fiction.

The pieces collected are presented in the preface as recordings of historical cases, and indeed several cases by Lan Dingyuan are included, along with selections from the classical essays of Feng Menglong, and from noted Qing writers such as Yuan Mei and Ji Yun. Once more there are selections from the *Strange Stories from a Chinese Studio*, indicating that a good plot, not historical veracity, was the guiding principle of selection. The compilers again categorize pieces by the type of ingenuity in the plot, though the kinds of stories are interspersed: judicial uprightness, itinerating among commoners to seek evidence, detection, ruses, ingenuity in applying the code, and breadth of knowledge. Two other categories are unjust cases and the "miscellaneous"—cases solved by mass action rather than officials. The stated aim of the book is educative; there is even a hope that the reader will learn how to judge cases for him or herself, which is yet another bolstering of adversarial values in post-Mao China. Yet clearly the chief merit of this book is the literary pleasure of the stories' ingenious crimes, detections, and plots.

Of medium difficulty were full reissues, sometimes for the first time since the communist revolution, of old novels in their original Ming-Qing idioms (sometimes an archaic vernacular). Even the first novelized version of the Judge Bao saga as told by Shi Yukun, the *Longtu erlu*, was reissued—in 80,000 copies. And yet the *Shi gongan* (Judge Shi's cases), for whatever reason, was originally for "internal distribution" only.

Materials in the modern vernacular are lower-end because they are accessible to readers with little education, and also because better-educated readers would probably prefer more sophisticated content. It would be interesting to know if intellectuals made an exception for, for instance, a novel-length write-up of a *tanci* performance in easy modern vernacular, Wu Dijun and Wang Guanlong's *Wan Qing diyi qi'an* (The top strange case in the late Qing), about the 1870 assassination of the high Qing official Ma Xinyi, who in his career had made enemies of Taiping rebels, pirates, usurers, and other commoners and officials.[188] The incident had appeared in a novel by Xiang Kairan during the early Republic.[189]

At the low end were books like *Bai an qi guan* (Strange tales: A hundred cases, ed. Zhang Chengfu). Its glossy cover has a montage of color scenes evidently from Hong Kong kungfu movies, with a backdrop of old imperial China. We see a pensive mandarin, a bloody woman's corpse, a swordsman and his servant, and a condemned man in a sealed cage for self-strangulation. Bold type on the back cover promises "Cases galore and crimes extraordinary! Ingenious detection that will make you slap the table and cry out in delight!"

The preface says that the book's sources are folklore, and the back cover identifies the general editor as a folklore researcher. He credits colleagues who helped him gather and process the material, whose names at the end of individual pieces are the only source attributions, as is common in Chinese folklore journal publication. The pieces are said to have been collected over the course of decades; one might surmise that they were published individually in provincial folklore journals during the 1980s, perhaps under the heading of "tales of upright officials," then pulled together for this book.

Styles and individual points of vocabulary vary from piece to piece, and so does the degree of specificity about time and place. Most pieces begin by telling the dynasty; some also indicate the reign period and a figure identifiable in history. In all of them the language is a very simple, eminently speakable vernacular without archaic touches, as is typical in modern Chinese folklorist publication. Probably these tales could be understood by readers with a grade-school education. The first piece opens: "One year in the time of the Song dynasty, in the summer, there was in a particular place a murder case. The details of the case were this: One evening, a monk entered the home of a villager." There are no notes. The main text tells the uneducated reader about bureaucratic procedure and what city was the capital in the relevant dynasty.

The stories may well have been taken down from storytellers, but most of this lore surely originated in the old casebooks and *biji* writings—which were in many cases based on hearsay and, for all we know, court gossip and professional storytellers' accounts themselves. Even a cursory inspection of the stories here reveals cases nearly the same as those in the *biji* collections above, the popular collection by Lu Fang'an discussed next, and indeed the *Parallel Cases* of the Song.[190] There are two stories about Judge Bao and one about Judge Di Renjie. Despite the usual throwaway claims about the knowledge that can be gleaned from the cases, the editor straightforwardly indicates that the chief interest for the reader is, first, the multifariousness of the crimes, and second, the cracking of the cases. These versions of familiar cases seem inferior to the *Parallel Cases* as literature primarily because the wonderful economy of the earlier tellings has been sacrificed. The five-sentence parable of the questioning of a fleece under torture, for instance (*Parallel Cases* no. 26B), is filled out by the modern storyteller with much inconsequential dialogue in a weak attempt to dramatize the disputant's arguments and questioning (260–62). The ingenious plot remains.

A model illustration in the present of the spirit of the old compilers of tales is *Jiu an xin shuo* (New tellings of old cases) by Lu Fang'an, who writes that he has been employed in "legal system propaganda work." Though its cases are all represented as real, this book shows the tension between an editor's desire both to pass on great plots and to give instruction. He selects twenty cases: seventeen from the Qing, one from the Song, one from 1947, and a 1923 hijacking of a railway train by mounted bandits that created an international crisis. The same incident inspired Zhang Xinxin's 1984 experimental detective novel *Feng pian lian* (Envelope, postcard, block-of-four).[191]

New Tellings of Old Cases is a relatively serious-minded and successful contribution among the lower-end works. No sources are given for the stories, but generally the reign period and the names of all the principals appear—judges, judicial supervisors, litigants, and witnesses. The space of ten or more pages per case allows the author to build plots in some detail. There are parenthetical explanations for the ignorant (explaining, for instance, that an "expectant official" is an official awaiting appointment [24]), and the language is a quite simple yet elegant vernacular. Judicious use of archaic expressions from the great vernacular novels, if not from old-style journalism—as in the rendering of dialogue, bureaucratic offices, judicial processes, and tortures—makes the stories more atmospheric and the setting more convincing. *Hua shuo* (the story goes . . .) is used sparingly. The author's favorite phrase is *qiliao* (how could one have expected that . . .). Another traditional touch is the use of couplet titles in literary Chinese, sometimes rhymed, to head subchapters. The stories are satisfying in their economy, management of suspense, and unsensational evocation of human interest. The ubiquity of questioning under torture is neither glossed over nor presented in a maudlin way.

Literary processing of the material includes, notably, supplied dialogue. Essentials about the characters' social position and character accompany their first appearance in the text, as material to explain their motivations. Steps in the legal process are also recounted. There is the accusation—perhaps a legitimate suspicion, unfortunately elaborated by certain parties into wild and unsubstantiated charges of heinous crimes so that the magistrate will take their complaint seriously; then the gathering of evidence; interrogation by torture; confession (usually false); sending of the case to higher levels in the bureaucracy for approval of the sentence; and so on. Sometimes the examining magistrate is himself rightly or wrongly caught up in the web of ruinous accusations. One gets a good sense of how cases could drag on for years owing to a lack of evidence or the disappearance of witnesses, and of the frequency with which cases were reopened because the original examining magistrate was rotated out. These elements impart a realistic and historical interest.

Lu Fang'an's didacticism, though Marxist, imparts a traditional flavor to his treatment of the cases. This is not a book dedicated to China's great tradition of upright officials. The editor's viewpoint is that China's "feudal" legal system was unjust, but feudal morality also caused legal tragedies. When a woman is raped and commits suicide, from shame, or as revenge in lieu of launching such a chancy thing as a lawsuit, or because her husband has been found guilty of a crime, or because she has been left without means of support following a state execution—the editor invariably condemns the "feudal" strictures of female chastity, the cheapness of woman's life, her lack of access to the courts, and the inadequacy of the presocialist system in sustaining orphans and widows.

Like Lan Dingyuan before him, Lu Fang'an also includes a case that lets him decry feudal superstition and the complicity of the legal system in it. Unlike magistrate Lan, though, who liked to brag about how he and his underlings acted the part of ghosts or mediums to scare commoners into spilling the beans, Lu Fang'an provides a marvelous mythic tale of a feud between two once friendly clans. A hint of jealousy between them that originated from a geomantic prophecy grows through the years into a mountain of distrust, mutual sabotage, and lawsuits, until finally the poorer but more populous clan burns the village of the richer but less numerous one and, more important, levels its ancestral graves—in 1911, just when the government was reluctant to antagonize clans that had excess manpower (who might join the revolutionaries; 206–15).

Most didactic commentary is isolated in an author's statement at the end—in a formal epilogue, in the first story—so that Lu Fang'an can condemn the feudal system and its unjust officials. If the book has the feel of a cross between old-style Republican tragic human-interest journalism and more ancient fiction (or histories), it is those final commentaries that swing the balance toward the latter, making this seemingly a book about "bad officials." But much of the interest of the cases, as of old, lies in the laudable ingenuity of the officials and the diabolical ingenuity of criminals needing to be corrected. Even these cases are followed by negative comment: What a tragedy this case would have been if by a miracle the crime victim had not been blessed with a wise official (146). This is little different from the ideology of old Chinese court case stories.

The chief criteria for selecting the cases—except for the more topical Republican-era and late Qing cases, which carry a heavier political burden—

lay in the plot interest. The evil deeds and travesties of justice are as interesting as the solutions. The sine qua non is marvelous coincidence—that
which in the premodern mind evoked a sense of fatedness, of the inevitable
presence of the inexplicable. Of equal interest is human ingenuity—the di-
abolicalness of the crimes and the serendipity if not intelligence displayed in
their solution. Consider the role of incredible (but evidently historical) coincidence in the first tale, "The Six-Fingered Man," which ends in injustice.
The *wrong* six-fingered man was executed, after a bride recalled that her
rapist had that abnormality. In addition to the unfortunate six-fingered man
locally known, a second one, a criminal, had come in from the outside the
very day of the wedding to steal the dowry. The editor-author's warning is
addressed to careless officials: the bride testified that the criminal (whom she
saw only vaguely in the dark) had six fingers on his right hand, but the local
man had an abnormal left hand!

A tale worthy of a classical Western detective story or Hitchcock film depends on the bizarre coincidence of two plots against one married woman.
Her husband has a friend plant a letter suggesting she is an adulteress, little
suspecting that someone else will soon murder her. Suspicion naturally falls
on the husband, but only belatedly, since at first he succeeds in framing the
friend who planted his false letter. He even remarries. When his lie is finally
exposed and he is about to fall into the trap he laid for himself, the real murderer finally goes too far, murdering his second wife. This draws attention to
the real culprit, his psychotic ex-girlfriend, who was betrothed to him and
loved him from childhood but never saw her love consummated (118–31).

Other stories have the traditional devices of the deceased "returning from
the dead," after being recognized by relatives from afar and brought back just
in time (or not) to keep his or her spouse from being unjustly executed for
the presumed murder. There is, of course, a logical explanation. Maybe the
"deceased" simply took off, nefariously to collaborate with another lover, or
perhaps only out of fear (92, 106). Or, maybe on her wedding night a bride
fell into a coma resembling death, was mistakenly laid out in a coffin for bur-
ial, was miraculously rescued by a passerby who heard her muffled cries before interment but then decided to carry her off as his own wife and filled
her coffin with the corpse of his uncle, who had joined in her rescue but objected too vociferously to the kidnapping! (92–105).

Three of the twenty tales involve murder or seeming murder of a newly-wed in the bridal chamber on the wedding night (1, 65, 92). There are repetitions of the common literary theme (though it also figures in genuine Qing cases in the *Conspectus of Penal Cases*) of brides or grooms, the latter perhaps in the socially humiliating position of having accepted a matrilocal marriage, conspiring or suspected of having conspired with an outside lover to do in their new legal mate. There is the case of a horde of bandits ambushing an official en route to his post in a secluded place, murdering and replacing all his retainers, assistants, and family (except his wife), then all of them taking up the respective positions at the post to plunder the taxes. They are not discovered as frauds for a year, since they kill all visitors from the real official's home town (147–55). Another case, with substitutions of corpses and comatose bodies, a lecherous monk, and remarkably opportune robbery-murders, complicated by false confessions from various parties incidentally entrapped, simply sounds like a fairy tale.[192] Lu Fang'an's cases appear to have a historical legal atmosphere, but here, more than ever, law cases have turned into page-turners. Elements of imagination and style from the past must have enriched the imaginations of China's writers of "legal system" fiction as it began to find its own voice in the later 1980s.

LITERATURE AS LAW?

Old formats go well with old cases, but what about contemporary cases? Even traditional "law case" narratives compiled for bureaucratic purposes emphasized facts—stories—more than legal reasoning. One might thus quibble that the preceding subject was "cases into literature," not "law into literature." And how could one ever come full circle and speak of "literature as law," since literary works are not "enforced"? (Roland Barthes came as close as anyone to saying that psychological preconceptions created by bourgeois fiction so influence language as to determine legal verdicts—he did so by writing up a couple of cases.)[193] But boundaries can blur.

An example of the continuing interpenetration of law and literature is a classified 1985 casebook from Jiangxi called *Zui yu fa* (Crime and the law).[194] Prepared by the provincial judiciary's propaganda section, a university law department, and the staff of a crime-and-law magazine published by a newspaper with a youth readership, it is supposedly restricted to use by "legal system propaganda personnel." Yet it clearly serves a curious general reading public—lower-end at that, judging by its sensational subject matter, crude style, and screaming didactic comments, all presented much like an old-style literary casebook. Perhaps it was classified "to protect the innocent" or for fear of giving would-be criminals "ideas" or insights into police methods and social resources. One case history tells of a bank employee who "pressed the xx," as if it were privileged information that banks have burglar alarms.

However, this popular reading matter, studded with advertisements, was published as instruction in the law and in morality. So says the commentary. Small wonder that the two are not distinguished; "law" here evidently includes police and provincial policies. Law and literature thus come full circle: true "law" cases (truer, at least, than ancient cases based on hearsay) are sugarcoated into moralistic (sub)literature, evidently in competition with books like those just mentioned—and published as legal texts to instruct cadres. Legal propaganda cadres did after all have to answer public derision of certain verdicts that gained notoriety on the public grapevine. The primitive and sensationalist "roots" of crime sought out by the authors here are in fact like those cited in other classified, all-too-serious books on criminology and criminal psychology.[195]

The "literary" (not professionally juridical) forms of *Crime and the Law* are what first meets the eye, but they run in opposite directions, toward the traditional literary and the trashy popular. The format is startlingly like the *Parallel Cases*, or the *Longtu gongan*. Most chapters are a pair of cases exemplifying a common theme. Always there is a "critical commentary" at the end, like Wu Na's for the Song dynasty anthology. The commentaries have their own subtitles, one of which is "Wrong! Wrong! Wrong!" Titles for chapters are not in couplets, but they are catchy: "The Murderer Who Had Read *La Dame aux camélias* (*Camille*, by Alexandre Dumas *fils*)" (mysterious and arty), "Strange Cases in Money Vaults" (intriguing and traditional), "The Repentance of a Master's Degree Student" (morally edifying and evoking an old interest in scholars as a class), "A Young Girl, Blind to the Law and Headed for Hooliganism" (bathetic and evoking the moral horror of fallen women). The paired cases are always preceded by a statute or excerpt from the constitution printed in boldface right after the title, as the invocation or "wedge." One thus sees retribution foreordained from on high; what follows are exemplifications in the world of crime below. Law is a warning, of retribution. Indeed, law here is high, as a literary manifestation. Law exists before the case, as if it were "natural"; and, towering above the immoral cases that follow, lofty state-executed law appears for once high in comparison with low, popular (often misconceived) "morality."

Ah, but the immorality! The old literary touches are drowning in subliterary and commercial lures. The cover has a "popular" line-drawing illustration of a handsome and poised uniformed policeman towering over a superimposed image of a fleeing criminal looking back in fear. Advertisements for local industrial firms (and a lawyers' firm) occupy the inside and back covers, and even free space between chapters—more space than in commercial magazines. The cases are sensational and the crimes are as interesting as the police and legal aftermaths. The reader is treated to gang crimes; a serial rapist-murderer who buries victims in Guizhou caves; and "The Second Biggest Embezzlement Case in All China," about a trade official who in 1960 forged Premier Zhou Enlai's name on a 200,000 yuan requisition to "restore a Lamaist temple" and kept the money but finally burned it, so scared was he of his own daring. The smell of burning ink gave him away.

The editors' preface admits that this book is "an experiment in propagandizing legal knowledge in popular (*tongsu*) form, melting information and curiosity value together in the same furnace." Cases are frankly categorized as "(1) Big cases, famous cases, and old [i.e., 1949–76] cases, edited for new significance. . . . (2) Disputed cases, difficult cases, and strange cases, made to reveal the new kinds of criminality. . . . (3) Murders of passion, cases of missing corpses, and juvenile criminality, framed as lessons about where the criminals first went astray." But promises of details on criminals' "new crime techniques, learned from outside," as in the case of break-in artists who skinned tigers right in a zoo, are unfulfilled. Those crooks just used rat poison. The plot interest lies in the crooks' boldness and lack of scruples.

Some cases begin like novels. Below are transcribed the front matter of two of them, to convey the cognitive dissonance—unless one takes statutes not as laws but as melodramatic warnings.

THE NEW "ANNA [KARENINA]"
IN THE POWER DEPARTMENT

Marriage, the family and mother and child are protected by the state.
(Constitution of the PRC, art. 49)

A marriage system based on the free choice of partners, on monogamy and on equality between man and woman shall be applied.

(Marriage Law of the PRC, art. 2)

This is the last interrogation before the case was sent to the procuratorate.

He looked at the preliminary hearing interrogator, abjectly begging for mercy. Tears streamed across his face. Sobbing, he said that since his children hadn't grown up yet, his book on nuclear power stations hadn't been published, and his new discovery hadn't been tested in production, he beseeched the government for mercy. . . .

Yes, you are the father of children not yet mature, you are the husband of a wife who still loves you though you cheated on her, you are an engineer and a graduate of a famous overseas chemical institute, you are deputy section chief of the energy department of the state science commission, and you went abroad to represent the state in conferences—you are only 41, your future was very bright, and the state desperately needed your services. But all that is past. Now you are a murderer! [11; this appears to be in the voice of the author, not an interrogator].

THE REPENTANCE OF A MASTER'S DEGREE STUDENT

Whoever intentionally kills another is to be sentenced to death, life imprisonment or not less than ten years of fixed-term imprisonment; when the circumstances are relatively minor, he is to be sentenced to not less than three years and not more than ten years of fixed-term imprisonment.

(Criminal Law of the PRC, art. 132)

On August 28, 1984, the god of death descended on Lu Peiying, riding the dense, early morning fog in the forest. On the north peak of Mt. Jiagedaqi in the Daxing'an Range of Manchuria, in the midst of beautiful scenery and the brisk autumn air, climbers went in quest of mushrooms, wood ear, and other mountain products. Suddenly, hidden below a pile of tree limbs, someone found the corpse of a woman. (26)

A poem of remorse penned by the atomic energy deputy section head before his execution is quoted, but the literary interests typically do not include well-managed suspense or ingenious applications of law. The chief (sub)literary interest is witnessing the tragedy of human beings laid low by their own criminality and the inevitable punishment of the law.

What then are the legal messages? They are disparate, but many of them reflect traditional legal attitudes and crimes that interested rulers and writers in imperial China. Each pair of cases has a common thread—usually a point of resemblance in the crimes, not necessarily in the law broken and cited after the title. The commentary often pursues yet a third subject. It may explain a point of law, moralize about the crimes, or psychologize about their origins. The aim is to learn a lesson about how to avoid evil and the shame of falling into the "net of the law." *Crime and the Law* is thus as much a book of warnings as a book of cases. It proffers morality, the stuff of Rites, as a first line of defense, and fear of the law as a second. If one is not "blind to law" (*famang*), one will realize the consequences for oneself of murdering and not commit it. But clearly that is only for people so far gone as to be unreachable by morality, for everyone knows that murder is immoral. As of old, social evil is the focus, not just lawbreaking. Ideally, one presumes, the warnings of legal system literature such as this (if sanitized and passed on in unclassified propaganda) might support rule of law by supplanting the need for actual arrests and disputations in court.

The moral warnings are simple and traditional—not the stuff of law codes, but repeated often enough to seem codified: one should not read bad books, associate with bad people (particularly gangs), have extramarital sex, gamble, take something for nothing, or think that one can get away with wrongdoing. One should control one's emotions, realize that one can reform if one errs, and recognize that young people are especially vulnerable. How these admonitions are exemplified in legal cases is the interesting part.

The problem of books is illustrated (1–5) by an adopted orphan who fell in love with his stepsister but murdered her and his stepmother with "bestiality" when the girl took a boyfriend. Then the murderer calmly read *La Dame aux camélias* at the crime scene. The editors take the book to be his pretext. Then there is the medical student who broke the rules and pursued a girl student, then murdered her so that no one else could have her when she tired of him. He had the audacity to blame his failure in love on communism and its alleged ruining of human relations, but really he was influenced by bad books: the Bible, which taught him the feudal idea of an afterlife (where he hoped to join the girl), and *The Golden Lotus*, which seduced him with bourgeois sybaritism. The law violated is art. 132, which bans murder, but that goes without saying. The statute is cited anyway, for its premonitory effect. The common theme that makes the cases interesting is not the legal one but the moral and literary one of improper and obsessive love inevitably leading to murder. The other lesson is the danger of bad books. If one behaves properly one will not get into trouble with the law.

Statutes against distributing pornography and on minors and their parents' legal responsibilities are cited at the head of a case (85–91) about a girl who was hounded by an overpoliticized class monitor, then fell in with the wrong people: a gang of Shanghai street thugs, including a girl called Rotten Orange who ruined her with dirty books and got her a boyfriend. The victim was estranged from her family until the party saved her in reform school. Here, as elsewhere (16–20, 81–84), the dangers of hanging out with the wrong crowd are manifest, but the main message is a call for leniency for minors (as in imperial law). They are still malleable. Statistics show, it is said, that the great majority of girl offenders have read bad books, and most committed crimes after reading them. The power of the word is great.

Crime and the Law is not friendly to women; they have a greater burden in enforcing morality and are a big proportion of the cited wrongdoers, contrary to reality. Take the case of the "Anna Karenina." Transferred to a power department, she had an affair with the deputy head. When she became a *Fatal Attraction*–type millstone (11–15), he strangled her to cover it up. The relevant statute is murder, cited at the start of the case story. But the main warning in the commentary is against self-pitying Annas who rationalize their way into becoming home-wreckers. "Isn't this just like the West?" says the main text. The commentary goes on to censure some bourgeois societies' "sexual freedom," calling it polygamy. In China adultery is illegal. (But not, in fact, criminal.)[196] Yet it is China's number one cause of murder. In one province in 1979, 40 percent of those executed had murdered in adulterous circumstances. May morality save us from wrong.

It is the same with gambling. "In Western society, some people take gambling to be an amusement. But our country has made it a banned activity (*weijin huodong*), because it is an unlawful way of getting property" (113). Again, it is not a crime,[197] which would bring an even greater degree of opprobrium (78–80). However, lawbreaking—gambling in particular—can lead to criminality. A jackpot of three cases is cited, the third providing a bonus "technical" lesson in real law, that theft is theft, even if one steals hot goods (e.g., gambling winnings).

The case lessons on controlling one's emotions (6–10) do lead to a point of law: where does self-defense end and murder begin? The substructure of one wrong leading to another remains. A woman's ex-boyfriend, released from prison, comes back and pulls a knife on her and her new boyfriend (the first crime). They smash his head with a stool. That is self-defense. But then they gouge out his eyes. That is a crime (the second). In the second case, a man rapes a young woman. When he returns and pulls a knife, she and her sister attack him with clubs, a shovel, and a hatchet. That is self-defense. But then one cuts off his penis and he bleeds to death. That is murder. The commentary inveighs against crimes carried out in the heat of passion and against vigilantism. The latter is a fine point, for "the criminal law of our country encourages citizens to bravely struggle against criminals" (9). But struggle is really a Maoist political emphasis.

Exhibiting police mentality and perhaps a whiff of the Maoist zest for preventive justice is a pair of cases (134–38) about girls raped after accepting rides in cars (they were doomed by their desire to get something for nothing, as were all the victims of the Guizhou serial killer). Again, the law cited is not particularly apropos, particularly to the unfortunate girls. It is art. 2 of the new criminal procedure code, which states that the code's task is to protect and serve. The commentary reasons that a major cause of the crimes was that the perps had got away with crimes before, or had seen other criminals escape the net of the law. "Many think the Public Security Bureau is not Sherlock Holmes and won't necessarily be able to crack every case." They also take advantage of their day job. Here, professional drivers were at an advantage in a society with few cars. "They forget that modern Public Security personnel have all the scientific apparatus and knowledge of modern criminal investigation and are conversant with jurisprudence, psychology, and logic, making them many times more formidable than Sherlock Holmes, armed only with his magnifying glass, tape measure, and pipe" (138). Such overconfidence can lead one to commit crime on top of crime—kill the woman one raped, to eliminate the witness. But that, of course, is just digging a deeper trench for oneself. Thus we see, in the parallel cases cited, that the driver who let his rape victim live went to reform-through-labor; the one "smart enough" to kill his victim got summary execution.

Although the commentaries often seek the psychological roots of crime, for preventive purposes, the theory is primitive. Rape is still assumed to be motivated by sexual desire and hedonism (36), and the "psychologies of criminality" are reductively codified into "hedonism, egoism, adventurism, revenge, megalomania, seeking the limelight, jealousy, suicidalism, brazenness, feelings of invincibility, decadence, impulsiveness, religiosity, copycat impulses, blind trust, curiosity, lust, etc." (137).

"Antifeudalism," or opposition to old Confucianized law, is an important cause championed by this book. A trio of cases is adduced to show that a father may no longer kill a son with relative impunity. Lack of filiality is no excuse, and even idiot sons have the right to life (21–25). Strangely, though, the first two cases, including a model Qing *Conspectus*-type case of a father ordering other sons to beat his eldest to death, lead to unspecified punishments; the third, in which a father and daughter do away with a son made an idiot by meningitis who peskily wants to get married—allegedly PRC eugenics law would prohibit that[198]—leads to their getting unspecified prison terms.

Forced marriage is rape; an exchange of gifts does not make it right, and there is no right of forced marriage even if it is "all in the family" (139–42). *Pace* Confucius, harboring a criminal relative is a crime. Two pairs of guilty fathers who became criminals by covering up for their sons are adduced (143–47).

Degrees of consanguinity are explained, and adopted children, particularly those who cared for their parents, trump blood relatives of the second degree of closeness in inheritance disputes. Here, *qing* (feelings) and the law agree. Marx is cited as approving of inheritance law, for it encouraged work. The moral lessons are that biology is not destiny, and that the lure of inheritance does cause young people to fake their identities, as it does people in capitalist countries to even commit murder. Hence a moral exemplar is cited—an adopted daughter (just in from the countryside) who won a disputed inheritance, then donated it to the state. A movie was made about her (148–55).

There is also a culturally interesting case of a boy who inveigled a girl into a mutual suicide pact without intending to keep his part of the bargain, so as to be rid of this woman who wanted to press her rightful claim to marriage.[199] She was saved by a girlfriend who knew something was up before the girl took her poisonous quaff (122–26). This case seems less typical and "traditional" than the editors' rather adventitious and sensational use of it to exemplify the difference between attempted murder and merely preparing for murder (as it might have been if the boy had taken his own poison and lived after throwing up).

Sensitive to new ideas from abroad, China is also at pains to prove that capital punishment is not feudal, as even some domestic critics allege; the sensational case of diabolically premeditated murder by a master's degree student (the opening is quoted above) is cited as evidence of the necessity of the death penalty. He was a smart boy, corrupted by Shanghai consumerism, who sliced up his wife with wire cutters, then stripped her corpse of its vulva, face, and scalp. The lesson: revenge is feudal, but neutralizing this kind of evil is necessary; it is not revenge.

The book is a little defensive also in supporting the concept of the crime of counterrevolution, which was finally deleted from the code in 1997. The pair of cases justifying constitutional vigilance against this crime are those of Lisa Wichser, unconvincingly alleged to be a CIA Mata Hari ("beautiful she-snake") who got men into bed to blackmail them into giving up "secrets" about Chinese people's attitudes toward the Cultural Revolution and the Gang of Four;[200] and a materialistic and lazy female worker who fell prey to a Taiwan intelligence recruiter because she worshipped the West. She looked so pitiful when she realized how low she had fallen (127–33). The tone could not be more paternalistic—as if the subject were children.

Perhaps the only new legal concept promoted by the book is consciousness of endangered species, now legally protected (156–60). Many chapters, whether representing reader interest, traditional state mentality, or the fact that vast resources are in official hands under socialism, deal with crime by officials, such as corruption and inside burglaries (43–62, 99–107). The book warns that recent amendments to the criminal law have made certain economic crimes subject to the death penalty (43).

What is the purpose of this book, then? It provides sensational pulp reading matter for the amusement of cadres and their friends and families, and perhaps a little sugarcoated legal education. The legal propagandists might have been expected to construct their own lectures and stories, if not fiction for magazines (like *Crime and the Law*, the periodical) from such materials. Alert cadres might then take note of real cases in their own bailiwicks and add them to the treasury of legal lore—in processed true case write-ups, or in fiction, for the edification of others. Here is another source of the new post-Mao legal system literature. Traditional law—and literature—were embedded still in lessons from modern life.

CONCLUSION

Law and literature should be a major research topic for any society as literary, precedent-conscious, and intent that the written word be turned to the cause of instruction as China. The major difficulty is not the difference in function between legal and literary texts. Sometimes it is difficult to draw the line between the two. Court cases appeared in many genres, at many levels, and for many purposes. The greater divergence is between written ideals and realities in the justice system. Yet stories about cases, even if intended for amusement more than instruction, do not always gloss over injustices, or even systemic flaws like judicial torture.

From this one can appreciate the official designation in 1984 of crime fiction as legal system literature, and also the seeming paradox that Perry Mason was of little influence. Traditionally, literary China has always looked at crime from the state's point of view. Truth never came from juries, those "specialists in epistemology" who operate like novelists in the opinion of Ian Watt.[201] It never came through the adversarialism of lawyer and prosecutor, only the opposition of judge and interrogatee, the latter kneeling abjectly and the judge on his high bench. The good judge of fiction was therefore more likely to uncover his truth by detection than by applying the law in "court," even if his method of detection was to ask tricky questions and set up clever ruses. But Chinese crime fiction, like all fiction, reflected literary conventions as well as judicial reality. The question remains—to what extent was literary creation implicated in maintaining the good and the awful aspects of Chinese justice? Did it shape what people thought they saw happening in the courtroom?

In the early twentieth century, the Western idea of detection by a private investigator unconnected to the state turned Chinese crime narration upside down, coming as it did precisely when intellectuals were bringing about the death of God, the classics, traditional morality, the classical language, and the literary forms that accompanied it. And yet, although the paradigm of the Western whodunit would loom large in Chinese crime writing ever after, the story of "cases"—a traditional, state-oriented paradigm—would never lose its grip. The "lowest" Chinese fiction about murder and mayhem is still considered a reflection on the legal system.

CHAPTER THREE

Shadows

To those old enough to remember, the Golden Age of the Chinese detective story will always be 1900–49. It was also the heyday of private, adversarial legal practice, though not of rule of law or of any fiction praising legal institutions. This chapter finds a partial explanation for that, and for the rise of the new fictional and legal practices themselves, in Western dominance. It led to resentment, and it was protected by treaty—Western-imposed law—when the Chinese government was weak. One upshot was that much of China's modern law was enacted mainly to persuade the West to give up extraterritoriality.[1] Another was a cynical "strategic use of law" by China's own practitioners because Western law seemed so hypocritical.[2] The West's literature, including its crime fiction, was in better repute. China's Golden Age of crime fiction was embodied in copious translations of Western classics and native Chinese series detectives in genre fiction. Chief among them was the Chinese Sherlock Holmes—Huo Sang—created by Cheng Xiaoqing (1893–1976). Another luminary was Lu Ping, a chivalrous outlaw whose very name suggests Arsène Lupin, the sleuthing gentleman-burglar and French anti-Holmes created by Maurice Leblanc (1864–1941). Lu Ping was created by Cheng Xiaoqing's friend, Sun Liaohong (1897–1958).

What were Cheng Xiaoqing and Sun Liaohong thinking when they imitated the West so blatantly? Many mystery writers in the West were just as imitative, but they were not as vulnerable to nationalistic and culturally polarized reproach. The Chinese writers preferred to rationalize their imitativeness rather than cover it up. They handled the national question by championing the modern analytical detective story as an international, not just a Western form. Their own works celebrate a lofty internationalist ethos of universal scientific principles and sportsmanlike equality among nations that implicitly reproves imperialism. To them, that went with the genre. In any case, their fiction had a high reputation among readers and genre critics of their day.[3] Moreover, the West's obsession with originality had never much troubled Chinese fiction writers in the past.[4] But Cheng Xiaoqing and Sun Liaohong were too Westernized to share that attitude. Like Agatha Christie, they took pains to make each of their works literally original and entertaining, and that was all their readers needed. But Cheng and Sun no more created a new individual or national subgenre or a distinctive reinterpretation of detective fiction as an international genre than did Christie.[5] And they were Chinese, not British. Why that mattered—even if it should not have— is a major subject of this chapter.

The initial heyday of Cheng Xiaoqing and Sun Liaohong was in the 1920s. They got involved in other activities in the 1930s, then enjoyed renewed popularity in the 1940s.[6] They even found minor creative jobs under communism. But their old Huo Sang and Lu Ping works were banned after 1949, and that is why China's crime fiction had to go through a second imitative phase in 1978–80 (described in Chapter One).[7] Only in the later 1980s were the cases of Huo Sang and Lu Ping reprinted. Chinese scholarship has not yet acknowledged their place in China's literary history.

All four heroes—Holmes, Lupin, Huo Sang, and Lu Ping—were series characters, and all were considered detectives, even the burglars. They all embodied the literary conceit that they were legends in their fictional worlds. Arsène Lupin is described in his first story as a burglar and pickpocket whose very name can send a *frisson* down the spines of the beautiful people as they cross the Atlantic on their luxury liners.[8] Luckily for Leblanc, Lupin did become a literary legend and an emblem of his nation like Holmes—but partly *because* Holmes was a national symbol.[9] Huo Sang and Lu Ping likewise came to represent China, at least to their authors and some readers.[10]

"Anxiety of influence"[11] of national proportions is thus a major theme of this chapter. Chinese writers of crime fiction, whose work was not automatically imputed patriotic motives like that of their equally Westernized counterparts in serious fiction, must have felt trepidations about borrowing culture from Britain and France. Those countries had taken the lead in humiliating China.

Arsène Lupin embodies both sides of the dilemma. He was a cultural influence in China. Not only did Sun Liaohong and others imitate him; Lupin made such a fool of Sherlock Holmes in Leblanc's stories that Cheng Xiaoqing tried to change the outcome by writing his own Holmes vs. Lupin stories. At the same time, Maurice Leblanc necessarily looked up to the British creator of Holmes. Leblanc was a fairly successful rival of Conan Doyle, but without Sherlock Holmes there would have been no Arsène Lupin. Leblanc wanted to even France's score with England, as did many of his countrymen on various grounds. But combat in the field of detective fiction necessarily evoked Britain's superiority over France, as over China. To be humbled here was bitterly ironic, for France and China had once "led" in this field, thanks to Vidocq, Gaboriau, and China's *gongan* writers. Moreover, Lupin came on the heels of another successful obverse of Holmes: A. J. Raffles, an English gentleman-burglar created in 1898 by Conan Doyle's brother-in-law, of all people, E. W. Hornung (1866–1921).[12] Raffles was the second most familiar and popular literary figure in England after Holmes himself. Leblanc's gusto in cutting Holmes down to size is more than just amusing, and he is unnaturally silent about Raffles. To suggest that Arsène Lupin is derivative of creations by lesser Anglo-Saxon lights than the great Conan Doyle or "Edgar Poe," honorary Frenchman,[13] is still to strike a Gallic raw nerve.

China's discomfiture before the West ran much deeper than France's vis-a-vis Britain. The early twentieth century was a time when Chinese intellectuals largely accepted the West's views of the Chinese people as backward and uncouth.[14] Cheng Xiaoqing and Sun Liaohong, like their colleagues writing "serious" fiction, were anti-imperialist, yet both kinds of writers favored an international hybrid culture instead of building a wall against "cultural imperialism." Like mainstream writing, detective fiction was adversarial and against paternalism, whether in China's "feudal" past or its politically weak present. Yet in this era, adversarialism and internationalism themselves looked like Western culture. Moreover, whereas Leblanc used his hero to even scores with a national rival, Cheng and Sun did not—not with the West or any nation in it. Why did they stray from Leblanc's path only here? Perhaps they felt that the modern culture they esteemed was too vulnerable to risk it. In view of the direction taken by the communist revolution, their fears were justified.

IN THE SHADOW OF A STRONGER NATION'S CULTURE

Readers in English need no introduction to Sherlock Holmes. That is not so true of Arsène Lupin. Perhaps it is because he ridicules the Anglo-Saxon world,[15] which has its own inferiority complex before French *culture*.

To search for Arsène Lupin's place in literature is to be immersed in cross-Channel rivalry. He can be placed within three "uniquely French" popular literary traditions. Like Rocambole before him and Fantômas close upon his heels, Arsène Lupin captures the reader's imagination not as a logician but as a magician—a man of a thousand faces. To steal another's name, even the whole social identity, is common enough, but the master criminals of French myth are "*voleurs de visage*," stealing so many faces and so perfectly that they have no identity of their own.[16] Lupin's chameleon-like nature verges on the metaphysical; Sun Liaohong would take the conundrum to that level in his own Lu Ping story, "Between Truth and Falsehood."

Another popular French literary tradition is for the crook to turn detective, either by actually switching sides, like Vidocq and M. Lecoq, or as a ruse, like Rocambole.[17] Jean-Claude Vareille finds the doubling of detective and criminal so integral a part of the *policier* formula as to give French roots to the double-plotted mystery that structuralists see as the essence of the detective story.[18] Others cite an earlier tradition of blurring the boundary between villainy and heroism in nineteenth-century French melodrama and adventure. The 1820s villain Robert Macaire, the Count of Monte Cristo, and Eugène Sue's Prince Rodolphe are the archetypes.[19]

Third, Arsène Lupin's ironic joie de vivre, which celebrates "*cambriolage* (housebreaking) as one of the beaux-arts,"[20] exemplifies the Belle Époque of his culture, not the Victorian era of Holmes. It resuscitates the decadence (called *dandysme* in French) common to both countries' aesthetic elites in the fin de siècle era just past. Ironically, *dandysme* was originally the philosophy of "the conqueror"—of English aristocrats whose ostentatious lifestyles in France after the defeat of Napoleon inspired "Anglomania" among French nobles. It was Baudelaire who transformed *dandysme* into a stoic, modernist spirit of revolt against the bourgeoisie. A half-century later, the natty clothes were worn by Leblanc himself, and the conceit of self-love as social criticism was imparted to his hero.[21] Lupin's chivalry is seldom altruistic; it creates a sense of style and independence. Lupin is an exponent of "*snobisme* or *contre-snobisme*," if not of Continental anarchism.[22] He is "the last of the dandies."[23]

And yet even French critics see the Arsène Lupin tales as detective stories (*romans policiers*) in the classical tradition, with Poe as founder and Conan Doyle the acknowledged master—despite Poe's debts to Vidocq, Sue, and Dumas, and Conan Doyle's to Gaboriau.[24] The Chinese, too, think of Lupin and Lu Ping as Sherlockian detectives. Leblanc's and Sun Liaohong's heroes do engage in analytical detection, and they are as concerned with treasures as with corpses. Leblanc denied that he really knew the works of Conan Doyle when inventing Lupin, though he claimed inspiration from Poe, the father of the genre.[25] In truth, Leblanc parodied Sherlock Holmes just a year after writing his first Lupin piece, and his first full-length Lupin novel, only a year after that, was *Arsène Lupin versus Herlock Sholmes*. It is Leblanc who indelibly linked the names of Holmes and Lupin.

In mystery fiction, the Belle Époque still belonged to Sherlock Holmes and the English, despite an international surge of gentleman-rogues and great criminal wits at the time.[26] Arsène Lupin was commercially conceived as a French hero to rival Sherlock Holmes, and Leblanc was promoted as "the French Conan Doyle." One can only speculate about the role of Raffles.[27] Gentleman-roguery never broke free of the detective/*policier* tradition, perhaps because it was such sport—where, too, the Anglo-Saxon was king.[28] In any case, Leblanc was determined that Lupin would beat Holmes, and *at his own game*.

Indeed, the Lupin stories trumpet a national desire to beat Britain in overt if also sardonic ways. The French, still licking their wounds from defeat in the Franco-Prussian War,[29] took pride in the "moral" victories of their "national thief."[30] (The Chinese might have recognized them as pyrrhic, "Ah Q victories.")[31] Lupin also compensates for Leblanc's provincial origins with his own fictitious Parisian, dandyish style, which Leblanc restores to the declining rural French aristocracy along the Paris-Rouen-coastal Norman axis of his boyhood.[32] At least the feelings of inadequacy of the provincial did not plague Cheng Xiaoqing and Sun Liaohong, who dwelt in "the Paris of the East."

Aspects of French *ressentiment* might even be called "postcolonial," now that the latter's problematique has broadened into its own discourse and undergone mitosis into postcolonial theory and postcolonial criticism.[33] But France, the neocolonial power par excellence, was never colonized—though Joan of Arc, Vercingétorix, and the comrades of Roland who succumbed to Islamic armies[34] might have begged to differ. On the other side of the Channel, mere close calls were not forgotten; Conan Doyle could think of no better epithet for Moriarty than "the Napoleon of crime"![35]

The point is that power relations affect "literary relations" even among Europeans. Such relations are subjective and do not require actual colonization. They also do not determine literary production and are not always germane to readers or even authors, though the latter may indeed fear having their minds colonized by the "Other."[36] Mimicry can be a symptom, and it can also be just mimicry; Holmes is mimicked in countries now stronger than Britain.[37]

Does this apply to China? It was the "central kingdom," the "core" indeed, and it was a colonizer, until in modern times it traded places with the "Other." The depth of that fall is what evokes the psychological force of having been colonized; the Marxist line is that China was "semicolonial" from 1840 to 1949. Borrowing foreign culture was not a problem in the Han and Tang dynasties, when China was strong.[38] If power alone were not enough to make Chinese intellectuals fear colonization of the mind, the omnipresence of Western academics and missionaries in their personal backgrounds must have been.[39] Moreover, China was bettered and oppressed by many nations, collectively, under international law. Mao expelled the imperialists, but after his death came the realization that Marxism too was Western, and that China's reemergence would not be so different from the postcolonial countries' after all.[40] And that was before the massive reentry into China of international capital. Perhaps the complexities of China's dilemma are best captured by the critics Liu Zaifu and Huang Ziping. They refer to China's being in the "shadow" of the Other—meaning chiefly the West.[41]

The most radical theories of cultural subordination come to mind when the paragons of China's great age of detection mimic not just Sherlock Holmes but the French anti–Sherlock Holmes.[42] Were Cheng Xiaoqing and Sun Liaohong "first stage" colonized native intellectuals as posited by Frantz Fanon, "proving that [they had] assimilated the culture of the occupying power" through works "we can easily link up . . . with definite trends in the literature of the mother country"?[43] Even the great mainstream writers of the age fit Fanon's "second phase" all too well, in which the native intellectual is alienated from his or her own people. "Past happenings of the bygone days of [the author's] childhood will be brought up out of the depths of his memory [Shen Congwen, Ba Jin]; old legends will be reinterpreted in the light of a borrowed aestheticism and of a conception of the world which was discovered under other skies [Lu Xun]."[44] Most Chinese writers then proceeded to Fanon's "third phase," "fighting" and revolution.

In his day, Huo Sang was called "the Oriental Sherlock Holmes," and Lu Ping "the Oriental Arsène Lupin." Neither Chinese author seems at first to have objected,[45] though later Sun Liaohong rebelled against such explicit subordination.[46] Did "Oriental" (*dongfang*) here reflect the kind of attitudes decried by Edward Said? Sorting out all the connotations of this word with its own history in Chinese is a task for the future; China's concept of the "Orient" did gain new currency in the 1920s from writings by Liang Qichao and Liang Shuming that were influenced by Henri Bergson, Rudolf Eucken, and Bertrand Russell's hopes for a pacifist "Orient" (China and India) that would redeem the warlike "West."[47] Yet to be the "Oriental Holmes" in Chinese was to be the master detective of all East Asia. Japan, ahead of China in "modernization" and perhaps Holmes mania,[48] used different Sino-Japanese characters (*kanji*) to write "Oriental" (they were pronounced *dongyang* in Mandarin; *tōyō*, in Japanese), in support of Japanese hegemony in Asia.[49] China's *dongfang* usage returned Japan to junior status in an "Orient" led by China.

Cheng Xiaoqing and Sun Liaohong did not reproduce Western "Orientalist" stereotypes, but they did depict the Chinese as "Western": as being as scientific, precise, technically advanced, and intellectual as the modern detective—and, by Chinese lights, individualistic and adversarial in spirit. Cheng and Sun may have, like Western Orientalists in Said's view, given their heroes virtues considered Western because of their "lamentable" absence in China, as "medicine" for their readers. King-fai Tam sees in the superiority of Huo Sang over his "Dr. Watson," Bao Lang, a privileging of the scientific over the literary mind. He also notes that Cheng tempered this by letting Bao Lang do some moral questioning,[50] which would be hybridity of the type prized by postcolonial critics.[51] The question remains: Did Cheng and Sun, or Leblanc, adopt Anglo-American conventions because they were consciously or unconsciously awed by the Anglo-Saxons' power?

Cheng Xiaoqing was forever measuring Chinese detective stories by the standards of the Western classics, and to China's disadvantage. He took the psychological edge off this by depicting the genre as new to China, which was his defense for Chinese inferiority; and new to the West, by which he explained detective stories' low status worldwide.[52]

Yet China had tales of clever detection and serial judge-detective characters centuries before the West.[53] The famous novelist Wu Jianren (Wu Woyao) meant to celebrate the superiority of real Chinese detection over Western detective fiction by putting out a collection of cases in the old *biji* style.[54] Other Chinese writers at the turn of the twentieth century pitted a facsimile of Holmes against Chinese ghosts and fox fairies.[55] But most twentieth-century Chinese detective stories ignored such native touches. Cheng Xiaoqing and Sun Liaohong took their genre and even many of their heroes' discretionary character traits straight from Europe. Granted that modern readers might have wanted new kinds of heroes, more unified and rapid-fire plots, and more modern gadgets than Chinese tradition had to offer, why not at least invent more original or "Chinese" heroes? Was this not the wholesale Westernization that nationalists railed at? By contrast, "El Sherlock Holmes Mexicano," based on a real detective, Valente Quintana, emerged as a distinctively national folk hero, "El Zorro."[56] Pastiches, parodies, and further adventures of Sherlock Holmes have been produced by Baker Street enthusiasts worldwide,[57] but Cheng and Sun did not write in that vein; they had pretensions to literary seriousness.

The fact that some Chinese have defended Cheng and Sun on ideological grounds raises more questions about Western influence. Sun Liaohong attacked modern corruption and materialism. Cheng Xiaoqing's hero claimed uniquely Chinese values from Mencius, Mozi, and knights-errant. Yet Mozi was newly rehabilitated, at a time when China sought parity with the West. Perhaps his ethic of universal love was disguised Christianity, which was more powerfully grounded in modern China. Cheng Xiaoqing was a churchgoing Methodist, and his sober habits showed it.[58]

Cheng Xiaoqing took the antitraditional side in the "two-line struggle" between Chinese and Western detection advanced by Wu Jianren. Cheng also wanted to make his own Great Detective's coadjutor, Bao Lang, a little more clever than Watson. This may have reflected a uniquely Chinese impetus to make him a bearer of moral and humanistic values. And yet, as a follower of the Western genre, Cheng Xiaoqing also felt that Bao Lang's reasoning really had to be distinctly inferior, to mislead the reader.[59]

Through didactic asides in his stories, Cheng applauded the logical analysis in Western works. When he went on to write his own brief history of the detective story, he confined himself to the West's "pure detective story," slighting what he called China's "sprouts of the detective story," which in his view were sidetracked by knight-errantry and ghostly doings. Hence the works failed to become logical and scientific. A similar explanation was used by some Chinese to explain the "backwardness" of their whole culture despite its head start, but most blamed imperialism as well as "feudalism" (native blockages such as superstition). Most critics agree with Cheng that the pleasures of *Three Heroes and Five Gallants* do not lie chiefly in detection, and many would second him when he argues the same point about the Ming *gongan* short stories.[60] Wu Jianren's old *biji* cases proved to modern readers the very opposite of what he intended: that Chinese tradition had nothing resembling the well-plotted Western detective story. The times were also unsympathetic to the traditional genre's enmeshment with imperial bureaucracy.[61] Perhaps *biji*-style case write-ups prevailed again in the early 1980s (as noted at the end of the previous chapter) only because they did not yet have much competition; mass (as opposed to scholarly) interest in them did not survive the decade.

These problems represent a larger Chinese cultural crisis if China's detective fiction is viewed as a popular affiliate of May Fourth literature (as Western scholars call the modern, socially engaged, serious literature of the time) rather than just as a continuation of "indigenous" popular fiction. Cheng Xiaoqing's stories resemble contemporary serious works in form and language (in an age when language often differentiated the serious from the popular), ideology, milieu (automobiles, not courtesans), and the author's view of creativity. The Huo Sang stories would be a specialized genre of the already very Westernized writing of their age, better plotted than most, middlebrow in reputation but better than middlebrow in execution, and attracting urbanites reading for pleasure as well as students. Such a perspective was inconceivable at the time, for mainstream authors condemned in practice the popular taste they praised in theory.[62] As May Fourth intellectuals elevated fiction, previously "low," to the serious literature of their age, the burden of proving that it truly was serious became heavy. Like the old high literature, May Fourth fiction needed lower forms to demonstrate that it was high. In fact, "mandarin duck and butterfly" love stories, the new fiction's major foil, evinced as much fascination with the West as May Fourth fiction. Critics from C. T. Hsia to Perry Link have shown that the gulf between them has been exaggerated.[63]

China's intellectual elite was in fact less censorious of detective fiction than of other popular genres, King-fai Tam finds, because of its obviously Western form and origins.[64] The genre was introduced as reformist fiction in the late 1890s. Its many years as a fiction in classical Chinese were attributable to interest in it by Liang Qichao and Lin Shu rather than affinity to old Shanghai popular genres. When vernacular and classical fiction traded places on the ladder of prestige, detective fiction made the transition to the new "high" vernacular—the language that Western-inspired genres seemed destined for all along.

The detective genre thus appeared to many readers intellectual, and its heroes active, individualistic, adversarial—against crime, tradition, and anything that might weaken China. Detectives embodied May Fourth norms. This was the Dorothy Sayers view of detective fiction as a favorite of thinkers and statesmen, hence not really "popular fiction." Only the story setups sinned—against the new Chinese god of literary realism, as when Cheng Xiaoqing's *private* eye sleuthed exotic "European-style" murders in bourgeois urban settings instead of "real crime" in the Zhabei slums, in the red-light districts, and on the docks; and when Sun Liaohong made his Shanghai burglar, who heads a criminal syndicate, a stranger to rackets, opium, the police, and Western fortune hunters.

Cheng Xiaoqing and Sun Liaohong did not plagiarize; plagiarists steal plots and disguise their deeds by erasing clues to the source. Traditional Chinese purveyors of good cases likewise appropriated plots, insouciantly changing details or not as the spirit moved them, in the absence of the concept of plagiarism. Such copying of narratives—whether of the first or second type it was hard to distinguish—was so common that Westernized Chinese critics of the early twentieth century regularly denounced the practice. Cheng Xiaoqing and Sun Liaohong, in contrast, exalted their treading in the footsteps of Western writers. Doing so may have helped sales. Or it may have been personal homage to the achievement of Conan Doyle, Leblanc, and their values. In this, Cheng Xiaoqing and Sun Liaohong represented the May Fourth era.

This chapter thus tackles three kinds of topics, still with a heavy burden of introducing unknown texts—which puts it in the familiar, quasi Orientalist position of restoring Chinese cultural history to China. There are the conventional questions of how the Chinese detective stories were constructed, what influenced them, and how good they are. More postmodern concerns lead to a hunt for sensitivities of the type addressed by postcolonial critics. A third and related subject is relations of law and literature in this first era "while China faced West."[65] This chapter concludes that China's crime fiction of the Republic, Westernized but nationalistic, embraced an adversarial spirit but rebuffed Western law. Both the embrace and the rebuff were related to China's being in the shadow of the West—a predicament not yet wholly past.

HOLMES AND LUPIN IN CHINA

Conan Doyle was one of China's five most frequently published foreign authors of 1896–1916. Soon Leblanc followed close behind. Holmes and Marguerite (of Dumas *fils*'s *La Dame aux camélias*—the work blamed for causing a crime in post-1949 Jiangxi, as told in the last chapter) were the best-known and most popular characters from foreign fiction in late Qing China, Chen Pingyuan observes; they were often mentioned together as personifications of Western novelistic art.[66] Four Sherlock Holmes tales were available in translation as early as 1896, in Liang Qichao's journal *Shiwubao* (The Chinese progress). Hence they began, and for more than two decades remained, a fiction in classical Chinese. But Liang's venue also embedded them in a context of reform, Westernization, nation-building, and international intrigue. The first Holmes work was "The Naval Treaty," about a copy of a secret Anglo-Italian pact feared to have been stolen for the French or

Russians. Knowledge of European diplomacy was the very sort of thing Liang wanted to impart to his readers. Printed as "*Biji* of Holmes," this story in Chinese blurred the distinction between Chinese and Western case write-ups. Some may have read it for information about scientific detection and thought it was nonfiction.[67]

Liang Qichao published more Holmes stories in his *Xinmin congbao* (New citizen journal) and *Xin xiaoshuo* (New fiction). In 1916, Zhonghua Publishers put out a *Fuermosi tan'an quanji* (The complete Sherlock Holmes) translated by ten established and younger masters of old-style fiction in the classical language, including Chen Diexian, Zhou Shoujuan, Liu Bannong, Yan Duhe—and young Cheng Xiaoqing.[68] By then, Conan Doyle had caught the attention of Lin Shu, China's greatest and most prolific translator of Western novels.[69] Besides *Micah Clarke* and five other Conan Doyle novels not in the Holmes series, Lin in 1908 published *A Study in Scarlet*, the 1887 novel that introduced Holmes to his English readers and thus became the foundational work of Sherlockiana.[70] Also favorable to Conan Doyle's reputation were the ease with which his Holmes tales could be imitated, coupled with the difficulty of actually equalling them. Like Bao, the original Holmes was a great series detective, his feats singular but reproducible.[71]

In the first decade of the twentieth century, detective stories outnumbered those of any other genre in China; at the Forest of Fiction Press, they constituted 70 to 80 percent of sales.[72] They were as much as one-third of all late Qing fiction in print.[73] Research has not pursued the question of whether these stories were wholly Westernized or had ghosts and touches of the *biji* or *gongan* traditions. But in the next decade, Cheng Shanzhi is said already to have written an antidetective crossover story, satirizing a teacher who, under the influence of too many detective stories, feels compelled to play detective in real life, with absurd results.[74]

The vernacular literary revolution began in 1917. Modern vernacular Chinese was used in a 1925 *New Cases of Sherlock Holmes* featuring nine stories that Conan Doyle published after the First World War. A new *Complete Works* (with 55 titles) came out in modern vernacular in 1927 from a translation team headed by Cheng Xiaoqing himself; most pieces were adapted from the classical Chinese versions. Conan Doyle's stories had by then inspired many Chinese imitations.

His Chinese followers included not just Cheng Xiaoqing but Lu Dan'an,

Chen Diexian, and lesser lights—at least 50, says Fan Boqun. Wei Shaochang counts the familiar "serious" writers Liu Bannong and Zhang Tianyi as among them.[75] Famous works not considered genre fiction but still influenced by the Western detective story included *The Strange Case of Nine Murders* (1906) and *Eyewitness Reports on Strange Things from the Past Twenty Years* (1910) by Wu Jianren himself,[76] Liu E's *Lao Can youji* (Travels of Lao Can; 1907), even Xu Zhenya's sentimental novel *Yulihun* (The jade pear spirit; 1912).[77] The scholar Chen Pingyuan feels that the Western detective story played a major role in introducing the inverted plot structure to China in the late Qing, although he laments that it did not more deeply influence Chinese fiction outside the detective genre.[78]

Edgar Allan Poe's detective stories also came to China in the late Qing. Zhou Zuoren translated "The Gold Bug" in 1905, at the behest of his brother, Lu Xun, in Japan. Dupin became known only later—after Rodolphe, for Eugène Sue's *Les Mystères de Paris* was serialized in 1904.[79] Western detective stories circulating in Chinese have not been counted, much less listed. Before 1949, Cheng Xiaoqing alone translated eleven Philo Vance mysteries by S. S. Van Dine (Willard Huntington Wright), ten books about The Saint by Leslie Charteris (Leslie Charles Boyer Yin), six Charlie Chan mysteries by Earl Derr Biggers, mysteries by Maurice B. Dix, K. S. Daiger, R. Austin Freeman, and Ellery Queen, and multiauthor crime story anthologies with introductions by Dorothy Sayers and others.[80]

Arsène Lupin was created only in 1905, but he too went to China in the early Republic, perhaps the late Qing. Key works were available in English by 1910, and China had many French speakers. Items available in Chinese by 1917 included *L'Aiguille creuse* (The hollow needle; first French edition 1909) and *813* (1910), rendered by Bao Tianxiao, who generally translated from Japanese texts; probably "Le sept de coeur" (The seven of hearts; 1907) and "Le Mariage d'Arsène Lupin" (The marriage of Arsène Lupin; 1912), done by Zhou Shoujuan; and *Arsène Lupin, gentleman-cambrioleur* (Arsène Lupin, gentleman-burglar; collected in French in 1907), *Le Bouchon de cristal* (The glass stopper; 1912), and *Arsène Lupin contre Herlock Sholmes* (Arsène Lupin versus Herlock Sholmes; 1908), rendered by others.[81] A *Yasen Luopin an quanji* (Complete cases of Arsène Lupin; 10 novels and 18 stories) came out in the vernacular in 1924, before the complete vernacular Holmes, from a team including Zhou Shoujuan, Shen Yuzhong—and Sun Liaohong. There was at least one other self-styled "Oriental Lupin" besides Lu Ping, a Lu Bin created by He Puzhai.[82]

So Cheng Xiaoqing and Sun Liaohong cut their teeth as creators of the Chinese Holmes and Chinese Lupin by working with the European prototypes. When Cheng first read Conan Doyle at the age of twelve or thirteen, he found him too difficult; it was when Zhou Shoujuan invited Cheng into his translation project that he began to delight in the plots and feel that he was also learning something. He went on to write both detective and romantic stories in classical Chinese. It is said that he published his first Huo Sang story, "Dengguang renying" (A human shadow in the lamplight; not extant), in 1914. The series began in earnest with "Jiangnan Yan" (lit., "Swallow of the South," the avian nickname of a criminal character), in 1919, in classical Chinese.[83] Sun Liaohong also wrote popular fiction in a variety of genres in the early 1920s and was still using classical Chinese in 1922.[84]

Just as original Western-style Chinese detective stories and other popular fiction in classical Chinese were scaling new heights, the May Fourth literary movement of 1917–19 stole their thunder—with intellectuals, not general readers—by stimulating creation of a whole new socially conscious Westernized literature in a "new language," the modern vernacular. Cheng Xiaoqing was able to make the transition and resurrect Huo Sang as a Chinese Sherlock Holmes in a vivid, modern, vernacular prose that could compete with Beijing's "serious" fiction from the literary revolution and with Shanghai's ever evolving popular fiction genres. Sun Liaohong likewise found his voice in a witty vernacular style. The "real" Holmes in translation also made the transition from a refined, activist, reformist (but still amateur) gentryman's "better self" to a new, modern, "scientific" professional-style amateur of modern times.

THE APPEAL OF SHERLOCK HOLMES

Holmes personifies logic, deduction, and ratiocination to readers of all nations, but his cases must also have appealed to traditional Chinese readers' interest in the "strange" or "uncanny" (*qi*).[85] The main story in a Holmes tale is often preceded by a short, brilliant, and basically irrelevant deduction ("preamble"). It may have reminded readers of the tale-before-the-tale in old *huaben* stories. Indeed, along a spectrum of works from those that tell the reader whodunit only on the last page to old Chinese tales whose detective interest lies in seeing the judge figure out whodunit, the Sherlock Holmes stories are somewhere in between.

Conan Doyle, who in his later years grew interested in spiritualism, was drawn to "the bizarre and the daring" "as a filing is drawn to its magnet."[86] That Lin Shu put the word *qi* into the title of his translation of *A Study in Scarlet* was characteristic of his free adaptation of Western fiction to Chinese taste, but the originals do traffic in the eerie, the uncanny, and the foreign mystery. Watson says in "The Adventure of the Speckled Band" that Holmes, "working as he did rather for the love of his art than for the acquirement of wealth, refused to associate himself with any investigation which did not tend towards the unusual, and even the fantastic."[87] This is in accord with Confucian attitudes toward law and literature. Chinese readers may have been quicker than Western critics to see Holmes's "marvelous" case solutions for what they were—not airtight deductions but flights of creative intuition.[88] This is clear especially in light of the more labored ratiocinations of Huo Sang, a purer, less confident epitome of modern, scientific, "anti-feudal" man. Dreams and cocaine belong to the worlds of Judge Bao and Sherlock Holmes, not Huo Sang. He is less eccentric than Holmes, and yet, because less romantic and flawed, less "human"—he has no weakness for a woman, no Irene Adler. A science teacher, Huo Sang might be able to replicate himself by training disciples. There is only one Holmes.[89]

The conflict between science and the uncanny may be more apparent than real, note literary historians commenting on Holmes's success with his original readers. Scientific references served reader curiosity about new things in their lives.[90] Conan Doyle was already attracting to the genre people who read for "information." Popular science writing, science fiction, and detective stories all enjoyed explosive growth in post-Mao China, which was experiencing a comparable fascination with the "new" Western technology displayed on television. Interest in science fiction and the classic Western-style whodunit then declined.[91]

Holmes, in the general reader's impression though not necessarily Watson's, better fulfills the "amateur ideal" of the Chinese gentry than Lord Bao himself, for Bao was little interested in hobbies. If Holmes were Chinese, he would spend time on calligraphy, painting, archery, herbal medicines, and tobacco (still using the pipe) in lieu of the violin and cocaine. In the post–May Fourth era, he would simply compose his poetry in the vernacular and continue his research in chemistry. The dilettante *complet* is Arsène Lupin, who can recite Homer in Greek and Milton in English.[92]

Holmes's friendship with Watson was appealing, too. Mutual understanding among friends (*zhiji*) was celebrated in chivalric novels. Bao Lang promotes the conceit that Huo Sang's readers, after meeting him in so many stories, are *zhiji* of the Great Detective like himself. China's original knights-errant were male and little attracted to women. The similar Western literary tradition of male bonding, undistracted by "domestic or amorous connection between the sexes," is found in adventure, frontier, and picaresque tales that place the heroes in danger, notes Edward Said, who traces the genealogy from Jason, Odysseus, and above all Don Quixote with Sancho Panza, to male pairs in *Huckleberry Finn*, *Moby Dick*, and *The Deerslayer*, down to Holmes and Watson and Batman and Robin.[93] But bonding did not keep Chinese chivalrous knights from establishing hierarchical relationships of service. Watson, too, "serves" an intellectually superior, patronizing, constantly instructing Holmes. That, coupled with the near invincibility of Holmes, evoked comforting images of the English detective as a *zhiji* who still functioned in time of crisis as a protective, mentoring father figure. Holmes is clearly the model for the Great Detectives in the post-Mao whodunits discussed in Chapter One, but perhaps he has a little of Judge Bao within himself.

Holmes and the law is a problematic subject. The detective was expert in and dedicated to the law, yet he sometimes acted outside it, like a knight-errant, even as a "final court of appeal."[94] Bao Lang pronounces Huo Sang expert in the law too,[95] but really he has little time for legal niceties.

Recent scholarship has also noted that the Sherlock Holmes stories partake of the romance of British imperialism; Conan Doyle has been cogently classified within a "genre of adventure-imperialism" with H. Rider Haggard, Charles Reade, and Vernon Fielding.[96] Britain was China's chief bugbear until 1915, when Japan "advanced." Yet Haggard and Conan Doyle, in Lin Shu's translations, gained tremendous currency in early-twentieth-century China. China shared Britain's sense of superiority over the "South Seas," part of which was once tributary to China—not politically colonized, but subject precisely to its "epistemic violence."[97] Perhaps modern Chinese readers were able to suspend their own national resentments and identify with Britain's imperialist burden in those realms.

HUO SANG, "THE ORIENTAL SHERLOCK HOLMES"

Cheng Xiaoqing's many stories and novellas, mostly set in Shanghai and outlying delta towns, treat Huo Sang as a celebrity who transcends the series. He has a past; habits and hobbies; a constant colleague; a China-wide reputation; regular nemeses who are left standing to fight Huo Sang another day, like Hairy Lion and his Five Blessings Gang; a mysterious underworld contact named Jiangnan Yan who may surface at any time as a nemesis or as an invisible guardian angel (in one story he performs a bit of bravado from the repertoire of Arsène Lupin);[98] and a repeating cast of colleagues and nuisances among the local police. Stories customarily begin Conan Doyle–style, with the police or a client coming to Huo Sang for help. A series memory of prior cases allows newer stories to refer to old cases. All that is lacking is a fixed chronology of cases and the aging of the detective in them. Yet Huo Sang's profession did not exist in China. In a Sun Liaohong story, Lu Ping ironically introduces Huo Sang to a friend as a Great Detective, pointing out also that he is China's *only* private detective![99]

Huo Sang's habits and eccentricities are Sherlockian, though one may suspect, given Cheng Xiaoqing's devotion to translating Philo Vance novels of the 1920s and 1930s, that in time he may have found that detective just as inspirational. Cheng was also attracted to Charteris's beyond-the-law character, The Saint (Simon Templar), but that hero made a splash chiefly in the 1930s and after.[100] It matters little. All are variations on Holmes. Vance is still more self-consciously erudite and pedantic, still more comfortable in his personal finances (so too the social circles he is called on to penetrate), still more dilettantish, in an aristocratic sense, as he helps the New York City police solve difficult cases. S. S. Van Dine provided interminable lists of the books in a character's library, multiple maps and plans of houses, even footnotes. That his detective sometimes takes the law into his own hands may have influenced later Huo Sang stories, but Cheng's early works already have "hard-boiled" interludes; guns are drawn in some of Holmes's adventures too. The Vance novels begin with prologues in which the amanuensis philosophically compares the case at hand with his hero's other cases, as in many Huo Sang tales. But again there were precedents for this in Conan Doyle, in "The Five Orange Pips," "The Adventure of the Speckled Band," and others.

Literary influence from Conan Doyle did not diminish the originality or interest of S. S. Van Dine's novels, "the most popular mystery novels of his era,"[101] any more than the similarity of later Holmes stories to earlier ones diminished theirs. Huo Sang is to Holmes simply what Vance is to Holmes. Still, notes King-fai Tam, Chinese readers would have considered Huo Sang's and Bao Lang's lifestyle very Westernized.[102] Conveniences of well-to-do Shanghainese may even be counted as part of the information dividend. This reader learned, for instance, that a Shanghai operator would give you the number, name, and address of the party who just telephoned you if you rang her up.[103] Cheng Xiaoqing no doubt felt a social responsibility to provide information. He has Huo Sang deliver short lectures on pop psychology from familiar Western thinkers like James Harvey Robinson, and in one story he provides a lesson in criminology, to wit, that eyewitnesses are unreliable. "Therefore when judges and detectives investigate a case, collection of supporting evidence and discrimination in interpretation are very important," advises the narrative, as if to instruct those functionaries.[104]

Cheng Xiaoqing liked to say that his hero's name was created by the editor who printed his first story, who either misread or deliberately changed the original name, "Huo Sen."[105] More important, characters in Huo Sang stories are given to identifying themselves by the first initials of their names in romanization. H. S. (Huo Sang) is an inversion of S. H., Sherlock Holmes. Liu Ts'un-yan (Liu Cunren), a disciple of Cheng's, opines that "Huo Sang" was "probably derived from Hawthorne in transliteration"—yet another Western derivation.[106]

Huo Sang lived in Shanghai, China's most international city, with a loyal servant and a cook who recur as minor characters, at No. 77 Aiwen Road (today, West Beijing Road; Cheng Xiaoqing knew that seven was lucky in the West, a significance it lacks in China). "Aiwen" literally means "loving culture"; when Sun Liaohong went on to write his anti–Huo Sang stories, he upped the literal meaning of the street a bit, calling it Aiwenyi Road— Loving Literature and the Arts Road.[107] Huo Sang addicts must surely have noticed the little dig.

Huo Sang's nearly constant companion, Bao Lang, is absolutely loyal and just as dedicated as Huo Sang to solving mysteries and achieving justice. His countless logical though inevitably wrong solutions are not stupid, but they are less insightful than his mentor's. He does enjoy prowess in Chinese boxing. Cheng Xiaoqing once (over)explained that Bao Lang's function is to lead the reader astray into myriad plausible but blind alleys.[108] As a writer, he is Huo Sang's equal socially, though it is not clear what he might have published other than Huo Sang stories. Like the original Watson, Bao Lang is the series narrator. Some stories open with passages evidently told by an omniscient narrator, but then Bao Lang breaks in to continue, explaining retrospectively that he has been relating the previous passage directly as it was told him by another person, typically Huo Sang himself. As in the Holmes stories, Bao Lang is also Huo Sang's sounding board. The early story "Jiangnan Yan" functions much like Conan Doyle's foundational work on Holmes, *A Study in Scarlet*, letting "the Watson" explain how he met the Great Detective and schematically introduce hobbies and eccentricities. As in the original Holmes saga, Bao Lang rooms with Huo Sang at first, marries, but moves back when his wife visits relatives. Huo Sang remains single, and like Holmes he is less a lady's man than his sidekick.[109] He is also financially comfortable; he often donates his detective fees to charity, though his means of support are not necessarily evident. Huo Sang and his friend and amanuensis are thus a perfect Holmes-and-Watson pair, and hardly the world's first.

The Westernization of Huo Sang and Bao Lang is apparent in their Western-style suits, ties, and concealed sidearms. Huo Sang wears a brimmed felt hat and smokes cigarettes (a cigar in "Jiangnan Yan"), not a pipe (which would be Sherlockian but also traditionally Chinese). He smokes incessantly, though Bao Lang tells us that "he used not to smoke at school; he only pulled out a cig when he was bored or deep in thought."[110] Here might be the origin of the smoking-equals-ratiocination cliché in the new Chinese whodunits of the early 1980s, if the authors had access to stored books from pre-1949 times. Huo Sang plays the violin but has no drug addiction. He and Bao Lang ratiocinate in the most up-to-date Chinese language, and they go to a club to relax, smoke, and read newspapers. (It is the Youth Club, indicative of sympathies with the New Culture movement.) They take taxicabs, though also rickshaws. And they go out for walks, even at night. Like Holmes, Huo Sang places want-ads in the paper if that will help solve his mystery, and carries makeup and knockout drops hidden in his cigars and shoes when going out to court danger.

Huo Sang's expertise is scientific and technological, but his knowledge of literature is not "nil," as Watson said of Holmes's; he appreciates the essence, the moral and ethical principles, of the old Chinese classics, without wasting his time on old-style memorization and exegesis.[111] He sounds, for all the world, like a modern ecumenical Protestant Christian, though Bao Lang identifies his chivalry and support of the poor and weak against the rich and powerful as coming from an appreciation of the "universal love" of Mozi. Of course Holmes is already the consummate "infracaninofile—helper of the underdog."[112]

Huo Sang, like Holmes, may be called in on a case by police who appreciate his brilliance or are just plain stumped. He can look at tire tracks and immediately know that they were made by Dunlops. Huo Sang takes every crime to be an offense against him personally. "Underworld gangs wholly beyond the law, shyster lawyers who turn right and wrong upside down, warlords and politicos who ride roughshod over the people with their power and wealth, evil merchants who will do anything for profit—all privileged classes, from the heartless rich to those who live outside the law—these are Huo Sang's mortal enemies," avers Bao Lang.[113] But there is no lack of well-bred clients calling at his home to seek his services, including mysterious and delicate young ladies. Huo Sang ignores rude and overbearing callers as if they were not there. That behavior calls for Bao Lang's best mediating skills. However, Huo Sang is much more humble than Holmes, and he comforts his Watson as often as he challenges or chides him.

Still, Huo Sang often keeps his own counsel, leaving Bao Lang in the dark, sometimes to protect him. This does not keep Huo Sang from enigmatically announcing, out of the blue, that he has solved a mystery. (He will explain later.) He also frequently pontificates. The first study of Cheng Xiaoqing from the PRC has extracted 56 adages and aphorisms from the lips of Huo Sang and Bao Lang, such as "Sitting and talking is not as good as getting up and acting," and "Some acts that are right are illegal; and some that are not illegal are not right."[114] Huo Sang is concerned above all for his reputation—as Lu Ping is aware, in Sun Liaohong's stories, for Lu Ping turns this bourgeois scruple against Huo Sang.

The plots too are in the Poe or Conan Doyle tradition. There is a mystery, usually of whodunit (not just howdunit or whydunit), and at first an intense interest in physical clues, with many irrelevant and misleading pieces of evidence leading to multiple red herrings proffered by Bao Lang, the police, and the suspects. False suspects are ruled out one by one, and new ones arise. Anonymous letters and other mysterious communications appear. The detectives go in disguise (like the great Chinese judges and Holmes), often turning the episode into a comedy of manners. Bao Lang, for instance, rehearses servility, the better to pass as Huo Sang's servant (in "Huangpu Jiang zhong" [On the Huangpu River]). A recap at the end explains everything, or a double recap relates how every crime and mysterious action was carried out and then how the Great Detective figured it all out. Every detail counts; few loose ends are left at the story's end.

Huo Sang's cases are prosaic in comparison with Holmes's "uncanny" ones. Every scene is set up with exact descriptions of furnishings, clothing, and the weather. This is common in Western novels (there are set descriptions of clothing and physiognomies also in China's great Ming and Qing vernacular novels), but not particularly in Conan Doyle, who is noted for economy of narration and dialogue. The Huo Sang stories steer clear of whimsy, and Cheng Xiaoqing overexplains how Huo Sang reads people's psychology. Every deduction comes honestly and arduously, not from creative, intuitive insight. If the West equals science, Huo Sang is more Western than Sherlock is himself.

Before examining Huo Sang as scientific man, let us get a sense of Cheng Xiaoqing's plots, from a simple but typical story (though it is set in Suzhou, not Shanghai)—"Jiangnan Yan," the *Study in Scarlet* of China's Great Detective.[115] Bao Lang at the start introduces Huo Sang, tells how they met, and, as his friend enters, draws from him a "preamble" of the Holmesian or *huaben* type. Having changed clothes and combed his hair, Bao Lang asks Huo Sang to deduce where he has been. Huo Sang at once reckons, from the sweat on Bao Lang's collar, his wet socks, and a remembrance that Bao Lang had to forgo an invitation for an outing two weeks earlier, that he has been boating, out of town. Bao Lang's recent reapplication of hair oil shows that he was rowing in heavy winds that do not blow in town. The deduction seems uncanny at first. Yet unlike the Holmes preambles, it is rather unremarkable when explained. Huo Sang's deductions are, however, more plausible—"scientific."

That proof completed, the companions take a stroll up on the Suzhou city wall and find a lost pearl. Huo Sang pronounces it booty dropped by the felon Jiangnan Yan, the "Swallow of the South" who burgled two homes of the rich in a single evening a fortnight ago. He must have escaped the city through this hole in the wall. Huo Sang concedes that the legal thing would be to turn the pearl in to the police; but it is too late to help them snare The Swallow now, so Huo Sang has a better use for it: he will sell it and give the money to charity. The property rights of the rich former owners count for nothing, and we hear no more of the pearl (a loose end). Huo Sang's keeping of Jiangnan Yan's secret does give the burglar some "face."

Now Bao Lang's student Mr. Sun rushes up and reports that Jiangnan Yan has robbed his house of 6,000–7,000 yuan, while his father, a wealthy former official named Sun Shougen, and his valet, Hong Fu, were at the opera. The father's concubine slept through it, and Jiangnan Yan scrawled his name on the wall as in the two previous robberies. The police, looking for an inside accomplice, have already hauled off the Anhui gatekeeper for questioning. That is the case. Reluctantly, Huo Sang accepts it, not knowing he will have a rival—the elder Sun's Pekingese valet, Hong Fu, who has cracked two cases for his master before and thinks himself superior to these locals.

Huo Sang examines, in this enormous compound, footprints, a lock pried open, a pond, a temple, and the house of the gardener, who gambled and was dismissed just two weeks earlier. He hears that the concubine is ill. The police detain the temple guard, another suspect, who says he saw a short man lurking outside a week ago. Long-gowned police detective Zhong De, who disapproves of Huo Sang and Bao Lang's Western suits, wonders why the cook, the maid, her little boy, and the gatekeeper all heard nothing. And Sun Shougen (Sun "Defend the Roots") forbids questioning of his sick concubine, so she is suspect too. Huo Sang and Bao Lang discuss the case. Huo Sang knows Jiangnan Yan was not involved, for the handwriting on the wall is not his, and he would pick a lock, not clumsily pry it open. Which insider went outside the compound to make a pretense of breaking in? The rickshaw man who took Sun and his valet to the opera knew that they were gone, and his brother, Dong Si, must have known too; but these, be warned, are just more red herrings.

Police protection is afforded the Suns after a threatening letter signed "Jiangnan Yan" warns them not to pursue him. Huo Sang has an insight, but he keeps it to himself. Using his remarkable knowledge of postal routes, he

determines that the letter was sent earlier than it appears, for it was mis-
routed.

Bao Lang and Huo Sang encounter the valet in a bathhouse, where Hong
Fu in a superior tone proffers his findings, and new evidence: a small shoe he
found in the grass—though Huo Sang has already observed that the far-apart
footprints betray a tall northerner's stride! These shoes, though, were castoffs
given to the dismissed gardener, who was literate enough to write a crude letter and moreover lived with the rickshaw boy and his brother. Hong Fu
seems to be progressing, whereas Huo Sang is behind in the game, clueless.
He sings and plays the violin to console himself, then gets an idea. He returns with a black thread in a parcel—"conclusive evidence," though heaven
knows why.

Huo Sang calls the police (who are so far behind that they are still seeking Jiangnan Yan) and asks them to cease surveillance. When the valet states
his intention to leave, to pursue the gardener—who has taken off for
Shanghai—Huo Sang dramatically announces: "The killer is in this room!"
He names Hong Fu, the trusted valet. Hong Fu attacks with his fists, but the
heroes are prepared. When the police enter, Huo Sang explains that the servant, long covetous of his master's valuables, made his move under cover of
Jiangnan Yan's notoriety; then, realizing that this would not hold up, he tried
to pin the deed on the gardener. Servants at the opera sit in a different class
of seats from their masters, so the valet was able to absent himself, break in
at home, and cover up his prints with the gardener's shoes, which he had
hidden in the compound pond. He threw them away the night of the break-
in, but "rediscovered" one when Jiangnan Yan's complicity became implausible. Huo Sang directs the police to the loot in a bucket atop the temple
flagpole. What evidence implicates the valet? Black threads from his inner
jacket are on the pole, and flagpole paint is on his jacket. How did Hong Fu's
plan go awry? The threatening letter he sent the family ("from Jiangnan
Yan") led to police surveillance, which left him unable to get the loot out of
the compound. There is another struggle and the valet almost gets away after
pulling a knife, but the heroes manage to knock him down, wounding Huo
Sang.

Huo Sang explains in the hospital how he figured it out. That the footprints went directly to the treasure and the pond indicated an inside job (belatedly Hong Fu realized this too), and the prints indicated a big man. Huo

Sang suspected the valet when he learned that the threatening letter was sent from near the theater, during the play, taking into account the misrouting delay. The encounter with the valet in the bathhouse was set up by Huo Sang, who knew his habits. Huo Sang's enigmatic enlightenment was his recall of the temple flagpole, which was colored like the dust on Hong Fu's jacket. Why did he never suspect the concubine? Shades of the Jiangxi *Crime and the Law* propagandists whose work wrapped up the last chapter—Huo Sang deduced her honesty from the moral purity of the reading matter by her bed! She slept through the robbery and felt sick the next day because she was chloroformed. QED.

Bao Lang asks permission to write up the case for posterity. It may not be as astonishing as cases in the West, he adds (true, though the plot is still *intriguing*), but it will be good for the Chinese people to see a case of their own that trades in reasoned analysis instead of ghosts and superstitions.

Hong Fu, though evil, has been a challenging adversary for Huo Sang. And Jiangnan Yan, the "subject of the story," is just a red herring. But he will turn up in later stories. In this one he sends Huo Sang a letter thanking him for clearing his reputation. He owes him one.

The Westernized delights of Cheng Xiaoqing's stories do not preclude Chinese touches, including outright didacticism, such as the criticism of superstition at the end of "Jiangnan Yan." In some stories, multiple cases come together, as if by fate (as in "Huo shi," "A Living Corpse"). The interest in physical evidence and whodunit is matched by the detection of hidden relationships in society. Sometimes the mystery is not a realized crime ("Xian hunyin," "Just Before the Wedding"); it may be an "uncanny" situation ("Bieye zhi guai," "Ghosts in the Villa"). Huo Sang protects Bao Lang from the sordid real world of violence like a father ("Bai shajin," "The White Handkerchief"; "Lun xia xue," "Blood Under the Wheels"). And like Judge Bao, after solving a case he may do some social engineering, like patching up human relationships and seeing that everyone has a means of support ("The White Handkerchief"; "Blood Under the Wheels"). Cheng Xiaoqing's condemnation of men who use the "new morality" to cheat women ("Yeban husheng," "The Cry at Midnight"), and the irresponsibility of the new press ("A Living Corpse") have traditionalist overtones. Some, though not all, of the Huo Sang stories (e.g., "Zi xinjian," "The Purple Letter") leave the reader hanging in high suspense at the end of chapters (most stories are divided into ten to twenty chapters), as in China's traditional chapter-driven novels, as well as some Western genre fiction.

But these continuities reflect China's major tradition of the great vernacular novels more than the minor traditions of "court case" stories and *biji* fiction. The status of the former, far more than the latter, was being raised in Republican times by New Intellectuals such as Hu Shi and Lu Xun. Cheng Xiaoqing drew from tradition only to improve his craft.

CHENG XIAOQING AS A MAY FOURTH WRITER

Let us ignore custom and look at Cheng Xiaoqing and his works as representative of China's New Culture movement. Cheng was an intellectual before 1917 and not particularly beholden to the old Confucian culture or society; he was a mostly self-taught marginal Shanghai literatus from a poor family. The modern vernacular he chose was ideologically linked to the overthrow of classical Chinese, the works and values expressed in it, and the old upper class. That Cheng, like Ye Shaojun, Zhang Tianyi, and Lu Xun, previously wrote in classical Chinese only makes his vernacular contribution more striking. Cheng Xiaoqing converted to the "cause" just a few years later than the May Fourth icons.

Cheng attended an old-style private school (*sishu*) in his home town, Shanghai, until his father died of epilepsy when Xiaoqing was about ten. At thirteen he learned the clarinet from an Italian musician, even played in bands. Two years later, in 1908, poverty cut short his formal schooling; at sixteen he sold watches in a shop. Taking free English lessons at the YMCA in 1910, and borrowing from a friend's private book collection, he taught himself to write salable ghost stories and romances. In 1915 he married, of his free will so far as we know, on the rebound from a tragic romance with a girl who considered him too poor. He moved his family to Suzhou, where he had found a job teaching Wu dialect to a foreigner. By exchanging language lessons with an American high school teacher, Cheng improved his English enough to work as a translator. And he began to see his creative works appear in major leisure-reading magazines such as the *Short Story Monthly* and *Saturday*. He found a post teaching Chinese at a Suzhou girl's normal school in 1916; joined the Methodist church the next year; and continued publishing ghost, romantic, and detective stories, the latter including original works and translations, until he found his niche with Huo Sang in 1919, the year of the May Fourth incident.[116]

Although Cheng Xiaoqing earned money from his writings and achieved fame because of them, he was always, like the typical May Fourth writer, a teacher who did a lot of writing, translating, and journal editing on the side. He wrote a few critical essays about detective fiction and took a course in criminology from an American correspondence school to improve his stories' realism. He tried to convey the latest research on psychology and criminology, as he imagined the fiction of S. S. Van Dine had done for him.[117] Some people thought of Cheng as a detective and asked him to help them solve thefts.[118]

The timing of Cheng Xiaoqing's conversion from writing in classical Chinese to the modern vernacular is unclear, and perhaps he wrote in both languages in the early 1920s. Research may also show that his well-made Huo Sang plots are indebted to his previous stories in the older language and in older genres. We do know that in the early 1920s Cheng Xiaoqing still wrote popular fiction without detective themes. Among the journals he helped edit was *Zhentan shijie* (The world of detectives, founded 1922), which published, at first in a stilted vernacular haltingly punctuated, detective criticism and news, *biji*-type stories about true crimes, and short fiction, including detective stories by Cheng himself but outside the Huo Sang series. Cheng joined the Green and Star Societies of Shanghai and Suzhou, respectively, whose core members are generally considered "popular" professional fiction writers. He was publishing his own stories in the modern vernacular verifiably by 1923, both inside and outside the Huo Sang series.[119]

Cheng Xiaoqing's classic plots are very "Western," and so is the richly detailed, descriptive texture of his writing. It answered the May Fourth call to write "realistically." His language too is very "May Fourth," Westernized and full of modern neologisms. His use of the standard new grammatical style, with vernacular sentence particles, clear subordination of parts of sentences, lengthy modifiers even in story subtitles (deleted in some post-Mao reprints), and recent coinages like the word *yi* (she) is striking when compared to the style of Sun Liaohong, who wrote in a modern vernacular more economical and indebted to China's classic premodern novels. Cheng's style might be criticized for the usual faults of the May Fourth writer. It is wordy,

with few subjects or objects left to the imagination. Some of his English neologisms are still shocking: *weizhe jingji shijian* (lit., "to economize [on]
time"); the word "economy," a neologism to begin with, was seldom used as
a verb.[120] His works have topical May Fourth concepts like "national character"[121] and quasi romantic references to supposedly Western gods of love,
death, the seasons, and so forth (which appear also in works by Sun
Liaohong).

New Intellectual consciousness is projected not just by vocabulary—the
Qing era so recently departed is called "the old society"[122]—but also in approving hints within Huo Sang's ideology. He is "patriotic"; not as patriotic
and supportive of the proletariat as post-1949 revisions suggest (readers be-
ware),[123] but Republican-era editions already point out that Huo Sang's
Western-style suits are cut from Chinese-made cloth. Huo Sang and Bao
Lang are better educated than Cheng Xiaoqing, having been classmates for
six years (indicating graduate study) at the fictitious Da Gong University and
Zhonghua (China) University. However, they evidently have not gone
abroad, unlike some of the immoral male characters and villains. In life, the
author too had patriotic credentials. He changed his name to avoid Japanese
and puppet attempts to get him to collaborate. Explicit anti-imperialist discourse is rare but not nonexistent in the Huo Sang tales: "I thought again of
how modern Shanghai society was getting worse with every change," Bao
Lang says in one story. "The devilish hands of the aggressors had got hold of
our heart. A pack of accomplices dependent on the foreign power, looting at
every chance, squeezing out the blood and sweat of the great masses," and so
on.[124] The narrative voice of "A Living Corpse" calls patriotic a terrorist organization of young Chinese who firebomb the shops of "evil merchants"
selling shoddy or Japanese goods. In "The Purple Letter," Huo Sang advises
a police friend not to recall a suspect young army officer back to town because it might interrupt his "revolutionary work," evidently for the KMT
Northern Expedition (also, his cop friend might end up being disciplined
for it, Huo Sang warns). In this story, set in a time when the KMT was revolutionary, Huo Sang sports a necktie with the party symbol.[125]

In "The White Handkerchief," Huo Sang is distracted from a murder
case by his consulting work for an official National Salvation Association investigating rice smugglers. The two cases finally merge, for the deceased is
one of the smugglers, and the person who shot him a female association spy

who acted in self-defense. Having solved the mystery to his own satisfaction, Huo Sang for once leaves his case officially unsolved—and both the police and the public in the dark—for the sake of the national interest. In contrast, the plot of "Blood Under the Wheels" is motivated by the presumed murder of a young socialist, Gu Ziyou ("Attending to Liberty"), alias Kong (like Confucius) Weixin ("Reforming"). Though Huo Sang discovers Gu is alive and has planned an insurance scam with his wife, he accepts them as heroes and lets them pull it off.

Ideological concerns are also abstractly expressed in the Huo Sang stories. May Fourth's most prominent antifeudal cause, after language reform, was the liberation of women. Bao Lang winces to hear an old fogy fulminate against that cause on the train.[126] And in "The Purple Letter" a man makes an ugly scene trying to break his sister's wedding engagement. Cheng Xiaoqing's handling of such issues is far from facile, though we know that in life he was "progressive"; he did not arrange the marriages of his sons or daughter.[127] A story about the disappearance of Bao Lang's fiancée "Just Before the Wedding" is a parable about the need for a husband and wife to communicate. The woman was misled by a doctored photograph and other false evidence alleging that Bao Lang had had a secret mistress and fathered a secret love-child.

Also in the antifeudal file is the assault on what Cheng called superstition, a new word, if not really a new concept among China's literati. A short and straightforward case is "Ghosts in the Villa," though the title is a teaser suggesting a ghost story. Phantom flute music and mysterious fires come from a newly built country mansion outside Shanghai. A big Shandongese sent to guard the empty house, who had thought he did not believe in ghosts, had quit after waking up one morning under the bed in which he went to sleep. This gives Huo Sang many chances to discourse on scientific approaches to life. He sets about smoking out the usual suspects—people who might want to buy the property cheap—by putting up a "for sale" sign. It turns out that the Five Blessings Gang hoped to rent the villa as a temporary base for their highway robberies. They staged sound effects and strange sightings and gassed the Shandongese to activate superstitions among the locals. This could serve as a "story about not fearing ghosts" of the sort later solicited by the communists.

A longer and twistier example is "The Cry at Midnight." Its police hero,

Ni Jinshou, runs into a boy, a petty thief absconding from an aborted robbery at the house of Professor Tian Wenmin ("Sensitive to Culture") of
Weixin ("Reform") University, who has a physics Ph.D. from the University
of Chicago. There is blood on the carpet, the professor is missing, and so is
a tablecloth big enough to wrap a corpse.

The cops have suspects galore, all red herrings—a man about to lend Tian
money and three other friends, plus Tian's rich fiancée and her three former
suitors. But they cannot find the corpse. Finally they call in Huo Sang; he
finds clues they overlooked, interviews postmen and rickshaw boys (learning
that a Mr. Yan of Huzhou, Tian's home town, visited him), and uses psychology to get the petty crook to give up his older accomplice. The older
man removed the tablecloth with the body in it from the crime scene, thinking the boy had wrapped the loot in it! The press speculates that anti-
reformers killed the professor to silence his advocacy of free marriage and
romance. Meanwhile Yan is found and detained in Huzhou. In a dramatic
courtroom scene at Yan's trial, the roles of criminal and victim are reversed.
It develops that Tian was already married to a Ms. Xu Huifang, who refused
him a divorce. So Tian forged a love letter seemingly from Yan to Huifang,
making them look like an adulterous pair, to give him grounds. Yan had
gone to Tian's house to make him destroy the letter. Into court rushes
Huifang herself, to confess that she shot her cheating husband and then escaped in his clothes. Miraculously, the corpse was stolen "for her." But Huo
Sang, who knows his bullet calibers, reveals that she shot a corpse. The
professor had already committed suicide with his own silenced gun—found
in the tablecloth by the old man who thought he had wrapped up a good
burglary.

The story is ideologically mixed. Huo Sang got on the right track early on
by scoping out Professor Tian as a hypocritical "modern man." Such men
were known in mandarin duck and butterfly fiction as well as that of the leftist icon Lu Xun.[128] Such bourgeois characters are long past traditional values.
Had Professor Tian married again without divorcing, his circle would have
called it bigamy, not polygamy. Lack of sentiment is what differentiates the
Huo Sang story from pulp romance. Huo Sang exposes the duplicitous
"modern man" and chivalrously rescues the wronged woman in the end; the
climax leads to an emotional anticlimax. The social milieu is interesting, but
the focus is still on solving the mystery.

Yet the story is framed, in the first and last chapters, within a larger "antifeudal" fable in the service of science and objectivity. Bao Lang is not in on this case; the initial focus is on the police detective Ni Jinshou, a series character. His little boy is ill with malaria, and his wife insists on "superstitiously calling in a shaman lady" (40). The boy is finally cured by a Western-medicine physician recommended by Huo Sang. This parable runs parallel to the main plot; the boy's sickness periodically distracts Detective Ni from his work, becoming the reason for calling in Huo Sang. In the end, "when his wife saw the efficaciousness of the cure, it gradually broke the hold of her superstition" (123). The cure of the son and Huo Sang's rescue of good people who hold old-fashioned values are mutually symbolic of the necessity for scientific thinking.

Science is Cheng Xiaoqing's avowed cause, and in his critical essays his alleged reason for promoting detective stories, which he called "popular scientific textbooks in disguise."[129] This may sound casuistic, but the idea that detective fiction trained the mind was common worldwide. Science was a Western and trans-Western discipline like Marxism that would end feudalism and build the nation's industrial and military strength to counter imperialism. Conan Doyle himself had united power and knowledge in the person of Holmes, elevating what was once the ignoble business of crime detection into almost "the respectability and order of the classics and chemistry."[130]

What Cheng meant by science was regard for evidence and research. Reading detective stories could develop one's powers of reasoning, theorizing, observation, imagination, analysis, and concentration. One had to train oneself to observe—to look at a person's eyes and notice their color, for instance. In May Fourth terms, the detective story developed habits of skepticism and curiosity necessary for China to progress and defeat superstition. Cheng also felt that detective fiction in China could be a mirror for police and judicial practice. Yet here he meant not that this fiction could cultivate favorable habits (of rule of law, as of scientific observation), but only expose how rotten and hopeless China's legal system was; the police investigated crimes against the rich and gave up on crimes against the insignificant poor. Cheng Xiaoqing was much more pessimistic about the utility of detective fiction in cultivating humanistic, democratic values than his successors in the 1980s.[131]

In fact, Cheng Xiaoqing's stories show an ideological ambivalence about the West typical of Chinese intellectuals. The conflict is conscious in "Jiangnan Yan." Likening the Neo-Confucian concept of *gewu* (investigation of things) to the modern scientific method, Huo Sang chides Bao Lang for being too impressed by what he has read in European and American fiction.[132] We must take from the West selectively rather than blindly, he says, even in detection. Chinese sleuths cannot rely as heavily as Westerners on footprints, for instance, for Western floors are shellacked, and Western shoes have more defined soles than Chinese cloth soles. Fingerprints too are far more useful in a society with a police bank of them. Chinese detectives, particularly private detectives, must cast their net wider. These comparisons actually set the stage for Chinese superiority. However, there is an irony. In this very story, footprints are key evidence. They tell Huo Sang that the robbery was an inside job, that it was done by a tall person who hid something in the pond, and that the valet, by proffering a small person's shoe, was working on a frame. Or was Huo Sang's initial statement on the limitations of footprint evidence intended to mislead?

Least controversial was the consensus against sybaritism, consumerism, and decadence: modern Western ways of conspicuous consumption, which differed from Chinese ways such as banqueting, gift-giving, patronizing the arts, endowing big ancestral temples, smoking, and hiring servants—the last a tail-end aristocratic tradition in the Western whodunit that was easily accepted in modern Chinese whodunits. Leisure-time pursuits of the wealthy class, not least of all their Westernized exponents who have studied abroad, come in for a drubbing. (Huo Sang realizes that the more traditional pastime of gambling can cause crime, but often as not, the trail of gambling leads away from the crime.)[133] The dance hall scene with its taxi dancers is especially evil and dangerous, as in "Wu gong moying" (Phantom of the dance palace) and "Wu hou de guisu" (After the ball). The villain of "A Living Corpse," Xu Zhiyu, has a sociology Ph.D. from New York University but is a murderer and a cad. He cheated his innocent ex-sweetheart, driving her to the suicide that early on makes her the story's namesake. Xu knows of the suicide, yet he goes on acquiring new girlfriends—multiple girlfriends—at the dance halls. At the end, Huo Sang abstracts these dance halls into symbols of China's decadence. They waste youthful energy that ought be used to fend off foreign bullies; the young are ensnared in the pursuit of leisure (a charge often leveled at detective fiction). "These places we call dance halls are demon lairs that devour our young people, places where 'living corpses' roam wild." (292).

"The Purple Letter" levels another broad attack at materialism, conceived as something new and modern because it is spreading from Shanghai with the construction of "new villages" in the country. The crime scenario is very like a classic one from the A.D. 1211 *Parallel Cases*. A man in the Huo Sang story named Xu finds the body of his enemy, Fu, dead on his doorstep. Xu looks guilty (115) but hopes to be cleared by the logic of the wise prefect who solved the original Song dynasty case (case no. 28A). The latter doubted the guilt of the man with the corpse on his doorstep: "When one has murdered someone and then leaves the body in front of one's own gate, is this not sufficient cause for doubt?" This doubt in the Huo Sang story leads to a comical situation in which three different theorists of whodunit jostle for dominance. The dead enemy is a former friend of Xu's who became his rival for the love of Xu's childhood sweetheart and cousin, Ms. Wang. Fu had got Ms. Wang to break off her engagement with Xu and promise to marry him, for he was much richer than Mr. Xu. Or might the killer be Ms. Wang's protective elder brother, a military man who despised Fu's decadent life and flew into a violent rage in an abortive attempt to annul the new engagement? Or a nineteen-year-old girl who visited Fu a few days before, perhaps a jilted lover of Mr. Fu (as traditional profligate)? Or a secret lover of Ms. Wang's, yet a third, who in one stroke killed his new rival and framed the old one? Finally it also dawns on the detectives to suspect relatives in competition with Mr. Fu to inherit his father's wealth. And Mr. Xu proffers his own, fifth, theory, at the very start: that Fu committed suicide on his doorstep to ruin him. This may sound absurd, and Huo Sang rules it out by analyzing the angle of the stab wound, but the guilty party was in fact the deceased in the Song case. Three sons persuaded their sick mother to let them kill her and lay her at the gate of their father's enemy, to get him executed by the law.

It *was* Mr. Xu who did away with his enemy for revenge, with the collaboration of a crooked cabbie and unexpected help from Ms. Wang's military brother, who so conveniently and publicly (in this little town) lashed out against their common opponent. Huo Sang's genius lies in reinterpreting the evidence that had become an obstacle to solution of the mystery, a letter on purple stationery. He discovers that the date, in this invitation to a tryst, has been cleverly altered to propose a meeting the night of the murder. Alteration of documents has also been a favorite challenge for Chinese detectives since the Song (as in *Parallel Cases*, no. 17B).

It is a wonderful plot (this is not the half of it), but the murder also has symbolic meaning, gradually adumbrated through symbolism and outright moralizing. Mr. Xu is the murderer, yet Huo Sang sympathizes with this honest engineer (a man of science) who committed an understandable crime of passion—though in this very story Bao Lang blames the Chinese for indulging their emotions too much (there are Neo-Confucian overtones, for he opposes emotions to reason; 258). It is Ms. Wang whom Huo Sang censures, for jilting Mr. Xu just to get a wealthier catch. He blames her for destroying two young men. This may reflect misogyny—asking for a double standard for men and women—or perhaps it inherits the logic of some *Longtu gongan* stories, as when a raped woman stays alive to bring her persecutor to justice but is still blamed for not choosing the higher morality of suicide, which would have kept her husband from searching for her and thus falling into the clutches of the evil rapist.[134] There is, in any case, in "The Purple Letter" as in older stories, a morality higher than the law. Fulfillment of the former is more important than catching criminals, even to Huo Sang. The cause of immorality is creeping materialism.

> Although Jiangwan was a few miles from Shanghai, the industrial and commercial enterprises that Chinese nationals were building in Shanghai were quickly spreading. In a few years this place, too, was bound to become another part of Shanghai. Because it was on a transportation line, the latent power of material civilization had already breached this zone of tranquillity and natural beauty. Thatched huts shaded by stands of bamboo were still to be seen in the neighboring villages, and water could still be heard flowing under its arched bridges. But the sweet dream of quiet and leisure was already dashed for the sincere and unaffected characters who dwelled in those huts. Now they wore masks of anxiety. The stream beneath the bridges had grown turbid. When the water was up, it rushed on with a frightening roar. No longer was it clear enough to see to the bottom, much less did it give off a tinkling music. The vanished quietude was like a sand pile upon a beach. When the raging tide of materialism surged over it, it would collapse in one heap; there was nothing else for it to do. (272)[135]

Mr. Xu was a construction engineer, which was scientific, but he built the new villages that literally sheltered exponents of the more sinister aspects of modern change.

POLICE, LAWYERS, AND WESTERNIZED LAW

Ridiculing police ineptness goes with the detective genre, even in the communist era, Chapter One has noted, as in "The Case of the Three Front Teeth." Denigrating the police in Cheng Xiaoqing's time was like beating a dead horse, so low had their status fallen. They were assumed to be lower-class roughnecks quick to anger and resort to beatings, and to have urban politicos, perhaps mobsters, as their bosses. Modern policing was a patently foreign cultural phenomenon from Japan and the West, and many Shanghai policemen worked for foreigners.[136] They still remind some Chinese of an era when they obeyed the laws of imperialists. It is not that China did not police its premodern cities. But that was a "watchman" style of policing, not a "legalistic" style, to use James Q. Wilson's distinction: the former relies on official paternalism, on patrolling and maintaining public order; the latter emphasizes the law itself and builds arrest records. Western-style modern police, proactive and armed with all the scientific technology envisaged by Cheng Xiaoqing, would be rather frightening.[137]

Cheng Xiaoqing's fictional police are an uneven lot. His early story, "Jiangnan Yan," really lets them have it; Huo Sang calls police detectives mostly *fantong* ("rice buckets," useless eaters) good only for solving petty thefts. Their prey have no way to defend themselves and often are tortured. The innocent go to jail; common folk have no redress (10). The cops' knee-jerk reaction in this story is to run in the Anhui gatekeeper. The lowly servants, all innocent, are scared to death of being questioned (25). The police detective in charge is an old fogy, but in the end he wises up. In a statement seemingly aimed *at* the prying police, Cheng Xiaoqing has him apologize to Huo Sang: "Eavesdropping is a crime, and I can't defend myself for doing it. Can you forgive me, sir?" (68–69). Invasion of privacy evidently troubled the author. In "The White Handkerchief," the narrative voice (technically Bao Lang's, but somewhat out of character) breaks into a short discourse about the evils of eavesdropping by people who claim to be educated. It appeals not to law but to morality, even good manners (161).

The police are not so sinister in later stories, like "The Cry at Midnight," perhaps because Cheng Xiaoqing was becoming more concerned about social order. The three wrong theories in "The Purple Letter," each blaming a different person for putting a corpse on engineer Xu's doorstep, are from three rival cops jostling to be proved right (all are wrong). One detective is so convinced that Ms. Wang has another secret lover—yet a third—who killed and framed the other two birds with one stone, that he illegally breaks into her house like a common burglar to get the evidence. The hypothesized third man does not exist, and the cop's rashness spoils Huo Sang's professional surveillance of the Wang house. Epitomizing police arrogance, he also destroys footprint evidence on the ground after drawing copies for himself. But he is fat and has a funny mannerism that makes him seem clownish. At odds with him is a more benign, Lestrade-like series cop who often cooperates with Huo Sang—Chief of Detectives Yao Guoying. Bao Lang damns him with faint praise. "His long and slender body, modest and amiable attitude, and neat uniform set him off from your typical police detective. And he is very dedicated to his duty. Pity is, he's not well enough educated. His formal learning leaves something to be desired, and he lacks the powers of observation and deduction detectives need. So sometimes his investigations go off track. That is his weakness" (212).

In "On the Huangpu River," Huo Sang has the fight of his life against a gang that kidnaps children for ransom and kills them even after the jig is up. Huo Sang arranges for police to keep an eye on them from a boat. But seeing no action, the lazy cusses just go home. By comparison, the criminal Jiangnan Yan lends Huo Sang a hand by tying up one of the bad guys. His main motive is to eliminate a rival gang and get their loot, but he also seems to have chivalric feelings toward the Great Detective, however unreliable, because Huo Sang after all is not a cop.

Yet Huo Sang himself uses dirty police tactics. He is not above lying when interviewing suspects, even misrepresenting himself as acting in an official capacity—as an insurance agent, in "Blood Under the Wheels." In "A Living Corpse" he mimics police tactics by telling the guilty party's manservant that his master has already been arrested for murder—a lie—and warns the servant that he will be implicated as an abettor if he does not come clean. In another story, he threatens exactly like a policeman: "If you don't admit it, okay, but later, when you've suffered the consequences and want to talk, it'll be too late—not so smart."[138] Huo Sang makes a threatening anonymous call to a suspect (a political-warfare tactic of KMT agents), and Bao Lang imitates him. All they are doing is getting "reactions."[139] Moreover, Huo Sang sometimes takes the law into his own hands; he truly becomes the police—

the judge, jury, and (passive) executioner. That this did not necessarily disturb Cheng Xiaoqing's readers may reflect the fact that Huo Sang does not represent the power of the state. Like Judge Bao, who did not typify "the system," he corrects the state's mistakes. Or was it rather the English derivation of Cheng's genre, a genre from a society that considered itself under rule of law and scarcely gave thought to good people like Holmes getting on the wrong side of it, that lulled Cheng Xiaoqing's readers into following the Great Detective wherever he led them?

Lawyers, whose very Western calling was already tarnished in China, are painted in unrelievedly dark and cynical tones by Cheng Xiaoqing, Sun Liaohong, and most Chinese writers. Lawyers are themselves rich and powerful; when the police check out the four cars in the town of Jiangwan, scene of the spreading materialism, one of them belongs to a lawyer. Worse, they offer their dangerous skills only to the rich and powerful, abetting crime by always getting them off. "You must understand," inveighs Huo Sang before a police colleague, "that in these years, a segment of those people we call Ph.D.s and lawyers have become a privileged class under a new feudalism!"[140] Professor Xu, one of the Ph.D.s, is able to launch counterattacks because his cousin is a big-time lawyer. Even exposing the cad in the press may not succeed. He might sue for libel. The lawyers' power lies in sophistry; Huo Sang assumes for his own profession (itself none too savory in reputation) an easy superiority when he tells a client, "When we carry out our professional duty, we are bound to rely on the truth. If what you want is verbal disputation based on fabrication, then please hire a lawyer. He'll be much better at that than we are."[141]

Ultimately Huo Sang is ambivalent about law itself, which in his view cannot possibly achieve justice. For a New Intellectual, however, the good society can no longer inhere in Rites; Cheng falls back on the ethic of the knight-errant. Says Bao Lang, "We investigate half to slake our thirst for knowledge, half out of duty to serve and uphold justice (*zhengyi*). In the realm of justice, we are never constrained by the wooden and unfeeling law (*daiban de falü*). Often we let people who break the law in the name of justice go scot-free. For in this society, which is gradually tending to surrender its core to material things, the spirit of the rule of law cannot be put into general practice, and the weak and ordinary people are aggrieved, more often than not unable to enjoy the protection of the law."[142]

Huo Sang's higher-than-the-law attitude is apparent in "Jiangnan Yan," when he finds a pearl and prefers not to find its owner, who must be rich enough already. In "Blood Under the Wheels," Huo Sang cleverly deduces that the corpse run over by his train was not the young socialist "Freedom" Gu, but a village bully who had designs on his wife, Aiquan ("In love with rights"). Gu accidentally killed the bully in self-defense, then laid him on the tracks in his own clothes. Huo Sang becomes the police and forgives them on his own authority. He lets the young socialists go and collect life insurance for Gu's alleged death; they want to be teachers, but the government is intolerant of them, so they need the money. This case remains on the books. The Gus are not criminals, but Huo Sang helps them commit insurance fraud. His rationale is that insurance companies, those modern, bourgeois institutions (personified in the story by a nosy appraiser), typically try to evade their social responsibility to pay, so it is poetic justice that they pay on this occasion. Moreover, Huo Sang has heard that this company is particularly crooked. Six months later the papers announce its bankruptcy. Huo Sang was right again. Or did he contribute to its failure?

Before one can call Huo Sang a leftist Robin Hood, though, he becomes "feudal" Judge Bao, rearranging social relations in the aftermath of the case. Of the 5,000 yuan of insurance money that Gu's wife will receive, Huo Sang will see that the mother of the actual deceased gets 1,000, as compensation— he the judge, jury, investigator, and social welfare case worker.

"A Living Corpse" also has a very clear moral. Criminals of the intellectual class are particularly difficult to snare in the net of the law; Huo Sang says so. In Bao Lang's words, genuine morality of the old school now holds sway only among the "ignorant class," like the good bellhop lad from Jiangbei (northern Jiangsu) who voluntarily risked his job to avenge an innocent girl (proving also that Jiangbei people are not as bad as Shanghainese think). "In present society," adds Bao Lang, "everything has become commodified (shangpinhua): friendship, marriage, relations between students and teachers, labor and capital."[143]

Huo Sang and Bao Lang twice stake out and later invade the lodgings of the evil and arrogant Professor Xu. The first time, another man standing outside Xu's door, unidentified, is shot to death in the street; the second, a bomb explosion damages all the neighboring houses, coincidentally blowing off half the face of Professor Xu trying to flee the long arm of Huo Sang. It was Xu, besieged by his own guilty fear, who murdered the stranger watching his house and then injured himself to make it look as if *he* were the intended victim. Xu is also guilty of a crime that may seem moot to us but sounds familiar from the Qing *Conspectus of Penal Cases*: homicide by pressing a person into suicide. Xu's victim was a young lady he had wronged in love, "the living corpse" who expired in Huo Sang's office from slow-acting poison that worked too fast for her to explain the wrong done her.

The key to the bizarre case, Huo Sang comes to realize, is that Xu was not the target of the surveillance and bombing; he only assumed he was. It was his misfortune to have as neighbor an unpatriotic coal firm, targeted by "patriotic" young terrorists who the first time were doing their own stakeout of the target. Huo Sang's surveillance there is of course subject to misinterpretation by the young firebrands, particularly since the other side, the sleazy merchants, approached Huo Sang at the start to ask him to protect them. Huo Sang insightfully makes the connection between the two randomly crossing paths of violence.

What is Huo Sang's conclusion? "Bao Lang, you scholar, you're too idealistic. Don't you realize how weak the law is in modern society? Privilege and power, 'face,' favors (*qing*), and money—the law has all these deadly enemies!" (168). Evidence, the key to learning who the bad people are, becomes an obstacle in bringing them to justice. Under the law, convicting evidence must be impossibly conclusive, or privileged scoundrels, with their clever lawyers, will get off and come after the good guys. And the law cannot help people like the wronged woman who died in Huo Sang's office. Law under the Republic is modern, more like Western than Qing law; pressing a person into suicide is no longer a crime. Xu's behavior toward her broke instead a higher law: morality, or what is left of it after the collapse of the Rites.

Justice must transcend the law. Bao Lang is sorry to hear that the professor is recovering from his wounds in the hospital. He would prefer him dead, for that is the only way to deal with a man beyond the law's reach—but not, perhaps, that of the press. The detectives will leak the story of the professor and the young girl, who turns out to have been pregnant. But no, this man is acquainted with lawyers; the press will not dare to tell the full truth. Then Bao Lang gets his first wish. Though the lawyer repeatedly succeeds in postponing Professor Xu's trial, he dies of infection. His new modern girlfriend never even visits him in the hospital.

And the bombers? Huo Sang considers them patriots, not criminals, obeying a higher law. However, Cheng Xiaoqing lets Bao Lang be the one to advocate revenge over law. Bao Lang is glad that the traitorous coal merchant and hypocritical professor got what they deserved. He mourns instead the "patriotic youth" the professor shot that night by mistake (277). Huo Sang, who values his reputation above all else, most fears not that he will appear oblivious to the law or incompetent, but unpatriotic. His most pressing final concern is to undo the patriots' misunderstanding of him as an enemy (283). They call to apologize for having mistaken his sympathies (292–93). It may be how the author hoped China's leftist young people would see him.

LU PING, "THE ORIENTAL ARSÈNE LUPIN"

The Lu Ping stories are fewer than the Huo Sang tales, but even more delightful. Less obligated to science, Sun Liaohong is not so prosaic, and his plots, which come from roguish resourcefulness more than solution of a mystery, are less predictable. In his unrestricted mission of entertaining readers, Sun moves in and out of various formulas, addressing the reader like a traditional storyteller here, gossiping, moralizing, setting a scene, staging a gunfight there—one never knows what to expect.

The style is more whimsical than Cheng's. It is breezy and informal, but the diction is also more ornate, with more classical figures of speech, onomatopoeia, slang, Shanghai dialect, underworld cant, and references to Hollywood and Walt Disney (in 1940s versions). Sun's vocabulary is larger and his syntax more varied than Cheng's, which opens up a May Fourth subject—does writing reach a wider audience through simplicity (limited vocabulary) or familiarity (traditional syntax)? Sun's syntax is more traditional than Cheng's—general readers might have thought Cheng's Westernized, if not mechanical—but both writers fit comfortably within the May Fourth mainstream.

The style of the text matches that of the hero. Lu Ping nonchalantly whistles (not so common for a Chinese hero) as he burgles, detects, or strolls into the jaws of danger. Sun engages the reader in badinage, in questions and conversation. He uses traditionally overt plot management. The language is ironic, given to *qiaopi hua* (wit, wisecracks, sarcasm), especially although not exclusively in passages of dialogue. The following flippancies come from a late 1940s novel that seems influenced by hard-boiled American detective stories or films.

> " 'Does she wear lipstick?'—'Does a sundae have a cherry on top?' "
> "She was a masterpiece of God and her dressmaker."
> "He loved women the way preachers love Jesus. . . . Or do they, really?" (Sun Liaohong was Buddhist, not Christian; this salvo surely has "postcolonial" overtones.)
> And, prefiguring Clint Eastwood: "Only then did he get it. The S&W coffee she'd prepared was S&W brand all right—a miniature Smith and Wesson revolver! This goddess of death in blue was beautiful when she held a gun."[144]

Influences on the Lu Ping stories thus include the hard-boiled tale; the classical whodunit, with its detection and careful observation of clues; the Chinese literary tradition of knight-errantry, in which the knight, unlike Hammett's and Chandler's heroes, can call on lesser heroes to help him out in fights; Shanghai modernism, with its attention to style, urban decadence, and description; and above all, Maurice Leblanc.

The unfortunate paradox for Sun Liaohong is that, in Leblanc's gentleman-rogue subgenre, plot is important, but the reader exults especially in the character of the rogue, and Sun was loath to tamper with it. He was no plagiarist; his plots are original, quoting and borrowing from other stories as genre works do, to the reader's delight. But Lu Ping is a lesser version of the French prototype.

Arsène Lupin is absolutely protean to begin with. Apart from his infinite wile and guile, humor and resourcefulness—intellectually and even physically—he has hardly any fixed traits that an anxiety-of-influence-ridden Chinese successor can redirect. He appreciates fine clothes, good manners, good art, and all aspects of high civilization. These can be sinicized, but they represent taste—class taste—not character. Absolute mutability is the sign of Lupin's genius and why he always gets away. An examining magistrate ruefully admits that Arsène Lupin came out of nowhere and has no record. He may have been the man Rostat who eight years earlier worked with the prestidigitator Dickson. Probably he was also the Russian student who six years earlier astonished a doctor at the St. Louis Hospital with his contributions to the theory of bacteriology; and the professor who introduced jujitsu to

Paris; and quite possibly the bicyclist who won the Grand Prix de l'Exposition, took his 10,000 francs, and disappeared forever.[145]

Arsène Lupin is so habituated to and expert at disguising himself that no one knows what he really looks like. Eyewitnesses observe that he changes even in stature and body build. (He uses newly invented drugs, not just makeup and prosthetics.) His telltale marks are blonde hair and a wound on his right forearm.[146] Just so, Sun Liaohong's hero wears a red tie and has a mole on his left ear. But hair color and ties are easily changed. Lupin's wound can be covered up by a shirtsleeve; Chinese pursuers find themselves chasing doubles of Lu Ping with bandages or makeup on the left ear. They may conceal a mole, or perhaps not.

Both rogues have innumerable pseudonyms and make up more as need calls. Lupin's are often distinguished and yet exotic, betraying eastern or southern European origins: the comte d'Andrésy (or d'Andrézy, suggestive of Slavic origins), the baron Anfredi, the chevalier Floriani, Don Luis Perenna of Spain, Prince Sernine of Russia; also Guillaume Berlat, Horace Velmont, Louis Valméras, and the slightly more raffish Jean Daspry—and one M. Lecoq.[147] Lu Ping's aliases are humorous: Fei Taimin ("Fees Too Nimble"; sounds like "Vitamin"), Shi Bing (Stony Ice), and Du Dade ("Du of Great Virtue," or D. D. T.; reminiscent of "Old Du," onetime head of the Shanghai underworld in life—he too a "gangster-philanthropist.")[148] Lu Ping reputedly has more than a hundred nicknames, such as "The Small-Change-Eating Tiger," referring to his willingness to settle for a modest percentage of pelf.[149] As to the Frenchman, some of his friends know him only by a pseudonym; they joke with him that he resembles descriptions of the dapper Arsène Lupin, evidently harboring fewer suspicions than Lois Lane has about Clark Kent.

To make the question of identity still more intriguing, even philosophically deep—and acknowledging that most readers of Sun Liaohong are formula readers familiar with the Lu Ping myth—some stories never identify their "red tie" character(s) or any other particular Lu Ping facsimile *as* Lu Ping. Protagonists are referred to only by attire, or in one story, figuratively as "the puppet." (A wooden puppet displayed in a store window is used to communicate to all Lu Ping cronies citywide the "Lu Ping costume of the day," so they will know if they encounter the real thing. Yet paradoxically, the puppet display also prevents their recognizing him, since it doubles as the cronies' key for disguising themselves as Lu Ping.) Lupin and Lu Ping were simulacra (copies of an original that was never real) before that new postmodern meaning was given to the word.

Both heroes can call up favors from a whole hidden-in-plain-sight underground of accomplices in every walk of Parisian and Shanghai life, monied and lumpenproletarian, blue collar and white collar (not to say that they all earn an honest living). In a crowd they may be summoned as decoys or to pay a house call, made up as Lupin or Lu Ping—if not as Herlock Sholmes or Huo Sang, or their faithful companions "Wilson" (Sholmes's "Watson") or Bao Lang, or their police inspector friends, or their landlady. The accomplices are loyal; Lupin and Lu Ping inspire honor among thieves.

A minor deviation from Leblanc back toward Conan Doyle is that Lu Ping's confreres include a first among equals, a fat but capable fellow named Meng Xing who waddles "like a Walt Disney duck." His name is reminiscent of Mencius, Master *Meng*, a great altruist; and Bao *Xing*, the servant and companion of Lord Bao in *Three Heroes and Five Gallants*. Loyal and jocular Meng Xing addresses Lu Ping as *Shouling* (Boss). Others use *Xiefu* (Fr.: *Chef*; Eng.: Chief).

Their ubiquitous associates provide the two heroes the daily "intelligence" that keeps them ahead of and simply beyond the comprehension of the police (or, in Shanghai, "real" criminals out to get Lu Ping). His business, Lu Ping says, is that of Shanghai's captains of industry and finance: *jieshou* (acquisition). Lupin and Lu Ping may install junior accomplices months in advance as governesses and housekeepers in the houses they wish to burgle. Or they take employment there as a clerk (Lupin) or chauffeur (Lu Ping) themselves. Lupin's "relentless enemy" Detective Justin Ganimard has a stable of officers himself, but the reader has low expectations of, say, Brigadier Folenfant ("Foolish child"). Ganimard himself is of superior sagacity "and even intuition," but "devoid of those flashes of genius that characterize Dupin, Lecoq, and Sherlock Holmes" (to cite two Frenchmen and one Englishman, in proper order!).[150] Lu Ping appears to face no danger from the police at all.

It is only certain that Lu Ping, like Lupin, will wriggle out of the most impossible dilemma in an amusing way. The original's disguises, spies, doubles, socially invisible bodyguards, and James Bond–like devices, not to mention secret tunnels and stairways, contravene the "fair play" of the whodunit, but these too are expected by the formula reader. Holmes himself might applaud Lupin's use of press disinformation, such as planting a news item that Ganimard is vacationing nearby, so that the local chateau owner whom Lupin has warned he will rob will hire that good detective—unfortunately for him, since the Ganimard closest at hand is really Lupin in disguise.[151]

Sun's gentleman-rogue in the Paris of the East is to this extent a carbon copy. But this does not diminish the reader's pleasure any more than it did that of Leblanc's readers. "Gui shou" (The ghost's hand) exemplifies Sun Liaoping's skill with the theme of disguised identity, in a tale that mixes and satirizes the detective, rogue, and ghost tale genres in a spirit of apolitical good humor characteristic of Leblanc. An anonymous man in a Sun Yat-sen suit smoking Turkish cigarettes (Lu Ping's favorites) tells the following story. The great-grandson of a Qing official who returned from study in Germany to build coastal defenses for Li Hongzhang, plus the man's wife and their regular companions, a female servant and a nervous young man, exchanged ghost stories late at night after watching Boris Karloff in *The Mummy's Hand* at a Shanghai cinema. They talked of walking corpses and of an evil lawyer who was killed by the ghost of a man whose death he caused for money. Made restless by these stories, the wife that night feels a "ghost" twice touch her throat as she sleeps. The next morning, chloroformed gauze lies beside her pillow.[152]

They call China's Great Detective, Huo Sang, to investigate. His willingness to take their case actually surprises them, as do his old clothes and gray hairs, the result of overusing his brain cells, quips the storyteller (with a trope from Agatha Christie). The family story is that the famous great-grandfather amassed a fortune in diamonds that were never found. Unable to speak as he lay dying of anger at China's defeat by Japan in the 1894–95 war, he pointed to his ear, mumbled "Datong" (Great Harmony, the name of his son), and traced the word "deaf," composed of the characters "dragon" and "ear." Huo Sang knows it is a rebus puzzle (like the playing-card puzzle Arsène Lupin figures out to open up double safes behind a Carolingian mosaic in "The Seven of Hearts"). He also brilliantly deduces that there were two intruders—inside and outside perpetrators with warm and cold hands respectively—and that they were after a dragon talisman really around the neck of the *husband*. Huo Sang recognizes its legs to be the teeth of a key. He searches and finds an altar, which the husband will not allow him to inspect, but Huo Sang tricks him into leaving. The altar has a little and a big bronze statue (a *datong*—it was not the son Datong that was meant), whose ear one twists while turning the dragon key. Huo Sang promises to return and solve the mystery in three days (his purpose is to make a new key from an impression he made in soap).

Huo Sang returns secretly at night two days later, with the maid (the insider) and the nervous young man (her boyfriend, the outsider) in tow, under duress. He whistles to himself while opening the safe in the statue. It yields a tiny 55-page book on building a modern Chinese navy that might have saved the day in 1894, and twelve diamonds, a gift from Bismarck, intended to help build it.

The storyteller admits to his incredulous listeners that it was really he, a professional thief, who took the original call for Huo Sang in his office (he had broken in there on other "business"), and he who after solving the mystery took the diamonds as his reward, recompensing the maid by not turning her in (perhaps he will use her another time), though he exposed the bad boyfriend. He also returned the little book to the master, who was too busy gambling and dancing to read it. A red mole on the storyteller's ear is visible as he disappears into the night.

Sun Liaohong's classic postwar novella "Lanse de xiangweishe" (The blue rattlesnake) demonstrates the versatility with which Lu Ping takes up different social roles. Coming near the end of Sun's career, its atmosphere is much more "noir"—opening with a shadowy figure in dark clothing (Lu Ping) skulking outside the house of a profiteer and collaborator with the Japanese on an inky night "bearing the stench of rain." Lu Ping is preparing to rob the house in the dark, in a chapter titled "In a Deep Black Atmosphere." Blackness is as symbolic of Shanghai, just after V-J Day, as of the scene. The novella is hard-boiled, showing pervasive moral corruption and having action scenes, though it also shows Lu Ping at his best as detective, collecting evidence, ratiocinating, and figuring out obscure codes in the dark—in mid-robbery—to crack the case of who killed his intended robbery victim and stole the money before he did. There is also a "dame," a sexy but dangerous woman who spies for the Japanese. As in the classic hard-boiled story, the hero is aroused but rebuffs her when she attempts to gain control over him.

In fact, the problem of sinifying Arsène Lupin is not limited to protean appearances, dialogue, or atmosphere. His style, character, code of ethics, and motivation are just as malleable. To continue the litany of lupinien identities recited by the French magistrate cited above: Arsène Lupin *may* have been the person who saved so many lives at the Charity Bazaar by spiriting them out of a little dormer window; "and, at the same time picked their pockets."[153]

Arsène Lupin's "chivalry" is a constant inconstant; it is always measured, if not offset in advance. He will go to any length to save a damsel in distress, but often he put her there, as his accomplice. He gives the proceeds of his thefts to charity, keeping some for himself. When he writes letters to the rich saying that on a certain date he will come calling to receive particular valuables of theirs—please have them ready, to avoid the mutual inconvenience of burglary followed by unsuccessful police response (a device used by Lu Ping in "Muou de xiju" or "A Wooden Puppet Play," and by Jiangnan Yan in a Huo Sang story)—he (and Lu Ping) ask only to borrow the valuables. Lupin and Lu Ping always keep promises made in honor, though otherwise they lie and deceive. The only rules are, Everything in moderation and with taste; and Do no lasting damage. Lupin never deliberately kills. Sun Liaohong likewise writes pointedly that Lu Ping never kills; he is a "nonformalist Buddhist," like the author.[154]

Consistency is the hobgoblin of Lupin's targets: aristocrats, wealthy shop owners, and beneficiaries of inherited wealth; also the Sûreté, Herlock Sholmes, felons outside his own network, and others who need to be taught a lesson. Lupin picks pockets mostly just as sport. From the upper class's chateaux and safes he selects jewels, furniture, medieval tapestries, and *objets d'art*—only the finest pieces, having a history of noble ownership that Leblanc relates in good quasi antiquarian detail. "The jewels Bismarck gave to build the Chinese navy" are an excellent Chinese facsimile. Plots in these cases are variations on the locked-room puzzle found in the classical detective story, as are Lupin's escapes from prison and from Sholmes in Lupin's chutes and ladders mystery house. In one story, though, Lupin returns all the loot he plundered from a chateau—in two trucks, driven by apparent military officers, to ensure safe passage through all the police investigators and curious townsfolk—because he is sweet on the Miss Nelly Underdown who caught him in the original act, and he doesn't want her to think ill of him. Here, reputation is the basis of Lupin's unpredictable chivalry, as it is of Holmes's and Huo Sang's rather more stable code.

Lupin's ultimate motivation seems often enough to be exhibitionism. He does the impossible just to show that it can be done; he calls in his rival Sholmes simply to demonstrate his superiority. The Englishman is something of an exhibitionist, too, but publicity does not excite him. Lupin uses *L'Echo de France* (which he partly owns) to print his self-celebratory, ostensibly third-person write-ups of his cases.[155]

Lu Ping's weakness as a character is that he has nothing to prove at all, not even Lupin's frivolous points of honor. He, too, robs and scams the wealthy and powerful, "the class with automobiles and foreign-style houses."[156] His chivalry delights and astonishes, but it is not to be taken at face value, and is always measured, with its own "economy." Sun Liaohong draws his own conclusion for the reader: "The Chief thought to himself, chivalric righteousness (*xiayi*), hmmh! I'm only chivalrous when there's money to be made."[157] And the narrator warns, at the end of another story: "In sum, our gentleman friend [Lu Ping] once again succeeded at his old 'rob from the rich and give to the poor' tricks. But I must explain that his character lacks any great 'sense of justice.' He doesn't rob from the rich to relieve the poverty of the poor! He only wants to relieve his own poverty."[158] And he exclaims, sarcastically, "When it came to fighting, Lu Ping wasn't afraid. He'd enjoyed exalted avocations all his life. Like meddling, lying, and stealing. Fighting was another one of them. For a while he took it to be his calisthenics, . . . as efficacious as MORNING EXERCISE."[159]

Sun Liaohong keeps an even greater moral distance between himself and his hero than do Cheng Xiaoqing and Maurice Leblanc. Sun still utilizes Lu Ping, amoral as he is (though movable by empathy), to make serious moral observations. After taking a job as chauffeur to a wealthy family in order to rob them, in "Zise de youyongyi" (The purple swimsuit), Lu Ping relents and goes to the aid of the mistress when he sees that she is deserted by her husband and oppressed by her mother-in-law. He helps the young woman recover a locket, the theft of which would prove that she has been gallivanting like a modern woman, against family rules. The thief who has the locket has been blackmailing her with it. "Ada," the family chauffeur, makes a duplicate locket and, with his cronies, steals it from her in a carjacking robbery to cover up the real locket's absence. The savior chauffeur is never identified as Lu Ping; only the M.O. and his nicknames give him away. His fee? Just the other baubles he stole in the carjacking! The story's title may be a tribute to "The Purple Letter," by Sun's friend, Cheng Xiaoqing.[160]

"SOCIAL EFFECTS" IN THE LU PING STORIES

Leblanc doesn't take Lupin's society too seriously; Sun Liaohong's wisecracks and ironies likewise suggest a cynical approach to life. In that, Sun as narrator and his character are as one. "There are fundamentally no honest people in the world," says Lu Ping. The narrator agrees: "In present society, it's difficult to distinguish between thieves and gentlemen (*shenshi*); sometimes thieves and gentlemen are one and the same."[161] And this cynicism appears justified.

Even women do not inspire dedication. Lu Ping notices women's beauty and it arouses him, but unlike Lupin, he would never put off a good heist because of a lady. Then again, the sirens he meets do not inspire admiration, like the original Lupin's Miss Nelly, or the oppressed Countess Yvonne d'Origny, whose plight must have been a model for the young woman's in Sun's "The Purple Swimsuit."[162] Lu Ping has no police nemeses, either. They seem beneath his notice.

The Shanghai and Parisian wealthy classes invite cynicism because of their hypocrisy, which both rogues feel entitled to prey upon, but the authors ascribe different meanings to and make different literary uses of it. In a typical Leblanc scenario, the world famous gems and tiaras Arsène Lupin steals from a count or countess turn out to be fake, as perhaps are their nobility, if not their titles. What Lupin has stolen is their honor: the mask behind which they live their duplicitous lives. They are no more what they appear to be than the gentleman-burglar. The absconding poseur after whom "Madame Imbert's Safe" is named turns the tables and frames Lupin as having the identity and criminality of her embezzling husband, since few people knew either of them;[163] this completes the symbolic circle. In Sun Liaohong's "A Wooden Puppet Play," it is intimated that a rich man's painting that Huo Sang must protect from Lu Ping may be fake. But the rich, however hypocritical, or even phony, are taken seriously by Sun himself, for at least three "serious" literary aims. One is social exposure, of the pessimistic, muckraking kind. The second is a more detached observation of human manners. The third is metaphysical depth.

"Tunyuganyouzhe" (The man who hoarded cod liver oil) is a story of the first type, exposing the criminal greed of the wealthy. Opening it with a brief revision of his 1925 tale "Yanweixu" (The handlebar mustache), which features an excursion into surrealistic terror and eerie gloom, Sun in 1943 lengthened and revised it into a story about wartime profiteering and corruption.[164]

One can at first sympathize with the disoriented protagonist Yu Weitang, a senior, wealthy man. He finds himself staggering down the street in an amnesiac stupor between drunkenness and sleepwalking, with no idea of where he is, what he has done, or where he is going. A strange, invisible voice behind him shadows him, advises that he is in danger, and warns him not to look back or board a rickshaw. Finally the phantom steers him into a coffee shop. Having already lost control of his actions and identity, Yu now discovers in the mirror that he is a different person. He is ten years younger; he has also exchanged his mustache and Chinese gown for a Western suit and leather shoes. There is a pistol in his pocket. Men chase him. Before he can fire his gun, they cuff him and put him in what seems to be a police wagon. It is all over so quickly.

The story suddenly switches from Gothic to comedy of manners, as the scene changes to the victim's house. His wife and two sons receive three odd phone calls from a self-styled concubine of Yu's of whose existence they've never heard. Then a stranger comes to the door, one Fei Taimin. The junior gentry find fault with his name card—too cheap—but let him in anyway because he is so well dressed, red necktie and all. Fei (Lu Ping) then negotiates the ransom of their father. The sons shamelessly try to barter, nonplussing "chivalrous" Lu Ping, who would not demean a magnate by asking for too little. After subtle threats have their effect, he walks off with the money (discounted 20 percent from the agreed-upon price by the skinflint young masters) in a briefcase, which he requested because of all the crime today, you know. Two family servants tail him, for the young gentrymen are too cowardly. After a long and difficult surveillance, the servants lose Lu Ping when a convenient "gang fight" unfolds before them (staged by cronies, *sans doute*). The red tie then reemerges—but from a police station. It is their master Mr. Yu, his appearance altered after he was kidnapped to resemble Lu Ping. It was that resemblance and a tip phoned in to the police that had got him hustled into the police van outside the café. The kidnapee has been safely in jail all the time.

That is right where he belonged. Lu Ping knew Mr. Yu to be a war profiteer seeking an illegal monopoly of medicine sales, so he set up a sting at Yu's hideaway by offering to sell him stolen Norwegian cod liver oil. It is only regrettable that Sun Liaohong also expressed *ressentiment* against merchant Jews. Lu Ping is disguised as one.[165]

That aside, Lu Ping chose his target patriotically. Yet it is precisely here that the author explicitly denies that Lu Ping has any great "sense of righteousness" (405). He picked Mr. Yu because Mr. Yu had picked on him, tried to goad the police into working harder to arrest Lu Ping. The debonair Chinese rogue has, on the other hand, exposed how much China's modern "gentlemen" resemble crooks like himself. Exactly who those people might be is unclear, but in a postwar story below, one encounters the name of T. V. Soong, from the uppermost circles of Chiang Kai-shek's regime.

In "Ye lie ji" (Night hunting), Sun Liaohong treats comic foibles rather than high crimes and treason, and with satire rather than condemnation. The story has a moral about truth and falsehood, though here it is more social than philosophical: One can never trust surface perceptions, least of all eyewitness accounts, for people lie and exaggerate about what they've seen. The narrator confides about his friend in the red tie: "He's a specialist in lying. When he runs out of stories, he tells me a lie. He says, 'This whole world is a lie. The greater a person, the better they lie, and the better they lie, the greater they are. Lying used to be evil; now it's a virtue.' In order to cultivate virtue, he learned how to lie. Whereupon he told me this uncanny (*liqi*), nearly absurd story. Maybe it's a lie" (155). Such prefatory remarks, with their hint of uncanniness, lend an air of suspense from traditional Chinese literature and suggest a bridge between the social and the metaphysical blurring of truth and fiction.

The absurd rumor is that a stuffed polar bear and a Shang dynasty dagger silently went missing one night from a locked room in a university museum. The night watchman saw the polar bear dancing outside, through a keyhole. Others began claiming that they, too, had previously seen the bear move—a red herring later explained with pop social psychology about copycatting and rumormongering. To confuse matters, another, unrelated copycat named Cao has read about the incident and decided to use the polar bear hysteria to scare his wife away from a gambling parlor where she is being seduced by a "bottle cap" (a flic; after the badge). Disguised in white furs, he descends upon the drunken gamblers. That coincidentally some of them are robbed when they go into shock simply feeds rumors that Shanghai has a night-stalking polar bear phantom. (Such hysteria was occasionally a social reality in twentieth century urban China.)

One learns all this in retrospect when Lu Ping admits that he committed the initial robbery, brandished the polar bear in front of a cop to scare him off, then figured out the further history of the rumors with his own investigations.[166] Helping *le Chef* in this case is a new and interesting kind of henchman, a college educated reporter who interviews the night watchman as a journalist and then checks out the gambling den rumors with his melancholic friend C. C., another Lu Ping associate, who lives across the street from Cao. Lu Ping helps them break into and enter Cao's home, which becomes for them an "arctic ocean" (a place for night prowling) just right for a polar bear. Cao is a good guy, maybe even a thief, so Lu Ping doesn't rob him. Lu Ping swears "by his tie" to keep Cao's secret. He might even come back to help him rip off the bottle cap—if there's enough money in it.

So the watchman saw Lu Ping brandishing the polar bear, right? No. His story was a lie. Lu Ping deduced this because there was no moon that night, as the watchman testified; the chief admonishes his journalistic aide not to be so sloppy in his research. Lu Ping repeats the moral at the end: "There are just too many unthinking people in this world of ours, and this allows the liars who inhabit every corner of the globe to go on fabricating their rumors on a daily basis" (201–202).

The ambiguity of identity with which the often disguised and doubled Lu Ping confronts the reader can be metaphysically elevated into an exploration of the relativity of truth; and so can the moral hypocrisy of the corrupt upper bourgeoisie. These two paths to ambiguity reinforce each other in "Zhen jia zhi jian" (Between truth and falsehood), in which Sun's art attains a new level of abstraction. A posh Christmas party in postwar Shanghai reveals a sharp contrast between the rich and the poor, and an uncharacteristic expression of class consciousness by the author, voiced through intimations of social malaise, resentment, and irony. "No one would have been able to explain what relation this tableau had to the birth of Jesus," comments the narrator (5). The location is a former Russian embassy. It was subsequently used by gamblers, then the Japanese, and finally it became a factory, until competition from American goods forced it out of business—another anti-imperialist salvo.

This *paidui* (party; *pah-tee* in Shanghainese) is a costume ball, attended by the sons and daughters of magnates. Master of ceremonies Ni Ming, "a giant in advertising," is dressed as Santa Claus. The son of a government minister performs magic tricks. The belle of the ball, nicknamed "Ms. Panda" and also "MISS UNITE," is married to a rich politician in T.V. Soong's camp who runs a few enterprises. He knows how to hoard, skim, and cheat. She admits to another guest that she doesn't love him, he's only her meal ticket. Unreality, masquerade, and magic set the stage for the best performance of all: a fake holdup of the guests by a man dressed as Lu Ping, with a red tie and a mole on his ear. As the guests' valuables disappear and turn up elsewhere, by magic, he pronounces a signature observation of the real Lu Ping: that he can never steal as much as the officials. Now, this "Lu Ping" is known to his friends as Rong Meng; but who here, after all, knows the real Lu Ping? Ms. Panda says she wishes he were the real one, tells him her safe combination, and allows as how she'd like Lu Ping to give her the publicity of a real theft—for the press has forgotten her since her marriage. Rong Meng exits, followed by a tall man in an overcoat who overheard them. That night her safe is indeed robbed, of US $1000 and all her jewelry.

Rong Meng, still in a red tie (he refuses to say if he's the real Lu Ping), summons Ms. Panda to a café the next day. Her jewelry was fake! He quotes Ni Ming to her: "this world lacks truth, goodness, and beauty—especially the first." Ms. Panda admits that the theft was a "smoke screen" to cover up her gambling losses. Rong Meng has his reward—the $1000. But now he is summoned to a booth where another man in a red tie waits. He has over-heard them again, and insists on being paid off. Yet Ms. Panda remains con-vinced that Rong Meng *is* the real Lu Ping, he is so cynical. "Dearest!" he says, "Life is but a game. Why take it seriously?" (29). And they begin to talk of love.

It is not clarified which of the "red ties," Rong Meng or his shadow, is the Real McCoy. Rong Meng keeps wearing his tie and playing the part forever after. Everybody credits him with being the Lu Ping that the police say broke into the politician's house—which may be at least half true. The narrator confesses at the end that even he doesn't know if this is the real Lu Ping of legend. There could now be two. But the narrator's didactic sarcasm unveils a larger truth. People always suspect the little thieves (those who steal ba-nanas), not the big ones (who steal whole countries). Hence people blame the theft at Ms. Panda's mansion not on Rong Meng, but on the other red-tied man at the party. Assuming that Rong Meng and Lu Ping are not the same, Lu Ping would be the "big thief," by honor and reputation, and Rong Meng the lesser copy. But the rich fellow would on the contrary be the big *thief*, like the others of his class. Lu Ping steals only bananas, doing no lasting harm, while the magnates subvert China. The implication is that rich people like Rong Meng can cash in even on Lu Ping's reputation, so they can steal yet a little more. Rong Meng may have beat Lu Ping to the theft—did not Ms. Panda say at the party that she hoped the *real* Lu Ping would come steal her jewelry?[167] The story, which is not a genre tale at all (it may be a *roman à clef*), may be read as a complete paradox of mirrors, with no identity ever finally fixed, or alternatively, as the ultimate condemnation of the rich. They can coopt and profit from even that small part of Lu Ping that exposes villains.

SUN LIAOHONG CONSIDERED AS A MAY FOURTH WRITER

Sun Liaohong's technique and "seriousness," cloaked in humor, entitle him to a place among the officially recognized mainstream writers of his day. His low status may be attributed to the genre magazines he published in, his use of generic detection, suspense, and roguery, and his nonallegiance, so far as we know, to any political group. Unfortunately Sun Liaohong's biography is more obscure than Cheng Xiaoqing's. Lu Runxiang, who visited Sun's surviving relatives, felt lucky just to retrieve a photograph of him and his probable year of death. It is said that his original name was Sun Yongxue and that his ancestors originated in Yin County, Zhejiang, near Ningbo, though the Suns had lived in Shanghai at least since Liaohong's grandfather opened a watch shop there. Hence Sun Liaohong, like Cheng Xiaoqing, may be called a native Shanghainese. He was publishing Lu Ping stories by at least November 1923, allegedly using gossip he picked up in Shanghai coffee shops. In name he edited the journal *Da zhentan* (Great detectives) in 1946, but gave it up after a year, due to chronic tuberculosis. He died of the disease in 1958, after finishing, evidently in the springtime of the Hundred Flowers campaign, an anti-spy novel titled *Qingdao miwu* (Miasma over Qingdao). In the early 1950s he also wrote plays. It is not known what he did during the war; the works of his that circulate in post-Mao China date mostly from the 1920s and 1940s.[168]

"The Blue Rattlesnake" and "Between Truth and Falsehood" surely attack the status quo, even the economic power of America, whose popular culture Sun loved. The plot of "The Man Who Hoarded Cod Liver Oil" is harnessed at the end to serve patriotism and the national interest—a very tricky thing when Sun revised it in 1943, possibly under the nose of Japan. "Night Hunting" (1942) is one of several stories declaring that the upper crust are equivalent to crooks. However, the radicalism in stories written or revised in the war and postwar years was not necessarily characteristic of Sun's work in the 1920s.

In the "antifeudal" file is the didactic conclusion to "Night Hunting," which attempts to represent the story as an exploration of why people are subject to superstition, falsehood, and mass superstitious hysteria (the night-prowling polar bear). Lu Ping commonly subverts science with "magic," but there is always science behind it. "A Wooden Puppet Play" presents Lu Ping's wife. She plays jazz piano and finds the old-style dress of Chinese gentry disgusting.

In "The Purple Swimsuit," in which Lu Ping rescues a modern young woman not only from her blackmailer but from an oppressive mother-in-law, the victim criticizes the traditional patriarchal family and its opposition to new life-styles. All sympathy is with her, a former swimming champion for China, since the restrictions on her are unreasonable: she must not ever swim again (swimsuits are too close to nudity), wear modern clothes, or go to movies. Or does Lu Ping help her for the traditional reason that she is in effect, like her mother-in-law, a widow? *Mais non*—that is simply why he decided not to burgle their house (351)!

The story indeed has an antichivalric message. Lu Ping finally observes, in a fit of conscience, "she must think me a great and good man, or something like a 'chivalrous knight.' [He remembers that his original motive was to rob her.] . . . I ask you, am I a good man? I ask you, is there such a thing as a good man on this earth?" (351). And yet, for once Lu Ping's chivalrous action is more purely altruistic than that of Arsène Lupin. One can make the comparison because "The Purple Swimsuit" is indebted to Leblanc's "The Wedding Ring," in which Lupin saves a countess who is imprisoned in her room from being blackmailed into a divorce by her husband. The count knows that she has replaced her wedding ring. The surprise is that Lupin had had a previous romantic attraction to the countess; it was her secret admiration for him that she commemorated by inscribing *his* name inside her wedding ring, and that is the Platonic affection that risks exposure.[169] In Leblanc's story, the mother-in-law will judge whether the marriage will last and the countess can keep her son. But in the Chinese case, Lu Ping rescues a total stranger, a once intended mark. His act is not self-interested at all. It is Lupin, not Lu Ping, who is motivated by—well, *guanxi* (personal relations).

Many feminists today see chivalry as in principle a threat to women's self-determination, though in "The Purple Swimsuit" it saves a modern woman from an old-style family. However, the victim did marry into the family for money, and Lu Ping does not actually free this "caged bird," as Lupin does the countess. Lu Ping reasons that "For now she doesn't want to fly; sometimes she even looks for reasons not to fly, and so she deceives herself. She is a woman of contradictory psychology. And that is why those able to seize hold of that psychology were able to victimize her." Sun Liaohong's social understanding is subtle, but his moral is clear: a person of any sex should be brave, know what he or she wants, and grasp it. The "contradictory psychology" of women in those times was a common topic in contemporary literature (350).

What allows special consideration of Sun Liaohong's work as an affiliate of China's "serious," May Fourth literature—diminished by being just too amusing—is its relation, even if parodic, to Shanghai modernism. The latter reveled in "Occidentalist" fascination with the West's fashions and new amusements. Dance halls, dance parties, coffee shops, nightclubs, jazz bands, fancy cars, modern buildings, chic department stores, museums, movies, dating, modern girls, modern dalliances in hotels, Misters and Misses, safes full of American dollars, and suitcases full of foreign books and magazines from study abroad are the emblems pursued by both Sun and the Shanghai modernists. Extravagance, ornamentation, speed, sin, connoisseurship, hobbies, trivial pursuits, *ennui*, self-amusement as an art form—these exhilarating and subconsciously worrying aspects of a new Shanghai life dedicated to foreign-derived, aesthetically decorated consumerism are the common values.[170]

Sun Liaohong's oeuvre proceeds into the social and leisure phenomena of decadence, particularly excesses of the sinful Shanghai elite amid a sea of poverty in "Between Truth and Falsehood." In "The Blue Rattlesnake," Lu Ping himself drives an Austin. One is told in that story that a cultured lady smokes only the first half of a cigarette, leaving the rest for the man (86). There are busts of Western composers in the coffee shops, torsos of alluring nude women in modern apartments. People call potential lovers "dear" and "darling" in Chinglish. Shanghai modernism had a fascination with social and aesthetic *décadence*—with a Baudelairean, dandyish, fin de siècle sensibility, with cities, fashion, the artificial, the new woman, and with corruption, dying—the beauty of dying.[171]

Shanghai modernism and Sun Liaohong were Francophile.[172] Shanghai's large French Concession was the city's chic and fashionable ward, bearing pretensions of cultural leadership and grandeur. There one found Chinese literary "salons," French street names, French cultural activities—and the major establishments of Old Du, Shanghai's *capo di tutti capi*. Devotees of Oriental fashion, the French projected the image of cosmopolitanism; did not Arsène Lupin himself bring Oriental martial arts to Paris? Conversely, a certain type of Chinese cosmopolite affected French identity.[173] The most famous literary outlet for Shanghai modernism, the journal *Xiandai*, took as its second title *Les Contemporains*.

Maurice Leblanc of the Belle Époque, gazing ironically at the bourgeoisie, nurturing his passion for the automobile, and playing with paradoxes of identity and the facelessness of modern life, looked out on the modernist movement, even if he was not a part of it. Francine Marill Albérès sees in him and his character a double affront to the bourgeoisie: a nostalgic, aristocratic contempt for propriety characteristic of the original, early-eighteenth-century dandies; and a protomodernist, antisocial embrace of a superman's aesthetic more in tune with the late-nineteenth-century dandies. Baudelaire was the bridge. Leblanc picked up, if nothing else, the sybaritic, "sporting" side of the aesthetic, embodied in speed, display, and extravagant expenditure. His hero was a trendsetter, driving an automobile, going by rail in *un sleeping*, finally by airplane.[174] This was the side of French modernity that was most obvious, if not most culturally avant-garde, in Shanghai.

Lu Ping has picked up the taste for waste and luxury, as well as the irony of it. In his world, a purple woman's swimsuit *is* exotic and erotic, suggestive of nudity, and also of China's new athletic heroes and beauty pageants (and Esther Williams in the movies). The urban night, which belongs to café habitués, Japanese collaborators, spies, and American sailors abroad in the streets, is the world of "The Blue Rattlesnake." But there is not a whiff of opium. Sun appears to have been on his guard against Shanghai decadence or roguery that fit Orientalist stereotypes from abroad. "Between Truth and Falsehood" offers the safe delights of fancy cars, fancy costumes, fancy repartee, and a locked safe full of U.S. greenbacks. Jazz enters the picture in "A Wooden Puppet Play."

Sun Liaohong's Occidentalism, with a few ironic downmarket touches, is parodic in "Ya mingsheng" (The call of a crow). It opens in the basement of a (discount!) department store, at a lunch counter where a man in a red tie sips an orange drink. Three amorous eighteen-year-old waitresses (gossiping "crows") try to guess his age (estimates range from 28 to 46), imagine he is throwing them a kiss, and wonder at how much he resembles Basil Rathbone.[175] He is dapper, like a Shanghai *langzi* (loafer), or a salesman of foreign products. The story is a tribute to, and satire of, many a formula. The hero's mission (he is never positively identified as Lu Ping) is like Dupin's in "The Purloined Letter." He must retrieve, from a strong French-made safe, old love letters from a dance hall girl to a prominent out-of-power statesman whose political comeback is endangered by the man who stole the letters for extortion. Taking a tip from foreign movies, Lu Ping looks behind mirrors and paintings for secret safes and also checks picture mountings.[176]

Foreign culture and even foreign women are not threatening to Lu Ping; he is up to date and financially comfortable without having dirtied himself through commerce; he merely appropriates what he needs. His love of decadence seems a reproof of the idea that "postcolonial" literature is a refuge from the decadence of the metropolitan center.[177] But what kind of mincemeat does he make of Western-style law enforcement? China had its own traditions glorifying outlawry, but Lu Ping's contempt for law and judicial process manage to break new ground.

Most noticeable is the surreal lack of a police presence. As Holmes needs Lestrade to sharpen his wits, so Arsène Lupin needs Ganimard. The great bureaucratic stable of Sûreté men Ganimard can send after Lupin evens up the odds and increases the fun. Lupin enjoys leading them around by the nose, mentoring them as "acolytes," that they may be more worthy opponents in future. Indications in the Lu Ping stories that Shanghai even has a police force are few, and they are double-edged. Lu Ping flashes a fake badge to intimidate the "Blue Rattlesnake." He threatens to turn the blackmailer in "The Purple Swimsuit" over to the law (just a threat), and reports to the police his carjacking staged to steal the fake locket. Anonymous, thug-like armed men who force Mr. Yu, the cod liver oil smuggler, into a van in the dark are only at the end authenticated as real police. And there is the salacious cop, the "bottle cap" of "Night Hunting," who tries to steal an honest thief's wife from under his nose. "A Wooden Puppet Play" says that the police of all Shanghai expended maximum effort to find the lair of the "chivalrous thief," diving in and bumping their heads against the wall wildly and aimlessly, "like a swarm of flies with their heads cut off," and with no more success than "looking for a tropical fish in the Arctic Ocean."[178] In that story, Huo Sang phones the police, initiating a vain attempt to arrest Lu Ping. But that is all, in the stories mentioned. The police are not seen collaborating with the wealthy elite, or with Lu Ping's associates, though Chinese readers knew the Shanghai underworld and police forces to be frequent collaborators, from top to bottom.

The real crime world of drugs, the rackets, and lower-class crime is similarly absent from the Lu Ping stories. Instead of prostitution, there is the cleaned-up world of dance halls and coffeehouses. This leads back to Leblanc. The more skilled, "artistic," or intellectual forms of crime, such as pickpocketing, cat burglary, fraud, and elaborate stings are more appropriate to detection and suit a particular genre taste. Still, the complete absence of "real crime" seems like magnificent sleight of hand—in Cheng Xiaoqing's works too. It looks particularly odd because many historians agree with Lu Ping that the Shanghai worlds of business and government were effectively criminalized.

Caution may have dictated self-censorship, particularly during the Japanese occupation. Surely national pride is also involved; the moviegoing Sun Liaohong surely knew that opium, banditry, and official corruption were signs of China's shame and degradation. *Ressentiment* at being in the shadow of the West is suggested also by the relative absence of another element present in the elite—and criminal—circles in which Lu Ping moves: foreigners.[179]

Lawyers hardly fare better. Three references to them appear in the stories above. In "The Ghost's Hand," the maid tells of a lawyer who had a man killed for money. The extortionist who tries to blackmail a politician with his indiscreet letters in "The Call of a Crow" is a tricky lawyer; Lu Ping gains en-

trance to his great mansion only by introducing himself as the Great
Detective Huo Sang. And when Lu Ping visits the man who is blackmailing
the young swimmer of "The Purple Swimsuit," he is accompanied by one
"Lawyer Meng," presumably his crony, Meng Xing. Lu Ping calls him
"Meng Da Lüshi" (Great Lawyer Meng), and the extortionist too adopts this
term of address toward a member of his social class, the class of wealth, corruption, and really big-time crime. The Great Lawyer performs up to stereotype. After showing the blackmailer that his side has a locket just like the one
stolen and can pin the carjacking on the extortioner by dealing with the matter "by law," "Lawyer Meng" and Lu Ping negotiate for the real locket and a
little extortion money for themselves. A lawyer does make a good blackmailer. Lu Ping is still just "Ada" the chauffeur; getting him admitted to the
apartment of the terribly respectable extortioner, who is on a social footing
equal to that of a Great Lawyer, takes some doing.[180]

Lu Ping gives us his take on the law as such in an interior monologue
while he detects in the dark, trying to solve who murdered the man on the
floor—and emptied his safe—before he, Lu Ping, could break in and get the
second-floor job done himself.

Well then, was he willing, in his capacity as thief, to represent the sanctity of
the law and catch the murderer? Yes, he would be quite happy to round up
that murderer. But he wasn't at all willing to boost the reputation of the law.
He'd always felt that the law was only something like an amulet that certain
smart guys had fabricated to get them out of embarrassing situations. Such
an amulet might be good for scaring away stupid people (lit., "stupid
ghosts"), but it couldn't threaten the violent, crafty, and arrogant evil ones.
Not only could it not scare them away, a lot of them hid right behind it to
work their evil tricks![181]

So much for progress through rule of law.

A CIRCUS OF INTERTEXTUALITY:
LU PING VS. HUO SANG VERSUS
SHERLOCK HOLMES VS. ARSÈNE LUPIN

Maurice Leblanc had his fun with the Sherlock Holmes legend, but there is
a double vision in his Holmes-Lupin rivalry. The two heroes represent their

nations and their cultural differences. Yet both heroes also adhere to a common gentleman's ethic of civility, *politesse*, and accommodation, of playing by rules they accede to by choice—from good breeding, not because they are mandated by law. This transcends differences from being on opposite sides of the law as well as the Channel. It is not the same as Lupin's (or Lu Ping's) "chivalry" ethic, which is contingent and measured. This transcendent ethic (like Rites, though less codified) is English; Leblanc calls his own hero, in *franglais*, a *gentleman-cambrioleur*. The foreign language heightens the irony, but Eugène Sue, too, preferred the English word "gentleman" to the French "*gentilhomme*."[182] Whereas the English word had undergone a semantic shift like the Chinese word "*junzi*" (nobleman => noble man), the French word retained connotations of nobility from bloodlines rather than behavior. But "incommoding" oneself for another is also a very French idea.

It is on these very grounds that Lupin manifests his superiority over Holmes, though both are "gentleman *junzi*." Whose wits are superior, in an endless game of to-and-fro, is bound to be moot. No one will ever beat Holmes at science. Though it always feels like Arsène Lupin wins in the end (all European Lupin vs. Holmes stories were written by Leblanc), it is Holmes who always walks away with the "loot"—literally, for his job is to return the stolen booty. In the higher civilizational arts of living and accommodating one's fellow man, the Frenchman has the edge, even if in the mundane world of the law he is a thief. This is not just playing to the gallery as usual, but nourishing the *ressentiment* of a Frenchman speaking as a Frenchman, in a game whose rules are international, and yet, in the right hands, favorable to the underdog, which may after all once have been the top dog. (The similarity to China is clear.) Perhaps, then, there is a third level to the France vs. England game. Always the underdog in the world of the material, the French developed strategies of cultural influence in trying to reach (some theorists might say colonize) the rest of the world.[183] But was this "soft" answer to "hard" power not a characteristic "postcolonial" strategy?

Cheng Xiaoqing and Sun Liaohong pitted Holmes against Lupin, or "the Oriental Holmes" against "the Oriental Lupin," in works of their own. Although Sun Liaohong added anti-Japanese themes to his story when he revised it in 1942 (which is the version analyzed below, because it is by far the fullest and most interesting "Oriental Lupin" vs. "Oriental Holmes" text), neither Chinese author originally embraced the barest theme of national rivalry, East-West rivalry, or national parody. Instead, they conveyed the gentleman's ethic, which like Confucianism calls for deference. In Sun's case, the gentleman's ethic is most noticeable in the 1942 revision, when he must have been burning with national shame and anger. In the end, both Chinese authors, Sun included, defer to the Holmes character or surrogate, letting him "win"; and both, Cheng included, let the Lupin character triumph in the higher duel of right conduct. If Holmes = science-and-law = the West, Lu Ping, who undermines the law, might easily have used his roguery symbolically to undermine the West. Perhaps that would too obviously have repeated an Orientalist perception that "the East" is essentially wily and roguish and must be tamed by the West with law, order, and science.

Whatever its origin, the commitment to a gentleman's ethic characteristic of Holmes, Lupin, and the *junzi* is visible in the stories of the two modern Chinese writers. Were they simply deferring again to the spirit of Conan Doyle and Maurice Leblanc? Or were they expressing a backlash against the West, reining in the evident superiority of its science and technology in the name of a higher international spiritual ethic they could more easily share in? Or did the magnanimous Chinese spirit of the Rites once more triumph over mean-spirited law? Perhaps all three.

Neither "side" wins, not Holmes or Lupin; the adversarial spirit, the argumentative sport, comes out on top. But there is a loser, and it is the *law*.[184]

Leblanc showed polite deference to Conan Doyle in the story that explains Arsène Lupin's origins,[185] but the double vision really begins in "Sherlock Holmes Arrives Too Late" (Fr. original, 1906), in which "Horace Velmont" solves a multifaceted riddle in order to rob a locked chateau of its treasures. Caught in the act by Miss Nelly, the woman he loves, he is embarrassed into returning everything at 3:00 P.M. the next day—a deadline that is self-imposed but imperative, since Sherlock Holmes is to arrive from England to solve the case at four. (Holmes was summoned a day ahead of time, so convinced was the chateau owner, Devanne, that Arsène Lupin would be present, solve the riddle when given one more clue, and take possession of his treasures overnight!)[186]

The loot is duly returned in two army trucks and Lupin beats a hasty retreat. He passes Holmes and M. Holmes asks for directions; his "imprisoning" stare has taken Lupin's "negative," Lupin senses. Holmes will forever know him, whatever his disguise. Thus does Lupin protect the Holmes legend. And he is overtly deferential, if slightly ironic. Identifying himself only as a friend of Devanne, in the interest of self-preservation, he tells Holmes that he has "no more ardent admirer than . . . myself."

Holmes arrives at the chateau. For the benefit of M. Devanne, who has for years pondered riddles about secret passageways in his castle, Holmes figures out in only ten minutes the solution to this locked-room puzzle and thus how Lupin made away with the booty. Holmes is therefore quite as smart as Arsène Lupin. It is not Holmes's fault that Devanne summoned him to arrive only after the last piece of the riddle was revealed to Lupin, whose own genius was sure to figure it out in one hour. (One may even deduce that Holmes is six times as quick as Lupin.) Holmes did recognize Lupin while encountering him on the road, but he chose not to arrest him. So Holmes has already met Lupin on the common ground of civility. The deference is mutual; both are gentlemen. Or perhaps Holmes is as much an exhibitionist as Lupin. As Holmes puts it, Holmes does not take advantage of "chance opportunities"; he insists on making them. (If he were a lawyer, he might not use improperly obtained evidence.) At the end, he pronounces that he and Lupin "must" have another round in the game.

However, Holmes is inferior at acting out his role (performing the proper *li*). His "commonplace appearance" disappoints the guests and detectives at the castle. He does not resemble the "romantic," "mysterious," and "diabolical" hero that the name evoked for them before. "The Englishman," as he is here called, is gruff, even a bit ungracious, not having taken the car sent to receive him, and telling his host that this is not the way he does "business" (a very English concept, "business").

Holmes's arrogance reaches its height when he orders an automobile to return him to the railway station one hour after his arrival at the chateau, since he calculates that if Lupin solved the riddle in one hour surely he can too. He is correct, and yet Lupin has again done him one better. A car is waiting for him ahead of time anyway, for Lupin surmised better than he how quickly he would succeed. It is again a compliment to the Great Detective, and Holmes is flattered: "Clever man! I knew as much when I saw him." But it is in the car that Holmes is given back his watch. Devanne roars with laughter: "Sherlock Holmes's watch stolen by Arsène Lupin! Mon Dieu! How funny! Please, excuse me—I can't help it!" (139). But the French one-upmanship relies partly on Holmes's reaction. His silence the rest of the way is "more violent than the wildest rage." He is not a good sport.

Leblanc's dual vision of the Holmes-Lupin rivalry developed into a novel, *Arsène Lupin versus Herlock Sholmes* (1908).[187] That the name of the Englishman is altered, sparing the "real" Holmes embarrassment, must have struck Holmes fans as itself an act of deference. In reality, Leblanc was obliged to drop the name of "Holmes" after Conan Doyle read "Sherlock Holmes Arrives Too Late" and wrote Leblanc an indignant letter to say that he had no right to the name of his character. But that was not known at the time. In any case, the logic of the situation demanded that Holmes stay on top as the world's most powerful intellect, or he would "not really be Holmes," and not just to his fans. A victory over a weak Holmes would prove nothing.[188]

The novel features linked mysteries of short-story length of the sort typical in the Lupin cycle. Three intriguing crimes, all connected to Lupin through a blonde lady, provoke the upper-crust victims jointly to call in Sholmes from England as a last resort. He succeeds by brilliantly deducing a fantastic plot: Lupin has over the years assisted an architect renovating fifteen of Paris's finest homes, fitting them out with secret tunnels and elevators known only to him and his love, the architect's daughter: The Blonde Lady. In the end Sholmes returns the diamond whose loss brought him to France. Lupin is arrested, but he escapes. He is the porter on the train to Calais who thanks M. Sholmes for the 50-centime tip. Sholmes returns to England, but Lupin lures him back, in the case of "the Jewish lamp." These are the cases that later moved Cheng Xiaoqing to try to redress the balance for Holmes.[189]

Lupin openly embraces national rivalry: "Arsène Lupin versus Herlock Sholmes . . . France versus England . . . Trafalgar will be avenged at last"! (98). Even Ganimard predicts that "the Englishman will be defeated" (90). England (as usual?) is the aggressor, which is why he will win, Lupin says. True, Sholmes has no equal as a detective. But he, Lupin, has an advantage: Sholmes is attacking and Lupin is only defending himself (97). "Oh, have no fear. I shall do credit to King and country, for I am an Englishman" (134), says "Wilson" (Watson), fatuously.

Both sides live for their reputations. What if the match were decided on points? Lupin locks up Sholmes and Wilson overnight in a house they are investigating; the police have to rescue them the next morning. Lupin had prepared them a good French supper ahead of time, and clues for Wilson, lest the English fall hopelessly behind. The sarcasm and *politesse* of the police, their "affectation of good will," are equally "exasperating" to these English. Lupin gets Wilson to turn over his luggage and detection tools to a porter who is of course Lupin's crony. The Frenchman "makes a fool of you with the utmost grace and delicacy," Sholmes mutters (124). He admits that he has lost the first round.

And that is before *L'Echo de France* reports these indignities, remarking on Lupin's kind hospitality and delivering a warning of stronger measures to come. Sholmes is abducted in his own taxi by Lupin himself and tied up in a boat headed back to England. The underdog status of the English does not gain them any sympathy, for Sholmes uncovers Lupin's architectural scheme by finding and intimidating The Blonde Lady—Lupin's lover. Not very sporting.

The duel between the two great men takes place not just on the battleground of wits (science), but of honor and style. And the battle is clearly joined. The day Sholmes and Wilson land in France, they face off against Lupin and his amanuensis in a café. Lupin appeals to a transnational ethic in national terms: "Come now, show me that you are a true Englishman and thus a good sport" (108). Declining to make the easy arrest, Sholmes orders drinks all around. He *is* a sport. The adversaries "sign a peace treaty," and Sholmes promises to have Lupin arrested in ten days. Just like a lawyer.

Sholmes is a gentleman, yes, but not as much as Lupin. Stuffy and making such a fuss about getting his sleep, he is always "business." Lupin says as much when Sholmes offers to buy the stolen diamond from him—"you really are an Englishman" (250). Sholmes is so unsporting as to call in the police when he feels it necessary. And he ignores the injuries of his friend Wilson—most ungracious, toward a loyal friend, particularly since Wilson is so stupid.[190] Lupin, by contrast, apologizes for the injuries (which he, after all, has inflicted [252]).

Lupin's biggest victory is in the reprise over the Jewish lamp, which contains hidden jewels. He stole it as a rare act of altruism, to help the lady who owned it fend off a blackmailing ex-lover. A maidservant valorously kept the secret and even took the blame for the theft. Sholmes, summoned back to France to solve the robbery, chases Lupin and suffers new humiliations—letters, newspaper articles, and anti-Holmes placards at the railway station. He shares a sinking boat with Lupin that seemingly drowns the latter. Lupin's high spirits, courtesy, and bravos to the police on shore as they try to shoot him while he drowns are almost cloying. He gives the Brits credit where it is due: "What do you think of that, Ganimard? That's a real revolver! A genuine English bulldog" (315)—stolen from Sholmes, who utters an oath when he belatedly discovers its loss. As he sinks, Lupin dictates a will (320) bequeathing all his property to Sholmes. Chivalrous deference to the adversary in the extreme!

The victory is when Lupin comes back from his supposed drowning and confronts Sholmes on the ferry to England. Sholmes brilliantly solved the theft of the Jewish lamp, but that meant exposing not primarily Lupin, but the lady in distress and the faithful maid who covered for her. The whole point was to keep the affair secret so that the lady's husband would not discover the blackmail. Sholmes has "sown the seeds of discord" in a family Lupin was protecting. In solving the crime, for the law, he has done a moral evil. He did not mean to, but in the end he is not as good as Arsène Lupin. The young maid confirms this by putting herself under the protection of Lupin, not Sholmes. "With the satisfied air of a gentleman who has fulfilled his duty," he bids Herlock Sholmes goodnight (349–50).

Let us consider Cheng Xiaoqing's "Zuanshi xiangquan" (The diamond necklace), a late-1930s translation by Cheng and his daughter of his own classical-language work "Juezhi ji" (Battle of wits), which started to become a series in *The Grand Magazine* in 1917 but stopped after two contributions. In the vernacular rendition twenty years later, which is faithful to the original, Cheng gave the two pieces the colorful name *Long hu dou* (Dragon vs. tiger), perhaps after Feng Menglong.[191] "The Diamond Necklace" is a rematch of Holmes vs. Lupin, this time narrated by Watson in the Conan Doyle fashion. Cheng is loyal to "his" man, Holmes; his preface says he meant for Holmes to come out better than in the Leblanc stories and also to redress the balance for Watson, who as Leblanc's Wilson is an irredeemable dolt, and smug besides. Cheng pronounces Leblanc's stories looser and less logical in plot than Conan Doyle's, lacking in deductive analysis—they are "in the realm of the supernatural, which is only masked by science" (191). Cheng could hardly have overlooked Leblanc's theme of national rivalry, for

Cheng's Watson boasts that Holmes's fame has spread abroad, "even to China and Japan" (201). Yet Cheng makes no explicit or symbolic use of national rivalry in his own story. Moreover, his man Holmes does not completely triumph. Did Cheng have a subconscious, perhaps nationalistic desire to subvert the victory of the Briton? The spiritual victory of Lupin under the pen of a Holmes idolater more likely represents the victory of a transnational, gentlemanly (and maybe anti-imperialist) ethic above both law and national boundaries.

In this story, Arsène Lupin summons Holmes from England to recover a diamond necklace Lupin has stolen from a duke, who must have it back by his daughter's twentieth birthday celebration. Besides the time limit, Cheng's Lupin adopts such familiar Leblanc devices as disguising himself as Ganimard, as the concierge for the Englishmen's intended secret rooms in Paris, and as Watson himself. There are also frequent sarcastic communications to Holmes from Lupin that pop up at the funniest times and in the least expected places; misleading letters putatively from authoritative others that were really written by Lupin; co-optation by Lupin of servants and others with whom the Englishmen must deal; and thoughtful arrangements for their premature return to England.

Holmes has acquired a map of Lupin's secret hideout, probably from a Lupin associate who sold him out, before a vital midnight meeting that is to take place there. Holmes plants a false map for Lupin to steal back. The bait does attract Lupin, but Watson loses his clothes to the rogue while guarding it, which allows Lupin to go anywhere he pleases as "Watson."

The constitutional framework of the geste is a gentleman's agreement between detective and thief of terms even more exacting than in Leblanc's novel. In a face-to-face meeting before the contest, the ever-affable Lupin greets Holmes as an old friend and suggests that they struggle with their wits. Arsène Lupin promises to return the necklace voluntarily at the end, providing Sherlock Holmes agrees not to arrest him. They shake hands on the deal.

Still, Lupin insists on twitting Holmes with false leads and taunting letters. Lupin will return the necklace only if Holmes and Watson are on the 11:00 P.M. ferry to England (that is, before the rumored midnight meeting). Once aboard, the English are tricked again. They are promised the necklace in London, but they must not search the ship; the necklace could be thrown overboard. Yet it is not waiting for them at Baker Street. Holmes finally realizes that it has been in a false bottom of Watson's briefcase all along, hidden there when Lupin knocked him out and stole the fake map.

So the necklace is peacefully returned—a good symbolic representation of the adversary system. Lupin almost becomes a "loyal opposition." Would that international relations were based on this, not Unequal Treaties. Holmes for his part repeatedly reassures Watson, despite every typically lupinien setback and humiliation dealt them, that Lupin will keep his promise, so they should keep up their end, even if it means staying on the ferry.

So far, this is a Leblanc-type story in which Lupin wins, even though Cheng had intended the opposite outcome. Holmes has "won" only because Lupin let him, after much ridicule. Cheng Xiaoqing evens it up only by revealing at the end that Holmes handed off the real map to Ganimard before departing France. That resulted in police encirclement of the hideout and a midnight raid that netted Lupin himself. Holmes gets the last laugh without violating his oath, since the arrest occurred after he left France. But this is "unrealistic," for Lupin always manages to elude Ganimard. And it is not gentlemanly. Holmes has kept his promise only by a "legal" technicality. Since he did not make the arrest, one wonders if he can even claim credit for it. In this unwitting way, Cheng Xiaoqing has proved again that *politesse—li*—is what life is about, not winning under the law. To observe only the letter of the law is not to follow a high Confucian or gentlemanly moral ethic. Having no doubt sensed that he tipped the balance unsportingly in Holmes's favor, Cheng Xiaoqing finishes with a typical Leblanc ending: Arsène Lupin escapes before the story ends. Cheng meant to change the formula, but the real gentleman wins again.

Watson's reputation is not much rehabilitated either. As in a Leblanc story, the Great Detective's loyal friend nearly upsets the best-laid plans. It is in the adventures of his own Huo Sang that Cheng was to spend a career "making it up to Watson," by creating in Bao Lang one of the intellectually most equal Watson figures in the whole Holmes tradition, even though he is always wrong.[192]

Sun Liaohong restaged the celebrated rivalry in a dual between *Chinese* geniuses: "the Oriental Holmes" versus "the Oriental Lupin," in "Kuileiju" (Puppet show; 1923), one of his earliest Lu Ping works, revised in 1942 as

"Muou de xiju" (A wooden puppet play). The "Oriental Holmes" is called Lü Lun in the 1923 text, and Huo Sang in the revision. By that time Cheng Xiaoqing's creation had earned the accolade in Sun's as well as the public's mind.[193] Sun naturally takes Lu Ping's side; we have seen in other stories how often Lu Ping disguised himself as Huo Sang, so as to fool the gullible and the evil (e.g., lawyers) into false confidence in Lu Ping's bourgeois respectability. So here the surprise is that, although the spiritual victory goes to the rogue as expected, formal victory still lies with the Oriental Holmes— with Huo Sang, in the revision, in deference to him and his creator, Cheng Xiaoqing. Fortunately for readers, this does not preclude parody of Huo Sang, Bao Lang (called Huo Sang's *bao*, "burden," 254), Suzhou (Cheng's adopted home), even Cheng's style. Thus the narrator reassures the reader that "the author will not at this point prepare a list of the furniture" (263). He also mimics Cheng's phraseology: "This event was shocking—moreover, you could say it was extremely shocking!" (230).[194]

The 1942 version is explained in a preface as the reworking of a twenty-year-old tale, from the days "when Huo Sang, Lu Ping, and the [anonymous] narrator were young." Writing a Lu Ping tale in his usual manner, Sun Liaohong deprives the detective of the advantage he typically enjoys at the hand of Cheng Xiaoqing or any other follower of Conan Doyle—narration by the detective's coadjutor. And the challenge for Lu Ping is familiar enough: an art collector named Han has hired Huo Sang to guard his painting of a Buddha by the Tang master Wu Daozi. Han wants to exhibit it because people suspect it is fake (another typical Leblanc mystification). Rumors have made him afraid it will be stolen. Huo Sang and Bao Lang suspect that Lu Ping is behind this in the wake of another Leblanc device—an outrageously presumptuous letter from an anonymous, self-styled connoisseur who asks to "borrow" the painting—would Han please have it wrapped and ready for him when he comes to take possession?

Huo Sang employs two stratagems, both comic. Since the collector will not entrust his masterwork to a bank vault, Huo Sang has him adopt "The Silver Teapot Stratagem" from a Peking opera: Han must put it in a cupboard and never take his eyes off it. Meanwhile Huo Sang goes investigating in disguise, as a preemptive measure. The fun is in the role Huo Sang selects for himself: a middle-aged *shenshi*, an old fogy gentryman in long gown, riding jacket, and flowing beard. When Huo Sang tests out his disguise on Bao

Lang, as Holmes was wont to do, Bao Lang mistakes Huo Sang for the Kuomintang elder statesman Yu Youren![195] Whatever the politics, in generational and sartorial terms Bao Lang's "misperception" of the putatively cosmopolitan Huo Sang puts him in his bourgeois, fuddy-duddy place.

Yet it is Huo Sang who slinks around like a thief (244), alarming hotel service personnel (254). He becomes rattled, and even so is vain and arrogant. He is a bit too positivist about searching for clues, and he spends a remarkable amount of time just relaxing and waiting for something to happen.

Lu Ping meantime runs circles around Huo Sang with his "12.5 stratagems" (one of his thirteen is slightly inferior, so Lu Ping sportingly deducts a half point; though old Chinese novels also number stratagems, Sun may be satirizing Cheng Xiaoqing's fondness for enumeration). The stratagems are characteristic Leblanc and traditional Chinese devices: press releases planted by Lu Ping publicizing things about Huo Sang best kept secret; leading Huo Sang to where Lu Ping wants him with a little boy, Lu Ping's son, whom he arranges for Huo Sang to save from a staged auto accident (shades of Mencius, one of Huo Sang's putative moral compasses); letting Huo Sang chase two Lu Pings (doubles); the old elevator trick; getting physical with Huo Sang; and putting Lu Ping in disguise himself. He leads Huo Sang on wild goose chases and into a trap where he is disarmed. Then he persuades Mr. Han willingly to surrender his precious scroll to Lu Ping made up as Huo Sang disguised as the gentryman. In the end, Lu Ping is disguised as Huo Sang in disguise and Huo Sang is disguised as Lu Ping according to his last description.

It is misleading to speak of Lu Ping disguising himself, though, for no one has ever seen his original appearance. He is "the man you cannot see," "the tenth planet" whose presence is only suspected (212, 215). The motif of multiple identity bears a symbolic and even a metaphysical meaning. Moreover, the character(s) actually dramatized are never referred to by name, but only as "the wooden puppet." There seem to be other men made up to look like puppets besides the real Lu Ping, plus an animated mannikin in a tailor shop that he uses to indicate to his legions of confederates the "Lu Ping disguise of the day."

The figure of "wooden puppets" turns wicked when the author uses the term to refer to Huo Sang, Bao Lang, and the police (262). This satirizes the genre (Cheng Xiaoqing's subgenre in particular) as a play in which the author woodenly manipulates his characters. But Lu Ping as puppet is a genius, moving from one identity to another, whereas Huo Sang is a dumbbell—wooden indeed, bourgeois, stuffy. *He* seems to be the puppet in the story subtitles: "Ridiculing Him as a Puppet" (chap. 1), "A Puppet That Alternates Between Youth and Old Age" (chap. 4), and "The Puppet's Scorched Earth Tactics" (chap. 10).

There is another gentlemen's agreement, but only at the end. Bao Lang and Huo Sang barge in on Lu Ping, pistols drawn (rather lacking in manners), Huo Sang disguised as Lu Ping, Lu Ping still as Huo Sang. Yet Lu Ping serves his guests tea, even lights their cigarettes. In the face of such deference, the three men begin to talk as friends. Huo Sang frees Lu Ping in order to get the painting, but the exhibition is held a day late and the painting now bears Lu Ping's seal. Still, Huo Sang has the formal victory.

This message is however supplemented, if not undermined, by symbolism added in 1942. In wartime, these peace talks, diplomacy, and gentlemen's agreements are just smoke screens, the stuff of puppetry. Both Huo Sang and Lu Ping tell lies to reach their final accommodation. Perhaps they are both puppets.[196] And in the third, more obvious kind of symbolism, the targets are the Japanese and their puppet regime. This was fortuitous, for the original story was already about puppets. References to scorched earth tactics, sleuthing as a form of combat, and peace talks were added during the war.

Lu Ping's defeat is "glorious," says the narrator in 1942, while Huo Sang's victory is "tragic." China was in truth defeated, in Sun's eastern part of the country, controlled by the Japanese puppet, Wang Jingwei. But China put up a fight—achieved a "glorious defeat." Or did it? The fifth chapter title fits the KMT war effort all too well: "The Wooden Puppet Stages a Planned Retreat." There is however no hint of national allegory in the original version of 1923; evidently the idea was thrust upon Sun Liaohong when the very word "puppet" lost its innocence. Using the detective plots for national allegories is the one element of the genre that both Chinese authors seem to have resisted as long as possible.

CONCLUSION

The genre stories of crime and detection that returned to China just after Mao's death, less given to direct quotation of Western authors than those of

Cheng Xiaoqing and Sun Liaohong, are politically more daring, but their plots are less impressive. The first half of the twentieth century is indeed the Golden Age of the Chinese detective story. What authors of that age enjoyed was unprecedented freedom. Freedom evidently had salutary effects much broader than just allowing authors to comment on social issues.

Yet Republican-era detective and rogue-detective stories (often called "counter-detective stories" in Chinese) are more ideologically complex than their present obscurity in China might suggest. If May Fourth writers had taken these stories seriously, they might have had a shock of recognition—seen in them their own antifeudalism and patriotism, their own "obsession with China,"[197] expressed in their very own language. This is not to say that Cheng Xiaoqing and Sun Liaohong could ever have been elevated to the ranks of Mao Dun, Ba Jin, Cao Yu, and Lao She—but those authors' reputations too have had their ups and downs, and will again in any truly post-communist age.

Unlike the cultural watchdogs who took power in 1949, Cheng Xiaoqing and Sun Liaohong took the detective story form to be an international currency with no cultural imperialist character. And an internationally exchangeable commodity it was—self-referential and formulaic. Conan Doyle was the first to imitate Conan Doyle, and he was indebted to Poe and several Frenchmen. Yet given the power of Anglo-American and French culture in the early twentieth century, Cheng Xiaoqing and Sun Liaohong's attraction to Western forms could never be seen in China as accidental. Cheng himself justified the detective story not simply because it was fun to read but because it would help China become more modern. In choosing a Western popular formula, he turned away from China's court case formula, and he did so militantly. It looked like more than a mere matter of his pleasure. But if Cheng Xiaoqing, Sun Liaohong, and others could have continued writing, Chinese culture might be very different today. It might have more Westernized outer forms, although with different inner meanings, as in Mickey Mouse–toting, Elvis Presley–worshiping Japan today. Maybe that will be China's future even so.

China's international weakness and social disintegration affected Cheng Xiaoqing's and Sun Liaohong's writings. One can see it in their exaggerated patriotism, and even in their reticence about imperialism and social conflict. China's press and legal profession were convenient surrogate targets. Legal protection of Chinese citizens was indeed in a sorry state. Yet the authors assailed phantoms: kingpin lawyers rather than militarists, playboys rather than party (KMT) hacks. Perhaps it was a backlash against imperialism or modernity, or faith in a new or even a traditional ethic of universal civility, that made them salute right conduct over laws and treaties conceived by what they saw as petty minds.

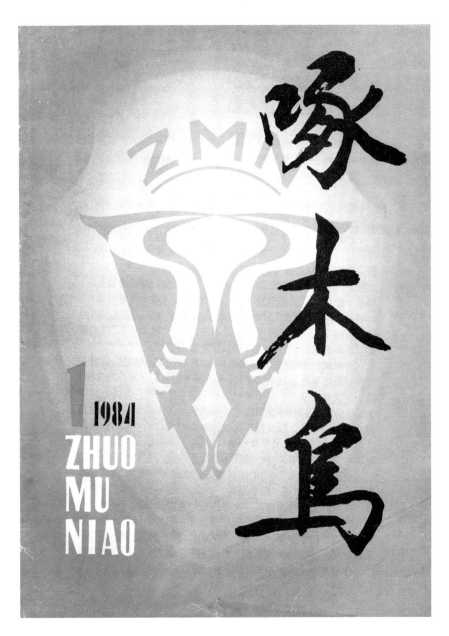

Woodpecker, second founding issue, February 1984, from Masses's Press, Ministry of Public Security. *Woodpecker* is an upholder of "serious" but conventional art. The two woodpeckers in profile make a bilaterally symmetrical policeman's shield.

Blue Shield, September 1989, from *Landun/Tianjin Daily News.* The cover evokes the high seriousness of modern abstractionism. This and *Woodpecker* were flagship police literary journals—upscale central periodicals with literary pretensions.

Jiangxi Public Security, July 1990, from the Provincial Public Security Department, Jiangxi. The sensational cover depicts policemen as they want to be seen: as brave action heroes, like their interservice rivals in the People's Liberation Army.

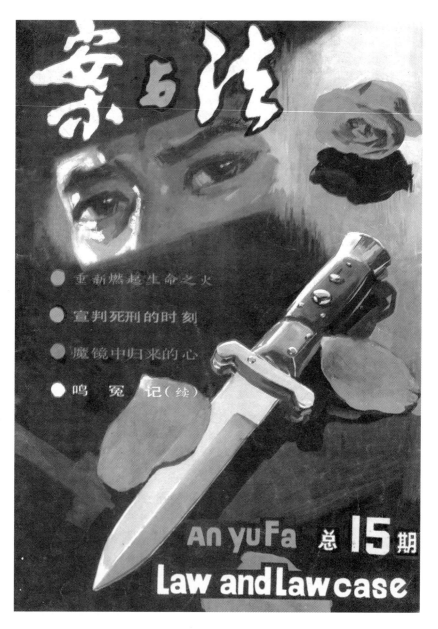

Cases and Law, December 1986, from the *An yu fa* Editorial Board, Xi'an. The cover capitalizes on the sensationalism of violent crime itself. The blood stain is in scarlet. This publication and *Jiangxi Public Security* were local, popular police magazines.

Great Chinese Detectives, June 1989, from Xuelin Press, Xining, edited by *Shanghai Stories* magazine and the Shanghai University College of Literature. The cover is violent chic for the masses.

风流男女
——法制故事大赛精选

Loose Boys and Unfettered Women, April 1988, from Yanbian University Press, Jilin. Here sex is the drawing card, however unrelated to content. The print run was 300,000. This publication and *Great Chinese Detectives* were one-time issues from the liberated late 1980s—slick but downmarket in reader appeal.

The Mystery of the Missing Person, November 1988, from Jiangxi People's Press, Nanchang. The print run of this pulp magazine was 100,000.

The Mad Profiteer and *The Widespread Kidnapping of Women for Sale in Old Cathay*,
February 1989, from Yishu Press, Beijing. Another pulp magazine, this publication had a
print run of 100,000.

Politics

How did communism change Chinese writing about crime, detection, and the law? This chapter finds that entire topics, genres, and strata of fiction were manipulated and annihilated by politics. Then the cadres presumed to create their own genres.

Political interventions affecting works of crime fiction were relatively benign after 1984 but still treacherous, for the police adopted writing about crime as their bailiwick.[1] This chapter discusses the predicament of Chinese crime fiction under communism in three periods: 1949–76 (the Mao years), 1977–83 (early in the Deng regime), and since 1984 (crime fiction's boom years). Each period is depicted in sections that variously present overviews, trends, or close readings of representative works and official ideal types.

The first section briefly summarizes the situation under Mao, from 1949 to 1976. It was dismal. More encouraging is the ingenuity of a crime novella analyzed in the next section. The novella is unusual, for it was written by Cheng Xiaoqing and published during a thaw, but its politics are typical. How Cheng had to adapt his old craft to serve socialism speaks volumes.

The next three sections discuss the aftermath of the new politics of 1979–

80. The opening segment surveys the initial cultural thaw under Deng Xiaoping, from its heyday in 1979 to its near collapse in 1983. That is followed in the next section by close readings of two works of China's critically acclaimed and relatively dissident "literature of introspection" of 1979–80. The argument is that some of these very political works were crime fiction—a socially esteemed, "high" crime fiction. But how were they like or different from the "popular" crime genres discussed in Chapter One? The next section necessarily asks just what was "high" and what was "low," socially and aesthetically. The concept of a lower or popular genre fiction was just dawning, but the whodunits and melodramas of Chapter One amply justified it. Seas of translated mysteries by Conan Doyle and Agatha Christie took the place of the native works in 1980–81, when it became politically inopportune again for Chinese to write about Chinese crime, even with formulas. Then the MPS suppressed foreign crime stories too.

The "literature of introspection" even now retains its reputation as serious literature, yet it is quite easy to read, melodramatic, and chockablock with formulas from both Western crime fiction and China's own classic "popular" fiction of the Ming and Qing.[2] The paradox is partly resolved if one remembers that, while China was emerging from a cultural desert, even "popular" formulas seemed new and original. When they had become banal again, the stage was set for differentiation of works by level as in other modern societies. China's more political and "introspective" crime fiction was, however, even less adaptable to chill winds after 1981 than the ordinary whodunits. A nadir for law and literature in every form arrived in late 1983, amid overlapping campaigns against spiritual pollution and against due process for accused criminals.

Yet the author Ye Yonglie prospered, so he is granted a section of his own. His simple appeals to scientific, patriotic, and police values gained him enough police protection to keep detective fiction with Chinese police heroes alive through the early 1980s—although even Ye was on the defensive in 1983. He set an example of how financially successful cooperation between the MPS and writers could be. Ironically, his works also appear in retrospect as transitional to a new age of subliterature.

The five sections making up the second half of this chapter reflect the about-face in cultural policy in 1984. Deng Xiaoping stoked the fires of reform again, and crime fiction came into its own. Indeed, its greatest popularity was at the start, in the mid-1980s. Readership declined steadily through the decade, finally stabilizing in the 1990s. Martial-arts fiction and other popular genres took the same course, and so did mainstream literature, which declined far more drastically.[3]

Hence the initial topic for the sections on the mid- and late-1980s is the explosion of crime fiction that began in 1984 and the forces that promoted it: the police, the judiciary, and new pulp writers competing with them from below. The arts were losing state subsidies and being forced onto a more commercial path; "private," fee-for-service practice came to writers well before it did to lawyers. Even so, politics remained the crux. The police gave crime fiction its muscle. They wrote and published it and tried to legislate a whole new police genre into existence. These developments account for the section subtitled "Politics and Genre."

But in 1984, the MPS had to face legitimate political and commercial competitors. The next section is thus called "The Birth Pangs of Legal System Literature"—not of "police literature." "Legal system literature" was a strange name that did not always fit the works, but its semantics evoked the compromises and conflicting hopes and fears of the age.

A more concrete idea of what was produced in the name of legal system literature is the subject of the last two sections. The first builds, by induction, a model of exactly what China's police and judicial cadres wanted works in their genre to be like. The second section compares the ideals for crime fiction espoused by official and dissident critics. It discovers considerable common ground. Many on both sides put political considerations first.

Close analysis of post-1984 writings themselves is left for Chapter Five. Some works truly were a legal system literature. The concept was unlikely from a communist viewpoint, but the full union of law and literature touched a chord in the Chinese soul. It was the new name, stirring up old fears of law and punishment now intensified by state control of law and literature, that caused many readers to shudder.

1949–76: ENEMIES TAKE THE PLACE OF CRIMINALS

The victory of modern Western forms over traditional Chinese ones that the New Culture movement and Cheng Xiaoqing had fought for was not undone by Mao's revolution, though Cheng's own stories were suppressed and bourgeois Western culture was denounced in an orgy of nationalistic excess. Traditional Chinese culture and literature were banned too, including fiction about wise judges, knights-errant, and other "feudal" characters. China's 1950s stories of police detection, such as they are, recall Western fiction far more than any Ming or Qing works. It was the line of descent that changed, from Conan Doyle to Soviet and Eastern bloc authors. In this, China's police fiction exemplified all literature under Mao. But law and literature in Mao's era are less known for foreign influence than for "self-reliance" and "politics in command."

Fiction reached unprecedentedly large audiences, through literacy campaigns, population growth, party organization, and "making it universal" (*puji*; "popularization")—that is, making it easier to read, or "dumbing it down" in the opinion of sophisticates. Deprived of choices, China's ever younger millions avidly read this fiction.[4] It was not called "popular" in Chinese (*su, tongsu*); that was a derogatory term for pulp, genre, and time-passing literature of "bourgeois" societies, like crime and love stories, which were supposed to disappear. Socialist fiction, however simple and formulaic, was neither a market-differentiated "popular fiction" homing in on particular reader tastes nor a folk literature from below. It was a "mass" literature from above—ideologically "serious" writing produced and distributed uniformly and in vast quantities by modern methods. Claiming the ideological importance of May Fourth literature, it allowed no genre writing below it, while itself plunging to basic literacy levels to gain a mass readership.

Adversarial legal practice was gone too, parodied by actions against "enemies" in party-led struggle sessions and self-criticisms. One became one's own adversary, to annihilate, not affirm, the self. Years of class struggle led many to want harmony at any cost. Ironically, Maoist fiction rarely depicts struggle sessions, despite the importance of confession and repentance in both traditional and Maoist society. Mass "trials" appear mostly in epic novels about land reform that extol revolutionary peasant vengeance instead of law enforcement.[5] Urban elites were accused and punished during the same years, but fictional description of this mostly awaited the years 1978–80, at which time it was "exposed" as a mistake. Traditional interest in the confession, punishment, conversion, and spiritual rebirth of criminals likewise revived only after Mao's death, in tales of tragedy about mistaken judgments.

Since popular genres and the very subject of crime were taboo, the closest approximation of crime fiction in Mao's era was stories showing detective work by nonmilitary heroes. There were many works about tracking down enemies in time of war and revolution; writ large, that was the theme of much mainstream fiction. But the mid-1950s also saw the translation and publication of Soviet and Eastern European "detective" novels. China rightly called them "anti-spy" (*fante*; counterespionage) and "suspense" fiction, for the crimes detected were treason and class sabotage. Chinese anti-spy stories likewise showed a topical devotion to real and fantasized conflicts with KMT agents from the surviving regime on Taiwan, with CIA spies, and finally with KGB agents. This focus now gives them a dated look. The same is true of mainstream novels, many of which replayed wars against Japan and the KMT that were already won.[6]

Public security cadres Gao Jianping and Zhang Zihong in 1990 made up a list of seminal Mao-era stories, plays, and films they deemed to be contemporary Chinese "police" or "public security literature." Most works concern ferreting out KMT agents and enemy spies, although a few are about domestic counterrevolutionaries.[7] A Tianjin writer and the authors of a textbook on composition for political-legal cadres cite the same 1950s and 1960s works as precursors of Chinese legal system literature—but not as genuine influences on it, so shallow were the art and ideology of the earlier works.[8] Police author-critic Wei Jun, who also likes the term legal system literature, stresses the Soviet influence. He speaks of a 1950s literature about exposing hidden counterrevolutionary elements that simply moved to a 1960s out-and-out anti-spy phase, until the Cultural Revolution terminated most writing even in that simple, nationalistic mode.[9]

Only seven of Gao and Zhang's representative works of the Mao years make Meishi Tsai's big general bibliography of influential Chinese fiction from 1949 to 1974.[10] Tsai catalogues another dozen-and-a-half "counterintelligence/sabotage" works not cited by Gao and Zhang, but some of them, indeed some works of Gao and Zhang's "public security literature," are about enemy agents operating before 1949 or the demise of spies at the hands of heroes who are not police detectives.[11] Gao and Zhang evidently included any work having a theme of detecting concealed enemies.

According to Gao and Zhang, the earliest works, of 1949–54, pitted police, border guards, and people's militia against spies, border infiltrators, and enemies gone underground after their defeat in the Civil and Korean Wars.

By all accounts, police and detection themes loomed larger in cinema than in fiction; Gao and Zhang cite seven films and no fiction at all. The filmmakers aroused hatred toward and constant vigilance against the enemy. That would continue as the highest official function of police literature even beyond the Mao years. The earliest films included *Wuxing de zhanxian* (The unseen front lines; 1949), directed by Yi Ming, and Xia Yan's *Renmin de juzhang* (The people's great power to strike back).[12]

New impetus for police detection in literature came with influence from the Soviet bloc and the 1955 campaign to Wipe Out (or Ferret Out) Hidden Counterrevolutionary Elements (*Suqing ancang de fangeming fenzi*), commonly called the Sufan movement (not to be confused with the prior Zhenfan movement to Suppress Counterrevolutionaries). The years 1955–59 are the second period of Chinese police literature according to Gao and Zhang, who slight the Hundred Flowers, Anti-Rightist campaign, and Great Leap Forward that most critics think set the course for mainstream Chinese literature. Perhaps works about security officers combating enemies were already so far "left" as to be immune from criticism.

"Shuangling matibiao" (The alarm clock with a second bell), by Lu Shi and Li Wenda, is often cited as the model public security story of the mid- and late-1950s. Other authors cited by Gao and Zhang are obscure today, except for old Cheng Xiaoqing, whose *Shengsi guantou* (The moment of life or death) portrays an enemy agent infiltrated in from Hong Kong who changes sides after witnessing the wonders of New China. In the modern drama, Gao and Zhang claim even Lao She's *Quanjia fu* (Happy home) and *Xi wang Chang'an* (Looking west toward Chang'an) for their genre. The latter has a corrupt cadre whose hidden KMT affiliation needs to be exposed. Film still dominates. Examples are *Xu Qiuying anjian* (The case of Xu Qiuying), about the murder of a female security officer who used to be a KMT agent, and *Tiedao weishi* (Railway guards), in which Public Security foils U.S. attempts to blow up trains and bridges during the Korean War.[13]

Films and plays remain dominant in Gao and Zhang's third period, 1960–66, which they characterize as beginning to treat "problems" in police work, themes of criminals reforming themselves, and relations between the police and the masses. But the "obvious evidence of the political function" limited the works' achievement, they admit, and the situation only worsened in the next ten years.[14]

So China lacked a crime fiction. But did it even have a "public security" or "police literature"? The term was not in use in the 1950s, although the old term "detective fiction" still was.[15] Genre fiction as such went unrecognized. Even mainstream fiction was about exposing enemies, though its heroes were mostly party members, basic-level and state cadres, poor peasants, workers, militia—and members of Public Security's far more prestigious rival, the People's Liberation Army (PLA). It was in film, where the police uniforms were visible, that "police art" had a chance. "Wiping Out Counterrevolutionaries" stories took definition as a subgenre only in 1978, when they were collected into a book according to that designation.[16]

Crime Story Conventions in an Age Without Crime Stories

As Heather Dubrow has noted, the "most obvious but hardly the least important signal" shaping genre expectations is the era of a work's composition.[17] Chinese readers under communism knew that bourgeois crime fiction was no longer tolerated, yet the novella *Dashucun xue an* (The bloody case at Big Tree Village) saw print in 1956, during a political thaw. The title promises a little old-fashioned criminal deviance, and the title page even bears a supertitle: "suspense novel." It is a unique work by China's past master of "bourgeois" detection, Cheng Xiaoqing. Yet the compromises Cheng was forced to make exemplify the impact of socialism. His vocabulary was always simple, but in this novella all the literary flourishes are gone. The plot and characters are also much simpler than in his classic stories. His new work seems written down for mass consumption and ideological innocuousness. This is formula fiction worthy of the name.

Cheng Xiaoqing stood his ground as much as he could; what makes *The Bloody Case at Big Tree Village* fascinating is that it grafts rather than mixes "bourgeois" and "socialist" genres, and so too separate discourses about what criminal offenses mean, what motivates them, and what counteracts them. Both capitalist and (in liberal eras) communist discourse admit such elements as an awful offense, a mystery about precisely who did it, detection by a professional, and several guilty-looking suspects. Hence Cheng's splice succeeds. In illiberal times it was intolerable to create any doubt, even for dramatic purposes, about which characters might be good or bad. Indeed, if literature is propaganda, the presence of multiple suspects would seem subtly to subvert the Maoist axiom that the overwhelming majority support the revolution. But then so might the socialist convention of sabotage committed by a whole counterrevolutionary conspiracy of malcontents in a village. Leave it to Cheng Xiaoqing to pin the crime on a conspiracy and still have suspects left over for red herrings.

In the story, a house in a Manchurian village has burned in the night, killing a three-generation family of eight: Lü Qingyun, his wife, his parents, and his four daughters. Arson is suspected. The main police investigator, sent from a subbureau of Public Security in Shenyang, is Jin Rukang, chief of criminal investigations. His paramilitary title is *xingjingdui duizhang* (head of the criminal brigade). Like Holmes or Poirot, he searches the crime scene for clues, using a magnifying glass to inspect butt ends of beanstalk straw that might have been used to set the fire. He overrules a premature deduction of his own as insufficiently "scientific"—a genuine Cheng Xiaoqing touch (9). Words like "deduction" and "deductive powers" from the old whodunit recur up to the end (29, 53, 65). Since the case is being solved by police instead of a private eye, though, the genre inevitably slides from the P.I. to the police procedural end of the detective formula. A team of eight uniformed policemen is jointly responsible: Jin, Ge Yang (his second in command—his Watson), and six others. Jin assigns them police duties in procedural fashion: preserving the crime scene, probing for clues, photographing the rubble, and sending the best-preserved body, the wife's, back to town for autopsy. The new theme of how overworked Chinese police are is already exemplified in this early story. The city policemen rise in the dead of night and come out to the sticks in jeeps to solve this case. They work hard, they sacrifice. Chief Jin is tall and dark, "steeled" by previous training in the People's Liberation Army (truly the typical origin of ranking policemen). Neither he nor the crime appears particularly political so far; the spell of the classical whodunit survives through the first two chapters.

In the end, the "crime" will turn out to be a political act of sabotage by a counterrevolutionary conspiracy of three men, all of whom have bad class backgrounds and really do hate socialism. So this is not just an entertaining tale in a discourse that transforms criminals into enemies. It is, like any Maoist fiction, "serious" writing to educate the reader to that view—not "popular fiction" at all. Enemies, of course, are best opposed by military strategies.

This is also a topical political novel, exposing how far class enemies will go to destroy the 1956 rural cooperativization movement. That is what motivated the arson-murders here. Cheng Xiaoqing responded to the political "needs" of the time as the party saw them, perhaps even wrote his novel to order. His old-fashioned "bourgeois" whodunit discourse of arson-murder as a crime of passion appears to have been just a red herring, a come-on to lure the reader into what is in the end an orthodox exercise in political education like any other story of the time.

In the second chapter, an overt two-line struggle, so to speak, develops between the incompatible bourgeois and socialist discourses of horrible individual criminal wrongdoing and a higher political reality. Was this an ordinary crime by a "bad element" or an act in a larger scheme of counter-revolution? Or might it have been just an accident? By the fourth chapter there is a list of suspects. Some had personal reasons to kill Lü Qingyun or his family; some had political motivations. But the political discourse is by now winning.

Two aspects of socialist discourse appear from the start, though they potentially conflict and are introduced too subtly to make it clear at first that straight-line class analysis will solve this arson. There is a focus on bureaucratic positions, inevitably hierarchical, and yet also on the power of spontaneous collective action. The first begins the night of the fire. One gets to know the whole village power structure: Zhang Zhishan, village head; Zhu Yingdun, head of the farming cooperative; and Yu Zhengyi, leader of the local production team within the co-op. This focus is not too obtrusive because, living up to their job expectations, these men perform as the chief activists in putting out the fire. The dousing of the fire by the whole village (or most of it) also provides a rousing opening metaphor of rural collectivism, with anxious emergency dialogue in the manner of Gorky's *Mother* and Ding Ling's *Flood*.

Soon one sees the three "chiefs" discussing the crime investigation collectively, taking over the function of Huo Sang and Bao Lang—not a duo now but a threesome, or foursome, once Chief Jin joins them. It is a major modification of the detective and even the procedural genre: Chief Jin will be the hero, but the crime really will be solved collectively by the local leaders and police. The locals represent the masses, without whom police could not function. Each leader will have his role to play, in imitation of the detective hero. But this is not at first apparent. It is natural that the readers should get to know the village before the police arrive, even its power structure. The political imperative that the case be cracked collectively will manifest itself only gradually.

It develops that the two houses in back of the arson site belong to questionable fellows, neither of whom belongs to the co-op. Wang Genfu was rejected for membership by the masses as too selfish and "backward." The other house belongs to Yin Zufu, who has been classified as a rich peasant. Both men have stacks of beanstalk straw out back. Yet the locals are still thinking locally, posing motives of petty gain or revenge. They have not yet put the political pieces together.

It is through Chief Jin that the political discourse becomes overt and emerges as the key to the case. Jin Rukang is a man of science, and yet his advanced appreciation, as a model party member, of the primacy of politics is the real badge of his intellectual superiority. There was a fire here once before, in a beanstalk pile. Jin already begins to suspect a counterrevolutionary conspiracy. The twin authorities of his rank and the privileged discourse of politics he represents reinforce each other, much as Huo Sang's legendary success as a series detective and his scientific discourse reinforced each other in Cheng Xiaoqing's old stories. This largely gives away the ending—one knows the motive for the crime without even knowing whodunit—but Cheng Xiaoqing still manages to leave the whodunit question in suspense.

The Maoist discourse is now explicit. After a Great Detective convention from the old genre—Chief Jin lifts up a finger while opening his eyes wide, this being his "mannerism," so to speak—he states the following "solemnly":

> No, we cannot see the question so simply. Co-op Leader Zhu, you're a Communist Party member, too, so you must realize that although the road we are now traveling is bright, it is not smooth. Certain people are dead set against our taking this path, for if we travel along it, they will have no road for themselves. This is where struggle comes from. Beanstalks are the property of the cooperative, and also of the people. The reason for burning them [referring to the earlier fire, which destroyed some of this collective property] may not be clear yet, but naturally it can't be a simple one. How can you count the damage as simply the loss of the value of the beanstalks? Forgive my saying so, but aren't you a little slow in bringing into play your vigilance as a revolutionary? (15–16)
>
> Yes, this is a life and death struggle! (19)

Because the enemy is so cruel, so cunning and evil, we must prepare well to completely exterminate it! (20)

After these authoritative blasts of Maoist rhetoric, the arson remains to be solved. Suspense is heightened through sightings of slinking figures in the night and new acts of sabotage—part of the burned-down house reerected by the police is mysteriously pulled down again one night. There are also new red herrings suggesting ordinary criminal motives, so that even the "two-line struggle" between the criminal and counterrevolutionary discourses is not wholly ended. Co-op planner Cao Zhaosheng, a Shandongese who drifted into Big Tree Village after the revolution, allows as how he once saw Lü's eldest daughter almost burn the house down in a cooking fire. He also reports a mysterious boat of outsiders docked not far outside of town. (This xenophobic suspicion has credibility when perpetrators are enemies.) Also, physical evidence and logical deductions still hold the stage. The doors and windows were all equally burned, suggesting multiple lightings at each place by an arsonist who wanted to prevent anyone from rushing in to put out the fire, Chief Jin notes. Or the Lüs from escaping, says the production team leader. But now the chief evidences his superior wits in the manner of the older discourse: more likely the former, for the victims must have been dead before the fire was set. They were not heard calling out during the fire, and one of them went to bed with her jacket on.

Cheng Xiaoqing draws out the suspense by using the evidence to seesaw. The autopsy of the wife finds smoke and dust in her windpipe, indicating that she was still breathing during the fire. But that is just one more clue to mislead us. The coroner was careless; Jin, with his superior insight, makes a special trip to Shenyang (a personal sacrifice, Cheng points out, satisfying the new pro-police discourse). He does it to get the job done right (reflecting his own, prerevolutionary discourse of investigative professionalism). The second time, they discover that she was raped and suffered a blow to the head.

While Jin does his duty in Shenyang, the rural leaders "mobilize the masses"; they interview them for intelligence about enemies of the Lüs and any suspicious doings they have seen. This is a populist and also a realistic touch. It is bona fide Maoist police procedure to get the masses to inform on each other.[18]

The result is a list of suspects in the fourth chapter, communicated to

Chief Jin upon his return. The four chiefs weigh each one, in dialogue that in form is not unlike that between Huo Sang and Bao Lang. But in substance, this could also be called a meeting in which the cadres try to understand the political relations among the masses—who hates whom and why.

Suspect One quarreled with Lü for calling him lazy, and he did not help put out the fire. Chief Jin asks his class status and is told he is a poor peasant (i.e., a good guy). So he cannot be guilty.

Yin Zufu, the rich peasant, lost some of his land to the Lüs during Land Reform (redistribution) and quarreled with them over a pot of silver dollars the Lüs dug up on it, evidently hidden by Zufu's father. Chief Jin realizes that the crux is the land, not a few dollars. How much land did he lose to them?, he asks.

Wang Genfu, the other non-co-op member in back of the Lüs, did work hard to put out the fire, but then he did not want it to spread to his place. He had quarreled with both Lü and his wife. There was a cavity in his beanstalk pile, and he was seen furtively trying to fill it in after the arson. At the risk of killing the "suspense," let us identify this peasant as a red herring, the primary false suspect from the start. The real culprit took his kindling from Wang's beanstalk pile to frame him.

Suspect Four is Cao Zhaosheng, the co-op planner from Shandong, whom Lü had castigated, rightly as it turned out, for setting production targets unrealistically high. Cao has volunteered some clues, about the cooking accident and the boatload of strangers, but these seem calculated to throw suspicion off the villagers. Jin asks the most important question again: What is his class status? Finding that he too is a poor peasant, Jin nonetheless keeps probing, and the village leaders join him in noting that Cao is "subjective" and also threatened people to force them to join the cooperative.

Finally there is a villager named Zhou who quarreled with Lü; a cobbler who yelled at Lü for not lending him money; and various people who did not help out at the fire. Other opinions from the masses appear to be rumors started by Cao. Two superstitious souls have concluded that "fox fairies" started the fire. Chief Jin still praises the masses for seeing clearly (39). One wonders whether Cheng Xiaoqing, past advocate of professional, scientific crime fighting, might be poking a little satiric fun not just at superstition but also at Mao's insistence that the masses cannot be wrong.

Now "sightings" by locals have linked (1) the rich peasant Yin Zufu to his cousin Yin Zugui one village over; (2) Yin Zugui to the crime scene; and (3) both men to Cao Zhaosheng. Chief Jin and Village Head Zhang still go to interview Wang Genfu, maintaining the multiplicity of suspects as long as possible. Wang is honest and has good answers for his behavior, and one learns from his wife that Yin Zufu hated the Lüs, and the Wangs too, since they withdrew from a mutual aid team (the collective form preceding the co-ops) because Yin Zufu took advantage of them in it. Yin Zugui also pressured them to stay in; the withdrawal of the Wangs was a big loss of face for both Yins, and it also explains the Wangs' continuing doubts about cooperative production. Thus the solution is Cheng Xiaoqing's favorite "killing of two birds with one stone" paradigm (as in "The Purple Letter"). Yin Zufu simultaneously killed his archenemy Lü Qingyun and pinned it on his other foe, Wang Genfu, by taking the kindling from Wang's beanstalk pile. So Wang is innocent. It would of course be a political mistake on Cheng Xiaoqing's part to choose a genuine poor peasant as his villain.

If the perpetrators are indeed *enemies*—as the discourse, the further sabotage, and the ratiocination of the main party hero all indicate—then one can expect some combat, which is characteristic of the Soviet and Chinese antispy and wiping-out-counterrevolutionaries stories. The four "detectives" divide up into two teams; the glory will be shared. And yet one reason for dividing up is that the old discourse is still strong enough for Chief Jin to want physical evidence to incriminate the enemy before making the arrest. While co-op leader Zhu stands guard, Chief Jin breaks into the Cao house and discovers beneath some straw on the floor (in the dark, by smell) bloodstains that Cao had not managed to wash away.

Cop Ge Yang and village head Wang meanwhile are eavesdropping on a secret meeting of the Yins at Yin Zugui's house in the next village. Cao, the third conspirator invited to the meeting, comes up behind the two officers and is about to do them in. But Chief Jin shoots Cao before he can do his foul deed. Presumably Jin shoots him from behind, but only in the leg, which seems sporting. A struggle ensues, and the village head and Ge Yang just avoid being blinded, if not dispatched (a typical role for the Watson in the old genre), by a deadly hurled teapot that crashes through the window! (Civilians have no guns in this society.) The two guns held by the police do finally "control" the two men. They were planning to poison the village head's water cistern and then the co-op leader's.

The good guys recover gold and silver jewelry stolen from Mrs. Lü and find Yin Zufu's bloody jacket, which he slyly hid by depadding it and wearing it under another jacket. Evidence and spoils in hand, Chief Jin restrains a village crowd from stoning the bad guys, calling for "law, not anarchy" (63), which is about as specific a meaning as the word "law" ever gets in this story.

Then comes the classic recap inherited from the older genre, reconstructing the crime and its motive—in this case, a political operation to overthrow the revolution. Cao was the head conspirator. After working as a cop for the Japanese in Shandong during the war, he fled to the countryside to escape the masses' justice for his evil past. Then he became a co-op administrator to sabotage the cooperatives from within, by setting quotas too high, driving out good people like the Lüs, and generally stirring up dissatisfaction with collectivization. In this he found two allies: Yin Zufu and Yin Zugui, the kulaks. They had engaged in minor sabotage of their own before, like setting straw piles on fire. Yin Zufu is the primary conspirator in the Lü Qingyun arson because he resented losing his land. Just as Chief Jin suspected, the three bad men got hold of Mrs. Lü first, gang-raped her and cracked her skull, dragged her home and beat the other family members to death, then set the fire to cover it up. Chief Jin, in a final reversion to the classical discourse, only regrets that he overlooked the cotton stuffing from Zufu's depadded jacket and did not search Zugui's house for the murder weapon, the blunt instrument used to crack Lü family skulls. We of course wonder why Mrs. Lü's second autopsy did not report semen that might be matched to the blood type of one of the three men.[19] Perhaps that would be divulging classified "information"; or perhaps Cheng feared being unable to maintain the mystery. But there is also a sexist bias. Even after the discovery of rape, no one thought to wonder if Mrs. Lü was the object of the crime.

To one used to Maoist formulas, Cheng Xiaoqing's stretching of this novel in "classic" directions is noteworthy and even courageous. Yet the socialist transformation of Cheng Xiaoqing is extensive. The party discourse seems to be speaking through him. One can picture him having to put the novel through different drafts—having to comply with suggestions to heighten the collective intelligence of the masses here, intensify the political message there, while maintaining suspense—but no, comrade writer, you must not let the bad guys have guns. That would go over the line.

In the end, even Cheng Xiaoqing's "best shot" under communism is not a crime novel, despite his efforts to make it look like one. It is an anti-counterrevolutionary melodrama, a political allegory of good versus evil. The enemy is simply hidden, like guerrillas, and some of its sabotage is so sly and subtle that it might have been mistaken for acts of nature. This is not a whodunit either. The perpetrators are not "least likely suspects" but "most likely" political enemies. There is suspense about their identity and their precise motives (as well as traditional chapter-driven suspense), but the larger class motives are no mystery. Combat, including counteroffensives and a final test of brute force, adds suspense, but the sides are not evenly matched in socialist melodrama, and Cheng Xiaoqing is not expert at writing combat scenes.

The socialist transformation of Cheng Xiaoqing's art is also manifest in style. Narration is not by a Bao Lang figure, but by the anonymous, omniscient, third-person narrator typical of Maoist fiction. Speculation about crimes and criminal motives has shrunk. Sometimes it looks like staged collectivism—affirmative action for alternative ratiocinators. Description still sets the stage, but it too is much diminished, except for the crime scene and gory close-ups of victims (8), evidently permissible during "combat." Characters—plain people all—are briefly described, mostly by a single trait—tall, short, dark. There are stock characters: the hero head cadre who educates others (the detective is, to be sure, no longer very mysterious himself) and the impulsive young revolutionary activist with a heart of gold (Yu Zhengyi). Dialogue is direct, and in short, simple, colloquial sentences. There are carryovers from Cheng Xiaoqing's old style, but the dialect is now the northern Chinese peasant dialect dominant in the communist novel.[20] The locale is Mandarin-speaking Manchuria, but that choice too is typical of the era. Cheng Xiaoqing has also graduated from the short story that was his forte (though he also wrote novellas) to the stand-alone book, though not the epic favored in these times.

The novel of liquidating enemies of the revolution is an epitome of paternalism as profound as the image of Judge Bao. Judge Bao was but one man. The collective security provided by the police and local officials stand for the paternal care of the whole Chinese Communist Party, with its gnostic vision of threats to social order and its promise of permanent solutions. There is, moreover, in *The Bloody Case at Big Tree Village*, a certain savvy about the paternalism of professional police action under Mao. The police, with the help of local leaders, invite the masses to come forward and tell what they know. The cadres sort it all out for them, the case is solved, and the people are "served." Adversarial, even independent action has no point.

1977–83: THE RISE AND FALL OF NEW LITERARY INFLUENCES AND INSTITUTIONS

China had hand-copied thrillers before Mao's death in 1976, but in 1979–80 Chinese authors could openly publish whodunits, penal law melodramas, and serious "literature of introspection," all with themes of contemporary Chinese crime. Private publishing also appeared. It was soon banned, but later it reemerged in tabloids (*xiaobao*). Readers had much catching up do, on banned works both from China's Old Society and from the entire outside world. For the first time in years, crime aficionados could read classic Ming and Qing fiction and cases, modern Western, Japanese, even Soviet detective fiction, and also *Crime and Punishment*, *Resurrection*, and in time, Kafka's *The Trial*. Remarkably, to stem the populace's burgeoning admiration of foreign capitalist societies and their comforts, the authorities in 1980 imported for general distribution the "B" movie *Nightmare in Badham County* (1976; when two UCLA co-eds have car trouble in a southern town, a bad sheriff, helped by his cousin the crooked judge, puts them in a prison camp on trumped-up charges and they experience atrocities). Thousands of Chinese were set to writing essays about the film in their political study classes; many presumed that the brave filmmaker had risked imprisonment for his frankness.[21] So closely do the film's themes resemble those of China's own "literature of introspection" that its "capitalist" atrocities surely suggested socialist analogues. Starlet Deborah Raffin assumed Elizabeth Taylor stature in a subsequent tour of China. *Kramer vs. Kramer*, which "exposed" the shakiness of the American family, also was imported and became a big hit.

That only a few foreign films were imported each year accounts for the disproportionate impact of the two mentioned. Meanwhile fiction was acquiring a new variety and also a mass-society repetitiveness. The number of literary journals mushroomed, but the time was not yet ripe for genre crime magazines. However, crime stories flourished in book form, and when native writing about Chinese crime was quashed again after 1980, foreign works that did not reflect on China took their place and expanded the genre readership even faster. According to the popular author Ye Yonglie, 29 Chinese publishers printed 89 books of foreign mystery fiction in 1981, 20 million copies in all—an average of 225,000 per title. Conan Doyle and Agatha Christie were ubiquitous. In 1980–81, almost 8.5 million volumes of Sherlock Holmes tales saw print, as well as 32 Agatha Christie titles in 8.2 million copies. That surpassed all the books by Maxim Gorky (20 titles, 2.45 million copies) printed in China since 1949. Of the foreign mysteries printed in 1981, 25 titles, in 6.72 million volumes, were published by the Masses' Press, whose total 1981 fiction and nonfiction list was 110 titles in 14.57 million volumes. This arm of the MPS had published only 33 foreign mysteries during the first 30 years of communism (1949–79; 1.317 million copies).[22]

Nonfiction also revived. In 1979, the year the Ministry of Justice was reestablished, professional law journals were founded, as was *Democracy and Legal System*, a monthly that provided popular entertainment and pointed out judicial errors in cases.[23] Meantime Liu Binyan and others exposed high crimes in reportage. It was not a new genre, but Liu Binyan restored to it real investigative journalism. The new publishing venues survived, but controversial works and authors were soon suppressed again.

Also in 1979 nearly every province founded (or declassified) its own legal system gazette (*fazhibao*). Many had literature columns. It was little noticed at the time, but the concept of *fazhi wenxue* or "legal system literature" was born about 1980. In 1981, MPS cadre Wei Jun organized a conference on it and also founded the Beijing Association for the Study of Legal System Literature. His story "Xin sheng" (Heartfelt wishes; 1981), about a female surgeon who operates to save the life of a hoodlum who once tried to rape her, won national fame as a representative work in the new genre.[24]

In 1980 the Masses' Press founded a literary crime and law enforcement journal called *Zhuomuniao* (Woodpecker). Cong Weixi, Liu Xinwu, Wang Yaping, and Li Wenda contributed to it. This prototype of a literary genre crime magazine did not use the term "legal system literature"; Wei Jun was almost alone in that. Indeed the magazine was terminated after two issues, and the legal system literature concept also expired. Both became viable again only in 1984. "Heartfelt Wishes" itself was criticized in 1982, for alleged "unhealthy" sex and violence and for letting the criminal have a change of heart without suffering punishment by "law"—which was still expected to be harsh and unmerciful.[25]

And yet a new force was alive, now that the morale of the Public Security was being rebuilt. Not just literary police cadres like Wei Jun, but also ordinary beat cops and detectives wanted to tell their "biggest cases" to the public. One result was *Jiekai shizong de mimi* (Uncovering the mystery of the missing person; 1980), in which Changsha cops collaborated with authors in a format not too different from the old 1950s "police" fiction. But here the malefactors are not political enemies but criminals—"bad people." The cases are framed as moral cautionary tales not unlike those in the later Jiangxi casebook *Crime and the Law* (1985) or indeed *The Newgate Calendar* (1773). "It's true," ends one Changsha tale, "crime does not pay. The people's dictatorship is omnipotent."[26]

However, the old Maoist paradigm of alternating freedom and repression was far from dead. Yu Haocheng, head of the Masses' Press, says his journal *Woodpecker* was done in by its link to the still illicit concept of "literature of the wounded," which he obliquely suggested himself in an afterword to the premier issue. Yu also coined the term "woodpecker literature" (pecking at social problems) as the antithesis of "parrot literature" (parroting slogans and party lines). The "wounded" slogan was legitimated only in 1984, by which time it was long passé. Most works considered to be in its category had not fared as badly as the name of the category itself. However, some legal cases that *Woodpecker* printed were in fact judged later to be too "sensitive"—though informants now remember the early issues as rather dull.[27]

"Literature of introspection," more daring than "literature of the wounded," faced stiffer condemnation. In the keynote speech at a January– February 1980 conference on playwriting, Party Secretary-General Hu Yaobang criticized Sha Yexin, Li Shoucheng, and Yao Mingde's play *Jiaru wo shi zhende* (What if I really were?) and two film scenarios, Wang Jing's *Zai shehui de dang'an li* (In the archive of society) and Li Kewei's *Nü zei* (The girl thief).[28] They remain banned today. It was not just literary works that suffered, but their forward momentum: the promise of more penetrating works in future, until no taboos were left. A Mao-style campaign of overkill against an exemplary negative work, Bai Hua's screenplay *Kulian* (Unrequited love), descended in April 1981. Finally came the attack on "spiritual pollution" in October 1983. Certain literary periodicals were suspended, closed down, or reorganized, and certain authors could not publish. One was Zhang Xinxin. Her response was to go slumming—ironically, to write a detective novel, to prove that she was *not* divorced from the masses—though hers was a modernist antidetective novel, and avant-gardism was also under attack.[29] Bourgeois "Western" violence as a whole was out of favor. Even science fiction was said to abet violence, sex, and belief in ghosts, and covertly to criticize socialism through utopianism.[30] China's new whodunits and penal law melodramas, already withering in 1981, looked unrevivable.

Meantime, a "strike hard" (*yanda*) campaign against crime in August 1983 had revived the old campaign style of law enforcement. There were frenzied mass arrests to fill quotas, followed by public executions in stadiums. Law and literature were linked: hard-liners said that writers increased the crime rate by "spreading doubts about socialism through their works and confusing the 'thought' of young people."[31]

Aware by 1984 that even his economic modernization reforms might be undone, Deng Xiaoping intervened on the opposite side again and progressives once more took heart. *Woodpecker* and legal system literature were quickly reborn. The reform thrust of Deng's new politics would in fact outlast his direct political crackdowns. After 1983, China experimented with making the arts self-sufficient, and then the urban economy as a whole, including finally even the practice of law. This set the stage for the reconceptualization of both law and literature (writing and lawyering) as private enterprises, and the stratification of writing about crime into the commercially popular and the "serious." Mainstream literature by famous authors was no longer best-selling—indeed, it was headed in commercially unpopular, avant-garde directions that hastened literary stratification.

In the early 1980s, publication was still easily controlled by quotas on paper and circulation and by distribution through state-owned bookstores and post offices. Local periodicals, which printed many of China's whodunits and melodramas, could not be exported. In 1984, when publishers and authors had to earn their pay, many of them went slumming. Tabloid publication also exploded, creating a subliterary "basement" until a spring 1985 crackdown. Even the great writers' conference of December 1984–January 1985, known for its liberalism, decried the tabloids.[32] The fiction of the future would be stratified by the market.

Notable Works: Literature of Introspection as Crime Fiction

Let us consider two famous works of "introspection," namely the two film scenarios singled out for attack in the 1980 conference on playwriting. The first, *In the Archive of Society*, is all too serious and was considered literature, and yet in style this easy-to-read piece resembles popular fiction. It may be called crime fiction, for it trades in multiple crimes, suspenseful revelations, self-conscious detection, sensational exposures of injustice, and hoodlum characters. It even has a "noir" sense of anomie.

The victim is a young and pretty army nurse named Li Lifang. In 1970, during the Cultural Revolution, she is raped by a marshal in the PLA at the seaside resort hospital for high military cadres where she nurses him. The man's younger son rapes her in his turn. Recovering from attempted suicide, she goes home to work in the same factory that her father works in. He persuades her to marry a much older medical doctor, who on their wedding night discovers that she is not a virgin and expels her. Suffering from factory gossip that he is a peddler of "damaged goods," Li's father in a drunken fury whips her. Leaving home and work for life on the street, Li Lifang becomes the moll of three hoodlums. Accosted one day by another, older son of the marshal who raped her, a good person with whom she had had a genuine summer seaside romance just months before her defilement, she spurns him and asks her new male cronies to "teach him a lesson." There is a knife battle and the hoodlums go too far. After lying wounded in the hospital for days, Wang Hainan, the good son, dies. Li Lifang finally admits the nature of his father's crimes against her, but she is sent to prison for "instigating murder" of the son, while the marshal goes free.

That is not the plot in its own order. The story as written begins with a dejected Wang Hainan sneaking across China's southern border. That was a crime even in 1970, when Vietnam was a fraternal communist country. In 1979 retrospect, with Vietnam an enemy, this scene provides a red herring suggesting that the film may be "anti-spy," which it is not. Taken to military headquarters, the boy is inexplicably released—so high in the military is his father, one infers. After further cinematic cuts one sees the same young man in the hospital, critically wounded, while Li Lifang and her three companions are held as suspects. That they committed the crime is confirmed only at the end, when the fight is dramatized in a hoodlum's flashback while he is being interrogated. Exactly how Li Lifang gave up on herself is also revealed gradually and by insinuation, as the police question her family and friends one by one. Episodes from Wang Hainan's diary are gradually dramatized too, filling in a narrative of Li Lifang's travails and ending in her "confession," which finally pulls away the veil of mystery about what happened in the army resort hospital.

This is a "popular" plot—sensational, sentimental, and with a love interest—the romance gone wrong of Li Lifang and Wang Hainan, the marshal's good son. The very mention of rape, let alone by a leader, was sensational in 1979, and the scenario calls for a shot of a male body bearing down upon the hapless girl. The audience is also treated to scenes of a hoodlum gang speaking their "black argot" (*heihua*); the three men fighting over Li Lifang; the girl being roughed up and slashed with a knife by the leader; a theft by the gang and an armed clash with another gang; Li Lifang's self-mutilation with a cleaver in lieu of submitting to mutilation by her man as punishment for her having kept him from molesting her younger sister; and the final violence that leaves Wang Hainan fatally wounded. There are also Li's drunken father's beatings of her after her return home from the unconsummated marriage. Once Li Lifang joins the hoodlums, her father takes to locking up her younger sister in their factory apartment just to keep her out of danger. And the hoodlum who finally confesses plays at being a raging madman before he submits to the state. All this leaves an impression of urban depravity, except that the sympathetic victim is a female martyr instead of the usual trapped male spiraling down into a noir world. This is the very scenario raised by the Jiangxi casebook *Crime and the Law*, about the gang moll Rotten Orange.

Other elements of popular appeal include good old-fashioned, indeed socialist, heroism; traditional fated coincidence; and a wicked stepmother. The good son, Wang Hainan, hates his father; as a Red Guard, he almost got his father into trouble by denouncing him—for just cause. Hainan had divided emotions because his mother, a high school principal, was locked up at school and tyrannized by bullying Red Guards (all of which is dramatized); he identified with her as a victim rather than with his father, who could do any wrong with impunity. That included divorcing his wife and leaving her to the mercies of the leftists while he married a younger woman. It was also a kind school principal who helped get Li Lifang into an army song-and-dance troupe, through audition. In fact, Li's benefactor *was* Wang Hainan's mother. (Wang preferred to take his mother's name rather than his father's.) That Li Lifang was assigned to be a mere nurse was the first betrayal of her by the PLA. The marshal's bad younger son is of course the progeny of the bad stepmother. But to return to the socialist heroism: Wang Hainan reconciled with his father—came to see him in the hospital in 1969, where he met and fell in love with his as yet undefiled nurse—only because he wanted to join the army, to fight the Russians after the Zhenbao / Damansky Island border clash. Disillusioned by the Cultural Revolution, his father's class privilege, and his own mixed class origins, he lives only to sacrifice—to seek a war where he can lay down his life. Clausewitz and Che Guevara's diary are his inspiration. When his father gets him a medical internship instead of a frontline assignment, the boy refuses it and goes north to join a militia brigade. There, after a baffling letter from Li Lifang breaks off their friendship (in the wake of her rape, which has made her unfit for marriage to any man, let alone an idealist), he renounces his chaotic motherland and, with Che's diary, goes to join the guerrillas of "a communist country to the south." He is arrested four times trying to cross the border and released four times on the say-so of his father. Li Lifang for her part is run in four times by Public Security for minor offenses.

Yet these martyrs occasioning "introspection" are not the characters with the most time on screen; that honor goes to a Public Security Bureau detective, Shang Qi. Like any police hero in the new whodunits, he is middle-aged, tired from overwork, and a chain-smoker, and he has a poker face. He also has the standard young-man sidekick who follows him everywhere. Shang is indeed a professional genre *detective*. By his superior powers of observation, he notes straight off the significance of a scar on Li Lifang's head, the result of a wound inflicted by the marshal during the rape; it is different from the knife scars left by Li's sadistic hoodlum boyfriend "protector" on the rest of her body. The main style of investigation, though, is police procedural, notably the systematic interviewing of subjects by which the two detectives knit the disparate pieces of the puzzle into a plot.

Shang Qi's allegiance to his own branch of service is key. An "army representative" is stationed in his office during this stage of the Cultural Revolution, when the PLA was charged with supervising the rehabilitation of old cadres and institutions. The army man leaps to condemn Li Lifang as the primary criminal under orders telephoned in by the marshal who raped her. Detective Shang Qi answers the PLA's class-struggle political discourse with a counterpoint of professional discourse. Impassively reciting the number of stab wounds on Wang Hainan's body and the three kinds of weapon, he concludes that Li's cleaver was not a murder weapon.

The setting during the ancien régime, which technically gives the film scenario political "cover" from charges that it is attacking the current regime, allows a maximal attack on army tyranny. The PLA man gives Shang Qi orders: a time limit for his investigation, during which he must prefer a predetermined charge and a directive to find the crime's motive in politics. Soon the army man threatens the good cop. This touch well reflects post-Mao police resentment of the continuing hegemony of the army over them and the PLA's greater social prestige.

Shang Qi also uses a common device of the penal law melodramas to assert the superiority of the police over the PLA; he reminds the PLA "representative" that so long as the procuracy remains disestablished, Public Security must observe legal procedures in its stead. Later, and more remarkably, he borrows a device from the alternative "detective story" genre, if not Agatha Christie's own playbook, by suspensefully gathering all of Li Lifang's relatives and acquaintances together in one room at the end of the story for a dramatic denouement.

But there is a twist that differentiates *In the Archive of Society* from generic crime writing and allows it to lay claim to a "higher," more serious—and abstract—critical commentary than the penal law melodramas. It quests not for whodunit but for the social origins of crime. This is quite a "model" theme. Instead of exposing a criminal, Shang Qi goes around the room accusing one person after another of having caused Li Lifang's behavior through the "social effects" of their negligence. He even begins, quite ungenerically, with an obvious victim and good person: principal Wang. She taught young people like Li Lifang only the good ideals of society, not the dark side, leaving young people unprepared to deal with darkness. Li's father beat her. And the doctor, overwhelmed by old-fashioned views on chastity, spurned her. This is all criticism of the system and of the culture. Then Shang glares at the marshal's younger son, the second rapist, now in PLA uniform himself and come to represent the interests of the rapists, and then at his own PLA "representative." He ends by speaking of the guilt of his own kind, for having allowed themselves and their public security mission to be shunted aside in the late leftist rebellion.

Though Li Lifang tells of her rape for the first time before the assembled witnesses, in a denouement typical of a genre crime story, it is she who is subsequently arrested, on Shang Qi's order. Then the PLA bursts into the room to arrest Shang Qi, evidently for allowing the girl to speak. Before he is arrested, Shang Qi performs an act of resignation that is hardly heroic. He asks that the record of his successful interrogation of Li Lifang be destroyed. "Destruction is the only possible fate for these materials," he tells his subordinate. "But all crimes are written in the archive of society and registered in the minds of the victims. Those cannot be destroyed!" (180). This voices a lack of confidence in both law and literature. The doctor protests that Shang's resignation to fate will prevent justice for the real criminal, the marshal. Shang Qi simply throws the responsibility back on society: "This is a question for you to answer, all of you!" (181).

The time is the Cultural Revolution, but the original and secondary crimes by the PLA are not peculiar to the times. A happy ending may not be possible under the current system. It leaves the reader in a state of doubt, indeed of "introspection," and this was intolerable to the Communist Party and state.

There are several conclusions. Corruption is pervasive; no sphere of life is untouched, not even the factory, where young men play poker instead of working. Young people have no hope for the future. Intellectuals are imprisoned. Workers are beset by civil war. Peasants die of famine. Even the privileged live meaningless lives. These indictments are more thorough than in genre fiction (168).

Worse, if justice is in principle unattainable even after the Cultural Revolution is over, other social flaws cannot be rectified—not cadre privilege, lack of respect for morality and proper procedure, or hypocrisy toward workers. Wang Hainan offers an ugly new conceptualization of his father's class as "a new kind of parasite" (167). And Li Lifang, asked to identify her rapists, lifts the crime onto an abstract plane: " 'It was him, it was them!' She pointed her hand upwards" (180).

Finally, this piece of "introspective" literature achieves seriousness through its symbolic reverberations. The scar on Li Lifang's head, Wang Hainan's ideal of war and glorious sacrifice, the ideals of Che Guevara—all lend layered meanings to the plot that go beyond the solution of the crimes at issue, the age, even the system. They speak to positive ideals. Crime itself is but the occasion. The focus is on something bigger: the political situation in which the law is enmeshed.

In stomping on *The Girl Thief,* the party dealt a blow to a more humorous and satiric kind of "literature of introspection." The second half of this film scenario capitulates to saccharine visions of criminals being shepherded back onto the path of goodness by education, understanding, reversal of wrong Cultural Revolution verdicts, and even a sympathetic lover (here, a judge's son). The text went through two rewrites in 1979; perhaps the ending became rosier in each revision, until finally it was innocuous enough to publish. The first half remains a picaresque comedy in which the girl thief, Blondie, is a sympathetic figure, and a municipal chief of public security, Chen Yitan, is the goat.

The first scene is the best. The chief uses kungfu to overcome a hoodlum gang that is riding a train without tickets and raising a ruckus. Meantime the girl thief, a gang member, picks his pocket so that when the others finally have to pay their fares they do so with the cop's money. Later she succeeds in breaking into the chief's house at night to return his stolen wallet, with a taunt and a present of "cakes" (of horse manure). She also breaks into the warehouse of a restaurant run by the cop's wife. He gives pursuit, but Blondie makes him look like a Keystone Kop. She is almost nabbed at a trade fair by a stakeout using multitudes of plainclothesmen, yet she outruns a jeep by fleeing on a horse stolen from the animal market; and so on. Even Chief Chen has to give her credit and accept a few jokes at his expense, making him perhaps the only cop with a sense of humor in his time. This is not "literature to make you think," but literature to make you laugh—with the hoodlums at the expense of the police. It keeps faith with "literature of introspection" by its creed that anything may be written. It is surely popular entertainment, with kungfu, crime scenes, chases, and hoodlums insulting cops in racy "black argot." With its celebration of hoodlum antics, *The Girl Thief* is in spirit the very antithesis of the later legal system literature. Some might call it anti–legal system literature, a way station between Sun Liaohong and Wang Shuo.

China's Serious Fiction Becomes Simultaneously More Serious and More Popular

The Mao era, in its liberal periods, tolerated weak semblances of crime fiction formulas, though the depiction of crime, indeed the *idea* of crime, was nearly banished. In 1979–80, fiction with crime themes was already di-

viding into what later would be recognized as "serious" and generic "popular" forms, though genre publishing, indeed the *idea* of "popular" literature,
remained banished. "Literature of introspection" was socially respected and
critically acclaimed high literature. Far "lower" were whodunits like those
analyzed in Chapter One, a new popular crime fiction that existed before the
name. The penal law melodramas were in between. Though they were as formulaic as whodunits and far more sentimental, Chinese critics proudly
ranked them above the allegedly more "escapist" whodunits. The law melodramas were "*our* [Chinese] detective stories," or "our *real* detective stories,"
since they not only raised visions of Bao rather than Holmes but assailed corruption as well[33]—even if it was still better and more courageous to bell the
cat without any concessions to popular taste.

Under communist dicta that lasted until the mid-1980s, in name all
Chinese fiction remained "serious" and nongeneric. The most simpleminded
mysteries, like love stories—another popular genre that ranged from the sentimental to the "engaged" (their fight was for romantic and finally sexual liberation)—appeared in putatively "high" literary journals, though typically in
the less prestigious local ones badly needing copy and readers. Journals devoted to genre fiction did not exist, except for the quickly aborted
Woodpecker. Genre designations were not printed in literary journals, except
for screenplay, opera, and the like.[34] Unofficially and in speech, one referred
to whodunits as "detective" (*zhentan*, the old term), "[criminal] investigative" (*[xingshi] zhencha*), "case-cracking" (*zhenpo*), "deductive" (*tuili*; after
Japanese usage), or "suspense" (*jingxian*) fiction. It was hard to know what
to call the works that this book has styled "penal law melodramas." In 1979,
names like "stories about upright officials" (*qingguan xiaoshuo*, or *gushi*) and
"law case (*anyu*) fiction" sounded "feudal." "Police fiction" and "crime
fiction" were still impolitic. The concept of legal system literature was
aborning, but as Wei Jun discovered, it sounded just too liberal.

Science fiction (*kehuan xiaoshuo*) was the exception, the popular genre
that was rehabilitated (in 1978) and officially named. It had several advan-
tages: an educational mission (science was one of the Four Modernizations),
a tendency to "look toward the future" instead of at past mistakes, authors
who were scientists, a target propaganda audience of young people, and a
precedent as a genre in the USSR and 1950s China itself.[35]

Yet popular crime fiction did exist, and even the more serious "introspective" fiction did not always "rise above" cop formulas or even Maoist formulas. It must have dawned on some writers that all their fiction—the generic, the Maoist, even the dissident—might be "popular" in a derogatory sense. Thirty years of Maoism had simplified and homogenized Chinese fiction's vocabulary, syntax, characterization, and subject matter. It was Mao who asked for peasants to write poetry, but the problem of pabulum was more pronounced after his death, when hundreds of new journals struggled to fill their columns with literary copy. The majority of works naturally appeared mediocre. In this context, works with "popular" Western touches like cops and robbers appeared fresh. It was not easy for cynosures of Maoist fiction such as Liu Shaotang and Hao Ran to adapt their literary skills to the new market era, but those two ultimately did.[36]

The public now wanted fiction that was both more popular (thrilling) and more serious (full of biting social themes). They did not always prefer the plainest Chinese, but often a more decorated prose with aphorisms, dialect, even clever four-character phrases adapted from the classical language in the manner of Gao Xiaosheng, Lu Wenfu, and Wang Zengqi. "Literature of introspection" sought popularity of that sort. It availed itself not just of the North China dialect used in Maoist fiction, but dialect from other regions, supplemented with humorous expressions from comic dialogues (*xiangsheng*), topical jokes, inversions of official slogans popular on the grapevine, rhetorical questions from the "storyteller," and aphorisms in classical syntax. Works with crime themes added street talk and hoodlum cant.

Another way that post-Mao literature became simultaneously more "popular" and more "serious" was by summoning up classics of the Ming and Qing. The new fiction featured characters, heroism, and friendships with a traditional flavor. Already in the "literature of the wounded," in Kong Jiesheng's "Yinyuan" (Marriage; 1978), a hero is nicknamed "Bao Qingtian" (7). The hero of Jiang Zilong's "Qiao Changzhang shangren ji" (Manager Qiao assumes his post) has the stern, uncompromising—indeed, heavy-handed—punishing ways of Judge Bao, though his "yamen" is a factory floor. He serves his bureau chief, Huo Dadao (Huo of the Great Way) as the Song prefect served his sovereign. At the end of the story, Jiang makes his ideal explicit, by having his hero sing Peking opera lyrics about "Bao Longtu, sitting in contemplation at Kaifeng fu" (72). Wang Hainan, the good son of *In the Archive of Society*, is tagged as Jia Baoyu (163). Liu Ke's "Feitian" (Angel

[Buddhist; lit., "Apsaras"]) mentions Lu Zhishen, the humorous "rough monk" of *Water Margin*, and calls him a knight-errant who can set things right for the oppressed—a claim that is incongruous, considering how unpardonable the crimes are in the modern story (136). The "girl thief's" mother is a Chinese opera singer. These characters nominally associated with tradition evoke not religious faith but marvelous traditional plot lines.[37]

Old-style episodic and picaresque plots reappeared, as in the first half of *The Girl Thief*, Gao Xiaosheng's "Li Shunda Builds a House," You Fengwei's "Qingshui yamen" (Clear water yamen), and a Jiang Zilong sequel called "Qiao Changzhang hou zhuan" (Supplementary biography for manager Qiao). The last piece's coverage of multitudinous bureaucratic ills in quick succession recalls muckraking novels of the late Qing. It manages to satirize the iron rice bowl, sloppy purchasing from collective funds, sabotage of a rival enterprise by blocking it from above through concurrent posts, misappropriation of enterprise property and cover-ups, gossiping, factionalism, special privileges, backdoor deals, foreign junketing, unreliable transportation (being blackmailed into financing a railroad's reconstruction to get it to ship your goods), long queues to buy goods, featherbedding and malingering, even bad institutional food. But it is in the original story, "Manager Qiao Assumes His Post," that Qiao appears as a Liu Bei defending himself from rival kingdoms with the help of a personal "strategist," a Zhuge Liang. A Lord Bao savior reappears also in the person of the preternaturally impassive Shang Qi of *In the Archive of Society*, and even as the newsman of "Clear Water Yamen," who resorts to stratagems to uncover a story of monumental corruption. For a traditional sense of the inescapability of fate, there is "Angel." Many stories further abandoned old realist and socialist realist conventions by opening with an old-style preface or "wedge." Some pieces had synopses of a character's life story upon his or her entrance. Modernist devices were few, except in stories by Wang Meng.

"Literature of introspection," silenced in persecutions of 1980–81, prepared the way for a Chinese fiction more serious than ever before, with the writer as a self-motivated, adversarial conscience of society as in the May Fourth era. Yet this was a more "popular" fiction than May Fourth fiction, in form and in the size of its readership. After 1984, popular and serious writing would be more differentiated. China's culture bureaucrats, including police littérateurs, saw it as their mission to put the two back together in a legal system literature. It would be less dissident than "introspective" fiction, but it would also encourage citizens (not writers) to act as adversaries—not to overthrow party rule but to found what would turn out to be a new adversary system. Moreover, the new works would find themselves positioned between a real, down-and-dirty tabloid fiction below, and an avant-garde literature unmistakably above them.

A Bridge Between Thaws and Genres:
The Detective Stories of Ye Yonglie

In the less favorable atmosphere for crime fiction between 1980 and 1984, the popular science writer Ye Yonglie loomed very large. Favored with an MPS contract to create a "suspenseful science fiction" police series, the prolific Ye almost single-handedly bridged two thaws, two genres (science fiction [SF], which was legitimate, and detective fiction, which was not yet), and two groups (officials and readers). The result was the first official Chinese detective fiction apparently willing to follow reader taste as low as it went. The MPS found itself in control of a whole subgenre of popular, perhaps young-adult reading matter. The cost to art and science was high, but then the MPS was suppressing the competition.

Like many a Chinese author, Ye Yonglie (b. 1940 in Wenzhou) was a precocious literary youth who had dreamed of becoming a great littérateur ever since a newspaper published his childhood poems. But he entered Beijing University as a chemistry major in 1957 and graduated a scientist in 1963. Meantime he discovered his calling: popular science writing. It began in the Great Leap Forward, when his class went down to Hunan to assist in smelting steel. Ye Yonglie's science essays were published locally and in Beijing. By 1960 he had a book, *Tan de yi jia* (The carbon family), and was principal author of the giant children's (and peasants') encyclopedia of basic and popular science, *Shiwan ge wei shenme* (A hundred thousand questions and answers). In a day when even literature was subject to "making it universal," popular science writing was truly elementary, though also read in newspapers by newly literate adults. Ye's output was genuine mass culture. By 1989 he took credit for 2,500 newspaper and magazine articles and 120 books, and for directing more than twenty films.[38]

In 1978 science fiction was rehabilitated, with youth as its target audience and "popularization" of scientific knowledge ("making it universal") as its mission, as in the 1950s. Adapting his skills to fiction, Ye was soon cranking out SF best-sellers alongside old hands like Zheng Wenguang and Tong Enzheng. Then he won a huge readership for a new subgenre, "suspenseful science fiction," which combined SF with mystery and counterespionage formulas. Its simple patriotic theme of future Chinese technical superiority and foreign envy of it was already established in Chinese SF.[39] Ye's 1979 story, "Shenmi yi" (Mystery clothes), exemplifies the new hybrid. As in most Chinese SF, the impact of science on the imagined new society and its technology is perfunctory—robots here and laser guns there; SF brings China up to world modernization standards without altering the old political standoff between the PRC, KMT, and USSR. The poverty of imagination about new science and technology is offset only by visions of a new world of, by, and for scientists.[40]

Thus in "Mystery Clothes," an Overseas Chinese scientist on a tropical island invents a chameleon suit that makes its wearer invisible and able to scale walls with suction devices. Though he developed it in the interest of observing wildlife, the potential misapplications of invisibility attract both a greedy Chinese loyal to the KMT and spies from a familiar unnamed country where people speak Russian. The "white" foreigners imprison the scientist and his suit in their embassy (in the tropics; they could get away with no such thing on Chinese soil), but he escapes through the suit's secret aviation and submarine capabilities, which allow him to fly to the PRC, on which he had always intended to bestow the suit as a gift.

This is simply an "anti-spy" story without police. Here the scientist saves himself, indeed solves the "case," as in China's "pure" SF formula. Ye Yonglie's contribution to the latter is anti-spy and whodunit themes, for as the story opens the scientist ponders the murder of his pro-KMT rival, who first stole his chameleon suit. The foreigners murdered him to get the suit for their own purposes of world domination.

"Suspenseful SF" was first named in Chinese as a subgenre in March 1979, says Ye.[41] Soon it was identified with him, and he took most of the heat for it when self-appointed guardians of SF in time launched attacks.[42] "Science fiction mysteries" have been a known quantity internationally since the 1950s, thanks to Isaac Asimov. He too saw detectives and scientists as fellow spirits driven to probe "mysteries" analytically. Asimov moreover con-

cluded that good "SF mystery" fiction must meld SF with the classical detective formula. But the latter required "fair play," whereas SF writers were
forever expanding technology and knowable reality itself. The trick was,
"You *don't* spring new devices on the reader and solve the mystery with
them. You *don't* take advantage of future history to introduce ad hoc phenomena. In fact, you carefully explain all facets of the future background
well in advance so the reader may have a decent chance to see the solution."[43]
Ye Yonglie, however, did not master the technique of the whodunit before
proceeding with hybrids; wrapping up his plots with ad hoc technological
advances is his weakness. Add to that the genre's puerile patriotic mandate
and the burden of resorting to made-up science to keep real science and real
police procedure secret, and one can appreciate the handicaps he labored
under. But readers were still undiscriminating. Ye's new subgenre attracted
hundreds of thousands in 1979, most of them young.[44]

His appeal caught the eye of the MPS. The ministry contracted with Ye
Yonglie to produce a five-book series to channel the SF interests of his mass
youth following into a *police* SF.[45] Jin Ming, "the scientific Sherlock
Holmes," was the series sleuth: chief of detectives of the Public Security
Bureau in Coastal City, a vision of Shanghai after a successful and prosper-
ous modernization.[46]

SF, post-Mao China's first legitimate popular genre, thus paved the way
for popular detective stories. In Ye Yonglie's hands, it was a genre too "popular" in grade level for many adults, but it was armed with "police protection" and thus able to weather political storms. However, when Ye decided
to make his social commentary a little more trenchant in *Hei ying* (The black
shadow), that Jin Ming novella drew fire at the Masses' Press and they
dropped it. It was however printed by the Beijing Geological Press; Ye's science connections had their uses.[47] By then (1981) he was publishing detection, SF, science popularization, history of science, and children's science in
local literary and science popularization journals from Liaoning to
Guangdong. In 1981, serial installments of Jin Ming stories in the million-
reader newspapers *Wenhui bao* of Shanghai and *Yangcheng wanbao* of
Guangzhou kept his name before readers for months on end. The four Jin
Ming books from the MPS carried Ye's subgenre into the difficult year of
1983.[48] There were also comic book adaptations, of which 7 million copies
were printed.[49]

Ye's shift to the police genre was opportune, for reader interest in "pure" science fiction was crashing. Growing sophistication and differentiation of taste may have been among the causes; the reasons Ye himself later suggested prophesy the fears that crime writers faced when their genre achieved official backing: withdrawal of government support; attacks on fictional works' realism by relevant professionals (for SF, by scientists; for crime fiction, by police); the failure of genre writing to gain status as real literature; weaknesses in the writing; and excessive political interference (SF was attacked in 1983).[50]

Putting police back into anti-spy stories to share the scientist heroes' glory was hardly original, but a Conan Doyle–type *detective* like Jin Ming gave official Chinese police fiction an energy it had lacked since the 1950s. Chinese SF was weak in technical imagination, and detection could make up for that. Ye's new subgenre was really "detective science fiction" or "science fiction of deduction," he admitted.[51] As in the 1950s, *crime* remained the odd element out. Ye Yonglie's mission was to see that police censorship did not throw out all the science too.

Contradictions and compromises abound in all three elements of Jin Ming's crime-story appeal: the hero, plots, and "information dividend." A fourth element peculiar to SF—an original romantic vision of a better future with a few surprises—was clearly dead on arrival.

The hero Jin Ming at first suggests anything but compromise. He is perfect—ideal for police ministry propaganda. But different kinds of perfection can work at cross purposes and defeat suspense. And why must the police be so perfect?, the reader asks. Because they are not?

Yet Jin Ming himself was the main attraction for many readers. They found his character inspiring, perhaps because it was so unexpected in a policeman.[52] It was of course fatuous to call Ye, writing sometimes at a junior high school level, a Chinese Conan Doyle (as some did), but he claimed the English author as his main inspiration, and clearly he was. The first Chinese Holmes, Huo Sang, remained eradicated from public memory until reprintings in 1986. The other books Ye cited as inspirations indicate the foreign mystery fiction (besides Holmes tales) available in Chinese at the end of 1979: Christie's *Death on the Nile* and *Murder on the Orient Express*, Wilkie Collins's *The Moonstone*, and Ellery Queen's *The Greek Coffin Mystery*.[53] Other meldings of scientist and detective, like Dr. John Thorndyke, R.

Austin Freeman's hero, were known to Cheng Xiaoqing's generation but not to Ye Yonglie's.

Ye Yonglie says he coined the name Jin Ming after *jingming* (shrewd, astute) and China's sage strategist of the ancient Three Kingdoms era, Zhuge Liang, or Zhuge Kong*ming*. "The Zhuge Policeman" is one of Jin Ming's nicknames. The name of his sidekick, Ge Liang, is also written with characters homophonous with Zhu*ge Liang*.[54] "Literature of introspection" had the same kind of allusions. Ge Liang is neither as equal to Jin Ming as Watson is to Holmes or Bao Lang to Huo Sang—nor as clumsy a coadjutor.[55] The hierarchical relationship between the detectives is like that in the whodunits with the "Chinese characteristics" of Chapter One.

"The Case of the Murdering Umbrella," the leadoff story in Ye's Masses's Press series, is the *Study in Scarlet* that introduces Jin Ming and his talents. Instead of a Dr. Watson or a Bao Lang, the impersonal, omniscient, third-person narrator conventional in China's socialist fiction narrates Ye's stories.

Not to put too fine a point on it, Jin Ming is just as intelligent, observant, scientific, clever, well-read, and up to date as Holmes, but even more talented and also less eccentric and better rounded (socially, as in his waltzing with the ladies; he is not a "rounded character").[56] The scientific analytic pursuits Jin Ming loves are pure, though derivative of Holmes's. Both heroes have science labs in their apartments and extensive libraries (Jin's is stored in miniaturized forms, via SF). Though he repeatedly says "elementary" in generic "preambles," Jin Ming is the more mature personality, never impolite, gruff, ironical, or patronizing. He is, after all, a communist cadre who must always serve the people, not be eccentric. In his forties, muscular but of average height, a little dusky, and slow in speech, he is above all experienced at his work (reflecting a professional police rather than the Conan Doyle ethos) and, thanks more to training than to genetics, "of acute senses and quick in his actions." Like Holmes and Judge Bao, he is serious, with a brow furrowed from frowning during ratiocination. More like a classical detective than a propagandizing 1950s socialist cop, Jin Ming speaks sparingly. His words are the more treasured.[57]

Watson rates Holmes's literary knowledge as "nil," whereas Jin Ming is at home in literature, the arts, and history. People call him "Dr. Policeman" and "the Ph.D. of policedom." He plays the violin and the *erhu* (two-stringed viol), this being a patriotic genre; indeed, his hobbies suggest leisure: the flute, mouth organ, poetry recitation, chess, swimming, soccer, figure skating, horseback riding, archery, photography, photo development, repair of electronics, and so forth. He is fluent in English, Russian, French, and Japanese. Holmes's knowledge of politics was "feeble"; Jin Ming likewise shows no interest or inclination in that direction!

Jin Ming's humanism and cosmopolitanism are so developed as to contradict old communist values. Fluency in the aforementioned foreign languages would have got a cop in trouble during the Cultural Revolution. Jin's openness counters the MPS's paramilitary, no-nonsense vigilance against saboteurs and spies. That requires a paranoia inconsistent with Jin Ming's urbanity.

Jin Ming is so bureaucratically unfettered—working on one case at a time and seemingly not burdened with meetings, reporting to superiors, participation in mass campaigns, or public service ("army literature" showed the PLA planting vegetables and fighting floods), that he seems an avatar of the "amateur professional," a model self-directing individual fighting injustice like a knight-errant. Encountering such idealized working conditions and self-images for scientists in post-Mao SF, Rudolf Wagner considered them wishful thinking, if not lobbying by the scientists writing it. Ye Yonglie the SF writer brings his police heroes into the same well-funded world, though their ethos also demands that they be shown working overtime, not enjoying themselves, and refusing meals even after long trips.[58]

Ye Yonglie was never a policeman,[59] and one suspects that an ex-cop would have been even more wary of showing real police activity such as the use of eavesdropping devices and secret cameras.[60] It might diminish reader sympathy for the MPS. Individualism and freedom are probably not in the policeman's utopia anyway. Jin Ming has a paramilitary side (he refers to himself as "[Badge] 606"), but then he is always dealing with inferiors. His stories are forever listing and even numbering measures he has "ordered" his subordinates to carry out.[61]

The plots evidence tortured compromises probably in consideration of the stories' "social effects." Offenses and perpetrators still favor anti-spy formulas: there are thefts of Chinese technological secrets and foul play by spies that threaten top Chinese scientists, space launches, the integrity of the currency, and other state interests. Though the time is the future and China is modernized, the continued danger from foreign powers conjures up a

dystopian world in which foreign powers are as threatening as ever. The political motives of sabotage and espionage are not the key to cracking the
cases, however, as in Cheng Xiaoqing's *The Bloody Case at Big Tree Village*.
Detection is so much in the Conan Doyle and Christie mode that Jin Ming's
scientific knowledge of spies' *methods*, and of the value of the technology
they want to steal, solves the case.

Detection is a proven audience-pleaser. But hidden ideological imperatives, or hasty writing, can lead to shocking results. Take "X-3 anjian" (The
X-3 case), which despite its compromises took flak in 1983.[62] An intriguing
mystery begins the tale: a scientist from a panda research institute returns
home from a research conference only to find, like Tom Sawyer, that his family is mourning his death. There had been mysteries already on his train ride
to the conference: (1) someone jumped from the train; (2) his compartment
mate left without a good-bye; and (3) when he got to the conference, the lecture notes in his travel bag had been replaced with waste paper.[63] It develops
that his compartment mate switched identical-looking travel bags with him
and jumped from the train, so disfiguring his face that he could not be
identified. It was the lecture notes in the stolen travel bag that misidentified
the deceased as the scientist hero of the story: Lin Ping.

Now it is up to Jin Ming to confirm that this is all a plot and that Lin
Ping's research was the object, and to find out what Lin knew that a foreign
spy might want. The national symbolism of the pandas ups the stakes. Ye
Yonglie has meanwhile forced some hard information down our throats: data
on how many pandas remain in the wild, information on the infrared photography that allows Lin Ping to count pandas at night by aerial photography—and what, by the way, is infrared light? Threats to pandas are not examined—not environmental change, neglect, poaching, panda diplomacy,
or anything that might reflect badly on China. On the contrary, a Japanese
memorial poem on the death of a friendship panda sent to Japan is cited.
But this is a diversion, for rare pandas are not the treasure at issue. Rather,
Lin Ping, in his efforts to stave off species extinction, has discovered cloning,
and then how to incubate whole fetuses in vitro until birth. The larger implications of his discoveries somehow escaped him!

Soon Ye's misuse of ad hoc SF devices and mindless patriotic appeals
begin to tell. Cloning technology is already plenty to motivate espionage. A
good mystery has been sustained so far without much reliance on SF; apart

from a miniaturized flashlight and other gadgets, cloning is the first miracle, and it was credible, near-future technology in 1980, if unoriginal in SF—not to speak of patriotic scholars who alleged that the idea of "cloning" first appeared in China's own *Journey to the West*. Lin Ping began by planting eggs into real mother panda uteruses, just as in the first actual cloning of a sheep in 1997.

But then Lin and Jin clone fully adult humans in vitro, without any convincing explanation of how. Not only are imaginary scientific explanations ignored, so are intriguing questions about whether the instant adult clones have memories, are psychologically "human," and what their moral, social, and philosophical status is. The jump to this stage of technology occurs six months after Jin Ming enters the case, probably (1) to give technology "time to advance"; (2) to emphasize, didactically, the need for patience in dealing with the "enemy" (six months is short for research but long in stakeouts); and (3) to establish a tendentious intellectual equivalence of cop and scientist. Jin Ming is such a quick study that he contributes to the final breakthrough. Without him, the final experiments would not have gone forward. It looks suspiciously as if a new generic requirement is that the police look indispensable.

More black-box "SF" devices follow. The purpose of cloning an adult human is to provide a copy of the professor himself, so that when the spy (a woman) comes to kill him, remove his brain with a scientific miracle knife, and freeze it to extract its memories by another invention, the spy can be caught without endangering the real Lin Ping. The spy makes her attempt on behalf of The Fat Man, an Ian Fleming–type villain like Dr. No, who is preparing on a private island for mass production of humans to fight in his army and work for free in his capitalist factories.

The concept of extracting ideas from a brain could have been convincing. However, despite hints that Ye extrapolated it from the experiments on transplanting rat RNA, in this story a vague and fantastic machine does the job. The adult clone of Lin Ping is an unnecessary device to close the story and leave readers gasping at the evil of the enemy and resourcefulness of the MPS—providing they can ignore the moral implications of cloning a human for sacrifice. (Lin Ping likewise regales Jin Ming with the thought that pandas will become so numerous that people will wear panda coats!) The inattention to moral, logical, and even scientific problems—for example, creating a panda population of weak genetic variability, which surely must have occurred to Ye Yonglie, who has written on genetics—suggests ultimately that what might have been a good (if not high-end) story of mystery, detection, *and* SF has gone very wrong. Mystification and edification have been swamped by the imperatives of besting the enemy even in deviousness. The moral superiority of "our side" that gives nationalistic fiction its energy is dissipated.

What about the "information dividend"? Ye Yonglie's readers wanted it, and he clearly wanted to satisfy them. But here the limitations of working with the police really tell. The MPS wanted to give the public "information" on its prowess and alertness, as well as enemy techniques to look for, without boosting readers' criminal capabilities. Such aims are contradictory, and the instinct of the secretive MPS was of course to withhold information on even such Hollywood commonplaces as invisibly sealing one's door with cellophane tape (to see if it is broken when one returns home). Such limitations, Ye claimed, drove him to use science *fiction* to solve Jin Ming cases[64]— meaning, evidently, his mind-reading machines, bloodless brain-extraction scalpels, and invisibility suits.

The mixed blessing of MPS cooperation would become a classic dilemma of major crime writers in the later 1980s. Ye proudly says that he lived in an MPS guest house in Beijing and had access to ministry case files; they inspired many of his stories. A Western reader might wonder where the influence is. But in the early 1980s, before China's information explosion, MPS files may have been the only available source on, say, the 1978 assassination in London of the Bulgarian writer and defector Georgi Markov by a KGB-trained Bulgarian agent who stuck him with an umbrella—a story well known in the West. This event was the basis for "The Case of the Murdering Umbrella," the first Jin Ming story. In Ye's story, as in life, an umbrella tip sticks a hollow iridium pellet filled with poison into the victim's thigh. The plot features a pretty Overseas Chinese woman working for a foreign power who tries to murder two major Chinese national security engineers. Ye says his police editors prevented him from naming the poison as ricin, the castor bean protein used on Markov; in the story, the venom is from an unidentified species of snake. Only in the freer atmosphere of 1985, in his nonfiction *Poan de xin yaoshi* (New keys for solving cases), could Ye name his poison.[65] The same poison had been used by Agatha Christie in a novel years earlier.[66]

Tours of MPS labs perhaps informed Ye's fiction and comic books about infrared light and radioactive argon isotope bombardment techniques for turning up latent fingerprints.[67] His *New Keys for Solving Cases* was not China's most technical unclassified book on forensic science, but really a book of science history, lore, and social statistics of just the sort he always loved to write. It became a best-seller, selling 100,000 copies in two printings.[68]

Typifying the book is Ye's chapter on "The Mysteries of Fingerprints." It starts with a scenario from a Chinese police thriller movie, proceeds to a capsule world history of discoveries about fingerprints, from ancient China to the Renaissance and scientific revolution in the West, and the first Chinese use, in 1913, of fingerprints to crack a case (no details). Then Ye discusses types of fingerprints and means of recovering obscure latent prints, mostly with anecdotes about amazingly old prints that cracked difficult cases. The rest is journalism: rundowns on computer banks of prints, an IBM lock that uses fingerprint scans, U.S. fingerprinting of children, and a Japanese case solved by "lip prints"; this answered press criticism of a story Ye had written that solved a crime by that method. There is a final reference to "voice prints,"[69] but not to the more important DNA technology. References to it are rare in Chinese crime fiction; one appeared in a 1989 one-time "periodical" of the very low-end type.

Ye's longest chapter, "Spies and Counterespionage," is the one best in accord with MPS needs; its subject is clever techniques used by *foreign* spy organizations, and these devices are not easily used by civilians. Surveillance techniques, eavesdropping devices, and so forth, are given short shrift; these are areas where the Chinese police are thought to be deeply invested. Perhaps even in 1985 many Chinese readers learned new things from Ye's accounts of World War II code-breaking (MAGIC), the KGB's "American village," electronic eavesdropping on the Russian who downed Korean Airlines Flight 007, microdots, assassinations, disguises, secret inks, satellites, industrial espionage, and other techniques. Always, Ye fleshes out scientific with social statistics: on the percentage of Ph.D.s in the CIA and the annual number of deaths from poisonous snakes in the United States and Brazil (but not in China). Much of his information is revealed as coming from publications of the "Free World."[70]

For all that, Ye Yonglie's "naive" belief in technology and criminological fixes allowed him to write of a case cracked by having mail routed from the post office to the police; the reading of unopened letters with infrared light; a meeting of postal employees convened to cast suspicion on all letters sent abroad; and interception on no particular grounds of a letter addressed to a foreigner. In another work, Ye conjures up a China in which everybody's fingerprints are in the computer.[71] It is science fiction, but only near-future; there may be some criticism in these stories, but there is no fear of a police will to power.

On the benefit side, Ye got, besides access to MPS files, a crack at many projects. He was asked to write a history of Chinese crime and detective fiction, starting with *gongan* fiction.[72] And he had the ministry's ear as its adviser. In March 1982, he helped persuade the MPS to clamp down on the proliferating translations of foreign mystery fiction, since many were unhealthy or prettified capitalism, and since different publishers were printing and distributing the same titles.[73]

Ye's concerns appealed to a vague but persistent idea in Chinese communist literary control that socialist publication must observe "proportions"—that topics, publishers, and geographical and bureaucratic venues should somehow be balanced. Ye also asked that publications serve social needs and the interests of the MPS, China's biggest publisher of foreign crime and mystery fiction. When provincial publishers competed with the MPS's own titles, it lost both control and much of the profits. In fact, foreign "imports" were outcompeting domestic crime fiction in the first place because of restrictions on materials that could be used in domestic manufacture. In any case, the flood of foreign mysteries was halted in 1982. Protection from foreign imports, and the MPS's determination to seize the initiative and create a "healthier" *Chinese* police fiction factory employing and glorifying its own cadres, seem in retrospect to have been preconditions for the birth of China's legal system literature as a protected literary industry.

Ye Yonglie redeemed himself a little with *The Black Shadow*, the Jin Ming story the MPS rejected. It epitomizes Ye's persistence in serving up to his readers any information he thought they needed, regardless of genre. Through him, the old Chinese tradition that fiction should be informational *and* amusing found its ultimate modern expression. Did he offer up trivia as a substitute for, even as repentance for, the hard facts about crime, police operations, even technology that he was not free to divulge? His zest to disclose inside dope on everything, and with a popular touch, followed in the footsteps of Soviet detective-story writers like Julian Semyonov, whose heroes dispensed tidbits from the Western memoir literature unknown to Russians about Khrushchev, Stalin, and the Kennedys, and more fanciful items about West German and U.S. corporations arming Mao Zedong with nuclear bombs and the like. Semyonov's characters, like Jin Ming's, discuss Pascal, Montaigne, and Kant "while Belgrade burns."[74] What one misses, besides the police lore Ye knew so well, is any reference to *legal* institutions.

The Black Shadow begins in a wilderness preserve in China's wild southwest, where an entomologist discovers a new species of mosquito that mysteriously has human blood in its system. But this area is uninhabited. So is it blood from a hermit? A spy? An extraterrestrial? A ghost? A legendary "hairy man" (the Chinese counterpart of a Yeti or Sasquatch)? The entomologist surmises that it is an enigmatic humanoid "black shadow" that he saw seep into the earth. This idea guides Jin Ming, who comes in to solve the mystery.

Using scientific analysis and above all computers to call up all previous world cases of "people disappearing through walls," Jin Ming finds leads. Some are simply entertaining: the computer pulls up a file on a Daoist immortal who passed through walls in Pu Songling's *Strange Stories from a Chinese Studio* (the seventeenth-century text mined by the *biji* anthologists discussed in Chapter Two). More research turns up a foreign case—Ali Baba. More recently, there is a police file on an unseen person who entered locked hotel rooms, food stores, and bank vaults at will in Coastal City during the Cultural Revolution. Shortly thereafter, attest newspaper clippings from the foreign city of Hamill, a Hamill bank vault was similarly penetrated. Is there a connection?

Jin Ming and his subordinates return to where the mosquito and the black shadow lived. They find a cave home with a mysterious book in code. Back to the computer terminal. Item: Samuel Pepys wrote a diary in code. Code can be used for personal memoirs. Item: An American wrote a book about breaking the Japanese naval code in World War II. Code has practical uses too. So the black shadow's code is broken and his identity is revealed, after several twists, turns, and a love interest.[75] The shadow is the long-lost boyfriend of the entomologist's now aged foster mother. The shadow is Chinese, the son of a man who invented a molecule-altering "wall-penetrating suit"; he had to flee China, deserting his sweetheart, when the Gang of

Four's police ran amok. Capitalist Hamill proved equally corrupt, full of spies out to get the suit. So the shadow chose a hermit's life of internal Chinese exile. For literary effect, his diary, written to his old sweetheart, is read into the text, sewing up all the loose ends in chronological order and providing all his motivations. There is a happy reunion; the invention is safely in China; and the bad guys were dealt with long ago, when the Gang of Four were arrested.

This novella partakes of SF romance more than Ye's other stories. The function of the wall-penetrating suit is to lead Jin Ming not into combat with enemies but into the realm of detection: to a classic locked-room mystery, a black fugitive whose identity and motives must be reconstructed, and, as the primary tool for that, a coded document. That the locked-room capers occurred with a futuristic suit is beyond "fair play" in the classical detective story, but the reader is carefully prepared for it, and the suit is not the means by which Jin Ming solves the case. The more implausible aspects of the plot, like conflicts between good and bad (Gang of Four) police, are social, and all in the past: in China's surreal, shadowy past, a terrain of long-repressed nightmares that the MPS evidently preferred to leave buried.

With the demonic spies relegated to the past, Jin Ming is humanized. Family ties are important, and the tone is light. As educator and father figure as well as genius cop, Jin Ming unlocks the creative deductive powers of others—his assistants, the entomologist and his mother (another scientist), and the black shadow himself. Science speaks *through* him, as do the world culture and community that China has so long been denied, from *Robinson Crusoe* (the shadow's inspiration to become a hermit) to the American memoir about MAGIC. For all his scientism, Jin Ming, like Sherlock Holmes and other great detectives, really solves cases not by scientific deduction but by making imaginative connections.[76] His genius is intuitive, humanistic, even artistic. In this novel, Jin Ming would as soon read Pepys and Defoe as a chemistry or criminology textbook.

The Chinese aficionado who reads for information delights in Jin Ming's literary citations; his tales about "hairy men," UFOs, specters, children raised by wolves, and postwar Japanese soldiers who lived as hermits rather than surrender; and his information on cryptoanalysis, blood types, entomology, the mounting of specimens, and wilderness survival. It is all gratuitous edification.

Ye also draws on exotica from China's *qi'an* (strange case) tradition. Mostly it is entertaining, but it also heightens a sense that there are more mysteries after this one. For once, science is science: not simply for technical solutions or national defense, but an invitation to seek further knowledge. Ye Yonglie never wholly forsook science education for its own sake. That may have been lost on the police. So, perhaps, was his little joke on them in *The Black Shadow*: the entomologist is such an expert on the kinds of mosquitoes and their haunts that he is referred to as "a veritable household-check policeman for the mosquitoes" (2).

Jin Ming flourished as long as the flow of information—and mysteries— was closed off. Later, when anyone could learn about spies, poisons, and assassinations in Western nonfiction, about scandals of the Chinese police, and about true crime—the "need" for novels like *The Black Shadow*—to borrow the Maoist concept of "need"—was over. "Information" would remain important in the appeal of crime fiction in China, as in the West. But Ye Yonglie's spies and inside dope for a closed society were throwbacks to the 1950s. In the later 1980s, he switched to a new genre of popular appeal, again with the help of MPS files: popular biographies of the Gang of Four.

SINCE 1984: THE SUDDEN EXPLOSION OF CRIME FICTION

It may be no contradiction to associate the new police fiction of 1984 with both the "strike hard" mentality, which showed that the CCP *wanted* citizens (but not foreigners) to see Chinese law as something to be feared (few Chinese sympathized with accused criminals), and also with its longer-lived "comprehensive management" strategy of foreseeing all social disturbances and crimes in order to manage and educate them away before they could spawn. When the cultural atmosphere became freer in 1984–85, crime fiction came roaring back in every venue high and low, and with its own genre magazines. The first were police magazines actually edited and published by the police with artistic pretensions—"police literary journals."[77] When the judiciary were allowed law enforcement magazines of their own (also with many police heroes), interservice rivalry was born.[78] The bureaucratic hierarchy simply structured it. Of first rank were crime and police journals edited by the central police and justice ministries in Beijing. Next were magazines put out by their subordinate branches in each province. Big-city newspaper staffs and legal associations printed "independent" journals like Tianjin's *Landun* (Blue shield). Literary and arts associations of lesser cities (like Anqing in Anhui province), answerable only to their local municipal CCP committee, entered the fray with humbler but less centrally supervised contributions. Then came the pulps or tabloids (*xiaobao*) of 1984, not printed by government units, or at least not by any unit authorized to do so. Above them all, prestigious literary journals like *Shiyue* (October) and *Huacheng* (Flower city) printed crime fiction by the likes of Shui Yunxian. Writing about crime was stratified, though most of it could be understood by high school and maybe junior high readers.[79]

There was money to be made. By 1985, officially sanctioned low-end "popular" (*tongsu*) publications took on the tabloids through (1) new legitimate journals of designated popular (*tongsu*) literature, "popular" meaning officially distributed entertainment catering to "lower" taste but guaranteed morally and politically harmless; (2) title-page classifications in the lower-ranking but by tradition still "literary" journals of their new content into popular genres and ad hoc subgenres like "martial-arts detective SF love story"; and (3) the mass desertion of local literary periodicals from the high end to the low. Many journals changed their names to make them more appealing. *Heilongjiang yishu* (Heilongjiang arts) became *Tiane* (Swan). Its new name symbolized rebirth in a more attractive form, but really it had reverted to what most Chinese would call an ugly duckling. Redesigned as pulps, the newborn journals attracted readers with sensational, unabashedly trashy front cover art (crude collages of guns, cops, and semiclad women), and still more revealing back and inside cover art with "artistic nudes"—more stylishly drawn, but more naked and more photographically realistic than the female portraits on the front cover. Sensational story titles often appeared on the front cover in bigger characters than the magazine title, if the latter appeared at all.[80]

Chinese crime editors and writers consider 1984 to 1986 the heyday of PRC crime fiction. They speak of (and perhaps are imagining) a "higher" crime fiction that reached its peak circulation in the mid-1980s, before pulp fiction and nonfiction of many kinds won the circulation war. They also cherish the latitude in the mid-1980s about what kinds of crimes could be discussed (e.g., those committed by high officials), and how much detail one could go into. Public interest in China's new legal institutions, legal technicalities, and lawsuits was at a peak.[81] To be sure, this is to judge literature primarily by its literal truth-telling capacity—still the norm of authors, critics (even police editors), and concerned readers in a nation in which literature was heavily censored. When reportage began to experience comparable freedom at the end of the decade, citizens' continuing sense of being starved for truth put reportage ahead of fiction as the preeminent crime genre at the high end of the spectrum. Why use disguised names if one could print the real ones?[82]

That was not Yu Haocheng's frame of mind when he spearheaded the revival of crime fiction by refounding *Woodpecker* in February 1984 as a bimonthly.[83] He took a positive view of his piece of the state apparatus as a tool for promoting human rights and reform of the rest of the apparatus. (The concept of "human rights" remained officially suspect in the PRC until the regime embraced the term, redefined to suit its own needs, in the 1990s.)[84] Furthermore, literature was propaganda, and fiction its highest form. Yu Haocheng's literary contribution was to see to it that crime was represented in creative *literature*, not just in high-class reportage and true-case write-ups as in *Democracy and Legal System* and the many legal system gazettes in the provinces. Yu's vision still reflected the May Fourth entrustment to fiction of the ancient function of the classics. Perhaps he also remained influenced by Marxist utilitarian ideas about writing. He was in trouble again by March 1986, after an interview with a Hong Kong magazine that offended the MPS party committee. But he continued as a force in legal system literature, and for a time his protégés Li Qingyu and Wang Yonghong remained *Woodpecker*'s editors.[85]

The inside cover of *Woodpecker*'s first 1984 issue spoke of the bird as a "guardian of the forest," "natural enemy of vermin," and "symbol of the people's public security warriors." A thick journal of 256 pages, not unlike the prestigious bimonthly literary "fat magazines" like *October*, *Woodpecker* would be "the friend of the broad masses of public security cadres and police, and of the people." "In the main," it would "reflect political-legal and public security subject matter."

Ironically, or perhaps not, readers remember that the inaugural 1984 issue caught fire owing to a lead item that was reportage: Li Honglin's "Zhuibu 'Er

Wang' jishi" (Pursuit and capture of the Two Wangs).[86] As in the 1980 issues, there were sections for reportage, fiction, poetry (not all of which was "public security poetry"—oxymoronic, if art is by nature unsettling), essays on crime fiction, and translations of foreign mystery fiction. There was back-cover art, obligatory in Chinese literary journals. In both the 1980 and 1984 issues the journal title appeared on the front cover in Mao Dun's calligraphy; in 1984 two woodpeckers faced each other sideways like twin dragons in a Shang dynasty *taotie* ("ogre mask") to form a bilaterally symmetrical gestalt of a policeman's shield. All issues omitted the editors' names. The secretive MPS printed their names only in 1988, by which time *Woodpecker* was publishing stories by the "hoodlum writer" Wang Shuo.

A flood of crime magazines followed in the next three years, and still more in 1988 (after the repressions of early 1987), though in the repression following the June 4, 1989, Beijing massacre, 11 percent of all magazines, police magazines included, were closed down. *Woodpecker* was and still is China's flagship police magazine, above those run by the Public Security Departments (Gongan Ting) of particular provinces and the Public Security Bureaus (Gongan Ju) of municipalities.

The newly refounded Ministry of Justice entered the fray with *Zhongguo fazhi wenxue* (Chinese legal system literature; founded October 25, 1985), run by its *Zhongguo fazhibao* (Chinese legal system gazette; 1986 circulation over 1.7 million).[87] Nearly every provincial Judiciary Department had a legal system gazette—there were more than 30 in the mid-1980s—and some had literary columns. The ministry's own four-page central gazette made room for a regular column of serial fiction, mostly by little-known authors, and for literary reportage by noted legal system writers such as Li Jian and Fu Xuwen that might fill the entire fourth page. Judiciary-run police-and-law magazines under provincial Judiciary Departments (Sifa Ting) were on a par with those run by the police in their provincial Public Security Departments.

Thus, in bureaucratic terms (and what state publisher did not think bureaucratically), many police-run journals were in competition with each other: these included *Shuijingshi* (Crystal; founded in Shenyang, January 1985) of the Liaoning Provincial Public Security Department; *Jian yu dun* (Sword and shield, founded March 1985), under the Shanghai Public Security Bureau; *Jingtan fengyun* (Police world; founded in Fuzhou, April 1986) of the Fujian Provincial Public Security Department; another Beijing police magazine, under the subordinate Beijing Public Security Bureau rather than directly under the MPS, *Jindun* (Gold shield; founded January 1988).They also competed with the judiciary's journals: *Fazhi yuekan* (Legal system monthly; declassified in Changsha, January 1984), under the Hunan Provincial Judiciary Department; *Ren yu fa* (Man and the law; founded fall 1985) under the Tianjin Judiciary Bureau; and others.

An influential journal that despite its name was apart from the ministries and, like the major journals listed above, devoted space to fiction in its early years, was *Landun* (Blue shield; founded in Tianjin, spring 1986). Its editorial officers overlapped the literary editorial staff of the *Tianjin ribao* (Tianjin daily). A noticeably more provincial magazine was the popular reprint journal *Fazhi wenxue xuankan* (Selections from legal system literature, founded in Anqing, late 1984), of the lowly Anqing Municipal Federation of Literature and Arts, which was under the Propaganda Department of the CCP Municipal Committee of Anqing. Even the most central journals were under the unitary control of the Communist Party at the top; it "led" state organs to begin with and had members on every editorial board, perhaps monopolized the positions, since top cadres in policing, justice, and propaganda were expected to join the party.

Often a crime magazine was hived off from a previously existing newspaper. On the judiciary side, the editors of *Man and the Law* were hard to separate from the *Tianjin fazhibao* (Tianjin legal system gazette), and on the public security side, *Sword and Shield* was in effect run by *Renmin jingcha* (People's police). Founded in 1949 as a classified publication, the latter went public in 1986. Back to the judiciary, Hunan's *Legal System Monthly* had its origins in 1981 in a classified newsletter about Hunan crime edited by one person (*Fazhi xuanchuan* or *Legal System Propaganda*). It emerged in January 1984 as a public and nationally distributed journal of police news, literary crime reportage, and fiction.

Down the bureaucratic and central/periphery food chain, fiction and "literary" flourishes gave way to crude true case write-ups (*anli*), lots of line drawings of police and criminals, and front and back cartoon stories. Local publications were often differentiated by whether they stressed police or legal subject matter. Mostly interested in true case write-ups like those in *Democracy and Legal System*, supposedly to popularize legal knowledge (and moral lessons about the inadvisability of, say, divorce), were journals like

Falü yu shenghuo (Law and life; Beijing) at the top, from the Ministry of Justice's Law Press; *Fazhi yu wenming* (Legal system and civilization; Shenyang), of the Liaoning Provincial Judiciary Department; *Shanghai fayuan* (Shanghai garden of the law; declassified January 1986?), under the Shanghai Judiciary Bureau; and *An yu fa* (Cases and law; Xi'an, founded 1985?). The MPS had its own journal of case write-ups and special features called *Falü zixun* (Legal consultation; founded January 1985 by Yu Haocheng). *Xiandai shijie jingcha* (Modern world police; founded March 1985), run by the MPS Research Institute on World Police, and after 1986 by the Chinese People's Police Officers University in Beijing, published news and photos of foreign police methods only. An intriguing and seemingly daring special-interest journal, partly literary, was *Da qiang neiwai* (Inside and outside the Big Wall; founded October 1988), about China's Gulag, run by the Shanghai Labor Reform Bureau.[88]

This is only a sample. Chinese libraries did not attempt to collect all of China's local literary periodicals, much less police and law magazines. There were too many. A few examples: *Fazhi wenzhai* (Digest of legal system literature; Taiyuan, founded February 1985?), under the Committee on Politics and Law of the Shanxi Provincial Committees of the Chinese Communist Party and Communist Youth League; *Jiangxi gongan* (Jiangxi public security; Nanchang, founded January 1989?), under the Jiangxi Provincial Public Security Department; *Jing di* (Police whistle; Wuhan), under the Hubei Public Security Department; *Jing tan* (Police investigations), of the Anhui Public Security Department; *Gongan* (Public security), under the Henan Public Security Department; *Dangdai jingcha* (Contemporary police), of the Hunan Public Security Department;[89] *Faxue jie* (The world of legal studies; Hefei, founded 1986?), under the Anhui Legal Studies Association; and *Fazhi* (Legal system; Guangzhou), of the Guangdong Provincial Judiciary Department. At the low end was *Fazhi huabao* (Legal system pictorial; Hebei?, founded May 1985?), which presented its cases in the form of cartoons.

A sub-basement of crime fiction in the mid-1980s was filled by ephemeral tabloids and underground magazines outside party scrutiny. Like illicit documents of dynasties past, they are now known primarily from official denunciations of them. By all accounts, they had few literary pretensions. In the late 1980s, legitimate presses and publishing enterprises in between were buying into the illicit business and catering to their "illicit" tastes. In 1986, railroad stations were already full of "legitimate" tabloids from presses of repute: *Wenxue gushibao* (Literary stories gazette), from People's Literature Press; *Gushibao* (Stories gazette), published in Fushun; a *Minzhu yu fazhi huabao* (Democracy and legal system pictorial), from the staff of Shanghai's *Democracy and Legal System* monthly; and a *Lianhuanbao* (Serial [cartoon] gazette) from the Anhui People's Press. The fare included historical fiction, stories about Chinese leaders, martial-arts fiction, and accident and disaster stories besides crime fiction and anecdotes.[90]

Seeking revenues, government organs, some already in the publishing business and some not, put popular literature of the harmless *tongsu* variety (in any genre that sold) into substantial magazines instead of throwaway tabloids. Crime and suspense fiction were staples, along with love stories, martial-arts fiction, and contemporary and legendary scandals. The MPS found it hard to defend the exclusive rights it had purchased to Cheng Xiaoqing's pre-1949 detective stories; copyright was ignored.[91] New "popular literature associations" boosted the legitimacy of *tongsu* enterprises. In the later 1980s the state decided that the masses needed more entertainment to relax them after their labors for modernization. A reader knew a journal had crime fiction when the front cover featured a collage of a smoking gun barrel, scowling cop faces, and seedy hoodlums sandwiched between obligatory seminude women and cowboys or swordsmen in dynastic costume indicating other genres featured. The obsolete Maoist concept of "mass" or "masses' " literature now took the same meaning as *tongsu*.

Designated popular fiction journals included *Xiandai tongsu xiaoshuo* (Modern popular fiction; Changchun, founded January 1985); *Liaoning qunzhong wenyi* (Liaoning masses' literature and art; Shenyang); *Tongsu wenyijia* (Popular entertainers; Yinchuan, Ningxia Hui Autonomous Zone Cultural Department); special magazine issues of the *Gushibao* (Stories gazette, from the Shenyang Press); and *Tongsu wenxue xuankan* (Selections from popular literature; Taiyuan, founded 1982?, survived through 1987), not to be confused with a magazine of identical title founded in September 1988 by the Chinese Folk Literature Association and Chinese Masses' Literature Association in Beijing. The "folkish," too, was becoming assimilated to the commercially successful "popular."

Intellectuals who looked down on all Chinese crime fiction admitted that they too read crime fiction—and not the middlebrow sort, but the very trashiest kind, based on sensational "true cases."[92] Different were ostensibly "popular" journals (as indicated by their titles) for intellectuals, such as *Jingu chuanqi* (Strange tales new and old; Wuhan). They let "popular" lack of seriousness run cover for stories and documentaries of satiric and topical import, including, after June 1989, some about the massacre in Beijing.[93]

"Popular" (*tongsu*) was originally a euphemism for the "vulgar" (*su*, *yongsu*), which pandered to reader taste, unlike the *dazhonghua* (made for the masses).[94] That the term *tongsu* was still patronizing is clear from apologetic *tongsu* singers interviewed by Andrew F. Jones: *tongsu* "is a form of art that's particularly easily accepted by the common people"; and, "I like to sing relatively complex, difficult songs, but I have to sing songs they'll understand."[95] Just so. To paraphrase a fiction editor—one of the few the present author ever met who was genuinely enthusiastic about crime fiction: "There's no strict definition of popular literature (*tongsu wenxue*), no strict line between it and pure literature. It's considered to be for people of a lower cultural level. Its emphasis is on the story, on the plot. It doesn't delve into new kinds of materials. There are no long descriptions of the scenery at the start; it gets right down to the point (*kaimen jianshan*)—to the murder." What then was "pure literature" in 1989? It had to be "exploratory" (*tansuo*), have new things in it. Works of the 1950s, though not "popular," "wouldn't qualify as pure literature today."[96] By the 1990s, even the word "cultural" (as in "cultural crime" or "cultural T-shirt") was a euphemism for the countercultural and salacious: pornography, nonintellectual dissidence—"attitude."

But not all officially sanctioned low-class literature was so under control. Old and new literary journals run by provincial-level organs or lower became unashamedly vulgar, particularly those far from the capital, but able now to ship and sell their wares to the urban littoral through individual peddlers (*getihu*), perhaps peasants living hand to mouth. Some critics put the Anqing *Selections from Legal System Literature* in this category. Its paper and printing were poor, and its early cover art was "popular." As regional disparities in literary control increased, a serious journal, like *Hainan jishi* (Hainan documentary), could likewise be published in a freer frontier area, while its editing and printing continued in Changsha, as arranged by its Hunanese editor, Han Shaogong.[97]

With front covers featuring recumbent women in nightgowns, wild criminals wielding bloody hatchets, and pistol-toting policemen (most Chinese police are unarmed, and those with guns often have no ammunition), local pulps in the guise of literary magazines promised half-pornographic delights. (The word *huang* [pornographic; lit., "yellow"] can refer to either sex or violence.)[98] The distant Guangxi Zhuang Nationality Autonomous Prefecture was noted for pushing the envelope, and crime stories helped stuff it. Nanning's *San yue san* (March the third; date of the minorities' youth mating day, the "water sprinkling festival") typified the risqué local journals that in the past would have printed low-grade socialist realist stories but now promised sensation, even exploitation, sometimes in issues exclusively devoted to crime and scandal. Such magazines might print the journal name on the cover in small characters, yielding to the sensational or salacious title of a constituent story in big characters: "On the Edge of Hell," or "Underground Criminals of Taiwan." In the crackdown of January 1987, *Jin cheng* (Golden city), from Hechi district, Guangxi, even managed to get itself closed down by the Guangxi government (though copies were still sold in Beijing two months later), for excessive murders and obscenity.[99]

Publication in particular provinces, especially frontier provinces, is prominent among the journals promising forbidden delights that were available in major eastern cities. But every region printed them: *Binglinghua* (Icicles; Jiamusi, Heilongjiang); *Tiane* (Swan; Haerbin); *Xiaoshuo lin* (Forest of fiction; Haerbin); *Lü ye* (Green wilderness; Jilin); *Changcheng wenyi* (Great wall literature and art; Beijing); *Wenxue gang* (Literary harbor; Ningbo); *Hua jing* (Path between the flowers; Nanchang); *Juanhua* (Azalea; Nanchang); *Xiaoshuo tiandi* (Universe of fiction; Nanchang); *Fu He* (Fu River; Fuzhou, Jiangxi); *Da shijie* (Wide, wide world; Changsha); *Wenyi chuang* (Window on literature and art; Changsha); *Wenyi shenghuo* (Literary life; Changsha); *Shantou wenyi* (Shantou literature and art; Shantou, Guangdong); *Zhanjiang wenxue* (Zhanjiang literature; Zhanjiang, Guangdong); *Wenyu shijie* (Entertainment world; Guiyang); *Xiaoshuo shijie* (World of fiction; Nanning, Guangxi); *Jin tian* (Golden fields; Yulin, Guangxi); *You Jiang wenyi* (You River literature and art; Baise, Guangxi). The popular also overwhelmed old-line literary journals once of a certain reputation, like *Chang'an* (Xi'an) and *Dongtinghu* (Dongting Lake; Yueyang, Hunan). *Wenxue daguan* (Literary magnificence; Liaoning) was published by a local branch of the Chinese Writers' Association. The youth market was supposedly served in *Qingnian wenxuejia* (Young littérateurs; Qiqihaer), but its content was rather "adult." It is unclear whether these local "literary" journals were counted as "popular literary journals," but an officer of the Chinese Writers' Association said that China had more than 190 of the latter in 1988.[100]

A crackdown on tabloids, private publishing, and dissident and pornographic content ensued in 1987, and a new central censorship system was set up under the State Press and Publications Administration (Guojia Xinwen Chubanshu). But in 1988–89, "official" publication loosened up as never before. Low-end "periodicals" were published ad hoc, on no particular schedule, as the columns filled up. Popular literature publishers anxious to make a buck borrowed, bought, or faked the publishing license of a legitimate press to bring out single-issue "periodicals," perhaps disguised as part of a series, with a racy, go-for-broke magazine cover about the selling of women and children or some such. Individual peddlers sold them in railway and subway stations and to newsstands.[101] "Legitimate" journals too, and the Ministry of Justice's own Law Press, used their printing authority to bring out one-shot sensational special issues, often with the title of a suitably shocking constituent fictional work as the apparent issue title.[102] Even first-rank provincial presses put out such magazines. From Hebei People's Press came *Xuelei fengchen nü* (A life of desperation makes a fallen angel; the title of a constituent story), a 30,000-copy 1988 publication. The Jiangxi People's Press published *Shenqi de zhuizong* (The miraculous pursuit of a missing person, after the title of a detective story) in 1988, in 100,000 copies. The cover art montaged a photo of a pretty girl, an artist's rendering of her voluptuous body in a slip, and in the shadows, a threatening man and cops on motorcycles. A main draw of a 289,500-copy imprint from Zhejiang People's Press in 1988 was the title, ostensibly the magazine's, *Xueran Zishijie: Pan Jinlian xin zhuan* (Amethyst Street stained by blood: The Pan Jinlian legend retold), collected with other tales of murder and mayhem from Chinese history and contemporary stories of international drug smuggling.

Decisions were made by marketers. When Hua Jian, an expert in the sociology of literature at the Shanghai Academy of Social Sciences, compiled a magazine of salable crime stories as part of a deal to help his publisher subsidize his scholarly books, the Yanbian University Press of Yanji, Jilin, brought out the former under the title *Fengliu nannü* (Loose boys and unfettered women; 1988; first printing, 300,000 copies). Hua's intended title, *Fazhi gushi da sai jing xuan* (The cream from a major competition in legal system stories), was just the subtitle. On the cover was a young woman in a nightgown fondling two distracted-looking naked young Caucasian men. Hua took many angry telephone calls from contributors.[103]

The whole literary industry was desperate for cash, and this only stoked the fires for a legal system literature under firmer control. The journals with a modicum of literary panache, like *Woodpecker* and *Blue Shield*, still enjoyed circulations that put the "pure literature" journals to shame. The circulation of both literary and genre magazines peaked early and steadily declined in the later 1980s, but the literary journals lost readers far more precipitously. *Woodpecker* led, selling 1.8 million copies at first, down to 200,000 (150,000 subscribers) in 1989 and 120,000 in 1990, post-massacre. That was far better than the "pure literature" journals, some of which enjoyed a circulation of around 100,000 in the mid-1980s but were under 10,000 by 1990.[104] Even the comparatively mediocre *Sword and Shield*, which printed relatively little fiction—at 900,000 readers in 1988 and still at 200,000 in 1989—outsold China's four biggest "fat" serious literary periodicals combined (*October*, *Harvest*, *Contemporary*, *Flower City*). Journals of reportage and documentary "literature" also held up far better than those dedicated to "pure literature." Han Shaogong's *Hainan Documentary* sold 200,000 copies an issue in 1989 before it was closed down.[105]

A notch below *Woodpecker* in prestige and presumed quality, *Blue Shield* had about 300,000 readers per issue at its height early on (and a record of 370,000 for one issue), but was down to 100,000 in 1989. The Anqing magazine, *Selections from Legal System Literature*, was poorly printed but envied for its vast mid-1980s circulation of 1 million.[106] *Police World* (Fujian Public Security Department), bolstered by its printing of a screenplay adapted from Lü Haiyan's very popular novel *Bianyi jingcha* (Plainclothes policeman), reached a top circulation of 600,000 copies in 1987.

Changsha's *Legal System Monthly* enjoyed a peak circulation of 200,000 in 1987, which declined to 120,000 in 1989.[107] *Gold Shield*, a new Beijing journal with a high fee scale, had a top circulation of 360,000 in 1988.[108] *Man and the Law* (of the Tianjin Judiciary) had 500,000 readers in 1985, 400,000 the next year, and 200,000 in 1987–88, before declining to somewhat over 100,000 in 1989.[109] Like *Sword and Shield*, Shanghai journals were still favored with relatively high circulations in 1989: *People's Police*, 140,000–150,000; *Shanghai Garden of Law*, 100,000; *Inside and Outside the Big Wall*, also 100,000 (200,000 at its debut in October 1988).[110] Nonpolice "popular fiction" journals also did well. *Selections from Popular Literature* (Beijing) once circulated 300,000 copies; it sold 100,000–150,000 in 1989 and still made money.[111]

Although police and law journals lacked the prestige of "pure literature," they hiked circulation by printing famous authors and paying better than the serious journals. In 1989, *Woodpecker* paid 20 yuan per 1,000 characters; *Gold Shield*, 30 to 40—double what the prestigious high-literary fat magazine *October* paid at the time (15 yuan).[112] By comparison, a murder suspect paid a lawyer a fee of 60 yuan for the whole case.[113]

After the 1989 massacre some of these periodicals were closed—for putative errors of their content or their staffs, or under the previously noted reasoning (or excuse) of proportionalism. It was decided—only in 1989—that a given unit could run only one mass publication; the Shanghai PSB kept *People's Police*, so *Sword and Shield* closed in July 1990. A newspaper (e.g., the *Zhongguo fazhibao*) was no longer allowed to run a journal, which meant the death of the Ministry of Justice's own *Chinese Legal System Literature* in January 1990. The popular Anqing magazine, *Selections from Legal System Literature*, which had printed reportage by the dissident Dai Qing and had a low-class air, was closed in the same month. *Inside and Outside the Big Wall*, after a long and initially promising bureaucratic fight, finally bit the dust in June 1990. Even some of the legal system gazettes were closed or merged. *Woodpecker*, *Blue Shield*, *Crystal*, *Gold Shield*, *Police Whistle*, and *Legal System Monthly* survived.[114] A major casualty in popular literary publication was Beijing's *Selections from Popular Literature*, which was terminated in January 1990. After the massacre, China's writers refused (or were afraid) to submit manuscripts. Finding good copy was harder than ever.

Politics and Genre

Before the new chaos of crime fiction in the mid-1980s stood the Chinese Communist Party and state. They already "guided" the new fiction with their police and law journals. It still needed organizations, standards, and a name—a purpose. China's officials reconstructed it as a whole new genre:

legal system literature. The cadres presumed to name and politically to construct "genres" even in popular music, Andrew F. Jones notes, and they used ideological more than stylistic considerations.[115] The unlikelihood of a "natural" genre being constructed by "positive" legislation was one familiar in Chinese law; it had the force of natural law, but one could see the emperor or CCP make it up as he (or it) went along.

"Legal system literature" was in principle less a genre than a *tifa* (formulation).[116] *Tifa* were not philosophically theorized in Chinese Marxism-Leninism but were still authoritative, and they had to be correct—scientific.[117] Some commentators did speak of legal system literature as a genre.[118] Certainly officials and academics debated it as if it were one. Many wanted the definition to be prescriptive as well as descriptive. They wrote books and curricula on how to compose its appropriate plots and characters.[119] A "planned literature" was being born, even as China's planned economy was on the wane.

The *name* "legal system literature" suggested a classification of works by subject matter. Dissidents and more orthodox critics considered such a manner of classification out of step with contemporary criticism, and they worried about its political implications. One well-meaning but evidently conflicted critic hailed Tolstoy's *Resurrection* as sublime legal system literature on one page and on the next distinguished legal system literature from "pure literature."[120] Chinese scholars in history had typically defined genres inductively. Yet they also searched obsessively for genre prototypes in ancient times.[121] The state encouraged such a quest for legal system literature, with the field broadened to include great foreigners such as Tolstoy and Dostoevski.

Yet political concepts were double-edged. Since prohibitions typically pertained to subject matter, so did "breakthroughs." The state, carrying over from its legislative practice, lined up subgenres in subordinate ranks under legal system literature. Each subgenre had its own field of authority in the service of instrumental control and indoctrination: there were "police literature," "customs inspection literature," even "Big Wall literature."[122] Might China not then have a subgenre of *lüshi wenyi* (lawyer literature and art)?, argued one person (perhaps a lawyer!). It would promote understanding of the new lawyer system and of how hard lawyers worked. It would also show that the lawyers' aim was *not* just to talk courts into letting the guilty go free.[123]

Legal system literature was already a broad swath of works targeted for police and judiciary supervision, but it could also function politically as a "united front," sanctioning all works supportive of legal reform on behalf of the common goal of modernization. If the formulation "popular literature" could protect low-grade works, "legal system literature" might likewise provide cover for stories expressing progressive ideas about crime and the law. United fronts had a hidden agenda of nudging the more reluctant allies into a more progressive stance.

An inclusive subject-matter formulation might even help Chinese crime fiction move beyond generic imitations and find its distinctive voice as a truly Chinese crime-and-law literature. A bridge between the high and popular could overcome old assumptions that no work could be both serious and popular; Chinese critics had no category for Dickens, whose serious fiction, some of it about crime and the law, sold well in his time. A focus on subject matter might also directly confront the prejudice that any hint of criminal subject matter made a work "low."[124] Moreover, good legal subject matter could overcome condescending attitudes toward the law as such. The bottom line, clear even to bureaucrats, was that no Chinese *Resurrection* was about to appear under existing conditions.

But subject matter was concrete, and Maoism had an unfortunate history of reifying elements of fiction as if they were ingredients in the baking of a propaganda cake. A work that was too plain needed a dollop of "art"; one too difficult could benefit by a dash of "making it universal" (by using, say, peasant dialect or folk songs). By analogy, popular bourgeois elements added just for taste, like cops, suspense, and trial scenes, needed the compensation of more nutritional and elevating legal education.

It was a time for new genres, and the government was in on many of the creations. China's "Western literature" (*xibu wenxue*), about frontier provinces like Xinjiang and Tibet, was suddenly acclaimed in 1984, after the critic Zhong Dianfei used the term for certain films.[125] It paved the way for a "literature seeking roots" (*xungen wenxue*) in 1985, which expressed complex if not inchoate intellectual and ideological tendencies; it cohered as a "wave" or genre mostly because its works described distinctive rural and regional cultures. Yet this "high" genre—unlike crime fiction—might not have existed without an official initiative to construct it. The name came first; the works second; critics dealt with the mismatch third.[126]

"Pure Politics": The Birth Pangs of "Legal System Literature"

The law of China's new crime fiction was passed down from on high, yet the formulation and interpretation of it betokened compromise. First were the compromises between the MPS, Ministry of Justice, academics, and legal associations. Second, hard-liners who wanted to propagandize law-and-order found common ground with liberals propagandizing for democracy and rule of law. Third, those who wanted crime fiction to be art found themselves working with people who saw it as a cash cow. It looked like a three-way compromise between official, liberal, and commercial interests, except that no "side" was pure. Among conservatives, the MPS was competing with Justice. Yu Haocheng of the MPS championed human rights. Professional writers wrote for the police. And all parties sought profit. Ideologically contradictory "coalitions" occur also in China's legislative process, a scholar notes.[127] Opposing liberal and conservative formulations of laws may put the idea of a law in play, even as they stymie final passage of any particular draft. "Legal system literature" was such a formulation. While opposing draft ideas of it were debated, diverse works of fiction were composed and read.

The public had its own semantics. One colloquial idea of legal system literature amounted to "trashy crime stories." Only bad people, after all, ever met the law. "Legal system" was sometimes a euphemism for punishment and control: "detective fiction" meant fighting crime with the mind, whereas "legal system fiction" meant fighting crime by force. To some liberals, "legal system" connoted class struggle. In a coy Beijing usage, "legal system" was what the police dished out to prostitutes and johns in vice raids. But the literal meaning was euphemistic. Tabloids claimed to be printing legal system literature in order to legitimate their wares.[128] All the more reason for officials to step in to protect the image of law enforcement.

The name "legal system literature" was evidently reinvented about 1984, with no acknowledgment of Wei Jun.[129] It was retroactively applied to all crime fiction since 1978 that meshed with the views of the post-Mao regime.[130] In 1984, *Selections from Legal System Literature* appeared in Anqing, which first put the phrase into a magazine title. The police naturally preferred *"gongan wenxue"* (police literature), but this term had no official track record either. The two terms were in "contention" in 1985. "Unity" was then achieved, and "legal system literature" became hegemonic. "Police literature" did not disappear, but it became a branch of "legal system literature."[131] By 1986, *Woodpecker* had the designation "legal system literature periodical" thrust upon it by authoritative organs of the Chinese Writers' Association. The new term wormed its way into the journal gradually.[132]

Yu Haocheng and many others had reservations about the term "legal system literature."[133] Conservatives worried that it might legitimate "crime fiction." They took up the old proportionality discourse; a story could be 80 to 90 percent about crime, with the criminal punished only in the last 10 to 20 percent.[134] But "legal system" was sufficiently suggestive of law-and-order that no police cadre could very well object to it in principle, particularly as legal institutions were being rebuilt in the mid-1980s. Wei Jun was an MPS cadre, and he raised the slogan in 1981 originally as an alternative to "detective fiction," which implied bourgeois private detection and had become derogatory, remembers Ye Yonglie. Legal system literature would reflect the reality of *police* work, not miraculous deductions. It would raise the position of detective stories, tame them, and make them more socialist.[135]

State intervention thus had mixed motives. Most obvious was the interest in controlling crime fiction to which Ye Yonglie had appealed in March 1982. "Healthy" domestic works under police control could replace foreign fiction, dissent, and pornography, while dedicated socialist Chinese cops replaced bourgeois foreign detectives.[136] Yes, admits a cadre, one effect of campaigns against "pornography" was to clear away some of ("legitimate") legal system fiction's competition.[137] The main thing was that all this stuff made money. New journals also provided editing and writing jobs for worthy judiciary and police cadres (the procuracy seems to have lost out).

Not only that, *police* heroes needed to stand out from PLA heroes, who usually got all the publicity. A senior *Police World* editor had called for a police counterpart to *Jiefangjun wenyi* (Liberation Army literature) on those grounds as early as 1980.[138] The literary inequality of the services deepened the police's inferiority complex before the PLA.

For cops, the new formulation meant an opportunity to write up their own cases, emerge from secrecy, and find a voice—to let the public realize, for the first time, their bravery, their sacrifices, their ingenuity in protecting the public. It would show that the police were a force not of irrational control, as under the Gang of Four, but of modernization. They had modern technology, just like the PLA. Moreover, an editor claimed, 4 percent of the population worked for the police, suggesting 40 million potential in-house readers.[139]

Legal system literature naturally was propaganda, with a place in the Five-Year Plan for Popularizing Common Knowledge of the Law announced by the central CCP Propaganda Department and the Ministry of Justice on December 4, 1985.[140] For some, it would teach citizens to "hate criminals," as 1950s detective stories had taught them to hate foreign spies. It would make readers more vigilant, perhaps more willing to report suspicious activities to the police.

For others, legal system literature would propagandize "legal system." There were conservative and liberal sides even to this. Fiction would keep people from being "oblivious to the law" (*famang*, lit., "blind to the law"), from breaking it because of unrealistic expectations about what they could get away with.[141] This might actually justify the very lowest crime fiction, as it did the *Crime and the Law* casebook from Jiangxi. The fiction could also raise a constituency for more legal reform, "democracy and legal system" (which some intellectuals equated), even human rights—topics about which mere journalists remained cautious.[142] It was useful that *fazhi*, "legal system," was homophonous with *fazhi* (rule of law); some felt that they were implicitly equated.[143] The police and judiciary might hope to enlist, even lead, China's most prominent and respected writers in this cause. Some enthusiasts claimed as foundational legal system literature every sort of historical work about justice, from *The Peacock Flies Southeast* to the *Longtu gongan* and *Water Margin*; cop classics "Sacred Duty" (Wang Yaping) and *Plainclothes Policeman* (Lü Haiyan); "legal" dramas like the play *Power vs. Law* and the film version of *Before the Bench and Behind the Scenes*; and "introspective" works about corruption and the Gulag, notably "People or Monsters?" (Liu Binyan), "Blood-Stained Magnolias Below the Big Wall" (Cong Weixi), and *Mimosa* (Zhang Xianliang). At least two who attended the Anqing conference discussed below dared to cite Liu Binyan's dissident "The Second Kind of Loyalty" as a foundational work of the genre.[144] Since writers were scapegoated in political campaigns, some actually hoped that legal system literature could promote the protection of writers' rights through the law.[145]

Some took a "literary" view; their mission was to elevate legal system literature and its social status—not simply deliver it from tabloid themes, but from the West's "merely popular" themes of crime, detection, and mystery for their own sake. This legal system literature would be a serious high literature like May Fourth fiction (without, perhaps, the dissidence), focusing on social problems, the roots of crime, and the potential for human rehabilitation under the penal system. Labor camp cadres wanted a voice too, and profits. Others claimed that Chinese, like Japanese, preferred a more social mystery fiction.

The new genre was to have a grand coming-out party and be officially ratified and embodied in a national organization of legal system authors and officials, at the National Research Conference on Legal System Literature in Anqing, October 8–10, 1986—exactly ten years after the arrest of the Gang of Four. The meeting was jointly sponsored by *Selections from Legal System Literature, Woodpecker, Blue Shield, Sword and Shield*, and *Chinese Legal System Literature*, whose combined circulation was 2.25 million even as individual "serious" journal circulations were plummeting from the high to the low 10,000s. Over 100 attended the conference, mostly police fiction cadres and writers like Wang Shuo, whose manuscripts editors wanted for their journals. Prominent liberals Liu Binyan, Wang Ruowang, and Yu Haocheng were invited as celebrities.[146] (Yu presented a paper in absentia; Wang Yonghong represented *Woodpecker*.[147] The meeting's backing by such liberals kept the editor of *Police World* from allowing his staff to go to Anqing.)[148] It was mostly an MPS operation; the Ministry of Justice had just staged a meeting of its own.[149] The liberals spoke freely and did not think of the meeting as a failure. It was still a liberal moment in 1986. It was the police who came away disappointed. They had not anticipated that a legal system literature might cut two ways.[150]

The main topic planned for discussion was how to raise the quality and "position" of legal system literature. *Les Misérables* and *Resurrection* were held up as ideals: China needed its own legal system literature like this! Liu Binyan, like Yu Haocheng, was not so keen on the "formulation." He thought it odd to sort literature by subject matter, and Tolstoy or no, the intent from above seemed to be to include as legal system literature "true crime" writing that was hardly literary. Why not improve the standards of real journalism instead, by removing restrictions? Another potential problem was exclusion of works about problems in the legal system that needed inclusion. Was it not hypocritical to speak of a legal system literature when the real legal system was far from under the rule of law?[151]

The meeting as recalled by the 1990 board of *Woodpecker* is that Zeng Zhennan and Zhang Qie spoke on the subject, whereas Liu Binyan and Wang Ruowang insisted on talking about other things. Liu's formal remarks in fact stressed liberation of the Chinese people, freedom of the press, and past injustices to Chinese of good will, and they contained his personal testament as a former Rightist; he said little about legal system literature as such.[152]

Memories differ as to whether a national association of legal system literature writers was founded or not. Evidently notices went out after the conference, asking authors to join. It was not founded in Anqing, got no recognition, and had few activities.[153]

Later, some blamed the setting as being unworthy of the state's ambitions for legal system literature. The hosts—*Selections from Legal System Literature*, its editor Geng Longxiang, the sponsoring Anqing Federation of Literature and Arts, and Anqing itself—were bit players on the national scene. The journal's priority in using the term "legal system literature," its runaway national circulation, and the proximity of Mt. Huang, which allowed big-name authors to do some postconference touring, had been in Anqing's favor. But Anqing was not an appropriate headquarters for a national association of writers, even genre writers. Some informants admit that regional prejudice and objections to the Anqing magazine as a mere reprint journal kept the hosts from playing a strong role.[154]

So legal system literature never reached its potential either as a unifier or as a tool of critique. Crime fiction was about to suffer again in early 1987, in the campaign against "bourgeois liberalization" that would kick Liu Binyan and Wang Ruowang out of the CCP; Liu left for the United States in March 1988. The proliferation of reading matter gave the leaders the impression of a problem of proportions again: there was simply too much crime fiction around, especially of the unedifying sort. But most journals, works, critiques, and the legal system literature formulation went on.[155] Its advocates even expanded the concept to include stories about divorce and inheritance law, including (retroactively) 1950s stories popularizing the era's new Marriage Law.[156]

That reformers did not give up is seen in their works; that the government did not flag is apparent from its activities, although many were in the name of police literature rather than legal system literature. After the Anqing meeting, *Woodpecker* and *Police World* arranged a *bihui* (writers' gathering) at a resort in the latter's home province of Fujian. The idea was for famous writers to gather for relaxation and touring as a sort of compensation in advance for articles they were to submit to the journals. The MPS had staged its own "gathering" in Qingdao; at the end of the 1980s, *Woodpecker* had them annually, and so did the *Renmin gonganbao* (People's public security gazette). Other magazines had them too, such as *Sword and Shield*. There were also training, lecture, and practice writing groups (*xunlianban, jiangxiban, lianxiban*) where younger writers heard famous writers lecture on how to write police fiction and had their compositions polished by more experienced hands. The MPS ran them, and the Anqing magazine is reported to have done so. There were even further attempts to set up associations of crime writers.[157] In the free atmosphere of January 1989, young Beijing writers of movie and TV screenplays, chiefly police dramas, founded a private association funded by a salon they ran (a bar, really).[158]

Outside critics were "mobilized" to write criticism of legal system literature; police and legal magazines "nurtured" theorists in order to produce books, anthologies and histories of police literature; they even sponsored conferences devoted to *pinglun* about it.[159] By 1990 the *People's Public Security Gazette* was cosponsoring a periodic column on "public security literature" in the Chinese Writers' Association's organ, the *Wenyibao* (Literature and arts gazette). It helped the concept of "police literature" achieve dominance over the "legal system literature" concept in the postmassacre era.

Political-legal institutes taught classes on legal system and police literature and how to write it.[160] There were books on it.[161] And inevitably there were prizes for discovering, developing, and bringing promising new authors to the genre. The first major competition, from March 1985 to March 1986, was sponsored by *People's Public Security Gazette, Blue Shield, Sword and Shield,* and *Crystal* for the best work of police literature. Subsequently the MPS sponsored "Gold Shield" contests every three years. Winners of the first prizes, in 1988, in short and medium-length fiction and reportage, were judged by the ministers of public security, justice, and culture (Wang Meng) and famous writers including Liu Xinwu and Chen Rong. After the magazine boards did an initial screening, the People's Public Security University and MPS did the second review. But the contest was initially conceived to honor the best work of "legal system literature." The *People's Public Security*

Gazette and *Literature and Arts Gazette* shared the dreadful task of running a prize competition for the best *pinglun* essays on police literature. That was during the dark days of 1990; promoting law and order in the wake of the massacre prompted all sorts of law enforcement activities, such as a three-month "Series of Activities on Legal System in the Film and Television Media" in Shanghai.[162]

The Ideal Product: An "Overdetermined" Genre, the More Beset by Contradictions

As usual, the state attempted to improve Chinese crime fiction through paternal regulation. Its habits of prescribing literary qualities and looking at art as a mixture of ingredients created an "overdetermined" legal system literature formulation whose specifications were so closely watched that they were often mutually contradictory. With the exception of Zeng Zhennan and a few others, the genre guardians were not content to stop at specifying subject matter, form, setting, style of heroism, intent (to make people less criminal), and effect (to do so by stirring up outrage at criminals and amazement at the ingenuity of their crimes—engaging both the "intellectual" puzzlement of the detective formula and the emotional catharsis of great literature).[163] The guardians wanted to specify and elevate legal system literature's social and literary position; send it down the path of "social realism"; and regulate the information dividend, as well as the literature's politics and morality—this too in the name of elevation. But neither the length nor the literary mode was specified; there could be legal system poems, plays, reportage, and "documentary fiction" (*jishi xiaoshuo*). The latter were not always distinguishable from fiction.

The result was not just a recipe for a genre, but for its ideal work. This too betrayed ambivalence; out of the muck of popular legal system literature would grow the lotus of its better essence. The object of the quest is here presented graphically as the intersection of ellipsoids representing genre characteristics. Actual works of legal system literature would be lesser versions of the ideal.[164]

Within each element subject to formularization, such as plot, characters, and heroism, were choices: "contradictions." Guardians of Chinese legal system, in their "united front" mode of accommodation, and according to the "mass literature" tendency to favor both high and low, always wanted to have it both ways. They wanted the delight of suspense *and* the realism of eschewing suspense. They wanted the plots to convey intriguing details about the legal system but also to cut to the chase. They wanted the police to be suspense heroes but also to help children cross the street. They wanted "good officials" as heroes but also a *system* that opposed "rule by men."[165] They wanted murders, maybe lots for them, to prove cop heroism and add hardboiled "realism"—but perhaps not, for that would be morally unedifying and not typical of Chinese society. Authors must write well enough to delight readers and yet not appear commercially adept.

The official discourse advocated that virtually every element of popular generic identity be transcended. The ellipsoids that constitute the following figure depict elements of legal system literature. Each ellipsoid is split down the middle into a complementary yin-yang pair. At the periphery yin prevails, the tried-and-true generic elements that make crime fiction popular. (The periphery represents all works of legal system literature, and it is not bad as a geographical metaphor—it might well have been in Guangxi.) This yin is squeezed to a minimum at the center, where the imaginary intersection of the constituent elements of the very best legal system literature takes place. Hints of the yin remain, must remain, but they have been sublimated by a "healthier" yang side of their particular story element that is merely latent in really popular fiction—though these yangs seem often enough to be defined simply as absence of yin. A Western critic might see the yang remediations on the original yin genre elements as political or ideological adulterations that weaken the story, but the moral, elevating intentions behind the ameliorations count for more in Chinese criticism. A further complication is that an elevated yang form (e.g., literary representation of law and order) may have more than one inferior-but-popular yin form—in this case either depiction of social anomie or a society of "too much law"—excessive contentiousness. Let us look, then, at the criteria as they seem to have been conceived officially in the 1980s. The larger aim is to reveal values pertaining to Chinese views of all literature and of the law.

Subject matter. Subject matter is second to form in most Western criticism, but it is principal where legal system literature is concerned, as in the genre construction of its nearest rival, "police literature," short for *gongan ticai*

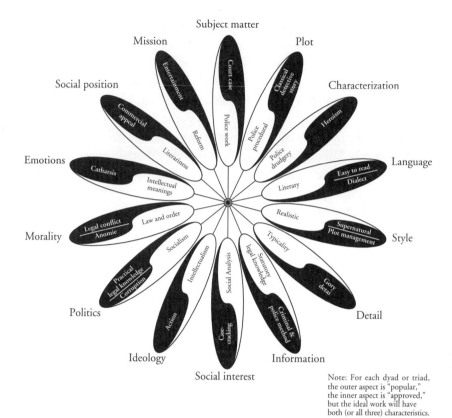

Note: For each dyad or triad, the outer aspect is "popular," the inner aspect is "approved," but the ideal work will have both (or all three) characteristics.

Legal System Literature: The Bureaucratic Ideal

wenxue (literature with public security [or police] subject matter [or themes]). The orthodox subject matter is not really so nebulous as correction of wrongdoing, as in a Chinese *Resurrection*. It is POLICE WORK and the work of judicial and other peace officers that is socially important. The lower subject matter from which this has been elevated is historic, Chinese, and popular: the COURT CASE, engendered by a covert, devious, often ingenious act of impropriety or violence that needs to be brought to light and punished by law. The case, indeed the crime, cannot be jettisoned if readers are to stay with the genre; and logically, police would have no work if there were no crimes (though espionage sufficed in Maoist times). The trick was to keep the "popular" attraction of court case subject matter while cleaning up its violence, even its ingenuity, since criminals must not be shown to be too smart,

certainly not smarter than cops (the sin of *The Girl Thief*). The subject need
not even be a crime; legal system literature had come to include "law stories"
about divorce and its social consequences, says a legal gazette reporter, and
also a case's "three extensions": Why did the criminal commit the crime?
How can he get a job after his release? What's the inner life of criminals?—
they make such beautiful handicraft paper eagles in prison.[166] Fiction about
labor reform is an official adjunct of crime fiction. One implies the other.

Yet legal system literature is more often about the work of cops than of
judges and lawyers. Chapter One explains that Chinese writers had no trouble imagining judges and procurators cracking crime cases. But the day of
fighting literary judges and procurators had ended for the time being, perhaps because so many cops were writing the new works, perhaps because of
the simple reality that the police, not the judiciary and procuracy, did most
of the work in the legal system, particularly the kind readers liked to read
about—catching crooks, analyzing evidence, locking people up, and sometimes judging and punishing them too. This kind of activity was all in the
MPS files for favored professional authors to use. As to trials, even lawyers
could not read the judicial files without special permission.

Plot. "Plottedness" (*qingjiexing*; plot ingenuity) was associated with "low"
and "popular" literature and was universally held to be one of the two or
three main attractions of Chinese legal system literature among the masses,
along with the satisfaction of seeing the good guys win.[167] A good legal system work must be a POLICE PROCEDURAL (or legal procedural) and not un-
duly stress plottedness. However, the historically much loved "popular" plot
formula from which the police procedural grew was the CLASSICAL DETEC-
TIVE STORY with its Sherlockian discoveries. The energy of that low form
should be kept. One might retain some amazing, "analytical" deductions
and suspenseful discoveries as concessions to popular taste. However, more
realism and less individualism is better.

Characterization. The characters in crime fiction are mostly given, but characterization offers choices. HEROISM is an audience-pleaser in the "low"
form, mixed with the cop's analytical detective brilliance. In the elevating
name of realism, and also to honor the police, the better legal system stories
must instead emphasize POLICE DRUDGERY and service: long hours and
sacrifice of family life.

This was a difficult point. Old-fashioned exciting and wish-fulfilling heroism was a staple of Maoism, one of its few assets. Heroism was also a staple of traditional Chinese fiction and the more hard-boiled forms of Western crime and spy fiction, and it was exploited in controversial "pure literature" novels by Ke Yunlu, author of *Xin xing* (New star), about the tribulations of a young civilian party member who comes to town and fights long odds to end corruption.[168] *New Star* was "serious" and "popular," as legal system literature aspired to be. Creation of a "savior," which in Maoist times had been considered a sign of bourgeois thinking, was now applauded by the police, who liked stories about good officials.[169] But savior officials were criticized by many legal system writers. They may have been jealous of Ke Yunlu's popularity and adaptability. Perhaps it was traditional popular taste that they feared.

Language. Language has crossover potential. The best legal system language is LITERARY, though to reach the masses it also must be EASY TO READ, or so officials imagined, perhaps too facilely. Beijing slang (*tuhua*) in Wang Shuo's late 1980s streetwise countercultural stories about petty criminals was socially "low" and understandable to the uneducated (he seldom mixed in "big words"), but also valued by intellectuals attracted to proletarian chic—hence "high" and trendy. Contrarily, DIALECT of all sorts might be "dangerous" enough to lend a story popular appeal, even if it were so obscure that most readers had to guess its meaning. Criminals contributed to slang with their "black argot." Through creative use of nonstandard vocabulary, works of legal system literature could attain an original and individual voice, drawing on genuinely "popular" culture and even criminal subculture.[170]

Style. A legal system story should be REALISTIC, providing scientifically and socially accurate scenes of the solution of crimes, and not pander to traditional PLOT MANAGEMENT, coincidence, and suspense. But the latter were of great popular appeal, and so were ghosts, the SUPERNATURAL, and the uncanny, which were simply taboo. However, one could introduce a fake ghost as a red herring and later show that it was not a ghost.

Detail. A writer with literary aspirations did not put all the GORY DETAIL about the crime or the detection into legal system literature.[171] One was not even allowed to provide details about crime techniques. The literally gory details about the corpse were what was left, so this very low aspect of the fiction often substituted for other details, making some legal system works exploitation fiction. One publisher of "popular literature" actually defended the printing of literally gory description as heightening the moral stakes of fiction.[172] In literature, the prejudice against "detail" had its most insidious effect not on technical disclosure, but on authors' imaginings—of cops' relations with their colleagues and criminals, for instance. Against detail was the old communist shibboleth of TYPICALITY. With police editors in the saddle, however, you could be sure that they would correct you if you confused, say, the color of the uniforms of the police with that of the judiciary.[173]

Information. Fears about excessive "detail" could mask competing ideas about what kind of education readers needed. A technical information dividend is a genre hallmark and a calculated means of attracting readers,[174] as writers of techno-thrillers know. Self-consciously dispensed technical information could remain in legal system fiction, but STATUTORY LEGAL KNOWLEDGE was better; perhaps it was the conceit of some cadres that scenes of police life—about their loss of sleep and their modern technology (in principle—details are seldom given)—were "information." But the kind of information that energized the original genres of crime, police, and detection was knowledge of CRIMINAL AND POLICE METHODS.[175] In the official view, this bespoke low, even criminal reader taste. Prisoners could subscribe to some legal system magazines in jail (e.g., *Blue Shield*),[176] but not to all; they did so allegedly to acquire "information" about the law. Unlike in America, prisons did not have big law libraries.

Social interest. Focus on society, or *shehuixing*—so admired in the Japanese detective story—was another axis of high and low value. Legal system literature should have it—should engage in abstract SOCIAL ANALYSIS of contemporary problems, notably those that lead to crime; vulgar, tried-and-true Western formulas only drew one into the trivial aspects of society (notably, crime itself) with their detection and cheap suspense. They focused merely on individual CASE-CRACKING. The ideal work would present a higher social truth while cracking the case that may have initially lured readers into reading the story.

Ideology. Legal system literature was supposed to have ideology, or thought (*sixiang*)—a higher understanding of how the law worked, as in its reform of people and society. Indeed, one of the new literature's purposes, opined Zeng Zhennan, departing from much official opinion, was to help one differentiate between law and morality.[177] This stress on deeper legal meanings would set Chinese legal system literature apart from vulgar Western detective fiction and from Chinese police literature, according even to one MPS cadre.[178] The Chinese genre would thus be known for INTELLECTUALISM—policy lessons, instead of simply ACTION.

Politics. Politics was not taboo, but it had to be correct. The ideal work would naturally prove that SOCIALISM was good. But legal system literature on vendors' stands sold out thanks to the "low" aspect of politics: CORRUPTION. Another appeal of tabloidized crime write-ups (as in *Democracy and Legal System*) was their unseemly interest in PRACTICAL LEGAL KNOWLEDGE— how to sue and make the law work for one's own selfish interests. This contradicted the higher aspects of socialist politics and morality. It was the wrong kind of detail. Legal knowledge was no longer secret, but this was not the legal knowledge that ought to be conveyed.

Morality. Legal system literature was in technique mainstream (*zhengtongde*) fiction with a "point," not avant-garde, like the fiction of the day most esteemed by literary critics.[179] The avant-garde was supposedly inaccessible to the mass reading public—elite by conception. Some thought legal system literature to be a form for educating the masses pure and simple. It needed clear morality, in accord with the premise that "to read it is to believe it," and frequent reader identification with protagonists. Many officials felt that crime fiction made people become criminals and that stories about good people tended to make people good.[180] The morality that was needed, in the official view, was one supportive of LAW AND ORDER, the spirit of a society run by laws and the ethic of human rehabilitation as trumpeted in Gulag and reform-school fiction.[181] Emphasis on accommodation and yielding was part of the old morality; here there was no conflict between the old (and popular) values and new high ones. But in modern times there was a new popular interest in moral confusion and ANOMIE. Wang Shuo and Liu Heng (*Black Snow*, after Simenon's *The Snow Was Black*?) exemplified it. It could add tang to stories about rudderless young people coming to see the light. The popular interest in real cases (*anli*) also bespoke an unseemly interest in LEGAL CONFLICT. Yet genre guardians encouraged write-ups of real cases as a form of popular genre reading matter. This left the door open to similar interests in creative legal system literature. Again, details about conflict that drew readers were pernicious, but they could at least be dressed up in legal terms.

Emotions. As in the West, emotions are distrusted; serious literature is thought to have INTELLECTUAL MEANINGS that distinguish it from popular fiction. Multilayered meanings are sanctioned in China, though not the utter indeterminacy that might betoken political doubt.[182] In contrast, popular fiction satisfies the reader with a profound emotional CATHARSIS; in crime fiction, this comes from seeing justice done and the bad guys caught. That can in fact be admirable, by Chinese lights. It is only in the modernist West that realism is low in relation to the avant-garde, with happy endings lowest of all. Somehow Chinese crime stories must be multilayered, "realistic," *and* have a happy ending, or at least one that does not lead to the depressing thought that justice is unattainable. This may seem like a debilitating contradiction left over from socialist realism, but it does legitimate the union of intellect and emotion.

Social position. The state wanted above all to manage the social position of legal system literature: to elevate it. This had implications for style, vocabulary, and other elements of what in propaganda work usually ran in the other direction, namely making it universal (*puji*). Legal system literature was to be known for its LITERARINESS. It was to be high, serious, and nongeneric, in view of the social importance of its theme. A Chinese *Resurrection* was the goal; the genre would include prestigious Gulag novels by Cong Weixi and Zhang Xianliang, which described suffering, and Ke Yan's long novel *Xunzhao huilai de shijie* (The world brought back), about reform school cadres sacrificing to remold juvenile delinquents. Though lacking in suspense and crime elements, these were traditional as well as MPS themes, and they may have made some readers cry.

Subliterary magazines put out exploitation fiction, known for its COMMERCIAL APPEAL. The legal system literature banner inadvertently protected and dignified such works. They (and also more Tolstoyan legal system fiction) mixed crime and love interests.[183] High and low remained under one umbrella; the idea was to make the literature serious while drawing on the "innate popular appeal" of cops and robbers—but better yet, leave out the robbers. An interesting lacuna, attested to by most informants (when asked), was satire of the legal system.[184]

Mission. Legal system literature had, in sum, a mission, like "pure literature." No one could define the latter's, or what literature was either, but everyone knew that literary callings were sacred. The mission of legal system literature was to aid in REFORM of the legal system, an idea that was broad enough to refer to systemic changes that some might consider subversive, or simply to efficiencies that stopped crime. The lower but acknowledged mission of legal system literature was ENTERTAINMENT.

The overlaps and contradictions of these categories are clear, but yet another difficulty was volunteered by Chinese critics: a serious genre should not dwell on the lifestyles of criminals and other lowlifes; it was not morally edifying. This was not a problem in the classical whodunit, where murders were committed on country estates and in people's parks, possibly by "the better sort." However, in the name of "realism" and edification, if not what Horace called genre "decorum," a work of Chinese legal system literature must not have a professor commit murder. Lowlifes did that sort of thing.[185] So the identity of the murderer too was overdetermined. Even if least likely, he must belong to the class of people most likely to murder according to social stereotype. But an unemployed youth's lifestyle was not good to talk about, so the plot strategy of keeping him and his guilt mysterious until the end worked out well. Yet it also ran counter to the interest in getting the inevitability of the beautiful reform of him into the open as soon as possible.

Variant Ideal Products:
Liberal Versus Official Literary "Seriousness"

The legal system literature formulation failed to catch fire at the 1986 Anqing conference and thereafter owing to increasing rifts in the party's moral-intellectual elite itself, between liberals and hard-liners. They agreed

THE "NATIONAL ESSENCE" OF CHINESE CRIME FICTION

	Old popular crime fiction	*Official new bureaucratic crime fiction*	*Dissident new bureaucratic crime fiction*
Crime	Petty gain	Social disorder	Official corruption
Treatment or solution of crime	Aestheticized	Socialist moral education	Dismantling socialist bureaucracy
Mode	Comedy/ melodrama	Tragedy: deterioration of public security	Tragedy: abuse of power
Criminals	Individuals	The lower, criminal class	Communist kleptocracy
Characterization	Stereotyped	Political-social	Political-moral
Detection	Technical, analytical	Social	Legal
Law	Law as a natural force	Paternal law	Adversary law

that writing about crime ought to be elevated, socially realistic, and morally and politically edifying. There simply were differences about what political direction China should take and about the nature of social reality—where the crime was coming from. The liberals had a vision of an open, adversarial society based on rule of law more like that in democracies of the West. Conservatives wanted continued paternalistic leadership. It was in a didactic and adversarial spirit that Liu Binyan himself attacked a formative piece of legal system literature in the Gulag subgenre, Cong Weixi's "Blood-Stained Magnolias Below the Big Wall," for lack of realism and of *needed* political-social-moral lessons. (The story has a savior official.)[186] But Liu also criticized avant-garde literature for uselessly pursuing art for art's sake. Likewise, he had no time for whodunits that showed no interest in the official roots of crime.

Hence this study presents a table showing the preferences of literature supposedly for pure entertainment (under the category "Old Popular"), the preferences of contemporary conservatives or officials (under the category

"Official New Bureaucratic"), and the preferences of contemporary liberals or dissidents (under the category "Dissident New Bureaucratic").

The crime. Desire for PETTY GAIN leads to crime in classic popular genres. Among the conservative bureaucrats, it is something more important: SOCIAL DISORDER, the result of failures in education. According to dissidents such as Liu Binyan, it is OFFICIAL CORRUPTION. But corruption could bring down the state, so conservatives also admitted it to crime fiction, depending on the political climate. It was better than a story about the murder of an unfaithful lover.

Treatment of crime. Crime is AESTHETICIZED in the old genres. Even old Chinese court case fiction, like Western whodunits, might emphasize the ingenuity of a crime at the expense of its immorality. The hard-boiled subgenre in the West, and the interest in pandemic injustice that surfaced in Chinese court case fiction, did not pretty up anything, but they did not extract due moral indignation either. The contemporary alternatives favor elevation. Conservative officials view crime as an occasion for SOCIALIST MORAL EDUCATION—didacticism; the liberals agree, but prefer lessons in DISMANTLING SOCIALIST BUREAUCRACY.

Mode. The Western crime story is often considered COMEDY—in its detection, which observes social manners, and in its risible portrayals of police. In other crime fiction, and perhaps Chinese *gongan* stories, MELODRAMA is the better characterization. The middle and right-hand side of the table show that TRAGEDY is the mode of the 1980s. For the conservatives, crime and DETERIORATION OF PUBLIC SECURITY lead to a bad end. For the liberals, ABUSE OF POWER does.

Criminals. Now for the professors. In the old genres, criminals are interesting, perhaps eccentric INDIVIDUALS with intriguing personal motives. Professors, aristocrats, and wealthy bourgeois make good criminals. For conservatives, the criminals are the LOWER, CRIMINAL CLASS, typified by "hooligans" (*liumang*—perpetrators of antisocial behavior, including vagrancy and sexual offenses). For liberals, the criminals are the COMMUNIST KLEPTOCRACY: high cadres.

Characterization. In the old genres, characterization is STEREOTYPED. Among the bureaucrats, both official and dissident, characterization is political. Socialist cadres (contemporary officials) stress upbringing and education. Hence they favor characterization along POLITICAL-SOCIAL lines. The Liu Binyans put the blame on greed and power-lust caused by the power configurations of socialism. The dissidents expect character to be delineated in POLITICAL-MORAL terms.

Detection. The old genres are full of TECHNICAL ANALYTICAL detection. For Chinese conservatives, detection is SOCIAL—mobilizing the masses to inform on each other. For liberals and dissidents, it is more likely to be LEGAL. Uncovering the trail of paper and money and the application of elementary concepts of rule of law reveal crimes within quotidian bureaucratic practice.

Law. In the old genres, the law is almost a NATURAL FORCE, an unfettered means of discovery and recompense of wrongdoing. Among conservative officials, it is PATERNAL LAW, a force restoring social order and retribution. For liberals, it is ADVERSARY LAW, a force of justice and retribution that discovers social conflicts and judges them in the open.

That was legal system literature, a gambit to control but also elevate crime fiction: something new but also very familiar. In the event, since literary officials did want their genre to be all things to all people, virtually anything was tolerated if it was not pornographic or critical beyond established norms of the party and state. It was not so much the literature itself as the name, "legal system literature," that nearly expired in the icy political winds ushered in by the June 4, 1989, massacre. The MPS had always preferred the term "public security" or "police literature"; the Ministry of Justice had always preferred "legal system literature." After the massacre the "two-line struggle" between the two genres or formulations broke out again, and in that restrictive climate "police literature" won.[187] The two major journals with "legal system literature" in their titles, the Ministry of Justice's *Chinese Legal System Literature* and the reprint journal *Selections from Legal System Literature,* bit the dust, whereas the only major police-run journal to expire was *Sword and Shield.* Whether the two formulations, "police" and "legal system," really suggested significantly different genres or subject matters was always moot. After 1989, books and articles traced the following precedents for "police literature" in a straight line of progression: (1) *gongan* fiction and whodunits; (2) anti-spy and suppressing-counterrevolutionaries books and films; (3) literature of the wounded; and (4) outstanding fiction and reportage of the 1980s ("the new era"). The field as a whole was defined to include nearly all actual works of the 1980s legal system literature except monumental works like *Resurrection* and the stories about divorce and inheritance law. Chinese works with Judge Bao in them were preferred to foreign ones. The usual observations were made about the merits and defects of the literature. Only the name changed.[188]

Yet the term "legal system literature" was not taboo. Wei Jun, the police cadre who first promoted it, got his book of genre history and criticism, *Legal System Literature and Creation*, published in 1990 (by the press he managed, to be sure). And the term made a noticeable comeback in the 1990s. In July 1992, *Blue Shield* began calling itself a "Monthly Journal of Legal System Literature" on its title page.[189] By the mid-1990s, with the renewed national emphasis on passing new laws and strengthening the legal system, important veteran culture bureaucrats in the party such as Feng Mu and Chen Huangmei referred very positively to legal system literature again, ignoring the concept of "police literature."[190] By then, some critics even spoke pridefully of the history of Chinese *detective* fiction.[191] Still, the ancestry of Chinese crime fiction, however designated, remains unsettled. Even before the massacre, Zeng Zhennan warned that the official preference for officials who were incorruptible "fathers and mothers of the people" was a holdover from feudal values.[192]

CONCLUSION

Politics, concern with genre—"rectification of names"—and a sense of high and low born of the assumed moral importance of literature have been constant companions of Chinese literature under communism, even since commercial forces were unleashed in 1984. Subject matter involving crime and the law (*she fa wenxue*) seemed to critics unavoidably low, even when on the next page they linked it to Tolstoy. Chinese officials tried to reclaim part of

China's fiction about crime and the law for the "high," morally important road—and for themselves, who laid down the law. This was impossible, not only because the late 1980s was a time of relative freedom, but because subject matter was king in their new "genre," and that very element was bound, in China, to send its reputation plunging. Crime fiction still meant sex and violence.

Since communism originally banished both law and literature as we know them, it is ironic that it later wedded them in an official genre. Both were educational in their bloodlines, but the union reinforced the need to keep their offspring respectable.

The parties who came to the wedding were the lower forms of law and literature: penal law and popular fiction. While the matchmaking was going on, the law in love with fiction was mostly known for his toughness, from his MPS associations. The fiction in love with the law was known for her shameless seduction of readers—in exchange for money—with illegal hawkers in the streets and railway stations as the pimps. Both partners were to emerge from the wedding reborn, aspiring to their higher selves, according to the pastor (the CCP, in an ecumenical ceremony representing all bureaucratic sects) and the ancient rite of ennoblement (ideologization) over which he presided.[193]

In union with literature, penal law would turn to higher truths of, if not exactly Rites, morality and public service. He would grow up and try some less violent, more complicated true *legal* cases of inheritance and divorce law. He might even do a little pro bono work in human rights, since that was educational and furthered modernization. Like any Chinese lawyer, he would remain a state employee. He must serve the law—and the truth—rather than go wherever his clients wanted to take him.

Fiction would become a little less wild after marriage, too; she would grow up, get an education, and learn a thing or two from the law about the beauties of a regulated life. She must keep her good looks and ought still to have lots of admirers—of the right kind—but now she had a career, in education. It was hoped she might accomplish something monumental, Tolstoyan. (No mere "volunteer work" or beauty pageants for her; she was a Chinese woman, her labor power liberated, so there was no reason why she could not contribute to truths as complete and beautiful as those of any political theoretician.) High literature might have a civilizing influence on all those boys in the MPS, fantasizing about the guns they were not allowed to fire in life.

Happily, the pastor left the couple alone after the wedding (more than usual), until they opted for a trial separation after June 4, 1989, still without renouncing the vows of 1984. Meantime, it had been a suitable marriage of convenience allowing each partner to experiment. Their offspring from 1978 to 1980, born before the marriage and without official parentage, were more acceptable in other societies than in their own. But the legitimate offspring, the works of the new legal system literature, were praised by officials and read by the public, and they developed stronger, more individualist personalities than their older, less legitimate siblings. The fact was that the bride and groom were much older than the pastor. They thought they remembered past lives going back thousands of years and prior marriages to each other. Were the preacher and his ceremony even necessary? Common-law marriage was on the rise, whereas the pastor's religion was fast dying out. There was a gulf between cultural theory and reality in the age of Deng Xiaoping, even when the two appeared to jibe.

CHAPTER FIVE

Fruition

This book finds, in closing, that Chinese fiction about crime and the law was not effectively killed. It is true that it suffered and still suffers from low status, limited freedom of expression, and ghettoization as a genre fiction in proportion to its very embrace by police magazines and popular fiction journals.[1] Many writers are actually proud of limiting their imaginations to "social reality"; they fetter themselves still more when the MPS gives them real case files to fictionalize. Yet the official prescriptions for legal system literature turned out to be nonbinding, even as the name provided protection for all sorts of deviations.[2]

Some writers escaped old formulas and new official formulations by taking an avant-garde path—though even experimentalism could become formulaic. Some pursued a realism beyond typicality, or probed taboo areas of official crime—though "critical realism" also had its Chinese formulas. Others escaped the mandate to educate. They wrote fiction as low as they thought readers wanted it. Even the many authors in the police force provided some quality along with all their quantity. "Social reality" was changing so fast that few could presume to figure it out from first principles any more. But these are topics for a sequel about Chinese writers' "escape from the law."[3]

The three famous fictional works (plus a Zhang Yimou film made from the last) that conclude this study are outside the aforementioned "escape" modes. All three plots contain some dissidence; Wei Dongsheng's story might have been considered avant-garde had it been published in a "pure literary" magazine instead of *Woodpecker*. But all three dance, consciously or not, within the chains of the legal system literature formulation. Even though it was created by bureaucrats, it reflected an inchoate national consensus about the good and bad of crime and law in literature.

One can evaluate these works from at least five standpoints. The state evaluation of them as legal system literature ought to be that they meet the many contradictory demands of the formulation: all are literary, not "genre fiction" in any narrow sense, and all attracted a mass urban readership. Each of the authors is a former professional or apprentice professional in the justice system. Still, one can imagine the MPS and party bureaucrats fussing over these works. Why could the authors not have selected brave policemen as heroes and shown them removing dangerous elements from society? Why make heroes of lawyers, a troubled cop, and a "legally blind" peasant woman of all people? The stories have messages, but are these the messages society needs? Why must "serious" stories always be so critical? Why does "rule of law" have to mean all of these things, instead of just getting people to follow rules and laws?

These stories really are about the law more than about crime: legal system literature. The first work makes heroes of activist lawyers. The second implicitly equates a cop and a criminal. The third could pass for an empathetic "law story"[4] about the hunger in society's lower ranks for a more formal and solemn justice than mediation and political compromise can provide. Perhaps the police were dreaming about legal system literature as a genre fiction after all, to make heroes of cops and "expose" the criminal element while somehow elevating those subjects' seriousness. It is doubtful that Georges Simenon or Dashiell Hammett (converted to the side of the police) could have written literary crime-and-law fiction to these specifications.

From the standpoint of readers and viewers seeking amusement—and many, in China no less than in the West, also wanted at least a sense of getting some information—these three works met all expectations, judging by their notoriety (there are no reader surveys). These works please by mixing art and entertainment, often with help from genre conventions. Some readers, however, probably found them too political, and Wei Dongsheng's piece too difficult; by this time it was easy to find stories that were full of danger and violence without the distraction of deeper cultural and political meanings.

From the standpoint of an American critic in a literature department or a newspaper reviewer of crime books, these works are flawed or middlebrow, except for Zhang Yimou's film. Even so, many Western readers might enjoy the stories if they could read them. But they would enjoy them only because of the exotic atmosphere, some critics might thunder back. Yes, but is it any different for the Chinese reader? Good crime fiction often succeeds by telling a good story (which is something more than just having a good plot, Symons reminds us) while taking the reader to new places, whether Victorian London or a southern U.S. courtroom. The works below transport one to the special worlds of a Chinese law firm, a cop's stressed-out home life, and a "new frontier" where urban-educated cadres must make their rules sound convincing to newly rich country folk suddenly filled with expectations of emancipation. These locales are exotic to Chinese readers too.

From the standpoint of a literary historian, these works show Chinese fiction about crime and the law leaving the imitative phase of the whodunits and melodramas described in Chapter One and finding its own voice. Having acquired ideology, which inevitably will date them, perhaps these pieces are bound one day to pass away, like Maoist fiction. Or maybe they will be dismissed not for having originated in the minds of bureaucrats but for appearing to be a Chinese kind of "sensational literature"—one the bureaucrats failed to tame when they gave it a name evoking legal reform. The best works of Dashiell Hammett, Truman Capote, and John Le Carré likewise have had trouble disassociating themselves from "the crime novel."

This study educes yet a fifth perspective: all three works imagine changes in China's legal culture. The early-1980s genre fiction discussed in Chapter One was satisfied to call adjudication by a good, paternal judge who played by the rules "rule of law"; the newer stories evidence more faith in and much deeper curiosity about the possible meaning of a truly adversarial law. Older concerns raised in Chapter Two, about whether enforceable norms are universal or class-bound, still appear, but the newer stories proceed to much more complicated questions of legal practice. Matters that intrigued readers of the 1990s were thought to be of interest only to lawyers a decade earlier.

SEEKING AN ADVERSARIAL LAWYER SYSTEM

The title of Wang Xiaoying's novel *Ni wei shui bianhu* (Whom do you defend; finished in 1987) suggests both legal defense and a moral question—whom would *you* "defend" among such characters—or among your friends in life? The title can even be read as an accusation hurled at the lawyers: What crooks are they getting off now? This is quintessential legal system literature, with genre interests in lawyers, detection subplots, and mystery, as well as a "serious" advocacy both ideological and legal: adversary law. The novel is too eclectic and literary to be called a formula; it has length, "style" (quotations from the Daoists and Tagore), and higher moral themes, though it was not avant-garde enough for the critics. Probably many Chinese readers liked Wang Xiaoying for the same reasons they did Sidney Sheldon and Irving Wallace.[5] Yet Wang's novel is a good fit with a subgenre of the full-length novel that Heather Dubrow for one takes as paradigmatically opposed to popular genre fiction: the *Bildungsroman*.[6] *Whom Do You Defend* is the *Bildung* of a generation of law students turned legal professionals in the 1980s, after two decades' suppression of legal defense, from 1959 to 1979.

At 744 pages (522,000 characters), Wang Xiaoying's novel does for lawyers what [Lü] Haiyan's *Plainclothes Policeman* (741 pages, 440,000 characters) did for cops. Haiyan's politically serious but best-selling *Bildungsroman* of a dedicated and reformist young policeman sent to jail was the consummate legal system novel since 1985—though the author insisted it was "pure literature." Haiyan belonged to the judicial system only in the broadest sense. He was an ex-cop, ex-prison guard, and assistant manager of the MPS's Kunlun Hotel. Colleagues saw his novel as their particular profession's testament.[7] Indeed, it is a police version of Ke Yunlu's *New Star* (the *Bildungsroman* of a civilian party reformer).

Haiyan's hero protagonist, like Ke Yunlu's, is male and a generation younger than the female Mei Zhen, the hero of *Whom Do You Defend*. Policing and party administration were careers fortunate enough to survive Maoism; Mei Zhen and her colleagues embody the "lost adolescence" of a lost profession—which, by force of history, is also a lost generation. Through flashbacks, the reader views their original education in law school in the 1950s. Their continuing education has always been and still is in politics. The revival of lawyering in the 1980s offers these middle-aged law professionals a second adolescence. In the process, Lawyer Mei becomes more assertive, as her teachers and bosses attest, and more sensitive to the barriers that all Chinese women face before the legal system. This is a feminist novel written by a woman.

Wang Xiaoying satisfies twentieth-century Chinese taste for the long, nineteenth-century French or Russian social novel of character and manners, which sums up an era through social conflicts and love interests. (Her favorite foreign reading matter included *Anna Karenina, Resurrection, Madame Bovary, Les Misérables, The Scarlet Letter,* and *The Gulag Archipelago*.)[8] *Whom Do You Defend* also suggests the traditional Chinese novel, with its myriad characters, subplots, and intriguing interlacings of heroes, villains, and stratagems; the reader is left in suspense at the end of each chapter. In the work's length and the breadth of its social panorama one finds echoes of the Maoist epic. And as a work of the 1980s, *Whom Do You Defend* is full of flashbacks and modernist passages with dream symbolism. Wang Xiaoying is of China's modernist generation and gender; she is a woman redefining herself in fiction after having paid her dues as a rusticated educated youth (*zhiqing*). With all its crusading for social reform, the novel ultimately fulfills the definition of an ideologically serious, reader-accessible novel of the old school in the manner, and with the middling critical and social status, of Charles Dickens, Anthony (and Joanna) Trollope, George Gissing, Edith Wharton, Louis Auchincloss, and Ke Yunlu.

Characterization defines the nineteenth-century novel. Mei Zhen anchors *Whom Do You Defend*'s plot and lawyerly ethos. Her drive and initiative are credible because she is the daughter of a famous lawyer who helped build China's first professional legal culture before all memory of it was erased by the 1949 revolution. Mei Zhen experienced its short-lived rebirth, under Russian influence, while training at a Political-Legal Institute in the mid-1950s. The profession's third springtime is in the novel's present, in the 1980s. Emblematic of how formerly "bourgeois" professions were being ideologically rehabilitated, Mei's melancholic and ineffectual, house-husbandly spouse, Zhuang Shitong (nicknamed Zhuang Zi, like the Daoist writer and philosopher who favored "nonaction"), has taken as his life mission the writing of a legitimating history of Chinese lawyers, centered on Mei Zhen's great father. (There is no hint that the concept of the national profession might be stretched to include any pre-twentieth-century native roots.) Mei Zhen herself, known as "Lawyer Mei" in the 1980s, is modeled after Wang Xiaoying's own boss while Wang was apprenticed as a part-time lawyer in 1985–86. Having handled 22 of the requisite 25 cases, Wang Xiaoying was nearly ready to be examined as a licensed lawyer, but her mentor pointed out that she was more cut out to be a writer; she too readily saw both sides of an argument. That a lawyer *should* cleave to one side of a case is the Western, "bourgeois" conception of a lawyer in adversary law.

Before writing this novel, Wang Xiaoying had seen the outside world, including America in 1986, and she had written fiction about Chinese students overseas.[9] Her mother was a high official on the Shanghai Municipal Court. But the cases in *Whom Do You Defend* are fictional. Wang's mentor emphasized the lawyer's duty to protect her clients' rights by keeping their cases out of literature[10]—a problem to which the MPS was less sensitive.

The other major characters in the novel are Mei Zhen's 1950s "law school" classmates. Now they are coworkers in a new lawyers' office (*lüshisuo*) of the 1980s, in Shanghai, one infers from bits of dialect. The lawyers are salaried state (central government) employees; the firm is a state-run office under the Municipal Judiciary Bureau, subordinate to the new Ministry of Justice. The local bureau is led on the spot by its own party committee, which, besides the press, is the group the director of the firm most wants to impress (117).

A flashback to a graduation party in 1956 is a guide to the lawyers' character today, though in the 1950s all were young and romantic, singing Russian songs, quoting Russian novels, and reciting love poems from Pushkin. He Jue, Lawyer Mei's rival in the 1980s, is class leader in 1956 and the class Communist, dangling sponsorship into the party before ambitious classmates. She will graduate and become a judge. Fang Boding, her future husband, is the handsomest one, a "Byron," head of the student association. He sings the praises of lawyers as public servants and, true to his ideals, becomes one. At the suggestion of Mei Zhen's famous lawyer father, he defends an accused counterrevolutionary, and so, by twisted official logic, is later assumed to be one. Judge He Jue will be induced to divorce him; unlike most characters in literature of the wounded, which put its heroes into just such dilemmas, she is complex enough to realize her mistake at the time.

Tian Shifei, also handsome and head of the school's Communist Youth League, is of rustic origins. By Maoist logic his class background is good, but he is professionally insecure—ignorant of Pushkin and yet still eager to be like Fang Boding. Tian dreams of becoming a procurator, but after graduation he will only be able to get a job as a lowly clerk in the procuracy. In post-Mao times too, he is destined for a default profession: legal journalism. To compensate, he will take "shortcuts," even as the editor of a legal gazette, compromising his ethics and disgracing himself.

Mei Zhen wants to be a lawyer like her famous father; so does Zhuang Zi, who has done a legal internship (like Wang Xiaoying's) with Mei's father. In 1956 that great lawyer of the Republican era had not yet had his comeuppance from the revolutionary left, but he would, shortly. Small wonder that Zhuang Zi became a cynic, though not Mei Zhen. Perhaps her father's dedication to following social "adverse currents"—defending innocent people charged by political rivals with counterrevolution—explains what is a mystery to her classmates: why Mei Zhen married Zhuang Zi, son of a "landlord and traitor," when she was pursued by Fang Boding, Tian Shifei, and a number of others.

These old love rivalries affirm the once beautiful (now middle-aged) Mei Zhen, not the more politically powerful He Jue, as the pivot of this fictional prosopography. The jealous He Jue used her political assets in 1956 to snag Mei's first love, Fang Boding. Then He Jue abandoned him for political and career reasons. In the 1980s, He Jue seeks to reconcile with the still handsome and popular lawyer Fang, but he is not interested. This renders He Jue incongruously powerless. Romances of the past intensify her rivalry with Mei Zhen, though the two women, "partners" at the same firm, are both proposed as model city lawyers by the firm's director. The old love interests also heighten continuing rivalry among the males—professional "adversaries" by training, schooled now by the hard knocks of political persecution, failing marriages (the morally weak Tian is having an affair with a nurse, Yan Yan, because his wife is ill), and collective disillusionment because of the decades-long disgrace of jurisprudence during their prime.

Mei Zhen is kept off balance too. Her husband, Zhuang Zi, dies in midnovel, leaving her available again. Fang Boding, seen with one possible new match after another as he keeps up his resistance to the wiles (and "masculine" charismatic power) of his ex-wife, He Jue, begins to appreciate anew the beauty of the Mei Zhen he knew in college—in the person of her twenty-year-old daughter, Zhuang Mei! *Whom Do You Defend* poses no happy solutions, certainly not for women. In love, one truly wonders whom to "defend."

The cases on which the plot turns in present time are mostly civil—inheritance disputes and divorces—for the protagonists are the Civil Group in their firm, which also has a Criminal, Economic, and new Patent Group (42). Divorces constitute "over half" of the firm's civil cases (308). But there is a criminal case too, to liven things up, provide mystery, and further a reformist argument of Wang's—that civil cases are as important as criminal and may lead to crime if left unresolved. That lawyers Mei and He work on several cases at once, leaving little time for a personal life, furthers the professional discourse in praise of lawyers. And their taking of unlikable clients makes *Whom Do You Defend* a brief for a true adversary legal system. Having many interlacing subplots also serves expectations from the nineteenth-century realistic and ancient Chinese "popular" novel genres.

Lawyer Mei's work begins with the Tang Shunü divorce case: a woman in her forties desperately seeks freedom from a thirteen-year marriage in which her husband has never been sexually available.[11] Mei Zhen represents Tang's plea for divorce, but it looks hopeless in the face of opposition from Tang's in-laws, her mother, all parties' work units, and various responsible social entities that really are not so responsible. Their only goal is to "preserve the family."

Meantime, Lawyer Mei represents the artist Wu Heng on the opposite end of another divorce case. Wu beats his wife, but the legal and social power structures (the parties' work units and their neighborhood association) will not grant him a divorce either. His wife, Ms. Dong—ably represented by He Jue—is opposed to divorce; the very thought of being cut loose turns her suicidal. When Ms. Dong is found stabbed to death, Wu needs a criminal defense. Confessing because he feels responsible, then retracting his confession, he claims that his wife committed suicide in front of him. Lawyer Mei stands by her client as his case enters a criminal phase.

Then there is a multiparty inheritance suit with courtroom drama more typical of Perry Mason than Chinese reality. It has revelations of new facts (which sometimes do occur in China's *civil* trials, Wang avers), colorful ad hominem attacks, and lawyers' objections, some of which are even sustained. Old Fan Yuanchu, an eldest son who inherited the family property before the revolution and sold it, becoming rich from the proceeds by building shoe factories abroad, is being sued by the brothers cut out of the inheritance. They allege that the old father's primogeniture solution was "feudal." Not too much moral outrage can be mustered for the main plaintiff, Fan Yuanlü, however, for the defendant sent him off to Hong Kong (not as good as America, though, where Fan Yuanchu sent his own son) and paid off the irresponsible Yuanlü's gambling and whoring debts. The Hong Kong plaintiff is represented by Lawyer He, who personally hates him but resolves to win the case in order to awe and thus "seduce" into marital reconciliation her exhusband, Fang Boding, who represents the defendant, Fan Yuanchu!

The case is settled in a compromise weighted toward the defendant, yet Wang Xiaoying entangles them in a reprise that pits Mei Zhen in a feminist battle. A widow, Yan, who always kept to herself but owned a house, dies intestate and without relatives, leaving the state to advertise for possible heirs to come forward before it seizes her property. Numerous frauds do surface, enriching the social comedy of the novel, and finally a much abused woman comes forward called Shen-or-Fan Huiting. Sold off long ago by her putative father to an unscrupulous ex-soldier who never even gave her the courtesy of a divorce (he now refuses it more than ever), she claims to be an illegitimate daughter of Fan Yuanchu's father. She became the all-but-adopted goddaughter of the widow Yan, who has just been identified as the old man's last concubine. The two despised women of the Fan family had sought refuge in each other's company; however, Huiting was a Red Guard for a time and had raided the Fans. Now the Fans also deny that they legally deeded over to the concubine, Ms. Yan, the house where she and Huiting lived. In comes Mei Zhen, to represent the disempowered and disowned Huiting, and also her godmother Yan's posthumous claim of Fan property, for Huiting's sake. Mei Zhen's first adversary is therefore the old Fan family lawyer—her still available old flame (indeed her boss, in a new firm, as will be explained)—Fang Boding. Her other opponent is Tian Shifei, no longer just a journalist at a legal gazette, although that job had put him under the Judiciary Bureau's jurisdiction as surely as if he were in a law firm. Now he is Mei's colleague in the new law firm. Tian has been blackmailed by the brother of his illicit lover, Yan Yan, into fraudulently representing him as a relative of the deceased widow Yan. "Like Zhuge Liang" (624), Tian must first ally with Mei Zhen (*his* former love object too), to prove that the widow Yan was a legal inheritor of Fan property, and then oppose Mei Zhen, to deny Huiting's connection to the widow Yan while upholding the spurious one of his own client named Yan.

These are by no means the only cases. Early in the novel, in a chapter called "A Day in the Life of a Female Lawyer," a married woman seeks Mei Zhen as counsel for a divorce case (Lawyer Mei refuses the case, for she knows her to be an adulteress), and a man wants representation against the housing bureau for leaving him homeless. He cannot get past the firm's receptionist because his papers (his "yellow ticket," Jean Valjean would say) mark him as an ex-con. Mei Zhen accepts this unattractive client after he sees her at her home. Taking his case earns her unexpected new enemies in the neighborhood where the ex-con used to live. The neighborhood committee writes malicious accusatory letters to Mei Zhen's boss, the director of the law firm, accusing her of abetting a criminal. (Not only do the committee members not want an ex-con back as neighbor; they also took possession of his rooms and do not want to relinquish them.) A later diversion that keeps the competitive, oratorical, and professional interests going is a moot court at the 1980s Political-Legal Institute. It tries yet another divorce case, which functions as an instructive play-within-the-play. Then there is the stream of clients who visit a newly founded law firm of Fang Boding's that sets up a booth in an open-air market to take a sample of all the victims of China's unformed legal system. Asks one victim, can a man (illegally) detained six months without being charged ask for his back wages? Answer: It depends; were you acquitted or was the prosecution simply called off? The police or a work unit may punish even an acquitted person administratively, outside the justice system, and therefore, it seems, all the more incontestably (379).

New cases complicate the lives of the other lawyers too. Fang Boding is pressured by the local court to represent a young prostitute who murdered a high cadre's son. He investigates and finds that it was revenge for the boy's having raped her years earlier. The rape caused her downfall in the first place. The boy was a gang leader—not an impossible scenario for a cadre son these days.

Meantime, Xiaotian, son of rising communist star He Jue, is accused in a corruption suit. He is Fang Boding's son too; will the estranged parents cooperate, and will such competitive people risk their own ascending careers to help him? (Answer: Within limits.) Complicating Xiaotian's case is the fact that he is a reformer perhaps facing political revenge, and that Tian Shifei, the journalist, is legal adviser to the factory where Xiaotian works. He wants to take Xiaotian's case for self-advancement.

But the plot is hardly so simple. And Wang Xiaoying attracts her readers from the start with devices from crime fiction. Her novel opens (in a sort of prologue or "wedge") with an unidentified youth, bloodied by a knife wound, who bursts in on a night watchman in a deserted alley, shouts "I didn't kill her," and then runs off. Even this quickly gets down to social comment, and it applies to societies other than China's. The watchman is annoyed that the police act more suspicious of him than of the perturbed youth.

The youth's identity is the initial mystery. When it is assimilated with the story of Lawyer Mei's long-standing divorce case client, the artist Wu Heng, whose wife turns up dead in an alleged suicide, the two mysteries form a traditional detective interest. They are gradually solved (between other subplots) by typical clue-gathering; Mei Zhen's apprentice lawyers interview suspects and look for the murder weapon as police in a procedural would do. Another conventional mystery threading through the novel is, Who is the insane man whom Lawyer Mei must visit in the hospital annually on a particular day in spring, to satisfy her father's deathbed wishes? (He is the father of an innocent boy sent away as a political criminal because Mei's father copped out and plea-bargained his case once he learned it had already been decided on political grounds before the trial; Mei Zhen continues her father's penance without knowing why.) Gang violence and muggings, their frequency made plausible by revenge motives within political-legal power struggles, punctuate the plot. The identity of apprentice lawyer Ma Haibo's muggers is food for Sherlockian inquiry because Ma has been working on several cases, including that of the homeless ex-con, who has more enemies than anyone knew. This is solved by a surprise near the end of the novel.[12] Lawyer Mei has her watch stolen during the moot court proceedings, evidently by a law student of the 1980s (the theft is also an omen of Zhuang Zi's death; 310).

Other devices include end-of-chapter suspense and courtroom drama—surely a fiction—in which new lawyers actually speak and new evidence is introduced, effecting surprise outcomes. By the novel's end, Wang has dramatized the Wu Heng trial, the Fan inheritance trial and reprise with Huiting's and the widow Yan's posthumous claims, plus the spurious one of the Yan man blackmailing Lawyer Tian (a tombstone has been altered, but Lawyer Mei finds the original with Fan Huiting's name on it), not to mention the moot court. The romances and possible reconciliations of exes evoke another popular genre, the love story. Emplotment with tragic Cultural Revolution fates (losing job and family, being beaten or becoming a political prisoner) is itself generic, often mixed with tragic love themes in works since the late 1970s, but surely it also evokes the older bathetic appeal (particularly when the victims are female) of weepy popular fiction from the first half of the twentieth century.

Much mystery comes from amazing plot turns and coincidences in the characters' mutual relations. There are romantic, revengeful, reconciliational, and cross-generational demarches, as well as terminal illnesses typical of the nineteenth-century European novel. Zhuang Zi is revealed to be terminally ill in mid-novel; he will leave Mei Zhen available, and he tearfully gives Fang Dingbo, his old rival, his blessing to pursue Mei when he is gone. Stratagems and intrigues fulfill interests from the traditional Chinese novel. Inspired by a foreign movie about surrogate mothers, Tang Shunü's mother-in-law forces a country cousin on her as a stud; this is rape, but there is no pregnancy, so soon it is rumored that Ms. Tang has an illness and that that is what has left her husband childless. Her case for divorce ought at this point to be very strong; but how can she pass her medical examination now that she is no longer a virgin?

The best lawyer is the one who wins the most cases. The party and its judiciary bureaucracy will construct the final ranking. *Whom Do You Defend* is thus a social novel, commenting on character; a novel of social realism, commenting on institutions; a *Bildungsroman*; a comedy of manners; a novel embodying fate more than character development, in which characters with European flaws achieve Chinese destinies; a typical 1980s political allegory of the evil of leftism and the goodness of reform; and, to be sure, an affirmation of law, hence legal system literature—but also, a "higher" social reform novel, given its "higher" feminist antifeudal discourse. Modernism appears in the characters' intertwining streams of consciousness and in Freudian touches like Mei Zhen's recurrent dream of a white bird, thought by Hainan superstition to be the soul of Mei's sent-down sister, the victim in Hainan of a political murder twenty years earlier.[13]

These many "serious" interests support adversarialism against paternalism. Mei Zhen argues on behalf of litigation itself: "I hope that the open trial process will dispel more and more citizens' sense of mystery, of dread, and of shame, in going to court." (680). The first chapter introduces only crimes and mysteries, leaving the first mention of lawyers and trials for the next chapter, by which time they clearly are needed—an ideological strategy as well as an appeal to formula crime readers. Wang suggests that lawsuits can be used to protect the environment or ensure government services like garbage removal, surely a novel idea then (27, 384).

A client flatters Mei Zhen—a lawyer!—as a "female Lord Bao of our time" (625).[14] In this imaginary society, reformer lawyers are cult heroes; high school girls seek their autographs (386). Lawyers are saviors of accused people in distress (289)—though the discourse of law being without mercy (*wuqing*) is still affirmed. Even the press sees the great Fan-Shen-Yan trial near the end of the novel as a contest between great lawyers, to be decided by their wits, not the merits of the case or the party's decision. By the late 1980s some Chinese were indeed beginning to see lawyers as people of status again, as educated professionals earning real money. But that impression is exaggerated, the novel protests: people fail to realize that lawyers' fees are taken by the state, with the lawyers themselves getting only modest salaries (23).

The novel endorses the idea of lawyers as celebrities, famous for oratorical powers and their personal win-loss records. Mei Zhen's father was such a one. The 1980s reader was asked to see irony in Lawyer Mei's riding a bus without being recognized. Such individualism and hero worship were once heresy. In this work, a client scares a witness into talking with the admonition, "You mustn't lie to a lawyer; she can sue you" (602). Wang more than once emphasizes lawyers' cross-examination skills as the crux of their success in the Chinese process. They expose lies and also promote justice beyond the client's interest (279, 637).

The young women law-school graduates just entering Mei's firm as interns do not, however, get assigned to Lawyer Mei, their role model. That privilege goes to an arrogant young man named Ma, a lady-killer with a politically powerful father. He makes a move on Lawyer Mei's rude and impressionable but pretty "modern" daughter, Zhuang Mei, after chancing to save her from a mugging in a deserted alley. *Whom Do You Defend* is Ma's *Bildung* too, and the daughter Zhuang Mei's. Ma wants only to handle high-profile corruption cases (he reads Judge Dee mysteries), but he finally shapes up after taking the housing case of the ex-convict, still another case of an undissolvable marriage, and other investigations. He comes to resent the affront to his dignity and the dignity of the law when people help him just because of his famous father. Zhuang Mei reexperiences her mother's generation's chastening by political injustice after she attends a meeting in Hainan that identifies the murderer of her mother's sister.

It was not of course by coincidence that golden boy Ma was assigned to Lawyer Mei. She is not only the young folks' favorite; she is also the firm's loose cannon and therefore might bear watching by politically more reliable people—or their offspring, like Ma. Case and personnel assignments are made by the firm's director, Xu, a heavy who gives orders as if he were still in the army. The firm is controlled by the Municipal Judiciary Bureau and the party, the latter personified by Xu. As the novel reveals his multiple transgressions against the rule of law, it opens a direct line of fire against paternalism. Having selected Mei Zhen and He Jue from his firm as model lawyers, director Xu is determined that they work the press and eschew losing cases. He arbitrarily removes Mei Zhen from the Wu Heng case. Lawyer Mei goes before the court and accepts the unattractive charge anyway, and director Xu's politics-over-law philosophy becomes clear when he explodes on hearing of her disobedience. The Wu Heng case is an officially designated major case; women's groups want to expose Wu's abuse and alleged murder of his wife. Xu's orders come straight from the bureau, he protests. Mei's duty is to get Wu Heng to confess and show how he became a criminal—he is an artist, so he must have been led astray by Western art. The trial will propagandize socialist legal system and prove that lawyers are as essential as the police in getting criminals to confess; Wu and Mei will discuss her "defense" later (271–74).

Indeed, Wu Heng's case is declared an "open" trial—a show trial for television. This is law as education, not justice. Xu threatens Mei Zhen, advising her that he got her nominated for model lawyer only by suppressing letters of complaint against her. He asks for her brief and insists that she rewrite it. When Mei Zhen continues her defense of Wu Heng through the last resort of leaving the government law firm, Xu starts investigating to see if he can build a corruption or scandal case against her; might she have stood behind her client because she has had special "relations" with him (534)?

In the Fan inheritance case, director Xu cavalierly invites in the press (Tian), since pressure might lead to a settlement out of court, a victory for "spiritual civilization." That is the state's paternal discourse again, not law, which in this case would be clearly adversarial. Finally, Xu threatens his own pet, He Jue, follower of the party. When her son, Xiaotian, is accused of an economic crime, she seeks well-connected counsel for him, including legal matriarch Mu Rong, just-retired president of the Political-Legal Institute (a head judge and law school professor of the 1950s and teacher to all local jurists), and then Tian Shifei. Both seek political solutions to Xiaotian's legal problem through the back door and *guanxi*. Xu finds this out and directs Lawyer He to "be a Communist." She can be "forgiven" if she writes a confession for the Judiciary Bureau and hands in any "gifts" her son might have received, as evidence against him. She buckles under and is rewarded: she is made the director's replacement when he is promoted into the bureau, and she is duly named model lawyer. This is the party's paternalism: forcing its children into line by forgiving them. But in the 1980s, "confession" seemed to suggest the equivalence of citizens with convicts.

It is later revealed that the letters accusing Mei Zhen, besides those from the ex-con's spiteful neighbors, came from Little Chen, a spacey judge in the local southern district who achieved political consciousness through a song praising the Maoist hero Lei Feng (a touch of black humor, this; 313). She confuses morality with law in divorce cases and dislikes Mei Zhen for reopening Tang Shunü's divorce suit after so many parties had almost succeeded in forcing her to withdraw it. This opens a second front in the novel, against paternalistic obscurantism in the judiciary itself (the first is against the paternalistic party). Judge Chen was secretly asked to write a letter against Mei Zhen by someone in Mei's own unit, but that cannot excuse her behavior. Her backward attitudes are partly due to the judiciary's lack of the most basic training. Little Chen, 40 now and with an old-style hairdo, was just a household registration cop (a service differentiated from the patrol officers and traffic cops) in this neighborhood. Having studied law for two years in a "special course" instituted after 1978, and having judged several dozen cases, she is now "experienced." But her flagging self-esteem also reflects a sexist society, for she thinks herself not hard enough to be a judge in this man's world, even as Mei Zhen's father considered the lawyer's profession too unfeminine for his daughter. It is Wang Xiaoying's mission to prove them wrong. As further evidence that formal justice is not a state priority, Wang describes the run-down temporary "courtrooms" in which it is dispensed.

Ah, but the trial verdicts. These come late (Wu Heng's is still undisclosed at the end), to keep up suspense about which litigant or lawyer wins and whether justice will be done. In the case of the two lowly women versus the Fans, Tian's fraudulent Yan claimant is exposed, but the Fans win victory over Huiting, although she is given court costs and a 2,000-yuan allowance for having cared for the widow Yan. Having in fact proven Huiting's Fan ancestry and the Fan's doctoring of the family tree, a crestfallen Lawyer Mei openly challenges the judge in court. The judge as much as admits that he decided the case not on its merits but to strengthen socialism. A Fan cousin is coming over to capitalize a joint venture; he must be assured that the law will protect his property (695). The Fans' being a People's Political Consultative Conference family surely did not hurt them. Appeal is impossible, for this has become another show trial. A verdict broadcast on television is fixed in stone. Mei Zhen falls ill.

Tian sinks in scandal, having used forged evidence, committed adultery with his client's sister, and even worse, earned "excessive" monthly fees of 500–600 yuan—though there is no rule defining excess.

Fang is ruined for defending the prostitute and murderer—he had the gall to point out that the victim was a criminal—and for conspiring with Tian to pump up his own new private law firm. A Judiciary Bureau special "investigative group" under conservative Mu Rong will probe that. Both offenses are affronts to Maoism and nothing more.

Oppressive paternal "feudalism," we know from Lu Xun, is particularly self-evident and absurd at the "Ah Q" level, where the lowest members in the pecking order find victims *they* can oppress. Here, a court recorder refuses on his own authority to record the defense spoken in court by golden boy Ma because he considers Ma's words not germane and because Ma is only a lawyer's apprentice (533).

But it is against a more insidious structural paternalism exercised directly against the adversarial principle itself that the novel opens up its major attack, on yet a third front, by dramatizing an open contention of the lawyers and their new sacred duty versus the legal system. In these reformist times, Fang Dingbo wins approval, by mid-novel, to set up a firm of lawyers not on state salary; they will earn their own fees. China did not have even a cooperatively run law firm until 1988, and Wang wrote in 1986–87.[15] Fang Dingbo seems to have gone further, with a *private* law firm organized personally by himself (*geren guapai* or *siren guapai*, "individually" or "privately" "hanging out a sign to do business"; 249). Lawyers solicit their own business and perhaps keep some of their own fees. Fang invites Mei Zhen and Zhuang Zi to join as partners and Tian Shifei the journalist to sign on part time, to build a united front against the Justice Ministry's paternal mismaneuvering of legal "defense." At the height of her dispute with director Xu, and believing Wu Heng to be innocent of murder whatever the feminists say, Mei Zhen jumps ship and joins the new enterprise. It will cost her the honor of being named a model lawyer.

The war is joined by the government—covertly, of course. The Judiciary Bureau oversees even private practice; its head calls in Fang to forbid him from naming the firm after himself, advertising, seeking press coverage (since his firm is just an "experiment"), or having a grand opening—for, aware of how the new reform economy works, Fang has printed up expensive invitations inviting important leaders and journalists to a party to be thrown by his firm. Fang and his partners are reduced to opening a legal information stall at market to advertise the services and the address of their real law offices—an ingenious ploy, and a good symbol of how socialism creates supercapitalism to counteract it. Later, two men from the judiciary will come to interview the lawyers about how much money they make, probing for evidence of economic crimes.

Mei Zhen's state-run law firm does allow her to transfer out to Fang's; indeed it initiates the move, since it calculates that her dissidence in the Wu Heng case will politically weaken the private firm. And is it any coincidence that Fang Dingbo is forced by the court to take up the unpopular defense of a prostitute who murdered a high cadre's son? When director Xu is promoted to the Municipal Judiciary Bureau, he will be able to wreak havoc and get the competition closed down—and suppress the very idea of competition.

Fang's private law firm represents the challenge of Western independent law practice in its internal management too. The lawyers are independent, able to pick their own cases and make their own professional and moral decisions (presumably even set their own fees). They will indeed *compete* with each other; that is part of the lawyer mystique, as it is of the new private enterprise system itself—and perhaps of adversary law as such. They will go at one another and shake hands afterward, abiding by the decisions of the courts (252). An element of comedy that comes with this innovation does not escape the novelist; in the three-ring circus of the Fan vs. Shen vs. Tian case (really Lawyer Fang vs. Lawyer Mei vs. Lawyer Tian), the court's formulaic bureaucratic piety enjoining the sides to mutually understand and respect each other sounds ironic (622).

In an adversary system, the lawyer puts the client first, letting "truth" emerge from alternative truths told in open debate. And this happens in the one case Lawyer Mei wins, Tang Shunü's. By the standards of socialist law, Mei Zhen is unethical. Aware of the criminal assault on Ms. Tang by the stud, Lawyer Mei does not disclose it to the court but instead uses it as a bargaining chip to help her client. She realizes the ethical problem, but for once her client does get justice. Adversarial justice is vindicated (339). We also see the converse. In the Wu Heng divorce case, He Jue tries to dig up dirt on Wu so that the press and public opinion jointly may prevent the divorce—and trial—that neither her client nor the state wants. Yet exposing the dirt makes reconciliation impossible. The state and He Jue did not foresee it, but Lawyer He's own client could have told her the outcome (510).

The novel also argues against paternalism in principle, in an impassioned speech by law student Fang Boding seen in flashback. Lawyers are important, he argues, and in foreign countries they are respected. Western bourgeois law broke the dictatorial hold on the justice system of China's judges, giving the accused the chance to defend themselves (the most fundamental aspect of adversary law, this book asserted in the introduction, citing Jerome A. Cohen). The lawyer system is part of the legal and democratic system, Fang protests. It is the very reflection of whether a country has law and democracy. China needs lawyers, to combat residual feudalism (145–46).

In the 1980s, Mei Zhen likewise defines the duty of the lawyer as protecting client rights while keeping faith with the facts and the law in order to serve the people's interest (174, 275, 289). That is about the biggest advance adversary law could make in the still-socialist 1980s. A more crystal-clear attack on paternalism is voiced by fictional Hong Kong lawyers, in the seemingly limited context of the unreasonable requirement that foreigners must hire native Chinese lawyers to represent their interests in China. Does not representation by a Chinese lawyer pose an inherent conflict of interest, since all Chinese law firms are under the government?, they ask (179, 250). But that argument would apply equally to domestic cases.

In 1956, He Jue rebutted Fang Boding by appealing to faith in party leadership, but the more tragic personification of party-state paternalism in the law is Mu Rong, mentor and role model of law students since the 1950s. The opposition to reform she symbolizes does not come from careerism or hunger for power, but sheer misguided communist principle and obedience. She opposes, in principle, the founding of private law firms: "If firms of lawyers can be made up of private entrepreneurs, then public security bureaus can turn into private investigating offices filled with Sherlock Holmeses" (249). That is, bounty hunters and mercenaries.

The problem with Mu Rong, a CCP guerrilla in her youth, is that her husband died saving her from enemies in wartime, though he was himself an enemy "Trostkyist" whom she had disowned and was escorting to a court-martial as proof of her loyalty to the CCP. Having lost him, twice, and then her baby, she lost the capacity to love anyone or anything but the party. It was she, once a head judge, who led Judge He Jue into the tragic mistake of divorcing Fang Boding in the late 1950s when he was political anathema. Mu Rong did not even ask He Jue to divorce him to save her career, but because the party wanted her to—believing that what the CCP wanted must be the right thing to do. Mu Rong is a hopeless idealist with outdated values. Observation of her generation occasions a wry comedy of manners, as when the novel observes how the judiciary cadres out jogging have all changed from their uniforms into comparably uniform workout pants of tolerable fashionableness (240).

The elders' confusion in the new era becomes clear when they, who are after all impoverished under the market reforms, dream of setting up their own law firm (241). Mu Rong means to head it. Yet given her poverty, perhaps it is not so contradictory that at the end of the novel she finds the young (i.e., middle-aged) lawyers traitors to socialist law—immoral and probably unlawful—because they earn too much. And they seek fame, that other false bourgeois idol. But Mu Rong's idol is still more obvious: the party.

In the end even He Jue, who compromises to advance her party career, has a tragic falling-out with her old teacher. She asks Mu to defend her accused son, Xiaotian. He Jue has discovered that the law that let Xiaotian be accused as an economic criminal is ex post facto. He was a public servant and a merchant on the side, but who could know that the law would change and make that a crime? Mu Rong will have none of this reasoning: listen to the organization; its decision is always right. And so the two party loyalists split. Neither old nor new socialist law will hold. The third way, an adversarial path, is the only option.

The press's role in justice is as dubious as Tian Shifei, its personification. He lives to make a name exposing corruption and writes in support of Fang Dingbo's experimental private law firm (since Fang invites him in). But the press is fickle. Tian advises Fang against inviting Mei Zhen into Fang's new firm, having heard of her conflict with director Xu and of Xu's future promotion. He thinks of jumping ship himself when the Judiciary Bureau kills his own newspaper article on Fang's firm. He takes it to be a warning.

Independent lawyers above all are wary of institutions that try cases out of court, particularly when they take the name of education. Just so the Court of Morality column in the local *Legal Information Gazette* (alluding to *Democracy and Legal System*), which reports actionable but above all sensationally immoral behavior so that readers may write in their opinions to the editor, lynching one side (or both) in a print version of American "tabloid television." An anonymous editor crucified Wu Heng in this Court of Morality before the death of Wu's wife, prejudicing or preventing any actual trial that might follow and ensuring an inherently unjust, educative show trial after the murder and the involvement of the women's groups. Moreover, the newspaper article usurped not just the power of the justice system but that of the party and society as well, for it caused Wu Heng to lose his career, even his living quarters. Mei Zhen is shocked to learn that the pen name is Tian Shifei's. He wrote the article on higher orders, of course. To that extent the press is simply a complicit arm of government policy like the justice system. But Tian emerges as a newsman with no scruples at all. His skill lies in information gathering and its unethical and twisted deployment in rumor-mongering. He even casts aspersions on the old Maoist Mu Rong, since he hopes to represent He Jue's accused son Xiaotian himself. Sure, all the judges are Mu Rong's former students, but might they not resent her now? And why did she retire after all? Like a journalist, a lawyer, or a cop interrogator, Tian uses a pretense of knowing everything to bluff his victims.

The novel's texture, or what readers take to be its information dividend, also subtly argues for a new legal culture of adversary law. There is a new language, as if from Erle Stanley Gardner: "clients," "conflicts of interest" (122), "political background checks" (a negative example; 143), "ad hominem attacks" (163), "leading questions" (526).

There are shabby courtrooms, the badges the lawyers wear at work, their makeshift quarters, and the various lower "law degrees" from inferior part-time institutions that are used to fill out the ranks of the lawyers while society finally gears up to educate more of them. They bring their own lunches instead of eating out (the text notes pointedly; 122). Fictional Hong Kong lawyers argue that Chinese lawyers lack the social dignity due them because cars are not assigned to bring them to public functions (179). However, songs on the radio appeal to good judges loved by the common people (which are ironic counterpoint to the inanities of Little Chen's jurisprudence, which the radio interrupts by penetrating the thin walls of her courtroom; 35). There are foreign detective films, Mei Zhen's daughter's dream of writing detective stories, and facetiously, "the latest legal system literature," *The Case of Taking the Headless Female Corpse by Strategy*.[16] An entire will is read into the text (the Fan will, 155–56). This may seem odd, but original editions of *Clarissa* (1748) printed a will that ran to fourteen pages.[17] No doubt eighteenth-century English and late-twentieth-century Chinese women found wills interesting for reasons of self-preservation.

There are lawyers' daily frustrations: seeking in vain for police permission to investigate crime scenes (68), having evidence sprung on them at trials, battling a press that airs confidences but is after all run by the government, yearning for the day when lawyers' offices may take foreign clients (78), listening to a judge say that it is all right to hold proceedings with one party's lawyer absent, since it is just a mediation and the lawyer has other cases (35). Wang Xiaoying depicts cadres of the police, procuracy, and judiciary all living in the same apartment complex (240).

There are, in contrast, concrete lawyer initiatives so breathtakingly bold that they seem unrealistic, dissident, or unethical even by American lawyers' standards. When apprentice lawyers interview witnesses without clarifying their professional stake in the case, even steal evidence (a possible murder weapon! 209), their actions might be chalked up to inexperience. But Mei Zhen herself, besides keeping secret her knowledge of the criminal rape of Tang Shunü, withholds from the court evidence she has discovered in the Fan-Shen-Yan trial (a tombstone; 681), and springs a surprise witness on the court during the trial of Wu Heng (the night watchman; 458). Then again, Fang Boding would never contravene the to us unjust prohibition on an accused having contact with counsel and family during his initial detainment (423). The law-versus-feelings (*qing*) discourse overrides the human rights discourse.

The author further explains that even in 1956 the procuracy preferred to hire demobilized soldiers over law school graduates. Procurators were to be sharp knives protecting socialism, whereas citizens trained in the law were considered in principle to have joined the Kuomintang legal culture. Most law students could not even pass a political background check; hence peasant-born Tian Shifei's hopes (unfulfilled) of becoming the exception. Background checks for judges were severe too. They excluded Zhuang Zi, who was "like Judge Bao" (143–44). Becoming a lawyer was the default profession for political-legal cadres of the 1950s.

In the realm of street talk—the modern version of sapient children's ditties in the old classic novels—the reader hears opinions that winning lawyers are those who have an "in" with the judges (33) and that lawyers are just "window dressing" (74). Judges prefer "two- or three-point lawyers," or those who only plead that, one, the facts are clear, two, the prisoner has confessed, and three, it is his first offense (447). The novel simply lobbies for the legal profession by having a character propose that a legal system gazette open a regular column on "hero lawyers" (116).

Yet *Whom Do You Defend* as a multifaceted social novel blames not just China's legal culture but all society for injustice. Since political intervention from above thwarts justice, one can achieve justice only by trumping it with even higher political interventions (556–57). But in law, the means are the end. Fang Boding is brought down by this catch-22. Only by seeking political intervention can he block an unjust verdict against the prostitute who murdered the criminal son of a cadre. But to seek such intervention is criminal behavior, so Fang's demise is easily arranged by simple "rule of law."

Neighborhood committees and work units are out of control too. They are unauthorized law enforcement agencies carrying out China's primary punishment—not incarceration but loss of one's job—and though low on the power scale they have the manpower to keep their prey under surveillance and maintain liaison with all enforcement units of society. Even party secretaries in work units "play Sherlock Holmes," stooping to investigate the marital lives of parties to a divorce (97). Through the CCP they have secret lines of communication to the party-run courts and law firms, as Mei Zhen discovers when the powers-that-be of the ex-con's neighborhood try covertly to poison her relationship with her boss. As if this were not enough, the Courts of Morality in the press have made anonymous denunciation endemic.

Social attitudes are still at fault. How can lawyers work when people think them abettors of the criminals they may represent (530)? Why can even a physically abused woman not get permission to "break up a family" and seek self-determination? The attorney for her husband need only produce old love letters indicating that he once loved her as proof that he can still love her. There is no room to consider the possibility of people changing or hurting the ones they love (195, 300). *Whom Do You Defend* thus separates law and morality. Let divorce be decided by the law alone, for ad hoc moral scruples will thwart justice. Let public opinion—the real court of morality—and political discipline take care of morality (303). In fact, Lawyer Mei Zhen is both a great lawyer and a saint. She arranges for Tang Shunü's husband, once he is remarried, to adopt a child, and in court she apologizes for her "moral lapse" in not having made it clear to Wu Heng's wife that her life would not be rendered meaningless if she were deprived of her husband (546). Or is this self-criticism really a skillful lawyer's strategy?

Whom Do You Defend does not have a rosy ending. Mei Zhen has lost the Shen Huiting inheritance case, her husband, and her second chance to wed Fang Boding. In the Wu Heng divorce case, she failed to achieve a separation quick and amicable enough to prevent the demise of his wife, not to mention the disgrace of her client. Did she at least get him off on the murder charge? The murder mystery remains a loose end, rather unusual for a plot that so skillfully manipulates suspense and solves even inheritance cases with discovered clues like missing tombstones. With the help of clues such as the knife that killed Ms. Dong, her diary, testimony from the night watchman about Wu Heng's state of mind after the wounding (the incident in the novel's prologue), and her own oratory, Lawyer Mei convinces the reader and the courtroom audience that Wu is innocent of that charge, but this contradicts the verdict that the judges have *already committed to writing before the trial is over*. They recess to reconsider it (547). We never learn of their decision; this ending, which simply by its looseness damns the legal system to the very core, might for all we know be due to censorship; Lawyer Mei's umbrage at the injustice in court is already softened by her moral disdain for her client and her own acceptance of guilt for the death of the troubled woman.

As to the endangered private law firm, Mu Rong, at the end, surprisingly reports that its achievements outweigh its faults. Xu, now ensconced in the Judiciary Bureau, decides to dissolve it anyway. Yet Mu Rong really has had a change of heart; after she argues with Xu, the bureau decides to spare the firm while putting it under new leadership: the loyal He Jue. The bureau's solution is an ingenious and believable compromise. Fang Boding can stay on as director of the firm he founded, but He Jue will control it as party secretary. The solution recreates their law school relationship, when He Jue was the class leader and party member and Fang Boding was head of the student association, the "natural" leader. Indeed, Fang Boding and He Jue will remarry; Mei Zhen weeps to hear of it. Officially, it will "help their work" (732).

Such manipulations were how the Dengists phased out the Maoists without taking away their titles. Hence it is unclear if the solution for the law firm is a symbol of reaction or of a hope that history, in a reform era, will inevitably be progressive when power is shared. There is one ray of hope. The He-Fang reconciliation will help not just their lives but also their "dialectical" issue, Xiaotian. He is a reformer, finally exonerated of alleged economic crimes, and his reformism, the wave of the future by historical and generational logic, may yet hope to prevail. Or is he on second thought too morally weak, having accepted so many gifts from his business partners? Wang Xiaoying's *zhiqing* generation may agree with He Jue and the older Mu Rong generation that young people have not been "tempered" by enough hardship—as the old communist discourse would put it.

The actual adversary trials that *Whom Do You Defend* portrays are less convincing, for all their attention to the forms and jurisprudential steps of "fact-finding," "defense," "debate," and so forth (533–36). It is the unsatisfied yearnings, the socially unsatisfied need for adversary law that offers hope in the novel. This is bolstered by Wang Xiaoying's portrayal of two sides to nearly every character, as well as to every social contention and litigation. Wang's own lawyer-mentor was right about that. Seeing both sides may put one at a disadvantage in courtroom practice, but it is a social prerequisite of adversary law, and certainly of the novelistic representation of multiple simultaneous truths.

Director Xu has no positive side, though he is a recognizable type, authoritarian and careerist; and Mei Zhen is impossibly exemplary, even if she does, in the heat of investigation at the end of the novel, commit a self-confessed elementary legal oversight.[18] But Fang Boding and He Jue are in the end quite human. Though he is an unstoppable innovator and reformer, and his subordination of means to ends in the cadre's son's murder case can be viewed as savvy realpolitik, he is weak when it comes to choosing his clients (the Fans) and particularly his women: young Zhuang Mei, and finally He Jue again. But he was after all persecuted, and his compromises may save his unique contribution to history: China's first private law firm. Neither is He Jue a moral cipher. Although she wavers before she helps her son—as does Fang Boding, the father—in a flash of self-insight and political-moral enlightenment, when she discusses the matter with Mu Rong, she sees herself becoming like Mu and withdraws from the brink. Speaking the truth from her heart "for the first time," He Jue reminds Mu that when she followed her advice before, sacrificing her marriage for the party, society itself found her lacking in conscience. "Don't you see how cold my thinking has become? I can become no cooler toward events than I already am. If my blood runs any colder than this I shall become a reptile" (433–34). What we know about He Jue is that she is sensitive to pressure. Now she is sensitive to pressure from outside the party. Repositioned, at the end, in a private law firm and trying to regain the trust of its founder, Fang Boding, can she—would she want to—wholly resist his reformist impulses? He Jue and Fang Boding, driven into each other's arms twice in a lifetime by ambition, deserve each other. Yet they might be able to complement each other's weaknesses.

The finest expression of Wang Xiaoying's dialogic imagination is her presentation of pressures that cause marital conflict. On the one hand they render divorce all the more necessary for some couples, and on the other hand, reconciliation all the more necessary in the eyes of other "interested parties." Tang Shunü feels she must divorce rather than separate, because mere separation would entail moving back home with her mother. Her mother is controlled by the shrewish wife of a son who lives with her. Lawyer Mei quickly dopes out the situation and silences Shunü's selfish sister-in-law by reminding her that, by law, a daughter (Shunü) has the same right to inherit property that a son (the shrew's husband) does.

The Wu Heng divorce-murder trial also has two sides. It develops that Wu Heng, a poor artist, married his wife, Ms. Dong, for her money and to further his career. He pushed for a divorce though he knew it would destroy his wife, and was frequently seen with the editor of an art magazine, a Ms. Feng who worshipped his art and did all she could to support his career. By the end of the trial, Mei Zhen despises her client and thinks it right that he be punished. Yet she continues to represent her client to the end and in front of all those women. She conveniently (and belatedly) retrieves Dong's moving diary, which reveals suicidal thinking and still more deep background. Dong's mother, abandoned by her own husband, has a neurotic hatred of men. Against her daughter's love match from the start because the groom was too poor (she was right about his motives despite herself), she maliciously and obsessively plotted to bring about discord even after the wedding. She "helped" her daughter learn of Ms. Feng's originally Platonic interest in her husband, sent spies, opened mail, got her daughter to rip up Wu's paintings, destroyed his brushes, and sent letters to the Court of Morality that prevented the divorce and also destroyed his career (the allegations of immorality caused him to lose his job and a place in an exhibition). Unfaithfulness became a self-fulfilling prophecy. The mother's neurosis is confirmed Perry Mason–style. She goes to pieces in the courtroom upon hearing expressions of audience sympathy with the man. We never hear the judgment. It is hard to imagine that Wu will not do more time, though he looks to be acquitted of murder. Through it all, Lawyer Mei continues to represent the client she hates. It is an object lesson in the difference between law and morality and of the principle of adversary legal process and just legal outcomes.

GIVING THE CRIMINAL A VOICE

Wei Dongsheng's "Xingjing duizhang yu sharenfan de neixin dubai" (Interior monologues of a head patrolman and a murderer; 1984) is our crossover.[19] Structured as a detective story, its mystery of the how and why of a murder is gradually disclosed in piecemeal streams of consciousness coming from two main "speakers," a suspect and a cop, until the chain of cause and effect is clear at the end, although the murder is never dramatized. The story's title and its original publication in *Woodpecker*, the uniformed hero, and the opening sentences describing a speeding police car all situate the work in "police story" territory.[20] Yet the style of narration just as quickly establishes Wei's piece as arty, avant-garde fiction. Soon the mystery takes on existential dimensions.

The opening elliptically sets the scene for discovery of a crime by describing a police siren with two sentence fragments; all text thereafter is printed as if drama, mostly as alternating soliloquies by a head patrolman, Yu Xiaolong, and his prey, the murder suspect Han Jiang. There is one spoken piece for Lu Qing, his wife. Her diary is also read into the text, but only as the policeman reads it.

Many suspense and mystery stories of the 1980s were already being written with movie adaptation in mind, perhaps including this one. The seriatim monologues of Yu Xiaolong and Han Jiang do not simply soliloquize their streams of consciousness, but give blow-by-blow descriptions of what they are seeing and doing in present time, sometimes with *nouveau roman*–style phenomenological description. These are interrupted by flashbacks, jump cuts, dreams, self-questioning, and self-psychoanalysis. In a movie, the alternating protagonists' texts would be read by the two men as alternating voice-overs during the action on the screen, "remembered" in sequence according to the idiosyncrasies of the subject's memory, but actually as necessary for the audience to piece together the story of how certain characters met and had a murderous falling-out. Yet Wei Dongsheng's work is a text, not a movie, without any screen images to provide visual orientation, much less fade-outs and changing camera angles as clues to temporal and point-of-view transitions. Ambiguities created by changes of time and setting render some scenes at first "difficult." Blow-by-blow ("present tense") first-person narration of the action, interspersed with flowery descriptions of the scene, thus lend a modernist, literary atmosphere that sets the story apart from popular fiction. The first Yu Xiaolong passage begins:

Yu Xiaolong—
Deep night, zero hour.

As rocket displays and exploding firecrackers surge to fill the empty night, each as if trying to outdo the other to greet the New Year—as their thunder merges in patterns of riotous color—I drag my weary legs back to the office.

No one is in the room.

A faint odor of wine wafts through the air. I see, spread out upon my work desk, an uncapped bottle of Shanxi wine and plates of snacks. I pluck a note from under the wine bottle: "Wishing the captain happy holidays!—The men of your brigade on holiday." . . .

I go to the window and throw it open. A gust of cold air blows in, mingling with the explosive sound of firecrackers. I feel the chill breeze grope me. Involuntarily I shiver, head to foot. Suddenly the frosty wind drives up a warmer current from the bottom of my stomach. It churns over and over in my throat. I am nauseous! (564–65)

The head patrolman has just returned, evidently in the speeding police car, from seeing the corpse. Momentarily a call from the chief will tell him that informants and material evidence have already led to a suspect, Han Jiang, and that Han has confessed everything and been formally arrested. (This is a story with a feel of procedural realism, unlike many other stories written by policemen; there is no concealment of how the hero orders his subordinates about in paramilitary fashion.) Whodunit is thus solved on the second page. The mystery is "who was 'done' " (through the first three-quarters of the story, to p. 594), and when that is answered, why and how. Even as a psychological whydunit (an Anglo-American formula of the 1990s), "Interior Monologues of a Head Patrolman and a Murderer" crosses over to higher literary and metaphysical themes. The cop's wife, a philosophy student, is heard discussing Sartre, Freud, and existentialism with a male friend—though not the cop (587)—and the chief reminds Yu Xiaolong from the start that "to be an outstanding public security officer, one doesn't just arrest the criminals. One must understand their criminal psychology and seek out the universal laws of why people commit crime in our time" (566).

Wei Dongsheng creates a noir, and in this context, avant-garde feel by depicting the patrolman's musings and aimless street wandering in dark and lonely night settings. The cop falls prey to disillusionment and nausea. There is constant precipitation—snow, as he unconsciously walks to his old apartment, where he lived happily with the wife from whom he is now separated—and soon after in the narrative, an uncharacteristic winter rain on the night, years ago, when he boorishly spoiled a surprise party his wife prepared for him on his thirtieth birthday; he did not realize it was for him until all the guests had gone home after he fell asleep in the bathtub (575–78).

This of course furthers the profession's discourse that cops are tired and overworked, even on holidays, which distresses their personal and family lives. The criminal understandably hallucinates about the past, owing to his unstable mental state, hunger, incarceration, and an attempted suicide in detention. Yu Xiaolong for his part nods off into semiconsciousness from sleep deprivation. He falls in and out of consciousness at his desk and into reverie when he strolls in the night air to revive himself. There is also the *zhiqing* (educated youths') lost-generation discourse of the 1980s: "our generation" has "nothing of its own, save politics-struggle, struggle-politics. We are not playthings, we are human beings. We need color, sunlight, learning, and love. Instead, our world is nothing but a blank" (567). These are the thoughts of the criminal-to-be Han Jiang, a writer, who speaks as well for his wife, for his old friend Li Guoqing, and, as it happens, for the cop's student wife and her intellectual friends—also, one imagines, for Wei Dongsheng, who is both a policeman and a writer. The only character alien to this discourse is the patrolman, Yu Xiaolong. He has only a junior high education. His wife's student friends thought him a poor pick. Besides, they distrusted *them*—the cops (575).

The case's basic conflicts are simple enough, though rendered complex by the crosscutting of time to each of several stages through which the conflicts have passed. Han Jiang is a fiction writer and literary magazine editor; his rather more hedonistic old friend Li Guoqing took advantage of the weakening of Han's marriage to make a move on Han's wife. Li paid with his life.

Dreaming and daydreaming in his cell, Han Jiang recalls how he met nurse Lu Qing by accident and married her for love. After marriage she found him far more interested in his work than her happiness, and he expected her to wait on him, the great author, like a servant. Their marriage dissolved into psychological games they played against each other. Then Li Guoqing came and gave Lu Qing "consolation." He also dated Han's sister, until she learned that Li had a reputation. About then, an old cadre directing Han Jiang's new play insisted that he give it a rosier ending; Han angrily withdrew it. Li sided with the old man, even insulted his friend in the press, while the old cadre destroyed Han's career forever by reporting him to the party's central Propaganda Department (here Wei Dongsheng sounds a dis-

senting, proauthor, anticonservative note typical of the progressive 1980s).
Yet these setbacks made Han all the more obsessed with the demands of career over family. His wife, despondent, had one last guilt-ridden fling with
Li. Ultimately, she commits suicide out of shame and despair, when she is
not allowed to apologize to Han Jiang in jail.

These sequential clues to whydunit (and confirmation of the murder itself) develop out of order, interspersed with Han Jiang's imprisonment, his
encounter with Head Patrolman Yu after Han attempts suicide in jail, the interrogations of him, and so forth. But this is only half the story, for interspersed with Han's soliloquies are the cop's. The interesting thing is that Yu
Xiaolong spends as much time thinking and reminiscing about his own
dashed marriage as about the murder of Li Guoqing. Small wonder, for the
two cases are structurally, psychologically, and ideologically (in feminist
terms) quite similar. Like Han Jiang, Yu Xiaolong met his wife by accident
and they married for love. He neglected her in proportion to his service to
the profession; when "his Li Guoqing" (in this case, his wife's philosophy
classmate, He Xiaoguang) filled the emotional and intellectual gap that he
left, Yu became jealous. An aggravating factor was that Yu, a cop, was too
straitlaced to dance and take his wife out for fun (575). But that is not wholly
an occupational fault.

Han Jiang, the intellectual, is similarly unable to relax and be a family
man. Tickets to good foreign films often come his way, but he will not go
with his wife, for technically she is unentitled, not being a member of the
Writers' Association—though Li Guoqing shows by his own example that a
writer may bring any date he pleases. Han Jiang is warned by Li Guoqing
that he is a male chauvinist and that his wife is ripe for conversion to feminism (something evidently akin to a disease). Head Patrolman Yu, having
read of this in Lu Qing's diary, recollects in daydream a talk on women's liberation given by his own putative "rival," He Xiaoguang—and how he, Yu,
nearly slept through the boring speech (584, 591–92). In the end, Yu admits
to learning from Han Jiang's mistakes not to be so self-centered or so jealous
of his wife's friendships with the opposite sex. Paradoxically, both Han's
tragic personal example and the ending of the play he would not change for
any reason featured a feminist heroine's choice not to rejoin her husband
even after he began to see the light.

Han Jiang, not the cop, is an educated man, a writer of fiction, and—like the author Wei Dongsheng—a magazine editor. Moreover, Han Jiang has the typical career background of a policeman, not a writer—he is a demobilized soldier. In this unusual conjoining of law and literature, Wei Dongsheng's own position is better represented by the criminal than by his fellow law enforcement professional.[21] Indeed, Wei had a reputation, in Chinese circles interested in gossip about writers, as a divorced friend of Wang Shuo who liked to talk low-down Beijing slang, join in media ventures to make money, and do other progressive, countercultural things. To the extent that Wei Dongsheng put his own emotions about career and divorce into the story, he may have identified with the criminal, and this may be his own confession.

Han Jiang is a sympathetic enough character. He is straitlaced, victimized by the party for the political progressivism of his fiction, and victimized by his hedonistic old friend. He rather crudely victimizes his wife, but she claims some of the blame for the family crisis for not having rejected Li Guoqing. Head Patrolman Yu, for his part, feels guilty about triggering Han's wife's suicide by not letting her see him in jail. The mingling of law and literature's missions is broached by the police chief, who asks his educationally challenged patrolman to understand "the universal laws of why people in our time commit crimes"—to be a good cop really by assuming the role of novelist.

The surprising result is an identification of writer and policeman, and even of policeman and criminal, roles that are not lightly reversed in China. The men share a common humanity, a common fate. They make the same mistakes. They are, in this manuscript, structurally and existentially equivalent beings.[22]

This image is softened when Yu Xiaolong indicates that the lesson he learned is to not take the "self" so seriously; his wife leaves him a quotation from Albert Einstein to that effect. The noir feeling is dispelled too, when Yu Xiaolong muses at the end how colorful is the new snow. This is a conservative moral that might have been tacked on to please higher-ups. In the end, Han Jiang is judged guilty and the cop is saved from damnation by Han's example, but during the story each defendant gets to speak his piece, each embracing part of the truth. It is, in the last analysis, an adversarial vision of temporary, partial truths running into each other headlong, with even the truth of the guilty party modifying the truth of the law enforcer. The equivalence of the law-enforcing detective and the lawbreaking criminal is old in the literary genre, but as an adversary ideology it is new in postrevolutionary China.

Chen Yuanbin (b. 1955) is yet another writer of the Red Guard or *zhiqing* generation, an Anhui native who was rusticated after he finished middle school. He became a professional writer and graduate of Beijing University, but as a former "legal worker" he also lists himself as a member of the Anhui Legal Society.[23] He does not write legal system literature exclusively, but Chen for one considers that portion of his writing his most important. His story "Tian xing" (Heaven's course) is a *Whom Do You Defend* in the space of a short story, with an all-male group of judges in a rural county taking the place of Wang Xiaoying's lawyers. Multiple cases crisscross and connect up, jurists try to fend off a journalist without alienating him, ironic injustices and misunderstandings run riot, and there is no promise in the end that justice will be done.[24]

But it is "Wan jia susong" (The Wan family sues) that made Chen famous, once Fifth-Generation director Zhang Yimou made it into the film *Qiuju da guansi* (Qiuju sues), starring Gong Li in the title role. (The film was distributed internationally as *The Story of Qiu Ju* and won the Golden Lion Prize at the 49th Venice International Film Festival.) The surname of the heroine's husband, assault victim Wan Shanqing, is hardly mentioned outside the title; there, its literal meaning, "ten thousand," allows a construction of the title as "Ten Thousand Families Sue," or "Everyperson Sues." "Qiuju," as the movie calls the heroine, is today a name of legendary proportions, so her character is referred to by that name below. In the original story she is He Biqiu, which is nearly homophonous with *hebi qiu* (why bother questing?).

Although Chen wrote "The Wan Family Sues" after the 1989 Beijing massacre, it explicitly criticizes paternalistic attitudes toward the law at local and higher levels. Qiuju's opinion is logical: Surely the state will not find itself guilty? Yet the story also makes ordinary citizens, certainly peasant women, look like pawns in need of paternal guidance. Who, then, is up to the task of ending state paternalism? The movie paints the heroine in even broader strokes, as a modern Dou E, a simple and traditional woman persevering in a stubborn quest for justice at any personal cost. It opens up another front against paternalism—but only by transcending the story's framing of the problem as a matter of law.

The plot line of "The Wan Family Sues" is simple for a legal story. In a remote Anhui village, an outlier so cut off from its own provincial authority that its people shop in Jiangsu, village head Wang Changzhu has kicked Qiuju's husband in the groin. This lays him up for months. When Qiuju confronts the offending village chief he refuses to apologize. So she makes an arduous journey to the township government to get justice, with full supporting evidence and clinical records. There she accuses (*gao*) the village head before a Public Security officer named Li. Although he is an old drinking buddy of the offender, after hearing the facts he decides on behalf of the Wans. They are to get medical expenses and sickness subsidies, half to be paid by village funds, half by the village chief himself. But when the time comes and it is just Qiuju and the chief, the latter raids the village treasury for all of the fine money and, far from apologizing—what Qiuju wanted most—he contemptuously throws the money on the ground. He says that in bowing to pick up the 30 bills, Qiuju will be 30 times apologizing to him.

So Qiuju kicks it back up to the township and then to the county-level police in the city. They simply send the case back down to the township, where the previous decision is affirmed. Qiuju pursues justice a step higher, with municipal-level police.[25] In vain she tries to contact the police chief himself, Captain Yan, a local hero. After months of delay, self-imposed hardship, and endless trips to the city where urban inflation makes her lodging ever more costly, Qiuju finally meets Captain Yan, who, though a man worthy of his reputation, has never personally followed her case. She can file suit in court if she is unhappy with how his office handled it, he says. She does, and there is a court trial—formally, *Qiuju v. Municipal Police*.

Despite sensible predictions from a kindly old innkeeper that Qiuju will win because hers is a model case, the first in which an ordinary citizen sues the government, Qiuju somehow actually loses in county court. Her action, in this 1991 story, seems to fall under the new Administrative Litigation Law, adopted on April 4, 1989, and put into effect on October 1, 1990. It formalized judicial review of state—but not party—administrative acts once they had gone through an administrative reconsideration (*fuyi*), in suits brought by citizens and juridical persons.[26] Yet, unusually for legal system literature, the statutory offense of the police or of the village head is never named. The aforementioned law was passed to oppose corruption and abuse of state power; it allowed courts to review the legality, not the substance, of administrative decisions, and it was not originally aimed at "judicial" decisions.[27] One can only surmise that Captain Yan and other officials are charged with dereliction of duty in their administrative reconsideration. (In life, it was China's ever-adversarial *writers*, like Wang Meng and Dai Qing, who in 1991 led the way in suing the government, though under previously enacted civil law.)[28]

Qiuju appeals again, this time to an intermediate level court. The appeal is accepted and two judges come down to the village to investigate. It develops that Wan Shanqing's debilitating shortness of breath is from cracked ribs, an overlooked subsidiary result of the beating. With the injury elevated in seriousness, thanks to X rays and who knows what other reasoning of the mysterious higher-ups, the village chief is finally led away in irons. Qiuju is dismayed. She only wanted an apology, a bit of face; she no more wanted to escalate the conflict into a jail term for the village chief than she had wanted to file those endless appeals.

"The Wan Family Sues" is not propaganda for the new Administrative Litigation Law. It may have inspired the story, but when a person of legal training depicts a political show trial, we must suspect deeper social criticism. And the trial provides humorous satire. Just before Qiuju gets her day in court, her friend the innkeeper regales her with the talk of the town: a mere peasant woman is going to sue the government! The state is putting on this first-ever trial just to show it can be done. Will she win?, Qiuju wonders. Of course!, says the innkeeper. Her case would not have been selected for a show trial if she were not in the right. Otherwise no one would ever dare sue the government again. That would be rather a negative example of how the new law works, he reasons.

The first joke is that this fearless and adventuresome peasant woman is Qiuju; she just does not know it yet. She thinks she is suing the village head, until the trial begins and the police, represented by her friend Captain Yan himself, are named defendant. It takes some time to explain it to her. The second joke is that, even though this is a show trial and the innkeeper's understanding of Chinese bureaucracy and politics is on the mark, she loses. It remains moot whether you really can sue the government and win. In China's legal culture, where trials are so often moral lessons rather than tools for finding facts, surely the government and its legal system should at least be sincere. Now even that is in question. The state wins even when it puts on a show trial for the predetermined purpose of finding in your favor.

Yet it is not just in this farcical passage that Qiuju plays the role of the fool. The author patronizingly says he wanted to write a story "from a country woman's limited perspective, related in colloquial language."[29] Indeed he did. We see the world through Qiuju's eyes, and when she looks at new, modern things, she breaks them down into simple, not very salient images: colors, shapes, buildings of such and such a size. She naively gapes at everything—at the growth and change of the township seat and the city, at new marketplace conventions, at new "morality," like women disporting themselves in bathing suits. On meeting officials, she tries to judge whether they are honest or crafty and wonders if they are laying a trap for her. Lawyers simply mystify her, as does, of course, their system of fees and expense account charges, though references to the latter satirize lawyers even as they patronize the peasant woman.

When Qiuju takes note of large and small characters on office doors instead of reading them, it is subtly, but coyly, conveyed that she is not even literate. She is at sea amid all the economic growth and social complications. She is brave but inadequate. That all the changes bespeak a new spirit of reform suggests that paternalism must be doomed, but also that peasant women can hardly be the instrument of change.

Yet excessive paternalism is just how Qiuju, in a very perspicacious moment, defines the problem. "The village head runs the people in the village like a big family. A household head can give orders to those below, beat them, curse them—that's all okay. But when he puts your life at risk, that's not proper" (368). These words can, of course, be viewed as acquiescence to paternalism. Qiuju only wants to limit it. In what might be a "feudal" view of justice, she wants an apology, face, blame-fixing—getting the other party to submit. She may be subject to the village head for life, so it may be true when she says that if she does not rectify her family's standing with him now, "they'll be unable to go on living" (378). She conjures up a blood feud, predicting that if the matter is not settled, sons and grandsons of the Wangs and Wans will be at odds forever. On hearing of a stabbing of Captain Yan in the big city (by hoodlums, in an unrelated case), she jumps to the conclusion that they too must have acted on revenge; the economic motive, in a new society with new inequalities of wealth, new levels of theft, and a new hoodlum stratum, is outside her imagination (384). She will not even ride with police because "police cars are for criminals" (406).

This is paternalism welling up from below, from the peasants. But Qiuju is not blind about those above; at one point she shows a sophistication about legal procedure that is hard to reconcile with her ignorance. The county court's written decision finding against her is transmitted to the offending village head to pass on to Qiuju. The state has an excuse for this—the courier who came to the village was new and unaware that the village head was party to the suit. But Qiuju has the sense to put it in legal language: it is improper procedure for her adversary to be asked to notify her of the decision (390).

Qiuju never gets to face the village head in court on the assault charge. She has only been able to accuse him to the paternal police that govern all parties like a family, and then question the rightness of the police decision— not argue things out with Wang Changzhu in an adversarial situation. The state calls its procedure mediation or "peace-making" (*tiaojie, daqiao*; lit., "building bridges"; 372). Proper mediation, even at the village level, ought to be done by a people's mediation committee, yet there is in truth a strong communist tradition of rural disputes being "mediated" by the police, who have the power to coerce.[30] The paternalism of mediation from above is masked in this case because it seems in the countryside opposed not so much to the (bourgeois) adversary trial as to a peasant woman's (feudal) desire to achieve face for her family while affixing blame on the other party. Mediation seems more modern than that.

Yet Qiuju's understanding of face is rather contemporary. She does not want to humiliate Wang Changzhu (by sending him to jail, which might really lead to a blood feud, especially if he became village head again after his term). Instead, she wants a slight adjustment of power relations between them, so that she *can* live out her life under his paternal direction, if necessary, without fear that he will have an old-fashioned slaveholder life-and-death power over her family. In effect, Qiuju has responded to the new spirit of modernization and simply claimed a share of it for leader-follower relations in the countryside. They may remain paternalistic, owing to continuing collective imperatives of the agricultural economy, but they need not be "feudal": overlords can curse, even beat, but they cannot *really* beat their wards: "times have changed," Qiuju says, who knows a thing or two about reform after all—"it's not like it was ten years ago; he can't beat people whenever he feels like it, much less kick them where it really hurts" (389).

The show trial is paternalism writ large. A citizen cannot have her day in court against a fellow citizen. The state will decide who is right without a trial, and if she disagrees, the state will take it "personally," as a criticism of itself. It was the state itself that picked Qiuju to sue it in the show trial, for the state's purpose of propagandizing a new law, not so that Qiuju could get justice. Then it had the gall to side with itself against her. Could it be that the state wants face? Why, indeed, has Qiuju even now not been allowed to go up against Wang Changzhu in open court on a simple assault charge?

In the end, the paternal state changes its mind and lets Qiuju win, but not through adversarial action on her part. When the two middle-level judges come down to reinvestigate and then reverse the verdict on Wang after discovering the cracked ribs, Public Security Officer Li is there again, down from the township, to escort them. Truly, "they" are all in on it; the state's high judges will not question a citizen without the mediation of those who as a matter of course exercise paternalistic authority over her at lower levels.

What about extenuating circumstances for the village chief? Why did he kick Wan Shanqing in the first place? Because Wan disobeyed an order to plant rape instead of wheat. All the villagers were to plant rape, on orders from agricultural officers above the village head, yet the Wans refused. As a result, their crop spoiled the vista of unbroken rape fields when inspectors came down to check, and the whole village was docked points for it. Hence the village head resorted to violence against Wan. And the logic of collective planting was correct, for the Wans lose their own precious wheat crop because they disobeyed. The rape is harvested first, then the rice planted in flooded fields. Seepage from surrounding fields waterlogs the Wan's lonely one and their wheat gets smut. The agricultural experts could have predicted that result; it was why everybody had been required to plant rape together.

Is this then an equivocal message on behalf of collective obedience, against Qiuju? Perhaps—and collectivism is always good to praise during political revanchism. But the logic of the full text is otherwise. Qiuju and her husband avow that they would have followed the collective mandate and planted rape too, avoiding conflict with the village head, if only he had explained the reason for the mandate. They were not dumb; they had planted rape on their land before and simply had not wanted to exhaust the soil. Wang Changzhu's fault lay precisely in his treating the Wans like children, expecting them to obey not out of self-interest but because he personified authority. He used force instead of persuasion. It was the village head who acted on the primitive, prelegal emotion of revenge, not Qiuju in her "stupid" quest to affix blame.

In one respect, Qiuju is a stubborn person ignorant of the big picture, marching forward pointlessly and without hope of effecting progress, eternally manipulated, even defending paternalism in principle. From another viewpoint, Qiuju exposes reactionary paternalism, opening up a possibility for reform.

Zhang Yimou's film, *The Story of Qiu Ju*, changes the focus to a more abstract one of justice versus law. It leads the viewer to contemplate ultimate questions of Chinese law and literature.

Zhang Yimou's adaptation is relatively faithful. The setting is changed to Shaanxi, Zhang's favorite locale, which only makes the countryside's backwardness next to the city starker. Now the Wans plant red chili peppers. They provide color and symbolize Qiuju's spirit. And Qiuju is pregnant, hence still more heroic, as well as stubborn—if not pigheaded—in her persistence. The pregnancy is useful in slowing down the beautiful Gong Li, who plays Qiuju, giving her a reason for being awkward other than stupidity or ineptness. A sister-in-law absent from the original story is now a constant helpmate for the burdened Qiuju as she makes her incessant, nerve-racking treks to the city.

Qiuju naturally has no idea what a trial is like, or why paying a lawyer might help her win a case she has always lost before, but Zhang Yimou does not patronize her as Chen Yuanbin did. The camera cannot convey the city subjectively, as Qiuju sees it. Shots of the city—Xi'an—show overcrowding, cacophony, and the ill-fitting and garish clothes of the urban nouveau riche, but this is not just a peasant's view. Although shots of Qiuju in the city show her standing around staring blankly, having her grope her way seems appropriate when the quest is to breach the walls of the state. Above all, the portrait of Qiuju's incompetence loses force in the face of constant comparisons with her far "stupider" sister-in-law. She has an even blanker look, always follows Qiuju, and still gets lost. Their backwardness is sublimated into a general cultural gap between town and country, and one with moral overtones, in which city folk gyp peasants, not vice versa.

A new theme is the importance of begetting a male heir, a social concern intensified by the new one-child policy. Qiuju's pregnancy brings this to full consciousness; one hears the family worry that the baby might not be male. They might then try again ("illegally," though "one child" really is only policy, not law). This for the first time lends logical weight to Qiuju's view of the kick to her husband's testicles as so important. Yet face also remains important, and its bearing becomes more cogent now that the biological overtones of the beating are clarified. In the film, the village chief has beat the husband not for getting him in trouble over planting but for a crude slur by Wan, who said that the chief could father only "hens" (he has no son and four daughters; they also prove that he has disobeyed population policy). Tempers rose to this point because the Wans wanted to build a shed to store chili peppers. The village head prevented it, calling it illegal but refusing to explain: he was the law. This keeps faith with the original legality-versus-paternalism theme of Chen Yuanbin. And building the shed, unlike planting one's own crop, which is only disobedient, is said to be actually against the law (really, it is against regulations—a case of building on cropland without authorization).

Although the film well conveys the chief's arrogant, above-the-law attitude, his refusal to admit errors, and his conscious refuge in a chain of privilege and power, it trivializes the latterly judged "unlawful" beating. In the film, Qiuju's husband quickly recovers; the injury was never very severe. This divorces Qiuju's desire for face—an apology—from practical power considerations, reducing it to personal and moral feelings (twice Qiuju silently weeps after being insulted) in opposition to a state system intent on mediation and monetary compensation as the instruments of justice—traditional remedies. A rift opens in Qiuju's own family when her husband becomes angry at her costly continued appeals. This makes Qiuju's case seem weaker on the merits, and Qiuju a quixotic woman.

In a movie, however, characters are necessarily concrete; the village head is flawed, but he does not seem spiteful. Off-base or not in her crusade, Qiuju *is* all the more powerful and colorful a heroine in her blind quest for an apology. She also wears the pants in her family. Her husband, already on his feet in the movie, wants to settle, not fight like a man, yet he is afraid his wife might object! And Qiuju wields authority as a demonstrated child-producer, a precious status that may explain the spell she casts over her sister-in-law.

But it is in the film's unique ending that the story's discourse of legal practice versus state paternalism is sidestepped—transcended, really. Qiuju goes into labor on New Year's Eve and faces death from hemorrhaging until the village head, responding to a knock in the middle of the night, mobilizes the villagers to get her to the hospital. He helps bear the stretcher to town, and mother and child are saved. The mood changes with the New Year. The gorgeous cinematography for which Zhang Yimou is famous finally emerges, in spectacles of the folk in gaudy opera costumes and of the Wan household as they prepare to celebrate the one-month anniversary of the baby's birth. Brilliant color is everywhere, and Gong Li finally appears beautiful and radiant. Previously, the characters have been socially contextualized through wide-angle shots, and the scenes, whether of overcrowded urban masses or arid, wintry countryside, have mostly been drab. Qiuju now experiences total victory: birth of a healthy baby *boy*, the whole village coming to congratulate her, including the village head's family as guests of honor, and, as it turns out, success in her suit that very day, from a reversal of verdict on the basis of the broken ribs. Her victory is total, but as in the story, she sees it otherwise. The village head is taken away for fifteen days of detention (a weasel word, that; perhaps he is not really "arrested," though the damage to his "face" is great—he is after all taken away in a police car). Qiuju is dumbfounded that her simple request for an apology has led to what is, more even than in the story, a legal overreaction.

Zhang Yimou's production makes the conflict more believably motivated on both sides, as it must be in a medium that cannot take refuge in abstractions. By trivializing the cause of the rift, while deepening its symbolic importance with reproductive concerns that heighten the heroine's victory, he has created a comedy: a tale of a small dispute ridiculously inflated until it rocks a province, and of a lovably obstinate woman. She no longer seems as wholly disempowered as her actual social status would suggest. It is in the village that Qiuju (in the film) seems ridiculously stubborn. As she makes ever higher and more solemn appeals, the very fact that she is taken seriously and not laughed off the stage—by the movie's saintly Captain Yan—lends a new dignity to her seemingly bizarre quest.

Yet the movie turns a question of what is legally (and politically) right into a question of what is morally right and sets the two in opposition. It is legally right for the village head to pay for his misdeed; the courts say so, and he has not yet learned to cure his little flaw of arrogance and paternalism, however much he may in fact serve the people. (The film, unlike the story, makes it clear that he lives far more comfortably than other villagers.) But here his moral goodness in serving his flock, including Qiuju, clearly out-weighs any harm done by his "crime." Qiuju naturally does not want the man who saved her baby locked up; but then, she no longer wants him to apologize to her either. That is to say, he has, with his kind act and "forgive-ness" of her roiling of the waters against him, indeed apologized to her, as far as she is concerned. So the movie seems to show that moral debts have sorted themselves out without the law, much less the ridiculous pursuit of the let-ter of the law in stuffy courtrooms far away and high above. The law comes in, mechanically and after the fact, wreaking havoc in its heavy-handed way, understanding nothing about where human relations really stand.

Law is not fine-tuned enough to make the right decision; this is an old Confucian critique of the law. Insofar as the village head has "rectified him-self," he is the good official who can act more justly in the future than would any overbearing and mechanical law imposed from above. Qiuju the peasant woman may not be so intellectually blank in the film version, but her stub-born questing has not led to justice, but to injustice—precisely because her "win" was through law, not a readjustment of human relations. But is Zhang Yimou really presenting a Confucian message? The critique of paternalism, including the show trial, remains. Perhaps it was the inherent "lowness" of legal discourse—the necessity to make his film transcend mere "legal system cinema"—that made him turn to higher, more abstract questions of justice beyond the law.

CONCLUSION

This book has told the story of a much-loved type of fiction that was virtu-ally obliterated but struggled incessantly, and in the end successfully, to be reborn. It is also the story of Chinese law and Chinese literature. It might be argued that crime fiction can hardly represent Chinese literature; what other Chinese writing was actually put under the authority of the police? Yet if Chinese "high" literature was so much freer, should it not be incomparably better than the works this book examines? It is easier to imagine that police control of writing about crime was an object lesson for all writers.

The emblems of China in the 1990s were private money-making, foreign investment, unabated consumerism, and oceans of pirated Hollywood movies on videotape. It was toward the end of the decade, when the roaring economy cooled, that the public took stock again of its freedom and culture. The general mood was upbeat, bringing hopes that in another ten or twenty years the political concerns of this book might appear quaint. The idea of stealing a wristwatch as a motive for murder is already quaint—though not the idea of a farmer being executed for stealing a few hundred yuan. In the cities, comprehensive surveillance and control of citizens by their work and residence units now belongs to that foreign country that is the past.

In the 1990s it was clear that law was up and literature was down. It was not that rule of law was achieved; neither the state nor the newly unleashed public showed much reverence for rules. But there was a boom in legal actions, notably liability lawsuits and proceedings against local public security bureaus and land-use offices.[31] Lawsuits were the talk of the town. Adversarial legal consciousness rode in with the new consumerism and a new sense of confidence in the individual's ability to withstand government retaliation.[32] Law cases were becoming popular culture. Spectacular crime too was becoming a spectator sport in print media.

Avant-garde literature seemed to have run out of steam. Moreover, the domestic movie industry, including Hong Kong's, was moribund. Popular fiction, television soap operas, and Hollywood blockbusters still thrived, but Wang Shuo was banned in 1996. Chinese crime fiction remained interesting because Chinese society was more complicated—and yet it was now more like the societies of other modern countries. Corruption was exposed—that was a priority of the CCP—but the popular media left deeper questions about the self and culture, and major political and social choices of the future, up to what remained of China's "pure literature." As ever, reportage, like *biji*, dressed up "true cases" (or aspects of them) in fancy narrative techniques. Writing about crime, in fact or fiction, lived (in the eyes of buyers) or died (at the hands of the censors) on the survivability of the smaller truths of its individual facts. High-culture critics, however, thought they observed traces of analytical detection everywhere, even in avant-garde fiction.

The line between fact and fiction was as hard to distinguish as ever, but "high" and "low" remained; capitalism in this age differentiates reading matter according to segmented reader tastes. Would the law, then, ever become a "high" subject in literature, film, or television? When Zhang Yimou avoided dramatizing the law according to its own discourse in *The Story of Qiu Ju*, was it because he thought the law incapable of generating sufficient dramatic tension or because he considered the law unworthy of his highest intellectual and artistic strivings? This book ends with higher expectations for law, literature, and their combination. Surely questions about the social and spiritual roles of them both will continue to intrigue and inspire creative authors even as—particularly as—China enters a more liberated era.

Notes

Introduction: The Revival of Law and Literature in China

1. Modern Chinese and most foreign crime fiction, traditional Chinese "court case fiction," and chivalric or martial-arts fiction were all banned, with minor exceptions during the Hundred Flowers and other thaws. The USSR by contrast tolerated even Nero Wolfe and Rex Stout in Russian editions, though hard-liners criticized the voice thus given to "typical representatives of decadent middle-class society." See "Crime Fiction (Moscow)," *Encounter* 57, no. 2 (August 1981): 26.

2. Link, "Hand-Copied Entertainment Fiction," pp. 19–21, reports that Sherlock Holmes stories and the Chinese novel *Terrifying Footsteps* circulated underground during the Cultural Revolution. The Chinese novel sounds like a thriller with detective, Gothic, xenophobic, and adventure interests. Its setting is nineteenth-century England and the detective is English.

3. Crime was called a leftover from capitalist exploitation in the Old Society. See Tao-tai Hsia, p. 30, citing a major 1963 Chinese book on law.

4. Dikötter's rare look at 1950s prison records shows that the PRC routinely arrested poor farmers and workers for petty theft and locked them up for ten to fifteen years. The Qing also viewed larceny as a threat to social order just a step down from rebellion; Antony, pp. 98–100. Conversely, there is a lingering doubt that it is right to use coercion to enforce judgments in civil conflicts, which are only "among the people"; see Clarke, "The Execution of Civil Judgments," p. 69, and Clarke and Feinerman, p. 136. The number of convicts imprisoned for counterrevolution in the PRC has always been secret, but in Heilongjiang in 1959 it was a little less than 60 percent of the total prison population; see *Human Rights Watch/Asia* 9, no. 4 (Apr. 1997): 31. Baum, p. 97, estimates 40 percent before the Cultural Revolution; 2 or 3 percent among Beijing and Shanghai criminal detainees in 1981–83.

5. Wagner, pp. 20, 41–42.

6. Since 1983, espionage and counterespionage activities have been hived off under a new Ministry of State Security. In the same year, armed police for border control and social disturbances became the People's Armed Police (PAP), supervised by the Ministry of Public Security (MPS) but directly under the Central Military

Commission and State Council. Forerunners of the PAP continually shifted between MPS and Army command (see Cheung). Chinese cadres stress that all security forces are under a unitary system, with the People's Liberation Army as the senior and dominating player. The main role of the Masses' Press (Qunzhong chubanshe) is printing technical police manuals like *Xingshi zhencha anli xuanbian*. Most are classified.

7. Yu Haocheng, then director of the editorial department of the Masses' Press, was investigated by Luo Ruiqing and the central CCP Propaganda Department after four Holmes volumes were published. During the Cultural Revolution a charge against Deng Xiaoping was that he had accepted a complete (used) set of Holmes adventures as a gift from Yu; int. 52. Ye Yonglie notes that before the Cultural Revolution, Holmes stories were printed only by the Masses' Press and China Youth Press; 340,000 volumes were issued in all, but only "internally"; ints. 17, 24. Cheng Xiaoqing asked in a May 21, 1957, *Wenhuibao* article for tolerance of "pure" (not smutty) detective stories in China. The Anti-Rightist campaign made that impossible; see Fan Boqun, pp. 219, 225.

8. *Cihai shixingben* (Trial edition of the *Sea of Words* dictionary; 1961), cited in Wei Shaochang, ed., 1: 120–21. The definition of *zhentan xiaoshuo* (detective fiction) in the *Cihai*, 1979 ed., 1: 545–46, is virtually identical, but it omits the sentence about sex and violence and adds, after mention of the Sherlock Holmes tales as the epitome of the genre, that "China in the early twentieth century had works imitating them." The entry in the *Cihai*, 1989 ed., 1: 625, is slightly longer. The beginning of the definition now clearly specifies that detective fiction was produced and flourished in Europe and America in the nineteenth century, which is why I feel confident using the past tense in translating the previous version. The 1989 entry cites Poe as well as Conan Doyle and adds a reference to Japan's "fiction of deduction." The 1989 version also adds that the genre is attractive to readers "but generally does not concern itself with the social origins of crime in capitalist society."

9. Fox Butterfield, "Crime-Conscious Peking Has First Bank Robbery," *New York Times*, Feb. 10, 1980, p. 9. On China's problematic representation of its crime rates, see H. Tanner, chaps. 4, 6. For a grim, classified update on crime rates from the MPS, telling of a 220 percent increase in bank robbery from 1983 to 1987, see "The Basic Character of Crime in Contemporary China," p. 166.

10. Symons, p. 57. Compare also "the Gongan" ("Public Security," the police) to "la Sûreté," now called the Police Judiciaire. The French terms have always referred only to France's central detective force.

11. A. Chen, p. 104.

12. "Fazhi wenxue yantaohui zai Wan juxing" (Research conference on legal system literature is convened in Anhui), *Renmin ribao*, Nov. 3, 1986, p. 7.

13. V. Li, *Law Without Lawyers*.

14. Simpson, p. 97, describes the key role of Cuba's Ministry of the Interior in the 1972 birth of a Cuban communist detective fiction (much of it, however, was

"anti-spy" or not about postrevolutionary Cuba). Western mystery fiction was available; Perry Mason appeared in a mystery by Juan Angel Cardi.

15. Originally named Dong Baohe, Yu Haocheng is of Manchu ancestry. He was born in 1925 in Beijing; arrested and held in the Qincheng Prison from 1968 to 1971; and detained for investigation within the MPS compound from June 1989 to December 1990. He came to the United States in 1994; int. 47.

16. Official repression of writers occurred again in 1996–97; H. Martin, pp. 294–98.

17. In 1989, the American TV series *Hunter* and a German series were favorites on Chinese TV, and Hong Kong cop shows on videotape were popular. Chen Mingqing of *Jingtan fengyun* wrote (Jan. 30, 1996) that he translated Erle Stanley Gardner's *The Case of the Daring Divorcee*, which I sent him in 1993. He was not aware of any earlier Perry Mason translations; int. 34.

18. The major exception is Wang Shuo's *Playing for Thrills*.

19. Borges, "The Analytical Language of John Wilkins," in *Other Inquisitions*, p. 103. Foucault gave this passage new life in *The Order of Things*, p. xv.

20. Herein I accept the all-inclusive view of genres as mental models, "options, alternatives, interrelations," within structures of textual practice, contracts with readers, or social, comparative cultural, or historical complexes, as Guillén puts it in *The Challenge of Comparative Literature*, pp. 109–16.

21. Rosmarin, p. 7. Most Western critics since Croce have disdained genre criticism; it differs from genre theory, Hernadi's concern, as Strelka, ed., makes clear, pp. vii–ix and 57; see also D. Bennett. Genre criticism is "thoroughly discredited by modern literary theory and practice," says Jameson, p. 105. Raymond Williams simply omits "genre" in *Keywords*.

22. See Manos and Rochelson, eds.

23. Todorov, *Genres in Discourse*, p. 14; Beebee, p. 12.

24. The crime novel has inspired crossovers, but not yet great "countergeneric" works like *Don Quixote*, which was provoked by the picaresque novel (Guillén, "Genre and Countergenre"), or *The Dream of the Red Chamber*, which was a response to the scholar-beauty romance; Zheng Shusen, p. 118.

25. Wellek and Warren, p. 232, call grouping by subject matter a "purely sociological classification" best suited for nonfiction, but they do not find it entirely irrelevant. Culler, p. 136, says that genre "is not simply a taxonomic class."

26. H. Zhao, p. 29 n. 27. On obsession with content, see L. Lee, "The Politics," p. 160; Moran, p. 148.

27. Huang Yanbo, p. 1; Meng Liye, pp. 3–5.

28. Dicks, "Compartmentalized Law," pp. 86–87; Vandermeersch, pp. 15, 22, 23.

29. Nivison, pp. 60–61.

30. Holman, p. 239.

31. Baldick, p. 91.

32. In fact Bruce D. Reeves, a Western critic, calls *Les Misérables* "essentially a de-

tective story in plot," though on the same page he provides the better judgment that it is "a unique combination of melodrama and morality"; see Magill, ed., 3: 1445. As a novel romanticizing revolutionaries fighting law and order, *Les Misérables* may be a precursor of the May Fourth love-and-revolution formula, if not Maoist fiction. It might even be a precursor of Chinese "prison literature."

33. Wright's book, for instance, shows that this does not even distinguish the crime story from the Western. Myth criticism finds "high" meanings in the "low" sensations we usually associate with crime fiction.

34. T. Roberts does add up all the genres and call them "junk fiction," though he submits that there is also a relatively nongeneric popular fiction, which he calls "plain fiction" (2). In the latter he includes *Gone with the Wind*, *Uncle Tom's Cabin*, and *The Godfather*. I think there is a category of subliterature below Roberts's junk fiction. Harlequin and Silhouette romances come to mind in America; in China there is the crime subliterature published by regional literary journals named in Chapter Four. The lowest writing serving the crime interest in the West may be crime nonfiction; on pulp crime fiction's decline since 1960, see Haut.

35. "Crime fiction" appeared in the title of a Hong Kong book: Cen Ying, ed., *Zhongguo dalu zuian xiaoshuo xuan*. I know of no other examples.

36. The terms "legal system literature" and "legal system fiction" were coined in the 1980s. The 1979 *Cihai* has no entry for these terms, and neither does the 1989 edition. Many languages now use a synecdoche originally denoting a subgenre, if not a specific popular formula, to stand for crime and mystery fiction in general. Hence, "detective fiction" (in English, originally "the tradition of Poe and Conan Doyle"); *roman policier* or *polar* (in French, lit., "police fiction"); *suiri shōsetsu* (in Japanese, lit., "fiction of deduction"); and *tuili xiaoshuo* (in Taiwan Mandarin, "fiction of deduction," a neologism from the Japanese). All four terms now refer to mystery fiction in general. Moreover, the terms "fiction" (Eng.), *roman* (Fr.), *xiaoshuo* (Mand.), and *shōsetsu* (J.) do not distinguish between the novel and the short story, or between literature and subliterature; the respective languages' terms for crime fiction do not do so either.

37. Auden, p. 24.

38. Shklovsky, pp. 101–16, discusses works of Dostoevski, Tolstoy, and Turgenev together with the Holmes tales. Apostolou, p. 324, indicates that Matsumoto Seichō asked Japanese writers to take *Crime and Punishment* as their model instead of Poe.

39. Graham Greene, Norman Mailer, C. Day Lewis, and Martin Amis are credibly portrayed as having strayed into crime mystery territory. Walter Mosley and P. D. James are sometimes cited as having gone the other direction. Tani cites, besides antidetective novels as such (what I would call crossovers), "deconstructive" and "metafictional" detective novels by Leonardo Sciascia, Thomas Pynchon, William Hjortsberg, Italo Calvino, and Vladimir Nabokov that, not being popular literature, would be "literature," though not necessarily monumental.

40. Dimock refers to the "self-imposed singularity of reference in criminal law and the self-flaunting multiplicity of reference in the novel" (26).

41. Richard Weisberg, in "How Judges Speak," says the novel is a form of law literature because it elevates legal practice into a linguistic, metalinguistic, or psychological construct, a form of modern *ressentiment*. In *The Failure of the Word*, Weisberg proceeds to make a case for Dostoevski's novels as "legal novels." Priestman's work shows similarities between detective fiction and "literature" while continuing to uphold a social division between them.

42. Posner, p. 218. Beebee, pp. 157–58, 171, conveys Barthes's views on how legal discourse is hegemonic and exclusive in legal processes, though it is itself constructed from nonlegal discourses.

43. Symons, pp. 15, 24, 25, 127–28, 238. Symons cites Faulkner as interested in the detective form, and so do Mick Gidley and Douglas G. Tallack, in Landrum, Browne, and Browne, eds., pp. 228–64.

44. Defoe wrote novels about the criminal life; see Faller.

45. By contrast, Roth, pp. 7–8, sees detective fiction as a "last bastion" of "sexual decency."

46. Porter, *The Pursuit of Crime*, p. 12.

47. Manos and Rochelson, eds., p. ix.

48. Vareille, pp. 8–72.

49. When Argentina imported the whodunit, it entered "high" culture. It was Borges's weapon against Peronist populism; see Simpson, p. 39.

50. Boileau-Narcejac, *Le Roman policier*, p. 122.

51. Camp comes to mind, but we also watch bad TV we do not consider camp.

52. Symons, p. 166.

53. Porter, *The Pursuit of Crime*, pp. 53–81. Panek, p. 111, notes that people read about hero crooks not just for the thrill of it but because of interest in criminal routines. See also T. Roberts, pp. 129–32.

54. See Borges, "On Chesterton," in *Other Inquisitions*, pp. 82–85.

55. Huang Yanbo, pp. 1–15.

56. Movies portraying capitalist justice as a criminal conspiracy are an exception, so perhaps Chinese translators just did not look hard enough. See Chapter Four on *Nightmare in Badham County*.

57. Paul, pp. 10, 23, citing a 1940s essay by E. M. Wrong. See also Panek, p. 3. On fascist bans, see Narcejac, pp. 205–6.

58. I often heard the statement that China has no law, as did Clarke and Feinerman (53). It means that officials are not bound by the law.

59. Taiwan critic Zhang Fang, p. 46, praises PRC author Lü Haiyan's *Bianyi jingcha*.

60. Zeng Zhennan, "Xuanyou bacui qujing yonghong" (Selecting the very best), *Zhuomuniao* 81 (May 1997): 98–99, reports on publication of the first five (of twenty) volumes of a *Dangdai Zhongguo gongan wenxue daxi* (Compendium of con-

temporary Chinese police literature). Gao Jianping's book could also be taken as a statement of a canon.

61. Porter, *The Pursuit of Crime*, p. 125. For dissenting views, see Stowe; Knight, "Radical Thrillers" (*pace* his own *Form and Ideology*); and Priestman, p. 105, who notes that several famous pre–World War I British detective novelists—Israel Zangwill, Arthur Morrison, E. C. Bentley, and G. K. Chesterton—"all displayed loosely socialist sympathies." There is also Dashiell Hammett.

62. Zhang Jinfan, Lin Zhong, and Wang Zhigang, pp. 23–24, call Chinese law "patriarchal" because of an alleged fusion of imperial law and "clan law." Marxist history ascribes patriarchal tendencies to a historicist concept of feudalism, a stage of history now past, but with remnants. Dutton sees patriarchal patterns in traditional and contemporary Chinese policing.

63. On possible futures of Chinese law, see Lubman; also Keith, *China's Struggle*, and "Legislating Women's and Children's 'Rights and Interests,' " for optimistic outlooks on "rule of law" and "rights," respectively. Definitive views of classical Western thought on rule of law are found in Polin.

64. Foucault, *Discipline and Punish*.

65. Quoted in Clarke and Feinerman, pp. 139–40. The defense is "co-author with the court of an 'archeology of truth,' " says Dutton, p. 263, in Foucaldian language.

66. Dworkin, *Law's Empire*, p. 13. As Beebee, a nonlawyer, puts it, p. 152, "Legal discourse constructs its own edifice and converses only with itself."

67. Cited by Richard Ford in "The Master of Ambiguity," *New York Times*, Oct. 17, 1996. Detection is the methodology of the scholar; see Winks, *The Historian as Detective*.

68. Watt, p. 31.

69. J. Cohen, Mentschikoff, and Lincoln, pp. 10–11; Alford, "Law, Law, What Law?"; Friedman treats changing American attitudes toward crime.

70. Lubman, p. 13.

71. Alford, *To Steal a Book*, pp. 7, 132–33 n. 27, 135 n. 30; Nicholas D. Kristof, "What's the Law in China? It's No Secret (Finally)," *New York Times*, Nov. 20, 1988; Dicks, "The Chinese Legal System," pp. 540, 561; Feinerman, p. 194.

72. Berman, p. 317.

73. Alford, "Double-Edged Swords"; Potter, "Riding the Tiger," pp. 325–26. The classic statement of this logic is the discussion of rule of law in E. P. Thompson, pp. 258–69.

74. Alford, "Tasselled Loafers"; Potter, "The Administrative Litigation Law," p. 273; Dicks, "The Chinese Legal System," p. 570.

75. Bourdieu, "The Force of Law." Moore, pp. 54–81, treats law as a "semiautonomous social field." See, in general, the *Journal of Legal Pluralism*.

76. Bhabha speaks of a "never" "implacably oppositional" "space of the adversarial" within a colonial situation, in "Signs Taken for Wonders" in *The Location of*

Culture, p. 109. The Guyanese novelist Wilson Harris also evokes the image of "adversarial contexts" in encounters between colonial and native cultures; see Maes-Jelinek, p. 55. Karl calls the eighteenth-century novel an "adversary literature," but he means by that a literature subversive of social norms.

77. Moran, pp. 180–88, 285–310, gives an interesting picture of reportage writers Su Xiaokang and Jia Lusheng as coming to appreciate adversarialism in legal and literary competition as a legitimate form of institution-building.

78. Hockx has done so. Bourdieu has indeed theorized literature (culture) in all societies as a "field," which further promotes analogies between law and literature; see *The Field of Cultural Production*, p. 9. However, in the present book, which describes poems and laws partly as ideas capable of having a life of their own, I prefer not to take such an absolutely sociological approach. Bourdieu, pp. 37–38, theorizes "the literary and artistic field" within a "field of power," which is within a "field of class relations." I consider that too deterministic.

79. "But poets . . . are not only the authors of language and of music, of the dance, and architecture, and statuary and painting; they are the institutors of laws and the founders of civil society. . . . Poets, according to the circumstances of the age and nation in which they appeared, were called in the earlier epochs of the world legislators or prophets . . . " Shelley, "A Defence of Poetry" (1821), in *Shelley's Prose*, p. 279.

80. Kingwell; B. Thomas, "Reflections"; White, "Law and Literature" and *Heracles' Bow*. White founded the current field with *The Legal Imagination*, a textbook on legal rhetoric. Seminal articles are in Ledwon, ed.; Levinson and Mailloux, eds.; J. Turner and Williams, eds.; *Law and Literature: A Symposium*; *Symposium: Law and Literature*; and Gemmette. Representative books include Richard Weisberg, *Poethics*; Dworkin, *Law's Empire*; B. Thomas, *Cross Examinations*; and Ward. See also Friedland, ed.; Minda; Douzinas and Warrington; and Dimock. A historical work is D. Cohen's.

81. Humanities courses are increasingly offered in medical schools for similar reasons.

82. For reviews, see Fish; Koffler; Teachout; West, "Law, Literature"; Richard Weisberg, "Entering with a Vengeance"; and Robert Weisberg. Books by West and Nussbaum frontally oppose Posner's approach.

83. West, *Narrative*, pp. 1–23.

84. Caryn James, "Information Please," *New York Times Magazine*, Mar. 29, 1998.

85. Clarke and Feinerman, pp. 140, 148.

86. Shen Jianming, a former law school professor at St. John's University who graduated from the Beijing University Law School, so characterized 1980s Chinese legal education. On the 1950s and 1960s, see Tao-tai Hsia. Many classroom materials were mimeographed and internal. The early 1980s had weak approximations of casebooks. The *Falü guwen* series presents cases in some detail, with discussion of

legal principles. Names of the accused and the venues are given, but not the names of injured parties. Even these teaching materials from the East China Institute of Politics and Law present no briefs or opinions in the words of the court or the parties; at the end there are instead statements of opinion by the editors. The book is a digest of cases, like the *Xing'an huilan* of the Qing, and internal. The *Anli fenxi* series is an early specimen, but classified, even though the book was prepared by the staff of the popular magazine *Democracy and Legal System*, presumably from its own journalism. Publicly distributed case digests were more numerous after the mid-1980s. The *Shuo anli, xue falü* (Learn the law through cases) series is a misnomer, for the emphasis is on legal principles, with skeletons of cases cited as exemplifications. The series was prepared for broadcast. Tao Mao et al., eds., is a fairly serious casebook, published by the MPS, but the cases are still in digest form. Names of the principals are represented by X's, and there are no direct quotations. One does not find here "case law," or law made during cases. Dicks, "Compartmentalized Law," p. 82, speaks of greater public availability of court decisions in the 1980s. A fuller compendium of the sort now published is the multivolume *Xingshi fanzui anli congshu* (1992). The Supreme People's Procuratorate now publishes a *Bulletin* too. H. Tanner, pp. 118–26, 148, discusses books of judicial interpretations (*sifa jieshi*), both classified and public, such as Xin Ru and Lu Chen, eds. (1991; a digest, though full names and many details are given), various classified collections of protested cases, and Ouyang Tao et al., eds., which strips cases to the bare bones and obscures the names of parties to the cases. Students read books like Gao Mingxuan, ed. (a history of Chinese criminal law) and *Zhonghua renmin gongheguo xingfa zongze jiangyi*.

87. N. Liu, p. 108; Liu believes that Supreme Court opinions actually are precedents.

88. W. Jones, "The Significance of the *Opinion* of the Supreme People's Court"; A. Chen, p. 102; Chen Guangfeng, "Supreme Court to Allow Publication of Decisions," *China Daily*, May 26, 1985. Steve Strunsky, "The Chinese Connection," *New York Times*, Mar. 16, 1997, New Jersey supplement, p. 4, quotes Haihai Duan Thompson, a founding partner of one of China's first private law firms: " 'American law, we call case law . . . You have a judgment based on a case and it becomes law. In China, we don't have that. We don't have juries and we don't have case law, we just have regulations. Everything is in this book.' "

89. Lubman, Introduction, in Potter, ed., p. 9.

90. Vandermeersch, pp. 3–25. *The Great Qing Code*, Introduction (by W. Jones), p. 10.

91. See Lo; see also Kinkley, "Chinese Crime Fiction and Its Formulas," pp. 128–29.

92. White, "The Judicial Opinion and the Poem," p. 13.

93. West, *Narrative*, pp. 89–176. The key articles in the "Fiss vs. Fish" face-off are in Levinson and Mailloux, eds., pp. 229–68.

94. West, *Narrative*, pp. 345–418.

Chapter 1: Origins

1. Donald A. Yates, Foreword, p. 9, in Stavans.

2. On Soviet mystery fiction, see Russell; Laqueur. In int. 52, Yu Haocheng mentioned the PRC's reprinting of Japanese mystery fiction. Another unresearched topic is to what degree Edogawa Rampo (a pen name transliterating "Edgar Allan Poe") and his Japanese compatriots were known in pre-1949 China. Lin Foer, p. 316, says they were not influential even in Taiwan, then a Japanese colony. Prewar Japanese whodunits, even more than postwar stories, were like the Anglo-American whodunit; see Rampo. Postwar stories are too. Lin Foer indicates that only in the mid-1980s was Matsumoto translated into Chinese for publication in Taiwan. Japan's well-organized mystery aficionados quickly sought Chinese links in the 1980s. On postwar Japanese works, see Nakajima; Itō; Queen, ed.; Matsumoto (two works); Apostolou; Schreiber. On Taiwan, see Zhang Dachun et al.

3. Brooks and Gewirtz, eds.; Bellow and Minow, eds., *Law Stories*. A look at law in early 1980s Chinese fiction is Clarke, "Political Power and Authority."

4. A. Chen, pp. 114–15. A procuratorate might mobilize people to write "letters to the editor" to criticize a judicial decision, whipping up public opinion to change the verdict; see Lo, p. 124.

5. Bai Hua, p. 44.

6. Int. 31; the *Beijing ribao* reported on a case of rape and murder in separate articles by Wang Lansheng and Yu Nengxiang.

7. Though most works in the category were noncontroversial by 1979, the *name* "literature of the wounded" was still dissident in 1980. The name was legitimated only in a 1984 speech by Zhang Guangnian; Yu Haocheng, *Ming chun ji*, p. 3. The officially "correct" term for famous "wounded" works by Liu Xinwu, Lu Xinhua, et al. was *chaotou wenxue* (new wave literature), a term that has now expired. Later the names "literature of the wounded" and "literature of introspection" were officially rendered innocuous when they were pictured as first and second steps toward a tamer third-stage "literature of reform." In 1984–85, that meant officially approved works of "constructive" social criticism. But in the late 1980s, "literature of reform" (referring to novels by Ke Yunlu, Zhang Jie, and Jiang Zilong) was retroactively radicalized and viewed as a follow-up to the daring "literature of introspection." See Wang Chungui; Zeng Zhennan presented the same view in int. 9. Jin Han et al., eds., also remember a wounded-introspection-reform sequence, but like others, they misremember reform literature as a movement of 1979–81, simultaneous with "literature of introspection" (530). See Kinkley, ed., *After Mao*, and Kinkley, "The New Chinese Literature," for references to works. Translations are available in Li Yi, ed., Li Yi and Bi Hua, eds., and Link, ed.

8. On 1980s control of literature, see Link, ed., pp. 1–28; J. Shapiro and Liang, pp. 92–120; Kinkley, Foreword.

9. Baum provides a good summary of Maoist legal history, with comparisons to the Soviet Union's.

10. A. Chen, pp. 120–23.

11. H. Tanner, pp. 72, 79–80; Epstein, p. 27; Clarke, "Dispute Resolution," p. 260; Leng with Chiu, pp. 72, 75, 82 n. 75; Berman, p. 316.

12. A. Chen, pp. 118–23; Barnett, pp. 194–97; Epstein, pp. 27–28. On the Republic, see Xu Xiaoqun.

13. Sentencing and executions are sometimes still done in batches, to maintain the old mass line and "educate" the people; see A. Chen, p. 113.

14. Leng with Chiu, p. 18.

15. Ibid. Bonavia, p. 153. On the origins of communist legal institutions, see Lötveit, pp. 106–44. Ladany relates later legal developments.

16. Leng with Chiu, pp. 17–28; Epstein, p. 36. Some statutes had been promulgated and published, but Bonavia (154) could not find them in bookstores in 1980, and they could not be consulted in libraries without special permission.

17. A. Chen, pp. 130–31; Alford, "Tasselled Loafers."

18. By 1997, China had 100,300 full-time lawyers and 8,265 law offices. Seven Chinese law firms had offices abroad, and 73 overseas firms had received permission to open offices in China. Li Bian, "Legal System Develops Apace," *Beijing Review* 40, no. 19 (Mar. 10–16, 1997): 23.

19. W. Jones, ed., p. xviii; W. Jones, "Some Questions," p. 309.

20. Epstein, p. 19.

21. *Fazhi yu renzhi wenti taolun ji*; Lo, esp. chap. 3; Eliasoph and Grueneberg; Keith, "Chinese Politics," pp. 108–12; on subsequent academic debates, see Keith, *China's Struggle*, pp. 1–38. See also Leng with Chiu, p. 18; Li I-Che [Li Yizhe], "Concerning Socialist Democracy and Legal System," in *China: The Revolution Is Dead*, pp. 213–41; Potter, "The Administrative Litigation Law," pp. 273, 294 n. 23.

22. Senger, pp. 171–74; Keith, *China's Struggle*, p. 120.

23. Epstein, p. 25.

24. Keith, "Chinese Politics," p. 110. See Keith, *China's Struggle*, pp. 12–13, on later mandates to differentiate policy and law.

25. Zeng Zhennan and Wang Shuo, int. 9. There were only the *pinglun* articles of Wei Jun and the two lone 1980 issues of *Zhuomuniao* (Woodpecker) discussed in Chapter Four.

26. See Zhao Guoqing; Su Ce; and Cong Weixi and Liang Jianhua. Philip F. Williams has a book in progress about such fiction. On the realities, see the books of Seymour and Anderson, H. Wu, Saunders, and Zhang Xianliang (*Getting Used to Dying*), and publications of Human Rights in China (*China Rights Forum*), Human Rights Watch, and Amnesty International.

27. Cited by James B. Harris, Translator's Preface to Rampo, p. vii.

28. See Symons; both books by Gilbert; Cawelti; Ousby; Sayers; Hilfer; Reddy; Klein; and Simons on pathologists' memoirs as fiction. On parody, see Kaye.

29. Porter, *The Pursuit of Crime*, p. 212; Eames, pp. 48–97.

30. Josephine Tey wrote a mystery about murders usually attributed to Richard III (*The Daughter of Time*); Umberto Eco and Ellis Peters have used medieval settings; Leonard Tourney and Edward Marston, Elizabethan England. Giffone discusses "neo-Victorian detective novels."

31. Symons, Hilfer, and Carr give an alternative history, stressing not the fractionating of the detective story to serve different subgeneric interests, but development toward a relatively open-ended, realistic crime novel, more psychological in its view of the killer or bureaucratic in its portrait of the detectives. Whether this fits the mass-market serial-murderer-versus-detective thrillers of today (by James Patterson, David Baldacci, Jonathan Kellerman, Robert K. Tannebaum, and others) is debatable. Barzun, a champion of the "detective story," is a noted opponent of Symons's view. Knight, *Form and Ideology*, argues the bureaucratic trend. The spy thriller has such conspiratorial and ideological villainy that it is usually theorized separately. See Cawelti, pp. 31–32; Palmer, *Thrillers*. However, Mandel, p. 85, and Symons include the spy thriller as a form of crime fiction.

32. Hanan, *The Chinese Vernacular Story*, pp. 39–44. I thank Patrick Hanan for the entire thumbnail sketch of *gongan*. On Yuan plays, see Perng.

33. Bao Zheng, *Bao Zheng wen ji*; Huang Yanbo, pp. 136–60; *Gongan xiaoshuo yanjiu ziliao*.

34. Hanan, *The Chinese Vernacular Story*, pp. 39–44, 72–74; Ma, "The Pao-kung Tradition"; Hayden, *Crime and Punishment*. On oral forms, see Blader, and Nienhauser, ed., p. 667 (entry by Susan Blader).

35. See Wang Hailin; Chen Pingyuan, *Qiangu wenren*; Wang Chungui; D. Wang, pp. 117–82. On chivalric novels with the word *gongan* in the title, see Huang Yanbo, pp. 226–44, and Meng Liye, pp. 119–34. Judge Bao also appeared in Qing novels like the *Ping yao zhuan* (Suppression of the sorcerers' revolt).

36. Hu Shi's actual trope, p. 441 (which Chang-tai Hung, pp. 89–90 says he took from Zhou Zuoren), is the straw figures in human form that the military strategist Zhuge Liang (A.D. 181–234) set up to draw enemy arrows.

37. Idema and Haft, pp. 241–43.

38. Symons, pp. 27–34; Grossvogel; Hollingsworth; Murch; Ousby; Porter, *The Pursuit of Crime*; Stavans, pp. 47–48; Cassiday, ed.

39. Knight, *Form and Ideology*, pp. 8–38.

40. Symons, pp. 27–63. See esp. Murch.

41. Higgins; Lehman; Murch.

42. In Japan since 1967, "Lupin III" (Rupan Sansei), a "grandson" of the Frenchman with Japanese gangster sidekicks and bureaucratic police nemeses, has been a popular *manga* and *anime* character. He has an international following and an animated Canadian cable television program, *Nighthood*. French authors have continued writing "new" Arsène Lupin adventures, notably, in the 1970s, "Boileau-Narcejac," the team of Pierre Boileau (b. 1906) and Thomas Narcejac (Pierre

Ayraud, 1908–98), the only ones authorized to use the Lupin name. An example is *La Poudrière*. Ruaud, pp. 90–95, lists pastiches and sequels. Georges Simenon, inspired by Lupin and writing under the name Georges Sim, penned *Les Aventures de Yves Jarry, gentleman cambrioleur*; see Derouard, p. 514.

43. PRC folklore journals in the 1980s regularly printed stories about ancient and modern upright officials (*qingguan*). See the compilations by Fan Mu and by Jiang Yuan with Qian Zhengjie.

44. Deng Shulin, "Old and New in Hefei," *China Reconstructs* (July 1982): 15–16.

45. Mao Zedong, 1: 32. In English, Mao Tse-tung, 1: 45, with a commendatory note identifying Lord Bao, p. 58 n. 21. The Chinese text lacks this annotation; no Chinese would need it.

46. Judge Bao is occasionally humiliated in Yuan dramas and the *Baijia gongan* (James St. André, personal communication).

47. Hanan, *The Chinese Vernacular Story*, pp. 72–74.

48. Chen Mingqing, int. 34.

49. It started in 1928 when Sayers gathered in London twenty writers who took an oath (see "The Detection Club Oath") forswearing reliance on "Divine Revelation, Feminine Intuition, Mumbo Jumbo, Jiggery-Pokery, Coincidence or Act of God." They also pledged to observe "a seemly moderation in the use of Gangs, Conspiracies, Death-Rays, Ghosts, Hypnotism, Trap-Doors, Chinamen, Super-Criminals and Lunatics" and to avoid "Mysterious Poisons unknown to Science." See Hone, pp. 54–55; Symons, pp. 93–97; Leitch, pp. 103–5; and Knox; see also S. S. Van Dine, who offers full "twenty rules" of his own.

50. Doyle, 1: 226, 2: 911. The "Red Circle" is a brotherhood said to be "allied with the old Carbonari." The Black Hand had been much in the press when Conan Doyle wrote the latter story in 1911. Chesterton inveighed against the whodunit's use of conspiracies in 1929; Roth, p. 227. On Conan Doyle as a writer of something other than "detective stories," see Leitch.

51. Deconstruction neither refutes nor supersedes other theories; Ellis, pp. 79–96.

52. Trotter, p. 66; see also Pyrhönen. Strangely, the Modern Language Association is known for resisting the study of crime and detective fiction. An antidote is the newsletter *Murder Is Academic: The Teaching and Criticism of Crime Fiction on Campus*, edited by B. J. Rahn of Hunter College.

53. Edmund Wilson, "Who Cares Who Killed Roger Ackroyd?" in Winks, ed., pp. 35–40. For good period criticism, see Ball, ed.; Haycraft; Haycraft, ed.

54. Shklovsky, pp. 101–46, 170; Todorov, *The Poetics of Prose*, pp. 42–52; Lacan, pp. 28–54, with commentary, pp. 55–98. Besides Eco's famous novel *The Name of the Rose*, he and other semioticians have written detective story criticism, as in Eco and Sebeok, eds. See also Sebeok and Margolis. Kristeva's novel is *Possessions*.

55. Irwin; Rosenheim.

56. Priestman, pp. 31, 48.

57. Holquist writes, p. 150, "What the structural and philosophical presuppositions of myth and depth psychology were to modernism (Mann, Joyce, Woolf, and so forth), the detective story is to postmodernism (Robbe-Grillet, Borges, Nabokov, and so on)." Tani discusses primarily crossovers and antidetective novels by the same authors. For recent theory, see Bargainnier and Dove, eds.; Benstock, ed.; Black; Champigny; Docherty, ed.; Hartman; Hühn; Knight, *Form and Ideology*; Leps; Lesser; Most and Stowe, eds.; Porter, *The Pursuit of Crime*; Priestman; Pyrhönen; Rader and Zettler, eds.; Spanos; Stavans; Suleiman; Jon Thompson; Walker and Frazer; Winston and Mellerski. On popular fiction, see Ashley; T. Bennett (two pieces); Levine; J. Palmer (two books).

58. Collins; During, ed.; Easthope. On feminism see Heilbrun; Irons; Klein; Kromm; Reddy; Sweeney. Paul examines theological overtones.

59. Gilbert, *The World of Mystery Fiction*, p. xiv, citing Robert A. W. Lowndes, "The Contributions of Edgar Allan Poe," in Nevins, ed., pp. 1–18.

60. T. Hall, pp. 91–143.

61. Ousby, pp. 3–18.

62. D. Wang, p. 118.

63. Cawelti, pp. 82–83, finds such conventions in other popular genres too.

64. Kromm, pp. 275–82.

65. Sweeney, pp. 40–41.

66. Holmes also displayed one-upmanship toward aristocrats. Kromm, pp. 273–74.

67. Mandel, pp. 78–80. Arthur Hailey, author of *Airport, Hotel*, and *The Evening News*, was thus attracted to the genre to write an arcanely "informative" police procedural, *Detective* (New York: Crown, 1997).

68. Frye, p. 46.

69. Symons, p. 104.

70. Roth, p. 27, instead argues that a generic boundary line excludes "social and political history."

71. See Charney.

72. Cawelti, p. 55; Boileau-Narcejac, *Le Roman policier*, p. 37.

73. John Kohut, "Sleuthing Comes to Shanghai," *Boston Globe*, Feb. 8, 1993, p. 2. The retired cops were picking up spare money by investigating economic cases not given priority by police and courts because the law was too ambiguous to firmly establish a crime. China's first security guard company, really a government-run economic entity, was organized in 1985. Guards were uniformed but presumably had no government badges. "China's First Security Service Company Established in Shenzhen," *Zhongguo fazhi bao*, Feb. 13, 1985, p. 1, translated in Foreign Broadcast Information Service (China), Mar. 5, 1985, p. K15. A more proactive service in Dalian arrested a gang of young thugs. Anthony Lewis, "Equality and Progress," *New York Times*, Aug. 22, 1985.

74. Dove, *The Police Procedural*, p. 3.

75. As early as 1988, Jiang Xi and Xia Guoqiang published a short story about a Chinese private detective—an ex-cop—sleuthing in post-Mao society.

76. Ints. 9, 11.

77. Binyon, pp. 9–46.

78. Cawelti, p. 96.

79. Gilbert, *The World of Mystery Fiction: A Guide*, pp. 126–27.

80. However, we can imagine murderers who might want to mutilate a corpse. Imperfect police work could account for the failure to find the hammer.

81. Gilbert, *The World of Mystery Fiction: A Guide*, p. 61.

82. Ji Ming, "Dai shoukao de 'lüke,' " p. 142.

83. C. Shih, *Injustice to Tou O*.

84. Rolston, pp. 126, 129. The *Analects* of Confucius says that the good reader (not just of fiction) is one who can furnish the other three corners of a square when the first is revealed. Rolston, p. 128.

85. The 62–story collection was culled from the 100–story *Longtu gongan*, which was in turn indebted partly to other court case collections whose heroes were originally other judges, and partly to a more colloquial but rarer collection of Bao cases whose 1594 and 1597 survivors are called the *Baijia gongan* (Hundred cases) for short. See Ma, "The Textual Tradition"; Hanan, "*Judge Bao's Hundred Cases* Reconstructed"; Ma, "The Pao-kung Tradition"; Huang Yanbo, pp. 136–60; Bauer; and most elegantly, Hanan, *The Chinese Vernacular Story*, pp. 72–74. Ma, "The Pao-kung Tradition," p. 139, discusses the *Bao Gong qi'an*, referred to by twentieth-century scholars Zhao Jingshen and Wei Juxian. Bauer, p. 442, refers to it as his "C3" version, an early copy of which was printed in Shanghai in 1934. Bauer, p. 447, believes that the stories are still paired by implication, but the subtlety may have escaped most readers. The text is divided into enormous run-on sentences, with commas separating one phrase from another. A 1993 TV series from Taiwan about Lord Bao's cases became a hit in the PRC. See Liang Hu Xueji, "Zoushang shentan de Bao Qingtian" (Blue Skies Bao ascends to godhood on the tube), *Jiushi niandai* 286 (November 1993): 100–101. English selections from the *Longtu gongan* are Comber, trans., and Ma and Lau, eds., pp. 456–62, 479–84. Chin, Center, and Ross, eds., has looser renditions.

86. My summary is indebted to the sources in the previous note and to Ma, "Themes and Characterization"; Hayden, "The Legend of Judge Pao"; the Translator's Preface to Comber, trans.; folkloric accounts of Judge Bao compiled by Fan Mu and others; the biographies of Bao recounted in Ma's dissertation, "The Pao-kung Tradition"; Judge Bao cases in the *T'ang-yin-pi-shih*; the novel *San xia wu yi*, its precursor *Longtu erlu*, and a successor, *Qi xia wu yi*; and helpful personal communications from James St. André. The late Qing Judge Bao novels were discussed early on in Lu Xun, *A Brief History of Chinese Fiction*. I differ with Ma's expert "Themes and Characterization," p. 179, when he differentiates Bao stories from

Western detective stories on the grounds that the former have, besides didactic teachings and supernatural interventions, solutions reached by coincidence. Critical opinion now stresses coincidence in the classical Western genre too. An early and influential comparison of Judge Bao and Sherlock Holmes in English appeared in a 1942 essay by Vincent Starrett that begins his *Bookman's Holiday*. His account appears to be secondhand, yet it is suprisingly accurate. Perhaps his source was Lin Yutang, whose authority Starrett cites on p. 25.

87. This is true in the three earliest *huaben* with crime case themes that Hanan has identified, in *The Chinese Vernacular Story*, pp. 40–44. Identifying the culprit from the start may have developed as a later convention.

88. See Donaldson.

89. As used below; Cawelti, pp. 44–45.

90. Huang Yanbo analyzes the *Longtu gongan* thematically, pp. 151–60.

91. Holmes also refreshes himself with sleep (and cocaine), and it may be that in these instances his subconscious mind is on the case. See Prchal. Sun Liaohong's "Muou de xiju" satirizes the time spent in sleep by Huo Sang, the Chinese Holmes.

92. In the Ming tale "Yaoshi" (The key), a poor young scholar is wrongly accused of murdering his paramour's maid. In a dream, Judge Bao sees an old scholar who makes the real criminal's name appear on a fortune-telling stick. The young scholar, who had summoned up his father in prayer and recognizes Judge Bao's vision as identical to his own, identifies the old scholar to Bao as his father. Judge Bao then realizes what the ghost was driving at; *Bao Gong qi'an*, p. 19. On Dou E, see C. Shih. Xi Xi's story "The Fertile Town Chalk Circle" imagines Judge Bao drifting off into the spirit world as a sort of dream process as conceived by modern psychology (99). It is a reevocation of an ancient play as an allegory for preretrocession Hong Kong, which was claimed by two masters, China and Britain.

93. Symons, p. 27.

94. *The Great Qing Code*, Introduction (by W. Jones), p. 10.

95. Buoye, p. 79.

96. Ma, "The Pao-kung Tradition," p. 64.

97. Knight, *Form and Ideology*, pp. 28–37. The title of the TV program *Hunter* was translated as *Shentan Hengte* (Marvelous detective Hunter).

98. *The Great Qing Code*, Introduction (by W. Jones), p. 10.

99. Ibid., p. 10. See also Kuhn; Vandermeersch, pp. 3–25.

100. Ma, "The Pao-kung Tradition," p. 80.

101. Huang Liu-hung, pp. 256–68 (esp. 321–22).

102. Meng Liye, p. 79.

103. *T'ang-yin-pi-shih*, case 46A, pp. 143–44.

104. Blader, p. 28.

105. *Celebrated Cases of Judge Dee (Dee Goong An)*, is said by Robert Van Gulik to have been written in the eighteenth century, which is late to begin with; Patrick Hanan notes (personal communication) that it was actually unknown before the

first surviving, late-nineteenth-century editions and probably was written about then.

106. Cawelti, pp. 44–45.

107. Under the May 15, 1996, Lawyers Law that took effect in January 1997, lawyers changed from "state legal workers" to "legal workers for society." No longer paid state salaries, they are now responsible for their own profits and losses in cooperative or private enterprises. The Ministry of Justice still oversees the lawyers' associations, and the duties of lawyers were not redefined.

108. H. Tanner, pp. 64–74.

109. Wagner, pp. 43–62.

110. *Stories About Not Being Afraid of Ghosts* (first Chinese-language edition, 1961).

111. Like Judge Shang Qin (Song Yuexun and Chen Dunde, 41). Chinese whodunit heroes are cops, so they too take pains to show their benevolence, like Ol' Gao, an "uncle cop" who carries candy in his pocket to give little girls (Wang Hejun, 14).

112. Judge Bao took on imperial enemies, and James St. André further notes that in some cases Bao is a young magistrate who has not yet acquired all his clout (personal communication).

113. See Tan Dazheng and Shen Qi, pp. 10–13, and the commentary by Hua Jian in that book.

114. See Y. Wu.

115. Compare with a case cited in Lo, p. 209.

116. The handling of petty theft and divorce, ca. 1982–83, is shown in *The Heart of the Dragon*.

117. Seymour and Anderson, pp. 171–73.

118. H. Tanner, pp. 89–106; Clarke and Feinerman, pp. 147–48. Shelter and investigation was to be terminated in 1997, not evidently by law, for neither the Criminal Procedure Law of 1979 nor the Decision of 1996 to amend that law mentioned it, but by the same sort of party fiat that established it above the law in the first place. See the articles by Yu Ping, Donald C. Clarke, and Yu Haocheng in the "Law and Human Rights" special issue (on the new 1995–96 laws) of *China Rights Forum* (Fall 1996).

119. A. Chen, pp. 24–25; Clarke and Feinerman, pp. 141–42; Ladany, pp. 135–36; Gelatt. For comparisons with Japan, see Bayley, and Tipton. Not only police, but even mere security departments of work units can punish people with reeducation-through-labor, although provincial judicial departments oversee these labor camps; Seymour and Anderson, p. 20.

120. J. Cohen, pp. 11–15; Leng with Chiu, pp. 68–72; see also the two articles by Ginsburgs and Stahnke.

121. Ginsburgs and Stahnke, "The People's Procuratorate," pp. 69, 77.

122. Tan Zhengwen, "Absorb Experience and Teaching, Impel a Great Leap

Forward in Procuratorial Work," *Zhengfa yanjiu* 3 (1958): 34–37, cited in J. Cohen, p. 383.

123. Leng with Chiu, p. 20.

124. Ibid., pp. 68–72.

125. J. Cohen, p. 378.

126. Leng with Chiu, p. 71, citing examples from 1981–82. Lo, pp. 107–10, 168–70.

127. Interview with Shen Jianming, New York, October 1996. Judges were no longer required to collect evidence for trial when the March 1996 Decision on Revisions to the Law of Criminal Procedure went into effect in 1997. On procurators, see Du Xichuan and Zhang Lingyuan, pp. 114, 129.

128. V. Li, "The Public Security Bureau," p. 53; see also Barnett, pp. 194–97.

129. V. Li, "The Public Security Bureau," p. 53.

130. Ibid., pp. 53–54; see also J. Cohen, p. 33.

131. H. Tanner, pp. 62–89 (stage fright, 70).

132. Leng with Chiu, p. 70, citing a "Work Report of the Supreme People's Procuratorate," Dec. 7, 1981. H. Tanner, p. 71, indicates that the conviction rate has remained well over 90 percent.

133. Clarke and Feinerman, p. 140.

134. *The Laws of the P.R.C., 1979–1982*, 1: 72, Art. 3.

135. Dicks, "Compartmentalized Law," pp. 94–95.

136. H. Tanner, p. 149.

137. J. Cohen, p. 16, quoting an approving 1959 article by Lin Zejun.

138. Leng with Chiu, p. 23, quoting a disapproving 1979 article by Liao Junchang (translation slightly modified). See also Clarke, "Dispute Resolution," pp. 261–63.

139. J. Cohen, p. 33.

140. *The Criminal Law and the Criminal Procedure Law of China* (1984), "Section 4, Search," makes no reference at all to a search when no one is present. Article 81 says that "When carrying out arrest or detention, if an emergency situation is encountered, a search may be conducted without the use of a search warrant" (139–40).

141. Leng with Chiu, pp. 21–22, 104–8.

142. The revolution reversed traditional penal codes, which allowed one to conceal one's kin's crimes and indeed punished one for accusing kin; see MacCormack, *Traditional Chinese Penal Law*, pp. 119–25, 161.

143. Not to be confused with the old leftist poet Wang Yaping (1905–83), whose name is identical.

144. Tan Dazheng and Shen Qi, pp. 25–28; commentary by Lin Huicheng.

145. The provincial police organ is called a bureau (*ju*) in the story, but I believe that as a provincial organ it should be a *ting* (department).

146. Page numbers refer to the translation under the title "Sacred Duty" by Geremie Barmé, in Barmé and Lee, trans., pp. 101–45.

147. Lu Xun, "Kuangren riji" (A madman's diary), in *Nahan*, p. 27.

148. J. Cohen, p. 15, citing legal articles from 1958.

149. Leng with Chiu, p. 94.

150. Huang Wei, "Amended Law Further Promotes Human Rights," *Beijing Review* 39, no. 43 (Oct. 21–27, 1996): 22–23, tells of three Liaoning lawyers arrested in 1984 for pleading a rape suspect innocent. Folsom, Minan, and Otto, pp. 139–40, tell of similar incidents from 1987. When dissidents used lawyers for a defense after the June Fourth massacre of 1989, lawyers had to submit their briefs to judicial authorities in advance for approval; see Yu Haocheng, "Positive Signals," *China Rights Forum* (Fall 1996): 15.

151. Clarke and Feinerman, p. 140; A. Chen, pp. 138–41.

152. "The Criminal Procedure Law of China" (adopted July 1, 1979, effective in 1980), Chap. 2, Sec. 1, Art. 110, in *The Criminal Law and the Criminal Procedure Law of China* (1984), p. 149. In the 1996 revision, a defendant was given all of two months in advance of the trial to hire and consult a lawyer; see Huang Wei, "Amended Law Further Promotes Human Rights," *Beijing Review* 39, no. 43 (Oct. 21–27, 1996): 23. This article makes an interesting slip; it says that before the law changed, "a lawyer was allowed to get involved in a case no earlier than seven days prior to the scheduled court session." That is a misreading of the law, but it could have been true.

153. Leng with Chiu, p. 94–95; quotation from Huang Wei, "Amended Law Further Promotes Human Rights," p. 25.

154. The narrator is at first revealed only as an interested spectator at the trial. Soon it is clear that he was a witness to something; then, that he is a relative of the procurator. Only later is his job revealed: he is on the staff of the prefectural party committee, where the Tangs hold sway.

155. Klein, pp. 223–25.

Chapter 2: Tradition

1. The Qin and Han also had complex codes, not fully extant today; see Hulsewé. Codes may date back to the Shang; see Creel, p. 29; and MacCormack, *Traditional Chinese Penal Law*, pp. 1–4. Somewhat correlative to the focus here, H. Zhao opines (216–17) that Neo-Confucianism—in the Song—caused Confucian ethics (Rites) to be newly applied to lower social strata, spurring a boom in moralistic vernacular fiction as a tool for that.

2. Wang Liqi, ed.; An Pingqiu and Zhang Peiheng, eds.; Guy; Alford, *To Steal a Book*. On abortive 1988–89 attempts to enact a press law, see Polumbaum.

3. Meng Liye, p. 76.

4. MacCormack, *The Spirit of Traditional Chinese Law*, p. 32; see also Escarra, p. 74; MacCormack, *Traditional Chinese Penal Law*, pp. 16, 290.

5. The Qing began drafting a modern code in 1904 and promulgated the first draft in 1907; Meijer, *The Introduction of Modern Criminal Law*, p. 11; Zhang Jinfan, Lin Zhong, and Wang Zhigang, pp. 88–90.

6. See Farmer; Furth; Smith; Kwang-ching Liu; Kai-wing Chow.

7. Chen Liang (1143–94) did find laws a moralizing influence; see Tillman, p. 16.

8. West, *Narrative*, pp. 1–23. Postmodern critics want to deconstruct the unity of law; Douzinas and Warrington, with McVeigh.

9. Peller, p. 1153.

10. White, "The Judicial Opinion and the Poem," pp. 23–25; Dworkin, "How Law Is Like Literature," pp. 3–33, 39–41; see also Dworkin, *Law's Empire*, p. 413.

11. Idema and Haft, pp. 31, 42–43, 47–53.

12. As stressed by Wong.

13. Attraction to fiction could be addictive or lead to neurosis; see Shen Congwen.

14. Premodern English upper classes so feared "light literature" that they opposed lower-class literacy, unlike the Chinese; see Symons, pp. 42–45.

15. Liang Zhiping, p. 58, says that the word *falü* came to China in the twentieth century from Japan, where the two-character compound was used in the nineteenth century and pronounced "*hōritsu.*" We know that "*falü*" was in official use by May 1904, when the Falü Bianzuan Guan (Chinese Bureau for the Compilation of Laws) was installed; Meijer, *The Introduction of Modern Criminal Law*, pp. 9–18. L. Liu, p. 272, agrees that *falü* was rediffused into China from Japan, but notes some classical Chinese uses of "*falü*" in the *Zhuangzi* and *Guanzi*, and also seventeenth-century Jesuit missionaries' use of the two characters to translate "law." It was glossed in that sense in Robert Morrison's 1815 *Dictionary of the Chinese Language*.

16. Bodde and Morris, pp. 11–12. "*Xing*" reverted to the meaning "penal law," and in recent centuries has meant "punishment." It also referred to the physical tortures a judge used to get a suspect—or witness—to talk. Zhang Jinfan, Lin Zhong, Wang Zhigang, pp. 1–8, give references to early words now meaning "law."

17. Bodde and Morris, p. 11. Recent scholarship has not only linked some of the most ancient Chinese concepts of law to concepts of the Dao, but opened up the question of whether *fa* was not originally closer to "standard" than law—that is, shorn of the connotations of punishment; unpublished paper by Chad Hansen, cited in K. Turner, p. 13.

18. Tillman, p. 28, citing John Knoblock's translation of the *Xunzi*.

19. Owen, p. 586.

20. Liang Zhiping believes that the Chinese *fa* has long been so inextricably bound up with the idea of punishment rather than rules of conduct that only in this century has "*fa*" become equivalent to our "law." Vandermeersch, p. 3, denies that China has ever had law in the Western juridical tradition, by which he means a tradition of law as a guarantor of rights (12–13). Impressed by the absolute sovereignty of the emperor and the fact that even in late imperial times substatutes (typically de-

creed by the emperor) always took precedence over codified statutes, he privileges edicts and rescripts as the law of China, and also ritual order, *li*. Statutes were mere administrative regulations below them. This in its own way confirms my sense of a hierarchy in Chinese norms, or law, broadly defined. Of interest to the law and literature field is his observation that anciently "sovereign decisions" ("laws") were "treated as a genre of literature" (7).

21. Starr, p. xviii; Pospísil, pp. 100–102; S. Roberts. Moore, pp. 1–31, provides a critical overview.

22. Bernhardt and Huang, eds.; P. Huang; Allee; MacCormack, *Traditional Chinese Penal Law*, pp. 61–67. Chang, pp. 308, 333 n. 105, says that customary law was not considered "law" in the Qing; it was first compiled in the 1930s. See also Escarra, pp. 125–27. On clan laws, which might themselves contain passages from the state code, see Chang, pp. 297–98; and Zhang Jinfan, Lin Zhong, and Wang Zhigang, pp. 23–24.

23. McKnight, "From Statute to Precedent"; Chang, pp. 308–09; See also Vandermeersch; MacCormack, *Traditional Chinese Penal Law*, pp. 56–60.

24. Moore, pp. 13–14.

25. "*Fa* overlaps ritual action (*li*) in that it too represents a formalized investment of meaning. That is, *li* and *fa* share a common starting point," say D. Hall and Ames, pp. 172–73, though they describe Rites as "negotiated and open-ended" "significating patterns" in the service of spontaneous harmony (168–69, 172). Rites were ideally tantamount to metalinguistic communication, Brian E. McKnight notes (personal communication). Vandermeersch, pp. 15, 22–23, suggests an ancient link between laws and music. Post-Mao Chinese legal scholarship speaks of a *lixing bingyong* (joint use of Rites and punishments) from the time of "slave society" (Xia, Shang, Zhou), but this is from a Marxist view in which Rites as well as laws are to begin with not so much rules as instruments to oppress people. Zhang Jinfan, Lin Zhong, and Wang Zhigang, pp. 141–48.

26. Brian E. McKnight and Robert E. Hegel reminded me of this; says *The T'ang Code*, 1: 51 ("General Principles," chap. 1), quoting the *Great Commentary on the Book of History*, "We receive heaven's great law (*lü*)." And, "A statute is similar to a measure or a model." See also Escarra, p. 37. On *li*, see Schwartz, p. 301; Tillman, p. 30. On *li* and music, see *Li Chi*, 2: 92–105, 125–27 (*Yue ji* or *Record of Music*). Owen, p. 51, retranslates *Li Chi*, 2: 93, thus: "Rites, music, government, and punishment are ultimately one and the same—a means to unify the people's minds and correctly execute the Way." On *wen*, see Owen, pp. 186–88, 594.

27. Escarra, pp. 70, 74. This view seems in part based on an etymological argument (p. 16 n. 25) that concludes too much from the origination of the word *fa* (law) in the ancient word *fa* (model).

28. MacCormack, *The Spirit of Traditional Chinese Law*, pp. 13–14, 45–51. Meijer, *The Introduction of Modern Criminal Law*, pp. 3–4, argues that punishments were "symbolic" restorations of natural order.

29. McKnight, *The Quality of Mercy*, p. 126. Somewhat in Escarra's vein, but referring only to the Han through Song, McKnight emphasizes "the system of acts of grace" in traditional Chinese justice (112).

30. B. Thomas, "Reflections," p. 526. See Wingate on Western crime fiction in which the criminal is punished by "poetic justice."

31. L. Yang; Eberhard; Brokaw. More orthodox ideas of ritual obligations also tended toward codification in late imperial China, even in simple household instructions. See Furth; Kai-wing Chow.

32. Liang Zhiping's theme is that China had no concept equivalent to justice (Latin: *jus*) beyond the law (Latin: *lex*); it had only *fa*, punishment. But the lack of a word does not always prove the lack of a concept.

33. Vandermeersch, p. 13.

34. *Li Chi*, 1: 90 (*Qu li* or *Summary of the Rites*). To Confucius, the *junzi* were a "moral aristocracy," not a blood aristocracy: "noble men" rather than "noblemen"; see Schwartz, p. 76. In fact, laws were not alternative to Rites but aimed at the same harmonious social result; D. Hall and Ames, p. 175.

35. Kai-wing Chow, p. 227.

36. J. Cohen, p. 4.

37. Bodde and Morris, pp. 16–17; see also Schwartz, pp. 326–28.

38. MacCormack, *Traditional Chinese Penal Law*, p. 35.

39. *Analects*, chap. XII, p. 13. *Shisan jing zhushu*.

40. Bodde and Morris, pp. 13–14. Zhang Jinfan, Lin Zhong, and Wang Zhigang, pp. 11–16, 20.

41. Van der Sprenkel, pp. 76–77.

42. Ibid., pp. 135–36, citing a 1926 collection by W. Scarborough.

43. Chang, pp. 294–97, 323 n. 7; Meng Liye, p. 26. Chang indicates that the Qing tests were not structured as tests of legal knowledge. See also Escarra, pp. 345–56.

44. Chang, pp. 300–14; Macauley.

45. P. Huang; Zelin.

46. Mair, "Language and Ideology," pp. 325–59.

47. *The Great Qing Code*, p. 89 (art. 61); MacCormack, *The Spirit of Traditional Chinese Law*, p. 214 n. 21.

48. *The Great Qing Code*, Introduction (by W. Jones), p. 6.

49. Baum, p. 100. Meijer, *Murder and Adultery*; McKnight, "From Statute to Precedent," pp. 111–16. Imperial decisions on individual cases could be so numerous that late Song law has been called precedent law by Miyazaki Ichisada; see McKnight, "From Statute to Precedent," p. 1.

50. Needham, 2: 532.

51. Kim, pp. 25–64. For a broader consideration of Chinese law as natural, see MacCormack, *Traditional Chinese Penal Law*, pp. 40–41, 291; and Zhang Jinfan, Lin Zhong, and Wang Zhigang, pp. 17, 20.

52. McKnight, *The Quality of Mercy*, pp. 17, 113. Hsu Dau-lin, pp. 111–25, emphasizes that violations of law were not tantamount to violations of the cosmic order. This might refer to the views of Bodde and Morris, pp. 4, 43–48; Meijer, *The Introduction of Modern Criminal Law*, pp. 3–4; and Escarra, pp. 7–10, 25. But Escarra's argument is partly based on the fact that many laws come from *li*. More support for the idea of "response" or "retribution" (*bao*) in Qin-Han law is given in Kroll. See also *The T'ang Code*, Introduction, 1: 15. MacCormack, in *Traditional Chinese Penal Law*, pp. 42–45, and *The Spirit of Traditional Chinese Law*, pp. 210–12, 292–94, weighs in against the cosmic harmony theory, while allowing that it may have a "core of truth" in certain instances. Silk manuscripts of the Huang-Lao school (a Warring States–era synthesis of Daoism and Legalism) unearthed at Mawangdui, Hunan, in 1973, indicate a view of law (*fa*) and policy-making as quintessential "natural law"—ideally guided by the Dao itself, to which the ruler is subject; see Peerenboom. The Mawangdui texts have prompted some contemporary Chinese scholars to interpret the Warring States as a time when "the rule of law, *fazhi*, replaced rule by rites, *lizhi*" (cited in K. Turner, p. 10). But one could as easily point to the resurgence of Confucian privilege in the Han.

53. *The Great Qing Code*, Introduction (by W. Jones), p. 3.

54. MacCormack, *Traditional Chinese Penal Law*, p. 53.

55. The Chinese texts are volumes 3, 4, and 5 respectively of *Shisan jing zhushu*.

56. Senger, pp. 204–5. On the Ming, see Farmer; on the Qing, Smith.

57. MacCormack, *The Spirit of Traditional Chinese Law*, p. 43, citing Ebrey, p. xiii.

58. *Li Chi*, 1: 238 (*Wang zhi*, or *The Royal Regulations*, chap. V); 1: 256 (*Yue ling*, or *Proceedings of Government in the Different Months*, chap. VI).

59. "[Officers] should (also) stimulate the wheat-sowing. (The husbandmen) should not be allowed to miss the proper time for the operation. Any who do so shall be punished without fail"; *Li Chi*, 1: 289 (*Yue ling*, Chap. VI). "The superior man framed . . . punishments to serve as a barrier against licentiousness"; *Li Chi*, 2: 284 (*Fang ji*, *Record of the Dykes*, chap. XXX).

60. "Where there had been neglect of the proper order of observances of the ancestral temple, it was held to show a want of filial piety, and the rank of the unfilial ruler was reduced. Where any ceremony had been altered or any instrument of music changed, it was held to be an instance of disobedience, and the disobedient ruler was banished"; *Li Chi*, 1: 217 (*Wang zhi*, chap. V).

61. *Li Chi*, 1: 285 (*Yue ling*, chap. VI).

62. *Li Chi*, 1: 236 (*Wang zhi*, chap. V); Dutton, p. 106.

63. Ch'ü, pp. 269–79; Bodde and Morris, pp. 27–29. Objections to this term are that filial piety predates Confucius, and also that Confucius himself, unlike those who later presumed to speak for him, thought that Rites should apply to commoners to begin with; see Creel, p. 39). Ocko provides interesting examples, without using the controversial term; local custom was not always "Confucianized."

64. Ch'ü, p. 279.

65. All cited in Ch'ü, pp. 279 and 54. Zhang Jinfan, Lin Zhong, and Wang Zhigang argue that Rites were anciently like law because they were enforced by punishment; cited in H. Tanner, p. 39. See Shaw for an account of how early Yi Korea haltingly assimilated the Ming code and Neo-Confucianism simultaneously, the latter's Rites understood legalistically as proper inspiration for Korean law.

66. In Part 3, article 107, the law against marriage between two people of the same surname is attributed to a principle in the *Zhou li*. *The Great Qing Code*, p. 128. Art. 3 also cites a Tang code subcommentary that in turn cites the *Zhou li* (Tang code, art. 7).

67. Ch'ü, p. 279. In *The T'ang Code*, one sees that the *Book of Rites* is both paraphrased without acknowledgment and cited as an authority in the code proper and in the commentaries.

68. Xu Xiaoqun, p. 3.

69. J. Liu, *The Chinese Knight-Errant*, pp. 7–8.

70. *Cihai* (1979), 2: 2071; translation inspired by Senger, p. 173. The passage quoted here is from the fourth of eleven definitions—or, I think we may say, from the definition of the fourth word of eleven words expressed with the phoneme *fa* and written with the same character. The first three mean, in English, "method," "standard," and "model oneself on"; subsequent ones include "dharma" and "France." The state law enacted by the Standing Committee of the National People's Congress itself takes other names besides *fa* or *falü*, including *tiaoli* and *jueding*. However, some of the subspecies of *fa* cited in the 1979 *Cihai*, apart from *falü*, *tiaoli*, and *jueding*, applied mostly to pre-1987 regulations issued by the State Council, and perhaps by lower organs; see A. Chen, pp. 88–89. The 1929 legal definition of "law" (*fa*) under the old Republic of China government (*fa* was uniformly replaced by *falü* in a 1935 constitution) spoke of *tiaoli*, *zhangcheng*, and *guize*, but they were regulations, not "laws"; Escarra, pp. 122–23.

71. The fourth definition of *fa* in the *Cihai* (1989), 2: 2362, begins:

Overall designation for behavioral norms formulated or approved by the state in accordance with the interests and will of the ruling class, and whose implementation is guaranteed by the state's coercive power. Identical to "*falü*" in the broadest sense. Any kind of written or unwritten law [*chengwen fa*, *buchengwen fa*], including constitutions, *falü* (in the narrow sense), decrees, administrative laws and regulations [*xingzheng fagui*], precedents, customary laws [*xiguan fa*], etc.

The definition goes on to differentiate between (1) the law of exploiting classes (slave, feudal, or capitalist), and (2) socialist law (*shehuizhuyi fa*).

72. Du Xichuan and Zhang Lingyuan, p. 35.

73. Senger, p. 176.

74. Zhang Youyu and Wang Shuwen, *Faxue jiben zhishi jianghua* (Talks on basic knowledge of law), 2d ed. (Beijing: Zhongguo qingnian chubanshe, 1980), p. 74, quoted in Senger, pp. 186–87.

75. Townsend, pp. 229–34.

76. Creel, p. 38; Schwartz, p. 76. On the current situation, see Senger, pp. 204–5.

77. J. Liu, *Chinese Theories*, pp. 7–8; Yuan Jin, *Zhongguo wenxue*, pp. 1–27; Owen, pp. 25, 186–93, 594; Plaks, "Towards a Critical Theory," pp. 309–52. Falkenhausen details theories of the most ancient uses of *wen*, including his own about the word as a ritual epithet—a usage more ancient than, and perhaps unrelated to, that of "pattern."

78. Owen, pp. 183–298.

79. J. Liu, *Chinese Theories*, p. 8.

80. Ibid., p. 106.

81. Nienhauser, "Some Preliminary Remarks on Fiction," p. 2.

82. D. Wang, p. 34.

83. H. Zhao, pp. 18–19, 184–86. R. Hegel points out, in *Reading Illustrated Fiction*, that fiction itself had its "high" and "low"; some was well printed, some was not, though the only absolute demarcation was between fiction that may have circulated in manuscript (high) and that which was entirely public.

84. On literary languages, see Hanan, *The Chinese Vernacular Story*, pp. 1–16.

85. Ibid., p. 12.

86. Rolston, p. 8.

87. Chang, p. 311. Woodside and Elman, p. 11, describe a Chinese scholar's view of local education as "war against 'subversive' popular culture."

88. Hanan, *The Chinese Vernacular Story*, p. 12.

89. Idema and Haft, pp. 212–13.

90. Hanan, *The Chinese Vernacular Story*, pp. 9–10, 12; Hegel, *The Novel in Seventeenth-Century China*, p. 3.

91. Plaks, "Full-Length *Hsiao-shuo* and the Western Novel."

92. Rolston, pp. 8–9, 25, 91. For comparison, see MacCormack, *Traditional Chinese Penal Law*, p. 52, on the complicated textual geography of interlinear commentary in an 1871 edition of the Qing code.

93. Plaks, *The Four Masterworks*; C. T. Hsia, "The Scholar-Novelist."

94. Lu Xun, in *A Brief History of Chinese Fiction*, combined all three approaches to defining fiction in his mission of rehabilitating Chinese fiction. Victor Mair's brilliant research finds Indian conceptions of creativity behind the presumably unprecedented *bianwen*. He sees these works as the start not only of China's tradition of vernacular drama and fiction but also of deliberate fictionality in the minds of creating authors; he implies that authors in the classical language of ancient eras who thought they were only recording, not inventing, were not writing fiction as we know it. Mair, "The Narrative Revolution in Chinese Literature," pp. 1–27, with re-

buttal on pp. 29–45 by DeWoskin, "On Narrative Revolutions." See also Mair's *T'ang Transformation Texts* and *Painting and Performance*.

95. Hägg; Doody.

96. Nienhauser, "The Origins of Chinese Fiction."

97. Hegel, "Traditional Chinese Fiction"; Ma, "Fiction," pp. 31–33.

98. Průšek, "History and Epics," argues that even Chinese history eschews a clear narrative flow.

99. DeWoskin, in "The Six Dynasties *Chih-kuai*," p. 27, sees "the birth of fiction"—in *zhiguai*—as "the divergence of fiction and history." He provides an interesting theory of the emergence of *zhiguai* as true fiction in tandem with the evolution of writing itself from a public, often collective event (writing history, or "recording" important events) to something private.

100. L. Wu, p. 340. Hou Zhongyi, pp. 1–4, attempts to derive a unified conception of *xiaoshuo* in the Han. See also Yuan Jin, *Zhongguo xiaoshuo*, pp. 1–22.

101. DeWoskin, "The Six Dynasties *Chih-kuai*," p. 45. He points out that *zhiguai* and *xiaoshuo* might in principle have been classed within a single genre, but instead the often discursive *xiaoshuo* were classed with philosophy; only *zhiguai* were lumped together with history, as lesser records. As the *zhiguai* developed into artfully shaped fiction, by the sixth century they were finally removed from the history category to join *xiaoshuo*. But the accession of *zhiguai* to the *xiaoshuo* category (under philosophy) was hardly a sign of its social importance. In the Tang it was still "petty talk," not entrancing stories, vulgar or not.

102. S. Lu, p. 5.

103. Song aficionados of vernacular literary and oral forms had previously used the term *xiaoshuo* for those works.

104. Idema, p. xliii. See also Hegel, "Traditional Chinese Fiction," p. 395, which notes the expanded use of the term *xiaoshuo* at the end of the Qing. In the late sixteenth century, the major bibliographer Hu Yinglin continued to envision *xiaoshuo* as an umbrella category for leftover works in classical Chinese. He excluded vernacular novels, though he surely knew them; L. Wu, p. 369 n. 67. Apart from his conservatism (unwillingness to purge a "genre" of works previously listed as belonging to it), this may indicate the low status of vernacular literature outside of its circle of friends.

105. H. Zhao, pp. 181, 182.

106. Idema and Haft, pp. 9, 56–60.

107. Rolston, p. 90.

108. Idema, pp. x–xi. The schlock novels were printed in inexpensive popular editions, and unlike the great vernacular novels they were not mentioned in literati essays. James St. André's paper notes a progression of *Three Heroes* from a relatively rare, ornamented, and more vernacular connoisseur's edition to a more prosaic edition in a more classical Chinese that is widely circulated today (and which Idema refers to).

109. Idema, p. liv. Hanan finds its idiom and invention duller than that of the *Hundred Cases*, though the *Longtu gongan* plots are of some interest. Its accusations, petitions, and formal verdicts are not necessarily in a debased novelese, but in legalese; see Hanan, *The Chinese Vernacular Story*, p. 73, and "*Judge Bao's Hundred Cases* Reconstructed," p. 303. C. T. Hsia finds the language of *Three Heroes* vivid; see his "The Scholar-Novelist," pp. 267–68 n. 4. Many Chinese critics classify both the *Longtu gongan* and *Three Heroes and Five Gallants* with, if not necessarily as, vernacular fiction because of resemblances in the larger forms, or because *Three Heroes* was rewritten from oral performances, recapitulating the presumed history of the vernacular novel; see Huang Yanbo; D. Wang. *San xia wu yi* is thought to be based on *Longtu erlu*, a listener's rendering of a performance by the storyteller Shi Yukun; Idema, pp. xi, xviii.

110. DeWoskin, "The Six Dynasties *Chih-kuai*," p. 51.

111. Exceptions include Hayden, *Crime and Punishment*; P. Li, pp. 104–25; Alford, "Of Arsenic and Old Laws," pp. 1180–1254; and Waltner.

112. *The Great Qing Code*, Introduction (by W. Jones), p. 1.

113. Bodde, "Age, Youth, and Infirmity," p. 137; MacCormack, *Traditional Chinese Penal Law*, p. 290.

114. *Qing* has other meanings too, such as "feelings" of love, and sentiment. The conflict between antipathy toward *qing* (feelings of obligation) in modern law and inclinations in favor of *qing* as romantic feeling is explicitly addressed in Geng Longxiang, p. 94. Romantic *qing* was an ascendant value over the past few hundred years. For a start, see Gong Pengcheng, pp. 101–35. Owen, pp. 585–86, indicates the range of meanings from a literary viewpoint.

115. Kim, pp. 68–75.

116. Bodde and Morris, p. 174.

117. "The accused has the right to defense" is in art. 41 of the 1978 constitution, which has only 60 articles. In the 1979 Law of Criminal Procedure, art. 26 provides for defense by lawyers; art. 27 says, "In cases in which a public prosecutor appears in court to bring a public prosecution" (a possible qualification), "and the defendant has not authorized anyone to be his defender, the people's court *may* designate a defender for the defendant" (my emphasis). Art. 8 also says that "the people's courts have the duty to guarantee that defendants obtain defence"; see *The Criminal Law and the Criminal Procedure Law of China* (1984), pp. 117, 122. The idea of legal aid came to China in 1994; see Huang Wei, "Noah's Ark for the Weak and Impoverished—Legal Aid in China," *Beijing Review* 39, no. 49 (Dec. 2–8, 1996): 11–14. In early 1997, 47 legal aid centers had handled fewer than 1,000 pro bono cases; see Li Bian, "Legal System Develops Apace," *Beijing Review* 40, no. 19 (Mar. 10–16, 1997): 23. But a national organization and funding body were established in May 1997; see "Free Legal Service Fund Established," *Beijing Review* 40, no. 24 (June 16–22, 1997): 5.

118. Two years later there appeared a book of groundbreaking reportage, *Shenpan*

qian de jiaoliang, which includes cases of massive negligence, such as the sinking of the Bohai No. 2 oil rig in 1980 (the title case, pp. 59–76). Although the write-up ends with a trial, this and other articles see the problems as political rather than legal. The accused is found guilty, but the legal grounds and the sentence (if any) are not recorded.

119. Articles 105 and 106 both begin "Whoever endangers public security by setting fires, breaching dikes,"and other similar crimes; they both end with graded punishments according to consequences: three to ten years' imprisonment where "serious consequences have not been caused" (art. 105), and death, life imprisonment, or not less than ten years if death or serious injuries, or major loss of property was caused (art. 106); further, "Whoever commits the crimes in the preceding paragraph negligently is to be sentenced to not more than seven years of fixed-term imprisonment or criminal detention." *The Criminal Law and the Criminal Procedure Law of China* (1984), pp. 39–40.

120. MacCormack, *Traditional Chinese Penal Law*, p. 134; Park, p. 969.

121. Art. 187, *The Criminal Law and the Criminal Procedure Law of China* (1984), p. 62: "State personnel who, because of neglect of duty, cause public property or the interests of the state or the people to suffer major losses are to be sentenced to not more than five years." Lo, pp. 203–4, examines a negligence case prosecuted under art. 187.

122. Escarra, p. 57. Confucius of course stressed the rectification of names in all governance.

123. This testimony might serve as an ironic Chinese confirmation of Robin West's caution, in a different arena, that the triumph of "legal storytelling" over "rights talk" need not be progressive; West, *Narrative*, pp. 419–39.

124. Kim, pp. 74–75, finds *qing* to have been the "natural laws" standing above the man-made (positive) laws.

125. G. Yang, pp. 92, 97.

126. The hero of *Power vs. Law* is, however, the *first* secretary of the municipal party committee, representing the newly rehabilitated modernizationist political forces of Deng Xiaoping, recently transferred in to take over leadership from, without being able to wholly neutralize (send into retirement), Gang of Four appointments such as villain Cao. Translations are my own, citing page numbers of the Chinese edition, with thanks to the unidentified translator in *Chinese Literature*.

127. In Cheng Xiaoqing, "Yeban husheng," 1: 113, the narrative voice uses this phrase when the "net of the law" closes in on an accused. He happens to be innocent.

128. Potter, "The Administrative Litigation Law," pp. 271–72. There was also a Ministry of Supervision, disbanded in 1959 but not refounded until 1986.

129. This was before judicial review of state actions under the Administrative Litigation Law of 1989 opened up a front of tort law besides the criminal prosecutions called for in "The Trial." Under this code, the party still is immune; Cao could

not be prosecuted for illegal actions as a party secretary, the only office we are sure he has; even now, one can only sue the *state's* administrators of relief and construction. The commission's leadership of the Supreme Court was apparent after the 1989 Beijing Massacre; see Dicks, "The Chinese Legal System," pp. 573–74. On the 1990s, see Lubman, pp. 10–11.

130. MacCormack, *The Spirit of Traditional Chinese Law*, pp. 16–17.

131. Ibid., p. 106.

132. Lu Xun, "Kong Yiji," in *Nahan*, p. 32.

133. "Punishment for Posting a Document," *China Focus* 5, no. 12 (Dec. 1, 1997): 4.

134. In traditional China, the necessity that a person accused of a serious crime confess was taken for granted. It was implied by substatutes but never explicitly required by statute or substatute. See MacCormack, *Traditional Chinese Penal Law*, pp. 85, 86.

135. Lo, chap. 5.

136. J. Cohen, p. 49.

137. It was in July 1997 that the Supreme People's Procuratorate published a book with 64 case studies of "people who were tortured to death while in police custody" and many other cases of false confessions under torture. It reported that 126 and 115 people were killed in police interrogations in 1993 and 1994 respectively. John Pomfret, "Burying a Taboo, China Gives Figures on Death by Police Torture," *International Herald Tribune*, June 29, 1998, p. 4.

138. Vogel, pp. 75–93. In traditional China, prevention of crime was considered superior to solving crimes already committed, but the point was that people should not be made so poor as to be reduced to crime (Huang Liu-hung, pp. 378–80); the purpose of the legal system was still to punish crimes.

139. MacCormack, *The Spirit of Traditional Chinese Law*, pp. 27–28; Meijer, *Murder and Adultery*, p. 1.

140. *The Great Qing Code*, p. 271.

141. Liu Hsieh [Liu Xie], p. 114.

142. See Buoye.

143. Abraham; Balkin; Peller.

144. Richard Weisberg, "How Judges Speak."

145. Huang Liu-hung, pp. 290–306.

146. I thank Leo Ou-fan Lee for suggesting that Qing legal codes could be read as narratives.

147. Posner, pp. 209–68.

148. *Li Chi*, 1: ix, "Suggested Study Guide." The *Yi li* deals entirely with ceremonies, not with the subject matter of criminal law; however, early portions have been attributed a "literary form" "of a terse gnomic order." *The I-li*, 1: xii (Introduction).

149. *Li Chi*, Introduction, 1: lvi–lxii.

150. Ibid., p. liii.

151. Wei Shouzhong, p. 133.

152. Also, chapters discoursing on philosophy have been granted a higher literary reputation than chapters more directly devoted to canons. *Li Chi*, "Suggested Study Guide," 1: xi, does cite chap. V of the *Wang zhi* as of the first literary rank and chap. XXX of the *Fang Ji* or *Records of Preventive Measures* as of the second rank, along with other books devoted to rituals.

153. The most developed example is *The Great Qing Code*; in Chinese, the *Da Qing lüli*; a useful edition for generalists is *Da Qing lüli tongkao jiaozhu*.

154. Gulik's introduction to *T'ang-yin-pi-shih*, p. vii, calls the phrase an "often-quoted saying"; perhaps he took this from Pelliot, p. 123, who attributes the same words, *On ne lit pas des codes*, to Su Shi (Su Dongpo, 1037–1101). Pelliot adds that Su opposed Wang Anshi's plan to institute examinations on the law, but Pelliot does not quote Su's words in Chinese, or the source, or link these particular words to the conflict between Su and Wang. (Escarra's influential book, p. 4, quotes Pelliot's citation, but without reference to Wang Anshi; Escarra only repeats the general inference that Chinese literati disdained law.) Alice Cheang found the source, a famous *shi* poem of 1071 titled "Xi Ziyou" or "Teasing Ziyou" (Su Shi, 7: 324). The sixth couplet reads, *Dushu wanjuan bu du lü / Zhi jun Yao Shun zhi wu shu* (Read books, myriad volumes, not read laws; Make prince Yao Shun, [you] know without method). The words had a specific meaning, which Cheang translates as, "You [Su Che, or Su Ziyou, Su Shi's brother] have read on thousands of subjects, all except the law, / Knowing that, for making our prince into a sage-ruler, [the law is] of no use." She understands this to be a satirical attack on the New Laws faction of Wang Anshi, which was in power and promulgated the study of legal codes; Su Shi was an official who had to implement the policies, whereas his brother was not. The poem was cited, with reason, as evidence in a court case accusing Su Shi of lèse-majesté. Possibly later Chinese literati detached the offending phrase from its context and used it as abstractly as Pelliot and Gulik imply, but I doubt that it was "often quoted," at least in this century. In Egan's reading, pp. 41–43, the line is still less amenable to abstraction.

155. MacCormack, *The Spirit of Traditional Chinese Law*, p. 49.

156. Hanan, *The Chinese Vernacular Story*, p. 26.

157. *The Great Qing Code*, Introduction (by W. Jones), p. 24.

158. Bodde and Morris, p. 360.

159. Ibid., p. 68.

160. *The Great Qing Code*, Introduction (by W. Jones), p. 3.

161. MacCormack, *The Spirit of Traditional Chinese Law*, pp. 210–12.

162. Bodde and Morris, pp. 165–66.

163. Idema and Haft, p. 162. Huang Yanbo, pp. 188–225, surveys *biji* cases, Pu Songling's *Liaozhai zhiyi*, and Lan Dingyuan's cases in a single chapter as crime fiction—like the anthologists discussed later.

164. The *Shiwubao* translates, from the *Memoirs of Sherlock Holmes*, "The Naval Treaty" (Doyle, 1: 447–69), in *Shiwubao* 6 (W. cal. Sept. 27, 1896), Taiwan reprint 1: 372–77; cont. in *Shiwubao* 7 (Oct. 7, 1896), Taiwan reprint 1: 442–47; *Shiwubao* 8 (Oct. 17, 1896), Taiwan reprint 1: 518–21; *Shiwubao* 9 (Oct. 27), Taiwan reprint 1: 586–88. Also from the *Memoirs*, "The Crooked Man," in Doyle, 1: 411–22, serialized in *Shiwubao* 10 (Nov. 5, 1896), Taiwan reprint 1: 656–59; *Shiwubao* 11 (Nov. 16, 1896), Taiwan reprint 2: 722–25; *Shiwubao* 12 (Nov. 25, 1896), Taiwan reprint 2: 792–95. And "The Final Problem," Doyle, 1: 469–80, serialized in *Shiwubao* 27 (May 22, 1897), Taiwan reprint 3: 1828–31; in *Shiwubao* 28 (May 31, 1897), Taiwan reprint 3: 1894–98; in *Shiwubao* 29 (June 10, 1897), Taiwan reprint 4: 1961–64; in *Shiwubao* 30 (June 20, 1897), Taiwan reprint 4: 2030–34. From the *Adventures of Sherlock Holmes* comes "A Case of Identity," in Doyle, 1: 190–201, serialized in *Shiwubao* 24 (Apr. 22, 1897), Taiwan reprint 3: 1623–26; in Shiwubao 25 (May 2, 1897), Taiwan reprint 3: 1692–95; in *Shiwubao* 26 (May 12, 1897), Taiwan reprint 3: 1758–62. There is a possibly true case from an English private detective (I cannot identify it as a Holmes story) in *Shiwubao* 1 (Aug. 22, 1996), Taiwan reprint 1: 46–51. In this venue, detectives are called "*baotan*," "consulting detectives." The phrase appears in the titles of both of the Holmes stories and that of the non-Holmes story in issue no. 1. Link, *Mandarin Ducks*, p. 129, supplied these leads, from a Chinese source—which evidently was forgotten by most researchers in the meantime, until Chen Pingyuan, *Zhongguo xiaoshuo*, p. 42. Chen's *Ershi shiji*, p. 28, identifies the unnamed translator of Conan Doyle as Zhang Kunde.

165. Sample translations are in S. Shapiro, pp. 52–68.

166. An unsympathetic guide to some of the literature is Posner, pp. 132–205.

167. See Chen Shunlie's edition.

168. *T'ang-yin-pi-shih*, Preface, p. ix. Gulik's influence on the modern Chinese whodunit was nil, but 1980s Chinese crime fiction aficionados embrace him as a major writer of Chinese crime fiction anyway.

169. Entry by Jaroslav Průšek: "*pi-chi hsiao-shuo*," in Průšek, ed., 1: 140.

170. In a cursory examination of post-Mao collections of case stories, I found three tellings of a nearly identical tale: a judge spots a new grave while touring the countryside to measure the temper of the people; gets suspicious of the young, newly enriched widow of the deceased; disinters and performs an autopsy on the corpse but finds nothing suspicious; is challenged by the widow; hence faces disgrace and punishment from superior officials but is given an extension to make further inquiries; goes in disguise as a fortune teller (like Kuang Zhong in *Fifteen Strings of Cash*); meets a commoner who witnessed the crime; learns that the wife and her lover arranged to have the husband bitten by a snake; and does a second autopsy, in which an entire snake (evidently missed the first time!) is found coiled up inside the belly. In all versions the dynasty is the Qing, yet in each case the judge is different and so is the province. See "Xin mu yi an" (The suspicious case of the new grave), in Lu Fang'an, pp. 134–46. "Ni Gong Chunyan" (Judge Ni Chunyan), in Liu Yeqiu

et al., eds., pp. 91–95. "She sha an" (The case of murder by snakebite), in Zhang Chengfu, ed., pp. 71–74.

171. Namely Wu Woyao, a promoter of *biji* court cases and also the famed author of a "new" novel in the old vernacular form, *Eyewitness Reports on Strange Things from the Past Twenty Years*, which was itself a sort of compendium of "cases."

172. As noted by Liu Yeqiu in the preface to the book he coedited, p. 3.

173. See *Ming Qing anyu gushi xuan*.

174. The Tang fiction, Lai Gu's "Persuasion Concerning Cats and Tigers," is construable into only about a dozen English sentences but manages to question the wisdom of the old book and poke fun at received wisdom as such. Nienhauser, "Some Preliminary Remarks," p. 11; *Li Chi*, 1: 431–32 (*Jiaodesheng* or *The Single Victim at the Border Sacrifices*).

175. *T'ang-yin-pi-shih*, Preface, p. ix, and notes on pp. 99, 177–78.

176. Fong, pp. 116–18. *Celebrated Cases of Judge Dee*, Preface (by Gulik), p. iv, mentions a novel of a different name as Wu Jianren's source and gives 1725 as the date of the crime.

177. Idema, p. xxxiv; *Traditional Chinese Fiction*, p. xxiii. See Chapter One on Sherlockian preambles such as "You have been in Afghanistan, I perceive" (Holmes to Watson on the first meeting; Doyle, 1: 18).

178. *Hai Gangfeng xiansheng juguan gongan zhuan*; Meng Liye, pp. 64–66.

179. "Qin mao da gong" (The general takes credit for the work of his troops), in *Bao Gong qi'an*, p. 121.

180. "Jie yi" (The borrowed clothes), in *Bao Gong qi'an*, p. 138.

181. Ibid., p. 137.

182. "Yaoshi" (The key), in *Bao Gong qi'an*, pp. 20–21.

183. Rolston, ed.; Ding; Sieber.

184. *Bao gongan*, with an initial printing of 100,000.

185. Legends about Bao Zheng, Hai Rui, and Kuang Zhong appeared in *Minjian wenxue* 167 (Dec. 20, 1983): 91–94; about Bao Zheng in *Minjian wenxue* 175 (Aug. 20, 1984): 30–35; and about assorted other good officials in *Minjian wenxue* 153 (Oct. 20, 1982): 91–98; and *Shanxi minjian wenxue* 15 (May 1984): 31–33. S. Shapiro, pp. 69–77, cites and translates from an early book of folklore cases, *Lidai yuanan pingfan lu* (Cases over the centuries of injustices righted; 1981), but it is unclear whether the book's sources are folklore or old books.

186. Chen Cun, quoted in Leung, p. 9.

187. Notably *Ming Qing anyu gushi xuan*, pp. 2–5.

188. The 1988 print run was 10,000, and the initial printings for the two following books discussed in this section were only 5,500 and 2,500. They were printed in 1990 and 1991, when readership for all literature was down, political control of print media was heightened, and books had to break even. The 1990s authors may have faced more competition from competing books too.

189. *Jianghu qixia zhuan* (Extraordinary knights roaming over rivers and lakes); see J. Liu, *The Chinese Knight-Errant*, p. 136.

190. For example, cf. Zhang Chengfu, ed., pp. 29–33, with *Parallel Cases* (*TYBS*) 16B, though the latter has fewer details; cf. pp. 41–42 with *TYBS* 46B, where the name of the official is slightly changed; cf. pp. 43–51 with Lu Fang'an, pp. 79–91; cf. pp. 52–53 with Liu Yeqiu, Yuan Yuxin, and Zhou Zhi, eds., p. 59 (a Wu Jianren tale), and also *Minjian wenxue* 183 (Apr. 20, 1985): 46, which names the wise judge as Kuang Zhong, unlike the other two tellings; cf. pp. 71–74 with Lu Fang'an, pp. 134–46, and also Liu Yeqiu , Yuan Yuxin, and Zhou Zhi, eds., pp. 91–95, citing an anonymous Qing work—the three retellings are remarkably close, but each has a different judge hero; cf. pp. 79–83 with Lu Fang'an, pp. 65–78; cf. pp. 103–106 with Liu Yeqiu, Yuan Yuxin, and Zhou Zhi, eds., pp. 72–74 (another Wu Jianren tale); cf. pp. 141–43 with *TYBS* 17B; cf. pp. 260–62 with *TYBS* 26B.

191. Analyzed in Kinkley, "The Cultural Choices of Zhang Xinxin," pp. 148–51.

192. See also Kuhn, *Soulstealers*.

193. Barthes, "The Dupriez Trial," in *The Eiffel Tower*, pp. 67–69; "Dominici, or the Triumph of Literature," in *Mythologies*, pp. 43–46. He writes, "Justice and literature have made an alliance, they have exchanged their old techniques, thus revealing their basic identity, and compromising each other barefacedly" (45). Referred by Beebee, pp. 151, 155, 171.

194. Zhu Yiqiang and Wu Nanfei, eds.

195. Bad books, bad friends, and loss of chastity, for example, appear just as simplistically in "studies" (some classified) of how female sex offenders are created; cited in H. Tanner, pp. 210–12. Cf. the Jiangxi stories below.

196. Illicit sexual relations are usually punished by the police noncriminally or under the law against hooliganism (art. 160). The *Zui yu fa* commentator's logic is that since the Marriage Law proclaims a system of monogamy, adultery is illegal. Bigamy, in fact, is a crime (art. 180), and so is knowing cohabitation with the spouse of a member of the armed forces on active duty.

197. Only assembling a crowd to reap profits from gambling, or making it an occupation, is criminal (art. 168).

198. This appears to be in error. A national eugenics law was proposed in the 1980s but withdrawn under criticism; even birth control was managed by provincial regulations, not law; M. Palmer, p. 128. China passed a eugenics law (called the Maternal Infant Health Care Law) only in 1994. It was internationally controversial.

199. Driving of a person to suicide was a focus of traditional criminal codes, particularly those of the Ming and Qing. MacCormack, *Traditional Chinese Penal Law*, p. 188.

200. Wichser was a 29-year-old University of Denver graduate student teaching English and studying Chinese agricultural policy. In 1982 she became the first American detained (and expelled) from the PRC in ten years of normalized U.S.-China relations. The United States denied she worked for any branch of the gov-

ernment; evidently her offense was simply collecting routinely classified ("internal") documents on agriculture for her thesis. The charge of seduction probably refers to her boyfriend. She had asked for official permission to marry him. That he was the son of a high CCP official, and that U.S.-China tensions were running high over U.S. arms sales to Taiwan, may have led to her to being singled out; the "capture" of this "spy" in her dorm room in the middle of the night was filmed by TV cameras. She was held incommunicado for days, in violation of a U.S.-China consular agreement, and treated in a fashion like that dramatized in 1997 by Richard Gere in the film *Red Corner*. *New York Times*, June 2, 1982, p. 7; June 4, pp. 1 and 3; June 5, p. 3; June 6, p. 15.

    201. Watt, p. 31.

Chapter 3: Shadows

    1. Xu Xiaoqun, p. 2.

    2. T. Lee, p. 5.

    3. PRC critics acknowledge that no one in China has yet equaled Cheng's mastery and domination of crime fiction; ints. 3, 34, 44. Several of China's successful mainstream writers also admit to having tried Cheng's genre and failed at it. He combed newspapers and listened to the radio daily for cases to inspire him, then drew up detailed plot outlines connecting all the clues with arrows. Shen Hongxin, "Zhongguo de Kenan Daoer—Cheng Xiaoqing" (China's Conan Doyle—Cheng Xiaoqing), *Beijing wanbao*, Summer 1988 (clipping from Cheng Yuzhen); Xu Bibo; int. 26.

    4. I thank Timothy C. Wong for this argument, which has much force.

    5. Who did? Consider Hammett, Chandler, Simenon, Matsumoto, Borges, Nicolas Freeling, Maj Sjöwall with Per Wahlöö, perhaps Elmore Leonard, Umberto Eco. This is not to say that they were (are) as accomplished in their subgenres or niches as Christie was in hers. Martial-arts fiction is a distinct Chinese popular genre, wholly different from crime or detective fiction. Jin Yong is its Agatha Christie.

    6. In the 1930s, Cheng was mostly occupied with teaching and translation and Sun faded from view, perhaps owing to illness or an unsettled life. But Cheng's works gained maximum exposure in pocket editions of the 1940s. Sun likewise regained popularity by writing new stories in the 1940s and revising old ones.

    7. In the Cultural Revolution, Cheng was charged with having conspired with fellow popular writers Zhou Shoujuan and Fan Yanqiao to form a "Three Family Village" of Suzhou, like the alleged counterrevolutionary conspiracy of Beijing intellectuals Wu Han, Deng Tuo, and Liao Mosha. Xu Bibo.

    8. Lupin had his debut in Leblanc, "L'Arrestation d'Arsène Lupin" (The arrest of

Arsène Lupin), English trans. in *The Extraordinary Adventures of Arsène Lupin*, pp. 1–11.

9. Albérès, p. 12. Redmond traces the fictional Holmes stories to real life influences.

10. On Huo Sang mania, Fan Boqun, p. 211. Zhao Tiaokuang plays with Huo Sang as a personality in his story.

11. Bloom.

12. Conan Doyle created his own inversion of Holmes in Moriarty.

13. The French call him Edgar Poe; Chinese in the Taiwan orbit call him Allan Poe (Ailun Po).

14. Fitzgerald, pp. 103–46.

15. Lupin was very popular in the early 1910s, when Americans, like the French, appreciated put-downs of the Brits.

16. Blonde.

17. Rocambole led a Parisian street gang, yet he had adventures in London, spoke English, and once posed as a Scotland Yard inspector. Murch, pp. 195–96.

18. Vareille, pp. 42–45.

19. Predecessors of Ponson du Terrail's (1829–71) hero Rocambole (1857) include Robert Macaire and his sidekick Bertrand, generic villains who first appeared in the 1823 melodrama *L'Auberge des Adrets*, and le Prince Formose, a gentleman-burglar of 1844 in a *roman-feuilleton* named after a protagonist created by Edmond Texier (Ruaud, 116). Macaire became famous in a cartoon series by Honoré Daumier (1808–79) in *Le Charivari*. Guilbert de Pixérécourt (1773–1844) also created memorable villains in melodramas; see Brooks, p. 33. Eugène Sue (1804–57) created Rodolphe in *Les Mystères de Paris* (1842–43). Also in the lineage are works by Alexandre Dumas (*père*; 1802–70): *The Count of Monte Cristo* (1844), *The Man in the Iron Mask* (see the duel in the Bois-Rochin), and *The Mohicans of Paris* (1854–57). See, generally, Veraille, pp. 11–72. Actually, French sources see early influence on their adventure novels from James Fennimore Cooper. Foundational works of the French *roman policier* are the memoirs, probably ghostwritten, of Eugène François Vidocq (1775–1857), a crook turned detective who became a model for Balzac's criminal Vautrin and Javert in Hugo's *Les Misérables*; the works of Sue; and the M. Lecoq tales by Émile Gaboriau (1833–73), France's first writer of admitted fiction of analytical detection. Vidocq made an impression on Leblanc (Derouard, 70), and of course he also read Gaboriau, Sue, and Dumas at an early age (Derouard, 50). Lamy, pp. 10, 175–78, stresses similarities between Lupin and Fantômas, created by Pierre Souvestre (1874–1914) and Marcel Allain (1885–1969), a more downmarket and truly evil "genius of crime" who nevertheless became a hero to the Surrealists. Rouletabille is also cited as an influence, but he was created by Gaston Leroux (1868–1927) only in his 1907 novel *The Yellow Room*. The Fantômas series began in 1909 (Tourteau, 97); the first books about him appeared in 1911. These characters might have influenced later Lupin stories, but Lupin sprang from Leblanc fully

formed at the start. Some readers still read into Lupin a dark side like that of Fantômas, contradicting his chivalry. Another often suggested influence, from life, is the French anarchist and *cambrioleur* Marius Jacob, head of the "Travailleurs de la Nuit" gang. He was sent to prison in March 1905; the first Lupin story appeared in July. Derouard, p. 267, denies that he was the *major* inspiration for Lupin.

20. Albérès, p. 17.

21. Dandyism began as a pose during England's Regency, epitomized by George Brummell—and Lord Byron too, in the mind of Baudelaire. *Le dandysme* and "Anglomania" became social forces in Paris after 1830, when Parisian *ton* for once came from the English lords who habituated it, and Brummell himself—then in full decadence, which the French construed as one more petal on his boutonniere—as he passed through Paris. Eugène Sue, "*le Fénimore Cooper français*," was one of the dandies and "Anglomaniacs," and so is his slumming German prince Rodolphe, modeled after not one but two faux-English Anglophilic dandies whom the public conflated into one legendary "milord Arsouille." Rodolphe has learned his sports in England, and his companion is an English servant, Murph, "whose sterling qualities are pure *Valtre-Scott*" [Sir Walter] (Moers, 118–19, 137). Musset, Gautier, and Balzac put the dandy into their own literary works, to critique contemporary French culture. In 1844, Barbey d'Aurevilly (like Leblanc a Norman, who took pride in the Norman intervention in English history), intellectualized the English cult of self-love and exclusivity (which was under Brummell already focused on aristocracy of *ton* to the point of undermining aristocracy by birth) into a philosophy of revolt against bourgeois mediocrity, through stoic self-control, detachment, and artificiality, en route to a philosophy of aestheticism and decadence, as in Huysmans. Baudelaire, a friend of Poe, was the key figure after 1844, and it was he who found dandyism "a modern thing" (Moers, 274). It was also "outside the laws," though having "rigorous laws of its own," to which its subjects must strictly submit; and a dandy did not forfeit his status by committing a crime, so long as it was not "born of a trivial source" (Baudelaire, 3: 483, 485). Yet the English (Bulwer-Lytton, in his novel *Paul Clifford*) had already invented the idea of dandies as criminals and criminals as dandies, as the French littérateurs knew, well before the figure of Paul Clifford evolved into the modern A. J. Raffles (France, ed., 219; Moers, 83). Maurice Leblanc, in the Belle Époque, was not so much affected by the literary reverberations of the "New Dandyism," which was more evident in fin de siècle England (of *The Yellow Book*) than in France, as by the affectations of dress of the original dandies and those of philosophy of the post-Baudelaireans. On stage and on many book covers, Lupin appears in evening clothes, with silk top hat, monocle, and dashing cape. That Lupin is at all chivalrous, with romantic implications and appreciation of the wiles of women, is perhaps his main departure from the classic dandy.

22. Tourteau, p. 67.

23. Albérès. Lupin turns patriotic and cooperates with the law after the Great War, which generally ended French dandyism.

24. Tourteau, who considers Lupin a "replica" of Holmes and Raffles (44), lists traits in the Lupin stories indicating that they are *polars*: deduction, suspense, locked-room puzzles, etc. (83–96). See also Vareille, pp. 39–72, 107–30; Boileau-Narcejac, *Le Roman policier*, pp. 57, 58, 59, 61; Cassiday; and Albérès, pp. 53–57, who sees Lupin as a cerebral character influenced by Poe.

25. Derouard, p. 267. Poe was more upmarket than Conan Doyle, more revered in France, and more Francophile. His detective Dupin was a Frenchman.

26. Penzler et al., p. 113; Panek, pp. 111–15. Grant Allen's Colonel Clay and Melville Davisson Post's Randolph Mason were famous turn-of-the-century rogue "detectives." Derouard observes (267) that the idea of the gentleman-rogue was abroad in France in July 1905, just as the first Lupin story appeared. The magazine *Lectures pour tous* (which *Je sais tout* was set up to rival) spoke of the new "*gentleman-cambrioleur*." For an international list of such types down to the present, see Ruaud, pp. 115–27.

27. Leblanc wrote the first Lupin story when Pierre Lafitte, prior to launching his new magazine *Je sais tout* in 1905, asked him to create a Holmesian story. And Leblanc had to be urged to continue. Derouard, pp. 231, 261–62, 269–71, 292. (Lafitte was once a reporter for *L'Echo de Paris*; cf. Lupin's mouthpiece, *L'Echo de France*.) Derouard, p. 303, dismisses the role of A. J. Raffles, Hornung's gentleman-burglar ("amateur cracksman") in the birth of Lupin, since Raffles was available in French translation only in July 1907. But surely Lafitte was aware of Raffles's commercial success. Lafitte published his own edition of Holmes stories in 1902 (261). One also wonders if Leblanc could read English; he was sent to Scotland during the Franco-Prussian War and later spent a year abroad in Manchester and Berlin. English and German are the two foreign European languages favored by Lupin (39–32; 81–84). The characters of Raffles and Lupin were popular on the Parisian stage as early as 1907–08—Raffles first. Sherlock Holmes, Rouletabille, and Lupin vs. Holmes adventures were all dramatized in Paris. In 1910–11, five ten-minute French films pitted Holmes against Lupin; Derouard, pp. 303, 317, 328, 347, 351.

28. Leblanc and Lafitte themselves enjoyed very "post-Raffaelite" British "sporting" pursuits. Lafitte was the epitome of a man about town ("*boulevardier*"), a publisher of "sporting magazines" devoted to his hobbies of bicycling and later motor touring. Leblanc had the same passions, met Lafitte in the same sports clubs, and was becoming known, at his pre-Lupin low point, as an author of *contes sportifs*. Arsène Lupin likewise was a sport. His father was a boxing instructor. (Conan Doyle, "a formidable all-round amateur sportsman" expert at cricket and billiards, was "one of the best amateur heavyweight boxers of his day"; T. Hall, 113). Rodolphe was too; the third page of *The Mysteries of Paris* describes Rodolphe's skills as worthy of "the most celebrated London boxers, . . . moreover, so completely out of the French mode of fighting, that the Slasher was mentally as well as bodily stunned by them." Lupin introduced jujitsu into France, in fiction; Conan Doyle really did introduce skiing into Switzerland (T. Hall, 113).

29. France's defeat renewed its overseas expansion. "France seemed literally haunted by Britain," eager particularly in the Orient "to catch up with and emulate the British," who were recolonizing Napoleon's old empire; Said, *Orientalism*, pp. 218–25; also Moore-Gilbert, p. 47.

30. On Lupin as a national treasure, see Lamy, p. 37, back cover, and the spoof by Comte-Sponville and George (real philosophers). Leblanc himself spoke of Lupin as the "national thief" in *The Blonde Lady*. French enthusiasts of Holmes point out that he had a French grandmother (see Doyle, 1: 435). T. Hall, pp. 55–69, deliberately or obtusely, sees the Lupin stories simply as a tribute to the excellence of the earlier British hero! Then again, a Frenchman has described Lupin as the "Robin des Bois de la Belle Époque," the *bois* in question being, *hélas*, not the Bois de Boulogne but Sherwood Forest. "La Page d'Arsène," www.cyber-espace.com/lupin (Sept. 1997).

31. Ah Q, hero of Lu Xun's famous short story "A Q zheng zhuan" (The true story of Ah Q), in *Nahan*, pp. 95–152, lost every battle, then tried to compensate by declaring a spiritual victory.

32. Leblanc's roots were in Normandy. His sister Georgette (a famous Paris stage comedienne, the "muse" and mistress of Maeterlinck) spiced up the family tree by claiming that their father was Italian-born and had naturalized for the sake of love. (Derouard, p. 20, refutes this.) Among Lupin's Italian affectations are his appearance as a chevalier Floriani in the story about his ancestry, "The Stolen Necklace." Leblanc fled the provinces and his conventional bourgeois family, like Georgette before him. The story goes that he went to the City of Light to become a Flaubert or a Maupassant, only to be "condemned," like Conan Doyle, to be eclipsed by his own light-fiction hero. Before inventing Lupin, from 1900 to 1905, Leblanc was "the most Parisian of journalists" (Albérès, 117). See Derouard, pp. 277, 310, 497–501.

33. Hutcheon, p. 200. See Christian, ed., and Schleh, ed. On the mitosis, see Moore-Gilbert, pp. 5–33. Marxists have assaulted postcolonial studies for dividing postcolonial theory from politics (Gandhi, ix). See Ahmad, pp. 159–219; Dirlik; San Juan Jr. Emphasizing hybrid works instead of literature ignoring or reviling the West, "postcolonialism" may mean "having known colonialism," not simply "after the termination of colonialism." This averts an objection that colonialism never really died (or dies), and also a philosophical objection that "discursive practices" and states of mind, once known, can never really expire, as can a person or institution; there is no "antecedent practice whose claims to exclusivity of vision is rejected" through postcolonial or indeed postmodern "artworks." Appiah, p. 119. One might call China postcolonial in the second sense, even though it fully terminated "semi-colonial" influences in 1949. But post-Mao China has welcomed international capital back. Elsewhere I have argued that the resurgence of Western forms and institutions in China in the 1980s, coupled with memories of real and imagined oppression and continued power disparities between China and the West, give all post-Mao literature a "postcolonial" flavor. Authors take the West as inspiration, as

object of dialogue, and as a force to struggle with for independence. Post-Mao crime fiction is a good example; what it resists is not just the Western detective story but what may seem to Chinese eyes a very intrusive "Western" police-judicial apparatus. An early application of the term "postcolonialism" to Chinese literature was my revision of a 1991 conference paper, "The Post-Colonial Detective in People's China" (1993). Christopher Lupke previously applied it to Taiwan literature.

34. Said, *Orientalism*, p. 59.

35. Doyle, 1: 471. This is a compliment as well as a condemnation.

36. One can theorize "epistemic violence" in weak countries, of natives "being prevailed upon to internalize as self-knowledge the knowledge concocted by the master" (Parry, 38), without assuming it to be ontologically irresistible or, on the contrary, requiring force, or assuming that native subjects wholly disappear or lose their voices as counterideologists, either owing to uniquely imperialistic subjugation by power or some postulated "construction" of subjectivity inherent in the human condition. Spivak's "Can the Subaltern Speak?," known for combining "postcolonial" with feminist study and identifying both of them with her own "position" (as in her book *The Post-Colonial Critic*), gives a classic pronouncement on "epistemic violence" done to subalterns, though the sources of her ideas in Derrida postulate constructed "subjectivity" as part of the human condition. Criticizing Spivak's emphasis on discourse, alleged incuriosity about material structures of power, and neglect of the efficacy of native resistance, is Parry. Recalling Fanon's assertion of effective anti-imperialist agency among the oppressed despite "epistemic violence" is Bhabha's "Remembering Fanon." A useful summary of the theoretical debates is Loomba's. Porter, in "Orientalism and Its Problems," sees incommensurability between reliance on theories of colonialism as "epistemic" or discursive "violence" (via Foucault) and theories of colonialism as hegemony through force and ideological "formations" (via Gramsci). Slemon, in "The Scramble for Post-Colonialism," schematizes theorists' varying emphases on domination through "institutional regulators" and "the semiotic field" ("textuality").

37. The role of mimicry in countries subject to Western power is controversial among the theorists. See Moore-Gilbert, pp. 181–84. The classic is Homi Bhabha's essay "Of Mimicry and Man: The Ambivalence of Colonial Discourse" in *The Location of Culture*, pp. 85–92. On colonial discourse in Western detective fiction, see Jon Thompson, and R. Thomas.

38. Huang Ziping, p. 206 (trans., p. 246).

39. Joseph Levenson contemplated these problems; see Meisner and Murphey, eds.

40. Liu Zaifu, p. 127.

41. Liu Zaifu; Huang Ziping critiques the term, adding that Chinese literature is in turn a "shadow" to the West.

42. Indeed, Chinese intellectuals had Anglophone and Francophone factions, depending on who had taught them.

43. Fanon, p. 40.

44. Ibid., p. 41.

45. Wei Shouzhong, p. 139, says that in 1923 Cheng published a work entitled "Dongfang Fuermosi de ertong shidai" (The early years of the Oriental Sherlock Holmes), though we cannot be absolutely sure it was not Cheng's editor who gave the piece its title. It is called "Huo Sang's Early Years" in the Masses' Press reprint, *Huo Sang tan'an ji*, 13: 306, but the editors of that edition have altered several of Cheng's titles. Calling Huo Sang "the Oriental Sherlock Holmes" was a compliment in his day. Cheng invited such appellations by having Huo Sang ask Bao Lang, in "Jiangnan Yan," 2: 68, if he wanted to be "the Oriental Watson." Cheng Xiaoqing liked Charlie Chan. He translated six books about him into Chinese. Sun Liaohong created a villainess spy for Japan nicknamed "The Yellow Mata Hari." Yellow also contrasts with her identity as "The Blue Rattlesnake" in the story so named, "Lanse de xiangweishe," *XDLP*, p. 149. Sun Liaohong and He Puzhai coauthored a *Dongfang Yasen Luopin an* (Cases of the Oriental Arsène Lupin) in May 1925, according to Lu Runxiang, p. 180. Sun's earliest Lu Ping stories bore the subtitle "recent cases of the Oriental Arsène Lupin."

46. In a 1925 story, Lu Ping "commands" his creator, "Sun Liaohong": "When in future I make new cases, your story [sub-]titles must only call them strange cases of Lu Ping, or stories about Lu Ping. You must not call them cases of the Oriental Arsène Lupin, for I am not willing to follow so closely in the footsteps of another." Yet the name Lu Ping is just as derivative. Sun Liaohong, *Xiao dao wen guai*, preface by Fan Boqun, p. 7.

47. Chow Tse-tsung, pp. 327–32; Liang Shuming (1921); Tang, pp. 193–96.

48. It could be, as Chen Pingyuan suggests in *Zhongguo xiaoshuo*, pp. 46–47, that Holmes came to China as quickly as he did Japan. Nakajima Kawatarō, pp. 75–79, and Itō Hideo, pp. 354–55, referred to me by Mark Silver, a Colgate professor writing on the Japanese detective story, and Tomoji Ohta's wonderful "THE GLORIA SCOTT Front Page," http://plaza15.mbn.or.jp/limelight/TGS1.html, agree that the first "faithful" Japanese translation of a Holmes opus (*A Study in Scarlet*) was serialized in 1899 in the *Mainichi Shimbun*—later, surprisingly, than the first Chinese translations of four stories in the *Shiwubao*, in 1896. Japan printed an adaptation (loose translation) of "The Man with the Twisted Lip" in 1894, but that is not much of a "head start." More important, Japanese interest in Holmes boomed with an 1895 series of adaptations from the *Adventures of Sherlock Holmes*, about a hero named Soroku Komuro, "the Magical Detective" (*Fushigi no Tantei*) (Ohta). It may have been (relative) scruples about copyright that slowed literal translations of the full canon in Japan. In 1914, says Dore, pp. 60–61, a Professor Yokoi Jikei complained that even in Japan's countryside young people were sporting Sherlock Holmes hats, evidently deerstalkers. (A measure of how much cultural memory was erased by the Cultural Revolution in China are the line drawings of Sherlock Holmes accompanying 1980s Chinese articles about him that show the English de-

tective with pipe and hat, but the "wrong" kind of hat.) Devotion to Holmes still reigns, Ohta notes, because of the Japanese love of the Victorian age, which they link to their own Meiji era. The Japan Sherlock Holmes Club is the largest Sherlockian society in the world. Silver reports, after Itō's book, that the first Japanese Arsène Lupin translation appeared on January 3, 1909, in the weekly magazine *Sandei* (Sunday). Derouard, p. 328, agrees that Lupin entered Japan before the war, but says that real translations appeared only in the 1920s. Again, China may have actually had the first complete translations owing to disregard for copyright, but Lupin mania was surely as strong in Japan, and it continued building in the postwar years, whereas communism ended Lupin's career in China.

49. Tanaka, pp. 1–28.

50. King-fai Tam, "The Detective Fiction," pp. 128–31. On "The Detective Novel and Scientific Method," see Agassi. On China as the imperial core, "Othering" the West, see Conceison, p. 99.

51. Ashcroft, Griffiths, and Tiffin, and Adam and Tiffin, eds. focus positively on hybrid discourses woven from strands of Western, colonial, native, and the anti- and postcolonial culture of colonized peoples. "Hybridization" is also a term used in British Cultural Studies, but differently, in reference to "signifiers" taken out of context in our postmodern world. See During, ed., Introduction, p. 7. Bhabha, in "Signs Taken for Wonders," in *The Location of Culture*, pp. 109–15, evokes a subversive hybridization, a "space of the adversarial," as a necessary production of colonialism. Mishra and Hodge accept *The Empire Writes Back*'s idea of a "postcolonialism" defined by the experience of colonialism itself rather than of its demise; they redefine it as postmodern but do not accept the idea of a unique hybrid discourse. H. Tiffin, "Post-Colonial Literatures," defends the idea of the hybrid. G. Lee dicusses Chinese hybridity.

52. Cheng Xiaoqing, "Zhentan xiaoshuo de duofangmian," pp. 68–71.

53. Ma and Lau, eds., pp. 531–74, add "The Master Thief" and "The Trickster" as stock figures in Chinese fiction, though there do not seem to have been serial thieves to match either Lupin or the Chinese judges and knights-errant.

54. Wu's book is *Zhongguo zhentan an* (Chinese cases of detection; 1906), discussed in Meng Liye, pp. 171–78. See also Yuan Jin, *Yuanyang*, pp. 83–84, 104, and Song Anna and Huang Zexin, p. 156. (A story of Wu Jianren's they mention appears in Liu Yeqiu et al., eds., pp. 40–41. A fuller write-up of the case, which perhaps was real, is in Lu Fang'an, pp. 13–23.) Note that Wu titled his cases *zhentan an*, not *gongan*. Meng Liye finds that even in this book Wu garbed his cases with Western plot elements; in spots he was reduced to arguing that Western techniques existed earlier in China.

55. According to Starrett, *Bookman's Holiday*, who evidently relies on Lin Yutang, cited on p. 25.

56. Stavans, p. 66.

57. See, e.g., Kaye, ed.

58. Ints. 26, 40. Wei Shouzhong, p. 135, says Cheng joined a Methodist church in Suzhou in 1917 and often attended services.

59. Cheng Xiaoqing, "Zhentan xiaoshuo de duofangmian" (1924), 1: 69. Bao Lang's surname is the same as Judge Bao's.

60. "Sprouts" appears in Cheng Xiaoqing's 1946 revision of ibid., called "Lun zhentan xiaoshuo" (Discussing the detective story), in Lu Runxiang, p. 157. King-fai Tam notes that Bao Lang expresses Cheng Xiaoqing's views on the respective Chinese and Western traditions in his story "Jiangnan Yan," 2: 68.

61. Chen Pingyuan, *Zhongguo xiaoshuo*, p. 46.

62. However, a cartoonist like Feng Zikai could be canonized providing he was politically correct.

63. C. T. Hsia, "Hsü Chen-ya's *Yü-li hun*"; Link, *Mandarin Ducks*. Y. Zhang, pp. 223–29, discusses Xu Xu's novel *Feng xiaoxiao* (The blowing wind; 1944) as a "serious" novel with "detectivism." It has an anti-Japanese spy theme, like some works by Sun Liaohong, which I would likewise place somewhere between serious and popular. Yuan Jin, *Yuanyang*, pp. 92, 195, offers an upward reappreciation of "mandarin duck and butterfly" fiction generally, as transitional from late Qing to May Fourth fiction, both of which he sees as serious. He finds a novel by Cheng Shanzhi fully up to May Fourth standards, if only its classical Chinese were changed into modern vernacular.

64. Tam, "Cultural Ambiguities."

65. This is the title of a book by James C. Thomson Jr.

66. Chen Pingyuan, *Ershi shiji*, pp. 11, 55, 99.

67. See p. 390 n. 164 for details and page references.

68. Wei Shaochang, *Wo kan*, p. 198.

69. L. Lee, *The Romantic Generation*, pp. 41–57.

70. Ma Tailai, "Lin Shu fanyi zuopin quanmu" (Complete list of Lin Shu's translations), in Qian Zhongshu et al., pp. 65–66.

71. Priestman, p. 91.

72. Link, *Mandarin Ducks*, p. 147; H. Zhao, p. 28. Cheng Xiaoqing, "Lun zhentan xiaoshuo," in Lu Runxiang, p. 160, lists these notable late Qing translators of Sherlock Holmes: Li Weige, Lin Weilu, Wei Yi, Chen Dalin, Chen Lengxue, Bao Tianxiao, Xu Zhuodai. According to an unsigned newspaper article clipped by Ye Yonglie, Zhou Guisheng (1862–1926, born in Shanghai) was one of the first translators of Holmes and coiner of the Chinese term for "detective story," *zhentan xiaoshuo*. The University of California at Berkeley library has Zhou's 1905 Xiaoshuolin Press translation, *Fuermosi zaisheng, Yi zhi wu an* (The return of Sherlock Holmes, Cases one through five), and a 1908 Commercial Press edition of Lin Shu's *Xieluoke qi'an kaichang* (A study in scarlet). On Zhou, see Chen Pingyuan, *Ershi shiji*, pp. 46, 98. Nick Carter stories were also available in the late Qing.

73. Chen Pingyuan, *Ershi shiji*, p. 99, citing a Japanese study.

74. Yuan Jin, *Yuanyang*, p. 105.

75. Fan Boqun, p. 212. Wei Shaochang, *Wo kan*, p. 201.

76. Fong; Chen Pingyuan, *Zhongguo xiaoshuo*, p. 49.

77. Plaks, "Towards a Critical Theory," p. 339 (Lao Can is referred to as a Sherlock Holmes near the end of Chapter 18 of Liu E's novel); also D. Wang, pp. 146–55; Link, *Mandarin Ducks*, pp. 44, 48. Meng Liye, pp. 163–92, cites other, lesser-known works.

78. Chen Pingyuan, *Zhongguo xiaoshuo*, pp. 49, 53.

79. Song Anna and Huang Zexin, pp. 155–56. Sue was translated by Chen Lengxue; Chen Pingyuan, *Ershi shiji*, p. 46.

80. Wei Shaochang, *Wo kan*, pp. 149, 199; int. 40. Cheng began translating Western detective stories early on, into classical Chinese—e.g., "Lingniu" (Collar button), by Arthur Train, in *Xiaoshuo daguan* (The grand magazine) 7 (1916).

81. Liu Yangti, p. 432. Zhou Shoujuan's preface to Cheng Xiaoqing, "Juezhi ji," the first story, *Xiaoshuo daguan* 9 (Mar. 1917), p. 1, and Cheng's own afterword, pp. 20–21. Because of liberties taken with the Chinese translations of the titles, some of these identifications are educated guesses. Yuan Jin, *Yuanyang*, p. 86, notes Bao Tianxiao's limitations in foreign languages.

82. Liu Yangti, p. 432; He Puzhai; Wei Shaochang, *Wo kan*, pp. 198, 201, cites He Puzhai and Yu Mugu as coauthors of Lu Bin stories; Lu Runxiang, p. 180, says that Sun Liaohong and He Puzhai collaborated in a 1926 book of cases involving "the Oriental Arsène Lupin."

83. Cheng Xiaoqing, "Zhentan xiaoshuo zuofa de guanjian," p. 3; Wei Shouzhong, pp. 133–36. Cheng also helped Liu Bannong translate fiction by the English author William Le Queux (1864–1927). I have not seen the works Wei refers to but have found a detective story of Cheng's set in Brooklyn and still in classical Chinese in 1919, "Shi shang ming" (The name on the stone). Cheng wrote poems in classical Chinese to the end of his days. His poetry collection *Jianlu shici yigao* was prepared posthumously by his daughter Cheng Yuzhen, now Mrs. Yu Tsung Woo, copublisher of *The United Journal*, a Chinese-language paper published in New York.

84. Sun Liaohong, *Xia dao wen guai*, preface by Fan Boqun, p. 7.

85. Zeitlin, esp. pp. 1–12.

86. The quoted statement, from Sir Max Pemberton, was endorsed by Conan Doyle's son Adrian; T. Hall, p. 122.

87. Doyle, 1: 257.

88. Roth, p. 212.

89. Knight, *Form and Ideology*, pp. 82, 87.

90. Keating, ed., p. 151.

91. "Science Fiction at a Low Ebb," *Beijing Review* 39.41 (Oct. 7–13, 1996): 30, notes a decline of science fiction publishing houses from twenty in the early 1980s to only one.

92. According to the Lupin novel *La Comtesse de Cagliostro*.

93. Bao Lang refers to the many fans who have sent mail to Huo Sang as his *zhiji* in "Wu hou de guisu," 3: 69. Said, *Culture and Imperialism*, p. 138.

94. Symons, pp. 22, 67.

95. Cheng Xiaoqing, "Jiangnan Yan," 2:1.

96. Said, *Culture and Imperialism*, p. 155; Jon Thompson, pp. 60–79.

97. The Chinese tribute system, often just a manipulation of natives' "discursive systems" or a fantasy of the metropolitan power (China), in theory resembled this famous description of colonialism: "The colonizer installs chiefs who support him and who are to some degree accepted by the masses; he gives these chiefs material privileges such as education for their elder children, creates chiefdoms where they did not exist before, develops cordial relations with religious leaders, builds mosques, organizes journeys to Mecca, etc." Cabral, p. 58.

98. In Cheng Xiaoqing, "Maoeryan," 9: 117, Jiangnan Yan informs Huo Sang by letter of his intention to come visit him in three days to relieve him of a precious bauble in his custody. Cf. Lupin's letter to Baron Nathan Cahorn in Leblanc, "Arsène Lupin in Prison," in *The Extraordinary Adventures*, pp. 13–14.

99. Sun Liaohong, *Xia dao Lu Ping qi'an* [*XDLP*], p. 277.

100. The books Cheng translated he ordered himself by mail from America; int. 40. Cheng praises S. S. Van Dine in "Zhentan xiaoshuo de duofangmian," p. 69, for his imagination, descriptions, beautiful style, and purveying of the latest findings in behavioral psychology and aesthetic knowledge. In the 1946 revision, "Lun zhentan xiaoshuo," in Lu Runxiang, p. 159, Cheng goes on to praise The Saint's above-the-law dedication to righteousness.

101. Penzler et al., p. 113.

102. Tam, "Cultural Ambiguities."

103. Cheng Xiaoqing, "Huo shi," 4: 129–31. Here the operator refuses to give the information, but that is considered unusual.

104. *CXQWJ* 1: 147. Robinson was an American historian interested in psychology and the primitive mind, a favorite authority of May Fourth figures Gu Jiegang and Shen Congwen.

105. Cheng Xiaoqing, "Zhentan xiaoshuo de duofangmian," p. 76; Cheng Yude, " 'Huo Sang' de laili" (The origin of the name "Huo Sang"), *Xin min wan bao*, Feb. 27, 1990.

106. Liu Ts'un-yan, ed., p. 32. Cheng must have known that the great rival of Arsène Lupin in Leblanc novels was "Herlock Sholmes." Liu says that Cheng translated works by Maurice Leblanc.

107. Sun Liaohong, *Xia dao Lu Ping qi'an* [*XDLP*], p. 206.

108. Cheng Xiaoqing, "Zhentan xiaoshuo de duofangmian," p. 72.

109. Cheng Xiaoqing, "Jiangnan Yan," 1: 1–3; Cheng Xiaoqing, "Huo shi," 4: 289.

110. Cheng Xiaoqing, "Jiangnan Yan," 2: 27; also 2: 66.

111. Ibid., 2: 1; cf. Doyle, 1: 21.

112. Christopher Morley, "In Memoriam Sherlock Holmes," preface to Doyle, 1: 10.

113. Cheng Xiaoqing, "Huo shi," 4: 126.

114. Lu Runxiang, pp. 126–30.

115. The story was translated into modern Mandarin by Cheng Xiaoqing's daughter, Cheng Yuzhen.

116. Wei Shouzhong, pp. 131–38.

117. Cheng discusses such research in "Zhentan xiaoshuo de duofangmian," p. 74; "Cong 'shi er bu jian' shuo dao zhentan xiaoshuo"; and a serialized article about the use of footprints, hair samples, code-breaking, reading facial expressions, and analysis of blood, paper, dust, inks, and fingerprints—"Kexue de zhentanshu."

118. Zheng Yimei, p. 389; Lu Runxiang, p. 143.

119. Wei Shouzhong, pp. 136–139. In June 1922, Cheng published a story I have not seen, titled "Mao Shizi" (Hairy lion), the name of a character known to Huo Sang.

120. Cheng Xiaoqing, "Yeban husheng," 1: 91.

121. Cheng Xiaoqing, "Huo shi," 4: 32.

122. Cheng Xiaoqing, "Zi xinjian," 1: 284.

123. Song Anna and Huang Zexin, p. 157, cite some leftist language in Cheng Xiaoqing's "Huo shi" that is only found in the communist-era revision.

124. "Qing jun ru weng," HSTAJ 10: 281, cited in Fan Boqun, p. 217.

125. Cheng Xiaoqing, "Zi xinjian," 1: 288, 291.

126. Cheng Xiaoqing, "Lun xia xue," 1: 2.

127. Int. 40.

128. Link, Mandarin Ducks, pp. 40–58; Lu Xun, "Shangshi" (Regret for the past), in Panghuang, pp. 144–72.

129. Cheng Xiaoqing, "Zhentan xiaoshuo de duofangmian," p. 70.

130. Said, Culture and Imperialism, p. 152.

131. Cheng Xiaoqing, "Tan zhentan xiaoshuo"; the expanded 1946 version is "Lun zhentan xiaoshuo," in Lu Runxiang, pp. 163–67. See also Cheng Xiaoqing, "Cong 'shi er bu jian' shuo dao zhentan xiaoshuo" and "Zhentan xiaoshuo he kexue."

132. Another "postcolonial" moment is when Huo Sang states that the Western view that "one's reputation is one's second life" is inferior to Mencius's view that reputation is more important than life itself. Cheng Xiaoqing, "Huo shi," 4: 97.

133. Like the gambling gardener Feng Er in "Jiangnan Yan," and victim Fu Xianglin's gambling in "Zi xinjian," which is later discovered only to have been for small stakes.

134. "Guan Yin Pusa tuo meng," in Bao Gong qi'an, p. 165.

135. Doyle, 1: 99 (The Sign of Four) similarly speaks of "monster tentacles which the giant city was throwing out into the country."

136. Kinkley, "The Post-Colonial Detective"; Wakeman; B. Martin.

137. Wilson; Slovak.

138. Cheng Xiaoqing, "Yeban husheng," 1: 65.

139. Cheng Xiaoqing, "Huo shi," 4: 192–94, 231–34.

140. Ibid., 4: 287.

141. Cheng Xiaoqing, "Bai shajin," 1: 132.

142. Ibid., 1: 172. Fan Boqun, pp. 217–20, also thinks Cheng Xiaoqing ambivalent about the law, but Fan faults him for his frequent cooperation with the authorities and for not having a more Marxist view of society.

143. Cheng Xiaoqing, "Huo shi," 4: 169–71. On prejudice against people from Jiangbei (or "Subei"), see Honig.

144. Sun Liaohong, "Lanse de xiangweishe," pp. 63, 83, 107, 143; Lu Runxiang, p. 188.

145. Leblanc, "The Escape of Arsène Lupin," in *The Extraordinary Adventures*, pp. 35–36. The first identity seems to be confirmed when Lupin himself tells his trusted narrator friend that he studied with a carnival magician for six months; "The Wedding Ring," in *The Confessions of Arsène Lupin*, p. 50. Arsène Lupin's name is by Leblanc's admission a "deformation" of the name of Arsène Lopin, a former Paris city councilman (Derouard, 265), but it also suggests Poe's French detective, Dupin, perhaps with a hint of the wolf (Fr.: *loup*).

146. Leblanc, "The Arrest of Arsène Lupin," p. 2, opening story of *The Extraordinary Adventures*.

147. For a list of four dozen, see Lamy, pp. 15–21, and Blonde, pp. 145–50. As M. Lenormand (Leblanc originated in Normandy), head of the Sûreté, Lupin pursues himself in *813*. Lupin's biography is reconstructed year-by-year in great detail at www.chez.com/hemmer/jdr/lupinbio.html.

148. Wakeman, p. 202; see also B. Martin.

149. Sun Liaohong, "Zise de youyongyi," p. 348.

150. Leblanc, *Arsène Lupin versus Herlock Sholmes*, p. 59.

151. Leblanc, "Arsène Lupin in Prison," in *The Extraordinary Adventures*, pp. 12–27.

152. Sun Liaohong, "Gui shou," pp. 452–76; the story title mimics the film title.

153. Leblanc, "The Escape," in *The Extraordinary Adventures*, p. 36; there was such a fire in real life.

154. Sun Liaohong, "Lanse de xiangweishe," pp. 76, 147. Arsène Lupin is a vegetarian, though not on grounds of religion but of "hygiene"; Leblanc, *Arsène Lupin versus Herlock Sholmes*, p. 92.

155. A good example is "The Mysterious Traveller," in Leblanc, *The Extraordinary Adventures*, pp. 45–57. Traveling in a railway compartment with Madame, the wife of the superintendent of the prison service, Lupin returns her purse after they are both robbed by another thief, who is dapperly dressed and naturally presumed to be Lupin. The real Lupin personally chauffeurs two gendarmes in pursuit of the false Lupin. Through it all, the real one is incognito but not in disguise;

French respect for authority—the superintendent's wife, who vouchsafes for her companion in distress—allows Lupin to escape suspicion. *L'Echo* reports, in summation, that Lupin effected the arrest of serial murderer Pierre Onfrey, returned to Madame her purse, "and gave a generous recompense to the two detectives who had assisted him in making that dramatic arrest." He keeps the bad man's cash and documents and Madame's jewels as compensation, for "business is business." It is a veritable "economy of chivalry," adding to regard for face a satiric moderation in greed, and camaraderie in one-upmanship.

156. Sun Liaohong, "Lanse de xiangweishe," pp. 36, 70.

157. Sun Liaohong, "Ye lie ji," p. 198. Lu Ping shows a sinister, Fantômas-like side in "The Sunglasses Society," forthcoming in a translation by Timothy C. Wong. Lu Ping is recognized by a person he is robbing who so fears Lu Ping's vengeance that he does not even unmask him to the others present.

158. Sun Liaohong, "Tunyuganyouzhe," p. 405.

159. Sun Liaohong, "Lanse de xiangweishe," p. 102; capitalized words appear in English in the Chinese original.

160. Lu Ping blackmails the blackmailer by altering the date of the latter's letter asking for ransom of the locket, as if it had been written after the carjacking, so that the blackmailer can be charged with the carjacking. The tribute to Cheng is hypothetical, for no one has yet researched the original date of publication of either of the "Purple" stories.

161. Sun Liaohong, "Ye lie ji," pp. 201, 189.

162. An editor who knew Sun Liaohong in the 1940s says that he had a wife but was not seen to live with her; see Chen Dieyi, p. 36. In literature, women were threatening not only to hard-boiled characters but also to dandies; see Garelick, pp. 5, 19, 25, 51.

163. Lupin naturally had hoped to rob the Imberts. Lupin cannot even recover his rent, for Mme. Imbert gave it to charity! Leblanc, *The Extraordinary Adventures*, pp. 99–107.

164. Sun Liaohong, "Yanweixu"; the original was in *Hong meigui* 2, nos. 12–13 (Sept. 21, 28, 1925).

165. Sun comments, flippantly but still anti-Semitically—and in 1943—that Yu should have known a Jew would not sell to him so cheaply; Sun Liaohong, "Tunyuganyouzhe," pp. 404–5.

166. Robbers disguised as monsters is an old Chinese theme seen, for instance, in *Three Heroes and Five Gallants*, chap. 84; D. Wang, p. 139.

167. It could be that Rong Meng is one of Lu Ping's assistants. Perhaps the real Lu Ping planted him as his surrogate at the party and let him undertake the theft of Ms. Panda's jewelry under his direction, with a percentage going to the "chief." After paying off the other red tie in the restaurant, Rong Meng calls him a "noble self-employed person" (27). He also mocks him, as if the other man were working for him, but perhaps he is just showing off before Ms. Panda. One can only speculate.

168. Lu Runxiang, pp. 179–93.

169. Leblanc, "The Wedding Ring," in *The Confessions of Arsène Lupin*, pp. 31–52. Sun Liaohong's "The Hand of a Ghost" may also have borrowed a plot element from this story. Leblanc's count chloroformed the countess as she lay in bed in order to extract the replacement wedding ring from her finger, but it was too difficult to remove without the intervention of a jeweler. Just so, the innocent lady of "The Hand of a Ghost" was chloroformed in bed by thieves in quest of an amulet.

170. See L. Lee, "Zhongguo xiandai wenxue de 'tuifei' ji zuojia"; Fruehauf; and S. Shih, who differentiates the Francophile and Japanophile Shanghai modernism of Liu Naou from May Fourth tradition.

171. L. Lee, ibid., pp. 39–41, cites the influence in Shanghai of dandyism, with Huysmans's fiction furnishing the main literary personality. Shao Xunmei was a model Shanghai dandy in dress and habits.

172. It is an indication of the obscurity into which Sun Liaohong has fallen that I could not learn if he read or spoke French. Leblanc was translated into English and Chinese; Sun might have picked up French words to spice up his stories in the French Concession.

173. Fruehauf, p. 145.

174. Albérès, pp. 84–91, 107–24.

175. Rathbone was famous for playing the lead in classic Sherlock Holmes movies.

176. Sun Liaohong, "Ya mingsheng," pp. 406–51.

177. Slemon, in "Modernism's Last Post," p. 1, takes as his epigraph David Trotter's words from "Modernism and Empire": "The remedy for decadence is a journey to the frontier." Baudelaire (3: 483, 485) found roots of dandyism (as he fancied Chateaubriand did) among the North American Indians!

178. Sun Liaohong, "Muou de xiju," p. 237; see also p. 273.

179. The "Blue Rattlesnake" siren gives orders to her henchmen in Japanese; but then, Lu Ping tries to psych out the Blue Rattlesnake by giving instructions in Japanese to *his* henchmen.

180. Sun Liaohong, "Zise de youyongyi," pp. 338–47.

181. Sun Liaohong, "Lanse de xiangweishe," p. 58.

182. Moers, p. 135.

183. Moore-Gilbert, p. 47, reading Said.

184. Even this ground was already trod by Europeans. Since Edward Bulwer in 1830 wrote *Paul Clifford* (Moers, 83), gentleman dandies have dabbled in criminality. To Baudelaire, dandyism, though having its own laws, was "outside" *the* law; Baudelaire, 3: 483.

185. Reappearing in aristocratic society in disguise as a chevalier Floriani of Sicily, Lupin shames the Comte de Dreux-Soubise for having groundlessly ruined Lupin's mother years before. The "chevalier" is an expert detective but humbly declines to identify himself with Sherlock Holmes. He has identified himself with C. Auguste

Dupin (Poe's chevalier)! Leblanc, "The Queen's Necklace," in *The Extraordinary Adventures*, pp. 58–71.

186. Leblanc, "Sherlock Holmes Arrives Too Late," in *The Extraordinary Adventures*, pp. 120–39.

187. The Chinese translation was called *Shuangxiong douzhi lu* (Two heroes' duel of wits).

188. When the narrator mentions Ganimard in comparison with the detectives Dupin, Lecoq, and Holmes, the original spelling of Holmes is retained, since here the fiction is that these are all real people (59). On Conan Doyle's letter, see Derouard, p. 277, who learned of it from Maurice Leblanc's son Claude. Leblanc also put "Sholmes" into a third work not analyzed here, *The Hollow Needle*. At the end, Lupin's wife interposes herself between Lupin and Sholmes's pistol; Sholmes fires and inadvertently kills her.

189. Cheng Xiaoqing, "Zuanshi xiangquan," in *Zhentan taidou*; preface by Fan Boqun, p. 199.

190. This is a bum rap; Holmes cares for Watson when he is shot in "The Adventure of the Three Garridebs."

191. Feng Menglong's collection *Gujin xiaoshuo* (Stories old and new) contains a piece called "Dragon Meets Tiger." My pagination cites the vernacular text, "Zuanshi xiangquan."

192. Cheng Xiaoqing, "Zhentan xiaoshuo de duofangmian," p. 72, anticipates this line of interpretation. He admits to Bao Lang's role as the one with limited insight who leads the reader astray, yet seems to think that this is unjust to Bao Lang.

193. The 1923 original is in a spare and stilted vernacular, with short sentences as in classical Chinese. Sun's humor, witty tone, and parody of Cheng Xiaoqing's style are not yet in evidence. However, the plot is very similar, although the original has fewer subplots. The draw between the Oriental Holmes and Oriental Lupin at the end is a little less friendly in the 1923 version.

194. Sun Liaohong may not have been the first to satirize Cheng. Cheng Xiaoqing, "Zhentan xiaoshuo de duofangmian" (1933), p. 77, reminisces that the detective story writer Zhang Biwu satirized Huo Sang by showing him up through a rival of Zhang's creation. Four readers wrote letters of complaint to Zhou Shoujuan for this disrespect toward Huo Sang. Zhang Biwu altered his original plan and awarded final victory to Huo Sang, just as Sun Liaohong ended up doing in his story.

195. Tongmenghui journalist (b. 1879) and editor in Shanghai during and after the anti-Manchu revolution; in 1942, head of the Control Yuan and member of the standing committee of the KMT Central Executive Committee. He was also a great painter.

196. For gratuitous war imagery, see Sun Liaohong, "Muou de xiju," pp. 215, 248, 252, 271, 284, 285, 286, 287, 288. Diplomats are ridiculed on p. 290, as in Sun Liaohong, "Tunyuganyouzhe," p. 379.

197. C. T. Hsia, "Obsession with China: The Moral Burden of Modern Chinese Literature," in *A History of Modern Chinese Fiction*, Appendix 1.

Chapter 4: Politics

1. Cf. Simpson, pp. 97–122. Cuba's Ministry of the Interior sponsored detective stories after 1972.

2. Chapter Two notes that the finer points of traditional "popular fiction" were accessible only to literati. However, the heroes, plots, and certain formulas of language were always accessible to people of less education, and by the 1970s there was mass literacy.

3. See Wang Chungui.

4. Link, "Fiction and the Reading Public," shows that Maoist fiction was popular into the 1980s.

5. D. Wang, p. 181, cites novels by Zhao Shuli, Zhou Libo, and Ding Ling.

6. Gao Jianping, p. 42. On Soviet thrillers, see Russell.

7. Gao Jianping, pp. 30–61. This material first appeared in an article Gao coauthored with Zhang Zihong in *Zhuomuniao* 39 (May 1990): 104–17, and there Zhang's name came first, so I credit both Gao and Zhang in my textual references. Gao (real name, Gao Jianping; "Jian" means "construct"), then in his early thirties, was a former teacher in the Jiangsu Public Security Academy (int. 45). Zhang (real name, Zhang Hong), in uniform in his magazine picture, was a teacher at the Shandong Public Security Academy (int. 45).

8. Zhang Chunsheng, p. 56. *Xiezuo gailun*, pp. 286–88.

9. Wei Jun, *Fazhi wenxue yu chuangzuo*, pp. 8–9.

10. Tsai, p. 407, cites Xie Tingyu's novella *Duanxian jiewang* (To catch a spy; 1956), about an enemy agent caught on the Korean border; Wanshi and Yongchen's novella *Kongshan bujianren* (No trace of anyone in the empty mountains; 1957), about enemy sabotage; Li Wenda's "Shuang ling matibiao" (The alarm clock with a second bell; 1955), about hidden counterrevolutionaries whose plot for a May Day riot is thwarted by Public Security, and his "Yi ben bijiben" (A notebook; 1956), also about counterrevolutionaries; and Yu Lin's "Bing fei xugou de gushi" (A story not at all fictitious; 1956), about the escape from a prison camp and recapture of a secret agent. Mulin and Hanxing's *Disilingqi hao tuzhi* (Draft no. 407; 1956) and Zhang Zhimin's *Feiyun gang* (Port Feiyun; 1957), both mentioned by Cai and by Gao and Zhang, are about KMT sabotage before 1949.

11. The works are about KMT saboteurs before and after the revolution, other spies and enemy agents operating particularly at the border (before and after 1949), landlord and counterrevolutionary saboteurs, foreign Catholic spies (Tsai, item 186: 6), and a member of the old Yiguandao (a secret society) who infiltrates back into China to overthrow the new regime (418: 1).

12. Gao Jianping, pp. 32–35. Zhang Chunsheng, p. 56, cites a 1954 Shanghai film directed by Wang Weiyi, "Shan jian lingxiang mabang lai" (Bells tell the approach of a horse caravan in the mountains), based on a story by Bai Hua.

13. Gao Jianping, pp. 35–39; Zhang Chunsheng, p. 56.

14. Gao Jianping, pp. 39–46.

15. Han Jiang. Fan Ping and Xiao Fan's story is about tracking down American agents at the border.

16. Ye Yonglie, ints. 17, 24. Wei Jun was assigned to edit this book—*Sufan xiaoshuo xuan*—in 1978. It and companion volumes of Sufan dramas and screenplays were all published by the Masses' Press; Wei Jun, *Fazhi wenxue*, pp. 31, 217.

17. Dubrow, p. 108.

18. Jin Rukang enjoins his men to "deeply go among the masses to gain understanding. . . . Only by relying on the masses can we resolve the matter" (13).

19. This novella was written long before there was DNA profiling, but over 80 percent of the population secretes antigens into body fluids that can be matched with their red blood cells' ABO type.

20. Characteristic phrases from Cheng Xiaoqing's old writing include *dun yi dun* (pausing; 7) and *tuwude* (abrupt; 13). Typical new phrases are *xiao huozi* (young fellow; 7), *duanlian* (to steel; 6), *jin yi bu* (a step further; 13), and all those associated with politics. Typical northern dialect is *chuanmen* (chat; 32).

21. J. Shapiro and Liang, p. 143.

22. Int. 18, citing research of March 4, 1982. Note that *Dr. Jekyll and Mr. Hyde* may have counted as a mystery. Ye made the same points in an unpublished conference paper of May 19, 1982 (rev. July 15).

23. Lo, p. x.

24. Nearly every province and provincial-level municipality had a *fazhibao* by the late 1980s, though not all had a *gonganbao*; of the latter, only the *Renmin gongan bao* of the MPS in Beijing was not classified. Experimentally started up in June 1984 and officially founded in October 1984, it was declassified in July 1987; int. 45. As Lu Ping put it, the *Shanghai fazhibao* was jointly managed by the Shanghai Sifaju and the CCP Shanghaishi Zhengfa Weiyuanhui (Political-legal committee); int. 21. Wei Jun, in *Fazhi wenxue yu chuangzuo*, pp. 32–33, says he was the first to raise "formally" the term "Chinese socialist legal system literature," in September 1981, at a meeting of the Standing Committee of the Beijing Literary Studies Association. The claim is backed by his editor, Zhang Weihua, p. 1, and Zhang's colleague Zhang Ce, int. 31. This does not literally contradict the claim of Jiang Yan, " 'Fazhi wenxue' suoyi" (A short discussion of "legal system literature"), *Fazhi ribao*, May 31, 1990, that the term "legal system literature" was commonly used in newspapers in 1980, making 1990 its tenth anniversary. Wang Yonghong, int. 48, considered Wei's claim presumptuous. Perhaps Wei Jun was the first to seize on a prior and unremarkable juxtaposition of "legal system" and "literature" and try to promote it as a literary

genre. Wei was the publisher (*shezhang*) and chief editor of the Police Officers Education Publishing House that printed his book; int. 44.

25. Criticisms of "Xin sheng" appear in *Zuopin yu zhengming* 17 (May 17, 1982): 57–60.

26. *Jiekai shizong de mimi*, p. 155; see also Kinkley, "Chinese Crime Fiction and Its Formulas," pp. 109–11.

27. Ints. 3, 9, 47; Yu Haocheng, *Ming chun ji*, p. 3; Zeng Zhennan, "Fazhan fazhi wenxue zhi wo jian," p. 93. Princeton's Gest Library holds *Woodpecker*, no. 1 (1980).

28. J. Shapiro and Liang, pp. 25–26; Li Yi and Bi Hua, eds., Afterword by Li Yi, p. 334.

29. *Feng pian lian*, analyzed in Kinkley, "The Cultural Choices of Zhang Xinxin," pp. 148–51.

30. J. Shapiro and Liang, pp. 107–9.

31. Ibid., p. 92; H. Tanner, chap. 6.

32. Lü Shi, "Zhongguo wentan de liangge chuntian zhi jian" (The Chinese literary world between two springtimes), *Zhengming* 88 (Feb. 1, 1985): 16–21; Shen Yuan, "Dalu baokan fanji 'laoshushi' " (Mainland periodicals and newspapers strike back at 'rat droppings') *Zhengming* 88 (Feb. 1, 1985): 22–23.

33. Interview with Wang Yaping, May 30, 1982.

34. Exceptions: Cen Zhijing and Wang Wenjin's "A Gold Buddha," lacking a generic title, is tagged a *xingshi zhencha xiaoshuo* (criminal investigation story) after the title. Guo Qiao and Xing Zhe's "The Strange Case on Taoyuan Street" is called a "deductive story." Li Di's "Bangwan qiaomen de nüren" is called a *zhenpo xiaoshuo* (case-solving story) on the contents page of *Zuopin yu zhengming* 52 (Apr. 1985): 3–40.

35. Chinese science fiction journals and a Chinese Association for the Popularization of Science were established; see Wagner, pp. 17–19.

36. Zhang Fang, p. 45.

37. Except for Kong Jiesheng's, stories mentioned in this and the next paragraph are in Li Yi and Bi Hua, eds.

38. Ye Yonglie, *Leng ruo bingshuang*, pp. 168–75, and the author's curriculum vitae. *Shiwan ge wei shenme* was designated a big poisonous weed during the Cultural Revolution; Ye Yonglie, " 'Pa gezi' de licheng," p. 409.

39. In 1920s Soviet suspense tales adapting detective story devices to battles of workers vs. capitalists, SF devices were commonly mixed in. See Russell, p. 394.

40. See Wagner, pp. 45–59.

41. Keating, ed., p. 14, cites *The Silver Bullet* by Arthur B. Reeve (1912) as the first SF-detection novel. Ye represents a 1940 story by Gu Junzheng (1902–80) as China's first story in the genre; Ye Yonglie, ed. (1981), p. 2 of Preface and pp. 1–27.

42. Zhao Shizhou, "Jingxian kehuan xiaoshuo zhiyi" (1983). Ye responded in "Jingxian kehuan xiaoshuo dayi."

43. Asimov, p. 12.

44. Ye's first "suspenseful SF" story, "Shengsi wei bu" (Fate unknown), began serialization in *Gongren ribao*, May 9, 1979. He followed it with stories in *Shaonian wenyi* and *Ertong wenxue*; Ye Yonglie, *Leng ruo bingshuang*, p. 163. On Western hybrids, see Gray.

45. Ye Yonglie publicly announced his intention to concentrate on suspenseful SF in February 1980; *Leng ruo bingshuang*, p. 164. His first volume for the Masses' Press, *Wuzhuang daban*, came out in November 1980. Probably Ye contracted to write for the MPS by early 1980. I do not know whether he came up with the idea of Jin Ming or the MPS asked him to create such a hero. Ye directed at least one film for the MPS; int. 17.

46. The dialects in which Jin Ming is said to be expert include Mandarin and the other major ones, even Subei dialect, but not Shanghainese; it must be his native tongue; Ye Yonglie, " 'Sharen san' anjian," *Qiaozhuang daban*, p. 3. In national cases, Jin is chief of detectives of the MPS.

47. Int. 18. During a subsequent campaign, at least one article by implication accused the novella of "spiritual pollution" for having a hero who allegedly has doubts about communism during the Cultural Revolution. See Gui Yi, "Sixiang shang de heiying" (A black shadow over ideology), *Zhongguo qingnianbao*, Nov. 3, 1983, p. 1.

48. *Qiaozhuang daban* (1980); *Mimi zongdui* (1981); *Buyierfei* (1982); *Ru meng chu xing* (1983).

49. Int. 18.

50. "Zhongguo de 'kehuan re' wei shenme xunsu xiaotui? Ye Yonglie laigao pouxi wu zhong yinsu" (Why did China's craze for science fiction suddenly wither? Five factors as analyzed in a submission by Ye Yonglie), *Wenyibao*, Apr. 2, 1988, p. 4. Ye says that SF declined by 1983.

51. Ye Yonglie, *Leng ruo bingshuang*, p. 165.

52. Japanese SF aficionados wrote in praise of Jin Ming's exemplary character. See Hai Ming, "Zhongguo de Fuermosi" (China's Holmes), *Guangzhou ribao*, Feb. 10, 1983; Liu Xin, "Zhongguo de 'Kenan Daoer' " (China's Conan Doyle), a newspaper clipping from Ye Yonglie, probably from the *Fazhi zhoubao*, ca. 1985.

53. Ye Yonglie, *Shenmi yi*, p. 1 of preface.

54. Ye Yonglie, *Leng ruo bingshuang*, p. 165.

55. Symons, p. 39.

56. In E. M. Forster's sense, p. 67.

57. Doyle, 1: 21; Ye Yonglie, " 'Sharen san' anjian," in *Qiaozhuang daban*, pp. 2–3.

58. See Ye Yonglie, "X-3 anjian," pp. 61–62; Wagner, pp. 45–59.

59. Int. 18.

60. Lü Haiyan, *Bianyi jingcha*, p. 145, shows police "in the days of the Gang of Four" using secret miniature cameras mounted on the belt to photograph protesters. The text disapproves of this, implying that it is a PLA tactic, not a police tactic.

61. In "X-3 anjian," for example.

62. Rewritten as a play, this reappears as the title work of Ye Yonglie, *Guobao qi'an*.

63. The scientist made his speech at the conference from memory in front of a big audience. That should have been sufficient to indicate that he did not die on the way there! Identical cases are switched on a train in a Simenon work, *Maigret and the Hundred Gibbets* (1931); Symons, p. 134.

64. Int. 17. The MPS felt that thieves learned from movies to use gloves while committing crimes. The Shanghai Public Security Bureau bemoaned a case in which thieves taped a window to keep the glass from falling on the floor while breaking it, as shown in a movie about guerrillas screened not long before. This technique also appears in Ye's "Zhi zui jin mi," p. 213.

65. Int. 17; " 'Sharen san' anjian," *Qiaozhuang daban*, pp. 1–33; *Poan de xin yaoshi*, pp. 109–13. In *Guiji duoduan* (comic book, 1982), p. 45, another plot resorts to a poison with a made-up name, "god of death no. 3." See Lin Jiaju for more of a *biji*-style write-up of a poisoning case in early post-Mao times.

66. Symons, p. 119. Ironically, " 'Sharen san' anjian," pp. 11–12, gloats that Jin Ming is a cop in socialist China with real science at his command, unlike Holmes, Cuff, and Poirot. On p. 13, Ye does do his best to inform readers of more common poisons like cyanide.

67. *Wuxing qiezei* (comic book), p. 33.

68. Int. 17. Zhu Jiazhen (1982, 1986) and Peng Wen (1989) are more technical yet unclassified. I do not know of a Chinese book on home detection and police procedure like Fallis and Greenberg, or Bintliff.

69. The connection with voice prints might seem dubious, but it is found in *The New Encyclopaedia Britannica, Micropaedia*, 15th ed., 4: 781, "fingerprinting" entry, signed "J. Edgar Hoover" (Chicago, 1997).

70. Ye Yonglie, *Poan de xin yaoshi*, pp. 196–97, discloses the questions that allegedly revealed Allyn Rickett to be a spy but shows no knowledge of the Ricketts' own *Prisoners of Liberation* (1973).

71. *Guiji duoduan* (comic book). Fingerprints of everybody in Coastal City over the age of eight are in the computer in *Zhi zui jin mi* (comic book), p. 14.

72. Int. 18. Ye never found the time to write it. From the scrapbook he made for his history, from which he generously let me photocopy, I gather that he intended to stress Conan Doyle's influence and include Robert Van Gulik as an honorary Chinese mystery writer. On Gulik, see Huang Yanbo, p. 254.

73. Int. 18.

74. Laqueur, p. 75.

75. It is broken by a code book in the possession of the shadow's old sweetheart, the entomologist's foster mother. One wonders if Ye felt he had to conceal the fact that computers can break codes.

76. Lehman, p. 78.

77. On crime control, see Wang Zhongfang; and H. Tanner, chap. 6. Li Tuo ret-

rospectively saw a big shift in high literary practice in "1985" in his article by that name—though for his purposes, "1985" began in 1984. Moran, p. 388, cites an anonymous but well-published informant who claimed that *Shidai de baogao* (Reports of the times) belonged to the MPS, 1980–83, and then, renamed *Baogao wenxue* (Reportage) after January 1984, to the Ministry of State Security, itself founded in 1983.

78. Int. 44.

79. Int. 34.

80. Montages of diverse artifacts of violence figure heavily on the covers of thrillers in Western supermarkets too. Beebee, pp. 6–7, says they are a reflection of the genre's plots, "which ask the reader to put the pieces together," and "a fetishistic image appropriate for the worship of violence."

81. Ints. 9, 15.

82. Moran, esp. pp. 2–3; Schell, pp. 293–310. Notable books of reportage with crime-fiction-style narrative are *Nan yi yuyue de pingzhang* and Ren Qun et al., eds.

83. Issue 1 of 1985 was numbered "no. 7," implying that issue 1 of 1984 (Feb.) was the first issue, as if those of 1980 never existed. In int. 44, informants claimed that the 1980 issues were not periodicals but part of a four-number collectanea (*congshu*) including *Xinxue* (Blood of the heart) and *Nuanfeng* (Warm wind). But the first 1980 issue's title page says "*diyi qi*" (issue no. 1).

84. "Human rights" was the target of denunciation in an official press campaign in 1979; see Davis, pp. 93, 136–38 (articles by Yu Haocheng and Zhu Feng). There was, however, much discussion of human rights in early 1989, a liberal period.

85. Yu Haocheng (int. 47) stressed his commitment from the start to using *Zhuomuniao* to further human rights. Wang Yonghong left the MPS for the Law Press, under the Ministry of Justice, since one could not leave China while in MPS employ. She emigrated to Canada in the summer of 1987; ints. 48, 50, 51.

86. The MPS had hated to reveal how very long it took them to bring these criminals to justice; int. 3. Articles on the case appeared in Hong Kong in *Zhengming*, no. 72 (Oct. 1, 1983): 8–13, and previously in no. 69. The inaugural issue of *Zhuomuniao* went into a fourth printing in July, as issue no. 4 was coming out.

87. "*Zhongguo fazhi wenxue* 10 yue 25 ri zai Jing chuangkan" (*Chinese Legal System Literature* is founded in Beijing on October 25), *Wenyibao* 457 (Nov. 9, 1985). I believe it did not start publishing until early 1986. The circulation figure is from Li Ti, "Fazhi wenxue de youshi" (The superior situation for legal system literature), *Zhongguo fazhibao*, Oct. 28, 1986, p. 4.

88. Int. 16.

89. Ai Qun kindly told me of the four last journals; int. 45.

90. Schell, pp. 297–310. See the reportage pieces by Jia Lusheng, and by Zhang Weihua and Zhang Ce. *Zuopin yu zhengming* frequently reprinted articles critical of the tabloids, as in no. 50 (Feb. 17, 1985).

91. Announcements by Gong Sha, legal adviser to the Masses' Press, and Cheng Yude, Cheng Xiaoqing's son, in *Zhuomuniao* 29 (Sept. 1988): 53.

92. Int. 35.

93. According to ancient-drama expert Wu Xiaoling, interviewed October 30, 1989. Zeng Zhennan (int. 9) agreed; Wang Shuo also brought up double meanings and allusions to the massacre in print; int. 19.

94. Ints. 35, 44.

95. A. Jones, p. 86.

96. Int. 10. Articles on *tongsu wenxue* are in *Zuopin yu zhengming* 54 (June 1985): 71–79, and other 1986–87 issues.

97. Han Shaogong had to go to Hainan to adopt a low profile during the repression following the June 4, 1989, massacre. His editorial board remained intact in Changsha.

98. Int. 19.

99. "Fazhi xiaoshuo gua yangtou mai gourou: Dalu tiewan sao 'jingshen laji' " (Legal system fiction a wolf in sheep's clothing: The mainland sweeps away 'mental trash' with its iron fist), *Huaqiao ribao* (New York), Apr. 4, 1987, citing the Hong Kong *Wanbao*.

100. Gao Tao, interviewed August 19, 1990, in Beijing.

101. Int. 17.

102. *Fazhi qi'an* (Strange cases from the legal system; Beijing), from the Falü chubanshe, 1990, 50,000 copies; *Dai guiguan de qiufan* (The convict who'd worn laurels; Tianjin), from the Bai hua chubanshe, 1988; *Fengkuang daoye* (The mad profiteer), whose "subtitle," "Shenzhou funü da guaimai" (The widespread kidnapping of women for sale in old Cathay), under a drawing of a howling, busty woman in shorts, is bigger than the "title" (Beijing? Shandong?), February 1989, 100,000 copies; *Qing huo* (Love perils; Changchun), 1987, 80,000 copies; *Dao guo zhuisha* (Pursuit to the death in an island nation; Tianjin), June 1989, 80,000 copies; *Liti youpiao an* (The case of the three-dimensional postage stamp), from "Farming Villagers' Reading Matter Press" (Nongcun duwu chubanshe), n.p., 1988; *Dangdai dianshi* (Contemporary television; Beijing) brought out a 1989 issue seemingly without any particular connection to television but packed with crime stories that it called, perhaps dubiously, *jishi wenxue* (documentary literature). Maybe some were TV scripts. Several times bigger than the ostensible periodical title were words emblazoned across the middle, seemingly *the* title: *Daan tean qi'an* (Big cases, special cases, strange cases). Similarly, *Xiju wenxue* (Dramatic literature; Jilin, 1987?) brought out an issue, not even numbered in periodical fashion, of crime stories whose ostensible title was really the title of a translated Japanese crime story within: *Yushi li de zuie* (The crime in the bathroom). *Yihai qiguan* (Strange things seen in the sea of art) of Wulumuqi, Xinjiang, which usually printed reportage about, e.g., scandals of the film director Zhang Yimou's love life (no. 22, June 1, 1989), published an extra issue in 1988 whose most prominent cover title was the name of a piece

within, *Yuhai fuzhou* (A boat overturned in a sea of lust); one contribution was classified as "chapter-driven," with chapter titles in couplets, though the story was in simple modern Mandarin. A 220,000-copy Xi'an *Shaonian yuekan* (Young people's monthly), probably of 1989, issued a very adult magazine whose most prominent front cover title is *Caihua dadao* (The great flower-plucking thief), after a work of "suspense Wulin martial-arts *chuanqi* fiction." It is joined by other formula stories. A magazine called *Shanghai gushi* (Shanghai stories), with the Shanghai University Institute of Literature, brought out a June 1989 *Zhongguo da zhentan* (Great Chinese detectives) with painted nudes on the back and inside front covers.

103. Int. 22. "Fengliu nannü" was the title of one of the stories.

104. Int. 16.

105. Int. 4. *Xiezuo gailun* (1988), p. 289, claimed that *Chinese Legal System Literature, Selections from Legal System Literature, Sword and Shield, Woodpecker*, and *Blue Shield* still circulated 2.5 million copies total.

106. Int. 11.

107. Int. 28.

108. Int. 31.

109. Int. 15.

110. Int. 16.

111. Int. 10.

112. Ints. 5, 31.

113. Int. 6.

114. Ints. 34, 38, 39, 41.

115. A. Jones, pp. 18–20.

116. Telephone conversation with Liu Binyan in Princeton, N.J., April 20, 1997; Du Yuanming, p. 126.

117. Schoenhals, pp. 6–15.

118. Du Ai, "Guanyu fazhi wenxue" (About legal system literature), *Zhongguo fazhibao*, Oct. 28, 1986, p. 4, calls legal system literature a *ti3cai2* (type) and a *pinzhong* (kind) as well as a *ti2cai2* (subject matter category).

119. A textbook on how to write it is *Xiezuo gailun*.

120. Zhang Qie (pronounced "Zhang Qi"), pp. 90 (Tolstoyan heights), 91 (distinct from pure literature). Lü Dai and Yi Hua, "Bu shi shengcun er shi fazhan zhuangda" (Not subsisting but developing and strengthening—casual criticism of some 1986 legal system subject-matter fiction and reportage), *Zhongguo fazhibao*, Mar. 5, 1987, p. 4, also upholds the seriousness of legal system literature but distinguishes it from pure literature. Yu Piao, p. 78, offers a typically broad definition of legal system literature, including *Les Misérables, Resurrection*, and *Eyewitness Reports on Strange Things from the Past Twenty Years*.

121. L. Wu, pp. 347, 356–58; see also Nivison, pp. 60–61.

122. Even Huang Yanbo considers the term "legal system literature" useful

(282). He implies that China's old *gongan* stories might be "ancient legal system literature" (2).

123. Shen Fujun, "Yougan yu 'lüshi wenyi' " (Feelings about "lawyer literature and art"), *Jiefang ribao*, Oct. 9, 1984.

124. Int. 9.

125. Zhu Hong, trans., p. viii. G. Lee, p. 117, likens China's literature about its exotic "West" to the West's "Orientalism" toward "the East."

126. Official literary meetings about seeking roots preceded the literary movement; Han Shaogong's seminal works were preceded by the Chinese Writers' Association Hunan Branch sending Han and other writers to West Hunan in 1985 expressly to search for "roots." Kinkley, "Shen Congwen's Legacy," p. 98. See generally J. Wang, pp. 180–86, 213–24.

127. M. Tanner, pp. 49–50, cites Polumbaum's study of China's attempt to pass a press law as an example.

128. Ints. 10, 37, 41. On class struggle, Mao Shian, int. 38; on Beijing usage, Wang Shuo, int. 9.

129. Ints. 11, 16.

130. Gao Hongshi, "Fazhi wenyi shi nian guankui" (My humble view of the ten years of legal system literature and art), *Fazhi ribao*, Dec. 29, 1988, p. 4.

131. Int. 32.

132. Ming Ying, "Wu jia kanwu faqi zhaokai fazhi wenxue yantaohui" (Five periodicals sponsor and convene a research conference on legal system literature), *Wenyibao*, Nov. 1, 1986, p. 2. "*Zhuomuniao* yu *Jingtan fengyun* lianhe juban Gulangyu bihui" (A writers' gathering jointly conducted by *Woodpecker* and *Police World* at Gulangyu), *Zhuomuniao* 19 (Jan. 1987): 91, uses the term "legal system literature" and calls police literature a branch of it. However, the article also implies that police literature covers the activities of both police and judicial cadres. *Woodpecker* attended the 1986 Anqing conference and published the reports of Zeng Zhennan and Zhang Qie, both of which had "developing legal system literature" in their titles. See Zhang Qie; and Zeng Zhennan, "Fazhan fazhi wenxue zhi wo jian." Zeng is a critic at the CASS Institute of Literature; his wife is on the editorial board of *Zhuomuniao*.

133. Yu Haocheng, "Chuangzao juyou Zhongguo tese de fazhi wenxue" (Create a legal system literature with Chinese characteristics), *Zhongguo fazhibao*, Oct. 28, 1986, p. 4. This is a summary of his speech, presented in absentia; Int. 47. See also Zhang Qie, p. 89; and Zeng Zhennan, "Fazhan fazhi wenxue zhi wo jian," p. 94.

134. Yue Ling, editorial: "Fazhi wenxue? Fanzui wenxue?" (Legal system literature or criminal activity literature?), *Wenyibao* 447 (Aug. 31, 1985): 1.

135. Ints. 17, 34, 37.

136. Int. 44. Mou Huaike, int. 16, said *Jian yu dun* was founded to provide a respectable alternative to the unhealthy tabloids, especially to win young readers away from them.

137. Int. 34; also int. 9 (Wang Shuo).

138. Chen Mingqing, int. 34. The leadership turned down his plea to found *Jingtan fengyun* in 1980.

139. Int. 34. I presume this includes all auxiliaries. Wang Zhongfang, pp. 481, 485, gives far lower numbers: 1.2 million professional police officers in 1987, and almost 7 million in public security small groups.

140. " 'Guanyu xiang quanti gongmin jiben puji falü changshi de wu nian guihua' zhaiyao" (Abstract of 'On the five-year plan to popularize common knowledge of the law generally among all citizens'), *Zhongguo fazhibao*, Dec. 6, 1985, p. 1 (citing a cable from Xinhua). See also Troyer, Clark, and Rojek, eds., pp. 73–76.

141. In int. 10, editors emphasized that their popular fiction could educate, say, *getihu* (individual entrepreneurs) selling blue jeans who break the law without even knowing it. A general defense of the informative aspects of legal system literature is in *Xiezuo gailun*, pp. 294–95.

142. Zeng Zhennan, "Fazhan fazhi wenxue zhi wo jian," p. 93, asserts that the general populace broadly associates democracy and rule of law. Also ints. 6, 7, 10, 11.

143. Int. 17; Epstein, p. 36; Keith, *China's Struggle*, p. 16.

144. Geng Longxiang, "Fazhi wenxue de yishu meili chutan" (Preliminary inquiry into the artistic fascination of legal system literature); and Li Ti, "Fazhi wenxue de youshi" (The superior situation for legal system literature), *Zhongguo fazhibao*, Oct. 28, 1986, p. 4 (these are summaries of their conference papers). Liu Binyan, *Di'er zhong zhongcheng*.

145. Zhang Qie, pp. 89–90; Xu Zhixiang, p. 79.

146. Ints. 3, 5, 9, 11, 17, 30, 34, 38, 44, 45, 47; Zhang Qie, p. 89. Circulation figures are from Li Ti, "Fazhi wenxue de youshi," *Zhongguo fazhibao*, Oct. 28, 1986, p. 4. This and articles on that page by Yu Haocheng, Yuan Ying, and Geng Longxiang summarize those authors' conference papers (Yu's was presented in absentia; an article by Du Ai, who did not attend, is also printed); see also the full speeches by Yuan Ying and Geng Longxiang. "Fazhi wenxue yantaohui zai Wan juxing" (Research conference on legal system literature is convened in Anhui), *Renmin ribao*, Nov. 3, 1986, p. 7, lists others who attended: Li Zhenjun, Cao Haibo, Chen Dengke, Ye Nan, Sun Jihuai. Also attending were Jiang Liu and Xu Xiaoyu, as well as representatives from the People's Armed Police and the Chinese Writers' Association (e.g., Zhang Qie); see Wu Ying, "Wu jia kanwu," *Wenyibao*, Nov. 1, 1986, p. 2, and *Zhongguo fazhi wenxue* 7 (Jan. 18, 1987): 91.

147. Wang Yonghong remembers that the conference was billed as the First All-China National Research Conference on Legal System Literature. There was no second conference; ints. 39, 51.

148. According to Ke Renchang, former manuscript editor of *Jingtan fengyun*, interviewed in New York, October 19, 1990. He referred to general editor Lin Zhangfu.

149. The Ministry of Justice, its *Zhongguo fazhibao*, and the Chinese Legal

Studies Association gathered young and middle-aged writers from all over China, apparently with little MPS input, in Beijing in September 1986. The session was billed as the First Conference for Creation of and Research on Legal System Literature. Bianjibu (pseud. homophonous with "editorial department"), "Shouci fazhi wenxue chuangyanhui jishi" (Report on the First Conference for Creation of and Research on Legal System Literature), *Zhongguo fazhi wenxue* 6 (Dec. 1986): 80, 26.

150. Another reason for the "failure" of the meeting alleged by some MPS cadres was that not everybody was invited who should have been; int. 44. Wei Jun was one not asked. Liu Binyan, in a telephone conversation, April 20, 1997, remembered the conference atmosphere as not bad.

151. Ints. 3 (on *Resurrection*), 30, 50. Telephone conversation with Liu Binyan in Princeton, N.J., April 20, 1997. Zhang Qie, p. 89, refers to the problems of slogan hypocrisy brought up at the meeting, presumably by liberals. Cong Weixi voiced the same reservations about "legal system literature" in int. 4; it did not address "the fundamental problem of the law."

152. Ints. 44, 51. Liu Binyan summarized his talk in "Ren de jiefang he yanlun ziyou."

153. Zeng Zhennan claims that the association was established; int. 3. Yu Haocheng (who was not at the meeting) claims it was never founded (int. 47), which is probably to say that it made no impression (ints. 5, 30). Wang Yonghong (int. 51) recalled postmeeting organizational activities that seem to be the reason for the confusion. She agreed that nothing much came of the organization. Three publications solicited for members for the organization, including *Zhuomuniao* and the *Zhongguo fazhibao*.

154. Ints. 11, 45, 50, 51. *Woodpecker* preceded *Selections* in printing content that fit the genre description; it was a bimonthly, so the Anqing journal proudly advertised itself as the first *monthly* of "legal system *literature*" ("literature" distinguishing it from monthly law magazines). Emphasis added.

155. Ints. 44, 45. There were representatives from the central CCP Propaganda Department and the state Ministry of Culture (then under Wang Meng), who remained silent at the meeting. They seem to have been a major avenue by which news of the meeting seeped out to Chinese intellectuals; int. 38.

156. See *Xiezuo gailun*, pp. 286, 287. Old cadres liked the fact that civil cases did not have all those awful crimes. Stories about divorce cases were favored by the many cadres who were themselves divorced.

157. There was a five-day MPS Fazhi Wenxue Yeyu Zuozhe Lianxiban (Training class for spare time writers in legal system literature) at Qingdao. Zeng Zhennan and others lectured and helped young authors, mostly policemen, revise their manuscripts. It was a vacation paid for by the MPS, so the authors were expected to send their manuscripts to *Zhuomuniao*; int. 3. At the First Public Security Literature Jiangxiban, September 5 to November 30, 1989 (after the massacre), run by the MPS

and Public Security Police Officers University, Dong Xuewen, Zhong Yuan, and Li Wenda taught; int. 45. On *Jian yu dun*, int. 39. On the meeting in Anqing, int. 17. After 1986 someone in Beijing tried to set up a Zhenpo Xiaoshuo Xiehui (Detective fiction league), but it failed; int. 34. Beijing in 1989 also had a Fazhi Wenxue Yanjiuhui (Lu Ping, int. 16); Zhong Yuan was a member. A Dazhong Wenxue Xuehui (Study association for masses' literature) was founded in Shanghai in 1989, with *Sword and Shield* as its main backer. But the journal itself was closed in 1990.

158. This was the Haima Yingshi Chuangzuo Zhongxin (Seahorse center for film and television creation), founded in Beijing on Jan. 23, 1989; int. 5. The *Zhuomuniao* (MPS) editor and fiction and screenplay writer Wei Dongsheng was a key member. Interviewees Wang Shuo, Su Lei, Ge Xiaogang, and Fu Xuwen (also MPS; int. 30) were members; Mo Yan and Ye Zhaoyan were among the other writers who helped set up the salon, the Haima Xiangcun Jiudian (Seahorse Country Style Pub), at 18 Zhaodengyu Rd. The authors were proud of having set up what they called "the first private group of authors, unlike the Chinese Writers' Association"; some even described it as a union (*gonghui*). It was more of a networking center, where writers compared notes on movie rights and other issues. It was still in existence at the end of 1989, after the crackdown.

159. E.g., a June 1990 conference in Taiyuan, Shanxi, sponsored by the *Renmin gonganbao*; int. 45. The history that was written is Gao Jianping's (with Zhang Zihong).

160. Yu Piao, p. 78.

161. Gao Jianping; *Xiezuo gailun*; Wei Jun, *Fazhi wenxue*.

162. "Fazhi wenxue yantaohui zai Wan juxing" (Research conference on legal system literature is convened in Anhui), *Renmin ribao*, Nov. 3, 1986, p. 7; int. 45. Winners of the first "Gold Shield" competition (for stories written from 1977 to 1987) were published in three volumes: *Jiaru shi ni zuoan*, *Nü minjing de kanke jingli*, and *Ruozhe, bushi nüren de mingzi* (Beijing: Qunzhong chubanshe, 1990). The Shanghai "series" was Aug. 28–Oct. 27, 1989; int. 41.

163. Zeng Zhennan, "Fazhi wenxue zhi wo jian," pp. 94–96, against overdefining the nature of legal system literature, argues that the genre has a component that ranges from high to low and a horizontal dimension (with socially panoramic legal system literature on one end and documentary legal system literature as well as detective-story legal system literature at the other end). Zeng also acknowledges (98) that this literature, however defined, must deal with the dark side—crime. In "Fazhi wenxue duanxiang" (1988), Zeng decided that he had been overeager to ask for legal system literature to soar to monumental heights. He was reconciled to it as a popular literature meeting current entertainment needs. Zhang Chunsheng (1986) is another exception; his strategy is to subcategorize legal system literature as deductive (detective), customs inspection, anti-spy, social-order (more sociological), and Court of Morality stories. The latter are about immoral behavior, not courtroom activity.

164. I think I was at first unconsciously influenced by graphic representations of "the legal system film" in Tan Dazheng and Shen Qi, eds., pp. 2–3. Tan taught the theory of and how to write legal system literature at the East China Institute of Politics and Law, Shanghai.

165. Int. 34; see also Yuan Ying, "Renmin huhuanzhe fazhi he fazhi wenxue (The people are calling for legal system and a legal system literature), *Zhongguo fazhibao,* Oct. 28, 1986, p. 4.

166. Lu Ping, int. 41. These recall the "three extensions" of labor reform work cited in H. Tanner, p. 339. Survivors of the *Golden Venture* boat wreck outside New York were famous for making eagles during imprisonment in York, Pennsylvania. Observers thought the eagles were "American."

167. Ints. 14, 17, 30, 31, 32, 34, 44.

168. Wang Shuo criticized Ke Yunlu for a "traditional" and yet opportunistic Red-Guard mentality that turned off his own (Wang's) younger generation; int. 9.

169. Int. 22.

170. Int. 30.

171. Int. 41.

172. Int. 10.

173. Int. 30.

174. Wang Shuo, int. 9.

175. Int. 44 acknowledged curiosity for information about police work as a legitimate reason for reading legal system literature. An Xingben gives a stark official justification of legal system literature because it provides "information."

176. Int. 11.

177. Int. 9. He felt that the Court of Morality in the periodical *Minzhu yu fazhi* was really counterproductive—antilegal in its principles—because it failed to separate law and morality. There may be seeds of a more Western high/low split here: law is intellectual, modern, and high; morality is popular, traditional, and low.

178. Ai Qun, int. 45.

179. Wang Shuo, int. 9.

180. Int. 9.

181. Zhou Yunfa (speech at the October 1986 Anqing meeting), pp. 5–8; ints. 6, 9 (Wang Shuo), 10, 11.

182. Zeng Zhennan, "Fazhi wenxue zhi wo jian," p. 94.

183. Int. 10.

184. Ints. 9, 11, 34, 37, 44. I know of no Chinese Rumpole. Only Fu Xuwen claimed that nearly all good legal system literature was bound to be satirical; int. 30. I believe he was speaking of Wang Shuo (see his *Xiangpiren* and *Yiban shi huoyan*) and criticizing avant-gardism. Editor of "low," "popular" crime fiction Wu Chao did argue that his selections often satirized the police; int. 10. Willard Huntington Wright inveighed against love interests in the classic detective genre (Symons, 14, 95), and the ban generally held.

185. The inadmissibility of a professor was cited independently in ints. 5 and 30; Fu Xuwen said editors enforced the principle.

186. Liu Binyan, "Stark Truth vs. 'False Realism': The Book That Stunned Beijing," *New York Times Book Review*, Nov. 6, 1988, p. 3. Liu confirmed Cong Weixi as the target at an April 2, 1991, talk at Princeton University.

187. Ints. 32, 34, 38.

188. Gao Jianping; Yan Xinrui.

189. *Landun* 88 (July 1992). No. 94 (Jan. 1993) broadened the self-designation to "Monthly Journal of Legal System Literature and Social Documentary."

190. Feng Mu (1994) was very positive about the literary concept and linked "legal system" to democracy and the aspirations of the people. [Chen] Huangmei's 1996 article was his talk at the "First All-China Research Conference on Legal System Literature and Art" (*fazhi wenyi*, including film as well as literature, whereas the first conference on *fazhi wenxue* was in 1986). The conference marked the founding of the Committee on Legal System Literature and Art under the Research Association for Popular Literature and Art. That pigeonholed "legal system" works as low, but Chen used the *old* term "legal system literature" (*fazhi wenxue*), which diminished distinctions between sublime, serious, and popular literature, thus challenging legal system literature to reach for the stars again. Du Yuanming (1996) allowed a space for "legal system literature," including police activities that concern the courts, though he claimed the major part of Chinese crime and case-cracking literature for "police literature." Meng Liye (1996), p. 1, speaks of both "legal system" and "police subject matter" works.

191. Song Anna and Huang Zexin; and Huang Zexin and Song Anna.

192. Zeng Zhennan, "Fazhi wenxue zhi wo jian," p. 97.

193. In defense of this metaphor I cite *The Happy Couple: Law and Literature*. Incidentally, crime magazine editors all said that the majority of their readers were male.

Chapter 5: Fruition

1. One can hear an editor saying: "You can publish *this* in *Sword and Shield*; why send it to us at *Shanghai Literature*?"

2. Int. 32. In int. 17, when I suggested that the idea of legal system literature offered official protection for writing about the dark side of society, Xiao Guanhong and Wang Xiaoying's reaction was, "Yes, you know you're right. This hadn't occurred to us before." As critical guardians of "high literature," they had seen only the dark side of the slogan.

3. Wang Meng's "Yaozi 8679 hao" is a satire of mystery stories. *Xingjing 803*, *Landun xiaoshuo ji*, and Wang Yonghong's "Fayi Yang Bo" and *Yinxing wugong* are standard police stories. Yu Hua writes avant-garde tales of murder and mayhem; see

his "Wangshi yu xingfa" and various translations in *The Past and the Punishments*. Try Li Jian for a more popular-style novel with violence. On pop culture, see Zha.

4. Massaro.

5. Wu Zhuyu, "*Ni wei shui bianhu*: Wang Xiaoying de ziwo bianhu" (*Whom Do You Defend*: Wang Xiaoying's self-defense), *Wenyibao* 684 (Mar. 31, 1990).

6. Dubrow, pp. 1–3.

7. Int. 37. People's Literature Press, which publishes "pure literature," printed this novel, not the MPS. Lü originally submitted the manuscript to the MPS, but they dallied with it.

8. Leung, p. 195.

9. Li Ziyun, "Wang Xiaoying bixia de liu Mei daluren" (Mainlanders studying in America as depicted by Wang Xiaoying), *Huaqiao ribao* (New York), Aug. 19, 1987.

10. Leung, p. 190; int. 17. Like Lü Haiyan, Wang Xiaoying disliked the concept of "legal system literature" (which to her meant vulgarity), and particularly the application of it to her novel. She said it was not about cases or cracking them, but about the fate of women.

11. Only in 1989 was "inability to carry out sexual intercourse" stipulated as grounds for divorce under the Marriage Law (rev. 1980), art. 25, by a ruling of the Supreme People's Court. M. Palmer, p. 113.

12. It turns out that the ex-con is hated not only by his neighbors but also by his brother; he beats up Ma for helping his sibling.

13. Bettelheim, p. 76, calls white birds a sign of the superego.

14. Shen Huiting's rotten husband says this, so it is ironic; he shows up only to share in whatever spoils Mei Zhen might get for his wife in a lawsuit.

15. In 1988 China experimented by removing state subsidies from one-fourth of its law firms; Cheng Gan and Yang Xiaobing, "Lawyers Win New Acceptance in China," *Beijing Review* 31, no. 28 (July 11–17, 1988): 19. The first genuine cooperative law office (in which lawyers divided up profits and losses) was set up in Shenzhen in 1988; by September 1992, there were 80 of them, mostly in big cities; "Reforms Demand More Lawyer Services," *Beijing Review* 35, no. 38 (Sept. 21–27, 1992): 12. The first in Beijing was the Jingwei Cooperative Law Office, set up in July 1988 (int. 6, with Wang Yiling and Zhang Chijun, October 1989), which elected its head and made decisions collectively. There were 24 such firms in July 1989; Zeng Shuzhi, "Cooperative Law Office in Beijing," *China Reconstructs* 38, no. 6 (June 1989): 19–20. In 1989, a J & H Law Office in Beijing claimed to have no leader, to be unaffiliated with a government agency, and to have self-employed partners, suggesting true private practice, except that each lawyer was paid "according to his contribution to the firm," which suggests at least some collectivizing of profits; Lou Xinyue, "Law Partners Tread New Path," *Beijing Review* 32, no. 36 (Sept. 4–10, 1989): 37–38. Foreign law firms were allowed to open offices in China in 1992; *Wall Street Journal*, Mar. 20, 1992. Things moved rapidly when the state saw that it could

unburden itself financially; the Lawyers Law of May 15, 1996, removed all lawyers from the state payroll.

16. The title is a triple parody, of a Maoist model opera (*Taking Tiger Mountain by Strategy*), trashy pulp fiction with the traditional theme of ghosts ("headless corpse"), and detective fiction ("the case of").

17. Beebee, p. 150.

18. Mei Zhen went to find witnesses to testify to Shen Huiting's birth under the Fan name but forgot to follow through. She realizes the extent of her negligence only in court (687).

19. Pagination from Li Jingchun and Gong Fan, eds., pp. 564–611.

20. *Zhuomuniao* 5 (Dec. 1984): 83–102. Wei's *Lü se de douhao* dates the story to May 1984.

21. Wei, who was in the army for three years before going to the MPS, was not yet divorced when he wrote this in 1984. His father had official pull; in 1990 he headed the Baseball Association in China; int. 33. Han Jiang has a famous, rehabilitated father at the vice-minister level.

22. Roth, pp. 152–61, discourses on the frequent identity of detective and criminal in crime fiction.

23. Chen Yuanbin, "Preface," *The Story of Qiuju*, pp. 7–10 and front matter; Chen Yuanbin, *Wan jia susong*, front matter. In "Qingnian zuojia tan fazhi wenxue," p. 93, Chen indicates that he has taken the lawyers' exam and defended some clients. In the English book, the title story is translated by Anna Walling.

24. "Tian xing"; translated as "Heaven's Course," *The Story of Qiuju*, trans. Eileen Cheng, rev. Esther Samson, pp. 149–95.

25. In this case, she would be dealing with the police at a prefectural or provincial municipality level.

26. See A. Chen, pp. 176–84; Potter, "The Administrative Litigation Law"; Keith, *China's Struggle*, pp. 79–86. The code's intended propaganda effect is apparent in Yang Xiaobing, "Civilians Can Sue Officials," *Beijing Review* 32, no. 19 (May 8–14, 1989): 7. Civilians had previously accused officials and got them punished by their bosses outside the legal system and had also won suits at law lodged with government-owned corporations. Note the title: "Small Potato Wins a Suit in Guangzhou," *China Daily*, Oct. 1, 1985. Administrative courts actually started up in 1986 to test what became codified in 1989; see Potter, p. 273. The first suit and then the first successful suit against public security bureau decisions were filed in 1987 and reported in *Minzhu yu fazhi*; see Lo, p. 230. A decade later, the local police were commonly defendants.

27. The 1986 revision of the Security Administration Punishment Regulations already provided for defendants, though not accusers of third parties, to appeal police verdicts to a people's court, whereas the 1989 law has been interpreted as not allowing citizens to sue the police, at least for wrongful *investigative* acts. See Clarke and Feinerman, pp. 142, 146.

28. On the famous 1990s suits of Wang Meng, Dai Qing, Nanjing University philosophy professor Guo Luoji, and Wang Juntao, see Alford, "Double-Edged Swords." These complainants were unsuccessful, but the new laws led to a "litigation fever" in the early 1990s; most suits were filed by entrepreneurs against the state.

29. Chen Yuanbin, "Preface," in *The Story of Qiuju*, p. 9.

30. Clarke, "Dispute Resolution," p. 269, citing a 1967 article by Stanley Lubman. Clarke's article stresses that Chinese "mediation" is broadly coercive, and we see this exemplified in court attempts to derail divorce trials and have dysfunctional couples make up through "mediation," as happened in Wang Xiaoying's novel.

31. Elisabeth Rosenthal, "A Day in Court, and Justice, Sometimes, for the Chinese," *New York Times*, Apr. 27, 1998, pp. A1, A6.

32. Craig S. Smith, "Chinese Discover Product-Liability Suits," *Wall Street Journal*, Nov. 13, 1997, p. B1.

Character List

Ai Qun　艾群

Aiwen (Aiwenyi)　愛文 (愛文藝)

An yu fa　案與法

Anhui wenxue　安徽文學

anyu　案獄

Ba Jin　巴金

Bai Hua　白樺

bao (burden)　包

bao (requital)　報

Bao Gong (Lord Bao)　包公

Bao Lang　包郎

Bao Tianxiao　包天笑

Bao Xing　包興

Bao Zheng (Bao Longtu)　包拯 (包龍圖)

Baogao wenxue　報告文學

baojuan　寶卷

baotan　包探

baoweizu　保衛組

Beijing wenxue　北京文學

bianwen　變文

bihui　筆會

biji (xiaoshuo)　筆記 (小說)

Binglinghua　冰凌花

Chang'an　長安

Changcheng wenyi　長城文藝

Changjiang wenyi　長江文藝

chaotou wenxue　潮頭文學

Chen Diexian　陳蝶仙

Chen Mengxiong　陳夢熊

Chen Mingqing　陳明慶

Chen Rong　諶容

Cheng Shanzhi　程善之

Cheng Yude　程育德

Cheng Yuzhen　程育真

chengwen fa　成文法

chuanqi　傳奇

Cong Weixi　從維熙

Da Lüshi　大律師

Da qiang neiwai　大牆內外

Da shijie　大世界

Da zhentan　大偵探

Daan tean qi'an　大案特案奇案

Dai Qing　戴晴

daiban de falü　呆板的法律

Dangdai 當代

Dangdai jingcha 當代警察

dangji guofa 黨紀國法

dangxing 黨性

Daode fating 道德法庭

Dazhong Wenxue Xuehui 大眾文學學會

dazhonghua 大眾化

"Dengguang renying" 燈光人影

Di Renjie 狄仁傑

Dianying chuangzuo 電影創作

Dianying xinzuo 電影新作

Dong Dexing 董德興

Dong Xuewen 董學文

dongfang 東方

Dongtinghu 洞庭湖

dongyang (tōyō) 東洋

Dou E 竇娥

Du Yuesheng 杜月笙

Edogawa Rampo 江戶川亂步

erhu 二胡

ermu 耳目

Ershiyi shiji 二十一世紀

fa 法

faling 法令

falü (hōritsu) 法律

Falü yu shenghuo 法律與生活

Falü zixun 法律諮詢

famang 法盲

Fan Yanqiao 范罗橋

fangzhen 方針

fansi wenxue 反思文學

fante 反特

Faxue jie 法學界

fazhi (legal system) 法制

fazhi (rule of law) 法治

Fazhi gushi da sai jing xuan 法制故事大賽精選

Fazhi huabao 法制畫報

fazhi wenxue 法制文學

Fazhi wenxue xuankan 法制文學選刊

Fazhi Wenxue Yanjiuhui 法制文學研究會

fazhi wenyi 法制文藝

Fazhi wenzhai 法制文摘

fazhi xiaoshuo 法制小説

Fazhi xuanchuan 法制宣傳

Fazhi yu wenming 法制與文明

Fazhi yuekan 法制月刊

fazhibao 法制報

Fei Taimin 費太敏

Feng Menglong 馮夢龍

Fengliu nannü 風流男女

Fu He 撫河

Fu Xuwen 傅緒文

Fuermosi tan'an quanji 福爾摩斯探案集

gao 告

Gao Jianping (orig. Jianping) 高澗平 (建平)

Gao Tao (Writers' Assn.) 高陶

gao wei 告為

Gao Xiaosheng 高曉聲

gaozhuang (-ren)　告狀 (人)

Ge Xiaogang　葛小剛

geren guapai, siren guapai　個人掛牌, 私人掛牌

getihu　個體户

gong jian fa　公檢法

Gong Li　鞏俐

gongan (genre; "court case")　公案

gongan (public security; police)　公安

Gongan Ju, Gongan Ting　公安局, 公安廳

gongan ticai wenxue　公安題材文學

gōngàn wénxúe (court case literature)　公案文學

gōngān wénxúe (police literature)　公安文學

gonghui　工會

Gu Junzheng　顧均正

Guangzhou wenyi　廣州文藝

guanli　慣例

guanxi　關係

guize　規則

Guojia Xinwen Chubanshu　國家新聞出版署

Gushi hui　故事會

Gushibao　故事報

Haima Yingshi Chuangzuo Zhongxin　海馬影視創作中心

Haima Xiangcun Jiudian　海馬鄉村酒店

Hainan jishi　海南紀實

Han Shaogong　韓少功

Hao Min　郝敏

Hao Ran　浩然

He Biqiu; hebi qiu　何碧秋; 何必求

He Puzhai　何樸齋

He Xilai　何西來

heihua　黑話

Heilongjiang yishu　黑龍江藝術

Heimao Jingzhang　黑貓警長

Hong meigui　紅玫瑰

Hua Jian　花建

Hua jing　花徑

hua shuo　話説

huaben　話本

Huacheng　花城

huang　黃

Huo Sang　霍桑

Huo Sen　霍森

Ji Yun　紀昀

Jia Baoyu　賈寶玉

Jian yu dun　劍與盾

Jiang Zilong　蔣子龍

Jiangnan Yan　江南燕

Jiangxi gongan　江西公安

Jiaru wo shi zhende　假如我是真的

Jiefangjun wenyi　解放軍文藝

jieshou　接收

Jin cheng　金城

Jin Ming　金明

Jin tian　金田

Jin Yong　金庸

Jindun　金盾

Jing di　警笛

Jing tan　警探

jingming　精明

Jingtan fengyun　警壇風雲

Jingu chuanqi　今古傳奇

jingxian　驚險

Jintian　今天

jishi xiaoshuo　紀實小説

Jiuming qiyuan　九命奇冤

Juanhua　鵑花

Juben　劇本

jueding　決定

junzi　君子

kaimen jianshan　開門見山

kanji (J.)　漢字

kehuan xiaoshuo　科幻小説

Kong Yiji　孔乙己

Kuang Zhong　況鍾

Kulian　苦戀

Landun　藍盾

langzi　浪子

Lao Can youji　老殘遊記

Lao She　老舍

Lei Feng　雷鋒

li (Rites)　禮

Li Honglin　李宏林

Li ji　禮記

Li Wenda　李文達

Li Xun　李遜

Li Yasha　李亞沙

Li Yizhe　李一哲

Liang Qichao　梁啓超

liangxin　良心

Lianhuanbao　連環報

Liaoning qunzhong wenyi　遼寧群眾
文藝

lifa, lilü　禮法, 禮律

Lin Bin　林斌

Lin Shu　林紓

Lin Zhangfu　林章富

liqi　離奇

Liu Bannong　劉半農

Liu Bei　劉備

Liu Cunren　劉村任

Liu Denghan　劉登翰

Liu E　劉鶚

Liu Heng　劉恒

Liu Shaotang　劉紹棠

Liu Xie　劉勰

Liu Xinwu　劉心武

Liu Zhiwu　劉志武

liumang　流氓

Lu Bin　魯賓

Lu Dan'an　陸澹盦

Lu Ping (the Chinese Lupin)　魯平

Lu Ping (legal reporter)　陸萍

Lu Shi　陸石

Lu Wenfu　陸文夫

Lü ye　綠野

Lu Zhishen　魯智深

Luoshen　洛神

lüshi wenyi　律師文藝

lüshisuo　律師所

Mao Shian　毛時安

Mao Shizi　毛獅子

Matsumoto Seichō   松本清張

Meng Xing   孟興

mingling   命令

Minjian wenxue   民間文學

Minzhu yu fazhi   民主與法制

Minzhu yu fazhi huabao   民主與法
制畫報

Mou Huaike   牟懷珂

paidui   派對

pan   判

panli   判例

Ping yao zhuan   平妖傳

pingfan   平反

pinglun   評論

pinzhong   品種

Pu Songling   蒲松齡

puji   普及

qi, qi'an   奇, 奇案

qiaopi hua   俏皮話

qiliao   豈料

qing (feelings)   情

Qingdao miwu   青島迷霧

qingguan (xiaoshuo, gushi)   清官
(小説, 故事)

qingjiexing   情節性

Qingming   清明

Qingnian wenxuejia   青年文學家

Qingtian   清天 (青天)

Qiuju   秋菊

quan   權

Quanjia fu   全家福

Qunzhong chubanshe   群眾出版社

Ren yu fa   人與法

Renmin de juzhang   人民的巨掌

Renmin gonganbao   人民公安報

Renmin jingcha   人民警察

San yue san   三月三

Sha Yexin, Li Shoucheng, Yao Mingde
沙葉新, 李守成, 姚明德

shang cheng, shang su, shang gao
上呈, 上訴, 上告

Shanghai fayuan   上海法苑

shangpinhua   商品化

Shanhu   珊瑚

Shantou wenyi   汕頭文藝

she fa wenxue   涉法文學

shehuixing   社會性

shehuizhuyi fa   社會主義法

shen (marvelous)   神

Shen Congwen   沈從文

shen de   審得

Shen Jiali   沈嘉立

Shen Yingci   申英次

Shen Yuzhong   沈禹鐘

Shengsi guantou   生死關頭

Shenqi de zhuizong   神奇的追踪

shenshi   紳士

shezhang   社長

Shidai de baogao   時代的告報

Shiwan ge wei shenme   十萬個為甚麼

Shiyue   十月

Shouhuo   收穫

Shouling 首領

"Shuangling matibiao" 雙鈴馬蹄表

Shuijingshi 水晶石

shuo (dao) 説 (道)

sifa jiguan 司法機關

sixiang 思想

su (plead), suzhuangren 訴, 訴狀人

su (vulgar), yongsu 俗, 庸俗

Su Lei 蘇雷

su wei 訴為

Su Xiaokang 蘇曉康

Sufan xiaoshuo xuan 肅反小説選

Sun Deping 孫德平

Suqing ancang de fangeming fenzi 肅清暗藏的反革命分子

Tam King-fai (Tan Jinghui) 譚京輝

Tan de yi jia 碳的一家

tanci 彈詞

tansuo 探索

taotie 饕餮

Teng Yun 滕雲

Tiane 天鵝

tiaojie, daqiao 條解, 搭橋

tiaoli 條例

tícái (subject matter category) 題材

tǐcái (type) 體裁

Tiedao weishi 鐵道衛士

tifa 提法

Tong Enzheng 童恩正

tongjian shafu zui 通奸殺夫罪

tongsu (wenxue) 通俗 (文學)

Tongsu wenxue xuankan 通俗文學選刊

Tongsu wenyijia 通俗文藝家

tuhua 土話

tuili (xiaoshuo); suiri (shōsetsu) 推理 (小説)

Wan xiang 萬象

Wang Ruowang 王若望

Wang Yiling 王以岭

Wang Zengqi 汪曾祺

weifa luanji 違法亂紀

weijin huodong 違禁活動

weizhe jingji shijian 為着經濟時間

wen 文

Wenxin diaolong 文心雕龍

wenxue 文學

Wenxue daguan 文學大觀

Wenxue gang 文學港

Wenxue gushibao 文學故事報

Wenxue yuekan 文學月刊

Wenyi chuang 文藝窗

Wenyi shenghuo 文藝生活

Wenyibao 文藝報

Wenyu shijie 文娛世界

wenzao 文藻

Wu Chao 吳超

Wu Han, Deng Tuo, Liao Mosha 吳晗, 鄧拓, 廖沫沙

Wu Jianren (Wu Woyao) 吳趼人 (吳沃堯)

Wu Na 吳訥

Wu Ningkun 巫寧坤

Wu Ruozeng　吳若增

Wu Xiaoling　吳曉鈴

Wu Zetian si da qi'an　武則天四大奇案

wuqing　無情

wuxia xiaoshuo　武俠小說

Wuxing de zhanxian　無形的戰線

Xi Ziyou　戲子由

Xia Yan　夏衍

Xiandai　現代

Xiandai shijie jingcha　現代世界警察

Xiandai tongsu xiaoshuo　現代通俗小說

Xiang Kairan　向愷然

xiangsheng　相聲

Xiao Guanhong　蕭關鴻

xiaobao　小報

xiaoshuo　小說

Xiaoshuo daguan　小說大觀

Xiaoshuo lin　小說林

Xiaoshuo shijie　小說世界

Xiaoshuo tiandi　小說天地

xiayi　俠義

xibu wenxue　西部文學

Xiefu　歇夫

xiguan fa　習慣法

Xin xiaoshuo　新小說

xing　刑

(xingshi) zhencha　（刑事）偵察

xingwei guize　行為規則

xingzheng fagui　行政法規

Xinmin congbao　新民叢報

Xiong Yuezhi　熊月之

Xiwang Chang'an　西望長安

Xu Qiuying anjian　徐秋影案件

Xu Ruisheng　許瑞生

Xu Zhenya　徐枕亞

Xu Zhuodai　徐桌呆

Xuefeng　雪峰

Xuelei fengchen nü　血淚風塵女

Xueran Zishijie: Pan Jinlian xin zhuan　血染紫石街: 潘金蓮新傳

xuetonglun　血統論

xungen wenxue　尋根文學

xunlianban, lianxiban, jiangxiban　訓練班, 練習班, 講習班

Yan Chasan　顏查散

Yan Duhe　嚴獨鶴

yanda　嚴打

Yasen Luopin an quanji　亞森羅蘋案全集

Ye Shaojun　葉紹鈞

yi　伊

Yi li　儀禮

Yi Ming　伊明

Yihai qiguan　藝海奇觀

yinlü　陰律

You Fengwei　尤鳳偉

You Jiang wenyi　右江文藝

yu (desires)　欲

Yu Mugu　俞慕古

Yuan Mei　袁枚

yuanzhang　院長

Yulihun　玉梨魂

zaju 雜劇

Zhang Biwu 張碧梧

Zhang Chijun 張赤軍

Zhang Hong 張宏

Zhang Jie 張潔

Zhang Tianyi 張天翼

Zhang Xianliang 張賢亮

Zhang Xuecheng 章學誠

Zhang Yimou 張藝謀

Zhang Zihong 張子宏

Zhanjiang wenxue 湛江文學

Zhenfan 鎮反

Zheng Wenguang 鄭文光

zhengce 政策

zhengce falü 政策法律

zhengtongde 正統的

zhengyi 正義

zhengzhi luxian 政治路線

zhenpo 偵破

Zhenpo Xiaoshuo Xiehui 偵破小說協會

zhentan (xiaoshuo) 偵探 (小說)

Zhentan shijie 偵探世界

zhifa 執法

zhiguai 志怪

zhiji 知己

zhiqing 知青

Zhong Yuan 鍾源

Zhongguo fazhi wenxue 中國法制文學

Zhongguo fazhibao 中國法制報

Zhongguo zhentan an 中國偵探案

Zhongguo zuojia 中國作家

Zhongpian xiaoshuo xuankan 中篇小說選刊

Zhou Guisheng 周桂笙

Zhou li 周禮

Zhou Shoujuan 周瘦鵑

Zhou Zuoren 周作人

Zhuge Liang (Kongming) 諸葛亮 (孔明)

"Zhuibu 'Er Wang' jishi" 追捕 "二王" 紀實

Zhuomuniao 啄木鳥

zidishu 子弟書

zuian xiaoshuo 罪案小說

Zuopin 作品

Zuopin yu zhengming 作品與爭鳴

Interviews and Works Cited

Interviews

1. Oct. 14, 1989. Wang Yonghong (a.k.a. Wang Hailun, Helen Wang; former co-editor of *Zhuomuniao*, in exile), in Vancouver, B.C.
2. Oct. 20, 1989. Liu Yangti (researcher on "mandarin duck and butterfly" literature, Chinese Academy of Social Sciences), in Beijing.
3. Oct. 24, 1989. Zeng Zhennan (critic, Institute of Literature, Chinese Academy of Social Sciences), in Beijing.
4. Oct. 25, 1989. Cong Weixi (author), in Beijing.
5. Oct. 27, 1989. Ge Xiaogang (author), Su Lei (author), Wang Shuo (author), Wei Dongsheng (author; editor, *Zhuomuniao*), in Beijing.
6. Oct. 28, 1989. Wang Yiling, Zhang Chijun (partners, Beijingshi Jingwei Lüshi shiwusuo [Beijing Jingwei Lawyers' Cooperative]), in Beijing.
7. Oct. 30, 1989. He Xilai (deputy head, Institute of Literature, Chinese Academy of Social Sciences, chief editor of *Wenxue pinglun*), in Beijing.
8. Oct. 31, 1989. Wei Dongsheng, in Beijing.
9. Nov. 4, 1989. Wang Shuo, with researchers at the Institute of Literature, Chinese Academy of Social Sciences, including Wang Hui and Zeng Zhennan, in Beijing.
10. Nov. 7, 1989. *Tongsu wenxue xuankan* (Selections from popular literature [Beijing]) editors: Wu Chao (chief editor), Li Yasha (editor and law student), in Beijing.
11. Nov. 13, 1989. *Landun* editors: Liu Zhiwu, Song Anna (also editor of the literary section of the *Tianjin ribao*), Zheng Yuhe (editorial director), in Tianjin.
12. Nov. 13, 1989. Xu Ruisheng (author), in Tianjin.
13. Nov. 13, 1989. Wu Ruozeng (author), in Tianjin.
14. Nov. 14, 1989. Tianjin Academy of Social Sciences, with Fu Zhenggu (critic), Teng Yun (director, Institute of Literature), Wang Changding (critic), Zhang Chunsheng (critic), others, in Tianjin.
15. Nov. 14, 1989. *Ren yu fa* editors: He Qiang (reporter; art director), Huang Zexin (researcher), Li Jiyuan (chief editor), Wei Junquan (deputy editor of *Tianjin*

fazhi bao; lawyer), Yang Wen (deputy editor), Zhang Chunsheng (author, re-searcher on films), Zhao Chun (literary editor), in Tianjin.

16. Nov. 20, 1989. Lu Haiguang (editorial committee, *Jian yu dun*; author), Lu Ping (editor and reporter, *Shanghai fazhi bao*), Mou Huaike (editorial director, *Jian yu dun*; reporter), Qiu Feng (chief editor, *Daqiang neiwai*; author), Sun Shufen (author), Xu Qingzhen (chief editor, *Shanghai fayuan*), Zhou Guang-wen (*Renmin jingcha* editorial board; uniformed), in Shanghai.

17. Nov. 22, 1989. Wang Xiaoying (author), Xiao Guanhong (deputy editor, *Wen-hui yuekan*), Ye Yonglie (author), in Shanghai.

18. Nov. 23, 1989. Ye Yonglie, in Shanghai.

19. Nov. 24, 1989. Huadong Zhengfa Xueyuan (East China Institute of Politics and Law) staff teaching a course on legal system literature: Qiao Maoyu, Shen Shun-hui, Tan Dazheng, Wang Hongwei, Xu Zaibin, Zhu Chunliang, in Shanghai.

20. Nov. 25, 1989. Institute of Literature, Shanghai Academy of Social Sciences, with researchers Dong Dexing, Wang Wenying, and others, in Shanghai.

21. Nov. 26, 1989. Lu Ping, in Shanghai.

22. Nov. 29, 1989. Shanghai Academy of Social Sciences, Chen Mengxiong (literary historian), Hua Jian (researcher on and compiler of popular literature publica-tions), Xiong Yuezhi (historian), others, in Shanghai.

23. Nov. 30, 1989. Zhou Yunfa (deputy editor, *Jian yu dun*; of the State Security Ministry), in Shanghai.

24. Dec. 1, 1989. Ye Yonglie (telephone interview), in Shanghai.

25. Dec. 1, 1989. Xiao Guanhong and Li Xun, in Shanghai.

26. Dec. 1, 1989. Zheng Yimei (95-year-old "mandarin duck and butterfly" author), in Shanghai.

27. Dec. 2, 1989. Shen Jiali (editorial director, *Minzhu yu fazhi*), in Shanghai.

28. Dec. 5, 1989. Editors of the *Hunan fazhi bao* and *Fazhi yuekan*: Chen Yisheng (editorial director of the daily), Liu Fuhua (editorial director, former chief editor of the monthly), Peng Cheng (former editorial director of both publi-cations, turned chief editor of *Lilun yu chuangzuo*), Shen Daoyue (chief and chief editor of both publications), Song Wugang (author; editor of *Da shijie*), Zhang Heping (editor, reporter, former responsible editor of the monthly). Also Lin He and Zhang Jingsong (chief editor and editorial director, respec-tively, of *Chu feng*), in Changsha.

29. Dec. 8, 1989. Editors and authors at the Hunan Wenyi Chubanshe (Hunan Literature and Arts Press), in Changsha.

30. Dec. 11, 1989. Fu Xuwen (author), in Beijing.

31. Dec. 14, 1989. Zhang Ce, Zhang Weihua (authors, reporters, editors of *Jindun*), in Beijing.

32. Dec. 16, 1989. Li Jian (author, literary department of the *Zhongguo fazhibao*), in Beijing.

33. July 29, 1990. Wei Dongsheng (author), in Beijing.

34. Aug. 1–2, 1990. Editors of *Jingtan fengyun*: Chen Mingqing (deputy editor and

translator), Lin Bin (author; uniformed), Lin Zhangfu (deputy chief and chief editor), Sun Deping, in Fuzhou.

35. Aug. 3, 1990. Fujian Academy of Social Sciences: Lin Bin, Lin Yan (deputy editor of *Wenhua chunqiu*), Liu Denghan (deputy head of the Institute of Literature; researcher), Wang Binggen (deputy editor, *Fujian wenxue*), Zhang Fan (researcher), in Fuzhou.

36. Aug. 6, 1990. Yu Hua (author), in Haiyan, Zhejiang.

37. Aug. 7, 1990. Lü Haiyan (author, general manager of the New Jinjiang Hotel), in Shanghai.

38. Aug. 9, 1990. Shanghai Academy of Social Sciences: Chen Mengxiong, Dong Dexing, Hua Jian, Mao Shian (deputy editor, *Shanghai wenlun*), in Shanghai.

39. Aug. 9, 1990. Chinese Writers' Association, Shanghai Branch: Huang Zhiyuan (author), Lu Ping, editors from *Renmin jingcha* and *Jian yu dun*, in Shanghai.

40. Aug. 11, 1990. Cheng Yude (son of Cheng Xiaoqing), in Suzhou.

41. Aug 14, 1990. Editors of *Shanghai fazhi bao*: Lu Ping, Shen Chen (chief editor), Shen Qi (deputy editor), in Shanghai.

42. Aug. 14, 1990. Dong Dexing, in Shanghai.

43. Aug. 15, 1990. Xiao Guanhong and Li Xun, in Shanghai.

44. Aug. 21, 1990. Editors of *Zhuomuniao*: Chang He (editor at the Masses' Press), Chen Hongxin (deputy editorial director of *Zhuomuniao*), Tao Heqian (deputy editor of the Masses' Press), Wang Lansheng (editorial director of *Zhuomuniao*), in Beijing.

45. Aug. 21, 1990. Editors of the *Renmin gongan bao*: Ai Qun (author and reporter), Li Changqun (chief and chief editor), and Yang Jin (responsible person for the literary section), in Beijing.

46. Aug. 22, 1990. Zhong Yuan (author), telephone interview, in Beijing.

47. Feb. 1, 1995. Yu Haocheng (exiled former head of the Masses' Press), in New York.

48. Apr. 11, 1997. Wang Yonghong, telephone interview, in Vancouver, B.C.

49. Apr. 16, 1997. Yu Haocheng, telephone interview, in Madison, Wisc.

50. Apr. 18, 1997. Yu Haocheng, telephone interview, in Madison, Wisc.

51. Apr. 20, 1997. Wang Yonghong, telephone interview, in Vancouver, B.C.

52. Dec. 28, 1998. Yu Haocheng, in Tempe, Ariz.

Works Cited

Abraham, Kenneth S. "Statutory Interpretation and Literary Theory: Some Common Concerns of an Unlikely Pair." *Rutgers Law Review* 32, no. 4 (Oct. 1979): 676–94.

Adam, Ian, and Helen Tiffin, eds. *Past the Last Post: Theorizing Post-Colonialism and Post-Modernism.* Calgary: University of Calgary Press, 1990.

Agassi, Joseph. "The Detective Novel and Scientific Method." *Poetics Today* 3, no. 1 (Winter 1982): 99–108.

Ahmad, Aijaz. *In Theory: Classes, Nations, Literatures.* London: Verso, 1992.

Albérès, Francine Marill. *Le Dernier des Dandies, Arsène Lupin* (The last of the dandies, Arsène Lupin). Paris: A.-G. Nizet, 1979.

Alford, William P. "Double-Edged Swords Cut Both Ways: Law and Legitimacy in the People's Republic of China." *Daedalus* 122, no. 2 (Spring 1993): 45–69.

———. "Law, Law, What Law?" *Modern China* 23, no. 4 (Oct. 1997): 398–419.

———. "Of Arsenic and Old Laws: Looking Anew at Criminal Justice in Late Imperial China." *California Law Review* 72 (1984): 1180–1254.

———. "Tasselled Loafers for Barefoot Lawyers: Transformation and Tension in the World of Chinese Legal Workers." In Lubman, ed., *China's Legal Reforms,* pp. 22–38.

———. *To Steal a Book Is an Elegant Offense: Intellectual Property Law in Chinese Civilization.* Stanford, Calif.: Stanford University Press, 1995.

Allee, Mark A. *Law and Society in Late Imperial China: Northern Taiwan in the Nineteenth Century.* Stanford, Calif.: Stanford University Press, 1994.

An Pingqiu 安平秋 and Zhang Peiheng 章培恒, eds. *Zhongguo jinshu daguan* 中國禁書大觀 (Historical overview of Chinese censorship). Shanghai: Shanghai wenhua chubanshe, 1990.

An Xingben 安興本. "Tan fazhi wenxue xinshang de teshuxing" 談法制文學欣賞的特殊性 (On the uniqueness of legal system literature appreciation). *Zhongguo fazhi wenxue* 11 (Sept. 18, 1987): 92–94.

Anli fenxi 案例分析 (Analysis of exemplary cases [series]). Vol. 1. Shanghai: Minzhu yu fazhi zazhishe, 1981. Internal.

Antony, Robert J. "Scourges on the People: Perceptions of Robbery, Snatching, and Theft in the Mid-Qing Period." *Late Imperial China* 16, no. 2 (Dec. 1995): 98–132.

Apostolou, John L. "A Yen for Murder: A Look at Japan's *Ichiban* Mystery Writer, Seicho Matsumoto." *The Armchair Detective* 20, no. 3 (Summer 1987): 322–25.

Appiah, Kwame Anthony. "The Postcolonial and the Postmodern." In Ashcroft, Griffiths, and Tiffin, eds., *The Post-Colonial Studies Reader,* pp. 119–29.

Ashcroft, Bill, Gareth Griffiths, and Helen Tiffin. *The Empire Writes Back: Theory and Practice in Post-Colonial Cultures.* London: Routledge, 1989.

———, eds. *The Post-Colonial Studies Reader.* London: Routledge, 1995.

Ashley, Bob. *The Study of Popular Fiction: A Source Book.* Philadelphia: University of Pennsylvania Press, 1989.

Asimov, Isaac. *Asimov's Mysteries.* New York: Fawcett Crest, 1977 [1968].

Auden, W. H. "The Guilty Vicarage." In Winks, ed., *Detective Fiction,* pp. 15–24.

Bai Hua. "Reaching Out to the World and to the Future." Tang Yiming and Marsha L. Wagner, trans. In Martin and Kinkley, eds., *Modern Chinese Writers,* pp. 42–46. 1986 speech.

Baijia gongan 百家公案 (Hundred cases [of Lord Bao]). 1594. Reprint, Taibei: Tianyi chubanshe, 1985.

Bakhtin, M. M. *The Dialogic Imagination: Four Essays.* Michael Holquist, ed.

Caryl Emerson and Michael Holquist, trans. Austin: University of Texas Press, 1981.

Baldick, Chris. *The Concise Oxford Dictionary of Literary Terms*. Oxford: Oxford University Press, 1990.

Balkin, J. M. "Deconstructive Practice and Legal Theory." *Yale Law Journal* 96 (1987): 743–86.

Ball, John, ed. *The Mystery Story*. New York: Penguin, 1978 [1976].

Bao Gong qi'an 包公奇案 (Strange cases of Lord Bao). Taibei: Wenguo shuju, n.d. [1996].

Bao gongan 包公案 (Cases of Lord Bao). Beijing: Baowentang, 1985. Based on the *Longtu gongan*, Ming edition with 100 stories in 10 *juan*.

Bao Zheng 包拯. *Bao Zheng wen ji* 包拯文集 (The works of Bao Zheng). Taibei: Jieyou chubanshe, 1993.

Bargainnier, Earl F., and George N. Dove, eds. *Cops and Constables: American and British Fictional Policemen*. Bowling Green, Ohio: Popular Press, 1986.

Barmé, Geremie, and Bennett Lee, trans. *The Wounded: New Stories of the Cultural Revolution, 77–78*. Hong Kong: Joint Publishing, 1979.

Barnett, A. Doak. *Cadres, Bureaucracy, and Political Power in Communist China*. New York: Columbia University Press, 1967.

Barthes, Roland. *The Eiffel Tower and Other Mythologies*. Richard Howard, trans. New York: Hill and Wang, 1979.

———. *Mythologies*. Annette Lavers, trans. New York: Hill and Wang, 1972.

Barzun, Jacques. "Detection and the Literary Art." In Nevins, ed., *The Mystery Writer's Art*, pp. 248–62.

"The Basic Character of Crime in Contemporary China." Michael Dutton, trans. *China Quarterly* 149 (Mar. 1997): 160–77. Originally prepared by the Ministry of Public Security Research Unit Number Five, 1989. Internal.

Baudelaire, Charles. "Le peintre de la vie moderne" (The painter of modern life). In *Oeuvres complètes*, Yves Florenne, ed., Vol. 3: 453–507. Paris: Le Club français du livre, 1966.

Bauer, Wolfgang. "The Tradition of the 'Criminal Cases of Master Pao' *Pao-kung-an (Lung-t'u kung-an)*." *Oriens* 23/24 (1974): 433–49.

Baum, Richard. "Modernization and Legal Reform in Post-Mao China: The Rebirth of Socialist Legality." *Studies in Comparative Communism* 19, no. 2 (Summer 1986): 69–103.

Bayley, David H. *Forces of Order: Policing Modern Japan*. Berkeley: University of California Press, 1991 [1976].

Beebee, Thomas O. *The Ideology of Genre: A Comparative Study of Generic Instability*. University Park: Pennsylvania State University Press, 1994.

Bell, Ian A., and Graham Daldry, eds. *Watching the Detectives: Essays on Crime Fiction*. Basingstoke, England: Macmillan, 1990.

Bellow, Gary, and Martha Minow, eds. *Law Stories*. Ann Arbor: University of Michigan Press, 1996.

Bennett, Donna. "The Detective Story: Towards a Definition of Genre." *PTL* 4 (1979): 233–66.

Bennett, Tony. "Marxism and Popular Fiction." *Literature and History* 7, no. 2 (1981): 138–65.

————. *Popular Fiction: Technology, Ideology, Production, Reading.* London: Routledge, 1990.

Benstock, Bernard, ed. *Art in Crime Writing: Essays on Detective Fiction.* New York: St. Martin's, 1983.

Berman, Harold J. "Soviet Perspectives on Chinese Law." In J. Cohen, ed., *Contemporary Chinese Law*, pp. 313–27.

Bernhardt, Kathryn, and Philip C. C. Huang, eds. *Civil Law in Qing and Republican China.* Stanford, Calif.: Stanford University Press, 1994.

Bettelheim, Bruno. *The Uses of Enchantment.* New York: Knopf, 1976.

Bhabha, Homi K. *The Location of Culture.* London: Routledge, 1994.

————. "Remembering Fanon: Self, Psyche and the Colonial Condition." In P. Williams and Chrisman, eds., *Colonial Discourse and Post-Colonial Theory*, pp. 112–123.

Bintliff, Russell. *Police Procedural: A Writer's Guide to the Police and How They Work.* Cincinnati: Writer's Digest Books, 1993.

Binyon, T. J. *Murder Will Out: The Detective in Fiction.* Oxford: Oxford University Press, 1989.

Black, Joel. *The Aesthetics of Murder.* Baltimore: Johns Hopkins University Press, 1991.

Blader, Susan Roberta. "A Critical Study of *San-hsia wu-yi* and [Its] Relationship to the *Lung-t'u kung-an* Song-book." Ph.D. diss., University of Pennsylvania, 1977.

Blonde, Didier. *Les Voleurs de visage: Sur quelques cas troublants de changement d'identité: Rocambole, Arsène Lupin, Fantômas et Cie* (Face-stealers: On some troubling cases of identity change). Paris: A.-M. Métailié, 1972.

Bloom, Harold. *The Anxiety of Influence.* New York: Oxford University Press, 1973.

Bodde, Derk. "Age, Youth, and Infirmity in the Law of Ch'ing China." In J. Cohen, Edwards, and Chen, eds. *Essays on China's Legal Tradition*, pp. 137–69.

Bodde, Derk, and Clarence Morris. *Law in Imperial China: Exemplified by 190 Ch'ing Dynasty Cases (Translated from the Hsing-an hui-lan).* Cambridge, Mass.: Harvard University Press, 1967.

Boileau-Narcejac. *La Poudrière* (The powder keg). Paris: Librairie des Champs-Élysées, 1987. Boileau-Narcejac is a pseudonym for Pierre Boileau and Thomas Narcejac; Narcejac is itself a pseudonym for Pierre Ayraud.

————. *Le Roman policier* (Detective fiction). Paris: Presses universitaires de France, 1975.

Bonavia, David. *The Chinese: A Portrait.* Harmondsworth, Eng.: Penguin, 1984 [1980].

Borges, Jorge Luis. *Other Inquisitions, 1937–1952.* Austin: University of Texas Press, 1964.

Bourdieu, Pierre. *The Field of Cultural Production: Essays on Art and Literature.* Randal Johnson, ed. and intro. New York: Columbia University Press, 1993.

———. "The Force of Law: Toward a Sociology of the Juridical Field." Richard Terdiman, trans. and intro. *Hastings Law Journal* 38, no. 5 (July 1987): 805–53.

Brand, Joseph L. "How Can We Know the Dancer from the Dance?" *George Washington Law Review* 57 (1989): 1018–28.

Brokaw, Cynthia J. *The Ledgers of Merit and Demerit: Social Change and Moral Order in Late Imperial China.* Princeton, N.J.: Princeton University Press, 1991.

Brooks, Peter. *The Melodramatic Imagination: Balzac, Henry James, Melodrama, and the Mode of Excess.* New Haven, Conn.: Yale University Press, 1976.

Brooks, Peter, and Paul Gewirtz, eds. *Law's Stories: Narrative and Rhetoric in the Law.* New Haven, Conn.: Yale University Press, 1996.

Buoye, Thomas. "Suddenly Murderous Intent Arose: Bureaucratization and Benevolence in Eighteenth-Century Homicide Reports." *Late Imperial China* 16, no. 2 (Dec. 1995): 62–95.

Cabral, Amilcar. "National Liberation and Culture." In P. Williams and Chrisman, eds., *Colonial Discourse and Post-Colonial Theory,* pp. 53–65.

Cao Yumo 曹玉模. "Nü tingzhang" 女庭長 (The female head judge). *Zuopin,* Feb. 1982, pp. 10–16.

Carr, John C. *The Craft of Crime: Conversations with Crime Writers.* Boston: Houghton Mifflin, 1983.

Cassiday, Bruce, ed. *Roots of Detection: The Art of Deduction Before Sherlock Holmes.* New York: Ungar, 1983.

Cawelti, John G. *Adventure, Mystery, and Romance.* Chicago: University of Chicago Press, 1976.

Celebrated Cases of Judge Dee (Dee Goong An): An Authentic Eighteenth-Century Chinese Detective Novel. Robert Van Gulik, trans. New York: Dover, 1976.

Cen Ying 岑螢, ed. *Zhongguo dalu zhentan xiaoshuo xuan* 中國大陸偵探小説選 (A selection of Chinese mainland detective stories). Hong Kong: Tongjin chubanshe, n.d. [1981?].

———. *Zhongguo dalu zuian xiaoshuo xuan* 中國大陸罪案小説選 (A selection of Chinese mainland crime stories). Hong Kong: Tongjin chubanshe, n. d. [1981?].

Cen Zhijing 岑之京 and Wang Wenjin 王文錦. "Yi zun jin foxiang" 一尊金佛像 (A gold Buddha). In Cen Ying, ed., *Zhongguo dalu zhentan,* pp. 46–56. Reprinted from *Guangzhou wenyi* 1980, no. 1.

Champigny, Robert. *What Will Have Happened: A Philosophical and Technical Essay on Mystery Stories.* Bloomington: Indiana University Press, 1977.

Chang, Wejen [Zhang Weiren]. "Legal Education in Ch'ing China." In Elman and Woodside, eds., *Education and Society in Late Imperial China,* pp. 292–339.

Charney, Hanna. *The Detective Novel of Manners: Hedonism, Morality, and the Life of Reason.* Rutherford, N.J.: Fairleigh Dickinson University Press, 1981.

Chen, Albert Hung-yee. *An Introduction to the Legal System of the People's Republic of China.* Singapore: Butterworths Asia, 1992.

Chen Dieyi 陳蝶衣. "Xia dao Lu Ping de suzaozhe—Sun Liaohong" 俠盜魯平 的塑造者──孫了紅 (The creator of the chivalrous thief Lu Ping—Sun Liaohong). *Wan xiang* 3 (Sept. 5, 1975): 36–38.

[Chen] Huangmei [陳] 荒煤. "Guanyu fazhi wenxue" 關於法制文學 (On legal system literature). *Zhuomuniao* 74 (Mar. 1996): 139–41.

Chen Pingyuan 陳平原. *Ershi shiji Zhongguo xiaoshuo shi; Diyi juan, 1897–1916* 二十世紀中國小說史；第一卷 (A history of Chinese fiction in the twentieth century; vol. 1: 1897–1916). Beijing: Beijing Daxue chubanshe, 1989.

———. *Qiangu wenren xiake meng: Wuxia xiaoshuo leixing yanjiu* 千古文人俠 客夢：武俠小說類型研究 (Age-old chivalric dreams of the literati: Typological study of martial-arts fiction). Beijing: Renmin wenxue chubanshe, 1992.

———. *Zhongguo xiaoshuo xushi moshi de zhuanbian* 中國小說敘事模式的轉 變 (The transformation of narrative styles in Chinese fiction). Shanghai: Shanghai renmin chubanshe, 1988.

Chen Shunlie 陳順烈. *Tangyin bishi xuan* 棠陰比事選 (Selections from the *Parallel Cases Solved by Just and Benevolent Officials*). Beijing: Qunzhong chubanshe, 1983.

Chen Yuanbin. *The Story of Qiuju*. Beijing: Panda, 1995.

———. 陳源斌. "Tian xing" 天行 (Heaven's course). In Chen Yuanbin, *Wan jia susong*, pp. 166–224.

———. *Wan jia susong* 萬家訴訟 (The Wan family sues). Beijing: Zhongguo qingnian chubanshe, 1992.

———. "Wan jia susong." In Chen Yuanbin, *Wan jia susong*, pp. 367–412. Reprinted from *Zhongguo zuojia* 1991, no. 3 (May 10, 1991): 4–20.

Cheng Xiaoqing 程小青. "Bai shajin" 白紗巾 (The white handkerchief). *CXQWJ* [*Cheng Xiaoqing wen ji*] 1: 124–208.

———. "Bieye zhi guai" 別墅之怪 (Ghosts in the villa). *CXQWJ* 4: 295–308.

———. *Cheng Xiaoqing wen ji: Huo Sang tan'an xuan* [*CXQWJ*] 程小青文集： 霍桑探案選 (Works of Cheng Xiaoqing: Selections from the cases of Huo Sang). 4 vols. Nanjing: Zhongguo wenlian chuban gongsi, 1986.

———. "Chuang" 窗 (Window). *HSTAJ* [*Huo Sang tan'an ji*] 7: 331–75.

———. "Cong 'shi er bu jian' shuo dao zhentan xiaoshuo" 從 "視而不見" 說 到偵探小說 (Considering the detective story from the standpoint of "looking without seeing"). *Shanhu* 2, no. 1 (Jan. 1, 1933): 1–7.

———. *Dashucun xue an* 大樹村血案 (The bloody case at Big Tree Village). Shanghai: Shanghai wenhua chubanshe, 1956.

———. "Huangpu Jiang zhong" 黃浦江中 (On the Huangpu River). *CXQWJ* 2: 1–46.

———. *Huo Sang tan'an ji* [*HSTAJ*] 霍桑探案集 (Collected cases of Huo Sang). 13 vols. Beijing: Qunzhong chubanshe, 1986–88.

———. "Huo shi" 活尸 (A living corpse). *CXQWJ* 4: 96–294.

———. "Jiangnan Yan" 江南燕 (Criminal's nickname; lit., "Swallow of the south"). *HSTAJ* 2: 1–69. Rendition in the vernacular by Cheng Yuzhen.

———. *Jianlu shici yigao* 蘭廬詩詞遺稿 (Posthumous poetry from the Humble Cocoon [Study]). New York: Lianhe yinshu gongsi, afterword 1982.

———. "Juezhi ji" 角智記 (Battle of wits), the first story. *Xiaoshuo daguan* 9 (Mar. 1917): 1–21. This story, not individually named in this periodical publication, was later translated into the vernacular by Cheng Yuzhen and the author and evidently reprinted in a work called *Long hu dou* 龍虎鬥, there named "Zuanshi xiangquan."

———. "Juezhi ji (2)" (Battle of wits, second story). *Xiaoshuo daguan* 10 (June 1917): 1–21. This story was not individually named in this periodical publication, but evidently was later translated into the vernacular and reprinted in a work called *Long hu dou.*

———. "Kexue de zhentanshu" 科學的偵探術 (Techniques of scientific detection). *Zhentan shijie* 18, 19, 20 (Feb.–Mar. 1923?).

———. "Lun xia xue" 輪下血 (Blood under the wheels). *CXQWJ* 1: 1–39.

———. "Maoeryan" 貓兒眼 (Cat's eye). *HSTAJ* 9: 111–30.

———. "Qing jun ru weng" 請君入瓮 (Come into my parlor . . .). *HSTAJ* 10: 281–99.

———. "Shi shang ming" 石上名 (The name on the stone). *Xiaoshuo daguan* 14 (1919).

———. "Tan zhentan xiaoshuo" 談偵探小説 (On detective fiction). *Hong meigui* 5, nos. 11, 12 (May 11 and 21, 1929).

———. "Wu gong moying" 舞宮魔影 (Phantom of the dance palace). *CXQWJ* 2: 303–94.

———. "Wu hou de guisu" 舞後的歸宿 (After the ball). *CXQWJ* 3: 69–281.

———. "Xian hunyin" 險婚姻 (Just before the wedding). *CXQWJ* 4: 1–43.

———. "Yeban husheng" 夜半呼聲 (The cry at midnight). *CXQWJ* 1: 40–123.

———. *Zhentan taidou: Cheng Xiaoqing* 偵探泰斗: 程小青 (The super detective: Cheng Xiaoqing). Fan Boqun 范伯群, ed. Taibei: Yeqiang chubanshe, 1993.

———. "Zhentan xiaoshuo de duofangmian" 偵探小説的多方面 (The many-sidedness of the detective story). In Rui Heshi, Fan Boqun, et al., eds., *Yuanyang hudie pai wenxue ziliao*, 1: 68–77.

———. "Zhentan xiaoshuo he kexue" 偵探小説和科學 (The detective story and science). *Zhentan shijie* 13 (Dec. 1922?).

———. "Zhentan xiaoshuo zuofa zhi guanjian" 偵探小説作法之管見 (My humble opinion on the art of the detective story). *Zhentan shijie* 1, 2, 3 (1923): 3–4, 7–8, 10.

———. "Zi xinjian" 紫信箋 (The purple letter). *CXQWJ* 1: 209–303.

———. "Zuanshi xiangquan" 鑽石項圈 (The diamond necklace). In his *Long hu dou* (Dragon vs. tiger). "Zuanshi xiangquan" only is reprinted in Cheng's *Zhentan taidou*, pp. 197–256. This story was originally written in classical Chinese and printed as the first story of a series called "Juezhi ji" (Battle of wits).

Cheung, Tai Ming. "Guarding China's Domestic Front Line: The People's Armed Police and China's Stability." *China Quarterly* 146 (June 1996): 525–47.

Chin, Yin-lien C., Yetta S. Center, and Mildred Ross, eds. *"The Stone Lion" and Other Chinese Detective Stories.* Armonk, N.Y.: M. E. Sharpe, 1992.

China: The Revolution Is Dead—Long Live the Revolution. The 70's, ed. Kan San, intro. Montreal: Black Rose Books, 1979 [1977].

Chow, Kai-wing. *The Rise of Confucian Ritualism in Late Imperial China: Ethics, Classics, and Lineage Discourse.* Stanford, Calif.: Stanford University Press, 1994.

Chow Tse-tsung. *The May Fourth Movement: Intellectual Revolution in China.* Stanford, Calif.: Stanford University Press, 1967 [1960].

Christian, Ed, ed. *The Post-Colonial Detective.* New York: St. Martin's, forthcoming.

Ch'ü, T'ung-tsu. *Law and Society in Traditional China.* Paris: Mouton, 1965.

Cihai 辭海 (Sea of words [dictionary]). 3 vols. Shanghai: Shanghai cishu chubanshe, 1979.

Cihai. 3 vols. Shanghai: Shanghai cishu chubanshe, 1989.

Clarke, Donald C. "Dispute Resolution in China." *Journal of Chinese Law* 5, no. 2 (Fall 1991): 245–96.

———. "The Execution of Civil Judgments in China." In Lubman, ed., *China's Legal Reforms,* pp. 65–81.

———. "Political Power and Authority in Recent Chinese Literature." *China Quarterly* 102 (June 1985): 234–52.

Clarke, Donald C., and James V. Feinerman. "Antagonistic Contradictions: Criminal Law and Human Rights in China." In Lubman, ed., *China's Legal Reforms,* pp. 135–54.

Cohen, Daniel A. *Pillars of Salt, Monuments of Grace: New England Crime Literature and the Origins of American Popular Culture, 1674–1860.* New York: Oxford University Press, 1993.

Cohen, Jerome Alan. *The Criminal Process in the People's Republic of China, 1949–1963: An Introduction.* Cambridge, Mass.: Harvard University Press, 1968.

———, ed. *Contemporary Chinese Law: Research Problems and Perspectives.* Cambridge, Mass.: Harvard University Press, 1970.

Cohen, Jerome Alan, R. Randle Edwards, and Fu-mei Chang Chen, eds. *Essays on China's Legal Tradition.* Princeton, N.J.: Princeton University Press, 1980.

Cohen, Jerome Alan, Soia Mentschikoff, and Ranlet Lincoln. "The Chinese Legal System." *Chicago Today* 3, no. 2 (Spring 1966): 10–14.

Collins, Jim. *Uncommon Cultures: Popular Culture and Post-Modernism.* London: Routledge, 1989.

Comber, Leon, trans. *The Strange Cases of Magistrate Pao: Chinese Tales of Crime and Detection.* Hong Kong: Heinemann (Asia), 1972 [1964].

Comte-Sponville, André, and François George. *Arsène Lupin: Gentilhomme-philosopheur* (Arsène Lupin: Gentleman philosopher). Paris: Éditions du Félin, 1996.

Conceison, Claire. "The Occidental Other on the Chinese Stage: Cultural Cross-Examination in Guo Shixing's *Bird Man.*" *Asian Theatre Journal* 15, no. 1 (Spring 1998): 87–100.

Cong Weixi 從維熙 and Liang Jianhua 梁劍華. "Daqiang xia de hong yulan" 大牆下的紅玉蘭 (Blood-stained magnolias below the Big Wall). In Cen Ying, ed., *Zhongguo dalu zuian*, pp. 255–83. Reprinted from *Dianying xinzuo* 1979, no. 6.

The Constitution of the People's Republic of China. Peking: Foreign Languages Press, 1975.

The Constitution of the People's Republic of China. Peking: Foreign Languages Press, 1978.

The Constitution of the People's Republic of China. Beijing: Foreign Languages Press, 1983.

Creel, Herrlee Glessner. "Legal Institutions and Procedures During the Chou Dynasty." In J. Cohen, Edwards, and Chen, eds., *Essays on China's Legal Tradition*, pp. 26–55.

The Criminal Law and the Criminal Procedure Law of China. Beijing: Foreign Languages Press, 1984.

Culler, Jonathan. *Structuralist Poetics: Structuralism, Linguistics, and the Study of Literature*. Ithaca, N.Y.: Cornell University Press, 1975.

Da Qing lüli 大清律例 (The Great Qing code). 1740.

Da Qing lüli tongkao jiaozhu 大清律例通考校注 (The Great Qing code, comprehensive compendium with annotations). Ma Jianshi 馬建石 and Yang Yutang 楊育棠, eds. Beijing: Zhongguo Zhengfa Daxue chubanshe, 1992.

Dangdai Zhongguo gongan wenxue daxi 當代中國公安文學大系 (Compendium of contemporary Chinese police literature). 20 vols. projected. Beijing: Qunzhong chubanshe, 1996–.

Davis, Michael C., ed. *Human Rights and Chinese Values: Legal, Philosophical, and Political Perspectives*. Hong Kong: Oxford University Press, 1995.

Derouard, Jacques. *Maurice Leblanc: Arsène Lupin malgré lui* (Maurice Leblanc: Arsène Lupin in spite of himself). Paris: Séguier, 1989.

"The Detection Club Oath." In Haycraft, ed., *The Art of the Mystery Story*, pp. 197–99.

DeWoskin, Kenneth J. "On Narrative Revolutions." *Chinese Literature: Essays, Articles, Reviews* 5, nos. 1/2 (July 1983): 29–45.

———. "The Six Dynasties *Chih-kuai* and the Birth of Fiction." In Plaks, ed., *Chinese Narrative*, pp. 21–52.

Dicks, Anthony R. "The Chinese Legal System: Reforms in the Balance." *China Quarterly* 119 (Sept. 1989): 540–76.

———. "Compartmentalized Law and Judicial Restraint: An Inductive View of Some Jurisdictional Barriers to Reform." In Lubman, ed., *China's Legal Reforms*, pp. 82–109.

Dikötter, Frank. "Crime and Punishment in Post-Liberation China: The Prisoners of a Beijing Gaol in the 1950s." *China Quarterly* 149 (Mar. 1997): 147–59.

Dimock, Wai Chee. *Residues of Justice: Literature, Law, Philosophy*. Berkeley: University of California Press, 1996.

Dine, S. S. Van. "Twenty Rules for Writing Detective Stories." In Haycraft, ed., *The Art of the Mystery Story*, pp. 189–93.

Ding, Naifei. "Tears of *Ressentiment*; or, Zhang Zhupo's *Jin Ping Mei*." *positions* 3, no. 3 (Winter 1995): 663–94.

Dirlik, Arif. *The Postcolonial Aura: Third World Criticism in the Age of Global Capitalism*. Boulder, Colo.: Westview, 1997.

Docherty, Brian, ed. *American Crime Fiction: Studies in the Genre*. New York: St. Martin's, 1988.

Donaldson, Norman. "R. Austin Freeman: The Invention of Inversion." In Nevins, ed., *The Mystery Writer's Art*, pp. 79–87.

Doody, Margaret Anne. *The True Story of the Novel*. New Brunswick, N.J.: Rutgers University Press, 1996.

Dore, Ronald Philip. *Land Reform in Japan*. London: Oxford University Press, 1959.

Douzinas, Costas, and Ronnie Warrington, with Shaun McVeigh. *Postmodern Jurisprudence: The Law of Text in the Texts of Law*. London: Routledge, 1991.

Dove, George N. *The Police Procedural*. Bowling Green, Ohio: Popular Press, 1982.

——. *Suspense in the Formula Story*. Bowling Green, Ohio: Popular Press, 1989.

Doyle, Sir Arthur Conan. *The Complete Sherlock Holmes*. Garden City, N.Y.: Doubleday, 1930 [1893, 1905].

Du Xichuan and Zhang Lingyuan. *China's Legal System: A General Survey*. Beijing: New World Press, 1990.

Du Yuanming 杜元明. "Wo guan 'gongan wenxue'" 我觀 "公安文學" (How I see "police literature"). *Zhuomuniao* 78 (Nov. 1996): 125–29.

Dubrow, Heather. *Genre*. London: Methuen, 1982.

During, Simon, ed. *The Cultural Studies Reader*. London: Routledge, 1993.

Dutton, Michael R. *Policing and Punishment in China: From Patriarchy to 'the People'*. Cambridge: Cambridge University Press, 1992.

Dworkin, Ronald. "How Law Is Like Literature." In Ledwon, ed., *Law and Literature*, pp. 29–46.

——. *Law's Empire*. Cambridge, Mass.: Harvard University Press, 1986.

Eames, Hugh. *Sleuths, Inc.: Studies of Problem Solvers: Doyle, Simenon, Hammett, Ambler, Chandler*. Philadelphia: J. B. Lippincott, 1978.

Easthope, Antony. *Literary into Cultural Studies*. London: Routledge, 1991.

Eberhard, Wolfram. *Guilt and Sin in Traditional China*. Berkeley: University of California Press, 1967.

Ebrey, Patricia Buckley. *Chu Hsi's Family Rituals: A Twelfth-Century Manual for the Performance of Cappings, Weddings, Funerals, and Ancestral Rites*. Princeton, N.J.: Princeton University Press, 1991.

Eco, Umberto, and Thomas A. Sebeok, eds. *The Sign of Three: Dupin, Holmes, Peirce*. Bloomington: Indiana University Press, 1983.

Egan, Ronald C. *Word, Image, and Deed in the Life of Su Shi*. Cambridge, Mass.: Council on East Asian Studies, Harvard University, 1994.

Eliasoph, Ellen R., and Susan Grueneberg. "Law on Display in China." *China Quarterly* 88 (Dec. 1981): 669–85.

Ellis, John M. *Against Deconstruction*. Princeton, N.J.: Princeton University Press, 1989.

Elman, Benjamin A., and Alexander Woodside, eds. *Education and Society in Late Imperial China, 1600–1900*. Berkeley: University of California Press, 1994.

Epstein, Edward J. "Law and Legitimation in Post-Mao China." In Potter, ed., *Domestic Law Reforms in Post-Mao China*, pp. 19–55.

Escarra, Jean. *Le Droit chinois: Conception et évolution; Institutions législatives et judiciaires; Science et enseignement* (Chinese law: Conception and evolution, legislative and judicial institutions, science and teaching). Pékin: Henri Vetch, 1936.

Falkenhausen, Lothar von. "The Concept of *Wen* in the Ancient Chinese Ancestral Cult." *Chinese Literature: Essays, Articles, Reviews* 18 (Dec. 1996): 1–22.

Faller, Lincoln B. *Crime and Defoe: A New Kind of Writing*. Cambridge: Cambridge University Press, 1993.

Fallis, Greg, and Ruth Greenberg. *Be Your Own Detective*. New York: M. Evans, 1989.

Falü guwen 法律顧問 (Legal consultant [series]). Vol. 6. *Qiangjiezui fali tantao* 搶劫罪法理探討 (Inquiry into the legal principles of the law of theft). Shanghai: Huadong Zhengfa Xueyuan faxue bianjibu, 1983. Internal.

Fan Boqun 范伯群. *Libailiu de hudie meng: Lun yuanyang hudie pai* 禮拜六的蝴蝶夢: 論鴛鴦蝴蝶派 (Saturday butterfly dreams: On the mandarin duck and butterfly school). Beijing: Renmin wenxue chubanshe, 1989.

Fan Mu 范牡, comp. "Bao Gong de chuanshuo" 包公的傳説 (Legends about Lord Bao). *Minjian wenxue* 175 (Aug. 20, 1984): 30–35.

———. "Minjian gongan gushi" 民間公案故事 (Folk stories about criminal cases). *Minjian wenxue* 167 (Dec. 20, 1983): 91–94.

Fan Ping 汎平 and Xiao Fan 曉凡. "Xiong zhang yin" 熊掌印 (Bear pawprints). *Wenxue yuekan* 10 (Apr. 1956): 42–45.

Fanon, Frantz. "On National Culture." In P. Williams and Chrisman, eds., *Colonial Discourse and Post-Colonial Theory*, pp. 36–52.

Farmer, Edward L. "Social Regulations of the First Ming Emperor: Orthodoxy as a Function of Authority." In Kwang-Ching Liu, ed., *Orthodoxy in Late Imperial China*, pp. 103–25.

Fazhi yu renzhi wenti taolun ji 法治與人治問題討論集 (Discussions on the question of rule of law versus rule by man). Beijing: Qunzhong chubanshe, 1981.

Feinerman, James V. "Chinese Participation in the International Legal Order: Rogue Elephant or Team Player?" In Lubman, ed., *China's Legal Reforms*, pp. 186–210.

Feng Mu 馮牧. "Guanyu 'fazhi wenxue' de suigan" 關於 "法制文學" 的隨感 (My feelings about "legal system literature"). *Zhuomuniao* 65 (Sept. 1994): 120–21.

Fish, Stanley. "Don't Know Much About the Middle Ages: Posner on Law and Literature." *Yale Law Journal* 97, no. 4 (Mar. 1988): 777–93.

Fitzgerald, John. *Awakening China: Politics, Culture, and Class in the Nationalist Revolution.* Stanford, Calif.: Stanford University Press, 1996.

Folsom, Ralph H., John H. Minan, and Lee Ann Otto. *Law and Politics in the People's Republic of China in a Nutshell.* St. Paul, Minn.: West, 1992.

Fong, Gilbert Chee Fun. "Time in *Nine Murders*: Western Influence and Domestic Tradition." In Milena Doleželová-Velingerová, ed., *The Chinese Novel at the Turn of the Century,* pp. 116–28. Toronto: University of Toronto Press, 1980.

Forster, E. M. *Aspects of the Novel.* New York: Harcourt, Brace, and World, 1927.

Foucault, Michel. *Discipline and Punish: The Birth of the Prison.* Alan Sheridan, trans. New York: Vintage, 1995.

———. *The Order of Things: An Archaeology of the Human Sciences.* New York: Pantheon, 1970.

France, Peter, ed. *The New Oxford Companion to Literature in French.* Oxford: Clarendon Press, 1995.

Friedland, M. L., ed. *Rough Justice: Essays on Crime in Literature.* Toronto: University of Toronto Press, 1991.

Friedman, Lawrence M. *Crime and Punishment in American History.* New York: Basic Books, 1993.

Fruehauf, Heinrich. "Urban Exoticism in Modern and Contemporary Chinese Literature." In Widmer and Wang, eds., *From May Fourth to June Fourth,* pp. 133–64.

Frye, Northrop. *Anatomy of Criticism: Four Essays.* Princeton, N.J.: Princeton University Press, 1957.

Furth, Charlotte. "The Patriarch's Legacy: Household Instructions and the Transmission of Orthodox Values." In Kwang-Ching Liu, ed., *Orthodoxy in Late Imperial China,* pp. 187–211.

Gandhi, Leela. *Postcolonial Theory: A Critical Introduction.* New York: Columbia University Press, 1998.

Gao Jianping 高涧平. *Shenmei de lixing yu jiqing* 審美的理性與激情 (Aesthetic reason and passion). Beijing: Qunzhong chubanshe, 1991.

Gao Mingxuan 高銘喧, ed. *Xin Zhongguo xingfa kexue jianshi* 新中國刑法科學簡史 (Brief history of the science of criminal law in New China). Beijing: Zhongguo Renmin Gongan Daxue chubanshe, 1993.

Garelick, Rhonda K. *Rising Star: Dandyism, Gender, and Performance in the Fin de Siècle.* Princeton, N.J.: Princeton University Press, 1998.

Gelatt, Timothy A. *Criminal Justice with Chinese Characteristics: China's Criminal Process and Violations of Human Rights.* New York: Lawyers Committee for Human Rights, 1993.

Gemmette, Elizabeth Villiers. *Law and Literature: Joining the Class Action.* Special issue of the *Valparaiso University Law Review* 29, no. 2 (Spring 1995): 665–859.

Geng Longxiang 耿龍祥. "Shidai zhi jiaozi" 時代之驕子 (Proud child of the age). *Zhongguo fazhi wenxue* 7 (Jan. 18, 1987): 93–95.

Giffone, Anthony. "The Representation of Victorian England in the Contemporary Detective Novel." In Putney, King, and Sugarman, eds., *Sherlock Holmes*, pp. 146–69.

Gilbert, Elliot L. *The World of Mystery Fiction*. Bowling Green, Ohio: Popular Press, 1983.

———. *The World of Mystery Fiction: A Guide*. San Diego: University Extension, University of California, San Diego, and Publisher's Inc., 1978.

Ginsburgs, George, and Arthur Stahnke. "The Genesis of the People's Procuratorate in Communist China, 1949–1951." *China Quarterly* 20 (Oct.– Dec. 1964): 1–37.

———. "The People's Procuratorate in Communist China: The Period of Maturation, 1951–54." *China Quarterly* 24 (Oct.–Dec. 1965): 53–91.

Gong Pengcheng 龔鵬程. *Jindai sixiangshi sanlun* 近代思想史散論 (Essays on modern intellectual history). Taibei: Dongda tushu gongsi, 1991.

Gongan xiaoshuo yanjiu ziliao 公案小説研究資料 (Research materials on court case fiction). Taibei: Tianyi chubanshe, 1983. *Zhongguo gudian xiaoshuo yanjiu ziliao huibian* 中國古典小説研究資料彙編 (Compendium of research materials on Chinese classic fiction), vol. 322.

Gray, W. Russel. "Future Sherlocks Meet Future Shock: Detectives in Science Fiction." In Putney, King, and Sugarman, eds., *Sherlock Holmes*, pp. 222–32.

The Great Qing Code. William C. Jones, with Tianquan Cheng and Yongling Jiang, trans. Oxford: Clarendon Press, 1994.

Greene, Douglas G. "John Dickson Carr: Fairplay Foremost." *The Armchair Detective* 28, no. 2 (Spring 1995): 160–66.

Grossvogel, David I. *Mystery and Its Fictions: From Oedipus to Agatha Christie*. Baltimore: Johns Hopkins University Press, 1979.

Guillén, Claudio. *The Challenge of Comparative Literature*. Cola Franzen, trans. Cambridge, Mass.: Harvard University Press, 1993.

———. "Genre and Countergenre: The Discovery of the Picaresque." In *Literature as System: Essays Toward the Theory of Literary History*, pp. 135–58. Princeton, N.J.: Princeton University Press, 1971.

Guo Qiao 果俏 and Xing Zhe 興詰. "Taoyuan Jie qi'an" 桃園街奇案 (The strange case on Taoyuan Street). In Cen Ying, ed., *Zhongguo dalu zhentan*, pp. 132–59. Reprinted from *Yalu Jiang* 1981, no. 1.

Guy, R. Kent. *The Emperor's Four Treasuries: Scholars and the State in the Late Ch'ien-lung Era*. Cambridge, Mass.: Council on East Asian Studies, Harvard University, 1987.

Hägg, Tomas. *The Novel in Antiquity*. Berkeley: University of California Press, 1983.

Hai Gangfeng xiansheng juguan gongan zhuan 海剛峰先生居官公案傳 (Account of Mr. Hai Rui's court cases while in office). Beijing: Zhonghua shuju, 1990. Preface by Li Chunfang 李春芳, 1606.

Hall, David L., and Roger T. Ames. *Thinking Through Confucius*. Albany: State University of New York Press, 1987.

Hall, Trevor H. *Sherlock Holmes and His Creator*. London: Duckworth, 1978.

Han Jiang 寒江. "Dui 'zhentan xiaoshuo' de yi dian yijian" 對 "偵探小說" 的 一點意見 (A humble opinion on "detective fiction"). *Wenxue yuekan* 11 (May 1956): 41, 79–80.

Hanan, Patrick. *The Chinese Vernacular Story*. Cambridge, Mass.: Harvard University Press, 1981.

———. "*Judge Bao's Hundred Cases* Reconstructed." *Harvard Journal of Asiatic Studies* 40, no. 2 (Dec. 1980): 301–23.

Hartman, Geoffrey H. "Literature High and Low: The Case of the Mystery Story." In *The Fate of Reading, and Other Essays*, pp. 203–22. Chicago: University of Chicago Press, 1975.

Haut, Woody. *Pulp Culture: Hardboiled Fiction and the Cold War*. London: Serpent's Tail, 1995.

Haycraft, Howard. *Murder for Pleasure: The Life and Times of the Detective Story*. New York: Appleton-Century, 1941.

———, ed. *The Art of the Mystery Story*. New York: Grosset and Dunlap, 1946.

Hayden, George A. *Crime and Punishment in Medieval Chinese Drama: Three Judge Pao Plays*. Cambridge, Mass.: Council on East Asian Studies, Harvard University, 1978.

———. "The Legend of Judge Pao: From the Beginnings Through the Yüan Drama." In Laurence G. Thompson, ed., *Studia Asiatica*, pp. 339–55. San Francisco: Chinese Materials Center, 1975.

He Puzhai 何樸齋. "Lu Bin ruyu" 魯賓入獄 (Lu Bin goes to prison). *Zhentan shijie* 10 (1923): 1–12.

The Heart of the Dragon (television film series). Alasdair Clayre, executive producer. London: Antelope-Sino-Hawkshead, 1984.

Hegel, Robert E. *The Novel in Seventeenth-Century China*. New York: Columbia University Press, 1981.

———. *Reading Illustrated Fiction in Late Imperial China*. Stanford: Stanford University Press, 1998.

———. "Traditional Chinese Fiction—The State of the Field." *Journal of Asian Studies* 53, no. 2 (May 1994): 394–426.

Heilbrun, Carolyn G. *Hamlet's Mother and Other Women*. New York: Columbia University Press, 1990.

Hernadi, Paul. *Beyond Genre: New Directions in Literary Classification*. Ithaca, N.Y.: Cornell University Press, 1972.

Higgins, Ellen F. "The Female Rivals of Sherlock Holmes: Alternative Sleuths, Alternative Heroes." In Putney, King, and Sugarman, eds. *Sherlock Holmes*, pp. 135–45.

Hilfer, Tony. *The Crime Novel: A Deviant Genre*. Austin: University of Texas Press, 1990.

Hockx, Michel. "The Literary Association (Wenxue yanjiu hui, 1920–1947) and the Literary Field of Early Republican China." *China Quarterly* 153 (Mar. 1998): 49–81.

Hollingsworth, Keith. *The Newgate Novel, 1830–1847.* Detroit: Wayne State University Press, 1963.

Holman, C. Hugh. *A Handbook to Literature.* 3d ed. Indianapolis: Bobbs-Merrill, 1972 [1936, 1960].

Holquist, Michael. "Whodunit and Other Questions: Metaphysical Detective Stories in Post-War Fiction." In Most and Stowe, eds., *The Poetics of Murder*, pp. 149–74.

Hone, Ralph E. *Dorothy L. Sayers: A Literary Biography.* Kent, Ohio: Kent State University Press, 1979.

Honig, Emily. *Creating Chinese Ethnicity: Subei People in Shanghai, 1850–1980.* New Haven, Conn.: Yale University Press, 1992.

Hou Zhongyi 侯忠義. *Han Wei Liuchao xiaoshuo shi* 漢魏六朝小説史 (A history of fiction in the Han, Wei, and Six Dynasties). Shenyang: Chunfeng wenyi chubanshe, 1989.

Hsia, C. T. *A History of Modern Chinese Fiction.* 2d ed. New Haven, Conn.: Yale University Press, 1971.

———. "Hsü Chen-ya's *Yü-li hun*: An Essay in Literary History and Criticism." In Liu Ts'un-yan, ed., *Chinese Middlebrow Fiction*, pp. 199–240.

———. "The Scholar-Novelist and Chinese Culture: A Reappraisal of *Ching-hua Yuan*." In Plaks, ed., *Chinese Narrative*, pp. 266–305.

Hsia, Tao-tai. "Chinese Legal Publications: An Appraisal." In J. Cohen, ed., *Contemporary Chinese Law*, pp. 20–83.

Hsu Dau-lin 徐道鄰. "Crime and Cosmic Order." *Harvard Journal of Asiatic Studies* 30 (1970): 111–25.

Hu Shi 胡適. "*San xia wu yi xu*" 三俠五義序 (Preface to *Three Heroes and Five Gallants*). In *Hu Shi wencun* 胡適文存 (Writings of Hu Shi), 3: 441–72. Taibei: Yuandong tushu gongsi, 1953 [1930].

Huang Liu-hung. *A Complete Book Concerning Happiness and Benevolence: A Manual for Local Magistrates in Seventeenth-Century China.* Djang Chu, ed. and trans. Tucson: University of Arizona Press, 1984.

Huang, Philip C. C. *Civil Justice in China: Representation and Practice in the Qing.* Stanford, Calif.: Stanford University Press, 1996.

Huang Yanbo 黃岩柏. *Zhongguo gongan xiaoshuo shi* 中國公案小説史 (A history of Chinese court case fiction). Shenyang: Liaoning renmin chubanshe, 1991.

Huang Zexin 黃澤新 and Song Anna 宋安娜. "Dui woguo zhentan xiaoshuo zou xiang shijie de ji dian sikao" 對我國偵探小説走向世界的幾點思考 (A few thoughts about the internationalization of our country's detective fiction). *Zhuomuniao* 77 (Sept. 1996): 135–41.

Huang Ziping 黃子平 (pseud. Hu Ang 胡昂). "Yu 'taren' gong wu" 與 "他人" 共舞. *Jintian* 16 (1992): 205–12. Translated as "Dances with the Other—Writing at a Critical Moment." Mei S. Chang de Huang, trans. In Henry Y. H. Zhao and John Cayley, eds., *Abandoned Wine: Chinese Writing Today*, pp. 245–54. London: Wellsweep, 1996.

Hühn, Peter. "The Detective as Reader: Narrativity and Reading Concepts in Detective Fiction." *Modern Fiction Studies* 33, no. 3 (Autumn 1987): 451–66.

Hulsewé, A. F. P. *Remnants of Han Law.* Leiden: E. J. Brill, 1955.

Human Rights in China. *China Rights Forum.* New York.

Human Rights Watch. *Human Rights Watch/Asia.* New York.

Hung, Chang-tai. *Going to the People: Chinese Intellectuals and Folk Literature, 1918–1937.* Cambridge, Mass.: Council on East Asian Studies, Harvard University, 1985.

Hutcheon, Linda. *A Poetics of Postmodernism: History, Theory, Fiction.* London: Routledge, 1988.

Idema, W[ilt] L. *Chinese Vernacular Fiction: The Formative Period.* Leiden: E. J. Brill, 1974.

Idema, Wilt, and Lloyd Haft. *A Guide to Chinese Literature.* Ann Arbor: Center for Chinese Studies, University of Michigan, 1997.

Idema, W[ilt] L., and E. Zürcher, eds. *Thought and Law in Qin and Han China.* Leiden: E. J. Brill, 1990.

The I-li, or Book of Etiquette and Ceremonial. John Steele, trans. Taipei: Ch'eng-wen, 1966 [1917].

Irons, Glenwood. "New Women Detectives: G Is for Gender-Bending." In Glenwood Irons, ed., *Gender, Language, and Myth: Essays on Popular Narrative,* pp. 127–41. Toronto: University of Toronto Press, 1992.

Irwin, John T. *The Mystery to a Solution: Poe, Borges, and the Analytic Detective Story.* Baltimore: Johns Hopkins University Press, 1994.

Itō Hideo 伊藤秀雄. *Kindai no tantei shōsetsu* 近代の探偵小説 (Modern detective fiction). Tokyo: San'ichi shobo, 1994.

Jameson, Fredric. *The Political Unconscious: Narrative as a Socially Symbolic Act.* Ithaca, N.Y.: Cornell University Press, 1981.

Ji Ming 紀明. "Dai shoukao de 'lüke'" 帶手銬的 "旅客" (The "passenger" in handcuffs). In Cen Ying, ed., *Zhongguo dalu zuian,* pp. 117–44. Reprinted from *Dianying chuangzuo* 1979, no. 9.

Jia Lusheng 賈魯生. "Di'er qudao" 第二渠道 (The second channel). *Baogao wenxue* 7 (July 1988): 2–15.

Jiang Xi 江西 and Xia Guoqiang 夏國強. "Siren zhentan diyi an" 私人偵探第一案 (A private investigator's first case). *Gushi hui* 4 (1988): 46–64.

Jiang Yuan 江園 and Qian Zhengjie 錢正杰. "Zhong Wanquan jiangshu de gu-shi" 鍾萬全講述的故事 (Stories told by Zhong Wanquan). *Minjian wenxue* 210 (July 20, 1987): 20.

Jiaru shi ni zuoan 假如是你作案 (If you were the offender). Beijing: Qunzhong chubanshe, 1990.

Jiekai shizong de mimi 揭開失踪的秘密 (Uncovering the mystery of the missing person). *Hunan gongan* 湖南公安 Editorial Board, ed. Changsha: Hunan renmin chubanshe, 1980.

Jin Han 金漢, Feng Yunqing 馮雲青, and Li Xinshou 李新守, eds. *Xin bian*

Zhongguo dangdai wenxue fazhanshi 新編中國當代文學發展史 (History of the development of contemporary Chinese literature, new edition). Hangzhou: Hangzhou Daxue chubanshe, 1992.

Johnson, David, Andrew J. Nathan, and Evelyn S. Rawski, eds. *Popular Culture in Late Imperial China.* Berkeley: University of California Press, 1985.

Jones, Andrew F. *Like a Knife: Ideology and Genre in Contemporary Chinese Popular Music.* Ithaca, N.Y.: Cornell University East Asia Program, 1992.

Jones, William C. "The Significance of the *Opinion* of the Supreme People's Court for Civil Law in China." In Potter, ed., *Domestic Law Reforms in Post-Mao China*, pp. 97–108.

———. "Some Questions Regarding the Significance of the General Provisions of Civil Law of the People's Republic of China." *Harvard International Law Journal* 28, no. 2 (Spring 1987): 309–31.

———, ed. *Basic Principles of Civil Law in China.* Armonk, N.Y.: M. E. Sharpe, 1989.

Kaemmel, Ernst. "Literature Under the Table: The Detective Novel and Its Social Mission." In Most and Stowe, eds., *The Poetics of Murder*, pp. 56–61.

Kao, Karl S. Y., ed. *Classical Chinese Tales of the Supernatural and the Fantastic: Selections from the Third to the Tenth Century.* Bloomington: Indiana University Press, 1985.

Karl, Frederick R. *The Adversary Literature: The English Novel in the Eighteeenth Century: A Study in Genre.* New York: Farrar, Straus and Giroux, 1974.

Kaye, Marvin, ed. *The Game Is Afoot: Parodies, Pastiches and Ponderings of Sherlock Holmes.* New York: St. Martin's, 1994.

Ke Yan 柯岩. *Xunzhao huilai de shijie* 尋找回來的世界 (The world brought back). Beijing: Qunzhong chubanshe, 1984.

Ke Yunlu 柯雲路. *Xin xing* 新星 (New star). *Dangdai* supplementary issue no. 3 (Aug. 1984).

Keating, H. R. F., ed. *Whodunit? A Guide to Crime, Suspense and Spy Fiction.* New York: Van Nostrand Reinhold, 1982.

Keith, Ronald C. *China's Struggle for the Rule of Law.* New York: St. Martin's, 1994.

———. "Chinese Politics and the New Theory of 'Rule of Law.'" *China Quarterly* 125 (Mar. 1991): 109–18.

———. "Legislating Women's and Children's 'Rights and Interests' in the PRC." *China Quarterly* 149 (Mar. 1997): 29–55.

Kim, Hyung I. *Fundamental Legal Concepts of China and the West: A Comparative Study.* Port Washington, N.Y.: Kennikat, 1981.

Kingwell, Mark. "Let's Ask Again: Is Law Like Literature?" *Yale Journal of Law and the Humanities* 6, no. 2 (Summer 1994): 317–52.

Kinkley, Jeffrey C. "A Bettelheimian Interpretation of Chang Hsien-liang's Concentration Camp Novels." *Asia Major*, 3d ser. 4, pt. 2 (1991): 83–113.

———. "Chinese Crime Fiction." *Society* 30, no. 4 (May/June 1993): 51–62.

———. "Chinese Crime Fiction and Its Formulas at the Turn of the 1980s." In Kinkley, ed., *After Mao*, pp. 89–129.

———. "The Cultural Choices of Zhang Xinxin, a Young Writer of the 1980s." In Paul A. Cohen and Merle Goldman, eds., *Ideas Across Cultures: Essays on Chinese Thought in Honor of Benjamin I. Schwartz*, pp. 137–62. Cambridge, Mass.: Council on East Asian Studies, Harvard University, 1990.

———. "Foreword." *Fiction* 8, nos. 2/3 (1987): 84–94.

———. "The New Chinese Literature: The Mainland and Beyond." *Choice* 31, no. 8 (Apr. 1994): 1249–65.

———. "The Politics of Detective Fiction in Post-Mao China: Rebirth or Re-extinction?" *The Armchair Detective* 18, no. 4 (Fall 1985): 372–78.

———. "The Post-Colonial Detective in People's China." In Christian, ed., *The Post-Colonial Detective*.

———. "Shen Congwen's Legacy in Chinese Literature of the 1980s." In Widmer and Wang, eds., *From May Fourth to June Fourth*, pp. 71–106.

———, ed. *After Mao: Chinese Literature and Society, 1978–1981*. Cambridge, Mass.: Council on East Asian Studies, Harvard University, 1985.

Klein, Kathleen Gregory. *The Woman Detective: Gender and Genre*. 2d ed. Urbana: University of Illinois Press, 1996 [1988].

Knight, Stephen. *Form and Ideology in Crime Fiction*. Bloomington: Indiana University Press, 1980.

———. "Radical Thrillers." In Bell and Daldry, eds., *Watching the Detectives*, pp. 172–87.

Knox, Ronald A. "Detective Story Decalogue." In Haycraft, ed., *The Art of the Mystery Story*, pp. 194–96.

Koffler, Judith Schenck. "Forged Alliance: Law and Literature." *Columbia Law Review* 89 (1989): 1374–93.

Kong Jiesheng 孔捷生. "Yinyuan" 姻緣 (Marriage). In *Zhuiqiu* 追求 (Pursuit), pp. 1–20. [Guangzhou]: Guangdong renmin chubanshe, 1980. Dated May 14, 1978.

Kristeva, Julia. *Possessions*. Paris: Fayard, 1996.

Kroll, J. L. "Notes on Ch'in and Han Law." In W. L. Idema and E. Zürcher, eds., *Thought and Law in Qin and Han China*, pp. 63–78.

Kromm, Sandra. "A Feminist Appraisal of Intellectual One-Upmanship in the Sherlock Holmes Stories." In Putney, King, and Sugarman, eds. *Sherlock Holmes*, pp. 267–86.

Kuhn, Philip A. *Soulstealers: The Chinese Sorcery Scare of 1768*. Cambridge, Mass.: Harvard University Press, 1990.

Lacan, Jacques. "Seminar on 'The Purloined Letter.'" Jeffrey Mehlman, trans. In Muller and Richardson, eds., *The Purloined Poe*, pp. 28–54.

Ladany, Laszlo. *Law and Legality in China: The Testament of a China-Watcher*. Marie-Luise Näth, ed. Honolulu: University of Hawaii Press, 1992.

Lamy, Jean-Claude. *Arsène Lupin: Gentleman de la nuit* (Arsène Lupin: Gentleman of the night). Paris: Bernard Grasset, 1983.

Lan Dingyuan 藍鼎元. *Luzhou gongan* 鹿洲公案 (Cases of [Lan] Luzhou). With trans. into modern Mandarin by Liu Pengyun 劉鵬雲 and Chen Fangming 陳方明. Beijing: Qunzhong chubanshe, 1985.

Landrum, Larry N., Pat Browne, and Ray B. Browne, eds. *Dimensions of Detective Fiction.* Bowling Green, Ohio: Popular Press, 1976.

Landun xiaoshuo ji 藍盾小説集 (Fiction from *Blue Shield*). Beijing: Falü chubanshe, 1986.

Laqueur, Walter. "Julian Semyonov and the Soviet Political Novel." *Society* 23, no. 5 (July/Aug. 1986): 72–80.

Law and Literature: A Symposium. Special edition of *Rutgers Law Review* 29, no. 2 (Winter 1976).

Laws of the People's Republic of China, 1979–1982. Beijing: Foreign Languages Press, 1987.

Leblanc, Maurice. *Arsène Lupin versus Herlock Sholmes.* George Morehead, trans. Chicago: M. A. Donohue, 1910.

———. *The Confessions of Arsène Lupin.* Joachim Neugroschel, trans. New York: Walker, 1967 [1913].

———. *The Extraordinary Adventures of Arsène Lupin, Gentleman-Burglar.* George Morehead, trans. New York: Dover, 1977 [1910].

Ledwon, Lenora, ed. *Law and Literature: Text and Theory.* New York: Garland, 1996.

Lee, Gregory B. *Troubadours, Trumpeters, Troubled Makers: Lyricism, Nationalism, and Hybridity in China and Its Others.* Durham, N.C.: Duke University Press, 1996.

Lee, Leo Ou-fan. "The Politics of Technique: Perspectives of Literary Dissidence in Contemporary Chinese Fiction." In Kinkley, ed., *After Mao*, pp. 159–90.

———. *The Romantic Generation of Modern Chinese Writers.* Cambridge: Harvard University Press, 1973.

———. [Li Oufan 李歐梵]. "Zhongguo xiandai wenxue de 'tuifei' ji zuojia" 中國現代文學的 "頹廢" 及作家 (Decadence and writers in modern Chinese literature). *Dangdai* (Taiwan) 93 (Jan. 1, 1994): 22–47.

Lee, Tahirih V. "Introduction: Coping with Shanghai: Means to Survival and Success in the Early Twentieth Century—A Symposium." *Journal of Asian Studies* 54, no. 1 (Feb. 1995): 3–18.

Legal Storytelling. Special edition of *Michigan Law Review* 87, no. 8 (Aug. 1989).

Lehman, David. *The Perfect Murder: A Study in Detection.* New York: Free Press, 1989.

Leitch, Thomas M. "The Other Sherlock Holmes." In Putney, King, and Sugarman, eds., *Sherlock Holmes*, pp. 102–16.

Leng, Shao-chuan, with Hungdah Chiu. *Criminal Justice in Post-Mao China: Analysis and Documents.* Albany: State University of New York Press, 1985.

Leps, Marie-Christine. *Apprehending the Criminal: The Production of Deviance in Nineteenth-Century Discourse.* Durham, N.C.: Duke University Press, 1992.

Lesser, Wendy. *Pictures at an Execution.* Cambridge, Mass.: Harvard University Press, 1993.

Leung, Laifong. *Morning Sun: Interviews with Chinese Writers of the Lost Generation.* Armonk, N.Y.: M. E. Sharpe, 1994.

Levine, Lawrence W. *Highbrow/Lowbrow: The Emergence of Cultural Hierarchy in America.* Cambridge, Mass.: Harvard University Press, 1988.

Levinson, Sanford, and Steven Mailloux, eds. *Interpreting Law and Literature: A Hermeneutic Reader.* Evanston, Ill.: Northwestern University Press, 1988.

Lewis, John Wilson, ed. *The City in Communist China.* Stanford, Calif.: Stanford University Press, 1971.

Li Chi: Book of Rites. 2 vols. James Legge, trans. Ch'u Chai and Winberg Chai, eds. New Hyde Park, N.Y.: University Books, 1967.

Li Di 李迪. "Bangwan qiaomen de nüren" 傍晚敲門的女人 (The woman who knocked at dusk). *Zuopin yu zhengming* 52 (Apr. 1985): 3–40.

Li Dong 李棟 and Wang Yungao 王雲高. "Shenpan" 審判 (The trial). In Cen Ying, ed., *Zhongguo dalu zuian,* pp. 5–14. Reprinted from *Changjiang wenyi* 1980, no. 5.

Li Jian 李建. *Nüxing de xueqi* 女性的血旗 (The bloody flag of womanhood). Beijing: Qunzhong chubanshe, 1990.

Li Jingchun 里景春 and Gong Fan 宮凡, eds. *1984 Zhongguo xiaoshuo nianjian: Zhentan xiaoshuo juan* 1984 中國小説年鑑: 偵探小説卷 (Yearbook of Chinese fiction 1984: Detective stories). Beijing: Zhongguo xinwen chubanshe, 1985.

Li Kewei 李克威. *Nü zei* 女賊 (The girl thief). In Li Yi and Bi Hua, eds., *Zhongguo xin xieshizhuyi wenyi zuopin xuan xubian,* pp. 211–36. Reprinted from *Dianying chuangzuo,* Nov. 1979.

Li, Peter. "In Search of Justice: Law and Morality in Three Chinese Dramas." In Richard Wilson et al., eds., *Moral Behavior in Chinese Society,* pp. 104–25. New York: Praeger, 1981.

Li Tuo 李陀. "1985." *Jintian* 3/4 (1991): 59–73.

Li, Victor H. *Law Without Lawyers: A Comparative View of Law in China and the United States.* Boulder, Colo.: Westview, 1978.

———. "The Public Security Bureau and Political-Legal Work in Hui-yang, 1952–64." In Lewis, ed., *The City in Communist China,* pp. 51–74.

Li Yi 李怡, ed. *Zhongguo xin xieshizhuyi wenyi zuopin xuan* 中國新寫實主義文藝作品選 (A selection of China's new realistic literary works). Hong Kong: Qishi niandai zazhishe, 1980.

Li Yi 李怡 and Bi Hua 璧華, eds. *Zhongguo xin xieshizhuyi wenyi zuopin xuan xubian* 中國新寫實主義文藝作品選續編 (A selection of China's new realistic literary works, sequel). Hong Kong: Qishi niandai zazhishe, 1980.

Liang Shuming 梁漱溟. *Dongxi wenhua jiqi zhexue* 東西文化及其哲學 (Eastern and Western civilizations and their philosophies). Taibei: Wenxue chubanshe reprint, 1979.

Liang Zhiping. "Explicating 'Law': A Comparative Perspective of Chinese and Western Legal Culture." *Journal of Chinese Law* 3, no. 1 (Summer 1989): 55–91.

Lidai yuanan pingfan lu 歷代冤案平反錄 (Cases over the centuries of injustices righted). Beijing: Zhishi chubanshe, 1981.

Lin Foer 林佛兒. "Dangdai Taiwan tuili xiaoshuo zhi fazhan" 當代臺灣推理小說之發展 (The development of fiction of deduction in contemporary Taiwan). In Meng Fan 孟樊 and Lin Yaode 林燿德, eds., *Liuxing tianxia: Dangdai Taiwan tongsu wenxue lun* 流行天下: 當代臺灣通俗文學論 (Rampant everywhere: On popular literature in Taiwan today), pp. 306–27. Taibei: Shibao wenhua chuban gongsi, 1992. Comments by Ye Yandu 葉言都, pp. 328–31.

Lin Jiaju 林家舉. "Pi yuan ji" 砒冤記 (Notes on an unjust attribution of poisoning by arsenic). In Cen Ying, ed., *Zhongguo dalu zhentan*, pp. 175–78. Reprinted from *Minzhu yu fazhi* 1980, no. 7.

Lin Xiao 林嘯. "Bai Yingying zhi si" 白盈盈之死 (The death of Bai Yingying). In Cen Ying, ed., *Zhongguo dalu zhentan*, pp. 57–67.

Link, Perry. "Fiction and the Reading Public in Guangzhou and Other Chinese Cities, 1979–1980." In Kinkley, ed., *After Mao*, pp. 221–74.

———. "Hand-Copied Entertainment Fiction from the Cultural Revolution." In Perry Link, Richard Madsen, and Paul G. Pickowicz, eds., *Unofficial China: Popular Culture and Thought in the People's Republic*, pp. 17–36. Boulder, Colo.: Westview, 1989.

———. *Mandarin Ducks and Butterflies: Popular Fiction in Early Twentieth-Century Chinese Cities*. Berkeley: University of California Press, 1981.

———, ed. *Stubborn Weeds: Popular and Controversial Chinese Literature after the Cultural Revolution*. Bloomington: Indiana University Press, 1983.

Liu Binyan 劉賓雁. *Di'er zhong zhongcheng* 第二種忠誠 (The second kind of loyalty). Taibei: Renjian chubanshe, 1987.

———. *People or Monsters? And Other Stories and Reportage from China after Mao*. Perry Link, ed. Bloomington: Indiana University Press, 1983.

———. "Ren de jiefang he yanlun ziyou—Zai Zhongguo fazhi wenxue yantaohui shang de fayan" 人的解放和言論自由——在中國法制文學研討會上的發言 (The liberation of humankind and freedom of speech: Presentation at the research conference on Chinese legal system literature). *Fazhi wenxue xuankan*, Jan. 1987, pp. 1–9.

Liu Heng. *Black Snow*. Howard Goldblatt, trans. New York: Atlantic Monthly Press, 1993.

Liu Hsieh [Liu Xie]. *The Literary Mind and the Carving of Dragons*. Vincent Yu-chung Shih, trans. New York: Columbia University Press, 1959.

Liu, James J. Y. *The Chinese Knight-Errant*. Chicago: University of Chicago Press, 1967.

———. *Chinese Theories of Literature*. Chicago: University of Chicago Press, 1975.

Liu Ke 劉克. "Feitian" 飛天 (Angel). In Li Yi, ed., *Zhongguo xin xieshizhuyi wenyi zuopin xuan*, pp. 136–159. Reprinted from *Shiyue*, Sept. 1979.

Liu, Kwang-Ching. "Socioethics as Orthodoxy: A Perspective." In Kwang-Ching Liu, ed., *Orthodoxy in Late Imperial China*, pp. 53–100.

————, ed. *Orthodoxy in Late Imperial China*. Berkeley: University of California Press, 1990.

Liu, Lydia H. *Translingual Practice: Literature, National Culture, and Translated Modernity—China, 1900–1937*. Stanford, Calif.: Stanford University Press, 1995.

Liu, Nanping. "'Legal Precedents' with Chinese Characteristics: Published Cases in the Gazette of the Supreme People's Court." *Journal of Chinese Law* 5, no. 1 (Spring 1991): 107–41.

Liu Ts'un-yan, ed. *Chinese Middlebrow Fiction: From the Ch'ing and Early Republican Eras*. Hong Kong: Chinese University Press, Renditions, 1984.

Liu Yangti 劉揚體. *Yuanyang hudie pai zuopin xuan ping* 鴛鴦蝴蝶派作品選評 (Selections from the mandarin duck and butterfly school, with criticism). Chengdu: Sichuan wenyi chubanshe, 1987.

Liu Yeqiu 劉葉秋, Yuan Yuxin 苑育新, and Zhou Zhi 周知, eds. *Biji xiaoshuo anli xuanbian* 筆記小說案例選編 (Selected and edited cases from *biji xiaoshuo* [literati jottings]). N.p. [Kaifeng?]: Zhongzhou shuhua she, 1982.

Liu Zaifu 劉再復. "Gaobie zhushen—Zhongguo dangdai wenxue lilun 'shijimo' de zhengzha" 告別諸神——中國當代文學理論 "世紀末" 的掙扎 (Farewell to all gods—The *fin de siècle* struggle in contemporary Chinese literary theory). *Ershiyi shiji* 5 (June 1991): 125–34.

[Liu] Zongdai [劉] 宗岱. *Gongan hun* 公安魂 (The soul of public security). Beijing: Qunzhong chubanshe, 1988.

Lo, Carlos Wing-hung. *China's Legal Awakening: Legal Theory and Criminal Justice in Deng's Era*. Hong Kong: Hong Kong University Press, 1995.

Longtu erlu 龍圖耳錄 (Longtu's saga, recorded as heard). 2 vols. Shanghai: Shanghai guji chubanshe, 1981.

Longtu gongan 龍圖公案 (Longtu's cases). Full cover title, *Xinjuan chunxiang shanben Longtu gongan* 新鐫純像善本龍圖公案 (Newly edited, fully illustrated rare edition of the cases of Bao Longtu). 3 vols. Guoli Zhengzhi Daxue gudian xiaoshuo yanjiu zhongxin, ed. Taibei: Tianyi chubanshe, 1985. One hundred stories in 10 *juan*.

————. Full cover title, *Xinping Longtu shenduan gongan* 新評龍圖神斷公案 (New critical edition of cases miraculously judged by Bao Longtu). 3 vols. Guoli Zhengzhi Daxue gudian xiaoshuo yanjiu zhongxin, ed. Taibei: Tianyi chubanshe, 1985. Sixty-two stories in 10 *juan*.

Loomba, Ania. "Overworlding the 'Third World.'" In P. Williams and Chrisman, eds., *Colonial Discourse and Post-Colonial Theory*, pp. 305–23.

Lötveit, Trygve. *Chinese Communism 1931–1934: Experience in Civil Government*. 2d ed. London: Curzon, 1979 [1973].

Lu Fang'an 陸方闇. *Jiu an xin shuo* 舊案新説 (New tellings of old cases). Shanghai: Shanghai renmin chubanshe, 1991.

[Lü] Haiyan [侶] 海岩. *Bianyi jingcha* 便衣警察 (Plainclothes policeman). Beijing: Renmin wenxue chubanshe, 1985.

Lu Runxiang 盧潤祥. *Shenmi de zhentan shijie: Cheng Xiaoqing Sun Liaohong xiaoshuo yishu tan* 神秘的偵探世界: 程小青孫了紅小説藝術談 (The mysterious world of detection: A discussion of the fictional art of Cheng Xiaoqing and Sun Liaohong). Shanghai: Xuelin chubanshe, 1996.

Lu, Sheldon Hsiao-peng. *From Historicity to Fictionality: The Chinese Poetics of Narrative.* Stanford, Calif.: Stanford University Press, 1994.

Lu Xun 魯迅 [pseud. of Zhou Shuren 周樹人]. *A Brief History of Chinese Fiction.* Yang Hsien-yi and Gladys Yang, trans. 2d ed. Peking: Foreign Languages Press, 1964 [1959].

———. *Nahan* 吶喊 (Outcry). Hong Kong: Xinyi chubanshe, 1967.

———. *Panghuang* 彷徨 (Hesitation). Hong Kong: Xinyi chubanshe, 1972.

Lubman, Stanley B. "Introduction: The Future of Chinese Law." In Lubman, ed., *China's Legal Reforms,* pp. 1–21.

———, ed. *China's Legal Reforms.* Oxford: Oxford University Press, 1996.

Luo Huajun 羅華俊 and Li Zaizhong 李在中. *Zhifazhe* 執法者 (Upholder of the law). In Cen Ying, ed., *Zhongguo dalu zhentan,* pp. 91–111. Reprinted from *Dianying xinzuo* 1979, no. 6.

Ma, Yau-woon. "Fiction." In Nienhauser, ed., *The Indiana Companion to Traditional Chinese Literature,* pp. 31–48.

———. "The Pao-kung Tradition in Chinese Popular Literature." Ph.D. diss., Yale University, 1971.

———. "The Textual Tradition of Ming *Kung-an* Fiction: A Study of the *Lungt'u kung-an.*" *Harvard Journal of Asiatic Studies* 35 (1975): 190–220. Chinese edition: Ma Youyuan 馬幼垣. *Zhongguo xiaoshuoshi jigao* 中國小説史集稿 (Collected manuscripts on the history of Chinese fiction), pp. 147–82. Taibei: Shibao wenhua chuban shiye youxian gongsi, 1983 [1980].

———. "Themes and Characterization in the *Lung-t'u kung-an.*" *T'oung Pao* 49 (1973): 179–202.

Ma, Yau-woon, and Joseph S. M. Lau, eds. *Traditional Chinese Stories: Themes and Variations.* New York: Columbia University Press, 1978.

Macauley, Melissa A. "Civil and Uncivil Disputes in Southeast Coastal China, 1723–1820." In Bernhardt and Huang, eds., *Civil Law in Qing and Republican China,* pp. 85–121.

MacCormack, Geoffrey. *The Spirit of Traditional Chinese Law.* Athens: University of Georgia Press, 1996.

———. *Traditional Chinese Penal Law.* Edinburgh: Edinburgh University Press, 1990.

Maes-Jelinek, Hena. "'Numinous Proportions': Wilson Harris's Alternative to All 'Posts.'" In Adam and Tiffin, eds., *Past the Last Post,* pp. 47–64.

Magill, Frank N., ed. *One Thousand Three Hundred Critical Evaluations of Selected Novels and Plays.* 4 vols. Englewood Cliffs, N.J.: Salem, 1978 [1976].

Mair, Victor H. "Language and Ideology in the Written Popularizations of the *Sacred Edict.*" In Johnson, Nathan, and Rawski, eds., *Popular Culture in Late Imperial China,* pp. 325–59.

————. "The Narrative Revolution in Chinese Literature: Ontological Presuppositions." *Chinese Literature: Essays, Articles, Reviews* 5, nos. 1/2 (July 1983): 1–27.

————. *Painting and Performance: Chinese Picture Recitation and Its Indian Genesis.* Honolulu: University of Hawaii Press, 1988.

————. *T'ang Transformation Texts.* Cambridge, Mass.: Council on East Asian Studies, Harvard University, 1989.

Mandel, Ernest. *Delightful Murder: A Social History of the Crime Story.* Minneapolis: University of Minnesota Press, 1984.

Manos, Nikki Lee, and Meri-Jane Rochelson, eds. *Transforming Genres: New Approaches to British Fiction of the 1890s.* New York: St. Martin's, 1994.

Mao Tse-tung [Mao Zedong]. *Selected Works of Mao Tse-tung.* Peking: Foreign Languages Press, 1965.

Mao Zedong 毛澤東. *Mao Zedong xuanji* 毛澤東選集 (Selected works of Mao Zedong). Beijing: Renmin chubanshe, 1990 [1966].

Martin, Brian G. *The Shanghai Green Gang: Politics and Organized Crime, 1919–1937.* Berkeley: University of California Press, 1996.

Martin, Helmut. "'Cultural China': Irritation and Expectations at the End of an Era." In Maurice Brosseau, Kuan Hsin-chi, and Y. Y. Kueh, eds., *China Review 1997*, pp. 277–325. Hong Kong: Chinese University Press, 1997.

Martin, Helmut, and Jeffrey Kinkley, eds. *Modern Chinese Writers: Self-Portrayals.* Armonk, N.Y.: M. E. Sharpe, 1992.

Massaro, Toni M. "Empathy, Legal Storytelling, and the Rule of Law: New Words, Old Wounds?" *Michigan Law Review* 87, no. 8 (Aug. 1989): 2099–2127.

Matsumoto, Seichō. *Inspector Imanishi Investigates.* Beth Cary, trans. New York: Soho, 1989 [1961].

————. *Points and Lines.* Makiko Yamamoto and Paul C. Blum, trans. Tokyo: Kodansha, 1970.

McKnight, Brian E. "From Statute to Precedent: An Introduction to Sung Law and Its Transformation." In McKnight, ed., *Law and the State in Traditional East Asia*, pp. 111–31.

————. *The Quality of Mercy: Amnesties and Traditional Chinese Justice.* Honolulu: University of Hawaii Press, 1981.

————, ed. *Law and the State in Traditional East Asia: Six Studies on the Sources of East Asian Law.* Honolulu: University of Hawaii Press, 1987.

Meijer, Marinus Johan. *The Introduction of Modern Criminal Law in China.* Batavia: De Unie, 1950. Reprint, Arlington, Va.: University Publications of America, 1976.

————. *Murder and Adultery in Late Imperial China: A Study of Law and Morality.* Leiden: E. J. Brill, 1991.

Meisner, Maurice, and Rhoads Murphey, eds. *The Mozartian Historian: Essays on the Works of Joseph R. Levenson.* Berkeley: University of California Press, 1976.

Meng Liye 孟犁野. *Zhongguo gongan xiaoshuo yishu fazhan shi* 中國公案小説藝術發展史 (A history of the artistic development of Chinese court case fiction). Beijing: Jing guan jiaoyu chubanshe, 1996.

Miller, D. A. *The Novel and the Police.* Berkeley: University of California Press, 1988.

Minda, Gary. *Postmodern Legal Movements: Law and Jurisprudence at Century's End.* New York: New York University Press, 1995.

Ming Qing anyu gushi xuan 明清案獄故事選 (Selected tales of cases from the Ming and Qing). East China Institute of Politics and Law, Language and Literature Teaching and Research Section, ed. Beijing: Qunzhong chubanshe, 1985.

Mishra, Vijay, and Bob Hodge. "What Is Post-Colonialism?" In P. Williams and Chrisman, eds., *Colonial Discourse and Post-Colonial Theory,* pp. 276–90.

Mitchell, W. J. T. "Postcolonial Culture, Postimperial Criticism." In Ashcroft, Griffiths, and Tiffin, eds., *The Post-Colonial Studies Reader,* pp. 475–79.

Moers, Ellen. *The Dandy: Brummell to Beerbohm.* Lincoln: University of Nebraska Press, 1960.

Moore, Sally Falk. *Law as Process: An Anthropological Approach.* London: Routledge, 1978.

Moore-Gilbert, Bart. *Postcolonial Theory: Contexts, Practices, Politics.* London: Verso, 1997.

Moran, Thomas Elton. "True Stories: Contemporary Chinese Reportage and Its Ideology and Aesthetic." Ph.D. diss., Cornell University, 1994.

Most, Glenn W., and William W. Stowe, eds. *The Poetics of Murder: Detective Fiction and Literary Theory.* San Diego: Harcourt Brace Jovanovich, 1983.

Muller, John P., and William J. Richardson, eds. *The Purloined Poe: Lacan, Derrida, and Psychoanalytic Reading.* Baltimore: Johns Hopkins University Press, 1988.

Murch, A[lma] E[lizabeth]. *The Development of the Detective Novel.* London: Peter Owen, 1958.

Nakajima Kawatarō 中島河太郎. *Nihon suiri shōsetsu shi* 日本推理小説史 (A history of Japanese fiction of deduction). Vol. 1. Tokyo: Tōkyo sōgensha, 1993.

Nan yi yuyue de pingzhang 難以逾越的屏障 (The impenetrable barrier). Beijing: Chunqiu chubanshe, 1988.

Narcejac, Thomas [pseud. of Pierre Ayraud]. *Une Machine à lire: Le roman policier* (A reading machine: Detective fiction). Paris: Denoël/Gonthier, 1975.

Needham, Joseph, with the research assistance of Wang Ling. *Science and Civilization in China.* Vol. 2. Cambridge: Cambridge University Press, 1970.

Nevins, Francis M., Jr., ed. *The Mystery Writer's Art.* Bowling Green, Ohio: Popular Press, 1970.

Nienhauser, William H., Jr. "The Origins of Chinese Fiction." *Monumenta Serica* 38 (1988–89): 191–219.

———. "Some Preliminary Remarks on Fiction, the Classical Tradition and Society in Late Ninth-Century China." In Winston L. Y. Yang and Curtis P. Adkins, eds., *Critical Essays on Chinese Fiction,* pp. 1–16. Hong Kong: Chinese University Press, 1980.

———, ed. and comp. *The Indiana Companion to Traditional Chinese Literature.* Bloomington: Indiana University Press, 1986.

Nivison, David S. *The Life and Thought of Chang Hsüeh-ch'eng (1738–1801)*. Stanford, Calif.: Stanford University Press, 1966.

Nü minjing de kanke jingli 女民警的坎坷經歷 (Rough sledding for a policewoman). Beijing: Qunzhong chubanshe, 1990.

Nussbaum, Martha C. *Poetic Justice: The Literary Imagination and Public Life*. Boston: Beacon Press, 1995.

Ocko, Jonathan K. "Hierarchy and Harmony: Family Conflict as Seen in Ch'ing Legal Cases." In Kwang-Ching Liu, ed., *Orthodoxy in Late Imperial China*, pp. 212–30.

Ousby, Ian. *Bloodhounds of Heaven: The Detective in English Fiction from Godwin to Doyle*. Cambridge, Mass.: Harvard University Press, 1976.

Ouyang Tao 歐陽濤 et al., eds. *Daoqiezui, guanqiezui* 盜竊罪, 慣竊罪 (Theft and habitual theft). Beijing: Zhongguo jiancha chubanshe, 1991.

Owen, Stephen. *Readings in Chinese Literary Thought*. Cambridge, Mass.: Council on East Asian Studies, Harvard University, 1992.

Palmer, Jerry. *Potboilers: Methods, Concepts and Case Studies in Popular Fiction*. London: Routledge, 1991.

———. *Thrillers: Genesis and Structure of a Popular Genre*. London: Edward Arnold, 1978.

Palmer, Michael. "The Re-emergence of Family Law in Post-Mao China: Marriage, Divorce and Reproduction." In Lubman, ed., *China's Legal Reforms*, pp. 110–34.

Panek, LeRoy Lad. *An Introduction to the Detective Story*. Bowling Green, Ohio: Popular Press, 1987.

Pang Taixi 龐太熙. "Poan zhi hou" 破案之後 (After cracking the case). In Cen Ying, ed., *Zhongguo dalu zuian*, pp. 218–25. Reprinted from *Zuopin* 1979, no. 1.

Park, Nancy E. "Corruption in Eighteenth-Century China." *Journal of Asian Studies* 56, no. 4 (Nov. 1997): 967–1001.

Parry, Benita. "Problems in Current Theories of Colonial Discourse." In Ashcroft, Griffiths, and Tiffin, eds., *The Post-Colonial Studies Reader*, pp. 36–44.

Paul, Robert S. *Whatever Happened to Sherlock Holmes: Detective Fiction, Popular Theology, and Society*. Carbondale: Southern Illinois University Press, 1991.

Peerenboom, R. P. *Law and Morality in Ancient China: The Silk Manuscripts of Huang-Lao*. Albany: State University of New York Press, 1993.

Peller, Gary. "The Metaphysics of American Law." *California Law Review* 73, no. 4 (July 1985): 1151–1290.

Pelliot, Paul. "Notes de bibliographie chinoise: II, Le droit chinois" (Notes on Chinese bibliography: II, Chinese law). *Bulletin de l'École Française d'Extrême-orient* 9, no. 1 (Jan.–Mar. 1909): 123–52.

Peng Wen 彭文. *Shiyong fayixue zhishi wenda* 實用法醫學知識問答 (Questions and answers on practical knowledge in forensic science). Beijing: Qunzhong chubanshe, 1989.

Penzler, Otto, et al. *Detectionary: A Biographical Dictionary of Leading Characters in Mystery Fiction*. Woodstock, N.Y.: Overlook, 1977 [1971].

Perng, Ching-hsi. *Double Jeopardy: A Critique of Seven Yuan Courtroom Dramas.* Ann Arbor: Center for Chinese Studies, University of Michigan, 1979.

Plaks, Andrew H. *The Four Masterworks of the Ming Novel: Ssu ta ch'i-shu.* Princeton, N.J.: Princeton University Press, 1987.

——. "Full-Length *Hsiao-shuo* and the Western Novel: A Generic Reappraisal." In William Tay, Ying-hsiung Chou, and Heh-hsiang Yeh, eds., *China and the West: Comparative Literature Studies,* pp. 163–76. Hong Kong: Chinese University Press, 1980.

——. "Towards a Critical Theory of Chinese Narrative." In Plaks, ed., *Chinese Narrative,* pp. 309–52.

——, ed. *Chinese Narrative: Critical and Theoretical Essays.* Princeton, N.J.: Princeton University Press, 1977.

Polin, Raymond. *Plato and Aristotle on Constitutionalism: An Exposition and Reference Source.* Aldershot, Eng.: Ashgate, 1998.

Polumbaum, Judy. "To Protect or Restrict? Points of Contention in China's Draft Press Law." In Potter, ed., *Domestic Law Reforms in Post-Mao China,* pp. 247–69.

Porter, Dennis. "*Orientalism* and Its Problems." In P. Williams and Chrisman, eds., *Colonial Discourse and Post-Colonial Theory,* pp. 150–61.

——. *The Pursuit of Crime: Art and Ideology in Detective Fiction.* New Haven, Conn.: Yale University Press, 1981.

Posner, Richard A. *Law and Literature: A Misunderstood Relation.* Cambridge, Mass.: Harvard University Press, 1988.

Pospíšil, Leopold. *Anthropology of Law: A Comparative Theory.* New York: Harper and Row, 1971.

Potter, Pitman B. "The Administrative Litigation Law of the PRC: Judicial Review and Bureaucratic Reform." In Potter, ed., *Domestic Law Reforms in Post-Mao China,* pp. 270–304.

——. "Riding the Tiger: Legitimacy and Legal Culture in Post-Mao China." *China Quarterly* 138 (June 1994): 325–58.

——, ed. *Domestic Law Reforms in Post-Mao China.* Armonk, N.Y.: M. E. Sharpe, 1994.

Prchal, Timothy R. "Secular Guardians of Sacred Justice: Fictional Detectives and Asceticism." In Putney, King, and Sugarman, eds., *Sherlock Holmes,* pp. 157–69.

Priestman, Martin. *Detective Fiction and Literature: The Figure on the Carpet.* New York: St. Martin's, 1991.

Průšek, Jaroslav. "History and Epics in China and in the West." *Diogenes* 42 (1963): 20–43.

——, ed. *Dictionary of Oriental Literatures.* Zbigniew Słupski, ed., Vol. 1: *East Asia.* New York: Basic Books, 1974.

Putney, Charles R., Joseph A. Cutshall King, and Sally Sugarman, eds. *Sherlock Holmes: Victorian Sleuth to Modern Hero.* Lanham, Md.: Scarecrow, 1996.

Pyrhönen, Heta. *Murder from an Academic Angle: An Introduction to the Study of the Detective Narrative.* Columbia, S.C.: Camden House, 1994.

Qi xia wu yi 七俠五義 (Seven knights and five gallants). Yu Yue 俞樾, ed. Beijing: Baowentang shudian, 1980 [1889].

Qian Zhongshu 錢鍾書 et al. *Lin Shu de fanyi* 林紓的翻譯 (Lin Shu's translations). Beijing: Shangwu yinshuguan, 1981.

"Qingnian zuojia tan fazhi wenxue" 青年作家談法制文學 (Young writers discuss legal system literature). *Zhongguo fazhi wenxue* 9 (May 18, 1987): 93–94.

Qiuju da guansi 秋菊打官司 (The story of Qiu Ju; film). Dir. Zhang Yimou 張藝謀. Screenplay by Liu Heng 劉恒. Starring Gong Li 鞏俐. Coproduced by SIL-Metropole Organisation Ltd. and Beijing Film Academy, The Youth Film Studio, 1992.

Queen, Ellery, ed. *Ellery Queen's Japanese Golden Dozen.* Tokyo: Tuttle, 1978.

Rader, Barbara, and Howard G. Zettler, eds. *The Sleuth and the Scholar: Origins, Evolution, and Current Trends in Detective Fiction.* New York: Greenwood, 1988.

Rampo, Edogawa [sic; in Japanese, "Edogawa Rampo" is an indivisible pen name]. *Japanese Tales of Mystery and Imagination.* James B. Harris, trans. Rutland, Vt: Charles E. Tuttle, 1956.

Reddy, Maureen T. *Sisters in Crime: Feminism and the Crime Novel.* New York: Continuum, 1988.

Redmond, Donald A. *Sherlock Holmes, a Study in Sources.* Montreal: McGill University Press; Kingston: Queens University Press, 1982.

Ren Qun 任群 et al., eds. *Pian: Shijiu qi zhapianan de zhenxiang* 騙: 十九起詐騙案的真相 (Stung: The real facts behind nineteen cases of fraud and swindling). Hebei: Guangming ribao chubanshe, 1989.

Rickett, Allyn, and Adele Rickett. *Prisoners of Liberation: Four Years in a Chinese Communist Prison.* Garden City, N.Y.: Doubleday Anchor, 1973 [1957].

Roberts, Simon. *Order and Dispute: An Introduction to Legal Anthropology.* New York: St. Martin's, 1979.

Roberts, Thomas J. *An Aesthetics of Junk Fiction.* Athens: University of Georgia Press, 1990.

Rolston, David L. *Traditional Chinese Fiction and Fiction Commentary: Reading and Writing Between the Lines.* Stanford, Calif.: Stanford University Press, 1997.

———, ed. *How to Read the Chinese Novel.* Princeton, N.J.: Princeton University Press, 1990.

Rosenheim, Shawn James. *The Cryptographic Imagination: Secret Writing from Edgar Allan Poe to the Internet.* Baltimore: Johns Hopkins University Press, 1997.

Rosmarin, Adena. *The Power of Genre.* Minneapolis: University of Minnesota Press, 1985.

Roth, Marty. *Foul and Fair Play: Reading Genre in Classic Detective Fiction.* Athens: University of Georgia Press, 1995.

Ruaud, André-François. *Arsène Lupin.* Pezilla-la-Rivière, France: DLM, 1996.

Rui Heshi 芮和師, Fan Boqun 范伯群, et al., eds. *Yuanyang hudie pai wenxue ziliao* 鴛鴦蝴蝶派文學資料 (Literary materials on the mandarin duck and butterfly school). Vol. 1. Fuzhou: Fujian renmin chubanshe, 1984.

Ruozhe, bushi nüren de mingzi 弱者，不是女人的名子 (Frailty, thy name is not woman). Beijing: Qunzhong chubanshe, 1990.

Russell, Robert. "Red Pinkertonism: An Aspect of Soviet Literature of the 1920s." *The Slavonic and East European Review* 60, no. 3 (July 1982): 390–412.

Said, Edward W. *Culture and Imperialism.* New York: Random House, 1994 [1993].

———. *Orientalism.* New York: Random House, 1994 [1978].

San Juan, E[pifanio], Jr. *Beyond Postcolonial Theory.* New York: St. Martin's, 1998.

San xia wu yi 三俠五義 (Three heroes and five gallants). Shi Yukun 石玉崑, ed. Taibei: Hele tushu chubanshe, 1980 [1879].

Saunders, Kate. *Eighteen Layers of Hell: Stories from the Chinese Gulag.* London: Cassell, 1996.

Sayers, Dorothy. "Aristotle on Detective Fiction." In Winks, ed., *Detective Fiction,* pp. 25–34.

Schell, Orville. *Mandate of Heaven.* New York: Simon and Schuster, 1994.

Schleh, Eugene, ed. *Mysteries of Africa.* Bowling Green, Ohio: Popular Press, 1991.

Schoenhals, Michael. *Doing Things with Words in Chinese Politics: Five Studies.* Berkeley, Calif.: Center for Chinese Studies, 1992.

Schram, Stuart R., ed. *The Scope of State Power in China.* London: University of London, 1985.

Schreiber, Mark. "The Agatha Christie of Japan: An Interview with Shizuko Natsuki." *The Armchair Detective* 20, no. 1 (Winter 1987): 54–60.

Schwartz, Benjamin I. *The World of Thought in Ancient China.* Cambridge, Mass.: Belknap Press, 1985.

Sebeok, Thomas A., and Harriet Margolis. "Captain Nemo's Porthole: Semiotics of Windows in Sherlock Holmes." *Poetics Today* 3, no. 1 (1982): 110–39.

Senger, Harro Von. "Recent Developments in the Relations Between State and Party Norms in the People's Republic of China." In Schram, ed., *The Scope of State Power in China,* pp. 171–207.

Seymour, James D., and Richard Anderson [pseud.]. *New Ghosts, Old Ghosts: Prisons and Labor Reform Camps in China.* Armonk, N.Y.: M. E. Sharpe, 1998.

Shapiro, Judith, and Liang Heng. *Cold Winds, Warm Winds: Intellectual Life in China Today.* Middletown, Conn.: Wesleyan University Press, 1986.

Shapiro, Sidney. *The Law and the Lore of China's Criminal Justice.* Beijing: New World Press, 1990.

Shaw, William. "The Neo-Confucian Revolution of Values in Early Yi Korea: Its Implications for Korean Legal Thought." In McKnight, ed., *Law and the State in Traditional East Asia,* pp. 149–72.

Shelley, Percy Bysshe. *Shelley's Prose.* David Lee Clark, ed. Albuquerque: University of New Mexico Press, 1954.

Shen Congwen. "Fiction and Society." Rey Chow and Ming-bao Yue, trans. In Martin and Kinkley, eds., *Modern Chinese Writers,* pp. 289–94.

Shen Zhiwei 沈志偉. "Zhifazhe" 執法者 (Upholder of the law). *Zuopin* 1981, no. 3, pp. 7–12.

Shenpan qian de jiaoliang 審判前的較量 (Tribulations before the trial). Beijing: Qunzhong chubanshe, 1981.

Shi gongan 施公案 (Judge Shi's cases). 3 vols. Beijing: Baowentang shudian, 1982. Internal.

Shi Tongxue 師彤雪. "Wuming biao qi'an" 無名表奇案 (The strange case of the watch that had no brand name). In Cen Ying, ed., *Zhongguo dalu zhentan*, pp. 112–31.

Shih, Chung-wen. *Injustice to Tou O* (Tou O Yüan): *A Study and Translation*. Cambridge: Cambridge University Press, 1972.

Shih, Shu-mei. "Gender, Race, and Semicolonialism: Liu Na'ou's Urban Shanghai Landscape." *Journal of Asian Studies* 55, no. 4 (Nov. 1996): 934–56.

Shisan jing zhushu 十三經注疏 (The thirteen classics, with notes and commentaries). 8 vols. [Ruan Yuan, ed.] Taibei: Yiwen yinshuguan, 1973 [1960].

Shiwubao 時務報 (The Chinese progress). Shanghai. 1896–98. Reprint, 6 vols., Taibei: Jinghua shuju, 1967.

Shklovsky, Viktor. *Theory of Prose*. Benjamin Sher, trans. Elmwood Park, Ill.: Dalkey Archive, 1990.

Shui Yunxian 水運憲. *Zhenpo an wailu* 偵破案外錄 (An unofficial story of how a case was solved). *Huacheng* 30 (Sept. 25, 1984): 124–64.

Shuo anli, xue falü 説案例, 學法律 (Learn the law through cases [series]). "Zhonghua renmin gongheguo jichengfa bufen" "中華人民共和國繼承法" 部分 (On the Inheritance Law of the People's Republic of China). Supreme People's Court and Zhu Fu 朱富, eds. Beijing: Zhongguo guangbo dianshi chubanshe, 1986.

Sieber, Patricia. "Rhetoric, Romance, and Intertextuality: The Making and Remaking of Guan Hanqing in Yuan and Ming China." Ph.D. diss., University of California, Berkeley, 1994.

Siegal, Larry J. *Criminology: Theories, Patterns, and Typologies*. 5th ed. St. Paul, Minn.: West, 1995 [1983].

Simons, John. "*Real* Detectives and *Fictional* Criminals." In Bell and Daldry, eds., *Watching the Detectives*, pp. 84–96.

Simpson, Amelia S. *Detective Fiction from Latin America*. Rutherford, N.J.: Fairleigh Dickinson University Press, 1990.

Slemon, Stephen. "Modernism's Last Post." In Adam and Tiffin, eds., *Past the Last Post*, pp. 1–11.

———. "The Scramble for Post-Colonialism." In C. Tiffin and Lawson, eds., *De-Scribing Empire*, pp. 15–32.

———. "Unsettling the Empire: Resistance Theory for the Second World." In Ashcroft, Griffiths, and Tiffin, eds., *The Post-Colonial Studies Reader*, pp. 104–10.

Slovak, Jeffrey S. *Styles of Urban Policing*. New York: New York University Press, 1986.

Smith, Richard J. "Ritual in Ch'ing Culture." In Kwang-Ching Liu, ed., *Orthodoxy in Late Imperial China*, pp. 281–310.

Song Anna 宋安娜 and Huang Zexin 黃澤新. "Zhongguo zhentan xiaoshuo fazhan de lishi huigu" 中國偵探小說發展的歷史回顧 (A historical review of the Chinese detective story's development). *Zhuomuniao* 73 (Jan. 1996): 155–59.

Song Ci 宋慈. *Xiyuan jilu jiaoyi* 洗冤集錄校譯 (Manual for redressing injustice, collated and translated). Yang Fengkun 楊奉崑, coll. and trans. [into modern Mandarin]. Beijing: Qunzhong chubanshe, 1980.

Song Yuexun 宋曰勛 and Chen Dunde 陳敦德. *Fating neiwai* 法庭內外 (Before the bench and behind the scenes). In Cen Ying, ed., *Zhongguo dalu zuian*, pp. 31–65. Reprinted from *Dianying chuangzuo* 1980, no. 1.

Spanos, William V. "The Detective and the Boundary: Some Notes on the Postmodern Literary Imagination." *boundary* 21, no. 1 (1972): 149–68.

Spivak, Gayatri Chakravorty. "Can the Subaltern Speak?" In P. Williams and Chrisman, eds., *Colonial Discourse and Post-Colonial Theory*, pp. 66–111.

———. *The Post-Colonial Critic: Interviews, Strategies, Dialogues*. Sarah Harasym, ed. New York: Routledge, 1990.

St. André, James. "'Getting Down Off a Tiger Isn't Easy': Editing *Wuxia* Fiction, 1870–1900." Paper presented at the Annual Meeting of the Association for Asian Studies, Washington, D.C., 1998.

Starr, June. *Law as Metaphor: From Islamic Courts to the Palace of Justice*. Albany: State University of New York Press, 1992.

Starrett, Vincent. "Some Chinese Detective Stories." In his *Bookman's Holiday: The Private Satisfactions of an Incurable Collector*. Freeport, N.Y.: Books for Libraries Press, 1971 [1942].

Stavans, Ilan. *Antiheroes: Mexico and Its Detective Novel*. Jesse H. Lytle and Jennifer A. Mattson, trans. Madison, N.J.: Fairleigh Dickinson University Press, 1997.

Stories About Not Being Afraid of Ghosts. Institute of Literature of the Chinese Academy of Social Sciences, comp. Preface by Ho Chi-fang. Yang Hsien-yi and Gladys Yang, trans. Peking: Foreign Languages Press, 1979 [1961].

Stowe, William W. "Critical Investigations: Convention and Ideology in Detective Fiction." *Texas Studies in Literature and Language* 31, no. 4 (Winter 1989): 570–91.

Strelka, Joseph P., ed. *Theories of Literary Genre*. University Park: Pennsylvania State University Press, 1978.

Su Ce 蘇策. "Tongfan" 同犯 (Fellow prisoner). *Xiaoshuo yuebao* 14 (Feb. 1, 1981): 2–12.

Su Dezhen 蘇德禎, Li Yangui 李延桂, and Lan Yangchun 藍陽春. "Beijing lai de jianchaguan" 北京來的檢察官 (Public procurator from Beijing). In Cen Ying, ed., *Zhongguo dalu zuian*, pp. 15–29. Reprinted from *Dangdai* 1980, no. 2.

Su Shi 蘇軾. *Su Shi shi ji* 蘇軾詩集 (The *shi* poems of Su Shi). Beijing: Zhonghua shuju, 1982.

Su Yunxiang 蘇雲翔. "'San ke menya' anjian" "三顆門牙" 案件 (The case of the three front teeth). In Cen Ying, ed., *Zhongguo dalu zhentan*, pp. 38–45. Reprinted from *Yalu Jiang*, 1979.

Sue, Eugène. *The Mysteries of Paris*. New York: Howard Fertig, 1987. Trans. from the French.

Suleiman, Susan Rubin. *Authoritarian Fictions: The Ideological Novel as a Literary Genre*. Princeton, N.J.: Princeton University Press, 1983.

Sun Liaohong 孫了紅. "Gui shou" 鬼手 (The ghost's hand). In *XDLP* [*Xia dao Lu Ping qi'an*], pp. 452–76.

———. "Kuileiju" 傀儡劇 (Puppet show). *Zhentan shijie*, Nov. 1923.

———. "Lanse de xiangweishe" 藍色的響尾蛇 (The blue rattlesnake). In *XDLP*, pp. 31–154.

———. "Muou de xiju" 木偶的戲劇 (A wooden puppet play). In *XDLP*, pp. 204–92.

———. "The Sunglasses Society." Timothy C. Wong, trans. Unpublished piece for a forthcoming anthology of popular Chinese fiction.

———. "Tunyuganyouzhe" 囤魚肝油者 (The man who hoarded cod liver oil). In *XDLP*, pp. 352–405.

———. *Xia dao Lu Ping qi'an* [*XDLP*] 俠盜魯平奇案 (Strange cases of the chivalrous thief Lu Ping). [Shanghai]: Wenhua yishu chubanshe, 1989.

———. *Xia dao wen guai: Sun Liaohong* 俠盜文怪: 孫了紅 (The literary marvel of the chivalrous thief: Sun Liaohong). Fan Boqun, ed. Taibei: Yeqiang chubanshe, 1993.

———. "Ya mingsheng" 鴉鳴聲 (The call of a crow). In *XDLP*, pp. 406–51.

———. "Yanweixu" 燕尾鬚 (The handlebar mustache). In Wei Shaochang and Wu Chenghui, eds., *Yuanyang hudie pai yanjiu ziliao*, pp. 1201–24.

———. "Ye lie ji" 夜獵記 (Night hunting). *XDLP*, pp. 155–203.

———. "Zhen jia zhi jian" 真假之間 (Between truth and falsehood). *XDLP*, pp. 1–30.

———. "Zise de youyongyi" 紫色的游泳衣 (The purple swimsuit). *XDLP*, pp. 293–351.

Sweeney, Susan Elizabeth. "The Other Side of the Coin in Arthur Conan Doyle's 'The Red-Headed League.'" In Putney, King, and Sugarman, eds., *Sherlock Holmes*, pp. 37–63.

Symons, Julian. *Bloody Murder: From the Detective Story to the Crime Novel: A History*. 2d ed. New York: Viking, 1985 [1972].

Symposium: Law and Literature. Special issue of *Texas Law Review* 60, no. 3 (Mar. 1982).

Tam, King-fai. "Cultural Ambiguities of Modern Chinese Fiction." In Christian, ed., *The Post-Colonial Detective*.

———. "The Detective Fiction of Ch'eng Hsiao-ch'ing." *Asia Major*, 3d ser. 5, no. 1 (1992): 113–32.

Tan Dazheng 談大正 and Shen Qi 沈栖, eds. *Zhong wai fazhi dianying shangxi* 中外法制電影賞析 (Analyses of Chinese and foreign legal system films). Shanghai: Shanghai kexue jishu wenxian chubanshe, 1991.

Tanaka, Stefan. *Japan's Orient: Rendering Pasts into History*. Berkeley: University of California Press, 1993.

The T'ang Code. Vol. 1: *General Principles.* Wallace Johnson, trans. Princeton, N.J.: Princeton University Press, 1979.

Tang, Xiaobing. *Global Space and the Nationalist Discourse of Modernity: The Historical Thinking of Liang Qichao.* Stanford, Calif.: Stanford University Press, 1996.

Tangyin bishi 棠陰比事 (Parallel cases solved by just and benevolent officials). Gui Wanrong 桂萬榮, ed. 1211.

T'ang-yin-pi-shih: Parallel Cases from Under the Pear-Tree: A Thirteenth Century Manual of Jurisprudence and Detection. R. H. Van Gulik, trans. Leiden: E. J. Brill, 1956.

Tani, Stefano. *The Doomed Detective: The Contribution of the Detective Novel to Postmodern American and Italian Fiction.* Carbondale: Southern Illinois University Press, 1984.

Tanner, Harold Miles. "Crime and Punishment in China, 1979–1989." Ph.D. diss., Columbia University, 1994.

Tanner, Murray Scot. "How a Bill Becomes a Law in China: Stages and Processes in Lawmaking." In Lubman, ed., *China's Legal Reforms*, pp. 39–64.

Tao Mao 陶髦, Wu Yanping 武延平, Fan Chongyi 樊崇義, Zhang Jiachun 張家春, and Li Baoyue 李寶岳, eds. *Xingshi susong anli* 刑事訴訟案例 (Cases exemplifying the Law of Criminal Procedure). Beijing: Qunzhong chubanshe, 1985.

Teachout, Peter Read. "Lapse of Judgment." *California Law Review* 77, no. 5 (Oct. 1989): 1259–95.

Thomas, Brook. *Cross Examinations of Law and Literature.* Cambridge: Cambridge University Press, 1987.

———. "Reflections on the Law and Literature Revival." *Critical Inquiry* 17 (Spring 1991): 510–39.

Thomas, Ronald R. "Revaluating Identity in the 1890s: The Rise of the New Imperialism and the Eyes of the New Detective." In Manos and Rochelson, eds., *Transforming Genres*, pp. 193–214.

Thompson, E. P. *Whigs and Hunters: The Origin of the Black Act.* New York: Pantheon, 1975.

Thompson, Jon. *Fiction, Crime, and Empire: Clues to Modernity and Postmodernism.* Urbana: University of Illinois Press, 1993.

Thomson, James C., Jr. *While China Faced West: American Reformers in Nationalist China, 1928–1937.* Cambridge, Mass.: Harvard University Press, 1969.

Tiffin, Chris, and Alan Lawson, eds. *De-Scribing Empire: Post-Colonialism and Textuality.* London: Routledge, 1994.

Tiffin, Helen. "Post-Colonial Literatures and Counter-Discourse." In Ashcroft, Griffiths, and Tiffin, eds., *The Post-Colonial Studies Reader*, pp. 95–98.

Tillman, Hoyt Cleveland. *Ch'en Liang on Public Interest and the Law.* Honolulu: University of Hawaii Press, 1994.

Tipton, Elise K. *The Japanese Police State: The Tokkō in Interwar Japan.* Honolulu: University of Hawaii Press, 1990.

Todorov, Tzvetan. *Genres in Discourse.* Catherine Porter, trans. Cambridge: Cambridge University Press, 1990 [1978].

————. *The Poetics of Prose.* Richard Howard, trans. Ithaca, N.Y.: Cornell University Press, 1977.

Tourteau, Jean-Jacques. *D'Arsène Lupin à San-Antonio: Le roman policier français de 1900 à 1970* (From Arsène Lupin to San-Antonio: French detective fiction from 1900 to 1970). Paris: Mame, 1970.

Townsend, Deborah E. "The Concept of Law in Post-Mao China: A Case Study of Economic Crime." *Stanford Journal of International Law* 24, no. 1 (Fall 1987): 227–58.

Trotter, David. "Theory and Detective Fiction." *Critical Quarterly* 33, no. 2 (1991): 66–77.

Troyer, Ronald J., John P. Clark, and Dean G. Rojek, eds. *Social Control in the People's Republic of China.* New York: Praeger, 1989.

Tsai, Meishi, with the assistance of I-mei Tsai. *Contemporary Chinese Novels and Short Stories, 1949–1974: An Annotated Bibliography.* Cambridge, Mass.: Council on East Asian Studies, Harvard University, 1979.

Turner, J. Neville, and Pamela Williams, eds. *The Happy Couple: Law and Literature.* Sydney: Federation Press, 1994.

Turner, Karen. "Rule of Law Ideals in Early China?" *Journal of Chinese Law* 6, no. 1 (Spring 1992): 2–44.

Van der Sprenkel, Sybille. *Legal Institutions in Manchu China: A Sociological Analysis.* London: Athlone Press, 1966 [1962].

Vandermeersch, Léon. "An Enquiry into the Chinese Conception of Law." In Schram, ed., *The Scope of State Power in China,* pp. 3–25.

Vareille, Jean-Claude. *L'Homme masqué, le justicier et le détective* (Masked men, avengers, and detectives). Lyon: Presses universitaires de Lyon, 1989.

Vogel, Ezra F. "Preserving Order in the Cities." In Lewis, ed., *The City in Communist China,* pp. 75–93.

Wagner, Rudolf G. "Lobby Literature: The Archaeology and Present Functions of Science Fiction in China." In Kinkley, ed., *After Mao,* pp. 17–62.

Wakeman, Frederic, Jr. *Policing Shanghai, 1927–1937.* Berkeley: University of California Press, 1995.

Walker, Ronald G., and June M. Frazer. *The Cunning Craft: Original Essays on Detective Fiction and Contemporary Literary Theory.* Macomb: Western Illinois University Essays in Literature, 1990.

Waltner, Ann. "From Casebook to Fiction: *Kung-an* in Late Imperial China." *Journal of the American Oriental Society* 100, no. 2 (April–June 1990): 281–89.

Wang Chungui 王春桂. "Bashi niandai dalu tongsu wenxue xingsheng zhi fengjiang—wuxia xiaoshuo re" 八十年代大陸通俗文學興盛之鋒將——武俠小說熱 (The leading edge in the flourishing of popular literature on the mainland in the 1980s—the mania for martial-arts fiction). In Danjiang Daxue Zhongwen xi, ed., *Xia yu Zhongguo wenhua* 俠與中國文化 (Chivalry and Chinese culture), pp. 57–73. Taibei: Xuesheng shuju, 1993.

Wang, David Der-wei. *Fin-de-Siècle Splendor: Repressed Modernities of Late Qing Fiction, 1849–1911*. Stanford, Calif.: Stanford University Press, 1997.

Wang Hailin 王海林. *Zhongguo wuxia xiaoshuo shilüe* 中國武俠小說史略 (Brief history of Chinese martial-arts fiction). Taiyuan: Beiyue wenyi chubanshe, 1988.

Wang Hejun 王賀軍. "Mousha fasheng zai Xingqiliu yewan" 謀殺發生在星期六夜晚 (The murder happened late on a Saturday night). In Cen Ying, ed., *Zhongguo dalu zhentan*, pp. 1–37. Reprinted from *Qingming* 1980, no. 2.

Wang, Jing. *High Culture Fever: Politics, Aesthetics, and Ideology in Deng's China*. Berkeley: University of California Press, 1996.

Wang Jing 王靖. *Zai shehui de dang'an li* 在社會的檔案裏 (In the archive of society). In Li Yi, ed., *Zhongguo xin xieshizhuyi wenyi zuopin xuan*, pp. 160–81. Reprinted from *Dianying chuangzuo* 1979, no. 10.

Wang Liqi 王利器, ed. *Yuan Ming Qing san dai jinhui xiaoshuo xiqu shiliao, zengding ben* 元明清三代禁毀小說戲曲史料 (Historical materials on the banning and destruction of fiction and drama in the Yuan, Ming, and Qing dynasties, expanded edition). Shanghai: Shanghai guji chubanshe, 1981 [1958].

Wang Meng 王蒙. "Yaozi 8679 hao" 要字 8679 號 (Number 8679). *Zhongpian xiaoshuo xuankan* 1988, no. 4, pp. 7–19.

Wang Shuo 王朔. *Kong zhong xiaojie* 空中小姐 (Airline stewardess). Beijing: Zhongguo qingnian chubanshe, 1988.

———. *Playing for Thrills: A Mystery*. Howard Goldblatt, trans. New York: William Morrow, 1997.

———. *Xiangpiren* 橡皮人 (Rubber man). In *Kong zhong xiaojie*, pp. 186–331.

———. *Yiban shi huoyan, yiban shi haishui* 一半是火焰, 一半是海水 (One part flame, one part sea water). In *Kong zhong xiaojie*, pp. 70–185.

Wang Xiaoying 王小鷹. *Ni wei shui bianhu* 你為誰辯護 (Whom do you defend). Beijing: Zuojia chubanshe, 1988.

Wang Yaping 王亞平. "Bianhuren" 辯護人 (Defender). In Cen Ying, ed., *Zhongguo dalu zuian*, pp. 145–61. Reprinted from *Guangzhou wenyi* 1980, no. 5.

———. "Shensheng de shiming" 神聖的使命 (Sacred duty). In Cen Ying, ed., *Zhongguo dalu zuian*, pp. 145–61. In Barmé and Lee, trans., pp. 101–45.

Wang Yonghong 王咏虹. "Fayi Yang Bo" 法醫楊波 (Medical examiner Yang Bo). In Li Jingchun and Gong Fan, eds., *1984 Zhongguo xiaoshuo nianjian*, pp. 444–503.

———. *Yinxing wugong* 隱形蜈蚣 (The hidden centipede). Beijing: Falü chubanshe, 1985.

Wang Zhongfang 王仲方. *Zhongguo shehui zhian zonghe zhili de lilun yu shijian* 中國社會治安綜合治理的理論與實踐 (Theory and practice of comprehensive management of public order in China). Beijing: Qunzhong chubanshe, 1989.

Ward, Ian. *Law and Literature: Possibilities and Perspectives*. Cambridge: Cambridge University Press, 1995.

Watt, Ian. *The Rise of the Novel*. Berkeley: University of California Press, 1957.

Wei Dongsheng 魏冬生 [pseud. Weiren 魏人]. *Lü se de douhao* 綠色的逗號 (Green commas). Beijing: Qunzhong chubanshe, 1987.

———. "Xingjing duizhang yu sharenfan de neixin dubai" 刑警隊長與殺人犯的內心獨白 (Interior monologues of a head patrolman and a murderer). In Li Jingchun and Gong Fan, eds., *1984 Zhongguo xiaoshuo nianjian*, pp. 564–611.

Wei Jun 魏軍. *Fazhi wenxue yu chuangzuo* 法制文學與創作 (Legal system literature and creativity). Beijing: Jingguan jiaoyu chubanshe, 1990.

———. "Xin sheng" 心聲 (Heartfelt wishes). *Zuopin yu zhengming* 17 (May 17, 1982): 51–56. Criticisms follow on pp. 57–60. Reprinted from *Luoshen* 1981, no. 4.

Wei Shaochang 魏紹昌. *Wo kan yuanyang hudie pai* 我看鴛鴦蝴蝶派 (The mandarin duck and butterfly school as I see it). Hong Kong: Zhonghua shuju, 1990.

———, ed. *Yuanyang hudie pai yanjiu ziliao* 鴛鴦蝴蝶派研究資料 (Research materials on the mandarin duck and butterfly school). Vol. 1. Shanghai: Shanghai wenyi chubanshe, 1962.

Wei Shaochang 魏紹昌 and Wu Chenghui 吳承惠, eds. *Yuanyang hudie pai yanjiu ziliao* 鴛鴦蝴蝶派研究資料 (Research materials on the mandarin duck and butterfly school). Vol. 2. Shanghai: Shanghai wenyi chubanshe, 1962. Internal.

Wei Shouzhong 魏守忠. "Cheng Xiaoqing shengping yu zhuyi nianbiao" 程小青生平與著譯年表 (Chronology of Cheng Xiaoping's life, works, and translations). In Lu Runxiang, *Shenmi de zhentan shijie*, pp. 131–56.

Weisberg, Richard H. "Entering with a Vengeance: Posner on Law and Literature." *Stanford Law Review* 41 (1989): 1597–1626.

———. *The Failure of the Word: The Protagonist as Lawyer in Modern Fiction.* New Haven, Conn.: Yale University Press, 1984.

———. "How Judges Speak: Some Lessons on Adjudication in *Billy Budd, Sailor* with an Application to Justice Rehnquist." *New York University Law Review* 57, no. 1 (Apr. 1982): 1–69.

———. *Poethics, and Other Strategies of Law and Literature.* New York: Columbia University Press, 1992.

Weisberg, Robert. "The Law-Literature Enterprise." *Yale Journal of Law and the Humanities* 1 (1988): 1–67.

Wellek, René, and Austin Warren. *Theory of Literature.* 3d ed. New York: Harcourt, Brace, and World, 1956 [1942].

West, Robin. "Law, Literature, and the Celebration of Authority." *Northwestern University Law Review* 83, no. 4 (Summer 1989): 977–1011.

———. *Narrative, Authority, and Law.* Ann Arbor: University of Michigan Press, 1993.

White, James Boyd. *Heracles' Bow: Essays on the Rhetoric and Poetics of Law.* Madison: University of Wisconsin Press, 1985.

———. "The Judicial Opinion and the Poem: Ways of Reading, Ways of Life." In Ledwon, ed., *Law and Literature*, pp. 5–28.

———. "Law and Literature: 'No Manifesto.'" *Mercer Law Review* 39 (1988): 739–51.

———. *The Legal Imagination: Studies in the Nature of Legal Thought and Expression*. Boston: Little, Brown, 1973.

Widmer, Ellen, and David Der-wei Wang, eds. *From May Fourth to June Fourth: Fiction and Film in Twentieth-Century China*. Cambridge, Mass.: Harvard University Press, 1993.

Williams, Patrick, and Laura Chrisman, eds. *Colonial Discourse and Post-Colonial Theory: A Reader*. New York: Columbia University Press, 1994.

Williams, Raymond. *Keywords: A Vocabulary of Culture and Society*. New York: Oxford University Press, 1985.

Wilson, James Q. *Varieties of Police Behavior*. Cambridge, Mass.: Harvard University Press, 1968.

Wingate, Nancy. "Getting Away with Murder: An Analysis." *Journal of Popular Culture* 12, no. 4 (Spring 1979): 581–603.

Winks, Robin W. *The Historian as Detective: Essays on Evidence*. New York: Harper and Row, 1968.

———, ed. *Detective Fiction: A Collection of Critical Essays*. Englewood Cliffs, N.J.: Prentice-Hall, 1980.

Winston, Robert P., and Nancy C. Mellerski. *The Public Eye: Ideology and the Police Procedural*. New York: St. Martin's, 1992.

Wong, Timothy C. "The *Xiaoshuo* Tradition and Modern Entertainment Fiction." Paper presented at the Annual Meeting of the Association for Asian Studies, Honolulu, 1996.

Woodside, Alexander, and Benjamin A. Elman. "Introduction." In Elman and Woodside, eds., *Education and Society in Late Imperial China*, pp. 1–15.

Wright, Will. *Six Guns and Society: A Structural Study of the Western*. Berkeley: University of California Press, 1975.

Wu Dijun 吳迪君 and Wang Guanlong 王瓘瓏 [performers]. *Wan Qing diyi qi'an: Zhang Wenxiang qi ci Ma Xinyi* 晚清第一奇案: 張文祥七刺馬新貽 (The top strange case in the late Qing: The seven stabbings of Ma Xinyi by Zhang Wenxiang). N.p. [Hangzhou?]: Zhejiang wenyi chubanshe, 1988.

Wu, Hongda Harry. *Laogai—The Chinese Gulag*. Ted Slingerland, trans. Boulder, Colo.: Westview, 1992.

Wu, Laura Hua. "From *Xiaoshuo* to Fiction: Hu Yinglin's Genre Study of *Xiaoshuo*." *Harvard Journal of Asiatic Studies* 55, no. 2 (Dec. 1995): 339–71.

Wu, Yenna. *The Chinese Virago: A Literary Theme*. Cambridge, Mass.: Council on East Asian Studies, Harvard University, 1995.

Xi Xi. "The Fertile Town Chalk Circle." In *Marvels of a Floating City*. Eva Hung, ed. Hong Kong: Renditions, 1997.

Xiezuo gailun 寫作概論 (General principles of writing). Zhang Jingtao 張靜濤, chief ed. Zhangjiakou: Falü chubanshe, 1988.

Xin Paian jingqi 新 "拍案驚奇" (The new *Slapping the Table in Amazement*). Ji'nan: Shandong wenyi chubanshe, 1987.

Xin Ru 辛茹 and Lu Chen 陸沉, eds. *Zhonghua renmin gongheguo falü lifa sifa jieshi anli daquan* 中華人民共和國法律立法司法解釋案例大全 (Compendium of legislative and judicial interpretations of the law of the People's Republic of China, with cases). Shijiazhuang: Hebei renmin chubanshe, 1991.

Xing Yixun 邢益勛. *Quan yu fa* 權與法 (Power vs. law). In Cen Ying, ed., *Zhongguo dalu zuian*, pp. 75–106. Reprinted from *Juben* 1979, no. 10. Trans. as "Power Versus Law." *Chinese Literature* 6 (June 1980): 31–91.

Xing'an huilan 刑案匯覽 (Conspectus of penal cases). Zhu Qingqi 祝慶祺, comp. 60 *juan*. 1834. Reprint, Taibei: Chengwen, 1968 [1886].

Xingjing 803 刑警 803 (Officer 803). Composed by the Shanghai renmin guangbo diantai wenyi tai (Shanghai People's Broadcasting Network Literary Station) and the Shanghaishi gonganju faxuanchu (Shanghai Public Security Bureau Legal Propaganda Department). Zu Wenzhong 祖文忠 and Qu Xinhua 瞿新華, eds. Shanghai: Shanghai wenyi chubanshe, 1992.

Xingshi fanzui anli congshu 刑事犯罪叢書 (Compendium of criminal case studies). Supreme People's Procuratorate, ed. Beijing: Zhongguo jiancha chubanshe, 1992.

Xingshi zhencha anli xuanbian 刑事偵察案例選編 (Selected cases of criminal investigation). Gonganbu sanju (Third Department of the Ministry of Public Security), ed. Beijing: Qunzhong chubanshe, 1980. Internal.

Xu Bibo 徐碧波. "Zhongguo de 'Kenan Daoer'—Wo suo renshi de Cheng Xiaoqing" 中國的 "科南道爾"——我所認識的程小青 (China's Conan Doyle—Cheng Xiaoqing as I knew him). *Wenhuibao*, Oct. 19, 1989, p. 4.

Xu Shaowu 徐紹武. "Jianchazhang renxuan" 檢察長人選 (The choice for head procurator). In Cen Ying, ed., *Zhongguo dalu zuian*, pp. 67–74. Reprinted from *Renmin wenxue* 1979, no. 8.

Xu Xiao 徐曉. "Yi ge nü yushenyuan de zishu" 一個女預審員的自述 (Statement from a female preliminary hearing interrogator). In Cen Ying, ed., *Zhongguo dalu zuian*, pp. 210–17. Reprinted from *Anhui wenxue* 1980, no. 1.

Xu Xiaoqun. "The Fate of Judicial Independence in Republican China, 1912–37." *China Quarterly* 149 (Mar. 1997): 1–28.

Xu Zhixiang 徐志祥. "Dui dangdai fazhi wenxue de sikao" 對當代法制文學的思考 (Reflections on contemporary legal system literature). *Zhongguo fazhi wenxue* 2 (Apr. 1986): 79–80.

Yan Xinrui 閻新瑞. "Gongan ticai xiaoshuo zhi wo jian" 公安題材小説之我見 (Fiction with police subject matter as I see it). *Zhuomuniao* 78 (Nov. 1996): 130–34.

Yang, Gladys. "'Power Versus Law'—a Courageous, Topical Play." *Chinese Literature* 6 (June 1980): 92–97.

Yang, Lien-sheng. "The Concept of 'Pao' as a Basis for Social Relations in China." In John K. Fairbank, ed., *Chinese Thought and Institutions*, pp. 291–309. Chicago: University of Chicago Press, 1967 [1957].

Yang Rongfang 楊容方. "Yuan Shui qi shi an" 沅水奇屍案 (The case of the strange Yuan River corpse). In Cen Ying, ed., *Zhongguo dalu zhentan*, pp. 160–74. Reprinted from *Xuefeng* 1980, no. 1.

Ye Yonglie 葉永烈. *Buyierfei* 不翼而飛 (Gone without a trace). No. 3 in series. Beijing: Qunzhong chubanshe, 1982.

———. *Guiji duoduan* 詭計多端 (Cunning as can be). Comic book. Guangzhou: Kexue puji chubanshe Guangzhou fenshe, 1982.

———. *Guobao qi'an* 國寶奇案 (The strange case of the national treasure). Shenyang: Liaoning renmin chubanshe, 1981.

———. *Hei ying* 黑影 (The black shadow). Beijing: Dizhi chubanshe, 1981.

———. "Jingxian kehuan xiaoshuo dayi" 驚險科幻小説答疑 (Response to doubts about suspenseful science fiction). *Zuopin yu zhengming* 29 (May 17, 1983): 71–73.

———. *Leng ruo bingshuang* 冷若冰霜 (Cold as ice). Fuzhou: Fujian kexue yishu chubanshe, 1982.

———. *Mimi zongdui* 秘密縱隊 (The secret column). No. 2 in series. Beijing: Qunzhong chubanshe, 1981.

———. "'Pa gezi' de licheng" "爬格子" 的歷程 (A career of "scribbling"). In *Zhong qing nian zuojia zizhuan* 中青年作家自傳 (Autobiographies of young and middle-aged writers), pp. 398–421. Changchun: Shidai wenyi chubanshe, 1988.

———. *Poan de xin yaoshi* 破案的新鑰匙 (New keys for solving cases). Ji'nan: Mingtian chubanshe, 1985.

———. *Qiaozhuang daban* 喬裝打扮 (In disguise). No. 1 in series. Beijing: Qunzhong chubanshe, 1980.

———. *Qiaozhuang daban.* Comic book. Guangzhou: Kexue puji chubanshe Guangzhou fenshe, 1981.

———. *Ru meng chu xing* 如夢初醒 (Like awakening from a dream). No. 4 in series. Beijing: Qunzhong chubanshe, 1983.

———. *Shenmi yi* 神秘衣 (Mystery clothes). Tianjin: Xin lei chubanshe, 1980.

———. *Wuxing qiezei* 無形竊賊 (The invisible thief). Comic book. Guangzhou: Kexue puji chubanshe Guangzhou fenshe, 1982.

———. "X-3 anjian" X-3 案件 (The X-3 case). *Zuopin yu zhengming* 29 (May 17, 1983): 57–68, 79.

———. *Zhi zui jin mi* 紙醉金迷 (Obsessed with gold and money). Comic book. Guangzhou: Kexue puji chubanshe Guangzhou fenshe, 1982.

———, ed. *Zhongguo jingxian kexue huanxiang xiaoshuo xuan* 中國驚險科學幻想小説選 (Selected Chinese suspenseful science fiction). N.p. [Nanjing?]: Jiangsu kexue jishu chubanshe, 1981.

Yu Haocheng 于浩成. *Dangdai zawen xuancui* 當代雜文選粹 (Selected contemporary essays). Changsha: Hunan wenyi chubanshe, 1986.

———. *Ming chun ji* 鳴春集 (Heralding the spring). Beijing: Qunzhong chubanshe, 1985.

Yu Hua. *The Past and the Punishments.* Andrew F. Jones, trans. Honolulu: University of Hawaii Press, 1996.

———. 余華. "Wangshi yu xingfa" 往事與刑罰 (The past and the punishments). *Beijing wenxue* 1989, no. 2 (Feb. 1989): 34–55.

Yu Piao 余飄. "Renmin xuyao fazhi wenxue, fazhi wenxue geng xuyao renmin" 人民需要法制文學, 法制文學更需要人民 (The people need legal system literature, and legal system literature needs the people even more). *Zhongguo fazhi wenxue* 8 (Mar. 18, 1987): 78–80.

Yuan Jin 袁進. *Yuanyang hudie pai* 鴛鴦蝴蝶派 (The mandarin duck and butterfly school). Shanghai: Shanghai shudian, 1994.

———. *Zhongguo wenxue guannian de jindai biange* 中國文學觀念的近代變革 (The modern transformation of the Chinese concept of literature). Shanghai: Shanghai shehuikexueyuan chubanshe, 1996.

———. *Zhongguo xiaoshuo de jindai biange* 中國小說的近代變革 (The modern transformation of Chinese fiction). Beijing: Zhongguo shehui kexue chubanshe, 1992.

Yuan Ying 袁鷹. "Renmin huhuanzhe fazhi he fazhi wenxue" 人民呼喚着法制和法制文學 (The people are calling for legal system and legal system literature). *Zhongguo fazhi wenxue* 7 (Jan. 18, 1987): 91–92, 96.

Zeitlin, Judith T. *Historian of the Strange: Pu Songling and the Chinese Classical Tale.* Stanford, Calif.: Stanford University Press, 1993.

Zelin, Madeleine. "Uncovering China's Contract Culture." *Columbia,* Fall 1997, pp. 12–13.

Zeng Zhennan 曾鎮南. "Fazhan fazhi wenxue zhi wo jian" 發展法制文學之我見 (My views on developing legal system literature). *Zhuomuniao* 19 (Jan. 1987): 89–98.

———. "Fazhi wenxue duanxiang" 法制文學斷想 (Judgment on legal system literature). *Jingtan fengyun* 25 (May 1988): 52–53.

Zha, Jianying. *China Pop.* New York: New Press, 1995.

Zhang Chengfu 張呈富, ed. *Bai an qi guan* 百案奇觀 (Strange tales: A hundred cases). Guilin: Li Jiang chubanshe, 1990.

Zhang Chunsheng 張春生. "Yi zhi hongxing chu qiang lai" 一枝紅杏出牆來 (A pink apricot pushes out through the wall). *Landun* 2 (1986): 56–59.

Zhang Dachun 張大春, Lin Foer 林佛兒, and Ye Yandu 葉言都. Special Supplement on Fiction of Deduction. *Zhongshi wanbao* 中時晚報 (Taibei), "Shidai wenxue" 時代文學 (China Times Express literary supplement), July 28, 1991.

Zhang Fang 張放. *Dalu xin shiqi xiaoshuo lun* 大陸新時期小説論 (On mainland fiction of the new era). Taibei: Dongda tushu gufen youxian gongsi, 1992.

Zhang Jinfan 張晉藩, Lin Zhong 林中, and Wang Zhigang 王志剛. *Zhongguo xingfashi xinlun* 中國刑法史新論 (A new history of Chinese criminal law). Beijing: Renmin fayuan chubanshe, 1992.

Zhang Qie 張鍥. "Youran zuoyun, peiran xiayu—Qian tan fazhi wenxue de xingqi jiqi fada" 油然作雲, 沛然下雨——淺談法制文學的興起及其發展 (As clouds gather, rain falls in profusion—Superficial thoughts on the rise and development of legal system literature). *Zhuomuniao* 19 (Jan. 1987): 89–98.

Zhang Weihua 張衛華 and Zhang Ce 張策. "Diankuang de shuchao" 顛狂的書潮 (Runaway book publishing). *Zhuomuniao* 27 (May 1988): 4–21.

Zhang Xianliang. *Getting Used to Dying*. Martha Avery, trans. New York: Harper-Collins, 1991.

———. *Mimosa and Other Stories*. Beijing: Panda, 1985.

Zhang Xinxin 張辛欣. *Feng pian lian* ☒☐⊞ (封片連) (Envelope, postcard, block-of-four). *Shouhuo* 52 (Feb. 1985): 4–92.

Zhang, Yingjin. *The City in Modern Chinese Literature and Film: Configurations of Space, Time, and Gender*. Stanford, Calif.: Stanford University Press, 1996.

Zhao Guoqing 趙國慶. "Jiujiu ta" 救救她 (Save her). In Cen Ying, ed., *Zhongguo dalu zuian*, pp. 172–209. Reprinted from *Gongren ribao*, Dec. 1979.

Zhao, Henry Y. H. *The Uneasy Narrator: Chinese Fiction from the Traditional to the Modern*. Oxford: Oxford University Press, 1995.

Zhao Shizhou 趙世州. "Jingxian kehuan xiaoshuo zhiyi" 驚險科幻小說質疑 (Queries about suspenseful science fiction). *Zuopin yu zhengming* 29 (May 17, 1983): 69–70.

Zhao Tiaokuang 趙苕狂. "Shui shi Huo Sang" 誰是霍桑 (Who is Huo Sang). *Zhentan shijie* 4 (1923): 1–8.

Zheng Shusen 鄭樹森 (William Tay). "Dazhong wenxue; xushi; wenlei—Wuxia xiaoshuo zhaji san ze" 大眾文學; 敘事; 文類——武俠小說札記三則 (Mass literature; narrative; genre—Reading notes on three issues about martial-arts fiction). *Ershiyi shiji* 4 (Apr. 1991): 113–19.

Zheng Yimei 鄭逸梅. "Cheng Xiaoqing" 程小青. In Rui Heshi, Fan Boqun, et al., eds., *Yuanyang hudie pai wenxue ziliao*, 1: 388–89. Dated 1925.

Zhonghua renmin gongheguo xingfa zongze jiangyi 中華人民共和國刑法總則講義 (Lecture notes on the general provisions of the Criminal Law of the People's Republic of China). Beijing: Qunzhong chubanshe, 1980.

Zhou Yunfa 周雲發. "Tantan fazhi wenxue de fazhan qushi" 談談法制文學的發展趨勢 (Talking about trends in the development of legal system literature). *Fazhi wenxue xuankan*, Nov.? 1986, pp. 5–8.

Zhu Hong, trans. *The Chinese Western: Short Fiction from Today's China*. New York: Ballantine, 1988.

Zhu Jiazhen 祝家鎮, Zhu Xiaoman 朱小曼, and Guo Jingyuan 郭景元. *Fayi yu poan* 法醫與破案 (Forensic science and solving cases). N.p. [Guangzhou?]: Guangdong keji chubanshe, 1986 [1982].

Zhu Yiqiang 朱一強 and Wu Nanfei 吳南飛, eds. *Zui yu fa* 罪與法 (Crime and the law). [Nanchang]: Jiangxisheng sifating fazhi xuanchuanchu (Department of Legal System Propaganda of the Jiangxi Province Judiciary), Jiangxi University Department of Law, and *Jiangxi qingnianbao* xinwenbu *Zui yu fa* bianxiezu (*Crime and the Law* Editorial Committee of the news bureau of the *Jiangxi Youth News*), n.d. Preface June 1985. Internal.

Index

In this index an "f" after a number indicates a separate reference on the next page, and an "ff" indicates separate references on the next two pages. A continuous discussion over two or more pages is indicated by a span of page numbers, e.g., "57–59." *Passim* is used for a cluster of references in close but not consecutive sequence.

Library of Congress Cataloging-in-Publication Data

Kinkley, Jeffrey C.
  Chinese justice, the fiction : law and literature in modern China
      p.   cm.
  Includes bibliographical references and index.
  ISBN 0-8047-3443-7 (alk.paper)—ISBN 0-8047-3976-5 (pbk. : alk.
  paper)
    1. Chinese fiction—20th century—History and criticism. 2. Legal
  stories, Chinese—History and criticism. 3. Law in literature.
  I. Title: Law and literature in modern China.   II. Title.

  PL2443 .K55 2000
  895.1'35209355—dc21   99-088186

Original printing 2000

Last figure indicates the year of this printing:
08 07 06 05 04 03 02 01 00

Typeset by BookMatters in 11/14 Adobe Garamond

DATE DUE